C000274302

The Mini

OXFORD

School

French

DICTIONARY

Editorial Manager: Valerie Grundy
Editor: Jennifer Barnes

OXFORD UNIVERSITY PRESS

Oxford University Press, Great Clarendon Street, Oxford OX2 6DP

Oxford New York
Athens Auckland Bangkok Bogotá Bombay
Buenos Aires Calcutta Cape Town Dar es Salaam
Delhi Florence Hong Kong Istanbul Karachi
Kuala Lumpur Madras Madrid Melbourne
Mexico City Nairobi Paris Singapore
Taipei Tokyo Toronto Warsaw

and associated companies in
Berlin Ibadan

Oxford is a trade mark of Oxford University Press

A CIP catalogue record for this book is available from the British Library

ISBN 0-19-910387-9

Typeset by Selwood Systems, Midsomer Norton

Printed and bound in Great Britain by
Omnia Books Ltd, Glasgow

INTRODUCTION

Learning a new language is an exciting experience. However, it can also sometimes seem confusing and difficult. Feeling secure and at ease in using a bilingual dictionary is essential to the building of confidence in understanding and using a foreign language.

This dictionary has been specially written for students who are preparing for exams. We have paid particular attention to making the dictionary as user friendly as possible. With the help of easy-to-follow signposts and examples, the right translation can quickly be found. French verbs on both sides of the dictionary are numbered to take the student straight to the appropriate pattern in the centre pages of the dictionary.

We have adopted a simplified version of traditional bilingual entry layout. This means that the dictionary is ideal for learning basic dictionary skills, which can subsequently be built upon as the student moves towards larger, more sophisticated dictionaries. We have done our best to make this dictionary a practical, easy-to-use tool for learning and understanding French.

Throughout the writing of this dictionary we have worked in close consultation with students, teachers, inspectors, and examining boards. We gratefully acknowledge the Northern Examinations and Assessment Board, the Southern Examining Group, the Midland Examining Group, London Examinations, and the Associated Examining Board, who have read and commented on the dictionary text.

HOW A BILINGUAL DICTIONARY WORKS

A bilingual dictionary is a dictionary that has two languages in it. When you look up a word in one of the languages, the dictionary gives the translation for that word in the other language. The two languages in this dictionary are English and French. This dictionary is divided into two halves separated by dark-edged pages in the middle. In the first half you look up French words to find out what they mean in English and in the second half you look up English words and find out how to say them in French.

In the first half of the dictionary you will find **French** words in alphabetical order from a to z and in the second half **English** words from a to z. In a dictionary, these are called **headwords** because each one of them comes at the **head** of an **entry**. In the entry you can find **translations** but also other sorts of information which you can use to make sure you get the correct translation. The different sorts of information are typed in different ways to help you see clearly which is which. Here is a guide to the different things you will find in an entry:

headword	a word you look up in the dictionary
translation	translations are the only things that are in 'ordinary' type in the dictionary. They are *always* typed like this, and something which is typed in a different way can *never* be a translation
noun	part of speech: tells you whether the word you are looking up is a noun, a verb, an adjective, or another part of speech. One headword can have more than one part of speech. For instance, **book** can be a noun *(she was reading a book)* or a verb *(I've booked the seats).*
(signpost)	helpful information: to guide you to the right translation, to show you how to use the translation, or to give you extra information about either the headword or the translation.
example	a phrase or sentence using the word you have looked up. If these appear in the entry you are looking at, you should read through them carefully to see if they are close to what you want to understand or say.
M	gender: after a French noun to tell you that it is masculine
F	gender: after a French noun to tell you that it is feminine
●	indicates a phrasal verb such as *to carry on*
★	shows an idiomatic expression such as *over the moon*
[27]	verb number – tells you which verb pattern to look at in the centre of the dictionary

vi

You can think of a dictionary entry as being made out of different sorts of building bricks. In the entries below you can see how they fit together to help you to find what you need. The more you use your dictionary the more confident you will feel about finding your way around it.

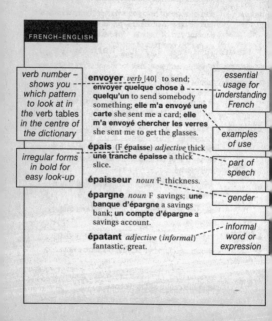

FRENCH–ENGLISH

verb number – shows you which pattern to look at in the verb tables in the centre of the dictionary

irregular forms in bold for easy look-up

envoyer *verb* [40] to send; **envoyer quelque chose à quelqu'un** to send somebody something; **elle m'a envoyé une carte** she sent me a card; **elle m'a envoyé chercher les verres** she sent me to get the glasses.

épais (F **épaisse**) *adjective* thick **une tranche épaisse** a thick slice.

épaisseur *noun* F thickness.

épargne *noun* F savings; **une banque d'épargne** a savings bank; **un compte d'épargne** a savings account.

épatant *adjective* (*informal*) fantastic, great.

essential usage for understanding French

examples of use

part of speech

gender

informal word or expression

A STEP-BY-STEP GUIDE TO FINDING THE TRANSLATION YOU NEED

Finding a word in the dictionary

You will be using this dictionary to do one of the following things:

1 look up a French word or phrase to find out what it means
2 look up an English word or phrase to find out how to say it in French.

1 Finding out what a French word means

First of all, look for it in the first half of the dictionary where you can find the French words and expressions with their English translations. You will see that the top of every page is marked like this.

No matter what you are using the dictionary to find out, you will always start by looking up a headword. Here are the French headwords **briller, brin, brindille, brioche** and **briquet** with their entries.

---

briller *verb* [1] to shine.

brin *noun* M 1 sprig (*of herb or plant*);
un brin d'herbe a blade of grass.

brindille *noun* F twig.

brioche *noun* F brioche, bun.

brique *noun* F 1 brick; 2 carton (*of fruit-juice, milk, etc*).

briquet *noun* M lighter.

Suppose you want to find out what the French word **matelas** means. You will look through the first half of your dictionary until you come to the bit which has all the French words beginning with **m**. You now need to find the page or pages containing French words beginning with **ma**, then **mat**, then **mate**. The dictionary helps you to do this by showing you the alphabetical range of words that you can find on the two pages you can see when you have the dictionary open.

For instance, if you look at pages 172–173, you will see **mariage** at the top of page 172 and **matin** at the top of page 173. This means that the first entry on page 172 is **mariage** and the last entry on page 173 is **matin**. The word you are looking for begins **mate-** so you will find it somewhere on these two pages.

If you look down the second column on page 173 you will find **matelas** between **match** and **matelassé**. Notice that hyphens, spaces between words, and accents on letters in French words make no difference to the alphabetical order.

> **mat** *adjective* matt.
>
> **mât** *noun* M mast; pole.
>
> **match** *noun* M match; **un match de foot** a football match; **faire match nul** to draw.
>
> **matelas** *noun* M mattress.
>
> **matelassé** *adjective* quilted.
>
> **matelot** *noun* M sailor.
>
> **matériaux** *plural noun* M materials; **les matériaux de construction** building materials.

When you look at the entry for **matelas** you will find the translation you are looking for: **matelas** means **mattress**.

> **matelas** *noun* M mattress.

You can also see that **matelas** is a *noun* and because all nouns are either masculine or feminine in French, you are given the gender M (F = feminine gender; M = masculine gender).

It often happens that a French word has more than one translation in English. If you look at the entry for **bouton** on page 36 you will see that it is divided into sections numbered **1** and **2**.

> **bouton** *noun* M **1** button; **2** spot, pimple.

The first translation is **button** and the second is **spot** or **pimple**. You will need to look at both translations and work out which one fits in best in the French sentence you are trying to understand. So:

> **il y a quatre boutons sur ma veste** *means* there are four buttons on my jacket
>
> BUT
>
> **j'ai un bouton sur le nez** *means* I've got a spot on my nose

You add an **-s** to most French nouns to form the plural, as in **boutons** in the sentence above. There are exceptions to this and where the plural is not **-s** you will find the plural form after the headword.

For instance, if you are trying to find out what the French word **animaux** means you can see immediately that it is the plural of **animal**:

> **animal** (*plural* **animaux**) *noun* M animal.

Similarly, you usually add an **-e** to French adjectives to make them feminine to agree with a feminine noun. Where this is not the case, you will find the feminine form straight after the headword if it follows alphabetically, like **gazeuse** here:

> **gazeux** (F **gazeuse**) *adjective* fizzy;
> **eau gazeuse** fizzy mineral water.

As with nouns, you usually add an **-s** to the masculine or feminine form of an adjective to make it plural, but again there are exceptions to this. If you are trying to find out what **normaux** means, you will find that it is the masculine plural of **normal**:

> **normal** (M *plural* **normaux**)
> *adjective* **1** normal; **2** c'est
> **normal** it's natural; **3** ce n'est pas
> **normal** it's not right.

French like English has certain words that you would use when chatting with friends but not in more formal situations. French words like this are marked *informal* in the dictionary, like **bouquin** here:

> **bouquin** *noun* M (*informal*) book.

Note that the usual word for **book** is **livre**.

2 Finding an English word and how to say it in French

You can see that it is quite easy once you know how the dictionary works to look up a French word and find out what it means. Students usually find it harder to use the dictionary to find out how to say something in French. This dictionary is written specially to help you do this and to make it easy to find the right way of saying things in French.

ENGLISH–FRENCH

Suppose you want to know how to say **garden** in French. Look up the word in the second part of the dictionary where the top of every page is marked like this.

If you follow the same method of going through the alphabetical order of the headwords as you did when you were looking up a French word, you will find **garden** on page 414.

> **gangster** *noun* gangster M.
>
> **gap** *noun* 1 (*hole*) trou M; 2 (*in time*) intervalle M; **a two-year gap** un intervalle de deux ans; 3 **an age gap** une différence d'âge.
>
> **garage** *noun* garage M.
>
> **garden** *noun* jardin M.
>
> **gardener** *noun* jardinier M; **he wants to be a gardener** il veut être jardinier.
>
> **gardening** *noun* jardinage M.
>
> **garlic** *noun* ail M.

Now you can see that the French word for **garden** is **jardin**. But if you want to make a sentence using a noun like **jardin** you need to know whether it is masculine or feminine. The **M** after **jardin** tells you that it is masculine so *in the garden* is **dans le jardin**.

It is not always as easy as this to know which French word you need. Sometimes there will be more than one French word for the English word you are looking up. When the dictionary entry gives you more than just one translation, it is very important to take the time to read through the whole entry. If you look up **plug** the entry looks like this:

> **plug** *noun* **1** (*electrical*) prise F;
> **2** (*in the bath or sink*) bonde F; **to**
> **pull out the plug** retirer la bonde.

You can see that **1** tells you that the French word for an electrical plug is **prise** and **2** tells you that the word for a bath plug or a sink plug is **bonde**.

Remember that information which is either in brackets or italics or both is there to help you, but it *will never be* the translation itself. Wherever there is more than one translation, depending on what meaning of the English word you are looking for, the dictionary will always help you to choose the right one.

Often it is not enough to find the translation of one word. In the case of more common words the dictionary also gives you a selection of common phrases you will often want to use. In the entry for **hair** below you can find out how to use the translation in different expressions:

> **hair** *noun* **1** cheveux M *plural*; **to have**
> **short hair** avoir les cheveux courts;
> **to brush your hair** se brosser les cheveux;
> **to wash your hair** se laver les cheveux;
> **to have your hair cut** se faire couper les
> cheveux; **she's had her hair cut** elle s'est
> fait couper les cheveux; **2 a hair** (*from the
> head*) un cheveu; (*from the body*) un poil.

How to use the verb table numbers

On the FRENCH–ENGLISH side of the dictionary all the headwords which are verbs look like this:

> **faire** *verb* [10]

On the ENGLISH–FRENCH side of the dictionary all the verbs given as translations of English verbs look like this:

> **frighten** *verb* effrayer [59]

If you look at the dark-edged pages in the centre of the dictionary, you will find tables showing you how to use the different types of French verbs. The verb **faire** above has the number 10. If you look at number 10 in the verb tables, you will see that because **faire** is a very common and very irregular verb it has a whole page to itself giving you all the tenses you will need.

The verb **effrayer** has number 59 after it. When you look up verb table number 59, you will see the verb **payer**. This means that the verb endings given for **payer** will also be the endings for **effrayer**. So **payer** is there to show you the pattern that other verbs like it, such as **effrayer**, will follow.

With practice you will soon be able to find your way easily around the dictionary and identify what you are looking for in an entry. Some entries may seem long and complicated at first glance. Reading carefully through the signposts and examples will lead you to the translation you need.

A a

a *verb* SEE **avoir**.

à *preposition* (*note that 'à + le'
becomes 'au' and 'à + les' becomes
'aux'*) **1** at; **à la maison** at home; **à
l'école** at school; **au bureau** at the
office; **à deux heures** at two
o'clock; **2** in; **à Londres** in London;
à la campagne in the country; **au
printemps** in the spring; **3** to; **aller
à Londres** to go to London; **donner
quelque chose à quelqu'un** to give
something to somebody; **4** by; **à la
main** by hand; **à vélo** by (or on a)
bicycle; **5** with; **une petite fille aux
yeux bleus** a little girl with blue
eyes; **6 à trois kilomètres d'ici**
three kilometres from here; **7 ce
bracelet est à Natalie** this bracelet
is Natalie's.

abandonner *verb* [1] **1** to give up;
elle a abandonné les maths she has
given up maths; **j'abandonne** I give
up; **2** to abandon; **un enfant
abandonné** an abandoned child.

abat-jour *noun* M lampshade.

abats *plural noun* M **les abats** offal
(*liver, kidneys, heart, etc*).

abattoir *noun* M slaughterhouse.

abattre *verb* [21] **1** to shoot down;
**deux policiers ont été abattus par
des gangsters hier** two policemen
were shot down by gangsters
yesterday; **2** to slaughter (*an
animal*); **3** to demolish (*a
building*).

abbaye *noun* F abbey; **l'abbaye de
Cluny** Cluny Abbey.

abbé *noun* M priest.

abcès *noun* M abscess.

abeille *noun* F bee; **une piqûre
d'abeille** a bee sting.

abîmer *verb* [1] **1** to damage; **la
pluie avait abîmé la porte** the rain
had damaged the door; **tu vas
t'abîmer les yeux** you'll ruin your
eyesight; **des fruits abîmés** fruit
which is going bad; **2 s'abîmer** to
get damaged; **les pommes vont
s'abîmer** the apples are going to go
bad; **la viande s'abîme vite** meat
goes off quickly.

aboiement *noun* M barking; **on
entendait des aboiements** we
could hear dogs barking.

abolir *verb* [2] to abolish.

abominable *adjective* abominable.

abondance *noun* F **une
abondance de** plenty of, lots of; **il y
a des fruits en abondance** there's
plenty of fruit.

abonné, abonnée *noun* M, F
1 season ticket holder;
2 subscriber (*to a magazine,
journal, etc*).
adjective **être abonné** to have a
subscription (*to a magazine, journal,
etc*); to have a season ticket (*for the
bus, train, theatre, etc*).

abonnement *noun* M
1 subscription; **2** season ticket.

abonner *verb* [1] **s'abonner à** to
subscribe to; **je me suis abonné
pour un an** I have a year's
subscription.

abord noun M **1** d'abord first; tout d'abord first of all; je vais d'abord faire du thé I'll make some tea first; **2** d'abord at first; j'ai d'abord cru qu'il était français I thought at first that he was French; **3** les abords the surroundings.

abordable adjective **1** des prix abordables affordable prices; **2** une personne abordable an approachable person.

aborder verb [1] **1** to tackle (a problem, a piece of work, a subject, etc); **2** to approach.

aboutir verb [2] **1** aboutir à to lead to; la rue aboutit à une petite place the street leads to a little square; **2** aboutir à to end up in; nous avons abouti à Paris we ended up in Paris; **3** to succeed, to be successful (of discussions or negotiations).

aboyer verb [39] to bark.

abrégé noun M summary. adjective la version abrégée the abridged version.

abréger verb [15] to shorten.

abréviation noun F abbreviation.

abri noun M **1** shelter; trouver un abri to take shelter; les sans-abri the homeless; **2** shed; **3** à l'abri de sheltered from; à l'abri du vent sheltered from the wind, out of the wind; à l'abri de la lumière in a dark place.

abricot noun M apricot; de la confiture d'abricots apricot jam; une tarte aux abricots an apricot tart.

abricotier noun M apricot tree.

abriter verb [1] **1** to shelter; **2** s'abriter to take shelter.

abrupt adjective **1** steep; une pente abrupte a steep slope; **2** abrupt.

abrutir verb [2] **1** to deafen; **2** to stupefy.

absence noun F **1** absence; pendant mon absence while I was out, while I was away; **2** l'absence de the lack of.

absent adjective **1** être absent to be out, to be away; je serai absent pendant une heure I'll be out for an hour; elle a été absente tout le mois de mai she was away for the whole of May; **2** absent; **3** absent-minded.

absenter verb [1] s'absenter to go out, to go away; je m'absente quelques minutes I'm just popping out for a few minutes.

absolu adjective absolute.

absolument adverb absolutely.

absorbant adjective **1** absorbing; un livre absorbant an absorbing book; **2** absorbent (material).

absorber verb [1] **1** to absorb; **2** to take (food or drink).

abstenir verb [81] s'abstenir de to refrain from.

abstrait adjective abstract.

absurde adjective absurd.

absurdité noun F absurdity; dire des absurdités to talk nonsense.

abus noun M abuse; l'abus d'alcool alcohol abuse.

abuser verb [1] **1 abuser de** to misuse; **abuser de l'alcool** to drink too much (*regularly*); **2 abuser de** to take advantage of, to exploit; **elle abuse de ta gentillesse** she's taking advantage of your kindness.

abusif (F **abusive**) *adjective* **1** excessive; **2** unfair.

acajou *noun* M mahogany; **une table en acajou** a mahogany table.

accablant *adjective* overwhelming.

accabler *verb* [1] to overwhelm.

accéder *verb* [24] **1 accéder à** to reach, to get to ; **pour accéder à la salle de bains, il faut passer par la chambre** to get to the bathroom you have to go through the bedroom; **2 accéder au pouvoir** to come to power.

accélérateur *noun* M accelerator; **appuyer sur l'accélérateur** to accelerate.

accélération *noun* F acceleration.

accélérer *verb* [24] **1** to speed up (*the rhythm, process, etc*); **2** to accelerate (*in a car*).

accent *noun* M **1** accent; **un accent étranger** a foreign accent; **parler français sans accent** to speak French without an accent; **2** accent (*on a letter in written French*); **un accent aigu** an acute accent; **un accent grave** a grave accent; **un accent circonflexe** a circumflex; **3 mettre l'accent sur quelque chose** to stress something.

accentuer *verb* [1] to emphasize.

acceptation *noun* F acceptance.

accepter *verb* [1] **1** to accept; **accepter une invitation** to accept an invitation; **2 accepter de faire** to agree to do; **elle a accepté de m'aider** she agreed to help me.

accès *noun* M **1** access; **accès interdit** no entry; **2 un accès de colère** a fit of anger.

accessible *adjective* **1** accessible; **un livre accessible** a book which is easy to read; **2 des prix accessibles** affordable prices.

accessoire *noun* M accessory; **les accessoires** accessories (*gloves, handbags, etc*). *adjective* incidental.

accident *noun* M **1** accident; **avoir un accident** to have an accident; **un accident de la route** a road accident; **2** hitch; **il y a eu un petit accident** there's been a slight hitch.

accidenté *adjective* **1** injured; **2** damaged; **3 'chaussée accidentée'** 'uneven road surface'.

acclamations *plural noun* F cheering.

accommodant *adjective* easy-going.

accompagnateur, accompagnatrice *noun* M, F **1** tourist guide; **2** courier (*for a group on a package holiday*); **3** accompanying adult (*with a child travelling alone*); **4** accompanist (*for example, a pianist accompanying a singer*).

accompagner *verb* [1] **1** to accompany; **je t'accompagne** I'll go with you, I'll come with you; **je t'accompagne jusqu'à chez toi** I'll see you home; **2 accompagné de** accompanied by; **elle est partie accompagnée de son frère** she left accompanied by her brother; **3** to accompany (*on the piano, for example*).

accomplir *verb* [2] to carry out (*a task, project, mission, etc*).

accord *noun* M **1** agreement; **2 d'accord** all right, OK; **je suis d'accord** I agree; **je suis d'accord avec Rosie** I agree with Rosie; **Paul est d'accord pour venir avec nous** Paul's agreed to come with us; **3** chord (*in music*).

accordéon *noun* M accordeon; **jouer de l'accordéon** to play the accordeon.

accorder *verb* [1] **1** to grant (*a favour, permission, etc*); **2** to tune (*a musical instrument*); **3 s'accorder** to agree.

accotement *noun* M verge (*on the edge of the road*); hard shoulder (*on the motorway*); **'accotements non stabilisés'** 'soft verges' (*as road sign*).

accouchement *noun* M childbirth, delivery.

accoucher *verb* [1] to give birth.

accoutumé *adjective* **1** usual; **2 accoutumé à** used to, accustomed to;

accoutumer *verb* [1] **s'accoutumer à** to become accustomed to.

accro *noun* M (*informal*) addict. *adjective* (*informal*) **être accro de quelque chose** to be hooked on something.

accroc *noun* M **1** tear; **tu as un accroc à ta jupe** you've got a tear in your skirt; **2** hitch; **sans accroc(s)** without a hitch.

accrocher *verb* [1] **1** to hang; **accrocher un tableau au mur** to hang a picture on the wall; **accroché au mur** hanging on the wall; **2** to catch, to snag (*something on a nail or thorn, for example*).

accroupir *verb* [2] **s'accroupir** to crouch (down), to squat.

accueil *noun* M **1** welcome; **un accueil chaleureux** a warm welcome; **2** reception desk; **Madame Jones est priée de se présenter à l'accueil** would Ms Jones please go to the reception desk.

accueillant *adjective* **1** (*of a person*) hospitable, welcoming; **2** (*of a place*) inviting, friendly.

accueillir *verb* [35] **1** to welcome; **2** to receive, to greet.

accumuler *verb* [1] **1** to collect; **2 s'accumuler** to pile up.

accusation *noun* F accusation.

accusé de réception *noun* M **envoyer une lettre avec accusé de réception** to send a letter recorded delivery.

accuser *verb* [1] to accuse; **il m'a accusé d'avoir volé son stylo** he accused me of stealing his pen.

acharner *verb* [1] **s'acharner à faire** to persist in doing.

achat *noun* M purchase; **je te montre mes achats** I'll show you what I've bought.

acheter verb [16] **1** to buy; je vais acheter du pain I'm going to buy some bread; **2** acheter quelque chose à quelqu'un to buy somebody something; je t'achète un sandwich? shall I buy you a sandwich?; je lui ai acheté un cadeau I bought him (or her) a present; **3** acheter quelque chose à quelqu'un to buy something from somebody; j'ai vendu ma voiture – c'est Lisa qui me l'a achetée I've sold my car – Lisa bought it from me.

acheteur, acheteuse noun M, F buyer.

achever verb [50] **1** to finish (a piece of work); **2** to finish off (meaning 'kill').

acide noun M acid. adjective sharp, sour.

acier noun M steel.

acné noun F acne.

acoustique noun F acoustics.

acquérir verb [17] to acquire.

âcre adjective pungent.

acrobate noun M & F acrobat.

acrobatie noun F acrobatics.

acte noun M act.

acte de naissance noun M birth certificate.

acteur, actrice noun M, F actor, actress.

actif (F active) adjective active; la vie active working life.

action noun F action, act; une bonne action a good deed.

activement adverb actively.

activer verb [1] **1** to speed up; **2** s'activer to hurry up.

activité noun F activity.

activité professionnelle noun F occupation.

actualité noun F **1** current affairs; **2** les actualités the news.

actuel (F actuelle) adjective present, current; la situation actuelle the present situation.

actuellement adverb at the moment; elle est actuellement à Rome she's in Rome at the moment.

adapté adjective **1** suitable; adapté à suitable for, suited to; **2** adapted.

adapter verb [1] **1** to adapt; **2** s'adapter à to adapt to, to get used to.

additif noun M additive.

addition noun F **1** addition; **2** bill (in a restaurant); l'addition, s'il vous plaît can I have the bill please.

additionner verb [1] to add up.

adhésif (F adhésive) adjective adhesive; ruban adhésif sticky tape.

adieu (plural adieux) noun M goodbye, farewell (the usual expression is "au revoir" since "adieu" is properly used to mean "goodbye for ever").

adjectif noun M adjective.

adjoint, adjointe noun M, F **1** assistant; **2** deputy.

admettre verb [11] **1** to admit; j'admets qu'elle a raison I admit that she's right; **2** admettre dans to admit to (*a restaurant, a club, etc*).

administratif (F administrative) *adjective* administrative.

administration *noun* F administration.

admiratif (F admirative) *adjective* admiring; des regards admiratifs admiring glances.

admiration *noun* F admiration.

admirer *verb* [1] to admire.

adolescence *noun* F adolescence.

adolescent, adolescente *noun* M, F teenager, adolescent. *adjective* teenage, adolescent.

adopter *verb* [1] to adopt.

adoptif (F adoptive) *adjective* un enfant adoptif an adopted child.

adoption *noun* F adoption.

adorable *adjective* adorable.

adorer *verb* [1] to adore, to love.

adresse *noun* F **1** address; quelle est ton adresse? what's your address?; se tromper d'adresse to get (or go) the wrong address; **2** skill; elle l'a fait avec beaucoup d'adresse she did it very skilfully; **3** speech, address.

adresser *verb* [1] **1** adresser une lettre à quelqu'un to send somebody a letter; **2** adresser la parole à quelqu'un to speak to somebody; **2** s'adresser à to enquire at; adressez-vous à la réception enquire at reception; **4** s'adresser à to be aimed at; le film s'adresse aux adolescents the film is aimed at teenagers.

adroit *adjective* skilful.

adulte *noun* M & F, *adjective* adult.

adverbe *noun* M adverb.

adversaire *noun* M & F opponent.

adverse *adjective* opposing.

aérer *verb* [24] to air.

aérobic *noun* M aerobics.

aéro-club *noun* M flying club.

aérogare *noun* F (flight) terminal (*in an airport*).

aéroglisseur *noun* M hovercraft.

aéronautique *noun* F aeronautics.

aéroport *noun* M airport; à l'aéroport at (or to) the airport.

aérosol *noun* M aerosol.

affaire *noun* F **1** matter, business; c'est une drôle d'affaire it's a funny business; c'est une autre affaire that's another matter; **2** affair, political crisis.

affaires *plural noun* F **1** les affaires business; un homme d'affaires a businessman; une femme d'affaires a businesswoman; un voyage d'affaires a business trip; **2** business; occupe-toi de tes affaires! mind your own business!; **3** belongings, things; tu peux laisser tes affaires dans la chambre you can leave your things in the bedroom.

affamé *adjective* starving.

affamer verb [1] to starve.

affecter verb [1] 1 to affect;
2 **affecter de faire** to pretend to do.

affection noun F affection; **j'ai
beaucoup d'affection pour lui** I'm
very fond of him.

affectueusement adverb
affectionately.

affectueux (F **affectueuse**)
adjective affectionate.

affiche noun F 1 poster; 2 notice.

afficher verb [1] to put up (a poster
or a notice).

affliger verb [52] 1 to distress, to
grieve; 2 **affliger de** to afflict with.

affluence noun F crowds; **aux
heures d'affluence** at peak times.

affolant adjective (informal)
frightening.

affoler verb [1] 1 **affoler
quelqu'un** to throw somebody into a
panic; 2 **s'affoler** to panic; **ne
t'affole pas** don't panic.

affreux (F **affreuse**) adjective
1 awful, dreadful; 2 hideous.

afin preposition 1 **afin de faire** in
order to do; 2 **afin que** in order that.

africain adjective African.

Africain, Africaine noun M, F
African.

Afrique noun F Africa; **en Afrique**
in (or to) Africa.

agaçant adjective annoying.

agacer verb [61] to annoy.

âge noun M age; **quel âge as-tu?**
how old are you?; **à l'âge de cinq
ans** at the age of five; **je ne sais pas
son âge** I don't know how old he (or
she) is; **il a l'âge de mon père** he's
the same age as my father.

âgé adjective 1 old; **les personnes
âgées** old people; 2 **âgé de** aged;
une femme âgée de trente ans a
woman aged thirty.

agence noun F 1 agency;
2 branch (of a bank).

agence de voyages noun F
travel agent's.

agence immobilière noun F
estate agent's.

agenda noun M diary.

agenouiller verb [1] **s'agenouiller**
to kneel down.

agent noun M 1 official; 2 agent.

agent commercial noun M sales
representative.

agent de police noun M police
officer; **une femme agent de police**
a woman police officer.

aggraver verb [1] 1 to make worse;
aggraver la situation to make
things worse; 2 **s'aggraver** to get
worse; **la situation s'aggrave** the
situation is deteriorating, things are
getting worse.

agir verb [2] 1 to act; 2 to behave;
3 **il s'agit de** it's about; **il s'agit de
ton frère** it's about your brother; **de
quoi s'agit-il?** what's it about?

agitation noun F 1 hustle and
bustle; 2 unrest; 3 restlessness.

agité adjective 1 restless, agitated;
2 rough (sea); 3 bustling (street);

4 **mener une vie agitée** to lead a hectic life.

agiter verb [1] to shake; **agiter la main** to wave your hand.

agneau (plural **agneaux**) noun M lamb; **un gigot d'agneau** a leg of lamb.

agrafe noun F 1 staple; 2 hook (on a garment).

agrafer verb [1] 1 to staple; 2 to fasten.

agrafeuse noun F stapler.

agrandir verb [2] to enlarge.

agrandissement noun M enlargement (of a photo).

agréable adjective pleasant, nice.

agréé adjective 1 registered; 2 authorized.

agréer verb [32] 1 to agree to; 2 **veuillez agréer l'expression de mes sentiments distingués** Yours faithfully, Yours sincerely (this is one of a number of fixed expressions used to end any formal or business letter).

agresser verb [1] 1 to attack; 2 to mug.

agresseur noun M attacker.

agressif (F **agressive**) adjective aggressive.

agression noun F 1 attack; 2 mugging.

agressivité noun F aggressiveness.

agricole adjective agricultural.

agriculteur, agricultrice noun M, F farmer.

ahuri adjective amazed, stunned.

ai verb SEE **avoir**.

aide[1] noun M & F assistant.

aide[2] noun F 1 help; **avec l'aide de Claire** with Claire's help; **venir à l'aide de quelqu'un** to help somebody; 2 aid (financial aid given to a person or a country).

aider verb [1] 1 to help; **il m'a aidé à mettre la table** he helped me set the table; **est-ce que je peux t'aider?** would you like some help?; 2 to give aid to (financial aid to a person, group, or country).

aigle noun M & F eagle.

aiglefin noun M haddock.

aigre adjective 1 sour; 2 sharp.

aiguille noun F 1 needle; **une aiguille à coudre** a sewing needle; **une aiguille à tricoter** a knitting needle; 2 hand (of a clock or watch).

aiguilleur du ciel noun M air traffic controller.

aiguiser verb [1] to sharpen.

ail noun M garlic.

aile noun F wing; ★ **voler de ses propres ailes** to stand on your own two feet (literally: to fly with your own wings).

ailleurs adverb 1 elsewhere, somewhere else; 2 **d'ailleurs** besides, moreover; 3 **par ailleurs** also, in addition.

aimable adjective kind, nice; **vous êtes très aimable** that's very kind of you.

aimant noun M magnet.

aimer verb [1] **1** to like; est-ce que
tu aimes les fraises? do you like
strawberries?; **aimer faire quelque
chose** to like doing something; elle
aime aller au cinéma she likes going
to the cinema; elle aimerait aller au
cinéma she'd like to go to the
cinema; **2** aimer mieux to prefer;
j'aime mieux les fraises que les
framboises I prefer strawberries to
raspberries, I like strawberries better
than raspberries; **j'aimerais mieux
aller au cinéma** I'd prefer to go to
the cinema, I'd rather go to the
cinema; **3** to love; **je t'aime** I love
you; **4** s'aimer to like each other, to
love each other.

aîné, aînée noun M, F l'aîné(e) the
eldest, the oldest (child).
adjective elder, older (of two);
eldest, oldest (of more than two);
leur fille aînée their elder (or eldest)
daughter.

ainsi adverb **1** thus; **2** in this way;
3 ainsi que as well as, along with.

aïoli noun M garlic mayonnaise.

air noun M **1** air; aller prendre l'air
to go out and get some fresh air;
2 un courant d'air a draught;
3 avoir l'air (...) to look (...);
avoir l'air bon to look good; avoir l'air
fatigué to look tired; **avoir l'air
de** to look like; il a l'air d'un policier
he looks like a policeman; **5** avoir
l'air d'être to look as if you are; elle
a l'air d'être perdue she looks as if
she's lost; **6** avoir l'air de faire to
look as if you are doing; il a l'air de
comprendre he looks as if he

understands; **7** sourire d'un air
heureux to smile happily; **8** tune.

air bag™ noun M air bag (in a car).

aire de jeu noun F playground.

aire de pique-nique noun F
picnic area.

aire de services noun F
motorway service station.

aise noun F être à l'aise to be
comfortable, to feel at ease; être mal
à l'aise to feel uncomfortable.

aisselle noun F armpit.

ajout noun M addition.

ajouter verb [1] to add; ajoutez un
œuf add an egg.

alarme noun F alarm; sonner
l'alarme to sound the alarm.

album noun M album.

album de bandes dessinées
noun M comic book.

album de photos noun M
photograph album.

album de timbres noun M stamp
album.

alcool noun M alcohol.

alcoolique noun M & F,
adjective alcoholic.

alcoolisé adjective une boisson
alcoolisée an alcoholic drink; une
boisson non alcoolisée a non-
alcoholic drink.

alcootest noun M Breathalyzer™.

alcôve noun F alcove.

alentours plural noun M
1 surroundings; **2** aux alentours

de in the vicinity (or neighbourhood) of.

algèbre noun F algebra.

Algérie noun F Algeria.

algérien (F **algérienne**) adjective Algerian.

algues plural noun F seaweed.

aliment noun M food.

alimentaire adjective des produits alimentaires food products; l'industrie alimentaire the food industry.

alimentation noun F 1 groceries; 2 diet.

allée noun F path, drive.

alléger verb [15] 1 to lighten; 2 to reduce.

Allemagne noun F Germany.

allemand noun M, adjective German.

Allemand, Allemande noun M, F German (person).

aller[1] verb [7] 1 to go; aller à Paris to go to Paris; je vais à Paris I'm going to Paris, I go to Paris; 2 (used with another verb in much the same way as 'going to' is used in English) je vais écrire à ma mère ce soir I'm going to write to my mother this evening; 3 (comment) ça va? how are you?; ça va bien I'm fine; comment va ta mère? how's your mother?; elle va bien she's fine; 4 to suit; cette robe te va bien that dress really suits you; est-ce que jeudi te va? does Thursday suit you?; 5 s'en aller to leave; je m'en vais! I'm off!

aller[2] noun M 1 faire des allers et retours to go to and fro; 2 un aller-simple a single ticket; un aller-retour a return ticket; Avignon aller simple, s'il vous plaît a single to Avignon please.

allergie noun F allergy.

allergique adjective être allergique à to be allergic to.

alliance noun F 1 wedding ring; 2 alliance.

alligator noun M alligator.

allô hello (only used on the telephone).

allocation noun F benefit, allowance.

allocation chômage noun F unemployment benefit.

allocations familiales plural noun F family allowance.

allonger verb [52] 1 to lengthen; 2 to extend; 3 s'allonger to lie down.

allumer verb [1] 1 to light; allumer le feu to light the fire; 2 to switch on; allumer la lampe to switch on the lamp; 3 to switch on the lights.

allumette noun F match; une boîte d'allumettes a box of matches.

allure noun F 1 speed; à toute allure at top speed; 2 appearance (of a person).

alors adverb 1 then, at that time; elle travaillait alors à Paris she was working in Paris then; 2 so; alors, comment ça va? so how are you?; 3 alors que while; alors qu'elle

faisait ses devoirs while she was doing her homework.

alouette noun F skylark.

Alpes noun F **les Alpes** the Alps.

alphabet noun M alphabet.

alphabétique adjective alphabetical; **dans l'ordre alphabétique, par ordre alphabétique** in alphabetical order.

alpin adjective alpine.

alpinisme noun M mountaineering.

alternatif (F **alternative**) adjective alternative.

altitude noun F altitude.

alu noun M (informal) aluminium; **du papier alu** kitchen foil.

aluminium noun M aluminium.

amalgame noun M mixture.

amande noun F 1 almond; 2 kernel (of a fruit stone).

amant noun M lover.

amateur noun M 1 enthusiast; **un amateur de musique** a music lover; adjective amateur; **un photographe amateur** an amateur photographer.

ambassade noun F embassy; **l'ambassade de France** the French Embassy.

ambassadeur noun M ambassador.

ambiance noun F atmosphere; **une bonne ambiance** a good atmosphere.

ambigu (F **ambiguë**) adjective ambiguous.

ambitieux (F **ambitieuse**) adjective ambitious.

ambition noun F ambition.

ambulance noun F ambulance.

ambulancier, ambulancière noun M, F ambulance driver.

âme noun F soul.

amélioration noun F improvement.

améliorer, s'améliorer verb [1] to improve.

aménagé adjective 1 equipped; **une cuisine aménagée** an equipped kitchen; 2 converted.

aménager verb [52] 1 to convert, to do up (a building, a room, etc); 2 to develop (an area); 3 to construct, to improve (a road or road system).

amende noun F fine; **une amende de 500 francs** a 500-franc fine.

amener verb [50] 1 to bring; **elle a amené son cousin** she brought her cousin (with her); 2 to take; **amener un enfant à l'école** to take a child to school.

amer (F **amère**) adjective bitter.

américain adjective American.

Américain, Américaine noun M, F American.

Amérique noun F America.

ami, amie noun M, F friend; **un ami à moi** a friend of mine; **un ami à Lisa** a friend of Lisa's. adjective friendly.

amiante noun M asbestos.

amical (M plural **amicaux**) adjective
friendly.

amicale noun F association.

amicalement adverb 1 in a
friendly way; 2 Best wishes (at the
end of a letter).

amitié noun F 1 friendship; **faire
quelque chose par amitié** to do
something out of friendship;
2 **amitiés** love (at the end of a
letter).

amortisseur noun M shock
absorber.

amour noun M love.

amoureux (F **amoureuse**) adjective
in love; **être amoureux de** to be in
love with.

amour-propre noun M self-
esteem.

amovible adjective detachable.

amphi noun M (informal) lecture
theatre (in a university).

amphithéâtre noun M
1 amphitheatre; 2 lecture theatre.

ample adjective 1 loose-fitting
(jacket, dress, etc); 2 ample
(quantity).

ampleur noun F size, scope.

ampli noun M (informal) amplifier.

amplificateur noun M amplifier.

ampoule noun F 1 light bulb;
2 blister.

amusant adjective 1 funny; **une
histoire amusante** a funny story;
2 entertaining.

amuse-gueule noun M **des
amuse-gueule** nibbles (crisps,
nuts, etc).

amuser verb [1] 1 to amuse; 2 to
entertain; 3 **s'amuser** to play;
4 **s'amuser** to enjoy oneself, to have
a good time; **on s'est bien amusé**
we really enjoyed ourselves, we had
a really good time.

an noun M year; **elle a dix ans** she's
ten (years old); **le nouvel an, le jour
de l'an** New Year's Day; ★ **bon an,
mal an** year in, year out (literally:
good year, bad year).

analphabète adjective illiterate.

analyse noun F 1 analysis; 2 **une
analyse de sang** a blood test.

analyser verb [1] to analyse.

ananas noun M pineapple.

anatomie noun F anatomy.

ancêtre noun M & F ancestor.

anchois noun M anchovy.

ancien (F **ancienne**) adjective
1 (coming before a noun) former;
l'ancien président the former
president, the ex-president; **mon
ancienne école** my old school; **un
ancien élève** a former pupil;
2 (coming after a noun) old; **une
maison ancienne** an old house; **une
table ancienne** an antique table.

ancien combattant noun M war
veteran.

âne noun M donkey.

anémone noun F anemone.

anesthésie noun F anaesthesia;
une anesthésie an anaesthetic.

anesthésiste noun M & F anaesthetist.

ange noun M angel; ★ être aux anges to be over the moon, to be absolutely delighted (*literally: to be at the level of the angels*).

angine noun F throat infection; avoir une angine to have a throat infection.

anglais noun M English; parler l'anglais to speak English.
adjective English.

Anglais, Anglaise noun M, F Englishman, Englishwoman; les Anglais the English; il y a une Anglaise dans notre classe there's an English girl in our class.

angle noun M 1 angle; un angle droit a right angle; 2 corner; à l'angle de la rue at the corner of the street; le magasin qui fait l'angle the shop on the corner.

Angleterre noun F England; en Angleterre in (or to) England; aller en Angleterre to go to England.

Anglo-Normande adjective les îles Anglo-Normandes the Channel Islands.

anglophone noun M & F English speaker.
adjective English-speaking.

angoisse noun F anxiety.

angoissé adjective anxious.

anguille noun F eel.

animal (*plural* animaux) noun M animal.

animateur, animatrice noun M, F 1 group leader; 2 organizer; 3 presenter.

animation noun F 1 liveliness, life; il y a beaucoup d'animation dans le quartier le soir there's a lot going on in the area at night; 2 organization (*of a group, a programme, etc*).

animé adjective 1 lively (*person or discussion*); 2 busy (*place*).

animer verb [1] 1 to run (*a course*); 2 to lead (*a group*); 3 to present (*a programme or a show*); 4 to liven up (*an occasion*); 5 s'animer to liven up.

anis noun M aniseed.

anneau noun M ring.

année noun F year; l'année prochaine next year; l'année dernière last year; les années 70 the seventies; Bonne année Happy New Year.

anniversaire noun M 1 birthday; fêter son anniversaire to celebrate one's birthday; Bon anniversaire, Joyeux anniversaire Happy Birthday; 2 anniversary.

annonce noun F 1 advertisement; les petites annonces the small ads (*in a newspaper*); 2 announcement; 3 sign.

annoncer verb [61] 1 to announce; 2 to forecast; ils annoncent de la neige pour demain snow is forecast for tomorrow.

annuaire noun M directory; l'annuaire téléphonique the telephone directory.

annuel (F **annuelle**) *adjective*
annual, yearly.

annuler *verb* [1] to cancel; **le vol a été annulé** the flight has been cancelled.

anonyme *adjective* anonymous.

anorak *noun* M anorak.

anorexie *noun* F anorexia.

anormal (M *plural* **anormaux**) *adjective* abnormal.

anse *noun* F handle (*of a basket, cup, jug, or teapot*).

Antarctique *noun* M
l'Antarctique the Antarctic.

antenne *noun* F 1 aerial (*for a radio or television*); 2 antenna (*of an insect, a radio mast, or a spacecraft*).

anthropologie *noun* F
anthropology.

antibiotique *noun* M antibiotic; **prendre des antibiotiques** to be on antibiotics.

antichoc *adjective* shockproof; **un casque antichoc** a crash helmet.

anticiper *verb* [1] to foresee, to anticipate.

antidérapant *adjective* nonslip, nonskid.

antidote *noun* M antidote.

antigel *noun* M antifreeze.

antillais *adjective* West Indian.

Antilles *plural noun* F **les Antilles** the West Indies.

antilope *noun* F antelope.

antipathique *adjective*
unpleasant.

antiquaire *noun* M & F antique dealer.

antiquité *noun* F antique.

antiseptique *noun* M, *adjective* antiseptic.

antitabac *adjective* antismoking.

antiterroriste *adjective*
antiterrorist.

antivol *noun* M anti-theft device.

anxieux (F **anxieuse**) *adjective*
anxious.

août *noun* M August; **en août, au mois d'août** in August.

apercevoir *verb* [66] 1 to catch sight of; 2 **s'apercevoir de** to notice; **s'apercevoir que** to notice that.

aperçu *noun* M 1 insight; 2 glimpse.

apéritif *noun* M drink (*usually alcoholic, before a meal*).

aphte *noun* M mouth ulcer.

aplatir *verb* [2] 1 to flatten; 2 to smooth out.

apostrophe *noun* F apostrophe.

apparaître *verb* [57] 1 to appear; 2 to seem; **il apparaît que** it seems that.

appareil *noun* M 1 device, appliance, piece of equipment; 2 telephone; **c'est Paul à l'appareil** it's Paul speaking; 3 **un appareil (dentaire)** a brace (*for teeth*).

appareil photo *noun* M camera.

apparemment *adverb* apparently.

apparence *noun* F appearance.

apparent *adjective* 1 visible, obvious; 2 apparent.

apparition *noun* F appearance.

appartement *noun* M flat; 'appartement à louer' 'flat to let'.

appartenir *verb* [81] **appartenir à** to belong to; **est-ce que ce stylo t'appartient?** is this pen belong to you?, is this pen yours?; **à qui appartiennent ces chaussures?** who do these shoes belong to?

appel *noun* M 1 call, appeal; **un appel d'aide** a call for help; 2 **un appel (téléphonique)** a telephone call; 3 **faire appel à** to appeal to; 4 **faire l'appel** to take the register (*at school*).

appeler *verb* [18] 1 to call; **ils l'ont appelé Roger** they called him Roger; 2 **s'appeler** to be called; **il s'appelle Frank** he's called Frank, his name is Frank; **je m'appelle Anne** my name is Anne; **comment t'appelles-tu?, tu t'appelles comment?** what's your name?; 3 to phone; 4 to call; **appeler un taxi** to call a taxi.

appendicite *noun* F appendicitis.

appétissant *adjective* appetizing.

appétit *noun* M appetite; 'bon appétit' 'enjoy your meal'.

applaudir *verb* [2] to applaud.

applaudissements *plural noun* M applause.

application *noun* F 1 care; 2 application.

appliquer *verb* [1] 1 to apply; 2 **s'appliquer** to take care; 3 **s'appliquer à** to apply to; **cela ne s'applique pas à vous** that doesn't apply to you.

apporter *verb* [1] to bring.

apprécier *verb* [1] to appreciate.

appréhender *verb* [1] 1 to arrest; 2 to dread.

apprenant, apprenante *noun* M, F learner.

apprendre *verb* [64] 1 to learn; **apprendre à lire** to learn to read; 2 to hear; **j'ai appris que tu vas partir** I hear you're leaving; 3 to teach; **apprendre quelque chose à quelqu'un** to teach somebody something; **elle leur apprend le français** she's teaching them French; **elle leur apprend à parler français** she's teaching them to speak French.

approche *noun* F approach.

approcher *verb* [1] 1 to move (something) closer; **approche ta chaise** move your chair closer; **approche ta chaise de la table** move your chair closer to the table; 2 **approcher quelqu'un** to go up to somebody; 3 **s'approcher de quelque chose** to go (or come) near to something.

approprié *adjective* appropriate.

approuver *verb* [1] 1 to approve of; 2 to approve (*a document, project, budget, etc*).

approximatif (F **approximative**) *adjective* approximate, rough.

approximativement adverb
approximately, roughly.

appui noun M support.

appuyer verb [41] **1** **appuyer sur quelque chose** to press something; **appuie sur le bouton** press the button; **2** to lean; **appuyer quelque chose contre le mur** to lean something against the wall.

après adverb afterwards, later; **une heure après** an hour later; **peu après** shortly afterwards; **longtemps après** a long time later; preposition **1** after; **après dix heures** after ten o'clock; **après l'école** after school; **2** **après avoir fait** after doing; **3** **après que** after.

après-demain adverb the day after tomorrow.

après-midi noun M or F afternoon; **cet après-midi** this afternoon; **demain après-midi** tomorrow afternoon; **hier après-midi** yesterday afternoon; **tous les après-midi** every afternoon.

aquarelle noun F watercolours; **une aquarelle** a watercolour (painting).

aquarium noun M aquarium, fish tank.

arabe noun M Arabic.
adjective **1** Arab; **2** Arabic.

Arabe noun M & F Arab.

araignée noun F spider; **une toile d'araignée** a spider's web.

arbitraire adjective arbitrary.

arbitre noun M referee, umpire.

arbre noun M tree.

arc noun M **1** bow (as in 'bow and arrow'); **2** arch.

arc-en-ciel noun M rainbow.

archéologie noun F archeology.

archéologue noun M & F archeologist.

archet noun M bow (for a musical instrument such as a violin).

archevêque noun M archbishop.

architecte noun M & F architect.

architecture noun F architecture.

Arctique noun M **l'Arctique** the Arctic.

ardoise noun F slate.

arène noun F **1** arena; **2** bullring.

arête noun F fishbone.

argent noun M **1** money; **dépenser de l'argent** to spend money; **2** silver; **une cuillère en argent** a silver spoon.

argent de poche noun M pocket money.

argot noun M slang.

aristocrate noun M & F aristocrat.

aristocratie noun F aristocracy.

arithmétique noun F arithmetic.

arme noun F weapon.

armé adjective **1** armed. **2** **armé de** armed with, equipped with.

arme à feu noun F firearm.

armée noun F army.

armée de l'air noun F Air Force.

armée de terre noun F Army.

armoire noun F 1 cupboard;
2 wardrobe.

aromates plural noun M herbs and
spices.

aromathérapie noun F
aromatherapy.

aromatisé adjective flavoured.

arôme noun M 1 flavouring;
2 aroma.

arracher verb [1] 1 arracher
quelque chose à quelqu'un to
snatch something from somebody;
2 to rip out, to rip off (a page or
pages); 3 to pull up (weeds or
vegetables).

arrangement noun M
arrangement.

arranger verb [52] 1 to arrange;
arranger une réunion to arrange a
meeting; 2 to arrange (flowers,
books, etc). 3 to sort out; 4 to fix;
5 s'arranger to get better; ça va
s'arranger it will sort itself out;
6 s'arranger avec quelqu'un to sort
it out with somebody; tu t'arranges
avec Paul sort it out with Paul.

arrestation noun F arrest.

arrêt noun M 1 stop; un arrêt de
bus a bus stop; 2 sans arrêt non-
stop.

arrêter verb [1] 1 to stop; arrêter la
voiture to stop the car; 2 to switch
off (an engine, a machine, etc);
3 arrêter de faire to stop doing; il a
arrêté de fumer he's stopped
smoking; elle n'arrête pas de
travailler she never stops working;
4 s'arrêter to stop; on va s'arrêter à

la boulangerie we'll stop at the
baker's.

arrhes plural noun F deposit;
verser des arrhes to pay a deposit.

arrière noun M back; à l'arrière in
the back (of a car); regarder en
arrière to look back.
adjective back (door, pocket, etc).

arrière-goût noun M aftertaste.

arrière-grand-mère noun F
great-grandmother.

arrière-grand-père noun M
great-grandfather.

arrière-grands-parents plural
noun M great-grandparents.

arrière-petits-enfants plural
noun M great-grandchildren.

arrivée noun F arrival.

arriver verb [1] 1 to arrive; arriver à
Londres to arrive in London, to get
to London; je suis arrivé à cinq
heures I arrived at five o'clock, I got
there (or here) at five o'clock;
j'arrive just coming!; 2 to
happen; un accident est arrivé an
accident has happened; tu sais ce
qui m'est arrivé? do you know what
happened to me?; 3 arriver à faire
to manage to do; je n'arrive pas à
tourner la clef I can't manage to
turn the key.

arrogant adjective arrogant.

arrondi adjective rounded.

arrondissement noun M
arrondissement; elle habite à Paris
dans le neuvième arrondissement
she lives in Paris in the ninth
arrondissement (large French cities

...e divided into numbered
administrative areas called
'arrondissements'.

arroser verb [1] to water; **arroser les
plantes** to water the plants; **on va
arroser l'anniversaire de mon frère**
we're going to have a few drinks to
celebrate my brother's birthday.

arrosoir noun M watering can.

art noun M art; **une galerie d'art** an
art gallery; **l'art de faire** the art of
doing.

art dramatique noun M drama.

artère noun F 1 artery; 2 arterial
road; 3 main road.

arthrite noun F arthritis.

artichaut noun M artichoke.

article noun M 1 article (*in a
newspaper, magazine, etc*); 2 item
(*for sale*); **articles de sport** sports
equipment; **articles de toilette**
toiletries; 3 article (*in grammar*);
l'article défini the definite article;
l'article indéfini the indefinite
article.

articulation noun F joint.

artificiel (F **artificielle**) adjective
artificial.

artisan noun M craftsman.

artisanal (M plural **artisanaux**)
adjective 1 traditional; 2 hand-
crafted.

artisanat noun M arts and crafts.

artiste noun M & F 1 artist;
2 performer.

as¹ verb SEE avoir.

as² noun M ace.

ascenseur noun M lift; **prendre
l'ascenseur** to take the lift.

asiatique adjective Asian.

Asie noun F Asia.

asile noun M 1 refuge; 2 **le droit
d'asile** political asylum.

aspect noun M 1 aspect;
2 appearance; **d'un aspect bizarre**
strange-looking; 3 side; **l'aspect
positif** the positive side.

asperger verb [52] to sprinkle.

asperges plural noun F asparagus.

asphyxier, s'asphyxier verb [1]
to suffocate.

aspirateur noun M vacuum
cleaner.

aspirine noun F aspirin.

assaisonnement noun M
1 seasoning; 2 dressing.

assaisonner verb [1] 1 to season;
2 to put the dressing on (*a salad*).

assassin, assassine noun M, F
murderer.

assassinat noun M murder.

assassiner verb [1] to murder.

assemblée noun F meeting.

assembler verb [1] 1 to put
together, to assemble (*a kit, a
machine, etc*); 2 to gather
together; 3 **s'assembler** to gather
(*of a group, crowd, demonstration,
etc*); ★ **qui se ressemble
s'assemble** birds of a feather flock
together (*literally: those who are
similar gather together*).

asseoir verb [20] s'asseoir to sit down; s'asseoir sur une chaise to sit down on a chair; assieds-toi take a seat; asseyez-vous do sit down; SEE ALSO **assis**.

assez adverb 1 assez de enough; assez de pain enough bread; 2 enough; elle ne mange pas assez she doesn't eat enough; 3 enough; est-ce que l'eau est assez chaude? is the water hot enough?; 4 quite; leur maison est assez grande their house is quite big; assez souvent quite often; assez joli quite pretty; 5 j'en ai assez (de) (informal) I'm fed up (with).

assiette noun F plate; une assiette plate a dinner plate; une assiette creuse, une assiette à soupe a soup plate; ★ je ne suis pas dans mon assiette aujourd'hui I'm not my usual self today.

assis adjective être assis to be sitting; elle était assise dans un fauteuil she was sitting in an armchair; rester assis to remain seated.

assistance noun F 1 audience; dans l'assistance in the audience; 2 assistance.

assistant, assistante noun M, F assistant.

assister verb [1] 1 to assist; 2 to aid (a country, the poor, etc); 3 assister à to be present at, to be at; j'ai assisté à leur mariage I was at their wedding.

association noun F association.

associé, associée noun M, F associate, partner.

associer verb [1] 1 associer quelqu'un à quelque chose to include somebody in something; 2 s'associer à un groupe to join a group; 3 s'associer pour faire to get together to do.

assommer verb [1] 1 assommer quelqu'un to knock somebody senseless; 2 assommer quelqu'un (informal) to bore somebody stiff; 3 être assommé par une nouvelle to be stunned by a piece of news.

assorti adjective matching; rideaux et coussins assortis matching curtains and cushions; une veste assortie à sa robe a jacket to match her dress.

assortiment noun M assortment, selection.

assortir verb [2] 1 to match; 2 s'assortir à to match.

assouplissant noun M fabric softener.

assourdir verb [2] 1 to deafen; 2 to muffle.

assourdissant adjective deafening.

assumer verb [1] 1 assumer la responsabilité de quelque chose to take responsibility for something; assumer une fonction to hold a position.

assurance noun F 1 confidence; avec assurance confidently; 2 insurance.

assuré adjective 1 confident; 2 insured.

assurer verb [1] 1 to assure; je vous assure que c'est vrai I assure you it's true; **2** to insure; **assurer sa voiture** to insure one's car; **3** to provide (*a service*); **4** to carry out (*a task or a responsibility*); **5 s'assurer** to make sure.

astérisque *noun* M asterisk.

asthmatique *adjective* asthmatic.

asthme *noun* M asthma.

asticot *noun* M maggot.

astiquer *verb* [1] to polish.

astrologie *noun* F astrology.

astrologue *noun* M & F astrologer.

astronome *noun* M & F astronomer.

astronomie *noun* F astronomy.

astronomique *adjective* astronomical.

astuce *noun* F **1** cleverness; **2 une astuce** a trick (*for managing to do something*); **il doit y avoir une astuce** there must be a trick to it.

astucieux (F **astucieuse**) *adjective* clever.

atelier *noun* M **1** workshop; **2** studio (*of an artist, a sculptor, etc*); **3** work group.

athée *noun* M & F atheist.

Athènes *noun* Athens.

athlète *noun* M & F athlete.

athlétique *adjective* athletic.

athlétisme *noun* M athletics.

Atlantique *noun* M **l'Atlantique** the Atlantic.

atlas *noun* M atlas.

atmosphère *noun* F atmosphere.

atome *noun* M atom.

atomique *adjective* atomic.

atomiseur *noun* M spray, atomizer.

atout *noun* M **1** trump card; **c'est atout pique** spades are trumps; **2** asset, advantage.

atroce *adjective* dreadful, terrible.

atrocité *noun* F **1** atrocity; **2** monstrosity.

attachant *adjective* lovable.

attache *noun* F **1** tie, string, strap; **2 attaches familiales** family ties.

attacher *verb* [1] **1 attacher ses cheveux** to tie (or fix) your hair back; **2 s'attacher** to stick (*to the pan*).

attaque *noun* F attack.

attaquer *verb* [1] **1** to attack; **2** to tackle (*a job*).

attarder *verb* [1] **s'attarder** to linger.

atteindre *verb* [60] **1** to reach; **2** to achieve.

atteint *adjective* **être atteint d'une maladie** to be suffering from an illness.

attendant *in phrase* **en attendant** meanwhile, in the meantime.

attendre *verb* [3] **1** to wait; **tu peux attendre deux minutes?** can you wait for two minutes?; **2** to wait for; **j'attends le bus** I'm waiting for the bus; **je t'attends dehors** I'll wait for you outside; **3 s'attendre à** to expect.

attendrissant *adjective* touching.

attentat *noun* M **1** un attentat (à la bombe) a bomb attack, a bombing; **2** assassination attempt.

attente *noun* F wait; une attente de vingt minutes a twenty-minute wait.

attentif (F attentive) *adjective* **1** attentive; **2** careful.

attention *noun* F **1** attention; **2** faire attention à to be careful of; **3** attention! watch out!

atterrir *verb* [2] to land.

atterrissage *noun* M landing.

attirant *adjective* attractive.

attirer *verb* [1] to attract; attirer l'attention de quelqu'un sur quelque chose to attract (or draw) somebody's attention to something.

attitude *noun* F attitude.

attraction *noun* F attraction.

attraper *verb* [1] **1** to catch; **2** attraper un rhume to catch a cold; **3** to catch hold of.

attrayant *adjective* attractive.

attrister *verb* [1] to sadden.

au SEE **à**.

aube *noun* F dawn; à l'aube at dawn.

aubépine *noun* F hawthorn.

auberge *noun* F inn; ★ on n'est pas sorti de l'auberge our problems are not over yet (*literally: we're not out of the inn*).

auberge de jeunesse *noun* F youth hostel.

aubergine *noun* F aubergine.

aucun *adjective* no; en aucun cas under no circumstances; sans aucun doute without any doubt. *pronoun* none; aucun des deux neither of them; aucun d'entre eux none of them.

aucunement *adverb* in no way.

audace *noun* F daring.

audacieux (F audacieuse) *adjective* daring.

au-delà de *preposition* beyond.

au-dessous *adverb* **1** underneath; **2** below; **3** au-dessous de underneath; au-dessous de la table underneath the table; **4** au-dessous de below; au-dessous de la limite below the limit.

au-dessus *adverb* **1** above; **2** au-dessus de above.

audience *noun* F audience.

audiovisuel (F audiovisuelle) *adjective* audiovisual.

auditeur, auditrice *noun* M, F listener.

audition *noun* F audition.

augmentation *noun* F increase; l'augmentation des prix the increase in prices; une augmentation de salaire a pay rise.

augmenter *verb* [1] **1** to raise, to increase; augmenter les prix to raise prices; **2** to rise, to go up; le prix a augmenté the price has gone up.

aujourd'hui *adverb* today; **nous sommes lundi aujourd'hui** today is Monday.

auparavant *adverb* before, beforehand.

auprès de *preposition* beside, next to.

auquel *pronoun* **le garçon auquel je parle** the boy I'm talking to.

aura, aurai, auras, aurez, aurons, auront *verb* SEE **avoir**.

au revoir *exclamation* goodbye.

aussi *adverb* **1** also, too; **moi aussi me too**; **j'ai aussi invité ton frère** I also invited your brother, I invited your brother as well; **2 aussi...que** as...as; **mon panier est aussi lourd que le tien** my basket is as heavy as yours; **3 aussi bien que** as well as; **les enfants aussi bien que les adultes** children as well as adults.
conjunction so, therefore.

aussitôt *adverb* immediately.

Australie *noun* F Australia.

Australien, Australienne *noun* M, F Australian.

australien (F **australienne**) *adjective* Australian.

autant *adverb* **1** as much, so much; **je n'ai jamais mangé autant** I've never eaten so much; **2 autant que** as much as, as many as; **tu en as autant que moi** you have as much (or as many) as me; **3 autant de...que** as much...as, as many...as; **tu as autant de problèmes que moi** you have as many problems as I do.

autel *noun* M altar.

auteur *noun* M author.

authentique *adjective* genuine.

auto *noun* F car.

autobiographie *noun* F autobiography.

autobus *noun* M bus.

autocar *noun* M coach.

autocollant *noun* M sticker.
adjective self-adhesive.

autodéfense *noun* F self-defence.

auto-école *noun* F driving school.

automate *noun* M robot.

automatique *adjective* automatic.

automatiquement *adverb* automatically.

automne *noun* M autumn; **en automne** in autumn.

automobile *noun* F car.
adjective **l'industrie automobile** the car industry.

automobiliste *noun* M & F motorist.

autoradio *noun* M car radio.

autorisation *noun* F **1** permission; **2** permit.

autoriser *verb* [1] **1** to allow, to authorize; **2 autoriser quelqu'un à faire** to allow somebody to do.

autorité *noun* F authority.

autoroute *noun* F motorway; **l'autoroute de l'information** the information super-highway.

avantage

auto-stop noun M hitchhiking;
faire de l'auto-stop to hitchhike.

**auto-stoppeur, auto-
stoppeuse** noun M, F
hitchhiker.

autour adverb 1 around; 2 **autour
de** round, around; **autour de la
table** round the table.

autre adjective 1 other; **l'autre
couteau** the other knife; **l'autre
jour** the other day; 2 **un/une autre**
another; **tu peux me passer un autre
verre?** can you pass me another
glass?; 3 **quelqu'un d'autre**
somebody else; **personne d'autre**
nobody else.
pronoun 1 **un/une autre** another
one; **donne-moi un autre** give me
another one; 2 **les autres** the
others; **où sont les autres?** where
are the others?

autrefois adverb in the past, in the
old days.

autrement adverb 1 differently;
autrement dit in other words;
2 otherwise.

autre part adverb somewhere else.

Autriche noun F Austria.

Autrichien, Autrichienne noun
M, F Austrian.

autrichien (F **autrichienne**)
adjective Austrian.

autruche noun F ostrich.

aux SEE **à**.

auxiliaire noun M & F,
adjective auxiliary.

auxquelles pronoun **les filles
auxquelles je parlais** the girls I was
talking to.

auxquels pronoun **les garçons
auxquels je parlais** the boys I was
talking to.

avalanche noun F avalanche.

avaler verb [1] 1 to swallow; 2 to
inhale.

avance noun F 1 advance,
progress; 2 **je suis arrivé dix
minutes en avance** I arrived ten
minutes early; **avoir dix minutes
d'avance** to be ten minutes early;
3 **être en avance** to be early; 4 **à
l'avance** in advance.

avancer verb [61] 1 to move
forward, to advance; 2 **avancer
quelque chose** to move something
forward; 3 **ma montre avance de
cinq minutes** my watch is five
minutes fast.

avant adverb 1 before; **longtemps
avant** a long time before;
2 forward; **plus avant** further
forward.
preposition 1 before; **avant Noël**
before Christmas; **avant six heures**
before six o'clock; **elle est arrivée
avant moi** she arrived before me;
2 **avant de faire** before doing; **avant
de partir, je vais téléphoner à ma
mère** before leaving (or before I
leave) I'll phone my mother;
3 **avant que** before.
noun M front.
adjective front; **la roue avant** the
front wheel.

avantage noun M advantage.

avantageux (F avantageuse)
adjective 1 des prix avantageux
attractive prices; 2 des conditions
avantageuses favourable
conditions.

avant-bras *noun* M forearm.

avant-dernier, avant-dernière
noun M, F l'avant-dernier the last
but one.
adjective second last, last but one.

avant-hier *adverb* the day before
yesterday.

avare *noun* M & F miser.
adjective mean, miserly.

avec *preposition* with; avec Marie
with Marie; avec un couteau with a
knife; avec ça? anything else? (*in a
shop*).

avenir *noun* M future; l'avenir the
future; à l'avenir in the future.

aventure *noun* F adventure.

avenue *noun* F avenue.

averse *noun* F shower.

avertir *verb* [2] 1 to inform; 2 to
warn.

avertissement *noun* M warning.

aveuglant *adjective* blinding.

aveugle *adjective* blind.

aveuglément *adverb* blindly.

aveugler *verb* [1] to blind.

avez *verb* SEE avoir.

aviation *noun* F 1 aviation;
2 aircraft industry; 3 flying; 4 air
force.

avion *noun* M aeroplane, plane;
aller à Paris en avion to go to Paris

by plane, to fly to Paris; par avion by
airmail.

aviron *noun* M 1 rowing; faire de
l'aviron to row; 2 oar.

avis *noun* M 1 opinion; à mon avis
in my opinion; 2 changer d'avis to
change one's mind; 3 notice.

avocat¹, avocate *noun* M, F
1 solicitor; 2 barrister.

avocat² *noun* M avocado (pear).

avoine *noun* F oats; des flocons
d'avoine porridge oats.

avoir *verb* [5] 1 to have (got); elle a
trois frères she has (or she's got)
three brothers; tu as beaucoup de
livres you have (or you've got) a lot
of books; 2 (*talking about age*)
avoir dix ans to be ten; Claudie a
dix ans Claudie's ten; quel âge a-
t-il? how old is he? 3 avoir chaud
to be hot; j'ai chaud I'm hot; j'ai
froid I'm cold; 4 (*used with another
verb, like 'have' in English, to form
past tenses*) j'ai perdu mon stylo
I have lost my pen; j'ai vu ta mère
hier I saw your mother yesterday;
5 j'en ai pour dix minutes it'll take
me ten minutes; 6 il y a there is,
there are; il y a un livre sur la table
there's a book on the table; il y a trois
livres sur la table there are three
books on the table; 7 il y a ago;
il y a trois ans three years ago;
8 qu'est-ce qu'il y a? what's the
matter?

avons *verb* SEE avoir.

avortement *noun* M abortion.

avouer *verb* [1] to confess, to admit.

avril *noun* M April; **en avril, au mois d'avril** in April.

azalée *noun* F azalea.

azote *noun* M nitrogen.

B b

babouin *noun* M baboon.

baby-foot *noun* M table football; **jouer au baby-foot** to play table football; **on va faire une partie de baby-foot** we're going to have a game of table football.

bac *noun* M 1 (*informal*) SHORT FOR baccalauréat; 2 tub.

bac à glace *noun* M ice tray.

baccalauréat *noun* M baccalaureate (*school-leaving certificate sat at the age of 17–18 and giving access to higher education*); **passer le baccalauréat** to sit the baccalaureate; **réussir au baccalauréat** to pass the baccalaureate.

bâche *noun* F tarpaulin.

badaud, badaude *noun* M, F passerby, onlooker.

baffe *noun* F (*informal*) slap.

baffle *noun* M speaker (*on a music system*).

bagage *noun* M **un bagage** a piece of luggage; **des bagages** luggage; **où sont tes bagages?** where is your luggage?; **j'ai fait mes bagages** I've packed.

bagarre *noun* F fight.

bagarrer *verb* [1] **se bagarrer** to fight.

bagnole *noun* F (*informal*) car.

bague *noun* F ring.

baguette *noun* F 1 baguette, French bread stick; 2 stick; 3 drumstick; 4 chopstick.

baguette magique *noun* F magic wand.

baie *noun* 1 bay (*on the sea*); 2 berry; 3 **une baie vitrée** a picture window.

baignade *noun* F swimming; 'baignade interdite' 'no swimming'.

baigner *verb* [1] **se baigner** to go swimming.

baignoire *noun* F bath.

bail (*plural* **baux**) *noun* M lease; **un bail de trois ans** a three-year lease.

bâiller *verb* [1] to yawn.

bain *noun* M bath; **prendre un bain** to have a bath.

baiser *noun* M kiss; **bons baisers** love and kisses (*at the end of a letter*).

baisser *verb* [1] 1 to lower; **baisser le store** to lower (or pull down) the blind; **baisser le volume** to turn down the volume; **baisser la lumière** to turn down the lights; **baisser les prix** to cut prices; 2 **se baisser** to bend down.

bal *noun* M dance; **un bal populaire** a village dance (or disco).

balade *noun* F walk, drive; **faire une balade (à pied)** to go for a walk; **faire**

une balade (en voiture) to go for a drive; **faire une balade à la campagne** to go for a walk (or drive) in the country.

balader *verb* [1] **1 se balader** to go for a walk (or a drive); **se balader en Écosse** to tour around Scotland; **2 balader quelque chose** to carry something around.

baladeur *noun* M Walkman™, personal stereo.

balai *noun* M broom, (long-handled) brush; **passer le balai** to sweep the floor.

balance *noun* F scales; **une balance de cuisine** kitchen scales.

Balance *noun* F Libra (*sign of the Zodiac*).

balancer *verb* [61] **1** to sway; **2** to swing; **3** (*informal*) to throw, to chuck; **balance-moi les clés!** chuck me the keys!; **4** (*informal*) to chuck out; **je vais balancer tous ces vieux bouquins** I'm going to chuck all these old books.

balançoire *noun* F **1** swing; **2** seesaw.

balayer *verb* [59] **1** to sweep; **balayer la cuisine** to sweep the kitchen floor; **2** to sweep up; **balayer les miettes** to sweep up the crumbs.

balayeur, balayeuse *noun* M, F roadsweeper.

balbutier *verb* [1] to mumble.

balcon *noun* M balcony.

baleine *noun* F whale.

baliser *verb* [1] **1** to signpost; **2** to mark out.

balle *noun* F **1** ball; **2** bullet.

ballerine *noun* F **1** ballerina; **2** ballerina shoe; **3** ballet shoe.

ballet *noun* M ballet.

ballon *noun* M **1** ball; **2** balloon; **3** (*informal*) Breathalyzer™; **souffler dans le ballon** to be breathalyzed.

balnéaire *adjective* seaside; **une station balnéaire** a seaside resort.

bambou *noun* M bamboo.

banal *adjective* ordinary; **peu banal** unusual.

banane *noun* F **1** banana; **2** bumbag.

banc *noun* M bench; **assis sur un banc** sitting on a bench.

bancaire *adjective* **1** banking; **2 une carte bancaire** a bank card.

bancal *adjective* **1** rickety; **2** wobbly.

bande *noun* F **1** group; **une bande de jeunes** a group of young people; **2** gang; **une bande de criminels** a criminal gang; **3** strip (*of fabric or paper*); **4** tape (*for recording*); **5** bandage.

bande-annonce *noun* F trailer (*for a film*).

bandeau (*plural* **bandeaux**) *noun* M **1** headband; **2** blindfold.

bande d'arrêt d'urgence *noun* F hard shoulder (*on motorway*).

bande de fréquence *noun* F wavelength (*on radio*).

bande dessinée noun F **1** comic strip; **2** comic book.

bande publique noun F Citizen's Band, CB radio.

bande rugueuse noun F rumble strip (*on motorway*).

bande sonore noun F **1** soundtrack (*of film*); **2** rumble strip (*on motorway*).

bandit noun M bandit.

banditisme noun M crime.

banlieue noun F **la banlieue** the suburbs; **une banlieue** a suburb; **une maison de banlieue** a house in the suburbs; **un train de banlieue** a commuter train.

banque noun F bank; **aller à la banque** to go to the bank.

banquette noun F **1** wall seat (*in a café or restaurant*); **2** seat (*in a car, bus, or train*).

banquier noun M banker.

baptême noun M christening.

baptiser verb [1] **1** to christen; **2** to name; **3** to nickname.

baquet noun M tub.

bar noun M bar.

baraque noun F (*informal*) house.

barbant adjective (*informal*) boring.

barbe noun F beard; ★ **c'est la barbe!** what a drag!; ★ **faire quelque chose à la barbe de quelqu'un** to do something behind somebody's back (*literally: to do something in somebody's beard*).

barbe à papa noun F candyfloss.

barbecue noun M barbecue.

barbelé noun M barbed wire.

barbouiller verb [1] **1** to smear; **tu es tout barbouillé de confiture** you've got jam all over your face; **2** to daub; **barbouillé de slogans** daubed with slogans.

barbu noun M **un barbu** a man with a beard.
adjective bearded.

barème noun M scale.

barmaid noun F barmaid.

barman noun M barman.

baromètre noun M barometer.

barque noun F rowing boat.

barquette noun F tub, container; **une barquette de fraises** a punnet of strawberries.

barrage noun M **1** dam; **2** roadblock.

barre noun F bar; **une barre de fer** an iron bar; **une barre de chocolat** a chocolate bar.

barreau (*plural* **barreaux**) noun M bar; **derrière les barreaux** behind bars (*in prison*).

barrer verb [1] **1** to block; '**route barrée**' 'road closed'; **2** to cross out; **barrer trois mots** to cross out three words; **3** **se barrer** (*informal*) to clear off, to leave; **je me barre!** I'm off!; ★ **on est mal barré** (*informal*) we're in trouble.

barrette noun F hairslide.

barrière noun F **1** fence; **2** gate.

bar-tabac noun M café (selling cigarettes, tobacco, and stamps as well as drinks and snacks).

bas noun M 1 bottom, lower part; **en bas de la page** at the bottom of the page; 2 stocking.
adjective (F **basse**) low.
adverb 1 low; **plus bas** further down; **parler plus bas** to lower one's voice; 2 **en bas** at the bottom; down below; downstairs; **les voisins d'en bas** the neighbours in the flat below.

bas-côté noun M verge (on the roadside).

basculant adjective **un camion à benne basculante** a dump truck.

bascule noun F 1 rocker; **un fauteuil à bascule** a rocking chair; **un cheval à bascule** a rocking horse; 2 seesaw.

basculer verb [1] to topple over.

base noun F 1 basis; **être à la base de quelque chose** to be at the root of something; 2 base; **à base de chocolat** chocolate-based; 3 **de base** basic; **les ingrédients de base** the basic ingredients.

base-ball noun M baseball.

base de données noun F database.

baser verb [1] to base; **basé sur** based on.

basilic noun M basil; **une sauce au basilic** a basil sauce.

basket noun M 1 basketball; 2 sports shoe, trainer; ★ **lâche-moi les baskets!** (informal) get off my back!

basketteur, basketteuse noun M, F basketball player.

basque noun M, adjective basque.

Basque noun M & F Basque (person).

basse noun F bass (in music).
adjective SEE **bas**.

bassin noun M 1 pond; 2 pelvis.

bassine noun F bowl.

bassiste noun M & F bassist.

bataille noun F 1 battle; **la bataille de Trafalgar** the Battle of Trafalgar; **la bataille du pouvoir** the battle for power; **une bataille de boules de neige** a snowball fight; 2 a card game (similar to beggar-my neighbour); ★ **avoir les sourcils en bataille** to have bushy eyebrows; ★ **elle avait les cheveux en bataille** her hair was all over the place.

bateau (plural **bateaux**) noun M boat, ship; **faire du bateau** to go boating (or sailing).

bateau de plaisance noun M pleasure boat.

bateau-mouche noun M pleasure boat (a large river boat for sightseeing trips).

bateau pneumatique noun M rubber dinghy.

bâti adjective built; **bien bâti** well-built.

bâtiment noun M 1 building; **les bâtiments de l'école** the school buildings; 2 **le bâtiment** the building trade; **travailler dans le**

bâtiment to work in the building trade; 3 ship.

bâtir verb [2] to build.

bâtisse noun F building.

bâton noun M stick.

bâton de ski noun M ski stick.

bâtonnet noun M stick.

bâtonnet de poisson noun M fish finger.

bâtonnet ouaté noun M cotton bud.

batte noun F bat (cricket, baseball, etc).

batterie noun F 1 battery; 2 drum kit, drums.

batterie de cuisine noun F pots and pans.

batteur noun M 1 drummer; 2 whisk.

battre verb [21] 1 to beat (in a game); Nicole m'a battu au tennis Nicole beat me at tennis; 2 to beat, to batter; battre un chien to beat a dog; 3 to beat (a mixture); battre les œufs to whisk the eggs; battre la crème to whip the cream; 4 se battre to fight; 5 battre des mains to clap your hands; 6 le cœur bat the heart beats; 7 la porte bat the door bangs.

bavard adjective talkative.

bavarder verb [1] to chat, to chatter.

baver verb [1] to dribble.

bazar noun M 1 general store; 2 (informal) mess.

B.D. noun F comic strip; SHORT FOR bande dessinée.

beau, bel (before a vowel or silent 'h') (F **belle**) (M plural **beaux**) adjective 1 beautiful, lovely; une belle maison a beautiful house; un bel homme a handsome man; fais de beaux rêves! sweet dreams!; 2 il fait beau it's a nice day; ★ faire le beau to sit up and beg (of a dog).

beaucoup adverb 1 a lot; tu m'en as donné beaucoup you've given me a lot; tu ne m'en as pas donné beaucoup you haven't given me much; cinquante francs c'est beaucoup fifty francs is a lot; 2 a lot; il lit beaucoup he reads a lot; il ne lit pas beaucoup he doesn't read much; 3 very much; j'aime beaucoup ta robe I like your dress very much, I really like your dress; j'aime beaucoup aller au cinéma I really like going to the cinema; 4 beaucoup de a lot of; beaucoup d'argent a lot of money; elle a beaucoup d'argent she has a lot of money; elle n'a pas beaucoup d'argent she doesn't have much money; il a beaucoup d'amis he has a lot of friends; il n'a pas beaucoup d'amis he doesn't have many friends; 5 beaucoup plus much more; beaucoup moins much less; beaucoup trop far too much; beaucoup trop court far too short.

beau-fils (plural **beaux-fils**) noun M 1 son-in-law; 2 stepson.

beau-frère (plural **beaux-frères**) noun M brother-in-law.

beau-père noun M 1 father-in-law; 2 stepfather.

beauté noun F beauty.

beaux-arts plural noun M fine arts; **école des beaux-arts** art school.

beaux-parents plural noun M parents-in-law, in-laws.

bébé noun M baby.

bec noun M beak.

bêche noun F spade.

bégayer verb [59] to stammer.

beige adjective beige.

beignet noun M 1 fritter; 2 doughnut.

bel adjective SEE beau.

belette noun F weasel.

belge adjective Belgian.

Belge noun M & F Belgian.

Belgique noun F Belgium.

bélier noun M ram.

Bélier noun M Aries (sign of the Zodiac).

belle noun F 1 **ma belle** darling; 2 **la Belle au bois dormant** Sleeping Beauty.
adjective SEE beau.

belle-famille noun F in-laws.

belle-fille (plural **belles-filles**) noun F 1 daughter-in-law; 2 stepdaughter.

belle-mère noun F 1 mother-in-law; 2 stepmother.

belle-sœur (plural **belles-sœurs**) noun F sister-in-law.

bénédiction noun F blessing.

bénéfice noun M profit; **faire un bénéfice de dix mille francs** to make a profit of ten thousand francs.

bénéfique adjective beneficial.

bénévole noun M & F voluntary worker.
adjective voluntary, unpaid.

bénir verb [2] to bless.

benne noun F skip (for rubbish).

béquille noun F crutch.

berceau (plural **berceaux**) noun M cradle.

bercer verb [61] to rock (a baby).

berceuse noun F 1 lullaby; 2 rocking chair.

béret noun M beret.

berge noun F bank (of a river or canal).

berger, bergère noun M, F shepherd, shepherdess.

berger allemand noun M Alsatian (dog).

besoin noun M need; **avoir besoin de quelque chose** to need something; **j'ai besoin d'un marteau** I need a hammer; **avoir besoin de faire** to need to do.

bestiole noun F (informal) creepy-crawly.

bétail noun M 1 livestock; 2 cattle.

bête noun F animal.
adjective stupid.

bêtise noun F stupidity; **faire une bêtise** to do something stupid.

béton noun M concrete.

betterave (rouge) noun F
beetroot.

beurre noun M butter; ★ **un œil
au beurre noir** a black eye (literally:
an eye with black butter).

beurrer verb [1] to butter.

bibelot noun M ornament.

biberon noun M (feeding) bottle.

bible noun F bible; **la Bible** the
Bible.

bibliothécaire noun M & F
librarian.

bibliothèque noun F 1 library;
2 bookcase.

bic™ noun M **un stylo bic™** a
Biro™.

biche noun F doe.

bicyclette noun F bicycle; **faire de
la bicyclette** to cycle.

bidet noun M bidet.

bidon noun M can.
adjective (informal) phoney.

bidonville noun M shanty town.

bidule noun M (informal) whatsit,
thingamajig.

bien noun M 1 good; **le bien et le
mal** good and evil; **ça te fera du
bien** that'll do you good;
2 possession; **tous leurs biens** all
their possessions.
adjective 1 good, nice; **des gens
bien** nice people; **ce sera bien de le
revoir** it will be nice to see him
again; 2 well; **je ne me sens pas
bien** I don't feel well; 3 happy,
comfortable; **on est bien ici** it's nice
here; **on est très bien dans ce**
fauteuil this chair's really
comfortable.
adverb 1 well; **elle chante bien** she
sings well; **bien joué!** well done!; **tu
vas bien?** are you well?; 2 well;
bien habillé well dressed; **cette
couleur te va bien** that colour suits
you; 3 very, really; **bien triste** really
sad; **bien chaud** really hot; 4 very
much; **j'aime bien ta robe** I like your
dress very much, I really like your
dress; **j'aimerais bien savoir** I'd
really like to know; **j'aimerais bien
aller au cinéma** I'd really like to go
to the cinema; **veux-tu du thé?** –
'oui, je veux bien' 'would you like
some tea?' – 'yes I'd love some'; **'tu
aimes le poisson?'** – **'oui, je l'aime
bien'** 'do you like fish?' – 'yes I do';
je veux bien le faire I'm quite happy
to do it; 5 much; **bien mieux** much
better; **bien plus chaud** much
hotter; 6 **bien de** many, a number
of; **bien des gens** many people;
★ **c'est bien fait pour elle!** serves
her right!

bien entendu adverb of course.

bien-être noun M well-being.

bien que conjunction although.

bien sûr adverb of course.

bientôt adverb soon; **à bientôt** see
you soon.

bienvenu, bienvenue¹ noun M,
F **soyez le bienvenu** (or **la
bienvenue**)! welcome!

bienvenue² noun F welcome;
bienvenue! welcome!; **bienvenue
en France!** welcome to France!;
souhaiter la bienvenue à quelqu'un
to welcome somebody.

bière *noun* F beer; **boire de la bière** to drink beer; **trois bières, s'il vous plaît** three beers, please.

bière blonde *noun* F lager.

bière brune *noun* F brown ale.

bifteck *noun* M steak.

bifurcation *noun* F fork (*in the road*).

bigoudi *noun* M hair curler.

bijou (*plural* **bijoux**) *noun* M jewel, piece of jewellery.

bijouterie *noun* F jeweller's (shop).

bijoutier, bijoutière *noun* M, F jeweller.

bilan *noun* M balance sheet;
★ **faire le bilan de quelque chose** to assess something.

bilingue *adjective* bilingual.

billard *noun* M 1 billiards; **jouer au billard** to play billiards; 2 billiard table.

billard américain *noun* M pool.

billard anglais *noun* M snooker.

billard électrique *noun* M pinball machine.

bille *noun* F 1 marble; **jouer aux billes** to play marbles; 2 billiard ball.

billet *noun* M 1 note, banknote; **un billet de cent francs** a hundred-franc note; 2 ticket; **un billet de train** a train ticket.

billion *noun* M billion.

biochimie *noun* F biochemistry.

biographie *noun* F biography.

biologie *noun* F biology.

biologique *adjective* 1 biological;
2 organically grown.

bip *noun* M beep; **'après le bip sonore'** 'after the tone' (*on an answering machine*).

biscotte *noun* F continental toast.

biscuit *noun* M biscuit.

bise *noun* F (*informal*) kiss; **faire la bise à quelqu'un** to kiss somebody on the cheek; **grosses bises** lots of love.

bissextile *adjective* **une année bissextile** a leap year.

bistro, bistrot *noun* M bistro, café.

bizarre *adjective* odd, strange.

blague *noun* F (*informal*) 1 joke; **sans blague!** no kidding!; 2 trick; **faire une blague à quelqu'un** to play a trick on somebody.

blaguer *verb* [1] (*informal*) to joke.

blaireau (*plural* **blaireaux**) *noun* M 1 badger; 2 shaving brush.

blâmer *verb* [1] 1 to criticize; 2 to blame.

blanc *noun* M 1 white; **peint en blanc** painted white; 2 white meat, breast; 3 white wine; 4 blank; **laisser un blanc** to leave a blank. *adjective* (F **blanche**) 1 white; 2 blank; **une feuille blanche** a blank sheet of paper.

blanche *adjective* SEE **blanc**.

Blanc, Blanche *noun* M, F white man, white woman.

blanchir *verb* [2] to whiten.

blé noun M wheat.

blessé, blessée noun M, F
injured person, casualty.
adjective injured.

blesser verb [1] **1** to hurt, to
injure; **2 se blesser** to hurt
oneself; **tu t'es blessé?** did you hurt
yourself?

blessure noun F **1** injury;
2 wound.

bleu[1] noun M, *adjective* blue; **peint
en bleu** painted blue; **bleu marine**
navy blue.

bleu[2] noun M bruise.

bleuet noun M cornflower.

bloc noun M **1** block; **un bloc de
ciment** a block of cement; **2 un
bloc de papier à lettres** a writing
pad.

bloc-notes noun M notepad.

blond *adjective* blonde, fair-haired.

bloqué *adjective* **1** blocked;
2 jammed; **3** stuck.

bloquer verb [1] **1** to block; **2** to
jam.

blouse noun F overall.

blouson noun M jacket.

blue-jean noun M jeans; **j'ai
acheté un blue-jean** I bought a pair
of jeans.

bobine noun F reel.

bocal (*plural* **bocaux**) noun M jar.

bœuf noun M **1** bullock; **2** beef;
est-ce que tu aimes le bœuf? do
you like beef?

bof *exclamation* (*informal*) **'c'était
bien hier soir?' – 'bof!'** 'did you
have a good time last night?' –
'nothing special'.

bohémien, bohémienne noun
M, F gipsy.

boire verb [22] to drink; **qu'est-ce
que tu veux boire?** what would you
like to drink?; **il n'y a rien à boire**
there's nothing to drink.

bois noun M wood; **une table en
bois** a wooden table; ★ **avoir la
gueule de bois** (*informal*) to have a
hangover (*literally: to have a mouth
made of wood*).

boisson noun F drink; **une boisson
fraîche** a cold drink.

boîte noun F **1** tin; **une boîte de
sardines** a tin of sardines; **2** box;
une boîte d'allumettes a box of
matches; **3** (*informal*) **une boîte de
nuit** a nightclub; **aller dans une
boîte** to go to a club; **4** (*informal*)
firm, company.

boîte aux lettres noun F post
box.

boiter verb [1] to limp.

bol noun M **1** bowl; **un bol de riz** a
bowl of rice; **2** (*informal*) **un
coup de bol** a stroke of luck; ★ **en
avoir ras le bol** (*informal*) to be fed
up (*literally: to have a bowlful*); **j'en
ai ras le bol d'attendre** I'm fed up
with waiting.

bombarder verb [1] **1** to
bombard; **2** to bomb, to shell.

bombe noun F **1** bomb; **2** spray
can (*containing hairspray, fly spray,
etc*).

bon

bon (F **bonne**) *adjective* **1** good; **un bon repas** a good meal; **bon en français** good at French; **2 un bon kilomètre** a good kilometre, at least a kilometre; **3** right; **le bon numéro** the right number; **la bonne adresse** the right address; **c'est bon** it's OK, it's fine.
noun **1** voucher; **2 cela a du bon** that has its good points; **pour de bon** for good.
adverb **sentir bon** to smell good (or nice); **il fait bon aujourd'hui** it's a nice day today; **il fait bon dans mon appartement** it's lovely and warm in my flat; SEE **bonne²**.

bon anniversaire *greeting* happy birthday.

bon appétit *exclamation* enjoy your meal.

bonbon *noun* M sweet.

bonbonne *noun* F **1 une bonbonne à gaz** a gas cylinder; **2** demijohn.

bond *noun* M leap; **se lever d'un bond** to leap to your feet.

bondé *adjective* crowded, packed; **bondé d'étudiants** packed with students.

bonheur *noun* M **1** happiness; **2** pleasure; **avoir le bonheur de faire** to have the pleasure of doing.

bonhomme (*plural* **bonshommes**) *noun* M fellow, man.

bonhomme de neige *noun* M snowman.

bonjour *greeting* hello, good morning, good afternoon; ★ **être simple comme bonjour** to be really

easy, to be as easy as pie (*literally: to be as simple as hello*).

bon marché *adjective* cheap.

bonne *noun* F maid.
adjective SEE **bon**.

bonne année *greeting* happy New Year.

bonne chance *exclamation* good luck.

bonne heure *in phrase* **de bonne heure** early.

bonne nuit *greeting* goodnight.

bonnet *noun* M hat, bonnet.

bon retour *exclamation* safe journey back.

bon sens *noun* M common sense.

bonsoir *greeting* good evening.

bonté *noun* F kindness.

bon voyage *exclamation* have a good trip.

bord *noun* M **1** edge (*of a table, cliff, etc*); **2** rim (*of a glass, cup, vase, etc*); **3** side, edge (*of a road, path, etc*); **au bord de la route** on the edge of the road; **4** bank (*of a stream or lake*); **5 au bord de la mer** at the seaside.

bordeaux *adjective* maroon.

border *verb* [1] **1** to line; **bordé d'arbres** tree-lined; **2** to edge, to trim.

bordure *noun* F **1** border; **2** edge; **3 en bordure de** on the edge of.

borne noun F 1 kilometre marker (*the equivalent of a milestone*); 2 bollard.

Bosnie noun F Bosnia.

bosse noun F bump.

bosser verb [1] (*informal*) to work.

botanique noun F botany. adjective **les jardins botaniques** the botanic gardens.

botte noun F 1 boot; **des bottes de cuir** leather boots; **des bottes de caoutchouc** wellington boots; 2 **une botte de foin** a bale of hay.

bottine noun F ankle boot.

bouc noun M billy goat.

boucan noun M (*informal*) din, racket.

bouc émissaire noun M scapegoat.

bouche noun F mouth.

bouche-à-bouche noun M mouth-to-mouth resuscitation.

bouchée noun F mouthful.

boucher[1] verb [1] 1 to cork (*a bottle*); 2 to block up, to fill (*a hole, gap, or crack*); 3 **se boucher** to get blocked up; 4 **se boucher le nez** to hold one's nose.

boucher[2], **bouchère** noun M, F butcher.

boucherie noun F 1 butcher's (shop).

bouchon noun M 1 cork; 2 screwcap; 3 traffic jam.

boucle noun F 1 buckle; 2 curl.

bouclé adjective curly.

boucle d'oreille noun F earring.

Bouddha noun M Buddha.

bouddhisme noun M Buddhism.

bouder verb [1] 1 to sulk; 2 **bouder quelque chose** to stay away from something.

boudin noun M black pudding.

boue noun F mud.

bouée noun F 1 rubber ring; 2 buoy.

bouée de sauvetage noun F lifebelt.

boueux (F **boueuse**) adjective muddy.

bouffe noun F (*informal*) food.

bouffée noun F **une bouffée d'air frais** a breath of fresh air.

bouffer verb [1] (*informal*) to eat.

bougeoir noun M candlestick.

bouger verb [52] to move.

bougie noun F 1 candle; 2 spark plug.

bouillabaisse noun F Mediterranean fish soup (*made with several varieties of fish and vegetables*).

bouillant adjective boiling; **faire cuire à l'eau bouillante** cook in boiling water.

bouillir verb [23] to boil; **faire bouillir le lait** to boil the milk; **le lait bout** the milk is boiling.

bouilloire noun F kettle.

bouillon noun M stock (*made with meat, fish, or vegetables*).

bouillon-cube *noun* M stock cube.

bouillotte *noun* F hot-water bottle.

boulanger, boulangère *noun* M, F baker.

boulangerie *noun* F bakery, baker's.

boule *noun* F bowl; **jouer aux boules** to play bowls.

bouleau *noun* M birch tree.

boule de neige *noun* F snowball.

boulette *noun* F pellet.

boulette de viande *noun* F meatball.

boulevard *noun* M boulevard.

boulevard périphérique *noun* M ring road.

bouleverser *verb* [1] **1** to overwhelm, to shatter; **être bouleversé** to be overwhelmed (or shattered) **2** to disrupt (*a schedule, plans, etc*); **3** to turn upside down.

boulot *noun* M (*informal*) **1** work; **j'ai trop de boulot** I've got too much work to do; **c'est un boulot immense** it's a huge amount of work; **2** job; **elle cherche du boulot** she's looking for a job.

boum *noun* F (*informal*) party.

bouquet *noun* M bunch, bouquet (*of flowers or herbs*).

bouquin *noun* M (*informal*) book.

bouquiner *verb* [1] (*informal*) to read.

bouquiniste *noun* M & F secondhand bookseller.

bourdon *noun* M bumblebee.

bourg *noun* M market town.

bourgeois, bourgeoise *noun* M, F middle-class person. *adjective* middle-class.

bourgeon *noun* M bud.

Bourgogne *noun* F Burgundy.

bourratif (F **bourrative**) *adjective* very filling.

bourré *adjective* **1** bourré de crammed with, stuffed with. **2** drunk.

bourrer *verb* [1] to cram.

bourse *noun* F grant.

Bourse *noun* F stock exchange.

bousculer *verb* [1] to push, to jostle.

boussole *noun* F compass.

bout *noun* M **1** end; **au bout de** at the end of; **2** tip (*of nose or finger*); **3** un bout de papier a scrap of paper; **un petit bout de fromage** a little bit of cheese; **4** au bout de after; **au bout d'une demi-heure** after half an hour.

bouteille *noun* F bottle.

boutique *noun* F shop.

bouton *noun* M **1** button; **2** spot, pimple.

bouton d'or *noun* M buttercup.

boxe *noun* F boxing.

boxeur *noun* M boxer.

bracelet *noun* M bracelet.

bracelet-montre *noun* M wristwatch.

braise noun F embers (of a fire).

brancard noun M stretcher.

branche noun F branch.

branché adjective (informal) trendy.

brancher verb [1] **1** to plug in (an iron, a television, etc); **2** to connect (electricity, gas, water, telephone).

bras noun M sleeve; **en bras de chemise** in one's shirtsleeves.

bras de fer noun M arm wrestling.

brasse noun F breaststroke.

brasserie noun F brasserie, café-restaurant.

brave adjective nice (person).

break noun M estate car.

brebis noun F ewe.

bref (F **brève**) adjective short, brief.

Brésil noun M Brazil.

Bretagne noun F Brittany.

bretelle noun F **1** strap; **2** slip road; **3 des bretelles** braces.

brevet noun M certificate.

bribes plural noun F bits, fragments.

bricolage noun M DIY, do-it-yourself

bricoler verb [1] to do DIY.

bricoleur, bricoleuse noun M,F DIY enthusiast.

brièvement adverb briefly.

brillamment adverb brilliantly.

brillant adjective **1** shiny; **2** brilliant.

briller verb [1] to shine.

brin noun M **1** sprig (of herb or plant); **un brin d'herbe** a blade of grass.

brindille noun F twig.

brioche noun F brioche, bun.

brique noun F **1** brick; **2** carton (of fruit-juice, milk, etc).

briquet noun M lighter.

brise noun F breeze.

briser verb [1] to break.

britannique adjective British.

Britannique noun M & F British person; **les Britanniques** the British.

brocante noun F **1** junk shop; **2** second-hand goods.

broche noun F **1** brooch; **2** spit (for roasting).

brochet noun M pike.

brochette noun F **1** skewer; **2** kebab; **une brochette de viande** a meat kebab.

brochure noun F **1** booklet; **2** brochure.

brocolis plural noun M broccoli.

broder verb [1] to embroider.

broderie noun F embroidery; **des broderies** embroidery.

bronchite noun F bronchitis; **avoir une bronchite** to have bronchitis.

bronzage noun M suntan.

bronzer verb [1] to tan.

brosse noun F brush.

brosse à cheveux noun F hairbrush.

brosse à dents noun F toothbrush.

brosser verb [1] **1** to brush; **2 se brosser les dents** to brush your teeth.

brouette noun F wheelbarrow.

brouillard noun M fog.

brouillon noun M rough draft.

bru noun F daughter-in-law.

brugnon noun M nectarine.

bruit noun M **1** noise; **entendre un bruit** to hear a noise; **entendre le bruit d'une voiture** to hear the sound of a car; **2** rumour.

brûlant adjective **1** boiling hot; **2** burning hot.

brûlé noun M **un goût de brûlé** a burnt taste; **ça sent le brûlé** there's a smell of burning.

brûler verb [1] **1** to burn; **2 se brûler** to burn yourself.

brûlure noun F burn.

brume noun F mist.

brun adjective **1** brown; **2** dark-haired.

brushing noun M blow-dry; **se faire faire un brushing** to have a blow-dry.

brut adjective **1** raw (material); **2** crude (oil); **3** gross (income); **4** dry (champagne).

brutal (M plural **brutaux**) adjective **1** violent, brutal; **2** sudden.

brutalement adverb **1** suddenly; **2** violently.

Bruxelles noun Brussels.

bruyant adjective noisy, loud.

bruyère noun F heather.

bûche noun F log.

bu verb SEE **boire**.

budget noun M budget.

buffet noun M **1** sideboard; **2** buffet.

buisson noun M bush.

buissonnière adjective **faire l'école buissonnière** to play truant.

Bulgarie noun F Bulgaria.

bulle noun F bubble.

bulletin noun M report, bulletin.

bulletin de salaire noun M payslip.

bulletin scolaire noun M school report.

bureau (plural **bureaux**) noun M **1** desk; **elle est à son bureau** she is at her desk; **2** office; **au bureau** **1** at (or to) the office.

bureau de poste noun M post office.

bureau de tabac noun M tobacconist's.

bureau de tourisme noun M tourist information office.

burin noun M chisel.

bus noun M bus.

buse noun F buzzard.

buste noun M bust.

but noun M **1** goal, aim, purpose;
2 goal (in football, hockey);
marquer un but to score a goal;
3 target.

buté adjective stubborn.

buvable adjective drinkable.

buvard noun M blotter; **du papier
buvard** blotting paper.

buvette noun F bar (at a dance,
village fair, etc).

buvez, buvons verb SEE **boire**.

C c

ça pronoun **1** that, this; **donne-moi
ça** give me that; **ça c'est un
moineau** that's a sparrow;
2 comment ça va?, ça va? how are
you?; **ça va bien merci** I'm fine
thanks; **3 c'est ça** that's right; **ça ne
fait rien** it doesn't matter.

çà adverb **çà et là** here and there.

cabane noun F hut, shed.

cabas noun M shopping bag.

cabillaud noun M cod.

cabine noun F **1** cubicle; **cabine de
douche** shower cubicle; **cabine
d'essayage** fitting room (in a
clothes shop); **2** cabin (on a ship).

cabinet noun M **1** office (of a
solicitor); **2** surgery (of a doctor or
dentist); **3 cabinet de médecins**
medical practice.

cabine téléphonique noun F
phone box.

cabinets plural noun M toilet.

câble noun M **1** cable; **2** rope.

câblé adjective **être câblé** to have
cable television.

cabosser verb [1] to dent.

cacahuète noun F peanut; **des
cacahuètes grillées** roasted
peanuts.

cacao noun M cocoa.

cache noun F hiding place.

caché adjective hidden.

cache-cache noun M **jouer à
cache-cache** to play hide and seek.

cachemire noun M **1** cashmere;
2 motif cachemire paisley pattern.

cache-nez noun M (thick) scarf.

cache-pot noun M flowerpot
holder.

cacher verb [1] **1** to hide; **cacher
quelque chose** to hide something;
**elle a caché son portefeuille dans
un tiroir** she's hidden her wallet in a
drawer; **2 se cacher** to hide; **il
s'est caché derrrière la porte** he
hid behind the door.

cachet noun M **1** tablet; **un cachet
d'aspirine** an aspirin; **2** official
stamp (made with a rubber stamp);
3 le cachet de la poste the
postmark.

cachette noun F **1** hiding place;
2 en cachette secretly, on the sly.

cachot noun M dungeon.

cactus noun M cactus.

cadavre noun M corpse, body.

caddie noun M trolley (*in the supermarket*).

cadeau (*plural* **cadeaux**) noun M present; **faire un cadeau à quelqu'un** to give somebody a present; **du papier cadeau** wrapping-paper; **je vous fais un paquet-cadeau?** shall I gift-wrap it for you?

cadenas noun M padlock.

cadence noun F rhythm.

cadet, cadette noun M, F younger child, youngest child. *adjective* younger, youngest.

cadran noun M 1 face (*of a watch or clock*); 2 dial (*on an instrument such as the speedometer in a car*).

cadran solaire noun M sundial.

cadre noun M 1 frame (*of a picture, mirror, or window*); 2 surroundings, setting; 3 executive (*a person with a management job in a company*); 4 frame (*of a bicycle*).

cafard noun M 1 cockroach; 2 depression; **avoir le cafard** to be down in the dumps.

café noun M 1 coffee; **café instantané, café soluble** instant coffee; **café moulu** ground coffee; **café en grains** coffee beans; **café au lait** coffee with milk; **prendre un café** to have a coffee; 2 café.

café-crème noun M white coffee.

caféine noun F caffeine.

cafétéria noun F cafeteria.

cafetière noun F 1 coffee pot; 2 coffee maker.

cage noun F cage.

cageot noun M crate.

cagnotte noun F 1 kitty (*of money*); 2 jackpot.

cagoule noun M hood.

cahier noun M 1 exercise book; 2 notebook.

caille noun F quail.

cailler verb [1] to curdle.

caillou (*plural* **cailloux**) noun M pebble, stone.

caisse noun F 1 till, cash register; 2 cash desk; 3 checkout (*in a supermarket*); 4 box, crate.

caisse à outils noun F toolbox.

caisse d'épargne noun F savings bank.

caissier, caissière noun M, F 1 checkout assistant; 2 cashier.

cajou noun **une noix de cajou** a cashew nut.

cake noun M fruit cake.

calamar noun M squid.

calamité noun F disaster, calamity.

calcaire noun M 1 limestone; 2 furring (*the sediment which clogs up kettles, steam irons, etc*). *adjective* 1 **eau calcaire** hard water; **l'eau ici est très calcaire** the water here is very hard.

calcium noun M calcium.

calcul noun M 1 calculation; 2 arithmetic.

calculatrice noun F pocket calculator.

FRENCH–ENGLISH 41 **camping**

calculer verb [1] to calculate, to work out.

calculette noun F pocket calculator.

caleçon noun M **1** boxer shorts; **2** leggings.

calembour noun M pun, play on words.

calendrier noun M **1** calendar; **2** schedule.

calepin noun M notebook.

caler verb [1] **1** to wedge; **2** to prop up; **3 ma voiture a calé** my car stalled.

calibre noun M **1** size, grade (of eggs, fruit, or vegetables); **2** calibre, bore (of a gun).

câlin noun M cuddle; **fais-moi un câlin** give me a cuddle (usually said to a child); **fais un câlin à ta grand-mère** give your gran a cuddle. adjective affectionate.

câliner verb [1] to cuddle.

calmant noun M sedative. adjective soothing.

calme noun M peace and quiet. adjective **1** calm; **2** quiet.

calmement adverb calmly.

calmer verb [1] **1 calmer quelqu'un** to calm somebody down; **2 se calmer** to calm down; **calme-toi** calm down; **3** to soothe; **l'aspirine a calmé la douleur** the aspirin soothed the pain.

calorie noun F calorie.

calque noun M **un calque** a tracing; **papier-calque** tracing paper.

calvados noun M calvados (apple brandy made in Normandy).

camarade noun M & F friend.

cambriolage noun M burglary.

cambrioler verb [1] **cambrioler une maison** to burgle a house; **ils ont été cambriolés** they were burgled.

cambrioleur, cambrioleuse noun M, F burglar.

caméra noun F cine-camera.

caméscope noun M camcorder.

camion noun M truck, lorry.

camion-citerne noun M tanker lorry.

camionnette noun F van.

camionneur noun M lorry driver, truck driver.

camp noun M camp.

campagnard, campagnarde noun M, F country person. adjective country; **la vie campagnarde** country life.

campagne noun F **1** country, countryside; **à la campagne** in the country, in the countryside; **aller se promener à la campagne** to go for a country walk; **2** campaign.

camper verb [1] to camp.

campeur, campeuse noun M, F camper.

camping noun M **1** camping; **faire du camping** to go camping; **2 un**

camping, un terrain de camping a campsite.

camping-car *noun* M camper van.

camping-gaz™ *noun* M camping stove.

Canada *noun* M Canada; **au Canada** in (or to) Canada.

canadien (F **canadienne**) *adjective* Canadian.

Canadien, Canadienne *noun* M, F Canadian.

canal (*plural* **canaux**) *noun* M canal.

canapé *noun* M sofa.

canapé-lit *noun* M sofa bed.

canard *noun* M duck.

canari *noun* M canary.

cancer *noun* M cancer; **avoir un cancer** to have cancer.

Cancer *noun* M Cancer (*sign of the Zodiac*).

candidat, candidate *noun* M, F **1** candidate; **2** applicant.

candidature *noun* F **poser sa candidature à un poste** to apply for a job.

cane *noun* F female duck.

caneton *noun* M duckling.

canette *noun* F **une canette de bière** a small bottle of beer.

canevas *noun* M canvas.

caniche *noun* M poodle.

canicule *noun* F scorching heat.

canif *noun* M penknife.

caniveau (*plural* **caniveaux**) *noun* M gutter.

canne *noun* F walking stick.

canne à pêche *noun* F fishing rod.

canne à sucre *noun* F sugar cane.

cannelle *noun* F cinnamon.

canoë *noun* M **1** canoe; **2 faire du canoë** to go canoeing.

canon *noun* M **1** gun; **2** barrel (*of a gun*); **3** cannon.

canot *noun* M small boat, dinghy; **un canot pneumatique** a rubber (or inflatable) dinghy.

canot de sauvetage *noun* M lifeboat.

cantatrice *noun* F opera singer.

cantine *noun* F canteen; **manger à la cantine** to have school lunch.

caoutchouc *noun* M **1** rubber; **des bottes en caoutchouc** wellington boots; **2** rubber band.

cap *noun* M **1** cape, headland; **2** course (*of a ship*).

capable *adjective* capable; **être capable de faire** to be capable of doing.

capacité *noun* F **1** ability; **2** capacity.

cape *noun* F cape, cloak.

capitaine *noun* M captain.

capital (*plural* **capitaux**) *noun* M capital (*financial*). *adjective* **1 d'une importance capitale** of major importance; **2 une question capitale** a key question; **3 la peine capitale** capital punishment.

capitale *noun* F capital city; **la capitale française** the French capital.

capot *noun* M bonnet (*of a car*).

câpre *noun* F caper.

caprice *noun* M **1** whim; **2** tantrum; **faire un caprice** to throw a tantrum.

Capricorne *noun* M Capricorn (*sign of the Zodiac*).

capsule *noun* F **1** cap, top (*of a bottle*); **2** capsule.

capter *verb* [1] **1 capter une chaîne (de télévision)** to get a (television) channel; **2 capter l'attention de quelqu'un** to catch somebody's attention.

captif, captive *noun* M, F captive.

captivant *adjective* **1** fascinating; **2** gripping, riveting.

captivité *noun* F captivity; **en captivité** in captivity.

capturer *verb* [1] to capture.

capuche *noun* F hood.

capuchon *noun* M **1** hood; **2** top, cap (*of a pen*).

capucine *noun* F nasturtium.

car¹ *conjunction* because.

car² *noun* M coach, bus; **voyager en car** to travel by coach; **un voyage en car** a coach journey.

carabine *noun* F rifle.

caractère *noun* M **1** character, nature; **avoir mauvais caractère** to

be bad-tempered; **2** character; **leur maison a beaucoup de caractère** their house has a lot of character; **3** character, letter; **en gros caractères** in large print.

caractéristique *noun* F, *adjective* characteristic.

carafe *noun* F carafe, jug (*for wine or water*).

caramel *noun* M **1** caramel; **2** toffee.

caravane *noun* F caravan.

carbone *noun* M **1** carbon; **2** carbon paper.

carbonisé *adjective* burnt to a cinder.

carburant *noun* M fuel.

carburateur *noun* M carburettor.

carcasse *noun* F carcass.

cardiaque *adjective* **une crise cardiaque** a heart attack.

cardinal (*plural* **cardinaux**) *noun* M **1** cardinal; **2** cardinal number.

carême *noun* M Lent.

caresser *verb* [1] to stroke, to caress.

cargaison *noun* F cargo.

caricature *noun* F caricature.

caricaturiste *noun* M & F caricaturist, cartoonist.

carie *noun* F **la carie dentaire** tooth decay; **avoir une carie** to have a hole in your tooth.

carillon *noun* M **1** church bells; **2** wind chimes.

caritatif (F **caritative**) *adjective*
charitable; **une association
caritative** a charity.

carnaval *noun* M carnival.

carnet *noun* M 1 notebook;
2 book (*of tickets or stamps*).

carnet de chèques *noun* M
chequebook.

carotte *noun* F carrot.

carpe *noun* F carp.

carpette *noun* F rug.

carré *noun* M, *adjective* square; **un
mètre carré** a square metre.

carreau (*plural* **carreaux**) *noun*
M 1 floor tile; 2 wall tile;
3 windowpane; 4 **du tissu à
carreaux** checked fabric; 5 **du
papier à carreaux** squared paper;
6 diamonds (*suit of playing cards*);
le roi de carreau the king of
diamonds.

carrefour *noun* M crossroads,
junction.

carrelage *noun* M 1 tiled floor;
2 tiling, tiles.

carrelet *noun* M plaice.

carrément *adverb* downright,
completely; **c'est carrément
malhonnête** it's downright
dishonest.

carrière *noun* F 1 career;
2 quarry.

cartable *noun* M 1 satchel,
schoolbag; 2 briefcase.

carte *noun* F 1 card; 2 playing
card; **jouer aux cartes** to play cards;

un jeu de cartes a pack of cards; a
card game; 3 map; 4 menu.

carte à jouer *noun* F playing card.

carte à mémoire *noun* F smart
card.

carte d'abonnement *noun* F
season ticket.

carte d'anniversaire *noun* F
birthday card.

carte de crédit *noun* F credit
card.

carte d'embarquement *noun* F
boarding card.

carte de séjour *noun* F resident's
permit.

carte de visite *noun* F business
card.

carte de vœux *noun* F greetings
card.

carte d'identité *noun* F identity
card.

carte postale *noun* F postcard.

carte routière *noun* F road map.

carte téléphonique *noun* F
phonecard.

carton *noun* M 1 cardboard; **une
chemise en carton** a cardboard
folder; **carton ondulé** corrugated
cardboard; 2 cardboard box.

cartouche *noun* F cartridge.

cas *noun* M 1 case; **au cas où tu
oublierais** in case you forget; **en
aucun cas** on no account; **en tout
cas** in any case, at any rate; 2 case;
trois cas de rougeole three cases of
measles.

cascade noun F 1 waterfall;
2 stunt.

cascadeur, cascadeuse noun
M, F stuntman, stuntwoman.

case noun F 1 square (on a board
game); 2 box (on a form); 3 hut.

casher adjective kosher.

casier noun M 1 pigeonhole;
2 locker; 3 rack.

casino noun M casino.

casque noun M 1 crash helmet;
2 safety helmet, hard hat;
3 headphones, headset.

casquette noun F cap; une
casquette de base-ball a baseball
cap.

casse-croûte noun M snack.

casse-noisettes noun M
nutcrackers.

casser verb [1] 1 to break; casser
un verre to break a glass; 2 se
casser to break; le verre s'est
cassé the glass broke; 3 se casser
la jambe to break your leg; ★ se
casser la tête to go to a lot of trouble;
(literally: to break your head); ne te
casse pas la tête! don't go to a lot
of trouble!

casse-pieds adjective (informal)
elle est casse-pieds! she's a pain in
the neck!

casserole noun F saucepan.

casse-tête noun M 1 puzzle;
2 problem.

cassette noun F cassette, tape.

cassis noun M blackcurrant; sirop
de cassis blackcurrant cordial.

cassoulet noun M oven-baked
beans (with meat and sausage).

castor noun M beaver.

catalogue noun M catalogue.

catastrophe noun F disaster,
catastrophe.

catch noun M wrestling.

catcheur, catcheuse noun M, F
wrestler.

catégorie noun F category.

cathédrale noun F cathedral.

catholicisme noun M (Roman)
Catholicism.

catholique noun M & F,
adjective (Roman) Catholic.

cauchemar noun M nightmare;
faire un cauchemar to have a
nightmare.

cause noun F 1 cause; la cause du
problème the cause of the
problem; 2 à cause de because
of; 3 la cause de quelque chose
the reason for something; fermé
pour cause de maladie closed for
reasons of illness; 4 cause; une
bonne cause a good cause.

causer verb [1] 1 to cause; 2 to
talk, to chat; causer de quelque
chose to talk (or chat) about
something; causer avec quelqu'un
to talk (or chat) to somebody.

caution noun F 1 deposit (when
renting a flat or house); 2 bail.

cavalier, cavalière noun M, F
rider.

cave noun F cellar.

caverne noun F cave.

CE noun F SEE short for Communauté Européenne EC.

ce¹, cet (before a vowel or mute 'h'), **cette** adjective **1** this, that; **ce stylo ne marche pas** this pen doesn't work; **cette semaine** this week; **ce couteau-ci** this knife; **2** that; **passe-moi cette assiette** pass me that plate; **cette chaise-là** that chair; **3** **cette nuit** last night; tonight.

ce², c' (before an 'e') pronoun **1** this, that, it; **qui est-ce?** who is it?; **c'est moi** it's me; **qu'est-ce que c'est?** what is it?; **c'est la première maison à gauche** it's the first house on the left; **2** he, she, they; **c'est un médecin** he's a doctor; **ce sont les enfants de Paul** they're Paul's children; **3** **ce qui** what; **mange ce qui reste** eat what's left; **4** **ce que** what; **prends ce que tu veux** take what you want; **5** **c'est tout ce qui reste** that's all that's left; **prends tout ce que tu veux** take everything you want.

ceci pronoun this; **ceci n'est pas à moi** this is not mine.

céder verb [24] **1** to give in; **2** **'cédez le passage'** 'give way' (at a road junction); **3** **céder sa place** to give up your seat; **4** **céder à quelque chose** to give in to something.

cédille noun F cedilla.

cèdre noun M cedar.

ceinture noun F **1** belt; **2** waistband; **3** waist.

ceinture de sauvetage noun F lifebelt.

ceinture de sécurité noun F seatbelt.

cela pronoun this, that, it ('cela' is used in the same way as 'ça' but is more formal); **cela ne me concerne pas** that does not concern me; **cela ne fait rien** that doesn't matter.

célébration noun F celebration.

célèbre adjective famous.

célébrer verb [24] to celebrate.

céleri noun M celery.

célibataire noun M & F bachelor, single woman.

celle pronoun SEE celui.

celle-ci pronoun SEE celui-ci.

celle-là pronoun SEE celui-là.

celles pronoun SEE ceux.

celles-ci pronoun SEE ceux-ci.

celles-là pronoun SEE ceux-là.

cellule noun F **1** (prison) cell; **2** cell (in biology and medicine); **3** unit.

celui, celle pronoun the one; **'quel livre?'** – **'celui qui est sur la table'** 'which book?' – 'the one on the table'; **'quelle casserole?'** – **'celle qui est sur la cuisinière'** 'which saucepan?' – 'the one on the cooker'.

celui-ci, celle-ci this one.

celui-là, celle-là pronoun that one.

cendre noun F ash; **les cendres** the ashes.

cendrier noun M ashtray.

Cendrillon noun Cinderella.

censé adjective supposed; **être censé faire/être** to be supposed to do/be; **je suis censé être là à dix heures** I'm supposed to be there at ten o'clock.

cent number a hundred, one hundred; **trois cents personnes** three hundred people; **deux cent cinquante personnes** two hundred and fifty people (note that there is no 's' on 'cent' when it is followed by another number).

centaine noun F **une centaine de personnes** a hundred people, a hundred or so people; **plusieurs centaines de personnes** several hundred people; **des centaines de lettres** hundreds of letters.

centenaire noun M centenary.

centième number hundredth.

centime noun M centime (the smallest unit of French money; there are 100 centimes to a franc).

centimètre noun M 1 centimetre; **un centimètre carré** a square centimetre; **un centimètre cube** a cubic centimetre; 2 tape measure.

central noun M **un central téléphonique** a telephone exchange.
adjective (M plural **centraux**) 1 central; 2 main.

centrale noun F power station; **une centrale nucléaire** a nuclear power station.

centraliser verb [1] to centralize.

centre noun M centre; **au centre de** in the centre of.

centre commercial noun M shopping centre.

centre sportif noun M sports centre.

centre-ville noun M town centre, city centre.

cependant adverb however.

cercle noun M circle; **en cercle** in a circle.

cercueil noun M coffin.

céréale noun F cereal, grain.

cérémonie noun F ceremony.

cerf noun M stag.

cerf-volant noun M kite.

cerise noun F cherry.

cerisier noun M cherry tree.

certain adjective 1 certain, sure; **être certain de** to be certain (or sure) of; 2 certain; **un certain nombre de** a certain number of; 3 some; **certaines personnes** some people.
pronoun some; **certains de mes amis** some of my friends.

certainement adverb 1 most probably; 2 certainly; 3 of course.

certes adverb admittedly.

certificat noun M certificate.

certifier verb [1] to certify.

cerveau (plural **cerveaux**) noun M 1 brain; 2 mind.

ces adjective 1 these; **c'est Sara qui m'a acheté ces fleurs** it was Sara who bought me these flowers; 2 those; **ces livres que je t'ai**

prêtés those books I lent you; **ces arbres-là** those trees.

CES noun M (*Collège d'enseignement secondaire*) secondary school (*from 11 to 15, when students can go on to a 'lycée' for a further 3 years*).

cesse noun F **sans cesse** constantly.

cesser verb [1] to stop; **cesser de faire** to stop doing.

cessez-le-feu noun M ceasefire.

c'est-à-dire phrase that is, that's to say.

cet, cette adjective SEE **ce**.

ceux, celles 1 the ones; **'quels livres?'** – **'ceux qui sont sur la table'** 'which books?' – 'the ones on the table'; **'quelles chaussettes?'** – **'celles que tu m'as prêtées hier'** 'which socks?' – 'the ones you lent me yesterday'; SEE **celui**.

ceux-ci, celles-ci these ones.

ceux-là, celles-là those ones.

chacal noun M jackal.

chacun, chacune pronoun 1 each; **ils ont chacun un billet** they each have a ticket; 2 everyone; **comme chacun sait** as everyone knows.

chagrin noun M grief.

chaîne noun F 1 chain; 2 channel (*on TV*).

chaîne hi-fi noun F hi-fi system.

chaîne laser noun F CD player.

chaîne stéréo noun F stereo system.

chair noun F 1 flesh; 2 meat; **la chair à saucisse** sausage meat; ★ **avoir la chair de poule** to have goose pimples (*literally: to have hen's flesh*).

chaise noun F chair.

châle noun M shawl.

chalet noun M chalet.

chaleur noun F heat, warmth.

chaleureux (F **chaleureuse**) adjective warm.

chambre noun F 1 bedroom; **dans ma chambre** in my bedroom; 2 (hotel) room; **une chambre pour une personne** a single room; **une chambre pour deux personnes** a double room; 3 **la musique de chambre** chamber music.

chambre d'amis noun F spare bedroom.

chambre de commerce noun F chamber of commerce.

chambres d'hôte plural noun F bed and breakfast.

chameau (*plural* **chameaux**) noun M camel.

champ noun M field.

champagne noun M champagne.

champ de bataille noun M battlefield.

champ de courses noun M racetrack.

champignon noun M 1 mushroom; **des champignons de**

Paris button mushrooms;
2 fungus.

champion, championne *noun*
M, F champion.

championnat *noun* M
championship.

chance *noun* F 1 luck; **un coup de
chance** a stroke of luck; **Bonne
chance!** Good luck!; **j'ai eu la
chance de pouvoir passer un an en
France** I was lucky enough to be able
to spend a year in France; **avoir de la
chance** to be lucky; **tu as de la
chance d'avoir une sœur pareille!**
you're lucky to have a sister like
that!; 2 chance.

chancelier *noun* M chancellor.

chandail *noun* M jumper.

chandelier *noun* M
1 candlestick; 2 candelabra.

change *noun* M exchange rate;
bureau de change bureau de
change (*for changing money*).

changeant *adjective* changeable.

changement *noun* M change.

changer *verb* [52] 1 to change; **tu
n'as pas changé** you haven't
changed; 2 **changer quelque
chose** to change something;
changer les draps to change the
sheets; **changer une prise** to
change a plug; 3 **changer quelque
chose** to exchange something (*in a
shop*); 4 **changer de** to change;
changer de train to change trains;
changer d'avis to change your
mind; **j'ai changé d'avis** I've
changed my mind; 5 **se changer** to
get changed, to change your clothes.

chanson *noun* F song.

chant *noun* M 1 singing; 2 song.

chantage *noun* M blackmail.

chanter *verb* [1] to sing.

chanteur, chanteuse *noun* M, F
singer.

chantier *noun* M 1 building site;
2 roadworks.

chantonner *verb* [1] to hum.

chaos *noun* M chaos.

chaotique *adjective* chaotic.

chapeau (*plural* **chapeaux**) *noun*
M 1 hat; 2 **chapeau!** well done!

chapeau melon *noun* M bowler
hat.

chapelle *noun* F chapel.

chapelure *noun* F breadcrumbs.

chapiteau (*plural* **chapiteaux**)
noun M 1 marquee; 2 big top
(*circus tent*).

chapitre *noun* M chapter.

chaque *adjective* each, every.

char *noun* M 1 (military) tank;
2 carnival float.

charabia *noun* M (*informal*)
gobbledygook, rubbish.

charade *noun* F riddle.

charbon *noun* M coal.

charbon de bois *noun* M
charcoal.

charcuterie *noun* F 1 pork
butcher's (*selling salads and ready-
prepared dishes as well as pork,*

bacon, ham, sausages, etc); **2** pork products (ham, salami, pâté, etc).

charcutier, charcutière noun M, F pork butcher.

chardon noun M thistle.

charge noun F **1** load; **2** responsibility; **avoir la charge de** to be responsible for; **3 charges** costs, charges.

charger verb [52] **1** to load; **2** to charge (a battery).

chariot noun M trolley (at the supermarket).

charité noun F charity.

charmant adjective charming.

charme noun M **1** charm; **2** spell.

charmer verb [1] to charm.

charnière noun F hinge.

charpentier noun M carpenter.

charrette noun F cart.

charrue noun F plough.

charte noun F charter.

charter adjective **un vol charter** a charter flight.

chasse noun F hunting, shooting.

chasse d'eau noun F (toilet) flush; **tirer la chasse d'eau** to flush the toilet.

chasse-neige noun M snowplough.

chasser verb [1] to chase off.

chasseur noun M hunter.

chat noun M cat.

châtaigne noun F sweet chestnut.

châtaignier noun M sweet chestnut tree.

châtain adjective **les cheveux châtains** brown hair.

château (plural **châteaux**) noun M **1** castle; **2** large country house.

château d'eau noun M water tower.

chatouiller verb [1] to tickle.

chatte noun F (female) cat.

chaud adjective hot, warm; **du lait chaud** hot milk; **un pull chaud** a warm jumper; **j'ai chaud** I'm hot; **il fait chaud ici** it's hot here.

chaudière noun F boiler; **une chaudière à gaz** a gas boiler.

chauffage noun M heating.

chauffage central noun M central heating.

chauffe-eau noun M water heater.

chauffer verb [1] **1** to heat, to heat up; **2** to warm.

chauffeur noun M **1** driver; **un chauffeur de taxi** a taxi driver; **2** chauffeur.

chaumière noun F thatched cottage.

chaussée noun F roadway.

chaussette noun F sock.

chausson noun M **1** slipper; **2** ballet shoe.

chaussure noun F shoe.

chauve adjective bald.

chauve-souris noun F bat.

chavirer verb [1] to capsize.

chef noun M 1 leader; 2 head;
3 boss; 4 chef de cuisine chef.

chef-d'œuvre noun M
masterpiece.

chemin noun M 1 country road;
2 track, path; 3 way; perdre son
chemin to lose your way; en
chemin on the way.

chemin de fer noun M railway.

cheminée noun F 1 chimney;
2 fireplace; 3 mantlepiece.

cheminot noun M railway worker.

chemise noun F shirt.

chemise de nuit noun F
nightdress.

chemisier noun M blouse.

chêne noun M 1 oak tree; 2 oak;
une table en chêne an oak table.

chenille noun F caterpillar.

chèque noun M cheque; un carnet
de chèques a cheque book.

chèque de voyage noun M
traveller's cheque.

chéquier noun M cheque book.

cher (F **chère**) adjective 1 dear;
Chère Anne Dear Anne;
2 expensive, dear; pas trop cher
reasonably priced.
adverb coûter cher to be expensive.

chercher verb [1] 1 to look for;
qu'est-ce que tu cherches? what
are you looking for?; je cherche mes
lunettes I'm looking for my glasses;
je cherche un emploi I'm looking for
a job; 2 chercher quelque chose
to look something up (in a
dictionary, for example); 3 aller

chercher to go and get (or fetch)
(somebody or something); je vais
chercher des verres I'll go and get
some glasses; 4 to pick up; je
viendrai te chercher à l'école I'll
come and pick you up from school;
5 chercher à faire to try to do.

chercheur, chercheuse noun
M, F scientist.

chéri, chérie noun M, F darling.

chérir verb [2] to cherish.

cheval (plural chevaux) noun M
1 horse; à cheval on horseback;
monter à cheval to ride a horse;
2 faire du cheval to go horseriding.

cheval à bascule noun M
rocking horse.

chevalet noun M easel.

chevet noun M 1 bedhead; au
chevet de quelqu'un at somebody's
bedside; un livre de chevet a
bedside book; une lampe de chevet
a bedside lamp; 2 bedside table.

cheveu (plural cheveux) noun M
1 un cheveu a hair; 2 les
cheveux hair; il a les cheveux
blonds he has blond hair; ★ avoir
un cheveu sur la langue to have a
lisp (literally: to have a hair on one's
tongue); couper les cheveux en
quatre to split hairs (literally: to cut
hairs in four).

cheville noun F ankle.

chèvre[1] noun F goat, nanny-goat.

chèvre[2] noun M goat's cheese.

chèvrefeuille noun M
honeysuckle.

chevreuil noun M 1 roe deer;
2 venison.

chez preposition 1 chez quelqu'un
at (or to) somebody's house; **je vais
chez Paul ce soir** I'm going to Paul's
this evening; **elle est chez les
Brown** she's at the Browns'; **viens
chez moi** come round to my place;
il est chez lui he's at home; **je rentre
chez moi maintenant** I'm going
home now; **fais comme chez toi**
make yourself at home; 2 **chez le
boucher** at (or to) the butcher's; **je
l'ai rencontrée chez le coiffeur
hier** I met her at the hairdresser's
yesterday; **je vais chez le coiffeur
demain** I'm going to the
hairdresser's tomorrow.

chic adjective 1 chic, well-dressed;
2 nice; **c'était vachement chic de
ta part** it was really nice of you;
3 Chic! (informal) Cool!

chicorée noun F 1 endive;
2 chicory powder (for adding to
coffee).

chien noun M dog; **'chien
méchant'** 'beware of the dog'.

chien d'aveugle noun M guide
dog.

chien de berger noun M
sheepdog.

chien de garde noun M guard
dog.

chienne noun F (female) dog,
bitch.

chiffon noun M 1 rag; 2 duster.

chiffre noun M figure; **un numéro à
cinq chiffres** a five-figure number.

chignon noun M bun, chignon.

chimie noun F chemistry.

chimique adjective chemical.

chimpanzé noun M chimpanzee.

Chine noun F China.

chinois noun M,
adjective Chinese.

Chinois, Chinoise noun M, F
Chinese man, Chinese woman; **les
Chinois** the Chinese.

chiot noun M puppy.

chips noun F crisp; **un paquet de
chips** a packet of crisps.

chirurgical (M plural chirurgicaux)
adjective surgical; **une intervention
chirurgicale** an operation.

chirurgie noun F surgery.

chirurgien noun M surgeon.

chirurgien-dentiste noun M
dental surgeon.

choc noun M 1 shock; **ça m'a fait
un choc** it gave me a shock;
2 crash.

chocolat noun M chocolate;
chocolat au lait milk chocolate;
chocolat blanc white chocolate;
chocolat en poudre drinking
chocolate; **un gâteau au chocolat** a
chocolate cake; **un chocolat chaud**
a hot chocolate.

chœur noun M 1 choir
(professional); 2 chorus.

choisir verb [2] to choose.

choix noun M 1 choice; **un bon
choix** a good choice; 2 **un grand
choix** a wide choice (or variety).

chômage noun M unemployment; **être au chômage** to be unemployed.

chômeur, chômeuse noun M, F unemployed person.

chope noun F beer mug.

choquer verb [1] to shock.

chorale noun F choir (*amateur*).

chose noun F thing; **les choses qui m'intéressent** the things that interest me; **j'ai plusieurs choses à te dire** I have several things to tell you; **je prends la même chose** I'll have the same.

chou (*plural* **choux**) noun M cabbage.

chouchou[1], chouchoute noun M, F teacher's pet.

chouchou[2] noun M scrunchy (*for holding back your hair*).

choucroute noun F sauerkraut (*pickled cabbage with different types of sausage, ham, and bacon*).

chou de Bruxelles noun M Brussels sprout.

chouette noun F owl.
adjective (*informal*) great; **c'est chouette!** that's great!; **leur maison est très chouette** their house is really lovely.

chou-fleur (*plural* **choux-fleurs**) noun M cauliflower.

chrétien, chrétienne noun M, F, adjective Christian.

christianisme noun M Christianity.

chrome noun M chromium.

chronique noun F **1** column, page (*devoted to a particular journalist in a newspaper*); **2** (radio) programme.
adjective chronic.

chronomètre noun M stopwatch.

chrysanthème noun M chrysanthemum.

chuchoter verb [1] to whisper.

chut exclamation shh!

chute noun F **1** fall; **faire une chute de 5 mètres** to fall 5 metres; **2 chutes de neige** snowfall; **chutes de pluie** rainfall; **3** fall, drop (*in price, value, temperature*).

chuter verb [1] to fall, to drop.

Chypre noun F Cyprus.

ci adverb **ce mois-ci** this month; **ces timbres-ci** these stamps; **ces jours-ci** these last few days.

cible noun F target.

ciboulette noun F **de la ciboulette** chives.

cicatrice noun F scar.

ci-contre adverb opposite.

ci-dessous adverb below.

ci-dessus adverb above.

cidre noun M cider.

ciel (*plural* **cieux**) noun M **1** sky; **au ciel** in the sky; **2** heaven.

cigale noun F cicada.

cigare noun M cigar.

cigarette noun F cigarette.

cigogne noun F stork.

ci-joint *adverb* veuillez trouver ci-joint please find enclosed (*in a letter*).

cil *noun* M eyelash.

ciment *noun* M cement.

cimetière *noun* M 1 cemetery; 2 graveyard.

cinéaste *noun* M & F film director.

ciné-club *noun* M film club.

cinéma *noun* M 1 cinema; aller au cinéma to go to the cinema; 2 (*informal*) play-acting; arrête ton cinéma! stop that nonsense!

cinéphile *noun* M & F keen cinema-goer.

cinglé *adjective* (*informal*) crazy.

cinq *number* five; Lucie a cinq ans Lucie's five; à cinq heures at five o'clock; le cinq avril the fifth of April.

cinquantaine *noun* F une cinquantaine (de) about fifty; une cinquantaine de personnes about fifty people; avoir la cinquantaine to be about fifty.

cinquante *number* fifty.

cinquantième *number* fiftieth.

cinquième *noun* F (*in a French school*) the equivalent of Year 8. *noun* M au cinquième on the fifth floor. *adjective* fifth.

cintre *noun* M clothes hanger.

cirage *noun* M shoe polish.

circonflexe *noun* M un accent circonflexe a circumflex.

circonstance *noun* F circumstance.

circuit *noun* M 1 circuit (*in an athletics stadium*); 2 tour; 3 (eléctrical) circuit.

circulaire *noun* F. *adjective* circular.

circulation *noun* F 1 traffic; il y a beaucoup de circulation ce soir there's a lot of traffic this evening; 2 circulation.

circuler *verb* [1] 1 to run (*of a bus or train*); ce train ne circule pas le dimanche that train doesn't run on Sundays; 2 to circulate.

cire *noun* F wax.

cirer *verb* [1] to polish.

cirque *noun* M circus; au cirque at (or to) the circus.

ciseaux *plural noun* M scissors; une paire de ciseaux a pair of scissors.

citadin, citadine *noun* M, F city dweller.

citation *noun* F quotation.

cité *noun* F 1 city, town; 2 housing estate; 3 une cité universitaire university halls of residence.

citer *verb* [1] to quote.

citerne *noun* F tank.

citoyen, citoyenne *noun* M, F citizen.

citron *noun* M lemon; une tarte au citron a lemon tart.

citronnade *noun* F still lemonade.

citronnier *noun* M lemon tree.

citron vert noun M lime.

citrouille noun F pumpkin.

civet noun M stew.

civil noun M 1 civilian; 2 **un policier en civil** a plain-clothes policeman.
adjective 1 civilian; 2 **un mariage civil** a civil wedding (as opposed to a church wedding).

civilisation noun F civilization.

civique adjective civic.

clair adjective 1 light; **bleu clair** light blue; 2 **la chambre est très claire** the bedroom is very light; 3 clear.
adverb clearly; **voir clair** to see clearly.

clair de lune noun M moonlight.

clairement adverb clearly.

clapier noun M rabbit hutch.

claque noun F slap.

claqué adjective (informal) exhausted, wiped out.

claquer verb [1] **claquer la porte** to slam the door.

clarifier verb [1] to clarify.

clarinette noun F clarinet; **jouer de la clarinette** to play the clarinet.

clarté noun F 1 light; 2 clarity.

classe noun F 1 class; **elle est dans ma classe à l'école** she's in my class (or year) at school; **en classe** in class; 2 classroom; 3 **première/deuxième classe** first/second class; 4 (social) class.

classement noun M
1 classification; 2 placing;
3 grading; 4 filing.

classer verb [1] 1 to classify; 2 to grade; 3 to file.

classeur noun M 1 ring binder, file; 2 filing cabinet.

classique adjective 1 classical; 2 classic; 3 usual; **c'est classique!** that's typical!

clavier noun M keyboard.

clé noun F 1 key; **fermer quelque chose à clé** to lock something; 2 spanner.

clef = CLÉ.

clémentine noun F clementine.

client, cliente noun M,F
1 customer; 2 client.

clientèle noun F customers.

cligner verb [1] **cligner des yeux** to blink.

clignotant noun M indicator (on a motor vehicle).

clignoter verb [1] to flash.

climat noun M climate.

climatisation noun F air-conditioning.

climatisé adjective air-conditioned.

clin d'œil noun M wink; **faire un clin d'œil à quelqu'un** to wink at somebody; ★ **en un clin d'œil** in a flash.

clinique noun F clinic, private hospital.

clip noun M **1** video clip; **2** clip brooch; **3** clip-on earring.

cliquer verb [1] **cliquer sur quelque chose** to click on something (using a computer mouse).

cliqueter verb [48] **1** to jingle; **2** to rattle.

clochard, clocharde noun M, F tramp, down-and-out.

cloche noun F bell.

clocher noun M **1** steeple; **2** bell tower.

cloison noun F **1** partition; **2** partition wall; **3** screen.

cloître noun M cloister.

clos adjective closed.

clôture noun F **1** fence; **2** close; **3** closing.

clou noun M **1** nail; **2** stud.

clou de girofle noun M clove.

clouer verb [1] **clouer quelque chose** to nail something down.

clown noun M clown.

club noun M club; **un club de foot** a football club.

cobaye noun M guinea pig.

Coca™ noun M Coke™.

cocaïne noun F cocaine.

coccinelle noun F ladybird.

cocher verb [1] to tick.

cochon noun M pig. *adjective* (F **cochonne**) (*informal*) dirty (*joke, story*).

cochon d'Inde noun M guinea pig.

cocktail noun M **1** cocktail; **2** cocktail party.

coco noun M **une noix de coco** a coconut.

cocorico noun M cock-a-doodle-do.

cocotte noun F **1** casserole; **2** hen (*in baby talk*); **3** chocolate hen (*traditionally sold at Easter*).

cocotte-minute™ noun F pressure cooker.

code noun M **1** code; **le code de la route** the highway code; **2 codes** dipped headlights.

code postal noun M postcode.

cœur noun M **1** heart; **2** hearts (*suit of playing cards*); **le roi de cœur** the king of hearts; **par cœur** by heart; **apprendre quelque chose par cœur** to learn something by heart; ★ **avoir mal au cœur** to feel sick.

coffre noun M **1** chest; **2** safe; **3** boot (*of a car*).

coffre-fort noun M safe.

cogner verb [1] to bump, to bang; **se cogner la tête** to bang your head.

coiffer verb [1] **se coiffer** to brush (or comb) your hair.

coiffeur, coiffeuse¹ noun M, F hairdresser.

coiffeuse² noun F dressing table.

coiffure noun **1** hairdressing; **2** hairstyle; **tu as changé de coiffure** you've changed your hairstyle.

coin noun M **1** corner; **au coin** in the corner; **au coin de** in the corner of; **2 le café du coin** the local café; **les gens du coin** the local people; ★ **au coin du feu** by the fireside (*literally: in the corner of the fire*).

coincé adjective stuck, jammed.

coincer verb [61] to jam.

coïncidence noun F coincidence.

col noun M **1** collar; **2** neck; **3** (mountain) pass.

colère noun F anger; **être en colère** to be angry.

colin noun M hake.

colique noun F diarrhoea.

colis noun M parcel.

collant noun M **un collant** (a pair of) tights. adjective sticky.

colle noun F **1** glue; **2** detention; **une heure de colle** an hour's detention.

collecte noun F collection (*of money*).

collection noun F collection.

collectionner verb [1] to collect.

collège noun M secondary school (*from 11 to 15, when students can either leave school altogether or go on to a 'lycée' for a further 3 years*).

collégien, collégienne noun M, F schoolboy, schoolgirl.

collègue noun M & F colleague.

coller verb [1] **1** to stick; **2** to stick down; **3** to glue; **4** to press.

collier noun M **1** necklace; **2** collar (*for a dog, cat, etc.*).

colline noun F hill.

collision noun F collision.

colombe noun F dove.

colonie noun F colony.

colonie de vacances noun F holiday camp (*for children*).

colonne noun F column.

colonne vertébrale noun F spine.

colorant noun M colouring.

coloré adjective **1** coloured; **2** colourful.

colorer verb [1] to colour.

colorier verb [1] to colour in.

coloris noun M colour; **existe en plusieurs coloris** several colours available.

combat noun M **1** fighting; **2 un combat de boxe** a boxing match.

combattant noun M **un ancien combattant** a war veteran.

combattre verb [21] to fight.

combien adverb **1** how much; **tu en veux combien?** how much do you want?; **c'est combien?** how much is it?; **ça coûte combien?** how much does it cost?; **je vous dois combien?** how much do I owe you?; **c'est combien?** how much is that? **2** how many; **tu en veux combien?** how many do you want?; **3 combien de** how much; **combien d'argent?** how much money?; **4 combien de** how many; **combien de tasses?** how many cups?; ★ **nous sommes le combien**

aujourd'hui? what's the date today? (*literally: we are the how many today*)?

combinaison noun F
1 combination; 2 jumpsuit; 3 overalls; 4 slip, petticoat.

combiné noun M receiver (*of a telephone*).

comble noun M 1 **le comble** the height of; **le comble du luxe** the height of luxury; 2 **ça c'est le comble!** that's the last straw!

comédie noun F comedy.

comédien, comédienne noun M, F actor, actress.

comestible adjective edible.

comique noun M comic, comedian.
adjective funny.

comité noun M committee.

commande noun F order; **sur commande** to order.

commander verb [1] 1 to order; **avez-vous commandé?** have you ordered?; 2 to be in charge.

comme preposition 1 like; **une montre comme la tienne** a watch like yours; 2 like; **comme ça** like this; 3 as a; **travailler comme serveur dans un café** to work as a waiter in a café; 4 **qu'est-ce que tu veux comme glace?** what kind of ice cream would you like?
conjunction 1 as; **comme tu veux** as you like; 2 as, since; **comme je suis malade** as (or since) I'm ill; 3 as; **comme je fermais la porte** as I was closing the door; 4 **comme si** as if.

adverb comme il est gentil! he's so nice!; **comme c'est bon!** it's so good!; **comme il fait chaud!** it's so hot!; ★ **blanc comme la neige** as white as snow; **fort comme un bœuf** as strong as an ox.

commencement noun M beginning, start.

commencer verb [61] 1 to begin, to start; **le film a commencé** the film has started; 2 **commencer à faire, commencer de faire** to start (or begin) to do; **elle a commencé à faire ses devoirs** she's started to do her homework; **je commence à comprendre** I'm beginning to understand; **il commence à pleuvoir** it's starting to rain.

comment adverb 1 how; **comment as-tu fait ce gâteau?** how did you make this cake?; **je ne sais pas comment le faire** I don't know how to do it; 2 **comment vas-tu?** how are you?; **comment ça va?** how are you?; **comment va ta mère?** how's your mother?; 3 **comment t'appelles-tu?** what's your name?; **il s'appelle comment, ton frère?** what's your brother's name?; 4 **pardon?**; 5 **comment est leur maison?, elle est comment, leur maison?** what's their house like?

commentaire noun M 1 comment; 2 commentary.

commenter verb [1] **commenter quelque chose** to comment on something.

commerçant, commerçante noun M, F shopkeeper.

commerce noun M 1 shop; 2 le commerce business; je fais des études de commerce I'm doing business studies; 3 le commerce trade.

commercial (M plural commerciaux) adjective 1 commercial; 2 un centre commercial a shopping centre.

commettre verb [11] 1 commettre une erreur to make a mistake; 2 commettre un crime to commit a crime.

commissariat noun M police station.

commission noun F 1 committee; 2 commission; 3 message; 4 errand; 5 faire les commissions to do the shopping.

commode noun F chest of drawers. adjective 1 convenient, handy; 2 easy.

commun adjective 1 common; 2 shared; 3 joint; 4 en commun in common; ils n'ont rien en commun they have nothing in common; 5 en commun jointly, together; 6 les transports en commun public transport.

communauté noun F community.

communication noun F 1 une communication téléphonique a telephone call; 2 communication.

communion noun F communion.

communiquer verb [1] 1 to communicate; 2 communiquer quelque chose to pass something on.

communisme noun M communism.

communiste noun M & F, adjective communist.

compact adjective 1 dense; 2 compact; 3 un disque compact a compact disc, a CD.

compagnie noun F 1 company, firm; 2 company; elle m'a tenu compagnie she kept me company.

compagnie aérienne noun F airline.

compagnon noun M companion.

comparable adjective comparable.

comparaison noun F comparison; en comparaison de in comparison with.

comparatif (F comparative) adjective comparative.

comparé adjective comparé à compared to (or with).

comparer verb [1] to compare.

compartiment noun M compartment.

compas noun M compass.

compatir verb [2] to sympathize.

compensation noun F compensation.

compenser verb [1] compenser quelque chose to compensate for something.

compétence noun F 1 ability; 2 skill; 3 competence.

compétent adjective competent.

compétitif (F compétitive) adjective competitive.

compétition noun F competition.

complémentaire adjective
further, supplementary.

complet noun M suit.
adjective (F **complète**)
1 complete; **2** total; **3** full
(speaking of a hotel or a train); **4 le
pain complet** wholemeal bread.

complètement adverb
completely.

compléter verb [24] **1** to
complete; **2** to fill in (a form).

complexe noun M,
adjective complex.

complication noun F
complication.

complice noun M & F accomplice.

compliment noun M compliment;
faire des compliments à quelqu'un
to compliment somebody.

compliqué adjective complicated.

compliquer verb [1] to complicate.

complot noun M plot.

comportement noun M
behaviour.

comporter verb [1] **1** to include;
2 to consist of; **3 se comporter** to
behave.

composé adjective **1 composé de**
made up of; **2 une salade
composée** a mixed salad.

composer verb [1] **1** to make up;
2 to put together; **3** to compose
(music); **4 composer un numéro
(de téléphone)** to dial a (telephone)
number.

compositeur, compositrice
noun M, F composer.

composition noun F composition.

composter verb [1] to punch (a
ticket); **'n'oubliez pas de
composter votre billet'** remember
to punch your ticket (in France it is
an offence to get on a train without
first punching your ticket in one of
the machines provided for this at
platform entrances).

compote noun F stewed fruit; **la
compote de pommes** apple puree.

compréhensible adjective
understandable.

compréhensif (F **compréhensive**)
adjective understanding.

comprendre verb [64] **1** to
understand; **je comprends** I
understand; **j'ai compris** I
understood; **j'ai mal compris** I
misunderstood; **2** to include; **3 se
comprendre** to understand each
other; **4 ça se comprend** that's
understandable.

comprimé noun M tablet.

compris adjective **1** included;
service compris service included;
non compris not included; **2 y
compris** including; **tout le monde y
compris les enfants** everybody
including the children.

compromis noun M compromise.

comptabilité noun F accounting,
accountancy.

comptable noun M & F
accountant.

compte noun M **1** account; **un compte bancaire** a bank account; **un compte d'épargne** a savings account; **j'ai cent livres sur mon compte** I have a hundred pounds in my account; **2 le compte est bon** the amount is correct; **3 se rendre compte de quelque chose** to realize something; **se rendre compte que** to realize that; **je me suis rendu compte que j'avais oublié mes clés** I realized I had forgotten my keys; **4 tenir compte de quelque chose** to take something into account; **5 en fin de compte** all things considered.

compter verb [1] **1** to count; **2 compter sur quelqu'un** to count on somebody.

compte rendu noun M report.

compteur noun M meter.

compteur de vitesse noun M speedometer.

comptine noun F nursery rhyme.

comptoir noun M **1** counter; **2** bar.

concentré adjective concentrated.

concentré de tomate noun M tomato puree.

concentrer verb [1] **se concentrer (sur)** to concentrate (on).

conception noun F design.

concernant preposition concerning.

concerner verb [1] to concern; **en ce qui me concerne** as far as I'm concerned.

concert noun M concert; **un concert de rock** a rock concert.

concessionnaire noun M & F dealer, agent.

concierge noun M & F caretaker.

conclure verb [25] to conclude.

conclusion noun F conclusion.

concombre noun M cucumber.

concours noun M competition.

concret (F **concrète**) adjective **1** concrete; **2** practical.

concurrence noun F competition; **il y a beaucoup de concurrence** there's a lot of competition.

concurrent, concurrente noun M, F competitor.

condamner verb [1] to sentence (a criminal).

condition noun F **1** condition; **en bonne condition** in good condition; **2 à condition de/que** provided that; **tu peux emprunter mon vélo à condition de me le rendre ce soir** you can borrow my bike provided you let me have it back this evening; **3 dans ces conditions** in that case.

conditionnel noun M conditional tense.

conditionner verb [1] to package.

conducteur, conductrice noun M, F driver.

conduire verb [26] **1** to drive; **apprendre à conduire** to learn to drive; **un permis de conduire** a driving licence; **je te conduis à la**

gare I'll drive you to the station;
2 to take; **je vous conduis à votre
chambre** I'll take you to your room;
3 se conduire to behave.

conduite noun F **1** behaviour;
mauvaise conduite bad behaviour.

conférence noun F **1** lecture;
2 conference.

confesser verb [1] **se confesser** to
go to confession.

confiance noun F **1** trust; **avoir
confiance en quelqu'un, faire
confiance à quelqu'un** to trust
somebody; **je te fais confiance** I'll
leave it to you; **2** confidence.

confiant adjective confident.

confidence noun F secret.

confier verb [1] **1 confier quelque
chose à quelqu'un** to entrust
something to somebody; **2 se
confier à quelqu'un** to confide in
somebody.

confirmation noun F
confirmation.

confirmer verb [1] to confirm.

confiserie noun F sweet shop.

confisquer verb [1] to confiscate.

confit adjective **les fruits confits**
crystallized fruits.

confiture noun F jam; **la confiture
d'abricots** apricot jam.

conflit noun M conflict.

confondre verb [69] to confuse, to
mix up.

confort noun M comfort; **tout
confort** with all mod cons.

confortable adjective comfortable.

confrontation noun F
1 confrontation; **2** clash.

confus adjective **1** confused;
2 embarrassed.

confusion noun F **1** confusion;
2 embarrassment.

congé noun M holiday, leave (from
work); **Robert est en congé
aujourd'hui** Robert's on holiday
today; **je pars en congé le dix** I'm
on holiday from the tenth; **prendre
une semaine de congé** to take a
week's holiday; **Sylvie est en congé
de maladie** Sylvie is on sick leave.

congélateur noun M freezer.

congeler verb [45] to freeze.

congère noun F snowdrift.

congestion noun F congestion.

congrès noun M conference.

conifère noun M conifer.

conjoint, conjointe noun M, F
spouse (husband or wife).

conjonctivite noun F
conjunctivitis.

conjugaison noun F conjugation.

connaissance noun F
1 knowledge; **tes connaissances en
français** your knowledge of
French; **2** acquaintance;
3 consciousness; **perdre
connaissance** to lose
consciousness.

connaître verb [27] **1** to know; **est-
ce que tu connais Gaby?** do you
know Gaby?; **je ne connais pas
Londres** I don't know London; **je la**

connais depuis trois ans I've known her for three years; **2 se connaître** to know each other; **on se connaît** we know each other; **3 s'y connaître en quelque chose** to know about something; **je ne m'y connais pas du tout en informatique** I know absolutely nothing about computers.

connecter verb [1] to connect.

connexion noun F connection.

connu adjective well-known; **elle est très connue en France** she's very well-known in France.

consacrer verb [1] to devote.

consciemment adverb consciously.

conscience noun F conscience; **avoir mauvaise conscience** to have a guilty conscience.

conscient adjective **1** aware; **être conscient de quelque chose** to be aware of something; **2** conscious.

conseil noun M **1** advice; **un conseil** a piece of advice; **des conseils** advice; **2** council.

conseiller¹, conseillère noun M, F adviser.

conseiller² verb [1] **1** to advise; **conseiller à quelqu'un de faire** to advise somebody to do; **je te conseille de voir un médecin** I advise you to see a doctor; **2** to recommend; **pouvez-vous me conseiller un dentiste?** Can you recommend me a dentist?

consentement noun M consent.

consentir verb [58] **consentir à quelque chose** to agree to something.

conséquence noun F **1** consequence; **2 en conséquence** consequently.

conséquent adjective **par conséquent** consequently.

conservateur, conservatrice noun M, F **1** conservative; **2** (museum) curator.

conservation noun F **1** conservation; **2 lait longue conservation** long-life milk.

conserve noun F **1 les conserves** canned food; **2 en conserve** canned; **des légumes en conserve** canned vegetables.

conserver verb [1] **1** to keep; **je t'ai conservé une place** I've kept you a seat; **'à conserver au frais'** 'keep in a cool place'; **2 se conserver** to keep; **ce fromage se conserve bien** this cheese keeps well.

considérable adjective considerable.

considérablement adverb considerably.

considération noun F consideration.

considérer verb [24] to consider.

consigne noun F **1** left luggage office; **2** deposit (on a returnable bottle); **3** instructions.

consistant adjective substantial; **un repas consistant** a substantial meal.

consister verb [1] consister en to consist of, to consist in.

consommateur, consommatrice noun M, F 1 consumer; 2 customer (in a café).

consommation noun F 1 consumption (of fuel, electricity, gas); 2 drink.

consommer verb [1] 1 to use (fuel); 2 to have a drink (in a café).

consonne noun F consonant.

conspiration noun F conspiracy.

conspirer verb [1] to conspire, to plot.

constamment adverb constantly.

constant adjective constant.

constater verb [1] to notice.

constipé adjective constipated.

construction noun F construction, building.

construire verb [26] to build; construire une maison to build a house; faire construire une maison to have a house built.

consul noun M consul.

consulat noun M consulate.

consultation noun F 1 consultation; 2 (doctor's) surgery hours.

consulter verb [1] 1 to consult; 2 to hold surgery.

contact noun M contact; prendre contact avec quelqu'un to contact somebody.

contacter verb [1] to contact.

contagieux (F contagieuse) adjective infectious.

contamination noun F contamination.

contaminer verb [1] to contaminate.

conte noun M tale, story; un conte de fées a fairy tale.

contempler verb [1] to look at, to contemplate.

contemporain, contemporaine noun M, F, adjective contemporary.

contenant noun M container.

conteneur noun M container.

contenir verb [77] to contain; 'ne contient pas de sucre' 'does not contain sugar'.

content adjective pleased, glad, happy; être content de quelque chose to be pleased with something; elle est très contente de son nouveau travail she's very pleased with her new job; je suis content de te voir I'm pleased to see you.

contenter verb [1] 1 to satisfy; 2 se contenter de faire to content oneself with doing.

contenu noun M contents.

contesté adjective controversial.

contester verb [1] to dispute, to challenge, to question.

contexte noun M context.

continent noun M continent.

continu adjective continuous.

continuation noun F
continuation.

continuer verb [1] to continue, to go
on (with); **continue!** go on!; **elle a
continué son histoire** she went on
with her story; **continuer à faire,
continuer de faire** to go on doing;
elle a continué à parler she went on
talking.

contour noun M outline, contour.

contourner verb [1] to go round.

contraceptif noun M
contraceptive.

contraception noun F
contraception.

contractuel, contractuelle
noun M, F traffic warden.

contradiction noun F
contradiction.

contradictoire adjective
contradictory.

contraindre verb [31] to force.

contraire noun M 1 **le contraire**
the opposite; **c'est le contraire de
ce que je pensais** it's the opposite
of what I thought; 2 **au contraire**
on the contrary.
adjective opposite.

contrairement adverb
contrairement à contrary to,
unlike; **contrairement à ce qu'il
nous a dit** contrary to what he told
us.

contrariant adjective annoying.

contrarier verb [1] 1 to upset;
2 to annoy.

contraste noun M contrast.

contraster verb [1] to contrast.

contrat noun M contract.

contravention noun F 1 parking
ticket; 2 speeding ticket.

contre preposition 1 against;
contre le mur against the wall;
2 **être contre quelque chose** to be
against something; **je suis plutôt
contre** on the whole, I'm against it;
3 **jouer contre quelqu'un** to play
against somebody; 4 versus;
5 **échanger quelque chose contre**
to exchange something for
(something else); 6 **par contre** on
the other hand; ★ **le pour et le
contre** the pros and cons.

contrebande noun F
1 smuggling; 2 smuggled goods.

contrebasse noun F double bass.

contredire verb [47] to contradict.

contreplaqué noun M plywood.

contribuable noun M & F
taxpayer.

contribuer verb [1] **contribuer à** to
contribute to.

contribution noun F
contribution.

contrôle noun M 1 control;
2 class test (at school); **j'ai un
contrôle de français cet après-
midi** I've got a French test this
afternoon; 3 **contrôle de police**
police check; 4 **contrôle des
passeports** passport control;
contrôle des billets ticket
inspection.

contrôle continu noun M
continuous assessment.

contrôler verb [1] **1** to check; **2** to control.

contrôleur, contrôleuse noun M, F ticket inspector.

controversé adjective controversial.

convaincant adjective convincing.

convaincre verb [79] **1** to convince; **je ne suis pas convaincu** I'm not convinced; **2** to persuade; **je l'ai convaincu d'acheter un ordinateur** I persuaded him to buy a computer.

convenable adjective **1** suitable; **2** decent.

convenir verb [81] **1 convenir à** to suit, to be suitable for; **est-ce que dix heures te convient?** does ten o'clock suit you? **2 convenir de faire** to agree to do.

convention noun F **1** agreement; **2** convention.

conversation noun F conversation.

convertir verb [2] to convert.

conviction noun F conviction.

convive noun M & F guest.

convivial (M plural **conviviaux**) adjective **1** friendly; **une atmosphère conviviale** a friendly atmosphere; **2** user-friendly.

convoi noun M **1** convoy; **2 'convoi exceptionnel'** 'dangerous load'.

convoquer verb [1] **1** to invite (to a meeting); **2** to summon.

coopératif (F **coopérative¹**) adjective cooperative.

coopération noun F cooperation.

coopérative² noun F cooperative.

coopérer verb [24] to cooperate.

coordonnées plural noun F address and telephone number.

coordonner verb [1] to coordinate.

copain noun M **1** friend, mate (male); **je sors avec les copains** I'm going out with my mates; **2** boyfriend; **elle est partie en vacances avec son copain** she's gone on holiday with her boyfriend.

copie noun F **1** copy; **2** paper (on which an exam or class exercise has been written); **j'ai un tas de copies à corriger ce soir** I've got a pile of marking to do this evening.

copier verb [1] to copy.

copieux (F **copieuse**) adjective hearty; **un petit déjeuner copieux** a hearty breakfast.

copine noun F **1** friend, mate (female); **je sors avec les copines** I'm going out with my mates; **2** girlfriend; **il est parti en vacances avec sa copine** he's gone on holiday with his girlfriend.

coq noun M cockerel.

coque noun F **1** hull (of a boat); **2** shell (of a nut); **3 un œuf à la coque** a soft-boiled egg.

coquelicot noun M poppy.

coqueluche noun F whooping-cough.

coquet (F **coquette**) adjective **1** flirtatious; **2** pretty.

coquetier noun M eggcup.

coquillage noun M 1 shellfish;
2 seashell.

coquille noun F 1 shell;
2 misprint.

coquille Saint-Jacques noun F
scallop.

coquin adjective cheeky, naughty.

cor noun M horn (musical
instrument).

corail (plural **coraux**) noun M
coral.

Coran noun M le Coran the Koran.

corbeau noun M crow.

corbeille noun F basket; une
corbeille à papier a wastepaper
basket; une corbeille à linge a linen
basket.

corbillard noun M hearse.

corde noun F 1 rope; 2 string (of a
racket, a bow, or an instrument such
as a guitar or violin); ★ pleuvoir
des cordes to be raining cats and
dogs (literally: to be raining ropes).

corde à linge noun F clothes line.

cordial (M plural **cordiaux**)
adjective warm, cordial.

cordialement adverb 1 warmly;
2 cordialement à vous Yours
sincerely.

cordonnerie noun F shoe
repairer's.

cordonnier noun M shoe repairer.

corne noun F horn.

cornemuse noun F bagpipes;
jouer de la cornemuse to play the
bagpipes.

cornet noun M 1 un cornet de
glace an ice cream cone; 2 un
cornet de frites a bag of chips (in
fact sold in a cardboard cornet).

cornichon noun M gherkin.

Cornouailles noun F Cornwall.

corps noun M body.

correct adjective 1 correct;
2 reasonable, fine; à un prix
correct at a reasonable price; le
repas était tout à fait correct the
meal was absolutely fine.

correctement adverb
1 correctly; 2 properly;
3 reasonably well.

correction noun F correction.

correspondance noun F
1 letters, correspondence;
2 acheter quelque chose par
correspondance to buy something
by mail order; 3 connection (a train
or flight); j'ai raté ma
correspondance I missed my
connection; un vol en
correspondance a connecting
flight.

**correspondant,
correspondante** noun M, F pen
friend.

correspondre verb [3] to
correspond.

corrida noun F bullfight.

corriger verb [52] 1 to correct;
2 to mark; elle est en train de
corriger ses copies she's doing her
marking.

corsage noun M 1 blouse;
2 bodice.

corse adjective Corsican.

Corse noun F Corsica.

corsé adjective full-bodied, strong.

corvée noun F chore.

cosmétiques plural noun M cosmetics.

costaud adjective strong, sturdy.

costume noun M 1 suit; 2 costume.

côte noun F 1 coast; 2 hill; 3 rib; 4 chop; **une côte d'agneau** a lamb chop.

côté noun M 1 side; **de l'autre côté (de)** on the other side (of); **de l'autre côté de la rue** on the other side of the street; 2 **d'un autre côté** on the other hand; 3 **à côté** nearby; **mon frère habite à côté** my brother lives nearby; 4 **à côté de** next to, beside; **elle était assise à côté de moi** she was sitting next to me.

Côte d'Azur noun F French Riviera.

côtelette noun F chop; **une côtelette de porc** a pork chop.

cotisation noun F 1 subscription; 2 contribution.

coton noun M 1 cotton; **un pull en coton** a cotton jumper; 2 sewing cotton; 3 cotton wool.

cou noun M neck.

couchage noun M **un sac de couchage** a sleeping bag.

couchant adjective **le soleil couchant** the setting sun; **au soleil couchant** at sunset.

couche noun F 1 layer; 2 coat (of paint); 3 nappy.

coucher verb [1] 1 to sleep; **tu peux coucher chez Sophie** you can sleep at Sophie's house; 2 **se coucher** to go to bed; **elle se couche à dix heures** she goes to bed at ten o'clock; 3 **coucher un enfant** to put a child to bed.

coucher de soleil noun M sunset; **un coucher de soleil magnifique** a magnificent sunset.

coucou noun M 1 cuckoo; 2 cowslip.

coude noun M elbow.

coudre verb [28] to sew; **coudre un bouton** to sew on a button.

couette noun F duvet, continental quilt.

couler verb [1] 1 to flow; 2 **avoir le nez qui coule** to have a runny nose; 3 **faire couler un bain** to run a bath; 4 to sink.

couleur noun F colour; **de quelle couleur est ta voiture?** what colour is your car?

couleuvre noun F grass snake.

coulisses plural noun F wings (in a theatre).

couloir noun M corridor.

coup noun M 1 blow; **il a reçu un coup à l'estomac** he was hit in the stomach; ★ **boire un coup** (informal) to have a drink; ★ **donner un coup de balai** to sweep the floor; ★ **un coup de peinture** a lick of paint; ★ **sur le coup** at first;

★ **tenir le coup** to last out; ★ **tout d'un coup**, all of a sudden.

coup de chance noun M stroke of luck.

coup de feu noun M (gun)shot.

coup de main noun M **donner un coup de main à quelqu'un** to give somebody a hand.

coup de pied noun M kick.

coup de poing noun M punch.

coup de soleil noun M **attraper un coup de soleil** to get sunburnt.

coup de téléphone noun M phone call.

coup de tonnerre noun M clap of thunder.

coup de vent noun M gust of wind.

coup d'œil noun M glance; **jeter un coup d'œil à quelque chose** to have a quick look at something.

coupable noun M & F culprit.
adjective guilty.

coupe noun F **1** cup (for sports); **la Coupe du Monde** the World Cup; **2** haircut; **3** fruit dish.

couper verb [1] **1** to cut; **se faire couper les cheveux** to have your hair cut; **2 se couper** to cut yourself; **se couper le doigt** to cut your finger; **3** to cut off, to turn off (gas, electricity); **4 excuse-moi, je t'ai coupé la parole** sorry, I interrupted you.

couple noun M couple.

coupon noun M **1** remnant (of fabric); **2** coupon.

coupure noun F cut; **une coupure de courant** a power cut.

cour noun F **1** school playground; **2** inner courtyard (in an apartment block or hotel); **3** court (of a king or queen); **4** law court.

courage noun M **1** courage, bravery; **2** energy; **avoir le courage de faire** to have the energy to do; **3 bon courage!** good luck!

courageux (F **courageuse**) adjective brave.

couramment adverb fluently.

courant noun M **1 être au courant de quelque chose** to know about something; **est-ce que ta sœur est au courant?** does your sister know?; **je te tiens au courant** I'll let you know what happens; **2** current; **3** electricity; **couper le courant** to cut off (or turn off) the electricity; **une panne de courant** a power cut.
adjective **1** common; **2** usual; **3** current.

courant d'air noun M draught.

courbe noun F curve.

courber verb [1] to bend.

coureur, coureuse noun M, F runner.

courge noun F (vegetable) marrow.

courgette noun F courgette.

courir verb [29] **1** to run; **traverser la rue en courant** to run across the street; **2 courir un risque** to run a risk.

couronne noun F crown.

courrier noun M mail, post.

courrier électronique noun M electronic mail, e-mail.

cours noun M 1 class, lesson; **le cours de français** the French lesson; **suivre des cours d'espagnol** to go to Spanish classes; 2 course (*of events*); **au cours de** in the course of.

course noun F 1 race; 2 running; 3 **les courses** shopping; **faire des courses** to do some shopping; **je fais mes courses à midi** I do my shopping at lunchtime.

court adjective short.

court-circuit noun M short-circuit.

court de tennis noun M tennis court.

couru verb SEE courir.

cousin, cousine noun M, F cousin; **mon cousin germain** my first cousin.

coussin noun M cushion.

coût noun M cost; **le coût de la vie** the cost of living.

couteau (*plural* **couteaux**) noun M knife; **un couteau à pain** a bread knife.

coûter verb [1] to cost; **ça coûte combien?** how much is it?; **ça coûte dix francs** it's ten francs; **coûter cher** to be expensive; **est-ce que ça t'a coûté cher?** was it expensive?

coutume noun F custom.

couture noun F 1 sewing, dressmaking; **faire de la couture** to sew; 2 seam.

couturier noun M fashion designer.

couturière noun F dressmaker.

couvent noun M convent.

couvercle noun M 1 lid; 2 screwtop.

couvert noun M place setting; **les couverts** the cutlery; **mettre les couverts** to set the table. *adjective* 1 covered; **un marché couvert** a covered market; 2 **couvert de** covered with; 3 overcast, cloudy.

couverture noun F 1 blanket; 2 cover (*of a book*).

couvre-lit noun M bedspread.

couvrir verb [30] to cover.

crabe noun M crab.

cracher verb [1] to spit.

crachin noun M drizzle.

craie noun F chalk.

craindre verb [31] to be afraid of.

crainte noun F fear.

crampe noun F cramp.

crâne noun M skull; **avoir mal au crâne** (*informal*) to have a headache.

crâner verb [1] (*informal*) to show off.

crapaud noun M toad.

craquement noun M creak.

craquer verb [1] 1 to split; 2 to creak; 3 (*informal*) to crack up; ★ **j'ai craqué** I couldn't resist it!

crasse noun F filth.

cravate noun F tie.

crawl noun M crawl (*in swimming*); **nager le crawl** to swim crawl.

crayon noun M pencil.

créatif (F **créative**) *adjective* creative.

création noun F creation.

crèche noun F 1 crèche, day nursery; 2 nativity scene (*as a Christmas decoration*).

crédit noun M 1 credit; 2 funding.

créer verb [32] to create.

crémaillère noun F chimney hook (*used in olden times to hang a pot for cooking over the fire*); ★ **pendre la crémaillère** to have a house-warming party (*literally: to hang the chimney hook*).

crème noun F, *adjective* cream.

crème Chantilly noun F whipped cream.

crémerie noun F cheese shop.

crémeux (F **crémeuse**) *adjective* creamy.

crêpe noun F pancake.

crépon noun M crepe paper.

crépuscule noun M twilight.

cresson noun M watercress.

creuser verb [1] 1 to dig; 2 to hollow out; ★ **se creuser la cervelle** (*informal*) to rack your brains.

creux noun M hollow. *adjective* (F **creuse**) 1 hollow; 2 **une assiette creuse** a soup plate.

crevaison noun F puncture.

crevé *adjective* 1 burst; 2 (*informal*) knackered.

crever verb [50] 1 to burst; **un pneu crevé** a burst tyre, a puncture; 2 (*informal*) to die; **je crève de faim!** I'm starving!

crevette noun F prawn.

cri noun M cry, shout.

criard *adjective* garish.

cric noun M (car) jack.

cricket noun M cricket; **jouer au cricket** to play cricket.

crier verb [1] 1 to shout; 2 to scream.

crime noun M crime.

criminel, criminelle noun M, F, *adjective* criminal.

criquet noun M grasshopper.

crise noun F 1 crisis; 2 attack (*of an illness*).

crise cardiaque noun F heart attack.

cristal (*plural* **cristaux**) noun M crystal.

critère noun M criterion.

critique[1] noun M critic.

critique[2] noun F 1 criticism; **les critiques** criticism; 2 review (*of a film, book, etc*).

critique[3] *adjective* critical.

critiquer verb [1] to criticize.

Croatie noun F Croatia.

croche-pied noun M faire un croche-pied à quelqu'un (informal) to trip somebody up.

crochet noun M 1 hook; 2 detour; 3 crochet.

crocodile noun M crocodile.

croire verb [33] 1 croire que to think that; je crois qu'il est parti I think he's left; tu crois que c'est trop tard? do you think it's too late?; je ne crois pas I don't think so; 2 to believe; je n'arrive pas à le croire I don't believe it; 3 croire à to believe in; 4 je n'en croyais pas mes yeux! I couldn't believe my eyes!

croiser verb [1] 1 to cross; croiser les jambes to cross your legs; croiser les bras to fold your arms; 2 croiser quelqu'un to bump into somebody (meet by chance); j'ai croisé Odile devant la banque I bumped into Odile outside the bank.

croisière noun F cruise.

croissance noun F growth.

croissant noun M croissant.

croître verb [34] to grow.

croix noun F cross.

Croix-Rouge noun F Red Cross.

croquant adjective crunchy.

croque-monsieur noun M toasted ham sandwich with cheese sauce on top.

croque-mort noun (informal) M undertaker.

croquer verb [1] to munch.

croquis noun M sketch.

crottes plural noun F droppings; des crottes de chien dog dirt.

croustillant adjective crispy.

croûte noun F 1 crust; 2 rind (of cheese).

croûton noun M crouton.

croyance noun F belief.

cru[1] verb SEE **croire**.

cru[2] adjective raw, uncooked.

cruauté noun F cruelty.

cruche noun F (large) jug.

crudités plural noun F raw vegetables (served with dips as a starter).

cruel (F **cruelle**) adjective cruel.

crustacé noun M shellfish.

crypte noun F crypt.

cube noun M cube. adjective cubic; un mètre cube a cubic metre.

cueillir verb [35] to pick (fruit or flowers).

cuiller noun F 1 spoon; 2 spoonful.

cuillère noun F = cuiller.

cuillerée noun F spoonful.

cuir noun M leather; des chaussures en cuir leather shoes.

cuir chevelu noun M scalp.

cuire verb [36] to cook.

cuisine noun F 1 kitchen; 2 cooking; faire la cuisine to cook, to do the cooking.

cuisiner verb [1] to cook.

cuisinier, cuisinière[1] *noun* M, F cook.

cuisinière[2] *noun* F cooker; **une cuisinière à gaz** a gas cooker; **une cuisinière électrique** an electric cooker.

cuisse *noun* F thigh.

cuisse de poulet *noun* F chicken leg, chicken thigh.

cuit *adjective* cooked; **bien cuit** well done (*meat*).

cuivre *noun* M copper.

cuivre jaune *noun* M brass.

culot *noun* M (*informal*) cheek; **quel culot!** what a cheek!, what a nerve!; **elle a du culot!** she's got a nerve!

culotte *noun* F **une (petite) culotte** knickers.

culpabilité *noun* F guilt.

cultivateur, cultivatrice *noun* M, F farmer.

cultiver *verb* [1] **1** to grow; **2** to cultivate.

culture *noun* F **1** farming; **2** growing; **de culture biologique** organically produced; **3** crop; **4** culture.

culturel (F **culturelle**) *adjective* cultural.

culturisme *noun* M body-building.

cure *noun* F course of treatment.

curé *noun* M parish priest.

cure-dents *noun* M toothpick.

curer *verb* [1] **se curer les ongles** to clean your nails; **se curer les dents** to pick your teeth.

curieux (F **curieuse**) *adjective* **1** strange, odd; **2** curious, inquisitive.

curiosité *noun* F curiosity.

curseur *noun* M cursor (*on a computer screen*).

cuvette *noun* F bowl; **la cuvette des wc** the lavatory bowl.

cyclable *adjective* **une piste cyclable** a cycle track.

cycle *noun* M cycle.

cyclisme *noun* M cycling.

cycliste *noun* M & F cyclist.

cyclone *noun* M hurricane.

cygne *noun* M swan.

cylindre *noun* M **1** cylinder; **2** roller.

cynique *adjective* cynical.

cyprès *noun* M cypress (tree).

D d

d' *preposition* SEE **de**.

dactylo *noun* M & F typist.

daim *noun* M **1** suede; **des chaussures en daim** suede shoes; **2** fallow deer.

dalle *noun* F paving slab.

daltonien (F **daltonienne**) *adjective* colour-blind.

dame *noun* F **1** lady; **2** queen (*in cards or chess*).

dames *plural noun* F draughts;
jouer aux dames to play draughts.

dancing *noun* M dance hall.

Danemark *noun* M Denmark; au
Danemark to (or in) Denmark.

danger *noun* M danger.

dangereux (F dangereuse)
adjective dangerous.

danois *noun* M,
adjective Danish.

dans *preposition* **1** in; elle est dans
la cuisine she's in the kitchen;
2 into; va dans la cuisine go into
the kitchen; **3** dans trois mois in
three months' time; **4** boire dans un
verre to drink out of a glass.

danse *noun* F **1** dance; **2** dancing;
faire de la danse to go to dancing
classes.

danse classique *noun* F ballet.

danser *verb* [1] to dance.

danseur, danseuse *noun* M, F
dancer.

date *noun* F date.

date de naissance *noun* F date
of birth.

date limite *noun* F closing date.

date limite de vente *noun* F sell-
by date.

datte *noun* F date (*fruit*).

dauphin *noun* M dolphin.

davantage *adverb* **1** more;
2 longer.

de, d' (*before a vowel or a silent 'h'*)
(*note that 'de + le' becomes 'du'*)
preposition **1** of; une boîte

d'allumettes a box of matches; le
pied de la table the leg of the table,
the table leg; **2** le père de Marie
Marie's father; la maison de tes
parents your parents' house;
3 from; elle vient de Paris she
comes from Paris; elle rentre du
bureau à six heures she comes
home from the office at six o'clock;
4 made from; une table de bois a
wooden table; **5** by; le prix a
augmenté de vingt francs the price
has gone up (by) twenty francs.
determiner du café (some) coffee;
veux-tu du café? would you like
(some) coffee?; je n'ai pas de café I
don't have any coffee; nous avons
des pommes et des oranges we
have apples and oranges; veux-tu de
l'eau? would you like some water?

dé *noun* M **1** dice; **2** un dé à
coudre a thimble.

dealer *noun* M drug pusher.

déballer *verb* [1] to unpack.

débardeur *noun* M camisole top,
vest-style top.

débarquer *verb* [1] **1** to
disembark; **2** to land;
3 (*informal*) to turn up; elle a
débarqué chez moi she turned up
at my place.

débarras *noun* M junk room;
★ bon débarras! good riddance!

débarrasser *verb* [1] **1** to clear out
(*a room*); débarrasser la table to
clear the table; **2** se débarrasser de
quelque chose to get rid of
something; je me suis débarrassé
de tous ces vieux bouquins I got
rid of all those old books.

débat noun M debate.

débattre verb [21] to discuss, to negotiate; **'prix à débattre'** 'price negotiable'.

débile adjective (informal) stupid, crazy; **tu es débile ou quoi?** are you stupid or something?; **c'est complètement débile!** that's completely crazy!

déblayer verb [59] to clear.

débordé adjective **être débordé** to be up to your eyes in work.

déborder verb [1] to overflow.

débouché noun M job prospect.

déboucher verb [1] **1** to uncork (a bottle); **2** to unblock (a drain or pipe); **3 déboucher sur** to lead into.

déboussoler verb [1] (informal) to confuse.

debout adverb **1** standing; **rester debout** to remain standing; **je suis resté debout toute la journée** I've been on my feet all day; **se mettre debout** to stand up; **tout le monde s'est mis debout** everybody stood up; **2** upright; **mettre quelque chose debout** to stand something upright; **3** up (out of bed); **je suis debout à six heures tous les jours** I'm up at six every day; ★ **ça ne tient pas debout** it doesn't make any sense (literally: it doesn't stand upright).

déboutonner verb [1] to unbutton.

débrancher verb [1] to unplug.

débris noun M **1** fragment; **2** piece of wreckage.

débrouiller verb [1] **se débrouiller** to manage; **je peux me débrouiller tout seul** I can manage by myself; **débrouille-toi!** get on with it!

début noun M beginning, start; **le début de** the beginning of; **au début** at the beginning, to start with; **on commencera début mars** we'll start at the beginning of March; **en début d'après-midi** in the early afternoon.

débutant, débutante noun M, F beginner.

débuter verb [1] to begin, to start.

décaféiné adjective decaffeinated.

décalage noun M **1** gap; **2** discrepancy.

décalage horaire noun M time difference (between time zones); **il y a une heure de décalage horaire entre la France et la Grande-Bretagne** there's an hour's time difference between France and Britain.

décaler verb [1] to move (forward or back).

décapiter verb [1] to behead.

décapotable adjective **une voiture décapotable** a convertible (car).

décéder verb [24] to die; **elle est décédée au mois de novembre** she died in November.

décembre noun M December; **en décembre, au mois de décembre** in December.

décemment adverb decently.

décennie noun F decade.

décent *adjective* decent.

déception *noun* F disappointment.

décès *noun* M death.

décevant *adjective* disappointing.

décevoir *verb* [66] to disappoint.

décharge *noun* F (public) rubbish tip.

décharger *verb* [52] to unload.

déchets *plural noun* M 1 waste; **les déchets nucléaires** nuclear waste; 2 rubbish.

déchiffrer *verb* [1] to decipher.

déchirant *adjective* heart-rending.

déchirer *verb* [1] 1 to tear; **j'ai déchiré mon pantalon** I've torn my trousers; 2 to tear up; **déchirer une enveloppe** to tear up an envelope; 3 to tear off; **déchirer une feuille** to tear off a sheet of paper; 4 to tear out; **déchirer une page** to tear out a page.

décidé *adjective* determined.

décidément *adverb* really.

décider *verb* [1] 1 to decide; **décider de faire** to decide to do; **j'ai décidé de vendre mon vélo** I've decided to sell my bike; 2 **se décider** to make up your mind; **il faut qu'on se décide une fois pour toutes** we must make up our minds once and for all; 3 **se décider à faire** to decide to do.

décimal (M *plural* **décimaux**) *adjective* decimal.

décimale *noun* F decimal.

décision *noun* F decision.

déclaration *noun* F 1 statement; 2 declaration.

déclarer *verb* [1] to declare.

déclencher *verb* [1] 1 to cause; 2 to set off; **déclencher l'alarme** to set off the alarm.

déclic *noun* M click.

décliner *verb* [1] to decline.

décollage *noun* M takeoff (*of a plane*).

décollé *adjective* ★ **avoir les oreilles décollées** to have sticking-out ears (*literally: to have ears which have come unstuck*).

décoller *verb* [1] 1 to take off (*of a plane*); 2 **décoller quelque chose** to peel something off; 3 **se décoller** to come unstuck, to peel off; **le papier peint est en train de se décoller** the wallpaper's peeling off.

décolleté *adjective* low-cut.

décolorer *verb* [1] **se décolorer** to fade; **se faire décolorer les cheveux** to have your hair lightened.

décombres *plural noun* M rubble.

décongeler *verb* [45] to defrost.

déconseillé *adjective* not recommended; **'déconseillé pour les enfants'** 'not recommended for children'.

déconseiller *verb* [1] **déconseiller à quelqu'un de faire** to advise somebody not to do; **nous lui avons déconseillé de voyager toute seule** we advised her not to travel alone.

décontracté adjective relaxed, laid-back; **mon patron est très décontracté** my boss is very laid-back.

décontracter verb [1] **se décontracter** to relax.

décor noun M 1 decor; 2 setting.

décorateur, décoratrice noun M, F interior designer.

décoratif (F **décorative**) adjective 1 ornamental; 2 decorative.

décoration noun F 1 decorating; 2 interior design.

décorer verb [1] to decorate.

découper verb [1] 1 to cut out; **découper un article dans un journal** to cut an article out of a newspaper; 2 to carve (meat); **c'est Marie-Laure qui va découper le poulet** Marie-Laure's going to carve the chicken.

décourageant adjective discouraging.

décourager verb [52] to discourage.

découvert noun M overdraft.

découverte noun F discovery.

découvrir verb [30] to discover.

décrire verb [38] to describe.

décrocher verb [1] 1 to lift the receiver (of a telephone); **'décrochez'** 'lift the receiver'; **il faut décrocher avant de composer le numéro** you have to lift the receiver before dialling; 2 to take down (a picture, curtains, etc).

déçu adjective disappointed; **nous sommes tous très déçus** we're all very disappointed.

dedans adverb inside; 1 **elle a ouvert la boîte mais il n'y avait rien dedans** she opened the box but there was nothing in it; 2 **là-dedans** in there.

dédommager verb [52] to compensate.

déduction noun F deduction.

déduire verb [26] 1 to deduce; 2 to deduct.

déesse noun F goddess.

défaire verb [10] 1 to undo; 2 **se défaire** to come undone; 3 **se défaire de** to get rid of.

défaite noun F defeat.

défaut noun M 1 flaw, defect; 2 **à défaut de** for want of.

défavorisé adjective underprivileged; **les défavorisés** the underprivileged.

défectueux (F **défectueuse**) adjective faulty; **une prise défectueuse** a faulty plug.

défendre verb [3] 1 to forbid; 2 to defend.

défendu adjective forbidden.

défense noun 1 **défense de fumer** no smoking; 2 defence; 3 protection; **la défense de l'environnement** the protection of the environment; 4 tusk (of an elephant).

défi noun M challenge.

déficit noun M deficit.

défigurer verb [1] to disfigure.

défilé noun M 1 parade;
2 procession; 3 march.

défiler verb [1] 1 to parade; 2 to
march; 3 to come and go.

définir verb [2] to define.

définitif (F **définitive**) adjective
final, definitive.

définition noun F definition.

définitivement adverb 1 for
good; 2 definitely.

défoncer verb [61] to smash in (a
door).

déformer verb [1] 1 to bend out of
shape; 2 to distort. 3 to stretch (a
garment or shoes).

défouler verb [1] 1 se défouler to
let off steam; 2 to unwind.

défunt noun M le défunt the
deceased.

dégagé adjective 1 clear; 2 casual.

dégager verb [52] 1 to clear; 2 to
free (a trapped person).

dégâts plural noun M damage.

dégel noun M thaw.

dégeler verb [45] to thaw.

dégénérer verb [24] 1 to
degenerate; 2 to go from bad to
worse.

dégivrer verb [1] 1 to defrost; 2 to
de-ice.

dégonfler verb [1] to let down (a
tyre, an airbed, etc).

dégouliner verb [1] to trickle.

dégourdi adjective smart, bright; un
gamin dégourdi a bright kid.

dégoût noun M disgust.

dégoûtant adjective 1 filthy; tes
mains sont dégoûtantes your hands
are filthy; 2 disgusting.

dégoûté adjective disgusted.

dégoûter verb [1] 1 to disgust;
2 dégoûter quelqu'un de quelque
chose to put somebody off
something; ça m'a dégoûté du
poisson that put me off fish.

dégrader verb [1] 1 to damage;
2 se dégrader to deteriorate.

dégraisser verb [1] to dryclean.

degré noun M degree.

dégringoler verb [1] (informal) to
tumble down.

déguisé adjective 1 in fancy dress,
in disguise; 2 une soirée déguisée
a fancy-dress party; 3 disguised.

déguiser verb [1] 1 to disguise;
2 se déguiser to dress up in fancy
dress.

dégustation noun F tasting;
'dégustation de glaces' 'a fine
selection of ice creams'.

déguster verb [1] 1 to savour, to
enjoy; 2 to taste (wine, cheese, etc).

dehors adverb 1 outside; je
t'attends dehors I'll wait for you
outside; j'ai passé toute la journée
dehors I've been outside all day;
2 en dehors de apart from; en
dehors de la salade, tout est prêt
everything's ready apart from the
salad.

déjà *adverb* 1 already; **tu pars déjà?** are you leaving already?; **je t'ai déjà dit de ne pas faire ça!** I told you not to do that!; 2 before; **tu es déjà venu ici?** have you been here before?

déjeuner *noun* M lunch; **petit déjeuner** breakfast.
verb [1] 1 to have lunch; **nous déjeunons à une heure** we have lunch at one o'clock; 2 to have breakfast.

délabré *adjective* dilapidated.

délacer *verb* [61] to unlace.

délai *noun* M period of time, waiting period.

délavé *adjective* 1 faded; 2 washed-out.

délecter *verb* [1] **se délecter à faire** to delight in doing.

délégué, déléguée *noun* M, F 1 delegate; 2 representative.

délibéré *adjective* deliberate.

délibérer *verb* [24] to discuss.

délicat *adjective* 1 delicate; 2 tactful.

délice *noun* M delight; **c'est un vrai délice!** it's absolutely delicious!

délicieux (F **délicieuse**) *adjective* delicious.

délinquance *noun* F 1 crime; 2 delinquency.

délinquant, délinquante *noun* M, F offender.

délirant *adjective* (*informal*) crazy; **c'est complètement délirant!** it's completely crazy!

délire *noun* M 1 (*informal*) madness; 2 frenzy.

délirer *verb* [1] (*informal*) to be crazy; **il délire!** he's crazy!

délit *noun* M criminal offence.

délivrer *verb* [1] to free, to liberate.

déloyal (M *plural* **déloyaux**) *adjective* disloyal.

deltaplane *noun* M 1 hang-glider; 2 **faire du deltaplane** to go hang-gliding.

déluge *noun* M 1 downpour; 2 **le Déluge** the Flood (*in the Bible*).

demain *adverb* tomorrow; **à demain!** see you tomorrow!; **après-demain** the day after tomorrow.

demande *noun* F 1 request; 2 application; **faire une demande d'emploi** to apply for a job; **'demandes d'emplois'** 'situations wanted'; 3 demand.

demandé *adjective* très demandé very much in demand, very popular.

demander *verb* [1] 1 **demander quelque chose** to ask for something; 2 **demander quelque chose à quelqu'un** to ask somebody (for) something; **demande à ton père!** ask your father!; **il m'a demandé ton adresse** he asked me for your address; 3 **demander à quelqu'un de faire** to ask somebody to do; **elle m'a demandé de téléphoner** she asked me to phone; 4 **se demander** to wonder; **je me demande ce qu'elle est en train de faire** I wonder what she's doing.

demandeur d'emploi *noun* M job-seeker.

démangeaison noun F itch.

démanger verb [52] ça me démange it itches.

démanteler verb [45] to dismantle.

démaquillant noun M make-up remover.

démaquiller verb [1] se démaquiller to remove your make-up.

démarche noun F 1 walk; 2 step.

démarrer verb [1] 1 to start (of engine or car); la voiture ne veut pas démarrer the car won't start; 2 to drive off; 3 to start up, to start off; le projet va démarrer en juin the project will start up in June.

démarreur noun M starter (in a car).

démêler verb [1] to untangle.

déménagement noun M (house) move, removal.

déménager verb [52] 1 to move (house); 2 déménager quelque chose to move something.

déménageur noun M removal man.

dément adjective crazy.

démentir verb [53] 1 to deny; 2 to refute.

démesuré adjective excessive.

demeurer verb [1] to reside, to live.

demi¹ adjective 1 half; trois et demi three and a half; elle a trois ans et demi she's three and a half; une heure et demie an hour and a half; 2 une demi-pomme half an apple; une demi-bouteille half a bottle;

3 à deux heures et demie at half past two; à trois heures et demie at half past three.

demi² noun M half (of beer).

demi-cercle noun M semicircle.

demi-douzaine noun F half a dozen.

demie noun F half-hour; à la demie on the half-hour.

demi-écrémé adjective semi-skimmed.

demi-finale noun F semifinal.

demi-frère noun M half brother.

demi-heure noun F une demi-heure half an hour; toutes les demi-heures every half hour.

demi-journée noun F half a day.

demi-litre noun M half a litre.

demi-pension noun F half board.

demi-sel adjective slightly salted.

demi-sœur noun F half sister.

démission noun F resignation; donner sa démission to resign.

démissionner verb [1] to resign.

demi-tarif adjective half-price.

demi-tour noun M faire demi-tour to turn back.

démocrate noun M & F democrat. adjective democratic.

démocratie noun F democracy.

démocratique adjective democratic.

démodé adjective old-fashioned.

demoiselle noun F young lady.

demoiselle d'honneur noun F
bridesmaid.

démolir verb [2] to demolish, to
wreck.

démolition noun F demolition.

démon noun M demon.

**démonstrateur,
démonstratrice** noun M, F
demonstrator (for products).

démonstratif (F **démonstrative**)
adjective demonstrative.

démonstration noun F
1 demonstration (of a product,
appliance, etc); 2 display.

démonter verb [1] to dismantle, to
take apart.

démontrer verb [1] to demonstrate,
to prove.

démoraliser verb [1] to demoralize.

démouler verb [1] to turn out (a
cake, mousse, etc, from a tin or
mould).

dénoncer verb [61] to denounce.

dénouer verb [1] to undo.

denrée noun F foodstuff.

dense adjective dense.

densité noun F density.

dent noun F tooth; **avoir mal aux
dents** to have toothache.

dentaire adjective dental.

dent de sagesse noun F wisdom
tooth.

dentelle noun F lace.

dentier noun M denture, false
teeth.

dentifrice noun M toothpaste.

dentiste noun M & F dentist.

déodorant noun M deodorant.

dépannage noun M repair;
'**dépannages**' 'emergency repairs';
le service de dépannage the
breakdown service; **un véhicule de
dépannage** a breakdown vehicle.

dépanner verb [1] 1 to fix, to
repair; 2 **dépanner quelqu'un**
(informal) to help somebody out.

dépanneuse noun F breakdown
truck.

départ noun M 1 departure; **je
t'appellerai avant mon départ** I'll
phone you before I leave; **elle m'a
appelé avant son départ** she
phoned me before she left; 2 **au
départ** at first, to start with.

département noun M
department. (As well as other sorts of
department, this is a French
numbered administrative area,
rather like a county in Britain. The
two numbers on the end of vehicle
registrations in France show the
number of the department where the
car is registered.)

dépassé adjective outdated, old-
fashioned.

dépasser verb [1] 1 to overtake;
2 to exceed; 3 **ça me dépasse!** it's
beyond me!

dépêcher verb [50] **se dépêcher** to
hurry up; **dépêche-toi!** hurry up!

dépendance noun F outbuilding.

dépendre verb [3] 1 **dépendre de**
to depend on; **ça dépend de l'heure**

it depends on the time; **ça dépend**
it depends; **2** to be dependent on.

dépenser verb [1] to spend.

dépenses plural noun F
1 expenses; **2** spending.

dépensier (F **dépensière**) adjective
extravagant.

dépilatoire adjective **une crème
dépilatoire** a hair-removing cream.

dépistage noun M screening.

dépit noun M **en dépit de** in spite
of.

déplacé adjective out of place.

déplacement noun M trip; **les
frais de déplacement** travel
expenses.

déplacer verb [61] **1** to move; **2 se
déplacer** to travel.

déplaire verb [62] **déplaire à
quelqu'un** to be displeasing to
somebody; **cela me déplaît** I don't
like that.

déplaisant adjective unpleasant.

dépliant noun M leaflet.

déplier verb [1] to unfold.

déporter verb [1] to deport.

déposer verb [1] **1** to put down;
2 to drop off; **il m'a déposé à la gare**
he dropped me off at the station;
3 déposer un chèque to pay in a
cheque.

dépôt noun M **1** warehouse;
2 depot; **3** deposit.

dépôt d'ordures noun M rubbish
tip.

dépoussiérer verb [24] to dust.

dépressif (F **dépressive**) adjective
depressive.

dépression noun F depression.

déprimant adjective depressing.

déprimer verb [1] **1** to depress;
2 to get depressed; **elle déprime en
ce moment** she's depressed at the
moment.

depuis preposition **1** since; **depuis
vendredi** since Friday; **je suis à
Paris depuis mardi** I've been in
Paris since Tuesday; **j'habite à
Londres depuis avril** I've been
living in London since April; **2** for;
**elle habite à Londres depuis cinq
ans** she's lived in London for five
years; **je le connais depuis
longtemps** I've known him for a
long time; **3 tu es là depuis
combien de temps?** how long have
you been here?; **tu le sais depuis
combien de temps?** how long have
you known?; **depuis quand es-tu à
Paris?** how long have you been in
Paris?
adverb **1** since; **je ne l'ai pas revu
depuis** I haven't seen him since;
2 depuis que since; **depuis que ton
frère est à Londres** since your
brother's been in London.

député noun M deputy (the French
equivalent of a member of
Parliament).

déraciner verb [1] to uproot.

déranger verb [52] to disturb; **'ne
pas déranger'** 'do not disturb';
excusez-moi de vous déranger
sorry to bother you; **est-ce que cela
vous dérange si j'ouvre la fenêtre?**
do you mind if I open the window?;

cela ne me dérange pas du tout I don't mind at all; **ça vous dérange de venir me chercher?** do you mind coming to pick me up?

déraper *verb* [1] **1** to skid; **2** to get out of control.

dérisoire *adjective* pathetic, trivial; **je l'ai acheté pour une somme dérisoire** I bought it for next to nothing.

dériveur *noun* M sailing dinghy.

dermatologue *noun* M & F dermatologist.

dernier (F **dernière**) *adjective* **1** last; **le dernier train part à minuit** the last train leaves at midnight; **jeudi dernier** last Thursday; **la semaine dernière** last week; **l'année dernière** last year; **leur dernier album** their latest album; **3 en dernier** last; **il est arrivé en dernier** he arrived last.

dernièrement *adverb* recently.

dérouler *verb* [1] **1** to unroll, to unwind; **2 se dérouler** to take place; **ça s'est très bien déroulé** it went very well.

déroutant *adjective* puzzling.

derrière *noun* M **1** back (*of an object or a house*); **2** bottom, backside.
preposition behind; **derrière la porte** behind the door.
adverb behind; **être derrière** to be in the back (*of the car*).

des *article* some, any; SEE **de**, **un**.

dès *preposition* **1** from; **dès l'âge de cinq ans** from the age of five; **2 dès que** as soon as.

désagréable *adjective* unpleasant.

désarroi *noun* M confusion.

désastre *noun* M disaster.

désavantage *noun* M disadvantage.

désavouer *verb* [1] **1** to deny; **2** to disown.

descendre *verb* [3] **1** to go down; **descendre les escaliers** to go down the stairs; **2** to come down; **je descends dans trois secondes!** I'll be down in a second!; **3** to get off (*a train or bus*); **je descends à Dijon** I'm getting off at Dijon; **4** to get down; **pouvez-vous descendre ma valise, s'il vous plaît?** could you get my case down for me, please?; **5** to take (or bring) downstairs; **je vais descendre mes bagages** I'm going to take my luggage downstairs; **est-ce que tu peux descendre une chaise de là-haut?** could you bring a chair down from upstairs?

descente *noun* F descent.

descriptif (F **descriptive**) *adjective* descriptive.

description *noun* F description.

déséquilibrer *verb* [1] **déséquilibrer quelqu'un** to throw somebody off balance.

désert *noun* M desert.
adjective deserted.

déserter *verb* [1] to desert.

désespéré *adjective* **1** desperate; **2** in despair; **3 une situation désespérée** a hopeless situation.

désespérer *verb* [24] to despair, to give up hope.

désespoir noun M despair.

déshabiller verb [1] **1 se déshabiller** to undress, to get undressed; **2 déshabiller quelqu'un** to undress somebody.

désherbant noun M weedkiller.

désherber verb [1] to weed.

déshérité noun M **les déshérités** the underprivileged.

déshériter verb [1] to disinherit.

déshydraté adjective dehydrated.

désigner verb [1] **1** to point out; **2** to denote.

désinfectant noun M disinfectant.

désinfecter verb [1] to disinfect.

désir noun M **1** wish; **2** desire.

désirer verb [1] to want; **que désirez-vous?** what would you like?

désobéir verb [2] **1** to be disobedient; **2 désobéir à quelqu'un** to disobey somebody.

désobéissant adjective disobedient.

désobligeant adjective unpleasant.

désodorisant noun M air freshener.

désolé adjective **être désolé** to be sorry; **je suis désolé** I'm sorry; **désolé de te déranger** sorry to disturb you.

désopilant adjective hilarious.

désordonné adjective untidy.

désordre noun M **1** untidiness, mess; **être en désordre** to be in a mess; **2** disorder.

désorganisé adjective disorganized.

désorienté adjective disorientated, confused.

désormais adverb **1** from now on; **2** from then on.

desquels, desquelles pronoun (= de lesquels, de lesquelles) which, whom.

dessécher verb [24] **1** to dry out; **2 se dessécher** to dry out.

dessert noun M dessert, pudding.

desservir verb [58] **le train dessert Vienne et Valence** the train calls at Vienne and Valence.

dessin noun M **1** drawing; **un cours de dessin** a drawing class; **2 un dessin** a drawing; **3** design.

dessin animé noun M (animated) cartoon.

dessin humoristique noun M cartoon.

dessiner verb [1] to draw.

dessous noun M **1** underside; **le dessous du pied** the sole of the foot; **2 les voisins du dessous** the neighbours below; **3 les dessous** underwear; **4 en dessous** underneath; **5 en dessous de** below.
adverb underneath.

dessus noun M **1** top; **le dessus du carton** the top of the box; **un pantalon gris et un dessus rose** grey trousers and a pink top; **2 les voisins du dessus** the neighbours above; **3 en dessus** above; **4 au-dessus de** above.

adverb on top; **quelqu'un a écrit dessus** somebody's written on it.

dessus-de-lit *noun* M bedspread.

destin *noun* M 1 fate; 2 destiny.

destinataire *noun* M & F addressee.

destination *noun* F destination; **le train à destination de Nice** the train for Nice; **les passagers à destination de Rome** passengers travelling to Rome.

destiner *verb* [1] 1 **destiner quelque chose à** to design something for; 2 **être destiné à** to be intended for; 3 **être destiné à faire** to be intended to do.

détachable *adjective* detachable.

détachant *noun* M stain remover.

détacher *verb* [1] 1 to untie; 2 to undo; 3 to tear off; 4 to remove; 5 to remove the stains from; 6 **se détacher** to come off, to come undone.

détail *noun* M 1 detail; **en détail** in detail; 2 **regarder quelque chose dans le détail** to look closely at something; 3 retail.

détailler *verb* [1] to detail, to itemize; **une facture détaillée** an itemized bill.

détecter *verb* [1] to detect.

détective *noun* M detective.

déteindre *verb* [60] 1 to fade; 2 to run (*in the wash*).

détendre *verb* [3] 1 to be relaxing; 2 to relax; 3 **se détendre** to relax.

détendu *adjective* relaxed.

détenir *verb* [81] 1 to detain; 2 to keep.

détente *noun* F relaxation.

détenu, détenue *noun* M, F prisoner, detainee.

détergent *noun* M detergent.

détériorer *verb* [1] **se détériorer** to deteriorate.

détermination *noun* F determination.

déterminer *verb* [1] to fix.

détestable *adjective* appalling, revolting.

détester *verb* [1] to hate.

détour *noun* M detour; ★ **ça vaut le détour** it's well worth seeing (*literally: it's worth the detour*).

détournement *noun* M **un détournement d'avion** a highjacking.

détourner *verb* [1] 1 to divert; 2 **détourner un avion** to highjack a plane; 3 **détourner les yeux** to look away.

détritus *plural noun* M rubbish, refuse.

détruire *verb* [26] to destroy.

dette *noun* F debt.

deuil *noun* M 1 bereavement; 2 mourning.

deux *number* 1 two; **deux enfants** two children; **elle a deux ans** she's two; **il est deux heures** it's two o'clock; 2 **deux fois** twice; 3 second (*in dates*); **le deux juin** the second of June; **4** both; **les deux frères** both brothers; **tous les deux, toutes les deux** both; **ils sont malades tous les deux, tous les deux sont malades** they're both ill, both of them are ill.

deuxième *number* second; **pour la deuxième fois** for the second time; **au deuxième** on the second floor.

deuxièmement *adverb* secondly.

deux-points *noun* M colon.

dévaliser *verb* [1] to rob.

dévaluer *verb* [1] to devalue.

devant *noun* M front.
preposition **1** in front of; **elle était devant moi dans la queue** she was in front of me in the queue; **il l'a dit devant ses parents** he said it in front of his parents; **2** outside; **devant la boulangerie** outside the baker's.

développement *noun* M development; **les pays en voie de développement** developing countries.

développer *verb* [1] to develop.

devenir *verb* [81] to become; **devenir médecin** to become a doctor.

déviation *noun* F diversion.

deviner *verb* [1] **1** to guess; **2** to foresee.

devinette *noun* F riddle.

devis *noun* M quote, estimate.

devises *plural noun* F (foreign) currency.

dévisser *verb* [1] to unscrew.

devoir *noun* M **1** exercise, test; **2 devoirs** homework; **faire ses devoirs** to do your homework; **3** duty.
verb [8] **1** to owe; **elle me doit vingt francs** she owes me twenty francs; **je vous dois combien?** how much do I owe you?; **2** to have to; **je dois partir à dix heures** I have to (or I must) leave at ten o'clock; **3 tu dois être fatigué** you must be tired; **elle doit avoir quarante ans** she must be forty; **il a dû oublier** he must have forgotten; **4 tu devrais partir** you ought to leave, you should leave; **tu aurais dû partir** you should have left; **5 elle doit arriver à cinq heures** she's supposed to arrive at five o'clock.

dévorer *verb* [1] to devour.

dévoué *adjective* devoted.

dévouement *noun* M devotion.

dévouer *verb* [1] **se dévouer à** to devote oneself to.

diabète *noun* M diabetes.

diabétique *noun* M & F, *adjective* diabetic.

diable *noun* M devil.

diabolo *noun* M ·fruit cordial and lemonade; **un diabolo menthe** a mint cordial and lemonade.

diagnostic *noun* M diagnosis.

diagnostiquer *verb* [1] to diagnose.

diagonal (M *plural* **diagonaux**) *adjective* diagonal.

diagonale *noun* F diagonal; **en diagonale** diagonally.

diagramme *noun* M graph.

dialecte noun M dialect.

dialogue noun M dialogue.

dialyse noun F dialysis.

diamant noun M diamond.

diamètre noun M diameter.

diapo noun F (informal) slide; SHORT FOR **diapositive**.

diapositive noun F slide.

diarrhée noun F diarrhoea.

dico noun M (informal) dictionary; SHORT FOR **dictionnaire**.

dictateur noun M dictator.

dictature noun F dictatorship.

dictée noun F dictation.

dicter verb [1] to dictate.

dictionnaire noun M dictionary.

dicton noun M saying.

diesel noun M diesel.

diététique noun F un magasin de diététique a health-food shop. adjective dietary.

dieu (plural dieux) noun M god.

Dieu noun M God; mon Dieu! good heavens!

différemment adverb differently.

différence noun F 1 difference; quelle est la différence (entre)? what's the difference (between)?; 2 à la différence de unlike.

différend noun M disagreement.

différent adjective 1 different; différent de different from; 2 various, different; différentes personnes various people, different people.

difficile adjective 1 difficult, hard; difficile à faire difficult to do; leur maison est difficile à trouver their house is difficult to find; c'est difficile à imaginer it's hard to imagine; 2 hard to please, fussy.

difficilement adverb with difficulty.

difficulté noun F difficulty; avoir de la difficulté à faire to have difficulty in doing; j'ai eu de la difficulté à vous joindre I had difficulty getting in touch with you.

difforme adjective deformed, misshapen.

difformité noun F deformity.

diffuser verb [1] 1 to broadcast; 2 to distribute; 3 to spread.

digérer verb [24] to digest.

digestif noun M (after-dinner) liqueur.

digestion noun F digestion.

digital (M plural digitaux) adjective digital.

digne adjective 1 worthy; digne de worthy of; digne de foi trustworthy; 2 dignified.

dignité noun F dignity.

digue noun F 1 sea wall; 2 dyke.

dilemme noun M dilemma.

diligent adjective diligent.

diluant noun M thinner.

diluer verb [1] 1 to dilute; 2 to thin (paint).

dimanche noun M 1 Sunday; **nous sommes dimanche aujourd'hui** it's Sunday today; **dimanche dernier** last Sunday; **dimanche prochain** next Sunday; 2 on Sunday; **je t'appellerai dimanche soir** I'll ring you on Sunday evening; 3 **le dimanche** on Sundays; **fermé le dimanche** closed on Sundays; 4 **tous les dimanches** every Sunday.

dimension noun F size.

diminuer verb [1] 1 to reduce; 2 to come (or go) down; 3 to decrease; 4 to die down.

dinde noun F turkey (as meat).

dindon noun M turkey (when alive).

dîner noun M dinner, supper; **inviter quelqu'un à dîner** to invite somebody to dinner.
verb [1] 1 to have dinner; **viens dîner chez nous ce soir** come to dinner with us this evening.

dingue adjective (informal) crazy.

dinosaure noun M dinosaur.

diplomate noun M & F diplomat.
adjective diplomatic.

diplomatie noun F diplomacy.

diplomatique adjective diplomatic.

diplôme noun M 1 diploma, certificate; 2 (university) degree.

diplômé adjective qualified.

dire verb [9] 1 to say; **elle dit qu'elle est malade** she says she's ill; 2 to tell; **dire quelque chose à quelqu'un** to tell somebody

something; **j'ai dit à Anne que tu l'appellerais** I told Anne you'd ring her; **dire à quelqu'un de faire** to tell somebody to do; **je leur ai dit de venir à cinq heures** I told them to come at five o'clock; **dire la vérité** to tell the truth; **dire l'heure** to tell the time; **dire des mensonges** to tell lies.

direct adjective 1 direct; 2 **en direct de** live from.

directement adverb 1 directly; 2 **aller directement à** to go straight to.

directeur, directrice noun M, F 1 director; 2 manager; 3 head (of a school).

direction noun F 1 direction; **en direction de** towards, in the direction of; 2 management; 3 steering (of a vehicle).

dirigeant, dirigeante noun M, F leader.

diriger verb [52] 1 to direct; 2 to manage; 3 to conduct (an orchestra); 4 **se diriger vers** to make for; **elle s'est dirigée vers la porte** she made for the door.

discerner verb [1] 1 to make out; 2 to detect.

discipline noun F 1 discipline; 2 subject (of study).

discipliner verb [1] 1 to discipline; 2 to control.

disco noun M 1 disco; 2 disco music.

discothèque noun F 1 disco, discotheque; 2 music library.

discours noun M speech.

discret (F **discrète**) adjective
1 discreet; 2 quiet; 3 subtle.

discrétion noun F discretion.

discrimination noun F
discrimination.

discussion noun F discussion.

discutable adjective questionable.

discuter verb [1] 1 to talk; on peut
discuter tranquillement chez moi
we can talk in peace at my house;
2 to argue; ça se discute it's
arguable; 3 discuter de quelque
chose to discuss something; on va
en discuter demain we'll discuss it
tomorrow.

disparaître verb [27] 1 to
disappear; 2 faire disparaître
quelque chose to get rid of
something; 3 to die.

disparition noun F
1 disappearance; 2 une espèce en
voie de disparition an endangered
species; 3 death.

disparu, disparue noun M, F
1 missing person; 2 les disparus
the dead.
adjective 1 missing; 2 lost;
3 dead.

dispenser verb [1] 1 to hand out;
2 to give; 3 dispenser quelqu'un
de to exempt somebody from.

disperser verb [1] 1 to break up (a
crowd or demonstration); 2 se
disperser to break up; la foule s'est
dispersée the crowd broke up.

disponibilité noun F availability.

disponible adjective available.

disposé adjective 1 arranged, laid
out; 2 être disposé à faire to be
willing to do.

disposer verb [1] 1 to arrange, to
lay out; 2 disposer de quelque
chose to have something (at your
disposal).

dispositif noun M 1 device;
2 system.

disposition noun F
1 arrangement, layout; 2 à ta
disposition at your disposal;
3 measure.

dispute noun F argument.

disputé adjective 1 contested;
2 controversial.

disputer verb [1] 1 se disputer to
argue; ils se sont disputés they had
an argument; 2 se disputer
quelque chose to fight over
something; 3 se faire disputer
(informal) to get told off; je me suis
fait disputer par mon patron I got
told off by my boss.

disqualifier verb [1] to disqualify.

disque noun M 1 record; passer un
disque to play a record (or CD);
2 disc; 3 (computer) disk.

disque compact noun M
compact disc, CD.

disque dur noun M hard disk (of a
computer).

disquette noun F (computer)
diskette.

disséquer verb [24] to dissect.

dissertation noun F essay.

dissident, dissidente noun M, F dissident.

dissimuler verb [1] to conceal.

dissocier verb [1] to separate.

dissolvant noun M **1** nail polish remover; **2** solvent.

dissoudre verb [67] **1 dissoudre quelque chose** to dissolve something; **2 se dissoudre** to dissolve.

dissuader verb [1] **1 dissuader quelqu'un de faire** to persuade somebody not to do, to put somebody off doing; **il m'a dissuadé d'y aller** he persuaded me not to go; **2** to deter; **pour dissuader les voleurs** in order to deter thieves.

distance noun F **1** distance; **une distance de cinq kilomètres** a distance of five kilometres; **c'est à quelle distance d'ici?** how far is it from here?; **à distance** from a distance; **l'enseignement à distance** distance learning; **2** gap.

distant adjective distant; **distant de** far away from; **un village distant de trois kilomètres** a village three kilometres away.

distiller verb [1] to distil.

distillerie noun F distillery.

distinct adjective distinct.

distinctif (F **distinctive**) adjective distinctive.

distinction noun F distinction.

distingué adjective distinguished.

distinguer verb [1] **1** to make out; **j'ai distingué un bateau à l'horizon** I made out a boat on the horizon; **2 distinguer entre** to distinguish between.

distraction noun F **1** entertainment; **on a besoin d'un peu de distraction** we need a bit of entertainment; **2** leisure; **3** leisure activity, form of entertainment; **4** absent-mindedness.

distraire verb [78] **1** to amuse, to entertain; **ça m'a distrait un peu** that cheered me up a bit; **2** to distract; **3 se distraire** to amuse yourself, to enjoy yourself.

distrait adjective absent-minded.

distribuer verb [1] **1** to hand out to distribute; **2 distribuer les cartes** to deal (*in a card game*); **3 distribuer le courrier** to deliver the mail.

distributeur noun M **1** distributor; **2 un distributeur automatique** a vending machine; **3 un distributeur de tickets** a ticket machine; **4 un distributeur de billets** a cash dispenser.

distribution noun F **1** distribution; **2** handing out; **3** delivery (*of mail*); **4** cast (*of a play*).

diverger verb [52] to diverge.

divers adjective various; **dans divers pays** in various countries.

divertir verb [2] **1** to amuse, to entertain; **2 se divertir** to amuse oneself.

divertissant adjective amusing, entertaining.

divin adjective divine.

diviser verb [1] to divide.

division noun F division.

divorce noun M divorce.

divorcer verb [61] to get divorced.

dix number ten; elle a dix ans she's ten; il est dix heures it's ten o'clock; le dix juillet the tenth of July.

dix-huit number eighteen; il a dix-huit ans he's eighteen; à dix-huit heures at six p.m.

dixième noun M au dixième on the tenth floor.
adjective tenth.

dix-neuf number nineteen; elle a dix-neuf ans she's nineteen; à dix-neuf heures at seven p.m.

dix-sept number seventeen; elle a dix-sept ans she's seventeen; à dix-sept heures at five p.m.

dizaine noun F 1 ten; 2 une dizaine de personnes about ten people.

docteur noun M doctor.

document noun M document.

documentaire noun M, adjective documentary.

documentaliste noun M & F librarian.

documentation noun F 1 documentation; 2 material; 3 research.

documenter verb [1] se documenter sur quelque chose to gather information on something.

dodo noun M faire dodo (baby talk) to sleep; on va faire dodo time to tuck up in bed.

dogmatique adjective dogmatic.

doigt noun M finger; se couper le doigt to cut your finger; avoir mal au doigt to have a sore finger; ★ être à deux doigts de to be within an inch of (literally: to be two fingers away from).

doigt de pied noun M toe.

domaine noun M 1 estate; 2 field, domain.

dôme noun M dome.

domestique noun M & F servant. adjective domestic.

domicile noun M 1 place of residence; 2 à domicile at home; travailler à domicile to work at home.

dominant adjective 1 dominant; 2 main.

dominer verb [1] 1 to dominate; 2 to control.

domino noun M domino; jouer aux dominos to play dominoes.

dommage noun M 1 c'est dommage it's a pity; c'est dommage qu'elle n'y soit pas allée it's a pity she didn't go; 2 les dommages damage.

dompter verb [1] to tame.

DOM-TOM SHORT FOR départements et territoires d'outre-mer (French overseas departments and territories).

don noun M 1 gift; faire don de to give; 2 gift, talent; elle a un don pour les langues she has a gift for languages; avoir le don de faire to have the gift of doing.

donc

donc *conjunction* so, therefore.

donne *noun* F deal (*in card games*).

donné *adjective* given; **étant donné que** given that.

donnée *noun* F 1 fact; 2 **données** data.

donner *verb* [1] 1 to give; **donner quelque chose à quelqu'un** to give somebody something; **elle m'a donné dix francs** she gave me ten francs; **donne-moi ton adresse** give me your address; **il a donné tous ses livres** he gave away all his books; 3 **ma fenêtre donne sur la rue** my window looks onto the street; 4 **se donner à quelque chose** to devote yourself to something.

dont *relative pronoun* whose, of which; **une personne dont j'ai oublié le nom** a person whose name I've forgotten; **la maison dont je parle** the house I'm talking about; **six verres dont l'un est cassé** six glasses, one of which is broken.

doré *adjective* 1 gold; 2 gilt; 3 golden.

dorénavant *adverb* from now on; **dorénavant je serai là tous les jours** from now on I'll be here every day.

dorer *verb* [1] 1 to gild; 2 **faire dorer** to brown (*meat or vegetables*).

dormir *verb* [37] to sleep; **tu as bien dormi?** did you sleep well?; **elle va dormir chez moi** she's going to spend the night at my house; **il dort** he's asleep.

dortoir *noun* M dormitory.

dos *noun* M back; **avoir mal au dos** to have backache; **faire quelque chose dans le dos de quelqu'un** to do something behind somebody's back; **elle me tournait le dos** she had her back to me; **il m'a tourné le dos** he turned his back on me.

dosage *noun* M 1 amount; 2 mixture.

dose *noun* F 1 dose; 2 measure.

dossier *noun* M 1 file; 2 application form; **remplir un dossier** to fill in an application form; 3 **dossier médical** medical records; 4 **le dossier d'une chaise** the back of a chair.

douane *noun* F **la douane** customs; **passer la douane** to go through customs.

douanier *noun* M customs officer.

double *noun* M 1 **le double (de)** twice as much, twice as many; 2 copy, duplicate; 3 double. *adjective* double.

doublé *adjective* 1 lined; 2 dubbed (*film*).

doublement *adverb* doubly.

doubler *verb* [1] 1 to double; 2 to overtake; **il m'a doublé dans un virage** he overtook me on a bend; 3 to line (*a garment*); 4 to dub (*a film*).

doublure *noun* F lining.

douce *adjective* SEE **doux**.

doucement *adverb* 1 gently; 2 slowly; 3 softly.

douceur noun F 1 softness; 2 gentleness; 3 mildness (of weather).

douche noun F shower; **prendre une douche** to take a shower.

doucher verb [1] **se doucher** to have a shower.

doué adjective gifted; **être doué pour quelque chose** to have a gift for something.

douillet (F **douillette**) adjective cosy.

douleur noun F 1 pain; 2 grief.

douloureux (F **douloureuse**) adjective painful.

doute noun M 1 doubt; 2 **sans doute** probably.

douter verb [1] 1 to doubt; **douter de** to have doubts about; 2 **se douter de** to suspect; **je m'en doutais** I thought as much.

douteux (F **douteuse**) adjective 1 doubtful; 2 dubious.

Douvres noun Dover.

doux (F **douce**) adjective 1 soft; 2 gentle; 3 mild; 4 sweet.

douzaine noun F 1 dozen; 2 **une douzaine (de)** a dozen or so.

douze number twelve; **elle a douze ans** she's twelve; **le douze juillet** the twelfth of July.

douzième noun M **au douzième** on the twelfth floor.
adjective twelfth.

dragée noun F sugared almond.

draguer verb [1] (informal) **draguer quelqu'un** to chat somebody up; **il est toujours en train de draguer les**

nanas he's always chatting up the girls; **se faire draguer** to get chatted up; **Carole s'est fait draguer par ton copain** Carole got chatted up by your mate.

dramatique adjective 1 tragic; 2 dramatic; **l'art dramatique** drama.

drame noun M 1 tragedy; 2 drama; **il en a fait tout un drame** he made a big scene about it.

drap noun M sheet.

drapeau noun M flag.

drap-housse noun M fitted sheet.

dresser verb [1] 1 to train (an animal); 2 to put up (a tent); 3 to draw up (a list); 4 **se dresser** to stand up.

drogue noun F drug; **la drogue** drugs; **les drogues douces** soft drugs; **les drogues dures** hard drugs.

droguer verb [1] 1 to drug, to give drugs to; 2 **se droguer** to take drugs.

droguerie noun F hardware shop.

droit noun M 1 right; **les droits de l'homme** human rights; 2 **avoir le droit de faire** to be allowed to do; **je n'ai pas le droit de sortir ce soir** I'm not allowed to go out tonight; 3 **avoir le droit de faire** to have the right to do; **tu n'as pas le droit de me critiquer** you have no right to criticize me; 4 **le droit** law; **un étudiant en droit** a law student; 5 fee; **les droits d'inscription** enrolment fees.
adjective 1 straight; **une ligne droite** a straight line; 2 right; **ma**

main droite my right hand; **3 un angle droit** a right angle.
adverb **straight; continuez tout droit** go straight ahead.

droite *noun* F **1** right; **à droite** on the right; **tourner à droite** to turn right; **à la droite** on your right; **2 la droite** the right (*in politics*).

droitier (F **droitière**) *adjective* right-handed.

drôle *adjective* **1** funny; **une histoire drôle** a funny story; **un film très drôle** a really funny film; **2** odd; **un drôle de film** an odd film.

drôlement *adverb* **1** (*informal*) really; **c'était drôlement bon!** it was really good!; **2** oddly, peculiarly.

du *article* some, any; see **de**.

dû, due, dus *verb* see **devoir**.

duc *noun* M duke.

duchesse *noun* F duchess.

duo *noun* M duet.

duplex *noun* M maisonette.

duquel *pronoun* (= **de lequel**).

dur *adjective* **1** hard; **2** tough (*meat*); **3** difficult, hard.
adverb **travailler dur** to work hard.

durée *noun* F length.

durement *adverb* harshly.

durer *verb* [1] **1** to last; **2 durer pendant trois mois** to go on for three months.

dureté *noun* F **1** hardness; **2** toughness; **3** difficulty.

duvet *noun* M sleeping bag.

dynamique *adjective* dynamic, lively.

dyslexique *noun* M & F dyslexic.

E e

eau *noun* F water; **est-ce que tu veux de l'eau?** would you like some water?; **un verre d'eau** a glass of water; **eau gazeuse** sparkling mineral water; **eau plate** still mineral water; **'eau potable'** 'drinking water'; **'eau non potable'** 'not drinking water'; ★ **tomber à l'eau** to fall through (*literally: to fall into the water*); **nos projets sont tombés à l'eau** our plans have fallen through; ★ **mettre l'eau à la bouche de quelqu'un** to make somebody's mouth water; **ta sauce sent tellement bon que ça me met l'eau à la bouche** your sauce smells so good it's making my mouth water.

eau de Javel *noun* F bleach.

eau de toilette *noun* F toilet water.

eau minérale *noun* F mineral water.

ébaucher *verb* [1] **1** to sketch; **2** to outline.

ébéniste *noun* M & F cabinetmaker.

éblouir *verb* [2] to dazzle.

éblouissant *adjective* dazzling.

éboueur *noun* M refuse collector.

ébouillanter *verb* [1] to scald.

ébranler *verb* [1] to shake.

ébullition *noun* F boiling point; **porter à ébullition** to bring to the boil.

écaille *noun* F 1 scale (*of a fish or reptile*); 2 tortoiseshell.

écailler *verb* [1] **s'écailler** to flake; **la peinture s'écaille** the paint's flaking.

écart *noun* M 1 gap, distance; 2 difference; 3 **à l'écart de** away from.

écarté *adjective* 1 **un village écarté** a remote village; 2 **les jambes écartées** with legs apart; 3 **les bras écartés** with arms outstretched.

écarter *verb* [1] 1 to move apart; **écarter les rideaux** to open the curtains; 2 to move back.

échafaudage *noun* M scaffolding.

échalote *noun* F shallot.

échange *noun* M exchange; **en échange (de)** in exchange (for), in return for.

échanger *verb* [52] to exchange, to swap; **nous avons échangé nos adresses** we exchanged addresses.

échantillon *noun* M sample.

échapper *verb* [1] 1 **échapper à** to escape, to escape from, to get away from; **le week-end nous échappons à la ville** at weekends we get away

from the town; 2 **s'échapper** to escape.

écharde *noun* F splinter.

écharpe *noun* F scarf.

échasse *noun* F stilt.

échec *noun* M failure.

échecs *plural noun* M chess; **jouer aux échecs** to play chess.

échelle *noun* F 1 ladder; 2 scale.

échelon *noun* M 1 rung; 2 grade.

échiquier *noun* M chessboard.

écho *noun* M 1 echo; 2 **des échos** rumours.

échographie *noun* F (medical) scan; **passer une échographie** to have a scan.

échouer *verb* [1] to fail; **échouer à un examen** to fail an exam.

éclabousser *verb* [1] to splash.

éclair *noun* M 1 flash of lightning; 2 **un éclair au chocolat** a chocolate eclair.

éclairage *noun* M lighting.

éclaircie *noun* F sunny interval.

éclairer *verb* [1] to light (up).

éclat *noun* M 1 splinter, fragment; 2 brightness; 3 splendour; 4 **un éclat de rire** a roar of laughter.

éclatant *adjective* brilliant; **des murs d'une blancheur éclatante** brilliant white walls.

éclater *verb* [1] 1 to burst; **un pneu a éclaté** a tyre has burst; 2 to shatter; **l'ampoule a éclaté** the bulb shattered; 3 to break out (*war or*

fighting); **4 éclater de rire** to burst
out laughing; **éclater en sanglots**
to burst into tears.

écluse noun F lock (on a canal or
river).

écœurant adjective sickly.

écœurer verb [1] to make
(somebody) feel sick.

école noun F school; **aller à l'école**
to go to school.

école maternelle noun F (state)
nursery school (age 2 – 6).

école primaire noun F primary
school (age 6 – 11).

écolier, écolière noun M, F
schoolchild.

écologie noun F ecology.

écologique adjective
1 ecological; **2** environmentally
friendly.

économe noun M potato peeler.
adjective economical.

économie noun F **1** economy;
2 economics; **3 les économies**
savings; **faire des économies** to
save up.

économique adjective
1 economical; **2** economic.

économiser verb [1] to save.

économiste noun M & F
economist.

écorce noun F **1** bark (of a tree);
2 peel (of an orange or a lemon).

écorcher verb [1] **s'écorcher le
genou** to graze your knee.

écorchure noun F graze.

écossais noun M tartan (cloth).
adjective **1** Scottish; **2** tartan; **une
jupe écossaise** a tartan skirt.

Écossais, Écossaise noun M, F
Scotsman, Scotswoman, Scot; **les
Écossais** the Scots.

Écosse noun F Scotland; **elle
habite en Écosse** she lives in
Scotland.

écouter verb [1] to listen to; **j'écoute
beaucoup la radio** I listen to the
radio a lot; **écoute-moi** listen to me.

écouteur noun M **1** receiver (on a
telephone); **2** headphones.

écran noun M **1** screen; **à l'écran**
on the screen; **le petit écran**
television; **2 la crème écran total**
sun block.

écrasant adjective overwhelming.

écraser verb [1] **1** to crush;
écrasez les noix crush the
walnuts; **2** to squash; **tu vas
écraser les pêches!** you'll squash
the peaches!; **3 écraser une
cigarette** to stub out a cigarette;
4 se faire écraser to get run over;
Attention! Tu vas te faire écraser!
Watch out! You'll get run over!;
5 s'écraser to crash; **leur voiture
s'est écrasée contre un mur** their
car crashed into a wall.

écrémé adjective **le lait écrémé**
skimmed milk; **le lait demi-écrémé**
semi-skimmed milk.

écrevisse noun F crayfish.

écrire verb [38] **1** to write; **elle m'a
écrit une lettre** she wrote me a
letter; **2 s'écrire** to write to each
other; **ils s'écrivent tous les jours**

they write to each other every day;
3 **s'écrire** to be spelled; **comment
ça s'écrit?** how do you spell it?

écrit noun M 1 (piece of) writing;
2 written paper (of an exam); **il a
réussi à l'oral mais il a raté l'écrit**
he passed the oral but failed the
written paper; 3 **à l'écrit** in writing.
adjective written.

écriture noun F handwriting.

écrivain noun M writer.

écrou noun M nut (screwed onto a
bolt).

écrouler verb [1] **s'écrouler** to
collapse.

écume noun F 1 foam, froth;
2 scum.

écureuil noun M squirrel.

écurie noun F stable.

eczéma noun M eczema.

EDF SHORT FOR **Électricité de France**
French electricity company.

Édimbourg noun M Edinburgh.

éditer verb [1] to publish.

éditeur noun M publisher.

édition noun F 1 publishing; **elle
travaille dans l'édition** she works in
publishing; 2 edition; **une édition
de poche** a paperback edition.

édredon noun M eiderdown.

éducateur, éducatrice noun M,
F special needs teacher.

éducatif (F **éducative**) adjective
educational.

éducation noun F education; **elle a
reçu une bonne éducation** she had
a good education.

éducation physique noun F
physical education, PE.

éduquer verb [1] to educate.

effacer verb [61] to rub out.

effaceur noun M correction pen.

effarant adjective amazing.

effarer verb [1] to alarm.

effectivement adverb indeed
(used to show agreement with what
someone has just said); **il est
effectivement extrêmement gentil**
he is indeed extremely nice; **oui, elle
m'a effectivement téléphoné hier**
yes, that's right, she did phone me
yesterday; **'Tu as oublié tes clés'** –
'Ah oui, effectivement!' 'You've left
your keys behind' – 'Oh yes, so I
have!'; **'Il est maintenant trop tard
pour y aller'** – 'Oui,
effectivement' 'It's too late to go
now' – 'Yes, so it is.'

effectuer verb [1] to make, to carry
out.

effet noun M 1 effect; 2 **en effet**
indeed (used to show agreement with
what someone has just said); **elle
avait en effet raison** she was indeed
right; **'il fait très froid'** – 'Oui, en
effet' 'It's very cold' – 'Yes, it is,
isn't it?'; **'Tu as laissé la porte
ouverte'** – 'Oui, en effet' 'You've
left the door open' – ''Yes, so I have.''

efficace adjective 1 efficient; **elle
est très efficace** she's very
efficient; 2 effective; **c'est un**

remède très efficace it's a very effective remedy.

efficacité noun F 1 efficiency; **il est connu pour son efficacité** he's known for his efficiency; 2 effectiveness.

effondrer verb [1] **s'effondrer** to collapse.

efforcer verb [61] **s'efforcer de faire** to try hard to do; **elle s'efforce de rester calme** she tries hard to remain calm.

effort noun M effort; **faire un effort** to make an effort; **il n'a même pas fait l'effort de m'appeler** he didn't even make the effort to phone me.

effrayant adjective frightening.

effrayer verb [59] to frighten.

effroi noun M terror.

effronté adjective cheeky.

effroyable adjective dreadful.

égal, égale (M plural **égaux**) noun M, F equal.
adjective 1 equal; **une distance égale** an equal distance; **des quantités égales** equal quantities; **être égal à** to be equal to; 2 **ça m'est égal** I don't mind; **'Tu veux aller au cinéma ou rester à la maison?'** – **'Ça m'est égal'** 'Do you want to go to the cinema or stay at home?' – 'I don't mind'.

également adverb also; **elle est également prof d'allemand** she's also a German teacher.

égaler verb [1] to equal; **trois plus cinq égale huit** three plus five ⌐⌐ls eight.

égalité noun F 1 equality; 2 **les deux joueurs sont à égalité** the two players are level.

égard noun M 1 **à l'égard de** towards; **à mon égard** towards me; 2 **à cet égard** in this respect.

égaré adjective stray; **un chien égaré** a stray dog.

égarer verb [1] 1 to mislay; **j'ai égaré mes lunettes** I've mislaid my glasses; 2 **s'égarer** to get lost; **nous sommes égarés dans les petites rues** we got lost in the back streets.

égayer verb [59] 1 to brighten up; **j'ai acheté quelques fleurs pour égayer la pièce** I've bought some flowers to brighten up the room; 2 to cheer up; **un peu de musique va nous égayer un peu** a bit of music will cheer us up a bit.

églantine noun F wild rose.

églefin noun M haddock.

église noun F church; **aller à l'église** to go to church.

égoïsme noun M selfishness.

égoïste adjective selfish.

égout noun M sewer.

égoutter verb [1] to drain (vegetables or pasta).

égratignure noun F scratch.

Égypte noun F Egypt.

eh bien exclamation well; **eh bien, ça me fait plaisir de te revoir** well, it's nice to see you again.

élancer verb [61] **s'élancer** to dash.

élargir verb [2] to widen.

élastique noun M 1 rubber band; 2 elastic.
adjective 1 elastic; 2 elasticated.

électeur, électrice noun M, F voter.

élection noun F election.

électricien, électricienne noun M, F electrician.

électricité noun F electricity.

électrique adjective 1 electric; 2 electrical.

électronique noun F electronics. adjective electronic.

élégant adjective elegant.

élément noun M 1 element; 2 part.

élémentaire adjective basic, elementary.

éléphant noun M elephant.

élevage noun M 1 farming (of livestock); 2 farm; un élevage de porcs a pig farm.

élève noun M & F student, pupil.

élevé adjective high; une note élevée a high mark.

élever verb [50] 1 élever un enfant to bring up a child; elle a été élevée en Écosse she was brought up in Scotland; 2 to breed (animals); 3 élever la voix to raise one's voice; 4 s'élever to rise.

éleveur, éleveuse noun M, F breeder.

éliminer verb [1] 1 to eliminate; 2 to rule out; nous ne pouvons pas éliminer cette possibilité we cannot rule out that possibility.

élire verb [51] to elect.

elle pronoun 1 she; où est Sylvie? – elle est dans la cuisine where's Sylvie? – she's in the kitchen; 2 her; Paul est avec elle Paul's with her; 3 it (when referring to an object which is feminine in French); où est ma tasse? – elle est sur la table where's my cup? – it's on the table;

elle-même pronoun 1 herself; elle me l'a dit elle-même she told me herself; 2 itself (referring to an object which is feminine in French) la pièce elle-même est jolie mais les meubles sont hideux the room itself is pretty but the furniture is hideous.

elles pronoun they, them; 1 they (referring to female people or feminine objects); elles sont arrivées they've arrived; 2 them; avec elles with them.

éloigné adjective distant.

éloigner verb [1] s'éloigner (de) to move away (from).

Élysée noun M the Élysée Palace (the official residence of the French President).

émail noun M enamel.

emballage noun M wrapping.

emballer verb [1] 1 to wrap, to pack; 2 (informal) to get enthusiastic; elle s'est vraiment emballée pour son nouveau boulot she's got really enthusiastic about her new job; ça ne m'emballe pas vraiment I'm not that keen.

embarquement noun M boarding; **une carte d'embarquement** a boarding card.

embarquer verb [1] 1 (informal) to go off with; **elle a embarqué toutes mes chaises** she's gone off with all my chairs; 2 **s'embarquer** to board.

embarrassé adjective 1 embarrassed; 2 cluttered.

embarrasser verb [1] 1 to embarrass; 2 to clutter up.

embaucher verb [1] to take on (an employee); **ils embauchent en ce moment** they're taking people on at the moment.

embêtant adjective annoying; **c'est vraiment embêtant!** it's really annoying!

embêter verb [1] 1 to annoy; **arrête de m'embêter!** stop annoying me!; 2 **s'embêter** to be bored; **on ne s'embête pas ici** there's plenty going on here; **on ne s'embête pas!** we're having a great time!

embouteillage noun M traffic jam.

embrasser verb [1] to kiss; **je t'embrasse** lots of love (at the end of a letter or said on the phone to a friend).

embrayage noun M clutch (in a vehicle).

émeraude noun F emerald.

émerger verb [52] to emerge.

émeute noun F riot.

émission noun F programme (on television or radio).

emménager verb [52] to move in (to a flat or house); **nous avons emménagé la semaine dernière** we moved in last week.

emmener verb [50] to take; **c'est sa sœur qui l'emmène à l'école** it's his sister who takes him to school; **tu veux que je t'emmène?** would you like a lift?

émotif (F **émotive**) adjective emotional.

émotion noun F emotion.

émouvant adjective moving.

emparer verb [1] **s'emparer de** to seize.

empêcher verb [1] 1 to prevent, to stop; **rien ne t'empêche d'essayer** there's nothing to stop you trying; 2 **elle n'a pas pu s'empêcher de rire** she couldn't help laughing.

empiler verb [1] to pile up.

empirer verb [1] to get worse.

emplacement noun M site.

emploi noun M 1 job; 2 use; **le mode d'emploi** instructions for use.

emploi du temps noun M timetable (at school).

employé, employée noun M, F employee.

employer verb [39] 1 to employ; 2 to use.

employeur, employeuse noun M, F employer.

empoisonné adjective poisoned.

empoisonner verb [1] to poison.

emporter verb [1] to take (away); 'plats à emporter' 'takeaway meals'.

empreinte noun F footprint.

empreinte digitale noun F fingerprint.

emprisonner verb [1] to imprison.

emprunt noun M loan.

emprunter verb [1] to borrow.

EMT noun (= éduation manuelle et technique) technology (at school).

ému adjective moved.

en preposition **1** in; elle habite en Écosse she lives in Scotland; en été in summer; en avril in April; un livre en anglais a book in English; habillé en noir dressed in black; j'étais en pyjama I was in my pyjamas; **2** into; aller en ville to go into town; traduire en anglais to translate into English; **3** to; aller en Italie to go to Italy; **4** by; en avion by plane; **5** made of; une table en bois a table made of wood, a wooden table; **6** en vacances on holiday; **7** en ami as a friend; **8** en rentrant à la maison j'ai rencontré Tom as I was coming home I met Tom; je me suis brûlé en repassant ma chemise I burned myself (while) ironing my shirt.
pronoun **1** j'en ai I've got some; je n'en veux pas I don't want any; tu en as combien? how many (of them) do you have?, how much (of it) do you have?; elle en a quatre she's got four; 'qui a un stylo?' – 'j'en ai un' who's got a pen?' – 'I've got one' (notice that in this sort of expression 'en' is often not translated

at all); **2** elle m'en a parlé she talked about it to me; **3** j'ai emprunté ton fer à repasser – est-ce que tu en as besoin? I borrowed your iron – do you need it?

encadrer verb [1] to frame.

enceinte adjective pregnant.

encens noun M incense.

encercler verb [1] to surround, to circle.

enchanté adjective delighted.

enchère noun F bid; une vente aux enchères an auction sale.

encore adverb **1** still; elle est encore au bureau she's still at the office; il reste encore de la viande there's still some meat left; **2** pas encore not yet; il n'est pas encore rentré he hasn't come home yet, he's not home yet; **3** again; je l'ai encore oublié I've forgotten it again; **4** more; encore un peu a little more; encore une fois one more time; attendre encore une semaine to wait for another week; **5** even; encore mieux even better.

encourageant adjective encouraging.

encouragement noun M encouragement.

encourager verb [52] to encourage; elle m'a encouragé à suivre des cours de dessin she encouraged me to go to drawing classes.

encre noun F ink.

encyclopédie noun F encyclopedia.

endive noun F chicory.

endommager verb [52] to damage.

endormi adjective asleep.

endormir verb [37] **1 endormir quelqu'un** to send somebody to sleep; **2 s'endormir** to fall asleep, to go to sleep.

endroit noun M **1** place; **un bon endroit pour** a good place for; **2** the right side (of a garment); **3 à l'endroit** the right way up.

énergie noun F energy.

énergique adjective energetic.

énervé adjective irritated, annoyed.

énerver verb [1] **1** to irritate, to annoy; **ça m'énerve!** this is getting on my nerves!; **2 s'énerver** to get annoyed.

enfance noun F childhood.

enfant noun M & F child; **un enfant unique** an only child.

enfantin adjective **1** easy; **2** childish.

enfer noun M hell.

enfermer verb [1] **1** to shut up; **2 s'enfermer** to shut yourself up; **elle s'est enfermée dans sa chambre** she shut herself up in her room.

enfiler verb [1] **1** to put on; **je vais juste enfiler mon pull** I'll just put my jumper on; **2 enfiler une aiguille** to thread a needle.

enfin adverb **1** at last; **je l'ai enfin fini** I've finished it at last; **2** finally; **elle a enfin réussi** she finally succeeded.

enflé adjective swollen.

enfoncer verb [61] **1** to push in; **2 s'enfoncer dans** to sink into.

engagement noun M commitment.

engager verb [52] **1** to take on (an employee); **2** to commit; **3 s'engager à faire** to promise to do; **je me suis engagé à organiser le repas** I promised to organize the meal.

engelure noun F chilblain.

engin noun M device.

engourdir verb [2] **s'engourdir** to go numb.

engrais noun M fertilizer.

engueuler verb [1] (informal) to tell off; **elle m'a engueulé** she gave me a telling off; **se faire engueuler** to get a telling off.

énième adjective umpteenth; **pour la énième fois** for the umpteenth time.

énigme noun F riddle.

enivrer verb [1] **1 enivrer quelqu'un** to make somebody drunk; **2 s'enivrer** to get drunk.

enjeu (plural **enjeux**) noun M **1** stake (in a gambling game); **2** what is at stake.

enlèvement noun M kidnapping.

enlever verb [50] **1** to take off (garment); **il a enlevé sa veste** he took off his jacket; **2** to remove; **enlever une tache** to remove a stain; **tu peux enlever les assiettes**

you can clear the plates; **3** to kidnap.

ennemi, ennemie noun M, F enemy.

ennui noun M **1** boredom; **2** problem; **avoir des ennuis** to have problems.

ennuyé adjective **1** bored; **2** embarrassed.

ennuyer verb [41] **1** to bore; **son discours m'a ennuyé** I found his speech boring; **2** to bother; **je t'ennuie?** am I bothering you?; **3** s'ennuyer to be (or get) bored; **j'ai fini par m'ennuyer** I got bored in the end; **on s'ennuie ici** it's boring here.

ennuyeux (F **ennuyeuse**) adjective **1** boring; **2** annoying; **ça c'est vraiment ennuyeux** that's really annoying.

énorme adjective huge.

énormément adverb **1** tremendously; **2** énormément de masses of; **j'ai énormément de choses à faire avant de partir** I've got masses of things to do before I leave.

enquête noun F **1** investigation; **2** inquiry; **3** survey.

enregistrement noun M **1** recording; **2** check-in (at airport).

enregistrer verb [1] **1** to record; **2** to register; **3** to check in (at airport).

enrhumer verb [1] **s'enrhumer** to catch a cold; **être enrhumé** to have a cold.

enrichir verb [2] **1** to make rich; **2** to enrich.

enrichissant adjective rewarding.

enrouler verb [1] to wind.

enseignant, enseignante noun M, F teacher.

enseigne noun F sign; **enseigne lumineuse** neon sign.

enseignement noun M **1** teaching; **2** education.

enseigner verb [1] to teach.

ensemble noun M **1** outfit; **j'ai acheté un joli ensemble pour le mariage** I've bought a lovely outfit for the wedding; **2** l'ensemble de the whole of; **3** dans l'ensemble on the whole.
adverb together; **on va y aller ensemble** we'll go together; **ils sont ensemble depuis trois ans** they've been together for three years.

ensoleillé adjective sunny.

ensommeillé adjective sleepy.

ensuite adverb then; **on va aller à la banque et ensuite chez Marianne** we'll go to the bank and then to Marianne's.

entamer verb [1] to start; **ce paquet n'a pas encore été entamé** this packet hasn't been started yet.

entasser verb [1] to pile up.

entendre verb [3] **1** to hear; **est-ce que tu l'entends?** can you hear it?; **se faire entendre** to make yourself heard; **2** j'ai entendu dire que...** I've heard that...; **3** to mean; **qu'est-ce que tu entends par là?**

what do you mean by that?;
4 **s'entendre bien** to get on well.

entendu *exclamation* 1 okay, fine;
2 **bien entendu** of course.

entente *noun* F 1 understanding;
2 agreement.

enterrement *noun* M funeral,
burial.

enterrer *verb* [1] to bury.

entêté *adjective* stubborn.

entêter *verb* [1] **s'entêter à faire**
to persist in doing.

enthousiasme *noun* M
enthusiasm.

enthousiasmer *verb* [1]
s'enthousiasmer to get
enthusiastic.

enthousiaste *adjective*
enthusiastic.

entier (F **entière**) *adjective* 1 whole;
une pomme entière a whole apple;
le monde entier the whole world;
2 **je n'ai pas lu sa lettre en entier** I
haven't read his letter right through;
3 **le lait entier** full-fat milk.

entièrement *adverb* completely,
entirely.

entorse *noun* F sprain; **se faire une
entorse à la cheville** to sprain your
ankle.

entouré *adjective* **entouré de**
surrounded by; **elle est entourée
d'amis** she's surrounded by friends.

entourer *verb* [1] to surround;
entourer de to surround with.

entracte *noun* M interval (*at the
theatre*).

entraînement *noun* M
1 training; 2 practice.

entraîner *verb* [1] 1 to lead to;
entraîner des problèmes to lead to
problems; 2 to take; **il m'a entraîné
chez sa copine** he took me off to his
girlfriend's; 3 **entraîner une
équipe** to train a team; 4 to drag;
5 **s'entraîner** to train; **elle
s'entraîne tous les matins** she
trains every morning.

entre *preposition* 1 between; **entre
la porte et la fenêtre** between the
door and the window; **on va le
partager entre nous** we'll share it
between us; 2 among; **entre eux**
among themselves; 3 **l'un d'entre
eux** one of them.

entrée *noun* F 1 entrance; **à
l'entrée de** at the entrance to;
billets à l'entrée tickets at the door;
2 hall(way); 3 admission;
4 starter, first course.

entremets *noun* M dessert.

entrepôt *noun* M warehouse.

entreprendre *verb* [64] 1 to
undertake; 2 to start.

entreprise *noun* F firm, business.

entrer *verb* [1] 1 to go in; **entrer
dans un magasin** to go into a shop;
entrer à l'hôpital to go into
hospital; 2 to come in; **entrer dans**
to come into; **Entrez!** Come in!

entre-temps *adverb* meanwhile.

entretenir *verb* [81] 1 to maintain
(*a building, a road, etc*); 2 to
support.

entretien *noun* M 1 interview; **elle
a été convoquée à un entretien** she's

been invited for interview;
2 discussion; **j'ai eu un entretien
avec mon patron** I had a discussion
with my boss; **3** upkeep; **l'entretien
de la maison** the upkeep of the
house.

entrevue noun F interview.

entrouvert adjective ajar, half-
open.

envahir verb [2] to invade.

enveloppe noun F envelope; **une
enveloppe matelassée** a padded
envelope.

envelopper verb [1] to wrap up.

envers noun M **1** wrong side; **2 à
l'envers** upside down; inside out;
back to front.
preposition towards, to.

envie noun F **1** urge; **avoir envie de
faire** to want to do, to feel like doing;
j'ai envie de te voir I want to see you;
j'ai envie d'aller au cinéma I feel
like going to the cinema; **2 avoir
envie de quelque chose** to feel like
something; **j'ai envie d'une glace** I
feel like an ice cream; **3 ces frites
me font envie** I fancy some of those
chips.

envier verb [1] to envy.

environ adverb about; **environ
trente personnes** about thirty
people.

environnement noun M
environment.

environs plural noun M
surroundings; **aux environs de**
near.

envisager verb [52] envisager de
faire to plan to do; **qu'est-ce que
vous envisagez de faire?** what are
you planning to do?

envoi noun M **1** dispatch; **faire un
envoi de** to send; **2** consignment.

envoler verb [1] s'envoler to fly
away.

envoyer verb [40] to send; **envoyer
quelque chose à quelqu'un** to send
somebody something; **elle m'a
envoyé une carte** she sent me a
card; **elle m'a envoyé chercher les
verres** she sent me to get the
glasses.

épais (F **épaisse**) adjective thick;
une tranche épaisse a thick slice.

épaisseur noun F thickness.

épargne noun F savings; **une
banque d'épargne** a savings bank;
un compte d'épargne a savings
account.

épatant adjective (informal)
fantastic, great.

épaule noun F shoulder.

épaulette noun F **1** shoulder
strap; **2** shoulder pad.

épave noun F wreck.

épée noun F sword.

épeler verb [18] to spell.

éphémère adjective fleeting.

épi noun M ear (of corn); **un épi de
maïs** a corn cob.

épice noun F spice.

épicé adjective spicy, hot; **je n'aime
pas les choses épicées** I don't like
spicy food.

épicerie noun F grocer's (shop); **à l'épicerie** at the grocer's.

épicier, épicière noun M, F grocer.

épidémie noun F epidemic.

épilepsie noun F epilepsy.

épiler verb [1] **s'épiler les sourcils** to pluck your eyebrows; **une pince à épiler** eyebrow tweezers; **s'épiler les jambes** to shave your legs (or use wax or cream to remove hair).

épinards plural noun M spinach; **est-ce que tu aimes les épinards?** do you like spinach?

épine noun F thorn.

épingle noun F pin; **une épingle de sûreté** a safety pin.

épingler verb [1] to pin.

éplucher verb [1] to peel.

épluchures plural noun F peelings.

éponge noun F **1** sponge; **2** towelling.

éponger verb [52] **1** to mop up; **2** to sponge.

époque noun F time; **à cette époque-là** at that time.

épouse noun F wife.

épouser verb [1] to marry.

épouvantable adjective dreadful.

épouvantail noun M scarecrow.

épouvante noun F terror; **un film d'épouvante** a horror film.

époux noun M husband.

épreuve noun F **1** test; **2** exam; **l'épreuve de français** the French exam; **3** event (sports); **4** ordeal.

éprouver verb [1] to feel, to experience.

éprouvette noun F test tube.

EPS noun (= éducation physique et sportive) PE.

épuisant adjective exhausting; **c'est un travail épuisant** it's exhausting work.

épuisé adjective **1** exhausted, worn out; **je suis épuisé** I'm worn out; **2** out of stock; **3** out of print.

épuiser verb [1] to wear out; **cette discussion m'a épuisé** that discussion's worn me out.

équateur noun M equator.

équestre adjective **un centre équestre** a riding school.

équilibre noun M balance.

équilibré adjective balanced.

équipage noun M crew.

équipe noun F team.

équipé adjective **1** equipped; **2 une cuisine équipée** a fitted kitchen.

équipement noun M equipment.

équipements plural noun M **les équipements sportifs** sports facilities.

équitation noun F riding.

équivalent adjective equivalent.

érable noun M maple tree; **le sirop d'érable** maple syrup.

errer *verb* [1] to wander.

erreur *noun* F mistake; **par erreur** by mistake.

es *verb* SEE **être**².

escabeau *noun* M stepladder.

escalade *noun* F rock-climbing.

escalier *noun* M 1 stairs; **dans l'escalier** on the stairs; 2 staircase; 3 **un escalier mécanique, un escalier roulant** an escalator.

escargot *noun* M snail.

escarpin *noun* M court shoe.

esclavage *noun* M slavery.

esclave *noun* M & F slave.

escorter *verb* [1] to escort.

escrime *noun* F fencing (*the sport*).

escroc *noun* M crook, swindler.

escroquer *verb* [1] to swindle.

espace *noun* M space.

espacer *verb* [61] to space out.

espadon *noun* M swordfish.

espadrille *noun* F espadrille.

Espagne *noun* F Spain.

espagnol *noun* M, *adjective* Spanish.

Espagnol, Espagnole *noun* M, F Spaniard; **les Espagnols** the Spanish.

espèce *noun* F 1 sort; **une espèce de** a sort of; **on a mangé du poisson avec une espèce de sauce épicée** we had fish with a sort of spicy sauce; 2 species; 3 **espèce d'idiot!** you idiot!; 4 **en espèces** in cash.

espérer *verb* [24] to hope; **ils espèrent pouvoir venir** they're hoping to be able to come; **j'espère qu'elle n'a pas oublié** I hope she hasn't forgotten; **j'espère bien!** I certainly hope so.

espiègle *adjective* mischievous.

espion, espionne *noun* M, F spy.

espionnage *noun* M spying, espionage.

espionner *verb* [1] to spy on.

espoir *noun* M hope.

esprit *noun* M 1 mind; **ça ne m'est pas venu à l'esprit** it didn't cross my mind; 2 wit; **avoir de l'esprit** to be witty.

esquimau™ (*plural* **esquimaux**) *noun* M ice lolly.

esquisse *noun* F sketch.

esquisser *verb* [1] to sketch.

essai *noun* M 1 trial; 2 test; 3 attempt, try.

essaim *noun* M swarm.

essayer *verb* [59] 1 to try; **essayer de faire** to try to do; **j'ai essayé de t'appeler** I tried to phone you; 2 to try on; **essayer une robe** to try on a dress; **voulez-vous l'essayer?** would you like to try it on?; 3 to test;

essence *noun* F 1 petrol; **essence sans plomb** unleaded petrol; 2 essential oil.

essentiel (F **essentielle**) *adjective* essential; **c'est l'essentiel** that's the main thing.

essentiellement *adverb* 1 mainly; 2 essentially.

essorage *noun* M spin-dry.

essorer *verb* [1] to spin-dry.

essoufflé *adjective* out of breath.

essuie-glace *noun* M windscreen wiper.

essuie-tout *noun* M (paper) kitchen towel.

essuyer *verb* [41] to wipe; **essuyer la vaisselle** to do the drying-up; **s'essuyer les mains** to dry your hands.

est[1] *verb* SEE **être**[2].

est[2] *noun* M east; **l'est de Paris** the east of Paris; **dans l'est de la France** in the east of France; **l'Europe de l'Est** Eastern Europe. *adjective* 1 east; 2 eastern.

est-ce que (*used for asking questions*) **est-ce qu'il pleut?** is it raining? **est-ce que Julie est partie?** has Julie left? **où est-ce qu'il habite?** where does he live?

esthéticienne *noun* F beautician.

estime *noun* F respect.

estimer *verb* [1] 1 to esteem; 2 to value; 3 **j'estime que...** I think that...

estival (M plural **estivaux**) *adjective* summer.

estivant, estivante *noun* M, F summer visitor.

estomac *noun* M stomach; **avoir mal à l'estomac** to have stomachache.

Estonie *noun* F Estonia.

estrade *noun* F platform.

estragon *noun* M tarragon; **une sauce à l'estragon** a tarragon sauce.

et *conjunction* and.

établir *verb* [2] 1 to establish; 2 **établir une liste** to draw up a list; 3 **s'établir à son compte** to set up in business.

établissement *noun* M 1 institution; **établissement scolaire** school; 2 organization.

étage *noun* M floor; **au premier étage** on the first floor; **au dernier étage** on the top floor; **à l'étage** upstairs.

étagère *noun* F 1 shelf; 2 set of shelves.

étain *noun* M 1 tin; 2 pewter.

étalage *noun* M window display.

étaler *verb* [1] 1 to spread; 2 to spread out; 3 to roll out (*pastry*).

étanche *adjective* 1 watertight; 2 waterproof.

étang *noun* M pond.

étape *noun* F 1 stage; 2 stopping place.

état *noun* M 1 state, condition; **en mauvais état** in a bad state; **en bon état** in good condition; **en état de marche** in working order; **être dans tous ses états** to be in a state.

État *noun* M state, State.

États-Unis plural noun M les États-Unis the United States; aux États-Unis in (or to) the United States.

été[1] verb SEE être[2].

été[2] noun M summer; en été in summer; l'été dernier last summer; des vêtements d'été summer clothes.

éteindre verb [60] 1 to turn off, to switch off; éteindre la lumière to turn out the lights; 2 to put out (a fire or cigarette); 3 s'éteindre to go out.

étendre verb [3] 1 to spread out; 2 to stretch out (your arms or legs); 3 étendre le linge to hang out the washing; 4 s'étendre to stretch; 5 s'étendre to spread.

éternel (F éternelle) adjective eternal.

éternité noun F eternity.

éternuer verb [1] to sneeze.

êtes verb SEE être[2].

ethnie noun F ethnic group.

ethnique adjective ethnic.

étinceler verb [18] to sparkle, to twinkle.

étincelle noun F spark.

étiquette noun F 1 label; 2 etiquette.

étirer verb [1] to stretch.

étoffe noun F fabric.

étoile noun F star; une étoile filante a shooting star.

étonnant adjective 1 surprising; 2 astonishing.

étonnement noun M 1 surprise; 2 astonishment.

étonner verb [1] 1 to surprise; ça m'a beaucoup étonné that really surprised me; ça ne m'étonne pas du tout that doesn't surprise me at all; 2 s'étonner to be surprised; s'étonner de quelque chose to be surprised at something.

étouffant adjective stifling.

étouffer verb [1] 1 to stifle; 2 to suffocate; 3 s'étouffer to choke.

étourderie noun F 1 absent-mindedness; 2 une étourderie a careless mistake.

étourdi, étourdie noun M, F scatterbrain.
adjective scatterbrained.

étourdir verb [2] to daze, to stun.

étourneau noun M starling.

étrange adjective strange.

étranger[1], **étrangère** noun M, F 1 foreigner; 2 stranger.
adjective foreign; un pays étranger a foreign country.

étranger[2] noun M à l'étranger abroad.

étrangler verb [1] 1 to strangle; 2 to choke.

être[1] noun M being; un être humain a human being.

être[2] verb [6] 1 to be; nous sommes dans la cuisine we're in the kitchen; elle est malade she's ill; c'est moi it's me; 2 elle est infirmière she's a nurse; **3 être à quelqu'un** to belong to somebody, to be somebody's; **ce livre est à Paul** this book is Paul's; **ce livre est à moi** this book is mine; **4 il est 6 heures** it's 6 o'clock; **5 nous sommes le 7 mars** it's the 7th of March (today); **6** (used with certain verbs to form past tenses: for a list of these, see the centre pages) **je suis allé à Paris** I went to Paris; **nous sommes rentrés à 7 heures** we got home at 7 o'clock; **7** (used to form the passive of verbs) **ses robes sont faites par sa mère** her dresses are made by her mother.

étroit adjective **1** narrow; **2** close.

étroitement adverb closely.

étude noun F **1** study; **2 études** studies; **faire des études de médecine** to study medicine.

étudiant, étudiante noun M, F student.

étudier verb [1] to study.

étui noun M case.

eu verb SEE **avoir**.

Europe noun F Europe; **en Europe** in (or to) Europe.

européen (F **européenne**) adjective European.

euthanasie noun F euthanasia.

eux pronoun **1** them; **avec eux** with them; **des amis à eux** friends of theirs; **2** they.

eux-mêmes pronoun themselves.

évacuer verb [1] to evacuate.

évader verb [1] **s'évader** to escape.

évaluer verb [1] to assess.

évanouir verb [2] **s'évanouir** to faint.

évaporer verb [1] **s'évaporer** to evaporate.

évasion noun F escape.

éveillé adjective awake.

éveiller verb [1] **1** to arouse; **2** to awaken.

événement noun M event.

éventail noun M fan.

éventualité noun F possibility.

éventuel (F **éventuelle**) adjective possible.

éventuellement adverb **1** possibly; **2** if necessary.

évêque noun M bishop.

évidence noun F **être en évidence** to be clearly visible; **de toute évidence** clearly; **de toute évidence il a oublié de venir** he's clearly forgotten to come; **mettre quelque chose en évidence** to reveal something.

évidemment adverb of course.

évident adjective obvious.

évier noun M sink.

éviter verb [1] to avoid; **éviter de faire** to avoid doing; **ça t'évitera de sortir** that'll save you having to go out.

évolué adjective advanced.

évoluer verb [1] **1** to develop; **nous ne savons pas comment la situation va évoluer** we do not know how the situation will develop; **2** to progress; **l'informatique a beaucoup**

évolué ces dernières années
computer science has progressed a
great deal in recent years; **3** to
change; les choses ont évolué
depuis things have changed since.

évolution noun F **1** development;
2 progress; **3** evolution.

exact adjective **1** correct; c'est
exact that's absolutely right;
2 exact, precise.

exactement adverb exactly.

exagéré adjective **1** exaggerated;
2 excessive.

exagérer verb [24] **1** to
exaggerate; **2** to go too far.

examen noun M **1** exam; passer
un examen to sit an exam; réussir à
un examen to pass an exam; un
examen blanc a mock exam; **2** un
examen médical a medical
examination.

examinateur, examinatrice
noun M, F examiner.

examiner verb [1] to examine.

exaspérant adjective exasperating.

exaspérer verb [24] to exasperate.

excellence noun F excellence.

excellent adjective excellent.

excentrique noun M & F,
adjective eccentric.

excepté preposition except.

exception noun F exception; à
l'exception de with the exception
of.

exceptionnel (F exceptionnelle)
adjective **1** exceptional; **2** special.

exceptionnellement adverb
exceptionally.

excès noun M excess.

excès de vitesse noun M
speeding.

excessif (F excessive) adjective
excessive.

excessivement adverb
excessively; il est excessivement
timide he's incredibly shy.

excitant noun M stimulant.
adjective exciting.

excitation noun F excitement.

excité adjective **1** frenzied; **2** over-
excited; **3** thrilled.

exciter verb [1] s'exciter to get
excited.

exclamation noun F exclamation.

exclamer verb [1] s'exclamer to
exclaim.

exclu adjective il n'est pas exclu
que... it's not impossible that...

exclusif (F exclusive) adjective
exclusive.

excursion noun F excursion, trip.

excuse noun **1** apology; présenter
ses excuses to apologize;
2 excuse.

excuser verb [1] **1** to forgive;
excusez-moi! sorry!; excusez-moi
de vous déranger sorry to disturb
you; **2** s'excuser to apologize; je
m'excuse I'm sorry; je m'excuse
d'être en retard sorry I'm late.

exécuter verb [1] **1** to execute;
2 to carry out.

exemplaire noun M copy; **six exemplaires du dictionnaire** six copies of the dictionary.

exemple noun M example; **par, exemple** for example; **donner l'exemple** to set an example.

exercer verb [61] **1** to exercise (a right); **2** to practise (an art or a profession); **3** to exert (authority); **4** s'exercer to practise.

exercice noun M exercise.

exhiber verb [1] **1** to show off; **2** to display.

exhibitionniste noun M flasher.

exigeant adjective hard to please.

exiger verb [52] **1** to demand; **2** to require.

exil noun M exile.

exilé, exilée noun M, F exile.

existence noun F existence.

exister verb [1] to exist.

exotique adjective exotic.

expansion noun F **1** expansion; **2** growth.

expédier verb [1] to send (off); **expédier un paquet** to send off a package.

expéditeur, expéditrice noun M, F sender.

expédition noun F expedition.

expérience noun F **1** experience; **avoir de l'expérience** to be experienced; **2** experiment; **faire une expérience** to carry out an experiment.

expérimenté adjective experienced.

expert noun M expert.

explication noun F explanation.

explicite adjective explicit.

expliquer verb [1] to explain.

exploit noun M **1** achievement; **2** feat.

exploiter verb [1] **1** to exploit; **2** to use, to make use of.

explorer verb [1] to explore.

exploser verb [1] to explode, to blow up.

explosif (F **explosive**) adjective explosive.

explosion noun F **1** explosion; **2** boom.

export noun M export.

exportateur, exportatrice noun M, F exporter.

exporter verb [1] to export.

exposé noun M talk; **Gaby a fait un exposé sur le Japon** Gaby gave a talk about Japan.
adjective **1** exposed; **2** on display.

exposer verb [1] **1** to exhibit; **2** to expose; **3** to explain.

exposition noun F **1** exhibition; **une exposition d'art africain** an exhibition of African art; **2** exposure.

exprès adjective express.
adverb **1** deliberately; **tu l'as fait exprès** you did it deliberately, you did it on purpose; **il a fait exprès de le casser** he broke it on purpose;

c'est fait exprès it's meant to be like that; **2** specially; **je suis venu exprès pour te voir** I've come specially to see you.

express noun M **1** fast train; **2** espresso coffee.

expression noun F expression.

exprimer verb [1] **1** to express; **2 s'exprimer** to express yourself; **je m'exprime mal** I'm expressing myself badly.

expulser verb [1] **1** to evict; **2** to expel.

exquis adjective exquisite, delightful.

extase noun F ecstasy.

extensif (F **extensive**) adjective extensive.

extension noun F extension.

extérieur noun M **1** outside; **à l'extérieur** outside; **2** exterior. adjective **1** outside; **2** outer.

externat noun M day school.

externe noun M & F day pupil.

extincteur noun M fire extinguisher.

extra adjective (informal) great, fantastic; **ta sauce est vraiment extra!** your sauce is really fantastic!

extraction noun F **1** extraction; **2** mining.

extraire verb [78] **1** to extract; **2** to mine.

extrait noun M extract.

extraordinaire adjective extraordinary, amazing.

extravagant adjective **1** eccentric; **des vêtements extravagants** eccentric clothes; **2** extravagant.

extrême noun M, adjective extreme.

extrêmement adverb extremely.

Extrême-Orient noun M the Far East.

extrémité noun F **1** end; **2** tip; **3** edge; **4** extreme.

F f

F SHORT FOR **francs; 30 F** 30 francs.

fabricant noun M manufacturer.

fabrication noun F manufacture.

fabriquer verb [1] to make; **fabriqué en France** made in France; **qu'est-ce que tu fabriques?** (informal) what are you up to?

fabuleux (F **fabuleuse**) adjective fabulous.

fac noun F (informal) university; **être en fac d'anglais** to be doing a degree in English.

face noun F **1** face; **face à face** face to face; **2 en face** opposite; **en face de l'école** opposite the school; **la maison d'en face** the house opposite; **le magasin en face de chez nous** the shop opposite our house; **3 faire face à quelque chose** to face up to something; **4 face à** facing; **face au mur** facing the wall; **5 pile ou face?** heads or tails?

fâché *adjective* 1 angry; **elle est fâchée contre moi** she's angry with me; 2 **il est fâché avec son frère** he's fallen out with his brother.

fâcher *verb* [1] 1 **se fâcher** to get angry; **se fâcher contre quelqu'un** to get angry with somebody; **elle s'est fâchée contre moi** she got angry with me; 2 **se fâcher avec quelqu'un** to fall out with somebody.

facile *adjective* easy; **c'est facile** it's easy; **c'est facile à comprendre** it's easy to understand.

facilement *adverb* easily.

facilité *noun* F easiness.

faciliter *verb* [1] to make (something) easier; **ça devrait nous faciliter les choses** that should make things easier for us.

façon *noun* F 1 way; **il y a plusieurs façons de le faire** there are several ways of doing it; **d'une façon extraordinaire** in an extraordinary way; **de quelle façon?** in what way?; 2 **de toute façon** anyway.

façonner *verb* [1] 1 to make; 2 to shape.

facteur¹ *noun* M factor.

facteur², factrice *noun* M, F postman, postwoman; **est-ce que le facteur est passé?** has the postman been?

facture *noun* F bill; **la facture d'électricité** the electricity bill.

facultatif (F **facultative**) *adjective* optional.

faculté *noun* F faculty.

fade *adjective* tasteless; **la sauce est un peu fade** the sauce is a bit tasteless.

faible *noun* M **avoir un faible pour** to have a soft spot for. *adjective* 1 weak; **elle est encore très faible** she's still very weak; 2 **elle est faible en chimie** she's not very good at chemistry; 3 **un faible bruit** a faint noise.

faiblesse *noun* F weakness.

faiblir *verb* [2] 1 to weaken; 2 **le vent a faibli** the wind's died down a bit.

faïence *noun* F earthenware; **des assiettes en faïence** earthenware plates.

faillir *verb* [42] **faillir faire** to nearly do; **j'ai failli tomber** I nearly fell; **j'ai failli rater le train** I nearly missed the train.

faillite *noun* F bankruptcy; **faire faillite** to go bankrupt.

faim *noun* F hunger; **avoir faim** to be hungry; **j'ai très faim** I'm really hungry; **je meurs de faim !** I'm starving!; **je n'ai plus faim** I've had enough to eat; **ces gâteaux me donnent faim** those cakes make me feel hungry.

fainéant *adjective* lazy.

faire *verb* [10] 1 to make; **faire un gâteau** to make a cake; **je vais me faire un café** I'm going to make myself a coffee; **faire du bruit** to make a noise; 2 to do; **qu'est-ce que tu fais?** what are you doing?; **il est en train de faire ses devoirs** he's doing his homework; **faire du français** to do French; **fais comme**

tu veux do as you like; **3 qu'as-tu fait du couteau?** what have you done with the knife?; **4 il fait froid** it's cold; **il fait chaud** it's hot; **5 quel temps fait-il?** what's the weather like?; **il fait beau** it's a nice day; **il fait beau en été ici** the weather's nice here in summer; **6 ça ne fait rien** it doesn't matter; **7 faire faire quelque chose** to have (or get) something done; **elle a fait réparer son vélo** she got her bike repaired; **il s'est fait couper les cheveux** he's had his hair cut; **8 faire chauffer de l'eau** to heat some water; **faire cuire quelque chose** to cook something; **9 ne t'en fais pas** don't worry.

faire-part noun M announcement (of birth, marriage, or death).

fais verb SEE faire.

faisan noun M pheasant.

faisons verb SEE faire.

fait[1] verb SEE faire.

fait[2] noun M **1** fact; **en fait** actually; **en fait je l'ai vu hier** in fact I saw him yesterday; **2 au fait** by the way; **au fait, est-ce que tu as fermé la porte?** by the way, did you shut the door?

fait d'actualité noun M news item.

faites verb SEE faire.

falaise noun F cliff.

fallait verb SEE falloir.

falloir impersonal verb [43] **1 il faut le faire** it has to be done, you must do it; **il ne faut pas faire ça** you mustn't do that; **il ne fallait pas faire ça** you shouldn't have done that; **il**

faudra partir à six heures we'll have to leave at six o'clock; **2 il me faut un stylo** I need a pen; **il leur faut une voiture** they need a car; **qu'est-ce qu'il te faut?** what do you need?; **3 il faut que tu le fasses** (subjunctive) you must do it; **il faut que tu prennes tes clés** you must take your keys; **4 comme il faut** properly; **tu ne l'as pas fait comme il faut** you haven't done it properly; **marche comme il faut!** walk properly.

famé adjective **un quartier mal famé** a rough area.

fameux (F fameuse) adjective **1** first-rate; **le repas n'était pas fameux** the meal wasn't great.

familial (M plural familiaux) adjective family; **la vie familiale** family life; **les allocations familiales** child benefit.

familiariser verb [1] **se familiariser avec** to become familiar with.

familiarité noun F familiarity.

familier (F familière) adjective familiar; **un endroit familier** a familiar place.

famille noun F **1** family; **un déjeuner en famille** a family lunch; **une famille nombreuse** a big family; **2** relatives; **j'ai de la famille à Londres** I have relatives in London.

fanatique noun M & F fanatic.

fané adjective withered; **les fleurs sont fanées** the flowers are withered.

fanfare noun F brass band.

fantaisie noun F 1 imagination;
2 des bijoux de fantaisie costume
jewellery.

fantaisiste adjective 1 unreliable;
il est un peu fantaisiste he's rather
unreliable; 2 une idée fantaisiste a
wild idea.

fantastique adjective fantastic.

fantôme noun M ghost.

farce noun F 1 practical joke; un
magasin de farces et attrapes a
joke shop; 2 stuffing (for a chicken,
for example).

farci adjective stuffed; des tomates
farcies stuffed tomatoes.

farcir verb [2] to stuff (a chicken, for
example).

fardeau (plural fardeaux) noun
M burden.

farfelu adjective bizarre; c'est un
type farfelu he's a bizarre bloke; elle
a toujours des idées farfelues she
always has crazy ideas.

farine noun F 1 flour; 2 baby
cereal.

fascinant adjective fascinating; son
histoire était absolument
fascinante his story was absolutely
fascinating.

fascination noun F fascination.

fasciner verb [1] to fascinate; ça me
fascine I find that fascinating.

fascisme noun M fascism.

fastidieux (F fastidieuse) adjective
tedious; c'est un travail fastidieux
it's tedious work.

fatal adjective 1 inevitable; c'était
fatal it was bound to happen;
2 fatal.

fatalité noun F fate.

fatidique adjective fateful.

fatigant adjective tiring.

fatigue noun F tiredness.

fatigué adjective tired; je suis
fatigué I'm tired; tu as l'air fatigué
you look tired.

fatiguer verb [1] 1 to tire
(somebody) out; la promenade m'a
fatigué the walk tired me out; 2 se
fatiguer to get tired.

faubourg noun M suburb.

fauché adjective (informal) broke;
je suis fauché cette semaine I'm
broke this week.

faucher verb [1] 1 to mow, to
scythe; 2 (informal) to nick;
quelqu'un m'a fauché mon vélo
somebody's nicked my bike.

faucon noun M falcon.

faudra, faudrait verb SEE falloir.

faufiler verb [1] se faufiler à travers
la foule to thread your way through
the crowd.

faune noun F wildlife.

faussement adverb wrongly.

fausser verb [1] 1 to distort; 2 to
bend.

faut verb SEE falloir.

faute noun F 1 mistake, error; faire
une faute to make a mistake; une
faute d'orthographe a spelling
mistake; 2 fault; c'est (de) ma

faute it's my fault; **c'est la faute de Sophie** it's Sophie's fault; **3 faute de** for lack of; **faute de temps** for lack of time; **faute de mieux** for want of anything better; **4 sans faute** without fail.

fauteuil noun M armchair.

fauteuil roulant noun M wheelchair.

fautif (F **fautive**) adjective faulty.

fauve noun M wild animal.
adjective tawny.

faux[1] (F **fausse**) adjective **1** wrong; **c'est faux** it's wrong; **2** untrue; **c'est totalement faux** it's totally untrue; **3** false; **une fausse barbe** a false beard; **4** imitation; **une table en faux marbre** an imitation marble table; **5 chanter faux** to sing out of tune.

faux[2] noun M fake, forgery; **cette pièce est un faux** this coin's a forgery.

faux[3] noun F scythe.

faux ami noun M false friend (a word in a foreign language which looks very like a word in your own language but does not mean the same thing at all).

faux-filet noun M sirloin.

faveur noun F favour; **en faveur de** in favour of.

favorable adjective favourable.

favorablement adverb favourably.

favori (F **favorite**) adjective favourite.

favoriser verb [1] to favour.

fax noun M **1** fax; **envoyer un fax** to send a fax; **2** fax machine.

fédéral (M plural **fédéraux**) adjective federal.

fédération noun F federation.

fée noun F fairy; ★ **avoir des doigts de fée** to have nimble fingers (literally: to have the fingers of a fairy).

féerique adjective magical.

feignant adjective (informal) lazy.

fêler verb [1] **se fêler** to crack.

félicitations plural noun F congratulations.

féliciter verb [1] to congratulate.

fêlure noun F crack.

femelle noun F,
adjective female (animal).

féminin noun M **le féminin** the feminine (in French and other grammars); **au féminin** in the feminine.
adjective **1** female; **le sexe féminin** the female sex; **2** feminine; **elle est très féminine** she's very feminine; **3** women's; **les vêtements féminins** women's clothing; **la presse féminine** women's magazines; **les questions féminines** women's issues.

féministe noun M & F feminist.

femme noun F **1** woman; **c'est une femme très intéressante** she's a very interesting woman; **2** wife; **la femme de David** David's wife.

femme au foyer noun F housewife.

femme de ménage noun F cleaning lady.

fendre verb [3] **1** to split; **2** to crack.

fenêtre noun F window; **regarder par la fenêtre** to look out the window; ★ **jeter l'argent par les fenêtres** to throw your money away (*literally: to throw money out of the windows*).

fenouil noun M fennel.

fente noun F **1** slit; **2** slot; **3** crack.

fer noun M iron.

fer à cheval noun M horseshoe.

fer à repasser noun M iron (*for ironing things with*).

fer forgé noun M wrought iron.

férié adjective **un jour férié** a public holiday.

ferme[1] noun F **1** farm; **2** farmhouse.

ferme[2] adjective firm.

fermé adjective closed; **'fermé le dimanche'** closed on Sundays.

fermenter verb [1] to ferment.

fermer verb [1] **1** to close, to shut; **peux-tu fermer la porte, s'il te plaît** shut the door please; **il a fermé les yeux** he closed his eyes; **2** to turn off (*the lights, the tap, the water, etc*); **n'oublie pas de fermer les robinets** don't forget to turn off the taps; **3 se fermer** to close, to shut.

fermeture noun F **1** closing; **heures de fermeture** closing times; **2** fastening (*on a garment*).

fermeture éclair noun F zip.

fermier, fermière noun M, F **1** farmer; **2 la fermière** the farmer's wife.
adjective farm; **produits fermiers** farm produce; **un poulet fermier** a free-range chicken.

fermoir noun M clasp.

féroce adjective **1** fierce; **2** ferocious.

ferraille noun F scrap metal.

ferroviaire adjective rail; **le réseau ferroviaire** the rail network.

fertile adjective fertile.

fertilité noun F fertility.

fesse noun F buttock; **fesses** bottom.

festival noun M festival.

fête noun F **1** public holiday; **2** party; **faire la fête** to celebrate; **3 les fêtes de fin d'année** the festive season; **4** fête, fair; **5** saint's name day (*in France each day of the year is associated with the name of a saint and many people still celebrate the day of the saint they are named after*).

fête des Mères noun F Mother's Day (*in France on the last Sunday in May*).

fête des Pères noun F Father's Day.

fête foraine noun F funfair.

Fête Nationale noun F Bastille Day.

fêter verb [1] to celebrate.

feu noun M 1 fire; **faire du feu** to light a fire; **prendre feu** to catch fire; 2 light; **as-tu du feu?** have you got a light?; 3 **les feux de signalisation**; the traffic lights; **un feu rouge** a red light; 4 **faire cuire à feu doux** cook on a gentle heat; ★ **il n'y a pas le feu** there's no hurry (*literally: there isn't a fire*).

feu d'artifice noun M 1 firework; 2 firework display.

feuillage noun M leaves.

feuille noun F 1 leaf; 2 **une feuille de papier** a sheet of paper.

feuilleté noun M savoury pasty. adjective **de la pâte feuilletée** puff pastry.

feuilleter verb [48] **feuilleter un livre** to leaf through a book.

feuilleton noun M serial, soap (*on television*).

feutre noun M 1 felt; 2 **un feutre** a felt-tip pen.

fève noun F broad bean.

février noun M February; **en février, au mois de février** in February.

fiable adjective reliable.

fiançailles plural noun F engagement (*to be married*).

fiancé, fiancée noun M, F fiancé, fiancée. adjective **être fiancé à quelqu'un** to be engaged to somebody.

fiancer verb [61] **se fiancer** to get engaged.

fibre noun F fibre.

ficeler verb [18] to tie up.

ficelle noun F 1 string; 2 thin baguette (*of French bread*).

fiche noun F 1 form; 2 index card; 3 plug.

ficher verb (*informal*) [1] 1 to do; **qu'est-ce que tu fiches?** what do you think you're doing?; 2 **je m'en fiche!** I don't care! 3 **fiche-moi la paix!** leave me alone!

fichier noun M file.

fichu adjective (*informal*) done for; **ma voiture est fichue** my car's had it.

fiction noun F fiction.

fidèle adjective 1 faithful; 2 loyal.

fier[1] (F **fière**) adjective proud.

fier[2] verb [1] **se fier à** to trust.

fierté noun F pride.

fièvre noun F fever; **avoir de la fièvre** to have a temperature.

figer verb [52] 1 **se figer** to congeal; 2 to freeze to the spot.

figue noun F fig.

figuier noun M fig tree.

figure noun F 1 face; 2 figure.

figurer verb [1] 1 to appear; 2 **se figurer** to imagine.

fil noun M 1 thread; **du fil à coudre** sewing thread; 2 wire, flex (*of a telephone or electrical appliance*); 3 **un coup de fil** (*informal*) a phone call; **passer un coup de fil** to make a phone call; **passe-moi un coup de fil** give me a ring.

fil de fer noun M wire; **fil de fer barbelé** barbed wire.

file noun F **1** une file d'attente a queue; **2** lane (on a road).

filer verb [1] **1** to speed along; **2** (informal) to give; **elle m'a filé deux CD** she gave me two CDs (which she didn't want any more).

filet noun M **1** net; **2** fillet; **un filet de poisson** a fish fillet.

fille noun F **1** girl; **une petite fille** a little girl; **une jeune fille** a young woman; **2** daughter.

fillette noun F little girl.

filleul, filleule noun M, F godson, goddaughter.

film noun M film.

film comique noun M comedy (film).

film d'épouvante noun M horror film.

filmer verb [1] to film.

film policier noun M thriller.

fils noun M son.

filtre noun M filter.

filtrer verb [1] to filter.

fin[1] noun F end; **à la fin** in the end; **à la fin du film** at the end of the film; **sans fin** endless.

fin[2] adjective **1** fine; **2** slender.

final (M plural **finaux**) adjective final.

finale noun F final, cup final.

finalement adverb **1** in the end, finally; **2** after all.

finance noun F finance.

financer verb [61] to finance.

fines herbes plural noun F mixed herbs.

finir verb [2] **1** to finish, to end; **le film finit à dix heures** the film finishes at ten o'clock; **2** finir de faire to finish doing; **j'ai fini de faire la vaisselle** I've finished doing the washing-up; **3** finir quelque chose to finish something; **as-tu fini tes devoirs?** have you finished your homework?; **j'ai fini le sucre** I've finished the sugar, I've used up all the sugar; **4** finir par faire to end up doing; **il a fini par accepter** he accepted in the end.

finlandais noun M, adjective Finnish.

Finlande noun F Finland.

firme noun F firm.

fisc noun M tax office.

fissure noun F crack.

fixe adjective **1** fixed; **2** un emploi fixe a steady job; **3** aux heures fixes at set times.

fixer verb [1] to fix.

flacon noun M (small) bottle.

flamant noun M flamingo.

flamand noun M, adjective Flemish.

Flamand, Flamande noun M, F Fleming (Dutch-speaking Belgian).

flamber verb [1] to blaze.

flamme noun F flame.

flan noun M custard tart.

flanc noun M side.

flâner *verb* [1] to stroll.

flaque *noun* F **une flaque d'eau** a puddle.

flash *noun* M 1 flash (*on a camera*); 2 newsflash.

flatter *verb* [1] to flatter.

flatteur (F **flatteuse**) *adjective* flattering.

flèche *noun* F 1 arrow; 2 spire.

fléchette *noun* F dart; **jouer aux fléchettes** to play darts.

fléchir *verb* [2] 1 to bend; 2 to weaken.

fleur *noun* F flower; **un tissu à fleurs** a flower-patterned fabric.

fleuri *adjective* 1 flowery; **du tissu fleuri** flowery material; 2 **ton jardin est très fleuri** you've got lots of flowers in your garden.

fleurir *verb* [2] 1 to flower, to blossom; 2 to flourish.

fleuriste *noun* M & F florist.

fleuve *noun* M river.

flexible *adjective* flexible.

flic *noun* M (*informal*) policeman, cop.

flipper *noun* M pinball machine.

flirter *verb* [1] to flirt.

flocon *noun* M flake; **un flocon de neige** a snowflake.

flocons d'avoine *plural noun* M porridge oats.

floral (M *plural* **floraux**) *adjective* floral.

flotter *verb* [1] to float.

flou *adjective* 1 blurred; **une image floue** a blurred image; 2 vague; **ses projets sont un peu flous** her plans are a bit vague.

fluide *noun* M, *adjective* fluid.

fluo *adjective* (*informal*) fluorescent; **vert fluo** fluorescent green.

fluor *noun* M fluorine.

fluorescent *adjective* fluorescent.

flûte *noun* F flute; **jouer de la flûte** to play the flute.

flûte à bec *noun* F recorder.

focaliser *verb* [1] to focus.

foi *noun* F faith.

foie *noun* M liver; **une crise de foie** an upset stomach.

foin *noun* M hay.

foire *noun* F fair.

fois *noun* F 1 time; **une fois** once; **deux fois** twice; **trois fois** three times; **trois fois dix** three times ten; **plusieurs fois** several times; **la première fois** the first time; **trois fois plus grand** three times as big; **2 à la fois** at the same time; **trois à la fois** three at a time; **3 une fois que** once; **une fois que j'aurai pris une douche** once I've had a shower; **4 j'ai vu une fois...** I once saw...; **il était une fois...** once upon a time...

folie *noun* F madness; **c'est de la folie!** it's crazy!

folk *noun* M folk music.

folle noun F,
adjective SEE **fou**.

foncer verb [61] (informal) to rush;
tout le monde a foncé vers la porte
everybody rushed for the door.

fonction noun F 1 job; **une voiture
de fonction** a company car;
2 function.

fonctionnaire noun M & F civil
servant.

fonctionnel (F **fonctionnelle**)
adjective functional.

fonctionnement noun M
working; **comprendre le
fonctionnement de quelque chose**
to understand how something
works.

fonctionner verb [1] to work.

fond noun M 1 bottom; **au fond du
lac** at the bottom of the lake; **au
fond de la bouteille** in the bottom of
the bottle; 2 back; **au fond du tiroir**
at the back of the drawer; **au fond de
la salle** at the back of the room;
3 end; **au fond du couloir** at the end
of the corridor; 4 background;
5 **au fond** basically.

fondamental (M plural
fondamentaux) adjective basic,
fundamental.

fondateur, fondatrice noun M,
F founder.

fondation noun F foundation.

fond de teint noun M make-up,
foundation.

fonder verb [1] 1 to found; 2 to
base.

fondre verb [3] to melt.

fondu adjective melted.

font verb SEE **faire**.

fontaine noun F 1 fountain;
2 drinking fountain.

fonte noun F cast iron; **une poêle en
fonte** a cast iron frying pan.

foot noun (informal) **un match de
foot** a football match; **jouer au foot**
to play football.

football noun M football.

footballeur noun M footballer.

footing noun M jogging; **faire du
footing** to go jogging.

forain noun M fairground worker.
adjective **une fête foraine** a funfair.

force noun F 1 strength; 2 force;
de force by force; 3 force; **force de
vente** sales force; 4 **à force de** by;
**à force de travailler toute la nuit,
elle a fini sa dissertation** she
finished her essay by working all
night.

forcément adverb 1 inevitably; **il
y a forcément une solution** there
has to be a solution; 2 **pas
forcément** not necessarily.

forcer verb [61] 1 to force; 2 **se
forcer** to force yourself.

forêt noun F forest.

forfait noun M fixed price.

forgeron noun M blacksmith.

formalité noun F formality.

format noun M format, size.

formation noun F training; **elle a
une formation d'infirmière** she's a
trained nurse.

formation continue noun F
continuing education.

forme noun F 1 shape, form;
2 **être en forme** to be on form; **tu as
l'air en forme** you're looking well.

formel (F **formelle**) adjective
1 positive, categorical; 2 formal.

formellement adverb strictly;
formellement interdit strictly
forbidden.

former verb [1] 1 to form; 2 to
train, to educate.

formidable adjective (informal)
great, fantastic; **le film était
formidable** the film was fantastic.

formulaire noun M form; **remplir
un formulaire** to fill in a form.

fort adjective 1 strong; **il est très
fort** he's very strong; **le café est très
fort** the coffee's very strong; 2 **être
fort en quelque chose** to be good at
something; **elle est très forte en
maths** she's very good at maths;
3 stout.
adverb 1 extremely; **c'était fort
bon** it was extremely good; 2 hard;
frapper fort to knock (or hit) hard;
3 loudly; **chanter fort** to sing
loudly; **parle plus fort** speak louder.

fortifiant noun M tonic.

fortifier verb [1] 1 to strengthen;
2 to fortify.

fortuit adjective accidental.

fortune noun F 1 fortune; **faire
fortune** to make a fortune; 2 **de
fortune** makeshift; **un lit de fortune**
a makeshift bed.

fossé noun M ditch.

fossette noun F dimple.

fou, folle noun M, F madman,
madwoman; **un fou m'a doublé
dans un virage** a madman overtook
me on a bend.
adjective 1 mad; **devenir fou** to go
mad; 2 crazy, amazing; **on a passé
une soirée folle** we had an amazing
evening; **il y avait un monde fou**
there were masses of people; 3 **être
fou de** to be mad about;
★ **attraper un fou rire** to get the
giggles.

foudre noun F lightning; **être
frappé par la foudre** to be struck by
lightning.

fouet noun M 1 whip; 2 whisk (for
eggs, cream, etc).

fouetter verb [1] 1 to whip; 2 to
whisk (eggs, cream, etc); ★ **avoir
d'autres chats à fouetter** to have
other fish to fry (literally: to have
other cats to whip).

fougère noun F 1 fern; 2 bracken.

fouille noun F search.

fouiller verb [1] 1 **fouiller
quelqu'un** to search somebody;
2 **fouiller dans quelque chose** to
rummage through something.

fouillis noun M mess.

foulard noun M scarf.

foule noun F 1 crowd; 2 **une foule
de** masses of.

four noun M oven; **cuit au four**
roasted, baked.

four à micro-ondes noun M
microwave oven.

fourche noun F garden fork, pitchfork.

fourchette noun F fork.

fourgon noun M van.

fourmi noun F ant; ★ avoir des fourmis dans les jambes to have pins and needles in your legs (*literally: to have ants in your legs*).

fourmiller verb [1] fourmiller de to be swarming with.

fourneau (*plural* fourneaux) noun M stove.

fournir verb [2] to supply.

fournisseur noun M supplier.

fournitures plural noun F stationery; les fournitures de bureau office stationery.

fourré adjective 1 filled; fourré au chocolat with a chocolate filling; 2 fur-lined.

fourrure noun F 1 fur; 2 fur coat.

foyer noun M 1 home; rester au foyer to stay at home (*rather than going out to work*); une femme au foyer a housewife; 2 hearth; 3 household; 4 hostel.

fracas noun M crash.

fracasser verb [1] to smash.

fraction noun F fraction.

fracture noun F fracture.

fracturer verb [1] 1 to break open; 2 to fracture.

fragile adjective 1 fragile; 2 frail.

fragment noun M fragment.

fraîche adjective SEE frais².

fraîcheur noun F 1 coolness; 2 freshness.

frais¹ plural noun M 1 expenses; les frais de déplacement travel expenses; 2 costs.

frais² (F fraîche) adjective 1 cool, cold; il fait frais ce matin it's a chilly morning; 2 cool; ★boissons fraîches' 'cool drinks'; servir frais serve chilled; conserver au frais keep in a cool place; 3 fresh; des légumes frais fresh vegetables; 'peinture fraîche' 'wet paint'.

fraise noun F strawberry; une glace à la fraise a strawberry ice-cream.

framboise noun F raspberry; un yaourt à la framboise a raspberry yoghurt.

franc¹ noun M franc (*the unit of currency in France, Belgium, and Switzerland; there are 100 centimes to the franc*).

franc² (F franche) adjective frank.

français noun M French; j'apprends le français I'm learning French; Laura parle français Laura speaks French.
adjective French; un film français a French film.

Français, Française noun M, F Frenchman, Frenchwoman; les Français the French.

France noun F France; aller en France to go to France; habiter en France to live in France.

franche adjective SEE franc².

franchement adverb 1 frankly; franchement, je ne le crois pas frankly, I don't believe him; 2 really;

le film était franchement nul the film was really awful.

franchir verb [2] to cross.

franchise noun F 1 frankness, honesty; 2 franchise.

francophone adjective French-speaking.

frange noun F fringe.

frangin noun M (informal) brother.

frangine noun F (informal) sister.

frangipane noun F almond cream.

franglais noun M Franglais (a mixture of French and English).

frapper verb [1] 1 to hit; 2 **frapper à la porte** to knock on the door; 3 to strike; **être frappé par** to be struck by; **ça m'a beaucoup frappé** that made a big impression on me; 4 **frappé par le chômage** hit by unemployment.

fraude noun F 1 fraud; 2 cheating.

fredonner verb [1] to hum.

freezer noun M freezer compartment (in a fridge).

frein noun M brake; **les freins** the brakes; **le frein à main** the handbrake.

freiner verb [1] 1 to brake; 2 to slow down.

frêle adjective frail.

frelon noun M hornet.

frémir verb [2] 1 to shudder; 2 to tremble.

frêne noun M ash tree.

fréquemment adverb frequently.

fréquence noun F frequency.

fréquenté adjective 1 busy; **un restaurant très fréquenté** a very busy restaurant; 2 **un quartier mal fréquenté** a rough area.

fréquenter verb [1] 1 to go around with (people); 2 to go often to (a place).

frère noun M brother.

fric noun M (informal) money.

frictionner verb [1] to rub.

frigidaire™ noun M fridge.

frigo noun M (informal) fridge; **au frigo** in the fridge.

frileux (F **frileuse**) adjective **être frileux** to feel the cold; **je ne suis pas frileuse** I don't feel the cold.

frime noun F (informal) **c'est de la frime!** it's all show!

fringues plural noun F (informal) clothes.

fripé adjective crumpled.

frire verb [74] **faire frire quelque chose** to fry something.

frisé adjective 1 curly; 2 curly-haired.

frisée noun F curly endive, frisée (a sort of lettuce).

friser verb [1] to curl.

frisson noun M shiver.

frissonner verb [1] **1** to shiver; **2** to shudder.

frit adjective fried.

frite noun F chip, French fry; **steak frites** steak and chips.

friture noun F **friture de poissons** fried fish.

froid noun M **1** **le froid** the cold; **2** **avoir froid** to be cold; **j'ai froid** I'm cold; **3** **il fait froid aujourd'hui** it's cold today; **4** **prendre froid** to catch a chill.
adjective cold; **tes mains sont froides** your hands are cold.

froidement adverb coldly.

froideur noun F coldness.

froisser verb [1] **1** to crease; **2** **se froisser** to crease; **la soie se froisse facilement** silk crushes easily; **3** **se froisser** to take offence.

frôler verb [1] to brush against.

fromage noun M cheese.

fromagerie noun F cheese shop.

froment noun M wheat.

froncer verb [61] **froncer les sourcils** to frown.

front noun M **1** forehead; **2** **faire front à** to face up to.

frontière noun F border.

frotter verb [1] to rub; **se frotter les yeux** to rub your eyes.

fruit noun M **les fruits** fruit; **acheter des fruits** to buy some fruit; **un fruit** a piece of fruit; **veux-tu un fruit?** would you like some fruit?

fruité adjective fruity.

fruits de mer plural noun M seafood; **une omelette aux fruits de mer** a seafood omelette.

frustrant adjective frustrating.

frustrer verb [1] **1** to thwart; **2** to frustrate.

fugue noun F **1** **faire une fugue** to run away; **2** fugue.

fuir verb [44] **1** to run away, to flee; **2** **fuir quelque chose** to run away from something; **3** to leak; **la bouilloire fuit** the kettle's leaking.

fuite noun F **1** flight; **2** **prendre la fuite** to flee; **3** leak.

fulgurant adjective dazzling.

fumé adjective smoked; **du saumon fumé** smoked salmon.

fumée noun F smoke; ★ **il n'y a pas de fumée sans feu** there's no smoke without fire.

fumer verb [1] **1** to smoke; **2** **fumer une cigarette** to smoke a cigarette; **il fume la pipe** he smokes a pipe; ★ **fumer comme un pompier** to smoke like a chimney (literally: to smoke like a fireman).

fumeur, fumeuse noun M, F smoker; **zone non-fumeur** no-smoking area.

fumier noun M manure.

funambule noun M & F tightrope walker.

funèbre adjective **1** funeral; **pompes funèbres** undertaker's; **2** gloomy.

funérailles plural noun F funeral.

funiculaire noun M funicular.

fur noun M 1 au fur et à mesure as you go along; je corrige les erreurs au fur et à mesure I correct the mistakes as I go along; 2 au fur et à mesure que as.

furet noun M ferret.

fureur noun F 1 rage, fury; 2 frenzy; ★ faire fureur to be all the rage; ces boucles d'oreilles font fureur en ce moment these earrings are all the rage at the moment.

furibond adjective furious.

furieusement adverb furiously.

furieux (F furieuse) adjective furious; elle est furieuse contre son copain she's furious with her boyfriend.

furoncle noun M boil.

fusain noun M charcoal (for drawing).

fuseau noun M ski pants.

fusée noun F rocket.

fusible noun M fuse.

fusil noun M gun.

fusiller verb [1] to shoot.

fût noun M cask, barrel.

futé adjective 1 crafty; 2 bright, clever.

futur noun M, adjective future; son futur mari her husband-to-be.

G g

gâcher verb [1] 1 to waste; gâcher la nourriture to waste food; 2 to spoil; ça m'a gâché la journée! that's spoiled my day!

gâchis noun M waste.

gadget noun M gadget.

gaffe noun F (informal) blunder; j'ai fait une gaffe I've done something stupid; ★ fais gaffe! watch out!

gage noun M forfeit (in a game).

gagnant, gagnante noun M, F winner. adjective winning.

gagner verb [1] 1 to win; il a gagné he's won; gagner le match to win the match; 2 to earn (money); elle gagne bien sa vie she makes a good living; 3 gagner du temps to save time.

gai adjective cheerful.

gain noun M 1 earnings; 2 c'est un gain de temps it saves time.

gaieté noun F cheerfulness.

galerie noun F gallery.

galerie marchande noun F shopping arcade.

galet noun M pebble.

galette noun F 1 biscuit; 2 round flat cake or loaf.

galette des Rois noun F Twelfth Night cake (a cake eaten on Twelfth

Night; it contains a 'fève', literally a bean, but usually a small ceramic figure; the person who gets this is the king or queen and is given a cardboard crown to wear).

Galles noun le pays de Galles Wales.

gallois noun M, adjective Welsh.

Gallois, Galloise noun M, F Welshman, Welshwoman; les Gallois the Welsh.

galoper verb [1] to gallop.

gamba noun F king prawn.

gamin, gamine noun M, F (informal) kid; elle a trois gamins she has three kids.

gamme noun F 1 range; la nouvelle gamme de produits de beauté the new range of beauty products; 2 scale (in music).

gammé adjective la croix gammée the swastika.

gangster noun M gangster.

gant noun M glove.

gant de ménage noun M rubber glove.

gant de toilette noun M facecloth.

garage noun M garage.

garagiste noun M & F 1 garage owner; 2 motor mechanic.

garantie noun F guarantee.

garantir verb [2] to guarantee.

garçon noun M 1 boy; 2 young man; un brave garçon a nice

chap; 3 waiter; 4 un vieux garçon a bachelor.

garçon de café noun M waiter (in a café).

garde noun M & F 1 guard; 2 nurse; 3 être de garde to be on duty; la pharmacie de garde the duty chemist's; mettre quelqu'un en garde to warn somebody;
★ prends garde! watch out, be careful!

garder verb [1] 1 to keep; est-ce que tu peux garder mon sac? can you keep my bag for me?; je t'ai gardé du gâteau I've kept you some cake; je t'ai gardé une place I've kept you a seat; 2 to keep on; elle a gardé son manteau she kept her coat on; 3 to look after; je garde mon petit-fils ce soir I'm looking after my grandson this evening; 4 garder la maison to guard the house.

garderie noun F day nursery.

garde-robe noun F wardrobe.

gardien, gardienne noun M, F 1 security guard; 2 caretaker; 3 attendant (in a car park or museum).

gardien de but noun M goalkeeper.

gardien de la paix noun M policeman.

gare noun F (railway) station.

garer verb [1] 1 garer une voiture to park a car; 2 se garer to park.

gare routière noun F coach station.

garni adjective bien garni full, well-stocked.

garnir verb [2] **1** to decorate; **2** to stock (shelves, fridge).

garniture noun F **1** side-dish; **2** trimming, decoration.

gars noun M (informal) guy.

Gascogne noun F Gascony.

gasoil noun M diesel (oil).

gaspiller verb [1] to waste.

gastronome noun M & F gourmet.

gastronomie noun F gastronomy.

gâteau noun M cake; un gâteau au chocolat a chocolate cake.

gâter verb [1] **1** to spoil; **2** se gâter to go bad; la viande se gâte the meat is going bad; le temps se gâte the weather's breaking.

gauche noun F **1** left; à gauche on the left; les Anglais conduisent à gauche the English drive on the left; tournez à gauche turn left; à ma gauche on my left; **2** la gauche the Left (in politics); des idées de gauche left-wing ideas. adjective left, left-hand; sa main gauche his left hand.

gaucher (F gauchère) adjective left-handed.

gaufre noun F waffle.

gaufrette noun F wafer.

gaz noun M gas; le chauffage à gaz gas central heating; nous nous chauffons au gaz we have gas heating.

gazeux (F gazeuse) adjective fizzy; eau gazeuse fizzy mineral water.

gazole noun M diesel (oil).

gazon noun M grass, lawn.

géant, géante noun M, F giant. adjective huge.

gel noun M **1** frost; **2** le gel des prix the price freeze; **3** gel.

gelé adjective frozen.

gelée noun F **1** jelly; œuf en gelée egg in aspic; **2** frost.

geler verb [45] to freeze; il gèle dehors it's freezing outside.

gélule noun F capsule.

Gémeaux plural noun M Gemini (sign of the Zodiac).

gémir verb [2] to moan.

gênant adjective **1** annoying; ce bruit est très gênant that noise is very annoying; **2** awkward; c'est une situation gênante it's an awkward situation.

gencive noun F gum (part of your mouth).

gendarme noun M policeman.

gendarmerie noun F police station.

gendre noun M son-in-law.

gêne noun F **1** embarrassment; **2** inconvenience; **3** discomfort.

gêné adjective embarrassed.

gêner verb [1] **1** to bother; est-ce que mon sac vous gêne? is my bag in your way?; **2** to embarrass; **3** to block (traffic); ta voiture gêne your car's in the way.

général (plural généraux) noun M general.

adjective general; **en général** in general, generally; **de façon générale** generally.

généralement *adverb* generally.

génération *noun* F generation.

généreux (F **généreuse**) *adjective* generous.

générique *noun* M (film) credits.

générosité *noun* F generosity.

genêt *noun* M broom (*the bush*).

génétique *noun* F genetics.

Genève *noun* F Geneva.

génial (M *plural* **géniaux**) *adjective* 1 brilliant; **une idée géniale** a brilliant idea; 2 (*informal*) great; **c'était génial!** it was great!

génie *noun* M 1 genius; 2 engineering.

genou (*plural* **genoux**) *noun* M knee; **avoir mal au genou** to have a sore knee; **être à genoux** to be kneeling; **se mettre à genoux** to kneel down; **sur mes genoux** on my lap.

genre *noun* M kind; **un genre de sauce épicée** a kind of spicy sauce; **un peu dans le genre de ton pull** a bit like your sweater.

gens *plural noun* M people; **beaucoup de gens** lots of people; **les gens disent que...** people say that...

gentil (F **gentille**) *adjective* 1 kind, nice; **elle est très gentille** she's really nice; 2 kind; **c'est très gentil de ta part** it's very kind of you; 3 good; **sois gentil et mange ta**

viande be a good boy and eat up your meat.

gentillesse *noun* F kindness.

gentiment *adverb* 1 nicely; **demande gentiment** ask nicely; 2 kindly.

géographie *noun* F geography.

géométrie *noun* F geometry.

gérant, gérante *noun* M, F manager, manageress.

gérer *verb* [24] to manage, to run.

germain *adjective* **un cousin germain** a first cousin.

gésier *noun* M gizzard.

geste *noun* M gesture.

gestion *noun* F management; **gestion de fichiers** file management (*on a computer*).

gibier *noun* M game (*for example, venison, pheasant*).

gifle *noun* F slap (*in the face*).

gifler *verb* [1] to slap (*in the face*).

gigantesque *adjective* huge, gigantic; **un repas gigantesque** a huge meal.

gigot *noun* M leg of lamb.

gilet *noun* M 1 cardigan; 2 waistcoat.

gilet de sauvetage *noun* M life-jacket.

gingembre *noun* M ginger.

girafe *noun* F giraffe.

gitan, gitane *noun* M, F gipsy.

gîte (rural) *noun* M holiday house.

glace noun F **1** ice cream; **une glace au chocolat** a chocolate ice cream; **2** ice; **3** mirror; **se regarder dans la glace** to look at yourself in the mirror; **4** window (*in a car*).

glacé adjective **1** icy cold; **j'ai les mains glacées** my hands are freezing; **2** **un thé glacé** an iced tea.

glacier noun M glacier.

glacière noun F cool-box.

glaçon noun M ice cube.

glissant adjective slippery.

glisser verb [1] to slip, to slide; **attention, ça glisse!** be careful, it's slippery!

global adjective (M plural **globaux**) total.

gloire noun F fame, glory.

glorieux (F **glorieuse**) adjective glorious.

glossaire noun M glossary.

gobelet noun M cup, tumbler; **un gobelet en carton** a paper cup.

godasse noun F (*informal*) shoe.

gogo (*informal*) **à gogo** as much as you like; **pizza à gogo** as much pizza as you can eat.

golden noun F Golden Delicious (apple).

golf noun M **1** golf; **jouer au golf** to play golf; **2** golf course.

golfe noun M gulf.

gomme noun F rubber.

gommer verb [1] to rub out.

gonfler verb [1] **1** to pump up (*tyres*); **2** to blow up (*a balloon*).

gorge noun F **1** throat; **j'ai mal à la gorge** I've got a sore throat; **j'avais la gorge serrée** I had a lump in my throat; **il chantait à pleine gorge** he was singing at the top of his voice; **2** gorge.

gorgée noun F sip; **une gorgée de thé** a sip of tea.

gorille noun M gorilla.

gosse noun M & F kid.

goudron noun M tar.

gourde noun F water bottle.

gourmand adjective greedy.

gourmandise noun F **1** greed; **2 elle aime les gourmandises** she likes sweet things.

gousse noun F **une gousse d'ail** a clove of garlic.

goût noun M taste; **ça a un goût bizarre** it has a strange taste; **de bon goût** in good taste; ★ **chacun ses goûts** it takes all sorts to make a world.

goûter noun M **1** teatime snack; **2** children's party.
verb [1] **1** to taste, to try; **est-ce que tu as goûté le gâteau?** have you tried the cake?; **2** to have a teatime snack.

goutte noun F drop; **une goutte de** a drop of; **goutte à goutte** drop by drop.

gouvernement noun M government.

gouverner verb [1] to govern, to rule.

grâce noun F grâce à thanks to; la soirée a été un grand succès grâce à toi the evening was a great success thanks to you.

gracieux (F gracieuse) adjective graceful.

grade noun M rank; monter en grade to be promoted.

gradins plural noun M terraces (in a stadium).

graduel (F graduelle) adjective gradual.

graffiti plural noun M graffiti.

grain noun M 1 grain; un grain de sable a grain of sand; 2 du poivre en grains peppercorns; 3 du café en grains coffee beans; 4 un grain de beauté a beauty spot; 5 un grain de raisin a grape.

graine noun F seed.

graisse noun F fat, grease.

grammaire noun F grammar.

gramme noun M gramme.

grand adjective 1 big; une grande maison a big house; c'est ma grande sœur she's my big sister; 2 tall; un grand arbre a tall tree; ton frère est très grand your brother's very tall; elle est plus grande que moi she's taller than me; 3 great; un grand artiste a great artist; un grand ami a great friend; 4 main; les grandes lignes main (railway) lines. adverb wide; la porte était grande ouverte the door was wide open.

grand-chose much; pas grand-chose not much; il ne reste pas grand-chose there's not much left.

Grande-Bretagne noun F Great Britain.

grande personne noun F grown-up.

grande surface noun F hypermarket.

grand magasin noun M department store.

grandes vacances plural noun F summer holidays.

grandeur noun F size; grandeur nature life-size.

grandir verb [2] to grow, to grow up.

grand-mère (plural grands-mères) noun F grandmother.

grand-père (plural grands-pères) noun M grandfather.

grands espaces plural noun M open spaces.

grands-parents plural noun M grandparents.

grange noun F barn.

grappe noun F une grappe de raisin a bunch of grapes.

gras (F grasse) adjective 1 fatty, greasy; 40% matière grasse 40% fat (on cheese or yoghurt label); 2 une peau grasse oily skin; ★ faire la grasse matinée to have a lie-in.

gratitude noun F gratitude.

gratte-ciel noun M skyscraper.

gratter verb [1] 1 gratter quelque chose to scratch something; 2 se

gratter to scratch (yourself); **3** to itch; **ça gratte** it itches.

gratuit adjective free; **le concert est gratuit** the concert's free; **'entrée gratuite'** 'entrance free'.

grave adjective **1** serious; **un grave accident** a serious accident; **2 ce n'est pas grave** it doesn't matter; **3** serious; **une expression grave** a serious expression; **4** deep; **une voix grave** a deep voice.

gravement adverb seriously; **elle est gravement malade** she's seriously ill.

gravure noun F engraving, print.

gré noun M **contre son gré** against his will.

grec (F **grecque**) adjective Greek.

Grec, Grecque noun M, F Greek (person).

Grèce noun F Greece.

grêle noun F hail.

grelotter verb [1] to shiver.

grenade noun F **1** grenade; **2** pomegranate.

grenadine noun F grenadine (pomegranate cordial).

grenier noun M attic, loft; **au grenier** in the attic.

grenouille noun F frog; **les cuisses de grenouille** frogs' legs.

grève noun F strike; **une grève des trains** a train strike; **le métro est en grève** the underground's on strike; **faire grève** to go (or be) on strike.

gréviste noun M & F striker.

grièvement adverb seriously; **grièvement blessé** seriously injured.

griffe noun F claw.

griffonner verb [1] to scribble.

grillade noun F grilled meat, meat for grilling; **une grillade de porc** a pork steak.

grillage noun M wire netting.

grille noun F **1** metal gate; **2** railings; **3** wire fence.

grillé adjective **1** grilled; **2** toasted; **du pain grillé** toast.

grille-pain noun M toaster.

griller verb [1] **1** to grill; **2** to toast.

grillon noun M cricket (the creature not the game).

grimace noun F **faire des grimaces** to make faces.

grimper verb [1] to climb; **grimper dans un arbre** to climb a tree.

grincer verb [61] to creak, to squeak.

grincheux (F **grincheuse**) adjective grumpy.

grippe noun F flu; **avoir une grippe** to have flu; **une grippe intestinale** gastric flu.

gris adjective grey.

grogner verb [1] **1** to growl; **2** to grumble.

gronder verb [1] **1 gronder quelqu'un** to tell somebody off; **se faire gronder** to get a telling-off; **2** to rumble (thunder, for example).

gros (F **grosse**) *adjective* **1** big; un gros morceau a big piece; un gros problème a big problem; **2** fat; un gros monsieur a fat man; **3** un gros rhume a bad cold; **4** un gros fumeur a heavy smoker; **5** un gros mot a swear word; **6** en gros roughly.

groseille *noun* F redcurrant.

groseille à maquereau *noun* F gooseberry.

grosse *adjective* SEE **gros**.

grossesse *noun* F pregnancy.

grossier (F **grossière**) *adjective* **1** rude; **2** crude; une idée grossière de a rough idea of; une erreur grossière a bad mistake.

grossir *verb* [2] to put on weight; **il a beaucoup grossi** he's put on a lot of weight.

grosso modo *adverb* roughly.

grotesque *adjective* ridiculous.

grotte *noun* F cave.

groupe *noun* M group.

grouper *verb* [1] **1** to group; **2 se grouper** to gather, to form a group.

groupe sanguin *noun* M blood group.

grue *noun* F crane.

guépard *noun* M cheetah.

guêpe *noun* F wasp.

guère *adverb* ne...guère hardly; je ne l'ai guère vu depuis Noël I've hardly seen him since Christmas.

guérir *verb* [2] **1** to cure; **le médecin l'a guéri** the doctor cured him; **2** to

get better; **j'ai été malade mais je suis maintenant guéri** I've been ill but I'm better now.

guérison *noun* F recovery (*from an illness or injury*).

guerre *noun* F war; **le pays est actuellement en guerre** the country is at war at the moment; **la Seconde-Guerre mondiale** World War II.

guetter *verb* [1] to watch out for.

gueule *noun* F mouth (*of an animal; considered rude if used of a person*); **(ferme) ta gueule!** (*rude*) shut up!

gueule de bois *noun* F (*informal*) avoir la gueule de bois to have a hangover.

gueuler *verb* [1] (*informal*) to yell.

gui *noun* M mistletoe.

guichet *noun* M **1** ticket office (*in a station or museum*); **2** box office (*in a theatre or cinema*); **3** counter, window (*in a bank or post office*).

guichet automatique *noun* M cashpoint.

guide *noun* M guide.

guider *verb* [1] to guide.

guidon *noun* M handlebars.

guillemets *plural noun* M inverted commas; **entre guillemets** in inverted commas.

guirlande *noun* F des guirlandes tinsel; des guirlandes en papier paper chains.

guirlande électrique *noun* F fairy lights, Christmas-tree lights.

guitare noun F guitar; **jouer de la guitare** to play the guitar.

guitariste noun M & F guitarist.

gym noun F (informal) PE, gymnastics.

gymnase noun M gym; **je te verrai au gymnase** I'll see you in the gym.

gymnastique noun F gymnastics, exercises.

H h

habile adjective clever; **elle est habile de ses mains** she's clever with her hands; **de manière habile** cleverly.

habillé adjective 1 dressed; **je ne suis pas encore habillé** I'm not dressed yet; 2 smart (for example, a dress or suit).

habiller verb [1] 1 **habiller quelqu'un** to dress somebody; 2 **s'habiller** to get dressed; **habille-toi vite!** get dressed quick!; 3 **s'habiller** to dress up; **s'habiller en clown** to dress up as a clown.

habitant, habitante noun M, F inhabitant.

habitation noun F house.

habiter verb [1] to live; **ils habitent à Paris** they live in Paris.

habitude noun F 1 habit; **c'est une mauvaise habitude** it's a bad habit; 2 **d'habitude** usually; **d'habitude il arrive à midi** he usually arrives at twelve; 3 **comme d'habitude** as usual; **j'ai pris le bus comme d'habitude** I took the bus as usual; 4 **avoir l'habitude de faire** to be used to doing; **j'ai l'habitude de travailler le soir** I'm used to working in the evening.

habitué, habituée noun M, F regular (in a café, shop, etc).

habituel (F **habituelle**) adjective usual.

habituer verb [1] **s'habituer à quelque chose** to get used to something; **je m'y suis habituée** I've got used to it.

hache noun F axe.

haché adjective chopped; **du bœuf haché** mince.

hacher verb [1] 1 to chop (vegetables); 2 to mince (meat).

hachis Parmentier noun M shepherd's pie.

haddock noun M smoked haddock.

haie noun F 1 hedge; 2 **les haies** hurdles (sport).

haine noun F hatred.

haïr verb [46] to hate.

haleine noun F breath; **être hors d'haleine** to be out of breath.

hall noun M 1 (entrance) hall; 2 concourse (in a station).

halles plural noun F covered market.

halogène adjective halogen; **une lampe halogène** a halogen lamp.

halte noun F stop; **halte!** stop!; **faire une halte** to stop somewhere.

halte-garderie noun F playgroup.

haltérophilie noun F
weightlifting.

hameau (plural **hameaux**) noun
M group of houses.

hameçon noun M fish hook.

hamster noun M hamster.

hanche noun F hip.

handball noun M handball; **jouer
au handball** to play handball.

handicap noun M handicap.

handicapé, handicapée noun
M, F handicapped person.
adjective handicapped, disabled.

hareng noun M herring.

haricot noun M bean; **haricot vert**
French bean; **haricot blanc** haricot
bean.

harmonica noun M mouth organ;
jouer de l'harmonica to play the
mouth organ.

harmonie noun F harmony.

harmoniser verb [1] to coordinate,
to harmonize.

harnais noun M harness.

harpe noun F harp.

hasard noun M 1 chance; **par
hasard** by chance; **je l'ai rencontré
par hasard** I met him by chance;
2 **au hasard** at random; **elle a choisi
un livre au hasard** she chose a book
at random; 3 **à tout hasard** just in
case; **prends un manteau à tout
hasard** take a coat just in case; 4 **à
tout hasard** on the off chance.

hasardeux (F **hasardeuse**)
adjective risky.

hâte noun F **à la hâte** hurriedly;
elle est partie à la hâte she left in a
rush.

hausse noun F increase, rise; **une
hausse des prix** a rise in prices; **les
prix sont en hausse** prices are
rising.

hausser verb [1] 1 to raise;
2 **hausser les épaules** to shrug
your shoulders.

haut noun M 1 top **le haut de
l'échelle** the top of the ladder;
regarder quelqu'un de haut en bas
to look somebody up and down;
2 **l'arbre fait 10 mètres de haut** the
tree is 10 metres high; 3 **en haut**
upstairs; **elle est en haut** she's
upstairs; 4 **en haut de** at the top of;
en haut de l'escalier at the top of
the stairs.
adjective 1 high; **la branche la plus
haute** the highest branch; 2 **à
haute voix** aloud; **lire à haute voix**
to read aloud.
adverb high; **plus haut dans l'arbre**
higher up the tree; **'voir plus haut'**
'see above' (in a book); **haut les
mains!** hands up!

hautbois noun M oboe.

hauteur noun F height; **la hauteur
de la pièce** the height of the room;
dans le sens de la hauteur upright;
l'avion prend de la hauteur the
plane's gaining height; **il n'est pas à
la hauteur de son travail** he's not up
to his job.

haut-parleur noun M loudspeaker.

Haye noun **La Haye** The Hague.

hebdomadaire noun M weekly magazine.

héberger verb [52] to put up; **Jess va nous héberger** Jess'll put us up.

hein exclamation (informal) what?, eh?

hélas unfortunately; **elle est déjà partie, hélas** she's already left, unfortunately; **hélas non** I'm afraid not.

hélicoptère noun M helicopter.

hémorragie noun F haemorrhage.

hennir verb [2] to neigh.

herbe noun F **1** l'herbe grass; **2** herb; **les fines herbes** mixed herbs; **les herbes de Provence** mixed herbs; **3** une mauvaise herbe a weed.

hérisson noun M hedgehog.

héritage noun M inheritance.

hériter verb [1] to inherit.

hermétique adjective airtight.

héroïne noun F **1** heroine; **2** heroin.

héros noun M hero.

hésitation noun F hesitation.

hésiter verb [1] to hesitate; **à ta place, je n'hésiterais pas!** if I were you, I wouldn't hesitate!; **j'ai beaucoup hésité avant d'accepter** I thought about it for a long time before I agreed; **j'hésite entre le poulet et le poisson** I can't decide whether to have the chicken or the fish.

hêtre noun M **1** beech tree; **2** beech wood.

heure noun F **1** hour; **une heure plus tard** an hour later; **deux heures de train** two hours in the train; **une demi-heure** half an hour; **une heure et demie** an hour and a half; **Londres est à une heure d'avion de Paris** London is an hour from Paris by air; **toutes les quatre heures** every four hours; **payé à l'heure** paid by the hour; **cent kilomètres à l'heure** a hundred kilometres an hour; **2** time; **quelle heure est-il?** what time is it?; **il est sept heures** it's seven o'clock; **à huit heures du matin** at eight o'clock in the morning; **tu te lèves à quelle heure demain?** what time are you getting up tomorrow?; **à neuf heures** at nine o'clock; **à six heures et demie** at half past six; **3** être à l'heure to be on time; **4** à l'heure du déjeuner at lunchtime; ★ de bonne heure early; **je me lève de bonne heure demain** I'm getting up early tomorrow.

heures d'affluence plural noun F peak time, rush hour.

heureusement adverb fortunately.

heureux (F **heureuse**) adjective **1** happy; **elle est heureuse d'être ici** she's happy to be here; **2** lucky, fortunate.

heurter verb [1] to hit, to bump into; **la voiture a heurté un camion** the car collided with a lorry.

hexagone noun M **1** hexagon; **2** l'Hexagone France (French journalists often refer to France as l'Hexagone as it has a six-sided shape on the map).

hibou (plural **hiboux**) noun M owl.

hideux (F **hideuse**) adjective hideous.

hier adverb yesterday; **je l'ai vue hier** I saw her yesterday; **hier matin** yesterday morning; **avant-hier** the day before yesterday.

hi-fi noun F hi-fi; **une chaîne hi-fi** a stereo system.

hippique adjective equestrian; **un concours hippique** a horse show; **un club hippique** a riding school.

hippodrome noun M racecourse.

hippopotame noun M hippopotamus.

hirondelle noun F swallow.

histoire noun F 1 history; **l'histoire française** French history; 2 story; **l'histoire de ma vie** the story of my life; 3 matter **c'est une histoire d'argent** it's a matter of money; ★ **faire des histoires** to kick up a fuss.

historique adjective 1 historic; **un monument historique** a historic monument; 2 historical.

hit-parade noun M **le hit-parade** the charts (pop music).

hiver noun M winter; **en hiver** in winter.

HLM noun M or F (= *habitation à loyer modéré*) council flat; **nous habitons dans un HLM à Valence** we live in a council flat in Valence; **les HLM** council housing.

hocher verb [1] **hocher la tête** to shake your head, to nod.

hockey noun M hockey; **jouer au hockey** to play hockey; **le hockey sur glace** ice hockey.

hollandais noun M, adjective Dutch.

Hollandais, Hollandaise noun M, F Dutchman, Dutchwoman; **les Hollandais** the Dutch.

Hollande noun F Holland; **en Hollande** in (or to) Holland.

homard noun M lobster.

homéopathique adjective homeopathic.

hommage noun M tribute, homage.

homme noun M man.

homme d'affaires noun M businessman.

homme d'État noun M statesman.

homogénéisé adjective homogenized.

homosexuel, homosexuelle noun, M, F, adjective homosexual.

Hongrie noun F Hungary.

hongrois noun M, adjective Hungarian.

honnête adjective honest, respectable.

honnêtement adverb 1 honestly, frankly; **honnêtement je ne sais pas ce que tu veux dire** I honestly don't know what you mean.

honnêteté noun F honesty; **en toute honnêteté** in all honesty.

honneur noun M honour.

honorer verb [1] to honour.

honte noun F shame; **avoir honte de quelque chose** to be ashamed of something; **j'ai vraiment honte** I'm really ashamed of myself; **tu n'as pas honte!** what a thing to say! (or do).

honteux (F **honteuse**) adjective disgraceful.

hôpital noun M hospital; **être à l'hôpital** to be in hospital.

hoquet noun M hiccup; **avoir le hoquet** to have hiccups.

horaire noun M timetable; schedule; **les horaires de train** the train timetable.

horizon noun M horizon; **à l'horizon** on the horizon.

horizontal (M plural **horizontaux**) adjective horizontal.

horloge noun F clock.

horodateur noun M parking ticket machine.

horoscope noun M horoscope.

horreur noun F 1 horror; **quelle horreur!** how awful!; 2 **avoir horreur de quelque chose** to hate something; **j'ai horreur d'être en retard** I hate being late; **j'ai horreur des escargots!** I can't stand snails!

horrible adjective horrible.

horrifier verb [1] to horrify.

hors preposition 1 **hors de** outside; **hors de France** outside France; 2 **les boutiques hors taxe** the duty-

free shops; ★ **être hors de soi** to be beside yourself; **j'étais hors de moi** I was beside myself.

hors-d'œuvre noun M starter (to a meal).

hortensia noun M hydrangea.

hospitalier adjective **un centre hospitalier** a hospital.

hospitaliser verb [1] **elle a été hospitalisée** she's been taken into hospital.

hospitalité noun F hospitality.

hostilité noun F hostility.

hôte[1] noun M host.

hôte[2] noun M & F 1 guest; **hôte payant** paying guest; 2 host.

hôtel noun M hotel; **passer deux nuits à l'hôtel** to spend two nights in a hotel.

hôtel de ville noun M town hall.

hôtesse noun F 1 hostess; 2 receptionist.

hôtesse d'accueil noun F receptionist.

hôtesse de l'air noun F air hostess.

housse noun F cover (for a chair or a machine); **une housse de couette** a duvet cover.

houx noun M holly.

hublot noun M 1 window (in a plane); 2 porthole (in a boat).

huile noun F oil; **huile de tournesol** sunflower oil; **huile d'olive** olive oil; **huile solaire** suntan oil.

huit *number* **1** eight; Paul a huit ans
Paul's eight; **le huit juillet** the eighth
of July; **2 huit jours** a week; **il y a
huit jours** a week ago.

huitième *noun* M; **au huitième** on
the eighth floor.
adjective eighth.

huître *noun* F oyster.

humain *adjective* human.

humanitaire *adjective*
humanitarian.

humeur *noun* F mood; **il est de
bonne humeur** he's in a good mood;
elle est de mauvaise humeur she's
in a bad mood; **je ne suis pas
d'humeur à faire ça** I'm not in the
mood to do this.

humide *adjective* damp.

humidité *noun* F damp.

humoristique *adjective*
humorous; **un dessin
humoristique** a cartoon.

humour *noun* M humour; **avoir de
l'humour** to have a sense of humour.

hurler *verb* [1] to yell, to howl.

hutte *noun* F hut.

hydratant *adjective* moisturizing.

hygiène *noun* F hygiene.

hygiénique *adjective* **1** hygienic;
2 une serviette hygiénique a
sanitary towel; **3 du papier
hygiénique** toilet paper.

hymne *noun* M hymn; **l'hymne
national** the national anthem.

hypermarché *noun* M
hypermarket.

hypermétrope *adjective* long-
sighted.

hypertension *noun* F high blood
pressure.

hypnotiser *verb* [1] to hypnotize.

hypocondriaque *noun* M & F,
adjective hypochondriac.

hypocrite *noun* M & F hypocrite.

hypothèse *noun* F hypothesis.

hystérie *noun* F hysteria.

I i

ici *adverb* **1** here; **il y a trop de
monde ici** there are too many
people here; **les gens d'ici** the local
people; **2 jusqu'ici** this far; **les bus
ne viennent pas jusqu'ici** the buses
don't come this far; **3 jusqu'ici** so
far; **jusqu'ici il a fait beau** so far the
weather's been good.

idéal (*plural* **idéaux**) *noun* M,
adjective ideal; **l'idéal serait de
louer une voiture** the ideal thing
would be to hire a car.

idée *noun* F idea; **quelle bonne
idée!** what a good idea!; **je n'ai
aucune idée** I've no idea; **se faire
des idées** to imagine things.

identifier *verb* [1] to identify.

identique *adjective* identical.

identité *noun* F identity; **une carte
d'identité** an identity card.

idiot, idiote *noun* M, F idiot; **ne
fais pas l'idiot!** don't fool around!

adjective stupid; **c'est vraiment idiot!** it's really stupid!

ignorance *noun* F ignorance.

ignorant *adjective* ignorant.

ignorer *verb* [1] **1** not to know; **j'ignore leur adresse** I don't know their address; **j'ignore les détails** I don't know the details; **2** to ignore; **ils l'ont ignoré** they ignored him.

il *pronoun* **1** he, it; **il parle français** he speaks French; **2** it; **'où est mon sac?'** – **'il est sur la chaise'** 'where's my bag?' – 'it's on the table'; **il pleut** it's raining.

île *noun* F island.

illégal (M *plural* **illégaux**) *adjective* illegal.

illimité *adjective* unlimited.

illisible *adjective* illegible.

illumination *noun* F floodlighting; **les illuminations de Noël** the Christmas lights.

illuminer *verb* [1] to floodlight.

illusion *noun* F illusion; **elle se fait des illusions** she's fooling herself.

illustration *noun* F illustration.

illustré *noun* M comic. *adjective* illustrated.

illustrer *verb* [1] to illustrate.

ils *pronoun* they; **ils sont en vacances** they're on holiday.

il y a SEE **avoir.**

image *noun* F picture; **il y a de belles images dans ton livre** there are some lovely pictures in your book.

imaginaire *adjective* imaginary.

imagination *noun* F imagination.

imaginer *verb* [1] **1** to imagine; **je n'arrive pas à l'imaginer** I can't imagine it; **elle va appeler, j'imagine** I suppose she'll phone.

imbattable *adjective* unbeatable.

imbécile *noun* M & F fool; **faire l'imbécile** to fool around. *adjective* idiotic.

imitation *noun* F imitation.

imiter *verb* [1] to imitate.

immangeable *adjective* inedible.

immatriculation *noun* F registration (*of a car*); **une plaque d'immatriculation** a numberplate.

immédiat *adjective* immediate; **dans l'immédiat** for the time being; **je n'ai pas de projets dans l'immédiat** I don't have any plans for the time being.

immédiatement *adverb* immediately.

immense *adjective* huge.

immeuble *noun* M **1** block of flats; **2** building; **un immeuble de six étages** a six-storey building; **3 un immeuble de bureaux** an office block.

immigration *noun* F immigration.

immigré, immigrée *noun* M, F immigrant.

immobile *adjective* motionless.

immobilier *noun* M property (*houses and land*); **une agence immobilière** an estate agent's.

immobiliser verb [1] to immobilise.

immodéré adjective excessive.

immoral (M plural **immoraux**) adjective immoral.

immuniser verb [1] to immunize.

impact noun M impact.

impair adjective odd; **un nombre impair** an odd number.

impardonnable unforgivable.

imparfait noun M imperfect (tense); **à l'imparfait** in the imperfect.
adjective imperfect.

impasse noun F dead end.

impatience noun F impatience.

impatient adjective impatient.

impeccable adjective 1 perfect; **un accent français impeccable** a perfect French accent; 2 spotless; **l'appartement est impeccable** the flat's spotless; 3 (informal) great; **'je viendrai te chercher chez toi à midi'** – **'impeccable!'** 'I'll come and pick you up at your place at twelve' – 'great!'

impensable adjective unthinkable.

imper noun M (informal) SHORT FOR **imperméable** raincoat.

impératif noun M imperative; **à l'impératif** in the imperative.

imperfection noun F imperfection.

imperméable noun M raincoat.

impertinent adjective cheeky.

impitoyable adjective merciless.

impliquer verb [1] 1 to mean; **cela implique que nous n'aurons pas assez d'argent** this means that we won't have enough money; 2 **être impliqué dans quelque chose** to be involved in something.

impoli adjective rude.

importance noun F importance; **ça n'a pas d'importance** it doesn't matter.

important adjective 1 important; **il est important de savoir que…** it's important to know that…; 2 considerable; **une réduction importante** a considerable reduction; **il y aura des retards importants** there will be considerable delays.

importations plural noun F imports.

importer verb [1] 1 to import (goods); 2 to matter; **'lequel veux-tu?'** – **'n'importe!'** 'which one do you want?' – 'it doesn't matter!'; **n'importe où** anywhere; **viens n'importe quand** come any time; **n'importe qui sait faire ça** anyone can do that; **il dit n'importe quoi** he's talking nonsense; **elle le fait n'importe comment** she does it any old how.

imposant adjective imposing.

imposer verb [1] 1 to impose; **imposer à quelqu'un de faire quelque chose** to make somebody do something; **la maman de Katy lui a imposé de rester à la maison** Katy's mum made her stay at home; 2 **s'imposer** to establish oneself.

impossibilité *noun* F
impossibility.

impossible *adjective* impossible;
noun **faire l'impossible** to do your
utmost; **nous ferons l'impossible
pour les contacter** we'll do our
utmost to contact them.

impôt *noun* M tax.

imprécis *adjective* vague.

impression *noun* F impression; **sa
première impression** his first
impression; **elle a fait très bonne
impression** she made a very good
impression; **j'ai l'impression qu'il
n'est pas heureux** I have a feeling
he's not happy.

impressionnant *adjective*
impressive.

impressionner *verb* [1] to impress.

imprévisible *adjective*
unpredictable.

imprévu *adjective* unexpected.

imprimante *noun* F printer (*for a*
computer).

imprimé *noun* M form (*to fill in*).
adjective printed.

imprimer *verb* [1] to print.

improviser *verb* [1] to improvise.

improviste *noun* **à l'improviste**
unexpectedly; **mon oncle est arrivé
à l'improviste** my uncle arrived
unexpectedly.

imprudent *adjective* **1** careless;
2 rash.

impuissant *adjective* helpless.

impulsif (F **impulsive**) *adjective*
impulsive.

inabordable *adjective*
1 inaccessible; **2 des prix
inabordables** prohibitive prices.

inacceptable *adjective*
unacceptable.

inaccessible *adjective*
inaccessible.

inachevé *adjective* unfinished.

inadapté *adjective* unsuitable.

inadmissible *adjective* intolerable.

inaperçu *adjective* **passer
inaperçu** to go unnoticed; **son
départ est passé inaperçu** her
departure went unnoticed.

inattendu *adjective* unexpected;
une visite inattendue an
unexpected visit.

inattention *noun* F lack of
attention; **une faute d'inattention** a
careless mistake.

inaudible *adjective* inaudible.

inauguration *noun* F
inauguration, opening.

inaugurer *verb* [1] **1** to open (*an
exhibition, a new building*); **2** to
unveil (*a monument*).

incapable *adjective* **1** incapable; **je
suis incapable de bouger!** I'm
incapable of moving!;
2 incompetent; **il est
complètement incapable** he's
completely incompetent.

incassable *adjective* unbreakable.

incendiaire *noun* M & F arsonist.
adjective **une bombe incendiaire**
an incendiary bomb.

incendie noun M fire; **l'incendie a détruit l'église** the fire destroyed the church.

incertain adjective **1** uncertain; **le résultat est toujours incertain** the result is still uncertain; **2** unsettled (weather).

incertitude noun F uncertainty.

incident noun M incident; **en cas d'incident** if anything should happen.

inciter verb [1] to encourage; **le père d'André l'a incité à apprendre la guitare** André's father encouraged him to learn to play the guitar.

inclure verb [25] **1** to include; **2** to enclose.

inclus adjective including; **il y aura trente invités, enfants inclus** there will be thirty guests, including children; **jusqu'à samedi inclus** up to and including Saturday.

incollable adjective **le riz incollable** easy-cook rice.

incolore adjective colourless.

incommode adjective **1** awkward; **2** uncomfortable.

incomparable adjective incomparable.

incompétent adjective incompetent.

incompréhensible adjective incomprehensible.

inconditionnel, inconditionnelle noun M, F devotee; **c'est un inconditionnel du jazz** he's a real jazz fan.
adjective unconditional.

inconfortable adjective uncomfortable.

inconnu, inconnue noun M, F stranger.
adjective unknown; **elle m'est inconnue** I don't know her.

inconsciemment adverb unconsciously.

inconscient adjective **1** unthinking; **2** unconscious (in a faint).

incontestable adjective unquestionable.

incontournable adjective unavoidable; **c'est un fait incontournable** it's an undeniable fact.

inconvénient noun M **1** drawback; **il y a plusieurs inconvénients** there are several drawbacks; **2** l'inconvénient, c'est que...** the difficulty is that...; **3 si vous n'y voyez pas d'inconvénient** if you have no objection.

incorporer verb [1] to blend in (ingredients in cooking); **incorporez l'huile une goutte à la fois** blend in the oil drop by drop.

incorrect adjective **1** incorrect; **2** rude.

incrédule adjective incredulous.

incroyable adjective incredible.

inculper verb [1] **inculper quelqu'un de** to charge somebody with (a crime); **elle a été inculpée de vol** she was charged with theft.

Inde noun F India; **en Inde** in (or to) India.

indécis *adjective* 1 undecided; **elle est toujours indécise** she hasn't decided yet; 2 indecisive.

indemne *adjective* unharmed.

indemniser *verb* [1] to compensate; **demander à être indemnisé** to demand compensation.

indéniable *adjective* undeniable.

indépendamment *adverb* independently.

indépendance *noun* F independence.

indépendant *adjective* 1 independent; 2 **cuisine indépendante** separate kitchen; 3 **une maison indépendante** a detached house.

index *noun* M 1 index; 2 forefinger.

indicateur *noun* M 1 timetable (*in a rail or coach station*); **l'indicateur des départs** the departures board; 2 street directory; 3 gauge (*for example, for oil levels*); 4 **un panneau indicateur** a road sign.

indicatif *noun* M 1 dialling code; **l'indicatif pour l'Espagne est 34** the dialing code for Spain is 34; 2 theme tune; 3 indicative (*of a verb*).

indications *plural noun* F directions.

indice *noun* M clue.

indien (F **indienne**) *adjective* Indian.

indifférent *adjective* indifferent.

indigène *adjective* native; **les indigènes** the locals.

indigeste *adjective* indigestible.

indigestion *noun* F indigestion; **avoir une indigestion** to have indigestion.

indignation *noun* F indignation.

indigne *adjective* 1 unworthy; 2 disgraceful.

indigner *verb* [1] **s'indigner** to get indignant.

indiqué *adjective* recommended; **ce n'est pas très indiqué** it's not a very good idea.

indiquer *verb* [1] to point out, to show; **pouvez-vous m'indiquer la gare?** can you show me the way to the station?; **le nom est indiqué sur un grand panneau** the name is on a big sign; **cela indique que...** this shows that...

indirect *adjective* indirect.

indiscipliné *adjective* unruly.

indiscret (F **indiscrète**) *adjective* 1 indiscreet; **ne le lui dis pas, elle est très indiscrète** don't tell her, she can't keep a secret; 2 **si ce n'est pas indiscret** if it's not being nosy.

indiscutable *adjective* unquestionable.

indispensable *adjective* essential; **les vêtements indispensables** essential clothing; **il est indispensable** it's essential.

indisposé *adjective* unwell.

individu *noun* M individual; **c'est un drôle d'individu** he's a funny bloke.

individuel (F **individuelle**) *adjective*
1 individual; 2 separate; **une chambre individuelle** a single room; **une maison individuelle** a detached house.

indolore *adjective* painless.

indulgent *adjective* indulgent; **notre prof de maths est trop indulgent avec nous** our maths teacher isn't strict enough with us.

industrialisé *adjective* **les pays industrialisés** the industrialized countries.

industrie *noun* F industry.

industriel (F **industrielle**) *adjective* industrial; **une ville industrielle** an industrial city.

inédit *adjective* unpublished.

inefficace *adjective* 1 inefficient; **en tant que patron il est très inefficace** as a boss he's very inefficient; 2 ineffective; **un remède inefficace** an ineffective remedy.

inégal (M *plural* **inégaux**) *adjective* 1 uneven; 2 unequal.

inespéré *adjective* unhoped-for; **un succès inespéré** an unhoped-for success.

inévitable *adjective* 1 inevitable; **c'était inévitable** it was bound to happen; 2 unavoidable; **des problèmes inévitables** unavoidable problems.

inexact *adjective* 1 incorrect; 2 inaccurate.

inexpérimenté *adjective* inexperienced.

infarctus *noun* M heart attack.

infect *adjective* foul; **le repas était infect!** the meal was foul!

infecter *verb* [1] 1 to infect; 2 **s'infecter** to go septic.

infection *noun* F infection.

inférieur *adjective* 1 lower; **sur une marche inférieure** on a lower step; **des prix inférieurs à la moyenne** lower than average prices; 2 smaller; **la taille inférieure** the smaller size; 3 inferior, worse; **de qualité inférieure** of a lower quality.

infernal (M *plural* **infernaux**) *adjective* frightful, dreadful.

infini *adjective* infinite.

infinitif *noun* M infinitive (*in grammar*); **à l'infinitif** in the infinitive.

infirme *noun* **les infirmes** the disabled; *adjective* disabled.

infirmerie *noun* F medical room.

infirmier, infirmière *noun* M, F nurse.

inflammable *adjective* flammable.

inflation *noun* F inflation.

influence *noun* F influence; **il a une bonne influence sur son frère** he's a good influence on his brother.

influencer *verb* [61] to influence.

informaticien, informaticienne *noun* M, F computer scientist.

information *noun* F
1 information; **une information très utile** a very useful piece of information; 2 **les informations**

the news (*on TV or radio*); **les informations sont à vingt heures** the news is at eight o'clock.

informatique *noun* F computer science, IT.
adjective computer; **un système informatique** a computer system.

informatiser *verb* [1] to computerize.

informer *verb* [1] 1 to inform; 2 **s'informer** to find out; **je peux m'informer si tu veux** I can find out if you like.

infrarouge *adjective* infra-red.

infusion *noun* F herbal tea.

ingénieur *noun* M engineer.

ingrat *adjective* 1 ungrateful; 2 **un travail ingrat** unrewarding work.

ingrédient *noun* M ingredient.

inhabité *adjective* uninhabited.

inhabituel (F **inhabituelle**) *adjective* unusual.

inhumain *adjective* inhuman.

inimaginable *adjective* unimaginable, unthinkable.

ininterrompu *adjective* 1 uninterrupted; 2 continuous.

initial (M *plural* **initiaux**) *adjective* initial.

initiale *noun* F initial; **mes initiales sont là-dessus** my initials are on it.

initiation *noun* F introduction (*to a new place or skill*); **une journée d'initiation** an introductory day (*to a course, for example*); **une initiation**

à l'anglais an introduction to English.

initiative *noun* F initiative.

initier *verb* [1] 1 **initier quelqu'un à** to introduce somebody to (*a skill*); 2 to initiate (*an idea or plan*); 3 **s'initier à quelque chose** to learn about something; **elle s'initie à la photo** she's starting to learn photography.

injecter *verb* [1] to inject.

injection *noun* F injection.

injure *noun* F insult.

injurier *verb* [1] to insult; **il m'a injurié** he swore at me.

injuste *adjective* unfair.

innocent *adjective* innocent.

innombrable *adjective* countless.

innovation *noun* F innovation.

innover *verb* [1] to break new ground.

inoccupé *adjective* empty.

inondation *noun* F flood; **des inondations** flooding.

inonder *verb* [1] to flood.

inoubliable *adjective* unforgettable.

inouï *adjective* incredible.

inox *noun* M stainless steel; **une casserole en inox** a stainless steel pan.

inoxydable *adjective* **un évier en acier inoxydable** a stainless steel sink.

inquiet (F **inquiète**) *adjective* anxious, worried.

inquiétant *adjective* worrying.

inquiéter *verb* [24] **1** to worry; **je ne veux pas t'inquiéter** I don't want to worry you; **ça m'inquiète un peu** I find that a bit worrying; **ce qui m'inquiète, c'est qu'elle n'a pas téléphoné** what I find worrying is the fact that she hasn't phoned; **2 s'inquiéter** to worry, to be worried; **elle va s'inquiéter si nous sommes en retard** she'll worry if we're late; **ne t'inquiète pas!** don't worry!

inquiétude *noun* F anxiety.

insatisfait *adjective* dissatisfied.

inscription *noun* F **1** enrolment (*for a course or in a school*); **2** registration.

inscrire *verb* [38] **1** to enrol, to register (*someone for a course or school*); **elle m'a inscrit pour l'examen** she's entered me for the exam; **2 s'inscrire** to enrol; **s'inscrire au club de foot** to join the football club.

insecte *noun* M insect.

insertion *noun* F **1** insertion (*of an advertisement in a paper, for example*); **2** integration (*when somebody joins a new community*); **l'insertion des jeunes dans la société** the integration of young people into society.

insignifiant *adjective* insignificant.

insister *verb* [1] **1** to insist; **il faut insister** keep on trying; **la clé est un peu tordue, il faut insister un peu**

the key's a bit bent, you have to push it really hard.

insolation *noun* F sunstroke; **attraper une insolation** to get sunstroke.

insolent *adjective* insolent.

insoutenable *adjective* unbearable.

inspecter *verb* [1] to inspect.

inspecteur, inspectrice *noun* M, F inspector.

inspection *noun* F **1** inspection; **2** inspectorate (*an official department*).

inspiration *noun* F inspiration.

inspirer *verb* [1] **1** to inspire; **ça ne m'inspire pas** that doesn't appeal to me; **2** to breathe in; **inspire fort!** breathe in deep!; **3 s'inspirer** to be inspired by; **il s'est inspiré de Picasso** he was inspired by Picasso.

instable *adjective* unstable; **il fait un temps instable** the weather's unsettled.

installation *noun* F **1** installation, putting in; **2** move (*to a house or town*); **avant son installation à Paris** before he moved to Paris; **3 des installations sportives** sports facilities.

installer *verb* [1] **1** to install, to put in (*central heating or a dishwasher, for example*); to connect (*gas, electricity, a phone*); **2 s'installer** to settle, to settle in; **installez-vous** do sit down; **je me suis installée à mon bureau** I settled down at my desk.

instant noun M moment; **pour l'instant** for the moment; **à tout instant** all the time.

instantané adjective instant; **du café instantané** instant coffee.

instinct noun M instinct.

institut noun M institute; **un institut de beauté** a beautician's.

instituteur, institutrice noun M, F primary school teacher.

institution noun F 1 institution; 2 private school.

institutrice noun F SEE instituteur.

instructeur, instructrice noun M, F instructor.

instruction noun F 1 education; **instruction civique** civics; 2 **instructions** instructions; **instructions de lavage** washing instructions.

instruire verb [26]. 1 to teach, to train; 2 **s'instruire** to learn.

instruit adjective educated.

instrument noun M 1 instrument; **un instrument de mesure** a measuring instrument; **les instruments de bord** the controls; 2 **un instrument de musique** a musical instrument; **un instrument à cordes** a string instrument.

insu noun **à mon insu** without my knowing.

insuffisance noun F shortage.

insuffisant adjective 1 insufficient; 2 inadequate; **c'est insuffisant** it's not good enough.

insultant adjective insulting.

insulte noun F insult.

insulter verb [1] to insult.

insupportable adjective unbearable; **je la trouve insupportable** I can't stand her.

intact adjective intact.

intégral (M plural **intégraux**) adjective complete.

intégrale noun F complete works (usually music); **l'intégrale des Beatles** the complete Beatles collection.

intellectuel, intellectuelle noun M, F, adjective intellectual.

intelligence noun F intelligence.

intelligent adjective clever, intelligent.

intendance noun F administration (in a school).

intense adjective intense.

intensif (F **intensive**) adjective intensive.

intention noun F intention; **avoir l'intention de faire** to mean to do; **j'avais l'intention d'y aller mais je n'ai pas pu** I meant to go but I wasn't able to.

interdiction noun F ban; **'interdiction de fumer'** 'no smoking'.

interdire verb [47] to forbid; **je t'interdis de le faire** I forbid you to do it.

interdit adjective forbidden; **'entrée interdite'** 'no entry'; **il est interdit de fumer dans la salle** smoking is forbidden in the theatre.

intéressant *adjective*
1 interesting; **c'est un film très intéressant** it's a very interesting film; 2 **à un prix intéressant** at a good price.

intéressé *adjective* interested; **être intéressé par quelque chose** to be interested in something.

intéresser *verb* [1] 1 to interest; **ça ne m'intéresse pas** that doesn't interest me; 2 **s'intéresser à** to be interested in; **elle s'intéresse beaucoup à l'informatique** she's very interested in computing.

intérêt *noun* M 1 interest; **ce livre est sans intérêt** this book is really boring; 2 **tu as intérêt à faire** you'd better do; **tu as intérêt à le finir avant ce soir!** you'd better get it finished by this evening!

intérieur *noun* M inside, interior; **l'intérieur du placard** the inside of the cupboard; **où est-elle? – à l'intérieur** where is she? – inside (*in the house*).
adjective inside, internal; **le côté intérieur** the inside.

intermédiaire *noun* M & F go-between.
adjective intermediate; **avez-vous la taille intermédiaire?** do you have the size in-between?

internat *noun* M boarding school.

international (M *plural* **internationaux**) *adjective* international.

interne *noun* M & F boarder (*in a school*).
adjective internal.

Internet *noun* M Internet; **sur Internet** on the Internet.

interpeller *verb* [1] 1 to call out to; 2 **la police l'a interpellé** the police have taken him in for questioning.

interphone™ *noun* M entry phone.

interprète *noun* M & F 1 (*in the theatre*) actor; (*in music*) performer, soloist; 2 interpreter.

interpréter *verb* [24] 1 to perform, to play (*a role in the theatre or a piece of music*), to sing (*a song*); 2 to interpret (*a language or a remark*).

interrogatif *noun* M interrogative.

interrogation *noun* F 1 test (*at school*); 2 questioning.

interroger *verb* [52] 1 to question, to ask; **il m'a interrogé sur mon séjour en France** he asked me about my stay in France; 2 to test (*at school*).

interrompre *verb* [69] to interrupt; **interrompre quelqu'un** to interrupt somebody; **il a interrompu son travail** he broke off his work.

interrupteur *noun* M switch.

interruption *noun* F 1 interruption; 2 **sans interruption** without stopping.

intervalle *noun* M 1 interval; 2 **dans l'intervalle** in the meantime.

intervenir *verb* [81] to intervene.

intervention *noun* F intervention.

interview *noun* F interview (*on TV, radio, for a magazine*).

intestin noun M intestine.

intime adjective intimate; **un journal intime** a diary (*kept by somebody*).

intimider verb [1] to intimidate.

intimité noun F 1 intimacy; **dans l'intimité** in private.

intolérable adjective intolerable.

intolérant adjective intolerant.

intoxication noun F poisoning.

intrigue noun F plot (*of a novel, play, etc*).

introduction noun F introduction.

introduire verb [26] 1 to introduce (*an idea, a measure, a new product*); 2 **s'introduire** to get into; **un cambrioleur s'est introduit dans l'appartement** a burglar got into the flat.

intrus, intruse noun M, F intruder.

intuitif (F **intuitive**) adjective intuitive.

intuition noun F intuition.

inusable adjective hard-wearing.

inutile adjective pointless; **il est inutile de l'appeler** there's no point telephoning him; **inutile de dire que...** needless to say...

inutilement adverb pointlessly; **je l'ai cherché inutilement** I looked for it in vain.

inutilisable adjective unusable.

invalide noun M & F disabled person.

invasion noun F invasion.

inventer verb [1] to invent.

invention noun F invention.

inverse noun M **l'inverse** the opposite; **l'inverse est vrai** the opposite is true.
adjective opposite; **en sens inverse** in the opposite direction; **dans l'ordre inverse** in reverse order.

investigation noun F investigation.

investissement noun M investment.

invisible adjective invisible.

invitation noun F invitation.

invité, invitée noun M, F guest; **nous avons des invités ce soir** we have people coming round this evening.

inviter verb [1] to invite; **ils m'ont invité à dîner** they invited me to dinner.

involontaire adjective unintentional.

invraisemblable adjective 1 unlikely; **une explication invraisemblable** an unlikely explanation; 2 (*informal*) amazing.

ira, irai, iraient, irais, irait, iras verb SEE **aller**.

iris noun M iris.

irlandais noun M, adjective Irish.

Irlandais, Irlandaise noun M, F Irishman, Irishwoman; **les Irlandais** the Irish.

Irlande noun F Ireland; **la République d'Irlande** the Republic of Ireland.

Irlande du Nord noun F Northern Ireland.

ironie noun F irony.

ironique adjective ironic.

irons, iront verb SEE **aller**[1].

irradier verb [1] to irradiate.

irréel, irréelle adjective unreal.

irréfléchi adjective thoughtless.

irrégularité noun F irregularity.

irrégulier (F **irrégulière**) adjective irregular.

irrésistible adjective irresistible.

irresponsable adjective irresponsible.

irritable adjective irritable.

irritation noun F irritation.

irriter verb [1] **1** to irritate; **cela m'irrite** that makes me cross; **2 s'irriter** to get irritated.

islamique adjective Islamic.

isolation noun F insulation; **isolation acoustique** soundproofing.

isolé adjective **1** remote; **2** lonely.

isoler verb [1] **1** to insulate (a room or building); **2** to isolate (a sick person or a prisoner).

Israël noun M Israel.

israélien (F **israélienne**) adjective Israeli.

issue noun F exit; **issue de secours** emergency exit; **une rue sans issue** a dead end.

Italie noun F Italy; **en Italie** in (or to) Italy.

italien noun M, adjective Italian.

Italien, Italienne noun M, F Italian (person).

itinéraire noun M route.

itinérant adjective travelling.

ivoire noun M adjective ivory.

ivre adjective drunk.

ivresse noun F drunkenness.

ivrogne noun M & F drunkard.

J j

j' pronoun SEE **je**.

jacinthe noun F hyacinth.

jalousie noun F **1** jealousy; **2** slatted blind.

jaloux (F **jalouse**) adjective jealous.

jamais adverb **1** never; **elle ne fume jamais** she never smokes; **on ne sait jamais** you never know; **jamais plus!** never again!; **2** ever; **plus grand que jamais** bigger than ever; **si jamais il pleut** if by any chance it rains; **à jamais** forever.

jambe noun F leg; **se casser la jambe** to break your leg.

jambon noun M ham; **jambon blanc** cooked ham; **jambon de pays** cured raw ham.

janvier noun M January; **en janvier, au mois de janvier** in January.

Japon noun M Japan; **au Japon** in (or to) Japan.

japonais noun M, adjective Japanese.

Japonais, Japonaise noun M, F Japanese (person).

jardin noun M garden; **Patrick est au jardin** Patrick's in the garden; **une chaise de jardin** a garden chair.

jardinage noun M gardening.

jardinier, jardinière[1] noun M, F gardener.

jardinière[2] noun F (large) plant pot.

jardin public noun M park (in a town).

jaune noun M **1** yellow; **2 un jaune d'œuf** an egg-yolk. adjective yellow; **une robe jaune** a yellow dress.

jaunisse noun F jaundice.

Javel noun **eau de Javel** bleach.

jazz noun M jazz; **j'aime le jazz** I like jazz.

J.-C. noun M short for Jésus-Christ; **200 avant J.-C.** 200 BC; **400 après J.-C.** 400 AD.

je, j' (before a vowel or silent 'h') pronoun I; **je sais où il habite** I know where he lives; **j'habite à Lyon** I live in Lyons.

jean noun M **1** (pair of) jeans; **j'ai acheté un jean** I've bought some jeans; **2** denim; **une jupe en jean** a denim skirt.

jet noun M **1** jet (of water or steam); **les jets d'eau de Versailles** the fountains at Versailles; **2** jet (plane).

jetée noun F jetty.

jeter verb [48] **1** to throw; **jette-moi le ballon** throw me the ball; **2** to throw away; **j'ai jeté ces vieilles chaussures** I've thrown away these old shoes; **3 jeter un coup d'œil** to have a look; **est-ce que tu peux jeter un coup d'œil aux pommes de terre?** can you have a look at the potatoes?

jeton noun M **1** counter (for a board game); **2** token (for a machine).

jeu (plural **jeux**) noun M game; **faire un jeu** to play a game; ★ **ce n'est pas du jeu!** (informal) that's not fair!

jeu-concours noun M competition.

jeu de cartes noun M **1** pack of cards; **2** game of cards.

jeu de mots noun M pun.

jeu de société noun M board game.

jeudi noun M **1** Thursday; **nous sommes jeudi aujourd'hui** it's Thursday today; **jeudi prochain** next Thursday; **jeudi dernier** last Thursday; **2** on Thursday; **je l'ai vu jeudi soir** I saw him on Thursday evening; **3 le jeudi** on Thursdays;

fermé le jeudi closed on Thursdays; **4 tous les jeudis** every Thursday.

jeune noun M & F young person; **une émission destinée aux jeunes** a programme aimed at young people. adjective young; **un jeune homme** a young man; **une jeune femme** a young woman; **une jeune fille** a girl.

jeunesse noun F **1** young people; **la jeunesse d'aujourd'hui** young people today; **2** youth; **dans ma jeunesse** in my youth.

jeu-vidéo noun M video game.

jogging noun M **1 faire du jogging** to go jogging; **2 un jogging** a track-suit.

joie noun F joy.

joindre verb [49] **1** to get hold of (often by telephone); **je n'ai pas pu la joindre** I wasn't able to get hold of her; **2** to enclose (in a letter or parcel); **3** to put together; **les pieds joints** feet together; ★ **joindre les deux bouts** to make ends meet (financially).

joli adjective pretty.

jonquille noun F daffodil.

joue noun F cheek.

jouer verb [1] **1** to play; **elle joue avec le chien** she's playing with the dog; **à toi de jouer!** your go!; **bien joué!** well done!; **2 jouer à** to play (a sport); **on va jouer au foot** we're going to play football; **3 jouer de** to play (an instrument); **Robert joue de la guitare** Robert plays the guitar; **4** to act; **il joue bien dans ce film** he's really good in this film.

jouet noun M toy.

joueur, joueuse noun M, F player.

jour noun M **1** day; **les jours de la semaine** the days of the week; **trois jours plus tard** three days later; **le jour où** the day when; **un de ces jours** one of these days; **2 de nos jours** nowadays; **3 mettre quelque chose à jour** to bring something up to date; **4** daylight, light; **il fait jour** it's daylight; **en plein jour** in broad daylight; **jour et nuit** night and day.

jour de l'an noun M New Year's Day.

jour férié noun M public holiday.

journal (plural **journaux**) noun M **1** newspaper, magazine; **le journal du soir** the evening paper; **du papier journal** newspaper (for wrapping); **2** news (on TV or radio); **le journal de vingt-deux heures** the ten o'clock news; **3 un journal intime** a diary.

journalisme noun M journalism.

journaliste noun M & F journalist.

journée noun F day; **toute la journée** all day, the whole day; **il est payé à la journée** he's paid by the day.

jour ouvrable noun M working day.

joyeux (F **joyeuse**) adjective happy; **Joyeux Anniversaire** Happy Birthday; **Joyeux Noël** Merry Christmas.

judicieux (F judicieuse) *adjective* sensible; **un choix judicieux** a wise choice.

judo *noun* M judo.

juge *noun* M judge.

juger *verb* [52] to judge.

juif, juive *noun* M,F Jew. *adjective* Jewish.

juillet *noun* M July; **en juillet, au mois de juillet** in July; **le quatorze juillet** Bastille Day (*July 14, a national holiday to celebrate the taking of the Bastille prison in Paris by the people at the beginning of the French Revolution in 1789*).

juin *noun* M June; **en juin, au mois de juin** in June.

juive *noun* F, *adjective* SEE **juif.**

jumeau (*plural* jumeaux), **jumelle** *noun* M,F twin.

jumeler *verb* [18] to twin (*towns*); **Oxford est jumelé avec Bonn** Oxford is twinned with Bonn.

jumelles *plural noun* F binoculars.

jument *noun* F mare.

jungle *noun* F jungle.

jupe *noun* F skirt.

jurer *verb* [1] to swear.

juridique *adjective* legal; **le système juridique** the legal system.

jury *noun* M 1 jury; 2 board of examiners.

jus *noun* M 1 juice; **un jus d'orange** an orange juice; 2 gravy.

jus de fruits *noun* M fruit juice.

jusqu'à *preposition* 1 as far as (*a place*); **ce train va jusqu'à Paris** this train goes as far as Paris; **nous avons marché jusqu'à la mer** we walked as far as the sea; **il m'a accompagné jusqu'à chez moi** he took me all the way home; 2 until; **elle reste jusqu'à mardi** she's staying until Tuesday; **jusqu'à quand reste-t-il?** how long is he staying for?; **jusqu'à présent, jusqu'à maintenant** up to now; 3 **jusqu'à ce que** until.

juste *adjective* 1 right, correct; **le mot juste** the right word; **ce que tu dis est juste** what you say is right; 2 fair; **ce n'est pas juste!** it's not fair!; 3 in tune; **elle chante juste** she sings in tune; 4 **c'est un peu juste** it's a bit tight; **une heure est un peu juste** an hour's a bit tight. *adverb* just; **juste à temps** just in time; **il vient tout juste d'arriver** he's only just arrived.

justement *adverb* 1 precisely; 2 just; **je parlais justement de toi** I was just talking about you; 3 correctly; **comme elle a dit très justement** as she so rightly said.

justesse *noun* F 1 correctness; 2 **de justesse** only just; **il a eu son avion, mais de justesse** he caught his plane, but only just.

justice *noun* F justice.

justifier *verb* [1] to justify.

juteux (F juteuse) *adjective* juicy.

juvénile *adjective* youthful.

K k

kaki *noun* M persimmon.
adjective khaki.

kangourou *noun* M kangaroo.

karaté *noun* M karate.

karting *noun* M go-karting.

kascher *adjective* kosher.

kermesse *noun* F (school) fête.

kidnapper *verb* [1] to kidnap.

kidnappeur, kidnappeuse
noun M, F kidnapper.

kilo *noun* M kilo; **deux kilos de
pommes** two kilos of apples; **j'ai pris
trois kilos** I've put on three kilos.

kilogramme *noun* M kilogramme.

kilomètre *noun* M kilometre; **à dix
kilomètres d'ici** ten kilometres
from here; **Paris est à combien de
kilomètres de Dijon?** how many
kilometres is it from Paris to Dijon?

kinésithérapeute *noun* M & F
physiotherapist.

kinésithérapie *noun* F
physiotherapy.

kiosque *noun* M kiosk.

kiwi *noun* M kiwi (*the bird and the
fruit*).

klaxon™ *noun* M horn (*on a car*).

klaxonner *verb* [1] to sound the
horn (*in a car*).

km SHORT FOR **kilomètre**; **km/h** kph
(*kilometres per hour*).

K.O. *adjective* 1 **mettre quelqu'un
K.O.** to knock somebody out (*in
boxing*); 2 **je suis complètement
K.O.** (*informal*) I'm completely
knackered.

kraft *noun* M **le papier kraft** brown
paper.

K-way™ *noun* M cagoule.

L l

la, l' (*before a vowel or silent 'h'*)
definite article,
pronoun SEE **le.**

là *adverb* 1 there; **est-ce que Paul
est là?** is Paul there?; **c'est là
qu'habite mon frère** that's where my
brother lives; 2 here; **viens là** come
here; **Danielle n'est pas là en ce
moment** Danielle's not here at the
moment; 3 then; **c'est là que j'ai
pensé à toi** that's when I thought of
you.

-là *adverb* **cette maison-là** that
house; **ces gens-là** those people; **à
ce moment-là** at that moment.

là-bas *adverb* 1 there; **qu'est-ce
que vous avez fait là-bas?** what did
you do there?; 2 over there; **notre
maison est là-bas** our house is over
there.

labo *noun* M (*informal*) lab.

laboratoire *noun* M laboratory.

laboratoire de langues *noun* M
language laboratory.

labourer *verb* [1] to plough.

labyrinthe noun M maze, labyrinth.

lac noun M lake; **le lac d'Annecy** Lake Annecy.

lacer verb [61] **lacer ses chaussures** to tie your shoelaces.

lacet noun M lace (for shoes); **des chaussures à lacets** lace-up shoes.

lâche adjective 1 cowardly; 2 loose (a belt or rope, for example).

lâcher verb [1] 1 to drop (an object); to let go of (a rope or branch); **lâche-moi!** let go of me!; **ne lâche pas la corde!** don't let go of the rope!; 2 to drop; **elle a lâché son sac** she dropped her bag; 3 to give way; **la corde a lâché** the rope gave way.

lâcheté noun F cowardice.

lacrymogène adjective **le gaz lacrymogène** teargas.

là-dedans adverb in there; **il y a un oiseau là-dedans** there's a bird in there; **il n'y a rien là-dedans** there's nothing inside.

là-dessous adverb under there; **les verres sont là-dessous** the glasses are under there.

là-dessus adverb 1 on there; **tu peux mettre les assiettes là-dessus** you can put the plates on there; 2 about it; **ils sont d'accord là-dessus** they agree about it; **a-t-il dit quelque chose là-dessus?** did he say anything about it?; 3 with that; **là-dessus il est sorti** with that, he went out.

là-haut adverb 1 up here, up there; **il est là-haut dans l'arbre** he's up

there in the tree; 2 upstairs; **maman est là-haut** Mum's upstairs.

laid adjective ugly.

laideur noun F ugliness.

laine noun F wool; **un pull en laine** a woollen jumper.

laine vierge noun F pure new wool.

laïque adjective **une école laïque** a state school.

laisse noun F lead (for a dog).

laisser verb [1] 1 to leave; **j'ai laissé mes clés chez toi** I've left my keys at your house; **bon, je vous laisse** right, I must be off now; 2 **laisser quelqu'un faire** to let somebody do; **laisse-le parler!** let him speak!; **laissez-la faire, elle reviendra** leave her alone, she'll come back; 3 **il se laisse insulter** he puts up with being insulted; **elle s'est laissée aller** she's let herself go.

laisser-aller noun M carelessness.

lait noun M milk; **un thé au lait** a cup of tea with milk; **un café au lait** a white coffee.

lait demi-écrémé noun M semi-skimmed milk.

lait écrémé noun M skimmed milk.

laitier (F **laitière**) adjective **les produits laitiers** milk products (such as yoghurt).

laitue noun F lettuce.

lame noun F blade.

lamelle noun F thin strip.

lamentable adjective awful.

lampadaire noun M **1** standard lamp; **2** street lamp.

lampe noun F lamp, light; **allumer la lampe** to turn on the lamp.

lampe de poche noun F torch.

lampe électrique noun F torch.

lancement noun M launch.

lancer verb [61] **1** to throw; **il m'a lancé le ballon** he threw the ball to me; **2** to launch; **ils vont lancer leur nouveau produit en juin** they're going to launch their new product in June; **3** **se lancer dans quelque chose** to embark on something.

landau noun M pram.

lande noun F moor.

langage noun M language, type of language; **le langage administratif** official jargon.

langouste noun F crayfish.

langue noun F **1** tongue; **tirer la langue** to stick your tongue out; **2** language; **une langue étrangère** a foreign language; **ma langue maternelle** my mother tongue; ★ **je l'ai sur le bout de la langue** it's on the tip of my tongue.

lanière noun F strap.

lapin noun M rabbit; ★ **il m'a posé un lapin** (*informal*) he stood me up.

laque noun F **1** hairspray; **2** lacquer, gloss paint.

laquelle pronoun SEE **lequel**.

lard noun M streaky bacon.

lardons plural noun M diced bacon; **salade aux lardons fumés** green salad with diced smoky bacon.

large noun M open sea; **au large** offshore.
adjective wide; **un large sourire** a broad smile; **deux mètres de large** two metres wide.

largement adverb **c'est largement suffisant** that's more than enough; **j'ai largement le temps** I've got plenty of time.

largeur noun F width.

larme noun F tear; **en larmes** in tears; **rire aux larmes** to laugh till you cry.

laryngite noun F laryngitis.

lasagnes plural noun F lasagna; **manger des lasagnes** to eat lasagna.

laser noun M laser; **une platine laser** a compact disc player.

lasser verb [1] **se lasser** to get tired.

lassitude noun F weariness.

latin noun M,
adjective Latin.

laurier noun M laurel; **un laurier commun** a bay tree; **une feuille de laurier** a bay leaf.

laurier-rose noun M oleander.

lavable adjective washable; **lavable en machine** machine-washable.

lavabo noun M washbasin.

lavage noun M **1** washing; **2** wash (on a *washing-machine programme*); **3** car wash.

lavande noun F lavender.

lave-linge noun M washing machine.

laver verb [1] **1** to wash; **2 se laver** to wash; **se laver les mains** to wash your hands; **se laver les dents** to brush your teeth.

laverie noun F launderette.

lave-vaisselle noun M dishwasher.

le, la, l', les definite article **1** the; **le chat** the cat; **la maison** the house; **les enfants** the children; **'quelle chemise?' – 'la verte'** 'which shirt?' – 'the green one'; **2** (les is often not translated) **je n'aime pas les chiens** I don't like dogs; **3 elle se lave les cheveux** she's washing her hair; **4 le père de mon ami** my friend's father; **5** a, an; **5 francs le kilo** five francs a kilo.
pronoun **1** him, her, it, them; **je la vois tous les soirs** I see her every evening; **je le vois tous les soirs** I see him every evening; **où est-ce que tu les as mis?** where did you put them?; **il l'a acheté chez Meyer** he bought it at Meyer's.

lécher verb [1] to lick.

lèche-vitrines noun M **faire du lèche-vitrines** to go window-shopping.

leçon noun F lesson; **une leçon de géographie** a geography lesson.

lecteur, lectrice noun M, F **1** reader (of a book); **2** foreign language assistant (in a university).

lecteur de cassettes noun M cassette player.

lecteur de disquettes noun M disk drive.

lecteur laser noun M CD player.

lecture noun F reading; **j'aime la lecture** I like reading; **le soir il fait de la lecture** he reads in the evenings.

légal adjective (M plural **légaux**) legal.

légende noun F **1** caption (to a picture); **2** key (to a map); **3** legend.

léger (F **légère**) adjective **1** light; **une veste légère** a light jacket; **un repas léger** a light meal; **2** slight; **un léger retard** a slight delay; **3** weak; **un café léger** a weak coffee; **★ faire quelque chose à la légère** to do something without thinking.

légèrement adverb **1** lightly; **légèrement parfumé** lightly perfumed; **2** slightly; **il est légèrement blessé** he's slightly hurt; **elle est légèrement plus grande que moi** she's slightly taller than me.

légèreté noun F lightness.

législatif (F **législative**) adjective legislative; **les élections législatives** the general election.

légume noun M vegetable; **des légumes verts** green vegetables.

lendemain noun M **le lendemain** the next day; **Marc est arrivé le lendemain** Marc arrived the next day; **le lendemain matin** the next morning; **le lendemain de**

l'accident the day after the accident.

lent *adjective* slow.

lentement *adverb* slowly.

lenteur *noun* F slowness; **avec lenteur** slowly.

lentille *noun* F 1 lentil; **soupe aux lentilles** lentil soup; 2 lens; **lentilles de contact** contact lenses; **elle met ses lentilles** she's putting in her contact lenses.

léopard *noun* M leopard.

lequel, laquelle, lesquels, lesquelles *pronoun* 1 which one?, which?; **'passe-moi les verres'** – **'lesquels?'** 'pass me the glasses' – 'which ones?'; 2 which, who; **la voiture dans laquelle ils roulaient** the car they were driving in, the car in which they were driving; **le monsieur avec lequel je discutais** the man to whom I was talking (*often not translated*) the man I was talking to.

les *definite article, pronoun* SEE **le**.

lessive *noun* F 1 washing; **faire la lessive** to do the washing; 2 washing powder, washing liquid.

lettre *noun* F 1 letter; **écrire une lettre** to write a letter; 2 letter (*of the alphabet*); **une lettre minuscule** a small letter; **une lettre majuscule** a capital letter; ★ **il prend tout ce qu'on lui dit à la lettre** he takes everything you say literally.

lettres *plural noun* F arts (*at university*).

leur *pronoun* them (*meaning 'to them'*); **je leur donne de l'argent** I give them money.
adjective (*plural* **leurs**) their; **leur voiture** their car; **leurs enfants** their children.
pronoun theirs; **le leur, les leurs** theirs; **ça, c'est notre maison, et ça, c'est la leur** that's our house and that's theirs; **nous avons appelé nos parents et ils ont appelé les leurs** we phoned our parents and they phoned theirs.

levant *adjective* **le soleil levant** the rising sun.

lever[1] *verb* [50] 1 to lift, to raise; **levons nos verres!** let's raise our glasses!; **levez la main!** put your hand up!; **il a levé les yeux** he looked up; 2 **se lever** to get up (*out of bed or from a chair*); **je me lève à sept heures** I get up at seven o'clock; **nous nous sommes levés tôt** we got up early; **quand le soleil se lève** when the sun rises.

lever[2] *noun* M **au lever du soleil** at sunrise.

lève-tard *noun* M late riser.

lève-tôt *noun* M early riser.

levier *noun* M lever.

lèvre *noun* F lip.

lévrier *noun* M greyhound.

levure *noun* F yeast.

lexique *noun* M word list.

lézard *noun* M lizard.

liaison *noun* F 1 link, connection; **une liaison routière** a road link; **une liaison radio** radio contact; **une**

liaison satellite a satellite link;
2 (love) affair.

liasse noun F wad, bundle (of papers or banknotes).

libellule noun F dragonfly.

libération noun F release, liberation; **la libération des femmes** women's liberation; **la Libération (de 1944)** the Liberation (of 1944) (the end of the German occupation of France).

libérer verb [24] **1** to free, to release (a prisoner or hostage); **2** to vacate (a hotel room or flat).

liberté noun F freedom.

libraire noun M & F bookseller.

librairie noun F bookshop.

librairie-papeterie noun F bookseller's and stationer's.

libre adjective free; **1 vous êtes libre de partir** you are free to go; **2** free (of a seat or chair); **est-ce que cette place est libre?** is this seat free?

librement adverb freely.

libre-service noun M self service, self-service shop or restaurant; **un libre-service bancaire** a cashpoint.

licence noun F degree (at university); **elle a une licence de chimie** she has a chemistry degree.

licencier verb [1] **licencier quelqu'un** to make somebody redundant.

lien noun M link; **mes liens avec la famille** my links with my family; **un lien d'amitié** a bond of friendship.

lierre noun M ivy.

lieu (plural **lieux**) noun M **1** place; **un lieu public** a public place; **date et lieu de naissance** date and place of birth; **lieu de travail** place of work; **2 en premier lieu** in the first place; **3 avoir lieu** to take place; **le mariage aura lieu en juin** the marriage will take place in June; **4 au lieu de** instead of; **au lieu de prendre le bus, il est parti à pied** instead of taking the bus, he went off on foot; **5 les lieux** the premises; **peut-on visiter les lieux?** can one visit the premises?; **la police est arrivée sur les lieux** the police are now at the scene.

lièvre noun M hare.

lifting noun M face-lift.

ligne noun F **1** line; **une ligne droite** a straight line; **une ligne blanche** a white line (on the road); **à la ligne!** new paragraph! (in a dictation); **2** line (of a bus or train); **la ligne Paris-Dijon** the Paris-Dijon line; **une ligne de chemin de fer** a railway line; **les grandes lignes** the main lines (sign at a railway station); **3** cable; **ligne électrique** electric cable; **4** (telephone) line; **la ligne est mauvaise** it's a bad line; **restez en ligne, monsieur** hold the line, sir; **5** figure; **pour garder la ligne** to keep your figure, to stay slim.

lilas noun M lilac.

limace noun F slug.

lime noun F file; **une lime à ongles** a nail file.

limite noun F 1 limit; **une limite d'âge** an age limit; 2 **la date limite** the closing date; 3 **sans limites** endless; **une patience sans limites** endless patience; 4 **à la limite** if it comes to it, at a pinch; **à la limite, je peux te prêter l'argent** if it comes to it, I can lend you the money; 5 **dans la limite de** within the limits of; **dans la limite des places disponibles** subject to available seating space; **dans la limite du possible** as far as possible; 6 boundary; **les limites du village** the village boundaries; 7 maximum, last; **vitesse limite** maximum speed; **âge limite** maximum age; **date limite de vente** sell-by date.

limiter verb [1] 1 to limit; 2 **se limiter** to limit oneself; **je me limite à deux cafés par jour** I limit myself to two coffees a day.

limonade noun F lemonade.

lin noun M linen; **une jupe en lin** a linen skirt.

linge noun M 1 linen (*sheets, towels, etc*); **linge de maison** household linen; **du linge sale** dirty linen; 2 washing; **as-tu du linge pour la machine?** have you any washing for the machine?; **une corde à linge** a washing line; ★ **elle était blanche comme un linge** she was white as a sheet.

lingerie noun F lingerie.

lion noun M lion.

Lion noun M Leo (*sign of the Zodiac*).

liqueur noun F liqueur.

liquidation noun F clearance sale, closing-down sale; **'liquidation totale!'** 'everything must go!'

liquide noun M 1 liquid; 2 cash; **payer quelque chose en liquide** to pay cash for something. adjective liquid.

lire verb [51] to read; **lire un roman** to read a novel; **elle sait lire maintenant** she can read now; **elle m'a lu une histoire** she read me a story; **un auteur qui est très lu** a popular author; **lire à haute voix** to read aloud; ★ **lire entre les lignes** to read between the lines.

lis verb SEE **lire**.

lisible adjective legible.

lisse adjective smooth.

liste noun F list; **faire une liste** to make a list; **faire la liste de** to make a list of.

liste d'attente noun F waiting list.

lit[1] verb SEE **lire**.

lit[2] noun M bed; **aller au lit** to go to bed; **faire son lit** to make one's bed; **un lit à une place** a single bed; **un lit à deux places** a double bed; **une chambre à deux lits** a twin-bedded room; **au lit!** bedtime!

literie noun F bedding.

litière noun F litter (*for an animal's bed*); **la litière pour chat** cat litter.

litre noun M litre; **un litre d'eau** a litre of water.

littéralement adverb literally.

littérature noun F literature; **la littérature française** French literature.

livraison noun F delivery; **'livraisons à toute heure'** 'we deliver any time'; **'livraisons à domicile'** 'we deliver'.

livre[1] noun M book; **un livre pour enfants** a children's book; **un livre de poche** a paperback.

livre[2] noun F 1 pound (in money); **une livre sterling** a pound sterling; 2 pound (in France = 500 grammes); **une livre de tomates** a pound of tomatoes.

livrer verb [1] to deliver, to hand over.

livret noun M booklet.

livret de famille M noun family record book (with details of births, marriages, and deaths).

livret scolaire M noun school report book.

local (plural **locaux**) noun M place (usually a building); **locaux commerciaux** business premises; **dans les locaux du lycée** on school premises.
adjective local; **un journal local** a local paper; **dix heures heure locale** ten a.m. local time.

locataire noun M & F tenant.

location noun F 1 renting; **un appartement de location** a rented flat; **'locations'** 'to rent'; 2 hire, rental; **location de voitures** car hire; **location de vidéos** video rental; 3 reservation, booking (of theatre seats).

locomotive noun F engine, locomotive.

loge noun F 1 lodge (for the caretaker in a block of flats); 2 (in a theatre) dressing-room (for an actor); box (for a spectator).

logement noun M 1 accommodation; **il a trouvé un logement tout près** he's found somewhere to live just nearby; 2 housing; **la crise du logement** the housing crisis.

loger verb [52] 1 to put up; **peux-tu me loger ce soir?** can you put me up tonight?; 2 to stay; **pour l'instant elle loge chez mes parents** for the moment she's staying with my parents.

logiciel noun M 1 software; 2 program (for a computer); **un logiciel de jeux** a games program.

logique noun F logic.
adjective logical.

loi noun F law.

loin adverb 1 (in distance) a long way, far off; **c'est loin** it's a long way; **c'est trop loin** it's too far; **c'est loin d'ici** it's a long way from here; **le cinéma est plus loin** the cinema is further on; 2 (in time) far off; **les vacances sont loin** the holidays are a long way off; **il n'est pas loin de midi** it's almost twelve; 3 **de loin** from a long way off; **on voit leur maison de loin** you can see their house from a long way off; 4 **de loin** by far; **c'est de loin le plus cher** it's by far the most expensive; 5 **au loin** in the distance.

lointain adjective distant.

loisirs *plural noun* M 1 spare time; **je dessine pendant mes loisirs** I draw in my spare time; 2 spare-time activities.

Londonien, Londonienne *noun* M, F Londoner.

Londres *noun* London; **à Londres** in (or to) London; **les rues de Londres** the London streets.

long *noun* M 1 **une corde de cinq mètres de long** a rope five metres long; 2 **le long de** all along; **le long de la route** all along the road; 3 **tout le long du film** all the way through the film.
adjective (F **longue**) long; **une longue vie** a long life; **un long silence** a long silence; **un long voyage** a long journey; **la rue la plus longue de Paris** the longest street in Paris; **une chemise à manches longues** a long-sleeved shirt; **la pièce est longue de quatre mètres, la pièce fait quatre mètres de long** the room is four metres long; ★ **marcher de long en large** to walk up and down; ★ **à la longue** in the long run.

longtemps *adverb* (for) a long time; **elle est restée longtemps** she stayed for a long time; **longtemps après** a long time after; **elle est là depuis longtemps** she's been here for a long time; **j'y suis allé, mais il y a longtemps** I've been there, but a long time ago; **ça fait longtemps qu'on ne s'est pas vu!** it's ages since we've seen each other!; **je n'en ai pas pour longtemps** I won't be long.

longuement *adverb* for a long time.

longueur *noun* F 1 length; **de quelle longueur est le couloir?** how long is the corridor?; 2 **avoir des longueurs** to drag; **le film est intéressant mais il a des longueurs** it's an interesting film but it drags in places.

longueur d'onde *noun* F wavelength.

lorsque, lorsqu' (*before a vowel or silent 'h'*) *conjunction* when; **lorsque j'étais petite** when I was a little girl.

lot *noun* M 1 batch; **un lot de trois boîtes** a pack of three cans; 2 prize (*in a lottery*); **elle a gagné le gros lot** she won the jackpot.

loterie *noun* F 1 lottery; 2 raffle.

lotion *noun* F lotion.

lotissement *noun* M housing estate.

loto *noun* M lottery.

lotte *noun* F monkfish.

louche[1] *noun* F ladle.

louche[2] *adjective* fishy; **il y a un type louche à la porte** there's a fishy-looking guy at the door.

louer *verb* [1] 1 to let (*a house or flat*); **pendant mon absence j'ai loué mon appartement** while I was away I let my flat; **'à louer'** 'to let'; 2 to rent; **nous avons loué un appartement à Lille** we've rented a flat in Lille; 3 to hire; **nous avons loué une voiture** we hired a car; 4 to praise.

loup *noun* M wolf; ★ **j'ai une faim de loup** I'm absolutely starving *(literally: I'm as hungry as a wolf);* ★ **quand on parle du loup (on en voit la queue)** speak of the devil *(literally: when you speak of the wolf (you see its tail))*.

loupe *noun* F magnifying glass.

louper *(informal) verb* [1] **1** to miss *(a train)*; **on a loupé le train de dix heures** we missed the ten o'clock train; **2** to fail; **elle a loupé son permis** she failed her driving test.

loup-garou *noun* M werewolf.

lourd *adjective* **1** heavy; **ta valise est très lourde** your case is very heavy; **le repas était un peu lourd** the meal was a bit heavy; **2 une lourde erreur** a serious mistake.

loutre *noun* F otter.

loyal (M *plural* **loyaux**) *adjective* faithful.

loyauté *noun* F loyalty.

loyer *noun* M rent; **payer le loyer** to pay the rent.

lu *verb* SEE **lire**.

lucarne *noun* F skylight.

luge *noun* F sledge.

lugubre *adjective* gloomy.

lui *pronoun* **1** him; **c'est lui** it's him; **Hélène travaille avec lui** Hélène works with him; **est-ce qu'il a aimé le bouquin que je lui ai prêté?** did he like the book I lent him?; **2** to him; **Pierre est en colère – qu'est-ce que tu lui as dit?** Pierre's angry – what did you say to him?; **3** to her; **Nadine est en colère – qu'est-ce que tu lui as dit?** Nadine's angry – what did you say to her?;

4 *(for emphasis)* lui, **il n'est jamais content!** he's never pleased!

lui-même *pronoun* **1** himself; **il l'a fait lui-même** he did it himself; **2** *(on telephone)* **'Monsieur Dubois?' – 'lui-même'** 'Monsieur Dubois?' – 'speaking'.

lumière *noun* F light.

lumineux (F **lumineuse**) *adjective* luminous; **un panneau lumineux** an electronic display board; **une enseigne lumineuse** a neon sign.

lunch *noun* M buffet *(lunch or supper)*.

lundi *noun* M **1** Monday; **nous sommes lundi aujourd'hui** it's Monday today; **lundi prochain** next Monday; **lundi dernier** last Monday; **2** on Monday; **je l'ai vu lundi soir** I saw him on Monday evening; **3 le lundi** on Mondays; **fermé le lundi** closed on Mondays; **4 tous les lundis** every Monday.

lune *noun* F moon; ★ **il est dans la lune** he's got his head in the clouds; ★ **il m'a promis la lune** he promised me the earth.

lune de miel *noun* F honeymoon.

lunettes *plural noun* F glasses; **une paire de lunettes** a pair of glasses; **mets tes lunettes!** put on your glasses!; **je porte des lunettes pour lire** I wear glasses to read.

lunettes de natation *plural noun* F swimming goggles.

lunettes de soleil *plural noun* F sun-glasses.

lutte noun F fight, struggle; **la lutte contre la drogue** the fight against drugs.

lutter verb [1] to fight, to struggle; **ils luttaient pour la liberté et contre l'oppression** they were fighting for freedom and against oppression.

luxe noun M luxury; **une voiture de luxe** a luxury car.

luxueux (F **luxueuse**) adjective luxurious.

lycée noun M secondary school (for ages 15–18).

lycéen, lycéenne noun M, F secondary school student.

M m

M. SHORT FOR **Monsieur; M. Dupont** Mr Dupont.

ma adjective my; SEE **mon.**

macaronis plural noun M macaroni; **manger des macaronis** to have macaroni.

mâche noun F lamb's lettuce.

mâcher verb [1] to chew.

machin noun M (informal) whatsit, thingumajig; **tu n'as pas un machin pour ouvrir les enveloppes?** don't you have a whatsit for opening envelopes with?

machine noun F 1 machine; **2 taper à la machine** to type.

machine à coudre noun F sewing machine.

machine à écrire noun F typewriter.

machine à laver noun F washing machine.

machine à sous noun F fruit machine.

mâchoire noun F jaw.

mâchonner verb [1] to chew.

maçon noun M 1 builder; 2 bricklayer.

Madame (plural **Mesdames**) noun F 1 **Madame Jones** Ms Jones, Mrs Jones; **2 Madame,...** Dear Madam...; 3 **bonsoir madame** good evening (when greeting a person you do not know well in French, it is polite to add 'Madame', 'Monsieur', or 'Mademoiselle' to the greeting).

Mademoiselle (plural **Mesdemoiselles**) noun F 1 Miss, Ms; **2 bonsoir mademoiselle** good evening; SEE ALSO **Madame.**

magasin noun M shop; **un grand magasin** a department store; **un magasin de vêtements** a clothes shop; **un magasin de sport** a sports shop; **faire les magasins** to go round the shops.

magazine noun M magazine.

maghrébin adjective North African.

Maghrébin, Maghrébine noun M, F North African.

magicien, magicienne noun M, F magician.

magie noun F magic.

magique adjective 1 magic;
2 magical.

magistral (M plural magistraux)
adjective un cours magistral a
lecture (at university).

magnétique adjective magnetic.

magnétiser verb [1] 1 to
magnetize; 2 to hypnotize.

magnétophone noun M tape
recorder.

magnétoscope noun M video
recorder.

magnifique adjective splendid.

magouille noun F (informal)
fiddling.

magret de canard noun M duck
breast.

mai noun M May; en mai, au mois
de mai in May; le premier mai May
Day.

maigre adjective thin, skinny;
★ maigre comme un clou as thin as
a rake (literally: as thin as a nail).

maigrir verb [2] to lose weight; il a
beaucoup maigri he's lost a lot of
weight.

maille noun F stitch (in knitting).

maillot noun M 1 shirt, jersey (in
sports such as football); 2 maillot
(de corps) vest.

maillot de bain noun M
1 swimsuit; 2 swimming trunks.

main noun F hand; avoir quelque
chose à la main to have something
in your hand; serrer la main à
quelqu'un to shake hands with
somebody; se serrer la main to

shake hands; nous nous sommes
serré la main we shook hands; se
donner la main to hold hands; haut
les mains! hands up!; donner un
coup de main à quelqu'un to give
somebody a hand; tu veux un coup
de main? do you want a hand?; fait
à la main handmade.

main-d'œuvre noun F labour.

maintenant adverb 1 now; il est
maintenant trop tard pour sortir it's
too late to go out now; 2 nowadays;
maintenant presque tout le monde
a le téléphone nowadays nearly
everybody has a phone.

maintenir verb [81] 1 to maintain;
2 to support.

maire noun M mayor.

mairie noun F 1 town hall; 2 town
council.

mais conjunction 1 but; j'ai essayé
de t'appeler mais tu n'étais pas là
I tried to phone you but you weren't
there; 2 mais oui yes of course;
mais non of course not.

maïs noun M 1 maize;
2 sweetcorn; 3 des épis de maïs
corn on the cob.

maison noun F 1 house; leur
maison est petite mais très
confortable their house is small but
very comfortable; 2 home; rester à
la maison to stay at home; rentrer à
la maison to go home.

maître, maîtresse noun M, F
1 master, mistress; 2 teacher.

maître-nageur noun M
swimming instructor.

maîtresse noun SEE maître.

maîtrise noun F 1 mastery;
2 command; **la maîtrise de soi** self-
control; 3 master's degree.

maîtriser verb [1] 1 to control;
2 to master.

majestueux (F **majestueuse**)
adjective majestic.

majeur adjective 1 major; 2 **être
majeur** to be over 18.

majorité noun F majority.

majuscule noun F capital (letter);
en majuscules in block capitals; **un
R majuscule** a capital R.

mal (plural **maux**) noun M 1 pain,
ache; **faire mal** to hurt; **se faire mal**
to hurt yourself; **avoir mal à la
gorge** to have a sore throat; **j'ai mal
au dos** my back hurts; **ça fait mal** it
hurts; 2 **faire mal à quelqu'un** to
hurt somebody; **aïe ! tu me fais mal !**
ouch ! you're hurting me !; 3 **avoir du
mal à faire** to have difficulty in
doing; **j'ai du mal à comprendre ce
qu'il dit** I have difficulty in
understanding what he says; **se
donner du mal à faire** to go to a lot
of trouble to do; **elle s'est donné
beaucoup de mal pour contacter
tout le monde** she went to a lot of
trouble to contact everybody;
4 evil.
adjective 1 **pas mal** not bad;
2 **être mal** to be uncomfortable.
adverb 1 badly; **écrire mal** to write
badly; 2 **je t'entends mal** I can't
hear you very well; 3 **j'ai mal
compris** I misunderstand; 4 **être
mal à l'aise** to feel uncomfortable.

malade noun M & F patient.
adjective ill, sick; **tomber malade** to
fall ill.

maladie noun F 1 illness;
2 disease.

maladresse noun F
1 clumsiness; 2 blunder.

maladroit adjective clumsy.

malaise noun M 1 **avoir un
malaise** to feel faint, to pass out;
2 **créer un malaise** to make people
feel uncomfortable; **ça a créé un
malaise** it made everybody feel
uncomfortable.

malaxer verb [1] 1 to knead; 2 to
cream.

malchance noun F bad luck.

mal de mer noun M **avoir le mal
de mer** to be seasick.

mal du pays noun M **avoir le mal
du pays** to be homesick.

mâle noun M,
adjective male.

malédiction noun F curse.

malencontreux (F
malencontreuse) adjective
unfortunate.

malentendu noun M
misunderstanding.

malfaiteur noun M criminal.

mal famé adjective **un quartier mal
famé** a rough area.

malgré preposition 1 in spite of;
malgré le froid in spite of the cold;
2 **malgré tout** all the same; **mais
malgré tout nous avons décidé d'y**

aller but we decided to go all the same.

malheur noun M misfortune; **porter malheur** to bring bad luck.

malheureusement adverb unfortunately; **Vincent était déjà parti, malheureusement** unfortunately, Vincent had already left.

malheureux, malheureuse noun M, F poor thing; **la malheureuse!** poor woman! adjective 1 unhappy; **avoir l'air malheureux** to look unhappy; **rendre quelqu'un malheureux** to make somebody unhappy; 2 unfortunate; **un choix malheureux** an unfortunate choice.

malhonnête adjective dishonest.

malice noun F mischief.

malicieux (F malicieuse) adjective mischievous.

malin (F maligne) adjective 1 clever; **ce n'était pas très malin ça** that wasn't very clever; **elle se croit maligne** she thinks she's clever; 2 malignant (tumour).

malle noun F trunk.

malodorant adjective smelly.

malpoli adjective rude.

malpropre adjective dirty.

malsain adjective unhealthy.

maltraiter verb [1] to ill-treat; **les enfants maltraités** battered children.

malveillance noun F malice.

malveillant adjective malicious.

maman noun F mum, mummy.

mamie noun F granny, gran, nan.

mammifère noun M mammal.

manager verb [52] to manage.

manageur noun M manager.

manche¹ noun M handle (of a tool).

manche² noun F 1 sleeve; **une chemise à manches courtes** a short-sleeved shirt; **sans manches** sleeveless; 2 leg (of a match).

Manche noun F **la Manche** the Channel; **le tunnel sous la Manche** the Channel Tunnel.

mandarine noun F mandarin orange.

mandat noun M money order.

manège noun M 1 merry-go-round; 2 riding school.

manette noun F lever.

mangeable adjective edible.

manger noun M food. verb [52] to eat; **qu'est-ce qu'on va manger?** what shall we have to eat?; **manger au restaurant** to go out for a meal; **j'ai déjà mangé** I've already eaten; **j'ai assez mangé** I'm full, I've had enough; **donner à manger à** to feed; ★ **manger ses mots** to mumble (literally: to eat your words).

mangue noun F mango.

maniaque noun M & F fusspot. adjective extremely fussy.

manie noun F 1 odd habit; 2 mania.

manier *verb* [1] to handle.

manière *noun* F **1** way; **une manière plus facile** an easier way; **on ne peut pas le faire d'une manière plus facile?** isn't there an easier way of doing it?; **de cette manière** like this, like that; **d'une autre manière** in another way; **d'une manière ou d'une autre** one way or another; **d'une certaine manière** in a way; **2 de toute manière** in any case; **3 de manière à faire** so as to do; **de manière à éviter de dépenser de l'argent** so as to avoid spending money; **4 manières** manners; **ne fais pas de manières!** don't make a fuss!

manifestant, manifestante *noun* M, F demonstrator.

manifestation *noun* F demonstration; **une manifestation contre le racisme** a demonstration against racism.

manifester *verb* [1] **1** to demonstrate, to take part in a demonstration; **2 manifester quelque chose** to express something.

manipuler *verb* [1] **1** to handle; **2** to manipulate.

manivelle *noun* F handle.

mannequin *noun* M **1** fashion model; **2** dummy (*either in a shop window or as used by a dressmaker*).

manoir *noun* M manor house.

manque *noun* M **manque de** lack of, shortage of; **leur manque d'imagination** their lack of imagination; **être en manque**

d'affection to be in need of affection.

manqué *adjective* **1** failed; **un acteur manqué** a failed actor; **2** missed; **une occasion manquée** a missed opportunity.

manquer *verb* [1] **1 manquer quelque chose** to miss something; **il a manqué son train** he missed his train; **2 manquer un examen** to fail an exam; **3 manquer à quelqu'un** to be missed by somebody; **tu me manques** I miss you; **Londres leur manque** they miss London; **4 il manque quelque chose** something's missing; **il manque trois fourchettes** there are three forks missing, we're three forks short; **5 manquer de** to lack; **nous ne manquons pas de verres** there's no shortage of glasses; **6 manquer de faire** to fail to do; **il a manqué de fermer la porte à clé** he failed to lock the door.

mansarde *noun* F attic room.

manteau (*plural* **manteaux**) *noun* M coat.

manuel *noun* M **1** manual; **2** textbook; **un manuel scolaire** a school book.
adjective (F **manuelle**) manual.

manufacture *noun* F **1** factory; **2** manufacture.

manuscrit *noun* M manuscript.
adjective handwritten; **un petit mot manuscrit** a handwritten note.

maquereau (*plural* **maquereaux**) *noun* M mackerel.

maquette *noun* F scale model.

maquillage noun M make-up.

maquiller verb [1] se maquiller to put on your make-up.

marais noun M marsh.

marathon noun M marathon.

marbre noun M marble; une cheminée en marbre a marble fireplace.

marc de café noun M coffee grounds.

marchand, marchande noun M, F 1 shopkeeper; la marchande de fromage the woman in the cheese shop; 2 stallholder (on a market).

marchand de journaux noun M newsagent.

marchander verb [1] to haggle (over).

marchandise noun F goods.

marche noun F 1 walking; faire de la marche to go walking; 2 march; 3 step; les marches d'escalier the stairs; attention à la marche mind the step; 4 mettre en marche to start up (a machine); être en état de marche to be in working order.

marche arrière noun F reverse; faire marche arrière to reverse.

marché noun M 1 market; aller au marché to go to market; le marché aux fleurs the flower market; un marché aux puces a flea market; le marché de l'emploi the job market; 2 deal.

marchepied noun M step (on a train).

marcher verb [1] 1 to walk; on va marcher jusqu'à la gare we'll walk as far as the station; 2 marcher dans quelque chose to tread in something; marcher sur quelque chose to tread on something; 3 to march; 4 to work; ça a marché it worked; la machine à laver ne marche pas the washing machine doesn't work; les trains ne marchent pas aujourd'hui the trains are not running today; 5 et ton boulot, ça marche? (informal) and is your job going all right?; ★ faire marcher quelqu'un to pull somebody's leg.

marcheur, marcheuse noun M, F walker.

mardi noun M 1 Tuesday; nous sommes mardi aujourd'hui it's Tuesday today; mardi prochain next Tuesday; mardi dernier last Tuesday; 2 on Tuesday; je t'appellerai mardi soir I'll ring you on Tuesday evening; 3 le mardi on Tuesdays; c'est fermé le mardi it's closed on Tuesdays; 4 tous les mardis every Tuesday.

Mardi gras noun M Shrove Tuesday.

mare noun F pond.

marée noun F tide; la marée monte the tide's coming in; la marée descend the tide's going out.

margarine noun F margarine.

marge noun F 1 margin; 2 en marge de on the fringe of.

marguerite noun F 1 marguerite; 2 oxeye daisy.

mari noun M husband; le mari de Claire Claire's husband.

mariage noun M 1 marriage;
2 wedding; **être invité à un
mariage** to be invited to a wedding.

Marianne noun F Marianne (*a
woman figure representing the
French Republic in statues and
paintings*).

marié, mariée noun M, F
bridegroom, bride; **les jeunes
mariés** the newlyweds.
adjective married.

marier verb [1] 1 **se marier** to get
married; **ils se sont mariés à
Londres** they got married in
London; **elle s'est mariée avec
Frank** she married Frank; 2 **le
prêtre qui les a mariés** the priest
who married them.

marin noun M sailor.
adjective sea.

marine *adjective* **bleu marine** navy
blue.

mariner verb [1] to marinate.

marionnette noun F puppet.

marjolaine noun F marjoram.

marketing noun M marketing.

marmelade noun F **marmelade
d'oranges amères** orange
marmalade.

marmite noun F cooking pot.

marmonner verb [1] to mutter, to
mumble.

Maroc noun M Morocco.

marocain *adjective* Moroccan.

maroquinerie noun F 1 leather
shop; 2 leather goods.

marquant *adjective* outstanding.

marque noun F 1 brand; **une
marque de nourriture pour chats**
a brand of cat food; 2 make; **c'est une
marque de jean bien connue** it's a
well-known make of jeans; 3 mark;
4 point.

marque déposée noun F
registered trademark.

marquer verb [1] 1 to mark; 2 to
write down; **j'ai marqué ton nom**
I've written down your name;
3 **marquer un but** to score a goal.

marqueur noun M marker pen.

marraine noun F godmother.

marrant *adjective* (*informal*) funny.

marre *adverb* (*informal*) **j'en ai
marre** I'm fed up; **j'en ai marrre
d'écrire** I'm fed up with writing.

marrer verb [1] 1 **se marrer** to have
a great time; 2 **se marrer** to have a
good laugh.

marron noun M 1 (sweet)
chestnut; 2 (horse) chestnut.
adjective brown; **des chaussures
marron** brown shoes; **marron clair**
light brown; **marron foncé** dark
brown.

marronnier noun M chestnut tree.

mars noun M March; **en mars, au
mois de mars** in March.

Marseillaise noun F **la
Marseillaise** the Marseillaise (*the
French national anthem*).

Marseille noun Marseilles.

marteau noun M 1 hammer;
2 doorknocker.

marteau piqueur noun M pneumatic drill.

marteler verb [45] to hammer.

martinet noun M swift.

martin-pêcheur noun M kingfisher.

martyrisé adjective un enfant martyrisé a battered child.

mascotte noun F mascot.

masculin noun M masculine (in French and other grammars); **au masculin** in the masculine. adjective **1** male; **le sexe masculin** the male sex; **2** men's; **les vêtements masculins** men's clothing; **3** masculine.

masque noun M mask.

masquer verb [1] to hide.

massacre noun M massacre.

massacrer verb [1] to massacre.

massage noun M massage; **faire un massage à quelqu'un** to give somebody a massage.

masse noun F **1** mass; **2** une masse de** (informal) masses of; **j'ai une masse de boulot à faire avant lundi** I've got masses of work to do for Monday.

masser verb [1] **1** to massage; **2 se masser** to assemble.

massif (F massive) adjective **1** solid; **une table en pin massif** a solid pine table; **2** massive.

mass media plural noun M **les mass media** the mass media.

mastic noun M **1** putty; **2** filler.

mastiquer verb [1] **1** to chew; **2** to putty (a window); **3** to fill (a crack).

mat adjective matt.

mât noun M **1** mast; **2** pole.

match noun M match; **un match de foot** a football match; **faire match nul** to draw.

matelas noun M mattress.

matelassé adjective quilted.

matelot noun M sailor.

matériaux plural noun M materials; **les matériaux de construction** building materials.

matériel noun M equipment; **matériel de sport** sports equipment.

maternel (F maternelle) adjective **1** motherly; **2** maternal; **ma tante maternelle** my aunt on my mother's side of the family.

maternelle noun F (state) nursery school (for ages 2 – 6); **aller en maternelle** to go to nursery school.

maternité noun F **1** motherhood; **2** pregnancy; **être en congé de maternité** to be on maternity leave; **3** maternity unit.

mathématiques plural noun F mathematics.

maths plural noun F maths.

matière noun F subject; **la matière que j'aime le mieux c'est l'histoire** the subject I like best is history.

matières grasses plural noun F fat.

matin noun M morning; **à quelle heure est-ce que tu te lèves le**

matin? what time do you get up in the morning?; **à six heures du matin** at six o'clock in the morning; **du matin au soir** from morning till night; **de bon matin** early in the morning.

matinal (M plural **matinaux**) adjective **1** morning; **2 être matinal** to be an early riser.

matinée noun F **1** morning; **au cours de la matinée** during the morning; **2** matinée.

matou noun M tomcat.

matraque noun F truncheon, club.

matrimonial adjective **une agence matrimoniale** a marriage bureau.

maturité noun F maturity.

maudire verb to curse.

maussade adjective **1** sullen; **2** dull, dreary (weather).

mauvais adjective **1** bad; **une mauvaise expérience** a bad experience; **ça sent mauvais ici** there's a nasty smell here; **ça a mauvais goût** it tastes horrible; **c'est du mauvais goût** it's bad taste; **2** wrong; **le mauvais numéro** the wrong number; **la mauvaise adresse** the wrong address; **3 il fait mauvais** the weather's bad; **4 elle a mauvaise mine** she doesn't look well.

mauvaise herbe noun F weed.

maux plural noun M **des maux de tête** headaches.

maximum noun M, adjective maximum; **au maximum** as much as possible; **au maximum** at the most; **faire le maximum** to do your utmost.

mayonnaise noun F mayonnaise.

mazout noun M fuel oil.

me, m' (before a vowel or silent 'h') pronoun me; **1 elle me déteste** she hates me; **il m'a vu** he saw me; **2** to me; **elle ne me parle jamais** she never speaks to me; **elle m'a donné son adresse** she gave me her address; **il me l'a donné** he gave it to me; **3** myself; **je me fais une salade** I'm making myself a salad; **je me suis blessé** I hurt myself; **je me lève à sept heures** I get up at seven o'clock; **je me brosse les dents** I brush my teeth (literally: I brush to myself the teeth).

mec noun M (informal) guy.

mécanicien, mécanicienne noun M, F **1** mechanic; **2** train driver.

mécanique noun F **1** mechanics; **2** mechanism. adjective **1** mechanical; **2** clockwork.

mécanisme noun M mechanism.

méchamment adverb spitefully, nastily.

méchanceté noun F **1** nastiness; **2** spite.

méchant adjective **1** nasty; **elle a été vraiment méchante avec moi** she was really nasty to me; **2** spiteful; **3** vicious; **'chien méchant'** 'beware of the dog'.

mèche noun F **1** lock (of hair); **2** wick.

méconnaissable *adjective* unrecognizable.

mécontent *adjective* dissatisfied.

mécontentement *noun* M 1 annoyance; 2 displeasure.

médaille *noun* F medal.

médecin *noun* M doctor; **aller chez le médecin** to go to the doctor's.

médecine *noun* F medicine; **faire des études de médecine** to go to medical school.

médias *plural noun* M **les médias** the media.

médiathèque *noun* F multimedia library.

médical (M *plural* **médicaux**) *adjective* medical.

médicament *noun* M drug.

médiéval (M *plural* **médiévaux**) *adjective* medieval.

médiocre *adjective* second-rate, poor; **un travail médiocre** a second-rate piece of work.

méditation *noun* F meditation.

méditer *verb* [1] 1 to meditate; 2 **méditer quelque chose** to mull something over.

Méditerranée *noun* F **la Méditerranée** the Mediterranean.

méditerranéen (F **méditerranéenne**) *adjective* Mediterranean; **la cuisine méditerranéenne** Mediterranean cooking.

méduse *noun* F jellyfish.

méfait *noun* M 1 crime; 2 **les méfaits de la pollution** the detrimental effects of pollution.

méfiance *noun* F suspicion.

méfiant *adjective* suspicious.

méfier *verb* [1] **se méfier de quelqu'un** not to trust somebody; **méfie-toi!** watch out!

mégère *noun* F shrew.

mégot *noun* M cigarette end.

meilleur *noun* M best; **c'est le meilleur** it's the best one; **le meilleur des deux** the better of the two. *adjective* better; **le climat est bien meilleur au sud** the climate's much better in the south; **meilleur que** better than; **ton écriture est meilleure que la mienne** your writing's better than mine; **c'est meilleur que l'autre** it's better than the other one.

mélange *noun* M mixture.

mélanger *verb* [52] 1 to mix; 2 to mix up; **j'ai mélangé les dates** I got the dates mixed up.

mélasse *noun* F black treacle.

mêlée *noun* F scrum.

mêler *verb* [1] 1 **se mêler à** to mingle with; 2 **se mêler de** to meddle in; ★ **mêle-toi de ce qui te regarde!** mind your own business!

mélodie *noun* F melody, tune.

mélomane *noun* M & F music lover.

melon *noun* M 1 melon; 2 **un chapeau melon** a bowler hat.

membre noun M 1 member;
2 limb.

même adjective 1 same; j'ai le
même anniversaire que toi I have
the same birthday as you; ils avaient
des chapeaux de la même couleur
they had the same colour hats; 2 en
même temps at the same time;
3 tout de même all the same.
adverb even; il n'a même pas
demandé he didn't even ask.

mémé noun (informal) F
1 granny; 2 une vieille mémé an
old lady.

mémoire noun F memory.

mémoriser verb [1] to memorize.

menace noun F threat.

menacer verb [61] to threaten.

ménage noun M 1 housework;
faire le ménage to do the cleaning;
une femme de ménage a cleaning
lady; 2 household.

ménager[1] verb [52] ménager
quelqu'un to handle somebody
tactfully.

ménager[2] (F ménagère) adjective
household; les appareils ménagers
household appliances; les travaux
ménagers housework.

mendiant, mendiante noun M,
F beggar.

mendier verb [1] to beg.

mener verb [50] 1 to lead; mener à
to lead to; le chemin qui mène à la
ferme the track which leads to the
farm; 2 mener une société to run
a company; 3 mener une
campagne to conduct a campaign.

méningite noun F meningitis.

menottes plural noun F handcuffs.

mensonge noun M lie; dire des
mensonges to tell lies.

mensualité noun F monthly
payment.

mensuel (F mensuelle) adjective
monthly.

mental (M plural mentaux)
adjective mental.

mentalité noun F mentality.

menteur, menteuse noun M, F
liar.
adjective untruthful.

menthe noun F mint; le sirop de
menthe mint cordial.

mention noun F 1 mention;
2 grade (in an exam or a degree); elle
a eu son bac avec mention bien she
got a grade B pass in her
baccalauréate.

mentionner verb [1] to mention.

mentir verb [53] to lie, to tell lies.

menton noun M chin.

menu[1] noun M menu; qu'est-ce
qu'il y a au menu? what's on the
menu?; le menu du jour today's
menu.

menu[2] adjective very small.

menuiserie noun F woodwork.

menuisier noun M joiner.

mépris noun M contempt.

mépriser verb [1] to despise.

mer *noun* F sea; **aller à la mer** to go to the seaside; **au bord de la mer** at the seaside.

mercerie *noun* F haberdashery.

merci[1] *exclamation* thank you, thanks; **merci beaucoup, merci bien** thank you very much; **merci de m'avoir rappelé** thank you for calling me back.

merci[2] *noun* F mercy.

mercredi *noun* M **1** Wednesday; **nous sommes mercredi aujourd'hui** it's Wednesday today; **mercredi prochain** next Wednesday; **mercredi dernier** last Wednesday; **2** on Wednesday; **je t'appellerai mercredi soir** I'll ring you on Wednesday evening; **3 le mercredi** on Wednesdays; **c'est fermé le mercredi** it's closed on Wednesdays; **tous les mercredis** every Wednesday.

mercure *noun* M mercury.

Mer du Nord *noun* F North Sea.

mère *noun* F mother; **la mère de Sophie** Sophie's mother.

merguez *noun* F spicy lamb sausage.

méridional (M *plural* **méridionaux**) *adjective* southern.

meringue *noun* F meringue.

mérite *noun* F merit.

mériter *verb* [1] to deserve.

merle *noun* M blackbird.

merveille *noun* F **1** wonder; **ton gâteau est une vraie merveille** your cake's absolutely wonderful; **2 à merveille** wonderfully.

merveilleux (F **merveilleuse**) *adjective* marvellous.

mes *adjective* SEE **mon**.

Mesdames *noun* SEE **Madame**.

Mesdemoiselles *noun* SEE **Mademoiselle**.

mesquin *adjective* petty, mean.

message *noun* M message.

messager, messagère *noun* M, F messenger.

messe *noun* F mass; **aller à la messe** to go to mass.

Messieurs *noun* SEE **Monsieur**.

mesure *noun* F **1** measurement; **prendre les mesures de la pièce** to take the measurements of the room; **2 sur mesure** tailor-made; **3** measure; **prendre des mesures pour faire** to take measures to do; **le conseil municipal va prendre des mesures pour contrôler la pollution** the town council is going to take measures to control pollution; **4 être en mesure de faire** to be in a position to do; **nous ne sommes pas en mesure de vous aider** we are not in a position to help you.

mesurer *verb* [1] to measure.

met *verb* SEE **mettre**.

métal (*plural* **métaux**) *noun* M metal.

métallique *adjective* metallic.

métallisé *adjective* metallic; **bleu métallisé** metallic blue.

météo noun F weather forecast.

méthode noun F 1 method; **une méthode de faire** a method of doing; 2 manual, tutor.

métier noun M 1 job; 2 **un métier à tisser** a weaving loom.

mètre noun M 1 metre; 2 metre rule.

métrique adjective metric.

métro noun M underground; **une station de métro** an underground station.

mets verb SEE **mettre**.

metteur en scène noun M 1 director (of a film); 2 producer (of a play).

mettre verb [11] 1 to put; **où as-tu mis le sel?** where have you put the salt?; 2 to put on; **je vais mettre mon manteau** I'm going to put my coat on; 3 to wear; **mets ta jupe rose** wear your pink skirt; 4 to turn on (radio, television, heating); **mettre le réveil** to set the alarm clock; 5 **mettre quelqu'un en colère** to make somebody angry; 6 **j'ai mis trois heures pour le faire** it took me three hours to do it; 7 **se mettre quelque part** to stand (or sit) somewhere; 8 **se mettre debout** to stand up; 9 **se mettre à faire** to start to do; **elle s'est mise à chanter** she started to sing.

meuble noun M 1 **des meubles** furniture; 2 **un meuble** a piece of furniture.

meublé adjective furnished.

meule noun F 1 millstone; 2 **une meule de foin** a haystack.

meurtre noun M murder.

meurtrier, meurtrière noun M, F murderer.
adjective 1 deadly; 2 fatal.

Mexico noun Mexico City.

Mexique noun M Mexico; **aller au Mexique** to go to Mexico.

mi- prefix 1 half-; **mi-clos** half-shut; 2 mid-; **à la mi-février** in mid-February.

mi-bas noun M knee sock.

mi-chemin noun à **mi-chemin** halfway.

micro noun M microphone.

microbe noun M germ.

micro-ondes noun M microwave; **faire cuire quelque chose au micro-ondes** to cook something in the microwave.

micro-ordinateur noun M microcomputer.

microscope noun M microscope.

midi noun M 1 midday, noon; **il est midi vingt** it's twenty past twelve; **je viendrai vers midi** I'll come around twelve; **je fais mes courses à midi** I do my shopping in my lunch hour.

Midi noun M **le Midi** the South of France.

miel noun M honey.

mien, mienne, miens, miennes pronoun **le mien, la mienne, les miens, les miennes** mine; **'à qui sont ces chaussures?'** – **'ce sont les miennes'** 'whose shoes are these?' – 'they're mine'; **Puis-je**

t'emprunter ton vélo? Le mien est chez moi Can I borrow your bike? Mine's at home.

miette noun F crumb.

mieux adjective,
adverb 1 better; **tu la connais mieux que moi** you know her better than I do; **je me sens mieux** I feel better; **mon père va mieux maintenant** my father's better now; **c'est mieux comme ça** it's better like that; 2 **il vaut mieux que tu restes chez toi** it would be better if you stayed at home. 3 best; **c'est le rouge que j'aime le mieux** I like the red one best.
noun M **le mieux est de revenir** the best thing is to come back; **au mieux** at best, at least; **pour le mieux** for the best.

mignon (F **mignonne**) adjective sweet.

migraine noun F headache, migraine.

mijoter verb [1] to simmer.

milieu noun M 1 middle; **au milieu de** in the middle of; 2 background; **il vient d'un milieu pauvre** he comes from a poor background; 3 environment.

militaire noun M serviceman.
adjective military; **le service militaire** military service.

mille number a thousand; **mille personnes** a thousand people; **deux mille personnes** two thousand people.

millefeuille noun M vanilla slice.

mille-pattes noun M centipede.

milliard noun M thousand million.

milliardaire noun M & F multimillionaire.

millier noun M thousand; **des milliers de francs** thousands of francs.

milligramme noun M milligramme.

millimètre noun M millimetre.

million noun M million; **deux millions de francs** two million francs.

millionnaire noun M & F millionaire.

mime noun M & F mime artist.

mimer verb [1] 1 to mime; 2 to mimic.

minable adjective (informal) 1 pathetic; **ses plaisanteries sont minables** her jokes are pathetic; 2 crummy; **un film minable** a crummy film.

mince adjective 1 thin; **une mince tranche de viande** a thin slice of meat; 2 slim; 3 **mince alors!** (informal) oh bother!

minceur noun F 1 thinness; 2 slimness.

mine noun F 1 **avoir bonne mine** to look well; **tu as mauvaise mine** you don't look well; 2 expression; 3 mine; **une mine de charbon** a coalmine; 4 pencil lead.

minéral (plural **minéraux**) noun M mineral.
adjective mineral; **eau minérale** mineral water.

minet, minette noun M, F
pussycat.

mineur[1] noun M miner.

mineur[2], **mineure** noun M, F
person under 18.
adjective **1** minor; **2** under 18.

minijupe noun F mini-skirt.

minimal (M plural **minimaux**)
adjective minimal.

minimiser verb [1] **1** to minimize;
2 to play down.

minimum noun M,
adjective minimum; **au minimum** at
the very least.

ministère noun M ministry.

ministre noun M minister.

Minitel™ noun M (Minitel is
France Telecom's online data service;
subscribers have a small computer
linked to the telephone and can use it
to access a large number of services
including the telephone directories).

minorité noun F minority.

minou noun M pussycat.

minuit noun M midnight; **à minuit**
at midnight.

minuscule noun F small letter (as
opposed to a capital letter).
adjective tiny.

minute noun F minute; **dans dix
minutes** in ten minutes; **dix
minutes plus tard** ten minutes later;
d'une minute à l'autre any minute
now.

minuterie noun F time-switch.

mirabelle noun F small yellow
plum.

miracle noun M miracle; **par
miracle** miraculously.
adjective wonder.

miraculeux (F **miraculeuse**)
adjective miraculous.

miroir noun M mirror; **au miroir** in
the mirror.

mis verb SEE **mettre**.

miser verb [1] to bet.

misérable adjective poor.

misère noun F destitution, extreme
poverty.

missionnaire noun M & F
missionary.

mistral noun M mistral (a strong
cold north wind which blows down
the Rhône valley to the
Mediterranean).

mite noun F clothes moth.

mi-temps[1] noun M part-time job;
travailler à mi-temps to work part-
time.

mi-temps[2] noun F half-time (in a
match).

miteux (F **miteuse**) adjective seedy,
shabby.

mitraillette noun F submachine
gun.

mixer verb [1] to mix.

mixte adjective **1** mixed;
2 coeducational.

Mlle SHORT FOR **Mademoiselle**.

Mme SHORT FOR **Madame**.

mobile noun M **1** motive;
2 mobile.
adjective **1** mobile; **2** feuilles

mobiles loose sheets (*as opposed to a pad of paper*).

mobilier *noun* M furniture.

mobylette *noun* F moped.

mocassin *noun* M 1 loafer; 2 moccasin.

moche *adjective* (*informal*) 1 awful; 2 ugly.

mode[1] *noun* F fashion; **être à la mode** to be fashionable.

mode[2] *noun* M way, mode.

mode d'emploi *noun* M instructions for use.

mode de vie *noun* M way of life.

modèle *noun* M 1 model; 2 style; **ce modèle existe en plusieurs coloris** this style is available in several colours.

modéré *adjective* moderate.

moderne *adjective* modern.

moderniser *verb* [1] to modernize.

modernité *noun* F modernity.

modeste *adjective* 1 modest; 2 humble.

modestie *noun* F modesty.

modifier *verb* [1] to change.

modiste *noun* F milliner.

module *noun* M 1 module; 2 kitchen unit.

moelle *noun* F marrow (*of bone*).

moelleux (F **moelleuse**) *adjective* 1 soft; 2 mellow.

mœurs *plural noun* F 1 customs; 2 morals.

moi *pronoun* 1 me; **c'est pour moi** it's for me; **pas moi** not me; 2 **moi, je pense que...** I think that...; 3 **à moi** mine; **ce n'est pas à moi** it's not mine; **un ami à moi** a friend of mine.

moi-même *pronoun* myself; **je l'ai fait moi-même** I did it myself.

moindre *adjective* slightest; **le moindre problème** the slightest problem; **je n'ai pas la moindre idée** I haven't the slightest idea.

moine *noun* M monk.

moineau (*plural* **moineaux**) *noun* M sparrow.

moins *preposition* 1 minus; **sept moins deux égale cinq** seven minus two equals five; 2 **il est dix heures moins cinq** it's five to ten. *adverb* 1 less; **tu en as moins que moi** you've got less than me; **de moins en moins** less and less; **il est moins grand que son frère** he's not as tall as his brother; **c'est moins loin** it's not as far; **j'aime moins le bleu** I don't like the blue one as much; 2 **le moins** the least; **le moins difficile** the least difficult; **le moins gros** the smallest; 3 **moins de** less, fewer; **moins de beurre** less butter; **moins de voitures** fewer cars; 4 **au moins** at least; 5 **du moins** at least; 6 **à moins que** (+ *subjunctive*) unless; **à moins qu'elle soit malade** unless she's ill.

mois *noun* M month; **au mois de mai** in May; **le mois dernier** last

moisi

month; **le mois prochain** next month.

moisi noun M mould.
adjective mouldy.

moisir verb [2] to go mouldy.

moisson noun F harvest.

moite adjective **1** damp; **2** muggy.

moitié noun F **1** half; **la moitié d'une pomme** half an apple; **donnemoi la moitié** give me half; **la moitié du temps** half the time; **2** à **moitié** half; **à moitié vide** half empty.

moitié-moitié adverb half-and-half; **partager moitié-moitié** to go halves.

molaire noun F molar, back tooth.

molle adjective SEE **mou**.

mollet noun M calf (of the leg).
adjective **un œuf mollet** a softboiled egg.

molleton noun M flannel, flannelette.

môme noun M & F (informal) kid.

moment noun M moment; **un moment, s'il vous plaît** just a moment please; **en ce moment** at the moment; **par moments** at times; **pour le moment** for the moment; **au moment où** at the time when; **à ce moment** just at that moment, just then; **j'ai attendu un bon moment** I waited for a good while.

mon, ma, mes adjective my; **mon fils** my son; **ma fille** my daughter; **mes enfants** my children.

monarchie noun F monarchy.

monastère noun M monastery.

monde noun M **1** world; **2** people; **il y a beaucoup de monde** there are a lot of people; **peu de monde** not many people; **tout le monde** everybody.

mondial (M plural **mondiaux**) adjective **1** world; **la Seconde Guerre mondiale** the Second World War; **2** worldwide.

monétique noun F electronic banking.

moniteur[1] noun M monitor.

moniteur[2], **monitrice** noun M, F **1** instructor (sports or driving); **un moniteur de ski** a ski instructor; **2** camp leader.

monnaie noun F **1** currency; **2 une pièce de monnaie** a coin; **3** change; **je n'ai pas de monnaie** I don't have any change.

monopoliser verb [1] to monopolize.

monotone adjective monotonous.

Monsieur (plural **Messieurs**) noun M **1 Monsieur Lejay** Mr Lejay; **bonsoir monsieur** good evening (when greeting somebody you do not know well in French it is polite to add 'Monsieur', 'Madame', or 'Mademoiselle' to the greeting); **2** man; **un grand monsieur** a tall man; **les deux messieurs assis à la table** the two men sitting at the table.

monstre noun M monster.
adjective huge; **un travail monstre** a huge amount of work.

monstrueux (F monstrueuse) *adjective* monstrous.

mont *noun* M mountain; le mont Blanc Mont Blanc.

montagne *noun* F 1 mountain; la montagne the mountains; 2 une montagne de a mountain of.

montagneux (F montagneuse) *adjective* mountainous.

montant *noun* M sum. *adjective* rising.

monter *verb* [1] 1 to go up, to come up; monter l'escalier to go (or come) up the stairs; monter la colline to go up the hill; monter se coucher to go up to bed; 2 monter dans to get on (*a bus, train, etc*); 3 monter quelque chose to bring (or take) something up; je vais monter tes valises I'll take your cases up; 4 to assemble (*a kit*); 5 to rise; les prix ont monté prices have risen; 6 to increase; 7 monter à cheval to ride a horse.

montgolfière *noun* F hot-air balloon.

montre *noun* F watch.

montrer *verb* [1] 1 to show; montrer quelque chose à quelqu'un to show somebody something; montre-moi ton cadeau show me your present; 2 to point out; montrer quelque chose du doigt to point to something.

monture *noun* F frames (*of glasses*).

monument *noun* M 1 monument; un monument aux morts a war memorial; 2 historic building.

moquer *verb* [1] 1 se moquer de to make fun of; tout le monde s'est moqué de moi everybody made fun of me; 2 se moquer de not to care about; je m'en moque I couldn't care less.

moquette *noun* F fitted carpet.

moqueur (F moqueuse) *adjective* mocking.

moral (*plural* moraux) *noun* M morale; je n'ai pas le moral I'm feeling really down. *adjective* 1 moral; 2 mental.

morale *noun* F 1 moral; 2 morality.

morceau (*plural* morceaux) *noun* M piece, bit; un morceau de pain a piece of bread; un morceau de sucre a sugar lump.

mordre *verb* [3] to bite.

mordu *adjective* être mordu de quelque chose (*informal*) to be mad about something.

morne *adjective* 1 gloomy; 2 dismal, dreary.

morsure *noun* F bite.

mort[1] *noun* F death; trois mois avant sa mort three months before he died.

mort[2]**. morte** *noun* M, F dead man, dead woman. *adjective* dead.

mort-aux-rats *noun* F rat poison.

mortel (F mortelle) *adjective* 1 deadly; 2 fatal.

morue *noun* F 1 cod; 2 salt cod.

mosaïque *noun* F mosaic.

Moscou noun Moscow.

mosquée noun F mosque.

mot noun M **1** word; **mot à mot** word for word; **2 un petit mot** a note.

motard, motarde noun M, F (informal) motorcyclist.

mot de passe noun M password.

moteur noun M engine.

motif noun M **1** motive; **2** pattern.

motiver verb [1] to motivate.

moto noun F motorbike.

motocycliste noun M & F motorcyclist.

mots croisés plural noun M crossword.

mou, mol (before a vowel) (F **molle**) adjective **1** soft; **2** flabby.

mouche noun F fly.

moucher verb [1] **se moucher** to blow your nose.

moucheron noun M midge.

mouchoir noun M **1** handkerchief; **2** tissue.

moue noun F pout; **faire la moue** to pout.

mouette noun F seagull.

mouiller verb [1] **1** to wet; **2 se mouiller** to get wet.

moulant adjective tight-fitting.

moule[1] noun M mould.

moule[2] noun F mussel.

mouler verb [1] to mould.

moulin noun M mill.

moulin à vent noun M windmill.

moulu adjective ground; **le café moulu** ground coffee.

moulure noun F moulding.

mourir verb [54] to die; **elle est morte en février** she died in February; **je meurs de faim!** I'm starving!; **je meurs d'envie d'y aller** I'm dying to go there.

mousquetaire noun M musketeer.

moussant adjective foaming.

mousse noun F **1** foam; **mousse à raser** shaving foam; **2** lather; **3** froth; **4 mousse au chocolat** chocolate mousse; **5** moss.

mousser verb [1] to foam.

mousseux (F **mousseuse**) adjective **du vin mousseux** sparkling wine.

moustache noun F moustache.

moustique noun M mosquito.

moutarde noun F mustard.

mouton noun M **1** sheep; **2** mutton.

mouvement noun M **1** movement; **2** activity, bustle.

mouvementé adjective hectic, eventful; **j'ai eu une semaine mouvementée** I've had a hectic week.

moyen noun M **1** means; **un moyen de transport** a means of transport; **un moyen de faire** a means of doing; **je n'ai aucun moyen de le contacter** I have no means of contacting him; **2 les moyens** the

means, the wherewithal; **je n'ai pas les moyens de m'acheter un ordinateur** I can't afford to buy a computer; **3** way.
adjective (F **moyenne**) **1** average; **2** medium-sized; **3** average.

moyenne *noun* F **1** average; **en moyenne** on average; **2 avoir la moyenne** to pass (*an exam*).

Moyen-Orient *noun* M Middle East.

muet (F **muette**) *adjective* **1** speechless, dumb; **2** silent.

muguet *noun* M lily of the valley.

mulet *noun* M mule.

multifonction *adjective* multipurpose.

multiple *adjective* **1** multiple; **2** various.

multiplication *noun* F **1** multiplication; **2 multiplication de** increase in the number of.

multiplier *verb* [1] **1** to multiply; **2** to increase.

municipal (M *plural* **municipaux**) *adjective* **1** local, town; **2** municipal.

municipalité *noun* F **1** town (or local) council; **2** municipality.

mur *noun* M wall.

mûr *adjective* **1** ripe; **2** mature.

mûre *noun* F blackberry.

mûrir *verb* [2] **1** to ripen; **2** to mature; **3** to develop.

murmure *noun* M murmur.

murmurer *verb* [1] to murmur.

musc *noun* M musk.

muscade *noun* F nutmeg; **une noix de muscade** a nutmeg.

muscle *noun* M muscle.

musclé *adjective* muscular.

musculation *noun* F bodybuilding.

museau (*plural* **museaux**) *noun* M muzzle, snout.

musée *noun* M museum.

musical (M *plural* **musicaux**) *adjective* musical.

musicien, musicienne *noun* M, F musician.

musique *noun* F music; **mettre de la musique** to put on some music.

musulman, musulmane *noun* M, F, *adjective* Muslim.

mutuel (F **mutuelle**) *adjective* mutual.

myope *adjective* short-sighted; ★ **être myope comme une taupe** to be as blind as a bat (*literally: to be as short-sighted as a mole*).

myopie *noun* F short-sightedness.

myosotis *noun* M forget-me-not.

myrtille *noun* F bilberry.

mystère *noun* M mystery.

mystérieux (F **mystérieuse**) *adjective* mysterious.

mystifier *verb* [1] to fool.

mystique *adjective* mystical.

mythe *noun* M myth.

mythologie *noun* F mythology.

N n

n' *adverb* SEE ne.

nacre *noun* F mother-of-pearl.

nage *noun* F swimming.

nager *verb* [52] to swim.

nageur, nageuse *noun* M, F swimmer.

naïf (F **naïve**) *adjective* naïve.

nain, naine *noun* M, F, *adjective* dwarf.

naissance *noun* F birth; date de naissance date of birth.

naître *verb* [55] to be born; elle est née en 1975 she was born in 1975.

nana *noun* F (*informal*) girl.

naphtaline *noun* F mothballs.

nappe *noun* F tablecloth.

narcisse *noun* M narcissus.

narine *noun* F nostril.

natal *adjective* native; mon pays natal my native country.

natalité *noun* F le taux de natalité the birthrate.

natation *noun* F swimming; faire de la natation to go swimming.

natif (F **native**) *adjective* native.

nation *noun* F nation.

national (M *plural* **nationaux**) *adjective* national.

nationaliser *verb* [1] to nationalize.

nationalité *noun* F nationality.

natte *noun* F 1 plait; 2 mat.

nature *noun* F nature. *adjective* yaourt nature plain yoghurt; un thé nature a cup of tea without milk or sugar.

naturel *noun* M 1 nature; 2 au naturel plain. *adjective* (F **naturelle**) natural.

naturellement *adverb* of course.

nausée *noun* F nausea; avoir la nausée to feel sick.

nautique *adjective* water; faire du ski nautique to go water-skiing.

navet *noun* M turnip.

navette *noun* F shuttle; j'ai pris la navette de l'aéroport I took the shuttle from the airport; faire la navette to travel back and forth.

naviguer *verb* [1] to sail.

navire *noun* M ship.

navré *adjective* sorry; je suis vraiment navré I'm terribly sorry.

ne, n' (*before a vowel or silent 'h'*) *adverb* 1 ne + pas not; je n'aime pas le lait I don't like milk; 2 ne + jamais never; je ne vais jamais à Londres I never go to London; 3 ne + que only; je n'ai que dix francs I only have ten francs; **4 ne + plus** no longer; **elle n'habite plus à Londres** she no longer lives in London; **5 ne + rien** nothing; **il ne mange rien** he eats nothing; **rien ne t'empêche d'y aller** there's nothing to stop you going; **6 ne + personne** nobody; **il n'y a personne** there's nobody; **personne n'a compris** nobody understood.

né, née verb SEE **naître**.

néanmoins adverb nevertheless.

nécessaire noun M **faire le nécessaire** to do the necessary. adjective necessary; **il est nécessaire de faire** it is necessary to do; **est-ce qu'il est nécessaire de réserver?** is it necessary to book?

nécessairement adverb necessarily.

nécessité noun F necessity.

nécessiter verb [1] to require.

néerlandais noun M, adjective Dutch.

nef noun F nave (of a church).

négatif noun M, adjective (F **négative**) negative.

négligé adjective scruffy.

négligent adjective careless.

négliger verb [52] **1** to neglect; **2 il a négligé de le faire** he didn't bother to do it.

négociant noun M merchant.

négocier verb [1] to negotiate.

neige noun F snow; **un bonhomme de neige** a snowman.

neiger verb [52] to snow; **il neige** it's snowing.

nénuphar noun M waterlily.

néon noun M neon.

néo-zélandais adject.ve New Zealand.

Néo-Zélandais, Néo-Zélandaise noun M, F New Zealander.

nerf noun M nerve.

nerveux (F **nerveuse**) adjective nervous.

n'est-ce pas? adverb **il fait froid ce soir, n'est-ce pas?** it's cold this evening, isn't it?; **il habite à Paris, n'est-ce pas?** he lives in Paris, doesn't he?; **tu as déjà mangé, n'est-ce pas?** you've already eaten, haven't you?

net (F **nette**) adjective **1** clear; **c'est très net** it's quite clear; **2** distinct; **une nette différence** a distinct difference; **une nette amélioration** a distinct improvement. adverb **1 s'arrêter net** to stop dead; **2 refuser net** to refuse flatly.

nettement adverb far; **nettement meilleur** much better.

nettoyage noun M cleaning; **le nettoyage à sec** dry cleaning.

nettoyer verb [39] to clean.

neuf[1] number nine; **il est neuf heures du matin** it's nine o'clock in the morning; **Julie a neuf ans** Julie's nine; **le neuf juillet** the ninth of July.

neuf[2] (F **neuve**) adjective new; **une voiture toute neuve** a brand new car.

neutre *adjective* neutral.

neuvième *noun* M, **au neuvième** on the ninth floor; *adjective* ninth.

neveu (*plural* **neveux**) *noun* M nephew.

nez *noun* M nose.

ni *conjunction* **ni...ni** neither...nor; **ni lui ni son frère** neither he nor his brother; **il n'y a ni pain ni lait** there's neither bread nor milk; **ni Frank ni Paul ne le sait** neither Frank nor Paul knows; **ni moi non plus** me neither.

niche *noun* F **1** kennel; **2** niche.

nid *noun* M nest.

nièce *noun* F niece.

nier *verb* [1] to deny.

n'importe *adverb* **1** either, it doesn't matter; **'tu veux une aile ou une cuisse?'** – **'n'importe'** 'do you want a wing or a leg?' – 'either, it doesn't matter'; **2** **n'importe qui** anybody; **n'importe qui peut le faire** anybody can do it; **3** **n'importe quoi** anything; **je ferai n'importe quoi pour t'aider** I'll do absolutely anything to help you; **elle a fait n'importe quoi** she's made a real mess of it; **tu dis n'importe quoi** you're talking complete rubbish; **4** **n'importe quand** any time; **tu peux m'appeler n'importe quand** you can ring me any time; **5** **n'importe comment** any old how; **tu peux jeter tous ces papiers dans un tiroir n'importe comment** you can throw all these papers into a drawer any old how; **6** **n'importe où** anywhere; **pose tes valises**

n'importe où put your cases down anywhere you like; **je ne peux pas habiter n'importe où** I can't live just anywhere.

niveau (*plural* **niveaux**) *noun* M level; **au même niveau** at the same level.

niveau de vie *noun* M standard of living.

noble *adjective* noble.

noces *plural noun* F wedding.

nocif (F **nocive**) *adjective* harmful.

nocturne *noun* F late-night opening.
adjective nocturnal.

Noël *noun* M Christmas; **Joyeux Noël** Merry Christmas; **un cadeau de Noël** a Christmas present; **le sapin de Noël** the Christmas tree.

nœud *noun* M knot; **faire un nœud** to tie a knot.

noir *noun* M **1** black; **2** **le noir** the dark.
adjective **1** black; **2** dark; **il fait noir** it's dark.

Noir, Noire *noun* M, F black man, black woman; **les Noirs** black people.

noirceur *noun* F blackness.

noircir *verb* [2] to blacken.

noisette *noun* F hazelnut.

noix *noun* F **1** walnut; **2** **une noix de beurre** a knob of butter.

noix de cajou *noun* F cashew nut.

noix de coco *noun* F coconut.

nom noun M 1 name; nom de famille surname; nom de jeune fille maiden name; 2 noun.

nombre noun M number; bon nombre de a good many.

nombreux (F nombreuse) adjective many; de nombreuses personnes many people; ils étaient nombreux there were a lot of them; ils étaient peu nombreux there weren't many of them; une famille nombreuse a big family.

nombril noun M navel.

nommer verb [1] 1 to appoint; 2 to name.

non adverb 1 no; elle a dit non she said no; 2 non seulement not only; non loin de not far from; moi non plus me neither.

non- combining form un non-fumeur a nonsmoker.

nord noun M north; le nord de l'Espagne northern Spain; le vent du nord the north wind. adjective north, northern; le côté nord the north side.

nord-est noun M north-east.

nord-ouest noun M north-west.

normal (M plural normaux) adjective 1 normal; 2 c'est normal it's natural; 3 ce n'est pas normal it's not right.

normalement adverb 1 normally; 2 according to plan; normalement, elle doit être à Rome actuellement if things have gone according to plan, she should be in Rome at the moment.

normand adjective Norman; la côte normande the Normandy coast.

Normandie noun F Normandy.

norme noun F 1 norm; 2 standard; selon les normes européennes according to European standards.

Norvège noun F Norway.

norvégien (F norvégienne) adjective Norwegian.

nos adjective SEE notre.

notaire noun M notary public.

notamment adverb in particular.

note noun F 1 bill; la note, s'il vous plaît can I have the bill please; 2 mark; j'ai eu une bonne note en allemand I got a good mark in German; 3 prendre des notes to take notes.

noter verb [1] 1 to write down; 2 to notice.

notice noun F instructions.

notion noun F 1 idea; 2 des notions basic knowledge; j'ai des notions d'espagnol I have a basic knowledge of Spanish.

notre (plural nos) adjective our; notre fille our daughter; nos enfants our children.

nôtre pronoun le nôtre, la nôtre, les nôtres ours.

nouer verb [1] to tie, to knot.

nougat noun M nougat.

nouilles plural noun F noodles, pasta.

nounours noun M (*baby talk*) teddy bear.

nourrice noun F childminder.

nourrir verb [2] to feed.

nourrissant adjective nourishing.

nourrisson noun M infant.

nourriture noun F food.

nous pronoun 1 we; nous apprenons le français we are learning French; 2 us; viens avec nous come with us; elle nous aide she helps us; elle nous a aidés she helped us; 3 to us; elle ne nous a pas parlé she didn't speak to us; elle nous a donné son adresse she gave us her address; 4 ourselves nous nous ferons une salade we'll make ourselves a salad; 5 (*reflexive*) nous nous levons à sept heures we get up at seven o'clock.

nous-mêmes pronoun ourselves.

nouveau, nouvel (*before a vowel or silent 'h'*) (F **nouvelle**) (M plural **nouveaux**) adjective 1 new; viens voir mon nouvel appartement come and see my new flat; 2 à nouveau, de nouveau again.

nouveauté noun F 1 novelty; 2 new release.

Nouvel An noun M New Year.

nouvelle adjective SEE **nouveau**. noun F 1 une nouvelle news; j'ai une bonne nouvelle! I've got good news!; 2 short story; nous étudions une nouvelle de Camus we're doing a Camus short story; 3 des nouvelles news; nous n'avons pas de nouvelles pour l'instant we have no news for the moment; as-tu des

nouvelles de lui? have you heard from him?

Nouvelle-Zélande noun F New Zealand.

novembre noun M November; en novembre, au mois de novembre in November.

noyau (*plural* **noyaux**) noun M 1 stone (*in fruit*); 2 nucleus.

noyer¹ verb [39] 1 to drown; 2 se noyer to drown, to drown oneself.

noyer² noun M 1 walnut tree; 2 walnut; une table en noyer a walnut table.

nu adjective 1 naked; 2 bare.

nuage noun M cloud.

nuageux (F nuageuse) adjective cloudy.

nuance noun F 1 shade (*of a colour*); 2 nuance.

nucléaire adjective nuclear; l'énergie nucléaire nuclear power.

nuisible adjective harmful.

nuit noun F 1 night; cette nuit last night, tonight; dans la nuit in the night; toute la nuit all night; travailler la nuit to work at night; 2 il fait nuit it's dark; avant la nuit before dark; la nuit tombe à sept heures it gets dark at seven o'clock.

nul (F nulle) adjective 1 (*informal*) hopeless, awful; le film était nul the film was awful; je suis nul en histoire I'm hopeless at history; 2 un match nul a draw.

nulle part *adverb* nowhere; **je ne trouve nulle part mon dictionnaire** I can't find my dictionary anywhere.

numéro *noun* M number; **ils habitent au numéro vingt-cinq** they live at number twenty-five.

numéro de téléphone *noun* M telephone number.

nu-pieds *noun* M open sandal.

nutritif (F **nutritive**) *adjective* nourishing, nutritious; **valeur nutritive** nutritional value.

nylon *noun* M nylon.

O o

obéir *verb* [2] **obéir à** to obey.

obéissance *noun* F obedience.

obéissant *adjective* obedient.

objectif *noun* M objective. *adjective* (F **objective**) objective.

objection *noun* F objection.

objet *noun* M object.

objets trouvés *plural noun* M lost property; **aller aux objets trouvés** to go to the lost property office.

obligatoire *adjective* compulsory.

obligé *adjective* **être obligé de faire** to have to do; **je suis obligé de partir** I have to go.

obliger *verb* [52] **obliger quelqu'un à faire** to force somebody to do.

obscène *adjective* obscene.

obscur *adjective* 1 dark; 2 obscure.

obscurité *noun* F 1 darkness; **dans l'obscurité** in the dark; 2 obscurity.

obséder *verb* [24] to obsess; **être obsédé par quelque chose** to be obsessed by something.

obsèques *plural noun* F funeral.

observateur, observatrice *noun* M, F observer. *adjective* observant.

observation *noun* F 1 comment; 2 remark.

observatoire *noun* M observatory.

observer *verb* [1] 1 to watch; **elle nous observait de loin** she was watching us from a distance; 2 to observe (*rules*).

obstacle *noun* M obstacle.

obstination *noun* F obstinacy.

obstiné *adjective* stubborn.

obtenir [77] to get.

occasion *noun* F 1 opportunity; **avoir l'occasion de faire** to have the opportunity to do; 2 **acheter quelque chose d'occasion** to buy something second hand; **une voiture d'occasion** a second-hand car; 3 bargain; **une bonne occasion** a good bargain; 4 occasion; **à l'occasion de** on the occasion of; 5 **à l'occasion** some time.

occasionner *verb* [1] to cause.

Occident *noun* M **l'Occident** the West.

occidental (M plural **occidentaux**) adjective western.

occupation noun F occupation.

occupé adjective 1 busy; **je suis occupé en ce moment** I'm busy at the moment; 2 engaged (of a telephone line or toilet); 3 **cette place est occupée** this seat is taken.

occuper verb [1] 1 to occupy; 2 **s'occuper** to keep yourself busy; 3 **s'occuper de** to deal with, to see to; **je vais m'occuper du dîner** I'll go and see to dinner; **je m'en occupe** I'll see to it; 4 **s'occuper de quelqu'un** to attend to somebody; **est-ce qu'on s'occupe de vous?** are you being attended to?

occurrence noun F 1 case; **plusieurs occurrences de typhoïde** several cases of typhoid; 2 occurrence.

océan noun M ocean.

octet noun M byte (in computing).

octobre noun M October; **en octobre, au mois d'octobre** in October.

odeur noun F smell; **des odeurs de cuisine** cooking smells.

odorat noun M sense of smell.

œil (plural **yeux**) noun M eye; ★ **cela saute aux yeux** it's obvious (literally: it jumps into your eyes).

œillet noun M carnation.

œuf noun M egg; **un œuf à la coque** a boiled egg; **un œuf dur** a hard-boiled egg; **un œuf mollet** a soft-boiled egg; **un œuf sur le plat** a fried egg; **des œufs brouillés** scrambled eggs.

œuvre noun F work (of art or literature); **une œuvre d'art** a work of art.

offenser verb [1] to offend.

office noun M 1 office; 2 **office religieux** religious service.

officiel noun M official. adjective (F **officielle**) official.

officier noun M officer.

offre noun F 1 offer; 2 **'offres d'emploi'** 'situations vacant'.

offrir verb [56] 1 **offrir quelque chose à quelqu'un** to give something to somebody; **elle m'a offert une montre pour mon anniversaire** she gave me a watch for my birthday; 2 **s'offrir quelque chose** to treat yourself to something; **je vais m'offrir un nouveau dictionnaire** I'm going to treat myself to a new dictionary; 3 to offer.

oie noun F goose.

oignon noun M onion.

oiseau (plural **oiseaux**) noun M bird.

olive noun F olive; **l'huile d'olive** olive oil.

olivier noun M olive tree.

ombragé adjective shaded (from the sun).

ombre noun F 1 shade; **à l'ombre** in the shade; 2 shadow.

ombre à paupières noun F eyeshadow.

ombrelle noun F sun umbrella.

omelette noun F omelette; **une omelette aux champignons** a mushroom omelette.

omoplate noun F shoulder blade.

on pronoun **1** we; **on va au cinéma** we're going to the cinema; **on a oublié de fermer la porte** we forgot to shut the door; **on a** oublié de fermer la porte; **on a** **de la terrasse on voit la mer** from the terrace you can see the sea; **on ne devrait pas mentir** you shouldn't tell lies; **3** **on leur a dit que...** they were told that...; **on a volé leur voiture** their car's been stolen.

oncle noun M uncle.

onde noun F wave (on radio).

ondée noun F shower (of rain).

onéreux (F onéreuse) adjective costly.

ongle noun M nail; **se faire les ongles** to do your nails; **je me suis coupé les ongles** I've cut my nails.

ONU noun F SHORT FOR **Organisation des Nations unies** UN, United Nations.

onze number eleven; **onze personnes** eleven people; **Marie-Ange a onze ans** Marie-Ange is eleven; **le onze juillet** the eleventh of July.

onzième noun F **au-onzième** on the eleventh floor.
adjective eleventh.

opéra noun M **1** opera; **2** opera house.

opérateur, opératrice noun M, F operator.

opération noun F **1** operation; **2** calculation.

opérer verb [24] to operate; **opérer quelqu'un** to operate on somebody; **se faire opérer** to have an operation.

opinion noun F opinion.

opposant, opposante noun M, F opponent.

opposé noun **l'opposé** the opposite.
adjective **1** opposite; **2** **être opposé à quelque chose** to be opposed to something.

opposer verb [1] **1** **le match de samedi prochain oppose les Anglais et les Français** the English are playing the French in next Saturday's match; **2** **s'opposer à quelque chose** to oppose something.

opposition noun F opposition.

opter verb [1] to opt.

opticien, opticienne noun M, F optician.

optimisme noun M optimism.

optimiste noun M & F optimist.
adjective optimistic.

option noun F option.

optionnel (F optionnelle) adjective optional.

or¹ noun M **1** gold; **une montre en or** a gold watch; **2** **une occasion en or** a golden opportunity.

or² conjunction now.

orage noun M storm.

orageux (F **orageuse**) *adjective*
1 stormy; 2 thundery.

oral (*plural* **oraux**) *noun* M oral
(exam); **l'oral de français** the
French oral.
adjective oral; **une épreuve orale**
an oral exam.

orange *noun* F.
adjective orange.

oranger *noun* M orange tree.

orbite *noun* F orbit.

orchestral (M *plural* **orchestraux**)
adjective orchestral.

orchestre *noun* M 1 orchestra;
2 band.

orchidée *noun* F orchid.

ordinaire *noun* M 1 2-star petrol;
2 **sortir de l'ordinaire** to be out of
the ordinary; **ça sort un peu de
l'ordinaire** it's a bit out of the
ordinary; 3 **à l'ordinaire,
d'ordinaire** usually.
adjective ordinary; **une journée
ordinaire** an ordinary day.

ordinateur *noun* M computer.

ordonnance *noun* F prescription.

ordonné *adjective* tidy.

ordonner *verb* [1] to order.

ordre *noun* M 1 order; **donner des
ordres** to give orders; 2 order; **par
ordre alphabétique** in alphabetical
order; **mettre de l'ordre** to tidy up;
mettre en ordre to tidy.

ordures *plural noun* F rubbish.

oreille *noun* F ear.

oreiller *noun* M pillow.

oreillons *plural noun* M mumps.

organe *noun* M organ (*of the body*).

organique *adjective* organic.

organisateur, organisatrice
noun M, F organizer.

organisation *noun* F
organization.

organiser *verb* [1] 1 to organize;
2 **s'organiser** to get organized.

organisme *noun* M
1 organization; 2 body;
3 organism.

organiste *noun* M & F organist.

orge *noun* F barley; **le sucre d'orge**
barley sugar.

orgeat *noun* M **le sirop d'orgeat**
barley water.

orgue *noun* F organ; **jouer de
l'orgue** to play the organ.

orgueil *noun* M pride.

orgueilleux (F **orgueilleuse**)
adjective proud.

Orient *noun* M **l'Orient** the East.

oriental (M *plural* **orientaux**)
adjective 1 eastern; 2 oriental.

orientation *noun* F
1 orientation; 2 **l'orientation
professionnelle** careers advice;
3 **avoir le sens de l'orientation** to
have a good sense of direction.

orienter *verb* [1] 1 to position;
2 to direct; 3 **s'orienter** to find
one's bearings; 4 **s'orienter vers** to
move towards; **Bernard s'oriente
vers les langues** Bernard's going in
for languages.

originaire *adjective* **être originaire de** to be a native of; **Giselle est originaire de Dijon** Giselle comes from Dijon.

original (*plural* **originaux**) *noun* M original.
adjective **1** original; **le film est en version originale** the film isn't dubbed; **2** eccentric; **c'est une vieille dame assez originale** she's rather an eccentric old lady.

originalité *noun* F **1** originality; **2** eccentricity.

origine *noun* F **1** origin; **2 elle est d'origine écossaise** she's Scottish; **3 à l'origine** originally; **à l'origine la maison appartenait à mon oncle** the house originally belonged to my uncle.

orme *noun* M elm tree.

orné *adjective* **orné de** decorated with.

ornemental (M *plural* **ornementaux**) *adjective* ornamental.

orphelin, orpheline *noun* M, F orphan.

orphelinat *noun* M orphanage.

orteil *noun* M toe; **gros orteil** big toe.

orthographe *noun* F spelling.

ortie *noun* F nettle.

os *noun* M bone.

osé *adjective* daring; **c'était un peu osé de dire ça** it was a bit daring to say that.

oseille *noun* F sorrel.

oser *verb* [1] to dare.

osier *noun* M wicker; **un panier en osier** a wicker basket.

otage *noun* M hostage; **être pris en otage** to be taken hostage.

OTAN *noun* F SHORT FOR **Organisation du traité de l'Atlantique Nord** NATO.

ôter *verb* [1] **1** to take off; **je vais ôter ma veste** I'll take off my jacket; **2** to take away; **3** to remove.

otite *noun* F earache; **avoir une otite** to have earache.

ou *conjunction* **1** or; **est-ce que vous voulez le fromage ou le dessert?** would you like cheese or dessert?; **2 ou…ou** either…or; **c'est ou dans ma chambre ou dans le salon** it's either in my bedroom or in the sitting-room; **3 ou bien** or else; **on peut se retrouver au cinéma ou bien chez moi, si tu veux** we can meet at the cinema or else at my place, if you like.

où *adverb* where; **où es-tu?** where are you?; **ton frère habite où?** where does your brother live?; **tu l'as trouvé où ton sac?** where did you find your bag?; **je sais où elle habite** I know where she lives.
pronoun **1** where; **le village où elle habite** the village where she lives; **la ville d'où il vient** the town he comes from; **2** when, that; **le jour où je suis arrivé** the day I arrived.

ouate *noun* F cotton wool.

oubli *noun* M **1** forgetfulness; **2 l'oubli de quelque chose** forgetting something; **3** oversight;

c'était un oubli I (or you etc.) forgot about it.

oublier verb [1] 1 to forget; **j'ai oublié leur adresse** I've forgotten their address; 2 to leave; **j'ai oublié mes clefs chez Jérôme** I've left my keys at Jérôme's.

ouest noun M 1 west; **à l'ouest de Paris** west of Paris; **dans l'ouest de la France** in the west of France; **l'Ouest** the West; **l'Europe de l'Ouest** Western Europe.
adjective 1 west; **le côté ouest** the west coast; 2 western.

ouf exclamation phew!

oui adverb yes; **elle a dit oui** she said yes; **dire oui de la tête** to nod.

ouragan noun M hurricane.

ourlet noun M hem.

ours noun M bear.

oursin noun M sea urchin.

outil noun M tool.

outre preposition in addition to.

outré adjective outraged.

outremer noun M,
adjective ultramarine.

outre-mer adverb overseas.

ouvert adjective 1 open; **laisse la porte ouverte** leave the door open; 'ouvert le dimanche' 'open on Sundays'; 2 **laisser le robinet ouvert** to leave the tap on.

ouvertement adverb openly.

ouverture noun F 1 opening; **les heures d'ouverture** opening hours; 2 openness; **ouverture d'esprit** open-mindedness.

ouvre-boîte noun M tin-opener.

ouvre-bouteille noun M bottle-opener.

ouvrier, ouvrière noun M, F worker.
adjective **la classe ouvrière** the working class.

ouvrir verb [30] 1 to open; **ouvrir la fenêtre** to open the window; 2 **ouvrir le robinet** to turn on the tap; 3 **elle n'a pas ouvert la bouche** she didn't say a word; 4 **s'ouvrir** to open; **ça s'ouvre comment?** how do you open it?

ovale adjective oval.

ovni noun M SHORT FOR objet volant non identifié UFO.

oxygène noun M oxygen.

ozone noun F ozone.

P p

Pacifique noun M **l'océan Pacifique** the Pacific Ocean.

pagaille (informal) noun F mess; **quelle pagaille!** what a mess!

page noun F page; **à la première/dernière page** on the first/last page; **les Pages Jaunes** the Yellow Pages.

paie (or **paye**) noun F pay; **un bulletin de paie, une fiche de paie** a payslip.

paiement noun M payment.

paillasson noun M doormat.

paille noun F straw.

pain noun M **1** bread; une tranche de pain a slice of bread; **2** un pain a loaf of bread; trois pains three loaves of bread; un petit pain a roll; ★ ils se vendent comme des petits pains they're selling like hot cakes (literally: like rolls).

pain au chocolat noun M chocolate pastry.

pain complet noun M wholemeal bread.

pain de mie noun M sandwich loaf.

pain d'épices noun M gingerbread.

pain de seigle noun M rye bread.

pain grillé noun M toast.

pair adjective **1** even (number); **2** au pair (number); une jeune fille au pair an au pair; travailler au pair to work as an au pair.

paire noun F pair; une paire de chaussures a pair of shoes.

paix noun F peace.

palais noun M **1** palace; **2** palate.

palais de justice noun M law courts.

pâle adjective pale; bleu pâle pale blue.

Palestine noun F Palestine.

palier noun M landing (on a staircase).

pâlir verb [2] **1** to turn pale; **2** to fade.

palme noun F flipper (for swimming).

palmier noun M palm tree.

palpitant adjective thrilling.

pamplemousse noun M grapefruit.

panaché noun M shandy. adjective une salade panachée a mixed salad.

pancarte noun F notice, sign.

pané adjective coated in breadcrumbs.

panier noun M basket.

panier à salade noun M salad shaker.

panique noun F panic.

paniquer verb [1] to panic.

panne noun F breakdown (of a car or machine); la voiture est en panne the car's broken down; la photocopieuse est en panne the photocopier's not working; tomber en panne to break down; nous sommes en panne d'essence we've run out of petrol; une panne de courant a power cut.

panneau (plural panneaux) noun M sign, notice board.

panneau indicateur noun M signpost.

panneau publicitaire noun M advertisement hoarding.

panorama noun M **1** panorama; **2** viewpoint.

pansement noun M **1** sticking plaster; **2** dressing.

panser verb [1] to put a dressing on (a wound).

pantalon noun M trousers; **mon pantalon gris** my grey trousers; **un pantalon neuf** a new pair of trousers; **deux pantalons** two pairs of trousers.

panthère noun F panther.

pantoufle noun F slipper.

paon noun M peacock.

papa noun M Dad, Daddy, father.

pape noun M pope.

paperasse noun F (informal) paperwork, bumph.

papeterie noun F stationer's.

papi noun M (informal) granddad.

papier noun M paper; **du papier blanc** white paper; **vos papiers, s'il vous plaît monsieur** your (identity) papers please, sir.

papier à lettres noun M writing paper.

papier aluminium noun M kitchen foil.

papier cadeau noun M gift wrap.

papier-calque noun M tracing paper.

papier hygiénique noun M toilet paper.

papier peint noun M wallpaper.

papiers d'identité plural noun M identity papers.

papillon noun M butterfly.

paquebot noun M liner.

pâquerette noun F daisy.

Pâques noun M Easter; **à Pâques** at Easter; **un œuf de Pâques** an

Easter egg; **les vacances de Pâques** the Easter holidays; **le lundi de Pâques** Easter Monday.

paquet noun M 1 packet; **un paquet de sucre** a bag of sugar; 2 parcel; **il y a un paquet pour vous** there's a parcel for you; 3 bundle (of clothes or papers).

paquet-cadeau noun M gift-wrapped parcel; **est-ce que je vous fais un paquet-cadeau?** shall I gift-wrap it for you?

par preposition 1 by; **par moi** by me; **par la poste** by post; **payer par chèque** to pay by cheque; **par accident** by accident; **par hasard** by chance; **deux par deux** two by two; **jeter quelque chose par la fenêtre** to throw something out of the window; **aller par Paris** to go via (or by) Paris; **par ennui** out of boredom; 2 in; **par endroits** in places; **par cette chaleur** in this heat; 3 per; **50 francs par personne** 50 francs per person; **deux repas par jour** two meals a day; **deux fois par semaine** twice a week.

parachute noun M parachute.

parachutiste noun M & F parachutist.

paradis noun M heaven.

paragraphe noun M paragraph.

paraître verb [57] 1 to seem; **ça me paraît étrange** that seems strange to me; **il paraît qu'il est mort** it seems he's dead; 2 **paraît-il** apparently; **elle est à Nice, paraît-il** she's in Nice, apparently; 3 to appear; **paraître en public** to appear in public; **4** (*of a book*) to come out, to be published; **le roman va paraître en juin** the novel will come out in June.

parallèle *adjective* parallel.

paralysé *adjective* paralysed.

parapente *noun* M **1** paraglider; **2** paragliding.

parapluie *noun* M umbrella.

parasite *noun* M **1** parasite; **2 des parasites** interference (*on TV or radio*).

parasol *noun* M parasol.

parc *noun* M **1** park; **aller au parc** to go to the park; **2** grounds (*of a large house*).

parc d'attractions *noun* M amusement park.

parce que *conjunction* because; **parce qu'elle est malade** because she's ill; **c'est parce que je t'aime** it's because I love you.

par-ci *adverb* **par-ci par-là** here and there.

parcmètre *noun* M parking meter.

parc naturel *noun* M nature park.

parcourir *verb* [29] to go all over, to travel all over; **j'ai parcouru l'Europe** I travelled all over Europe.

parcours *noun* M **1** route (*for a bus or a traveller*); **2** course (*for a race*).

par-derrière *adverb* from the back, behind; **elle est passée par-derrière** she went round the back.

par-dessous *adverb* underneath.

pardessus *noun* M overcoat.

par-dessus *adverb* **1** on top; **2** over it; **il a sauté par-dessus** he jumped over it.
preposition over; **elle a sauté par-dessus le ruisseau** she jumped over the stream; **j'aime ça par-dessus tout!** I like that best of all!

par-devant *adverb* by the front.

pardon *noun* M **1** pardon, forgiveness; **je te demande pardon** I'm sorry; **2** excuse me, sorry.

pardonner *verb* [1] to forgive.

pare-balles *adjective* bullet-proof; **un gilet pare-balles** a bullet-proof vest.

pare-brise *noun* M windscreen.

pare-chocs *noun* M bumper (*on a car*).

pareil (F **pareille**) *adjective* **1** the same; **les deux voitures sont presque pareilles** the two cars are almost the same; **c'est toujours pareil** it's always the same; **mais ce n'est pas du tout pareil!** but it's not the same at all!; **2** such; **je n'ai jamais dit une chose pareille** I never said any such thing; **tu ne peux pas sortir par un temps pareil** you can't go out in weather like this.

parent *noun* M **1** parent; **mes parents** my parents; **2** relation; **parents et amis** friends and relations.

parenthèse *noun* F bracket; **entre parenthèses** in brackets.

paresse *noun* F laziness.

paresseux (F paresseuse)
adjective lazy.

parfait *adjverb* perfect.

parfaitement *adverb* **1** perfectly;
tu le sais parfaitement! you know
perfectly well!; parfaitement faux
totally wrong; **2** parfaitement!
absolutely!

parfois *adverb* sometimes.

parfum *noun* M **1** perfume;
2 flavour; tu veux quel parfum de
yaourt? what flavour yoghurt would
you like?

parfumé *adjective* **1** perfumed,
fragrant; parfumé à la lavande
lavender-scented; **2** flavoured; une
glace parfumée au chocolat a
chocolate ice-cream.

parfumerie *noun* F perfume shop.

pari *noun* M bet; faire un pari to
make a bet.

parier *verb* [1] to bet.

Paris *noun* Paris; à Paris in (or to)
Paris.

parisien (F parisienne) *adjective*
1 Parisian; **2** Paris; un restaurant
parisien a Paris restaurant.

parking *noun* M car park; dans le
parking in the car park.

Parlement *noun* M Parliament.

parler *verb* [1] **1** to speak; parler (le)
français to speak French; parler en
italien to speak in Italian; parler
fort/doucement to speak
loudly/softly; parler à quelqu'un to
speak to someone; **2** to talk; il parle
très vite he talks very fast; parler
cinéma to talk (about) films;
3 parler de to talk about, to
mention; tout le monde en parle
everyone's talking about it; non, il
n'en a pas parlé no, he didn't
mention it; n'en parlons plus! let's
say no more about it!; **4** se parler
to talk to each other; ★ tu parles!
(*informal*) you must be joking!

parmi *preposition* among; parmi les
invités among the guests.

parole *noun* F **1** les paroles the
lyrics; les paroles de la chanson
the lyrics of the song; **2** elle m'a
donné sa parole she gave me her
word; **3** speech; perdre la parole to
lose the power of speech.

parquet *noun* M **1** wooden floor;
2 parquet.

parrain *noun* M godfather.

parrainer *verb* [1] to sponsor.

parsemer *verb* [50] to sprinkle.

part *noun* F **1** portion, helping; une
part de pizza a portion of pizza;
2 share; il a payé sa part he paid his
share; elle a fait sa part du travail
she did her share of the work; **3** side;
de toutes parts from all sides;
4 pour ma part, je pense que... for
my part, I think that...; **5** à part
separate, separately; une chambre à
part a separate bedroom; j'ai mis
l'argent à part I put the money
aside; à part ça, qu'est-ce qu'il t'a
dit? apart from that, what did he
say?; **6** de la part de quelqu'un on
behalf of somebody, for somebody;
c'est de la part de qui? who's

calling?; **dis-lui bonjour de ma part** say hello to him from me.

partager verb [52] **1** to share (possessions or food); **2** to divide; **je partage mon temps entre mon travail et les enfants** I divide my time between my job and the children.

partenaire noun M & F partner.

parterre noun M **1** flower bed; **2** stalls (in a theatre).

parti noun M **1** party, group; **le parti communiste** the communist party; **2** side.

participation noun F participation.

participe noun M participle; **participe passé** past participle.

participer verb [1] **participer à quelque chose** to take part in something.

particulier noun M private individual.
adjective (F **particulière**) **1** special; **rien de particulier** nothing special; **2** private; **une voiture particulière** a private car; **3** **en particulier** in particular; **rien en particulier** nothing in particular; **4** **en particulier** in private.

particulièrement adverb particularly.

partie noun F **1** part; **une partie de ma vie** part of of my life; **la première partie** the first part; **2** **en partie** partly; **3** **faire partie de quelque chose** to be part of something; **ce bâtiment fait partie du musée** this building is part of the museum; **elle**

fait partie de la famille she's one of the family; **4** game; **faire une partie de tennis** to have a game of tennis; **gagner la partie** to win the game.

partir verb [58] **1** to leave, to go; **partir à pied** to go on foot; **tu pars déjà?** are you leaving already?; **elle est partie en Italie** she's gone to Italy; **il est parti à Londres** he's gone to London; **elle est partie au travail** she's left for work; **partir en vacances** to go on holiday; **elle est partie pour huit jours** she's gone away for a week; **ils sont partis en courant** they ran off; **2** **à partir de** from; **à partir de lundi** from Monday (onwards).

partition noun F score (in music).

partout adverb **1** everywhere; **j'ai cherché partout** I've looked everywhere; **2** **trois buts partout** three goals all.

parvenir verb [81] **1** **parvenir à** to reach; **2** **parvenir à faire** to manage to do; **il est parvenu à ouvrir la porte** he managed to open the door.

pas¹ adverb **1** (used with 'ne' to put verbs into the negative) **je ne suis pas** I am not; **je n'ai pas de stylo** I don't have a pen; **je ne pense pas** I don't think so; **ils n'ont pas le téléphone** they haven't got a phone; **2** not; **c'est lui qui paie, pas moi** he's paying, not me; **pas du tout** not at all; **pas vraiment** not really; **une radio pas chère** a cheap radio; **pas de chance!** bad luck!; **pas possible!** I don't believe it!

pas² noun M **1** step; **faire un grand/petit pas** to take a big/small step; **j'habite à deux pas d'ici** I live very near here; **2** pace; **ralentir le pas** to slow down; **'roulez au pas!'** 'dead slow' (road sign).

passage noun M **1** traffic; **une rue où il y a beaucoup de passage** a street where there's a lot of traffic; **passage interdit** no through traffic; **2** visit; **je peux te prendre au passage** I can pick you up on my way.

passage à niveau noun M level crossing.

passage pour piétons noun M pedestrian crossing.

passager, passagère noun M, F passenger.
adjective passing, temporary.

passage souterrain noun M subway (under a road).

passant, passante noun M, F passer-by.

passé noun M **1** past; **c'est dans le passé** it's in the past now; **2** past tense; **le passé composé** the present perfect.
adjective **1** **l'année passée** last year; **2** past; **il est dix heures passées** it's past ten o'clock.

passeport noun M passport.

passer verb [1] **1** to pass; **le temps passe vite** time passes quickly; **2** to spend (time); **j'ai passé deux jours à Paris** I spent two days in Paris; **3** en passant in passing; **4** passer quelque chose à quelqu'un to pass somebody something; **passe-moi le sel** pass me the salt; **5** to cross; **passer le pont** to cross the bridge; **6** to drop

in; **Pierre est passé ce matin** Pierre dropped in this morning; **est-ce que le facteur est passé?** has the postman been?; **je passerai te prendre à huit heures** I'll pick you up at eight; **7** to get through; **laissez passer l'ambulance!** let the ambulance through!; **8** to go; **passer à la caisse** to go to the checkout; **passons au salon** let's go through to the sitting room; **le film est passé à la télé lundi** the film was on telly on Monday; **9** to give; **il m'a passé son vélo** he gave me his bike; **je te passe Michel** I'll put you on to Michel (on the telephone); **10** to put (on) (a garment); **11** passer l'aspirateur to vacuum; **12** to take, to sit (a test or an exam); **13** passer par to go through; **nous sommes passés par Paris** we went through (or via) Paris; **14** se passer to happen; **qu'est-ce qui se passe?** what's happening?; **ça s'est passé en Chine** it happened in China; **15** se passer de to do without; **se passer d'un manteau** to do without a coat.

passerelle noun F **1** footbridge; **2** gangway.

passe-temps noun M hobby.

passif noun M passive (in grammar).
adjective (F **passive**) passive.

passion noun F passion.

passionnant adjective exciting.

passionné, passionnée noun M, F enthusiast; **c'est un passionné de tennis** he's a tennis enthusiast.
adjective keen; **c'est une**

musicienne passionnée she's a keen musician.

passionner verb [1] l'histoire me passionne history fascinates me.

passoire noun F strainer.

patate (informal) noun F potato.

pâte noun F 1 pastry; **pâte feuilletée** puff pastry; 2 dough; 3 batter; **pâte à crêpes** pancake batter; 4 paste; 5 **les pâtes** pasta; **on va manger des pâtes ce soir** we're having pasta tonight.

pâte à modeler noun F Plasticine™.

patience noun F patience.

patient, patiente noun M, F, adjective patient.

patienter verb [1] to wait; **patientez, s'il vous plaît** would you hold the line please?

patin noun M skate.

patinage noun M skating; **patinage artistique** figure skating.

patin à glace noun M ice skate.

patin à roulettes noun M roller skate.

patiner verb [1] to skate.

patinoire noun F ice rink.

pâtisserie noun F 1 cake shop; 2 cake.

patois noun M dialect.

patrie noun F homeland, country.

patron¹ noun M pattern (for dressmaking).

patron², patronne noun M, F boss.

patronner verb [1] to sponsor.

patte noun F 1 paw; 2 leg (of an animal); ★ **à quatre pattes** on all fours.

paume noun F palm (of the hand).

paumer verb [1] (informal) 1 to lose; 2 **se paumer** to get lost.

paupière noun F eyelid; **le fard à paupières** eyeshadow.

pause noun F 1 break; **faire une pause** to take a break; **la pause café** the coffee break; 2 pause.

pauvre noun M & F poor man, poor woman; **les pauvres** the poor; **le pauvre!** poor thing! adjective poor.

pauvreté noun F poverty.

pavé noun M cobblestone.

pavillon noun M 1 detached house; **un pavillon de banlieue** a house in the suburbs; 2 wing (in a hospital).

payant adjective 1 (of a show or event) not free; **c'est payant?** do you have to pay to get in?; **un parking payant** a pay-and-display car park; 2 **un hôte payant** a paying guest.

paye noun F wages.

payer verb [59] 1 to pay (a bill or a person); **c'est moi qui paie** I'm paying; **être mal payé** to be badly paid; **être payé à l'heure** to be paid by the hour; 2 to pay for; **il a payé le repas** he paid for the meal; 3 (informal) **je te paie à boire** I'll buy you a drink; 4 **je me suis payé**

une semaine à Paris I treated myself to a week in Paris.

pays noun M 1 country; **la France est un beau pays** France is a beautiful country; **des fruits du pays** locally grown fruit.

paysage noun M landscape.

paysan, paysanne noun M, F farmer.

Pays-Bas plural noun M **les Pays-Bas** the Netherlands.

pays de Galles noun M Wales; **au pays de Galles** in (or to) Wales.

PC noun M PC, personal computer.

péage noun M 1 toll; **autoroute à péage** toll motorway (motorists have to pay to travel on motorways in France); 2 tollbooth.

peau (plural **peaux**) noun F 1 skin; **avoir la peau sèche** to have dry skin; 2 peel (of fruit); **peau d'orange** orange peel.

pêche noun F 1 peach; 2 fishing; **aller à la pêche** to go fishing.

péché noun M sin.

pêcher[1] verb [1] 1 to fish for (trout, salmon, etc); 2 to catch; **Denise a pêché trois truites** Denise caught three trout.

pêcher[2] noun M peach tree.

pêcheur noun M fisherman.

pédagogique adjective educational; **méthode pédagogique** teaching method.

pédale noun F pedal; ★ **perdre les pédales** (informal) to lose your grip.

pédaler verb [1] to pedal.

pédalo™ noun M pedalo, pedal boat.

pédestre adjective **faire une randonnée pédestre** to go walking (on a long-distance public footpath).

peigne noun M comb.

peigner verb [1] 1 to comb; 2 **se peigner** to comb your hair.

peindre verb [60] to paint.

peine noun F 1 effort, trouble; **se donner de la peine** to go to a lot of trouble; **il n'a même pas pris la peine d'appeler** he didn't even take the trouble to ring; 2 **ce n'est pas la peine** it's not worth it; 3 difficulty; **elle a eu beaucoup de peine à trouver un logement** she had a lot of difficulty finding somewhere to live; 4 **faire de la peine à quelqu'un** to upset somebody; 5 penalty (in law); **sous peine d'amende** offenders will be fined; 6 **à peine** hardly, scarcely; **je le connais à peine** I hardly know him; **il était à peine cinq heures** it was barely five o'clock.

peine de mort noun F death penalty.

peintre noun M painter.

peinture noun F 1 paint; **'peinture fraîche'** 'wet paint'; 2 painting; **faire de la peinture** to paint; 3 **une peinture** a painting.

pelle noun F 1 spade; 2 shovel.

pelle à poussière noun F dustpan.

pelle mécanique noun F mechanical digger.

pellicule noun F 1 film (*for a camera*); **une pellicule couleur** a colour film; 2 **les pellicules** dandruff.

pelouse noun F lawn; **'pelouse interdite'** 'keep off the grass'.

peluche noun F soft toy.

pencher verb [1] 1 to tilt; 2 **se pencher** to bend down; 4 **se pencher par la fenêtre** to lean out of the window.

pendant preposition 1 for; **je t'ai attendu pendant deux heures** I waited for you for two hours; 2 during; **pendant l'hiver** during the winter; 3 **pendant que** while; **pendant que les enfants sont à l'école** while the children are at school.

pendentif noun M pendant.

penderie noun F wardrobe, hanging cupboard.

pendre verb [3] 1 to hang; 2 **pendre quelque chose** to hang something up; 3 to hang down.

pendule noun F clock.

pénétrer verb [24] 1 **pénétrer dans** to enter; **un voleur a pénétré dans le bureau** a thief got into the office; 2 to penetrate.

pénible adjective 1 difficult, hard; 2 **il est pénible** he's a pain.

péniche noun F barge.

pénis noun M penis.

pensée noun F 1 thought; 2 pansy.

penser verb [1] 1 to think; **je pense que tu as raison** I think you're right; **oui, je pense** yes, I think so; **je ne pense pas** I don't think so; 2 to intend; **il pense arriver mardi** he's intending to arrive on Tuesday; 3 **penser de** to think of; **qu'est-ce que tu penses de mon idée?** what do you think of my idea?; 4 **penser à** to think about; **à quoi penses-tu?** what are you thinking about?; 5 **cette chanson me fait penser à ta mère** this song reminds me of your mother; **pendant que j'y pense** while I remember; **fais-moi penser à acheter des citrons** remind me to buy lemons.

pension noun F 1 boarding school; 2 boarding house; 3 pension; 4 **pension complète** full board; **demi-pension** dinner, bed and breakfast.

pensionnaire noun M & F boarder.

pente noun F slope; **en pente** sloping.

Pentecôte noun F Whitsun; **à la Pentecôte** at Whitsun.

pépin noun M 1 (grape) pip; 2 (*informal*) slight problem.

perçant adjective 1 piercing; 2 sharp.

perce-neige noun M or F snowdrop.

percer verb [61] to pierce; **avoir les oreilles percées** to have pierced ears; **se faire percer les oreilles** to have your ears pierced; **percer un trou** to make a hole.

perceuse noun F drill.

perdant, perdante noun M, F
loser.

perdre verb [3] **1** to lose; **notre
équipe a perdu** our team lost;
2 perdre quelque chose to lose
something; **j'ai perdu mes clefs** I've
lost my keys; **j'ai perdu mon chemin**
I've lost my way; **3 être perdu** to be
lost; **4 se perdre** to get lost; **je me
suis perdu dans les petites rues** I
got lost in the back streets; **5 perdre
du temps** to waste time.

perdu adjective **1** lost; **un enfant
perdu** a lost child; **2** stray; **un chien
perdu** a stray dog; **3 c'est du temps
perdu** it's a waste of time.

père noun M father; **le père Noël**
Father Christmas.

perfectionner verb [1] to perfect.

performant adjective **1** efficient;
2 high-performance.

périmé adjective out-of-date.

période noun F period.

périphérique noun M ring road.

perle noun F **1** pearl; **2** bead.

permanence noun F **1** service;
'**permanence de 8h à 19h**' 'open
from 8 a.m. to 7 p.m.'; **2 en
permanence** permanently, all the
time.

permanent adjective
1 permanent; continuous.

permettre verb [11] **permettre à
quelqu'un de faire** to allow
someone to do; **elle leur a permis de
partir** she allowed them to leave;
permettez-moi de vous aider let me
help you.

permis noun M permit, licence.

permis de conduire noun M
driving licence; **passer son permis**
to sit your driving test.

permission noun F
1 permission; **2** leave (from the
army).

perroquet noun M parrot.

perruche noun F budgie.

perruque noun F wig.

persécution noun F persecution.

persévérer verb [24] to persevere.

persil noun M parsley.

persister verb [1] to persist.

personnage noun M **1** character
(in a book, film, or play); **2** figure,
person; **un personnage célèbre** a
famous person.

personnalité noun F personality.

personne[1] pronoun **1** nobody;
personne ne sait nobody knows;
2 anybody; **je ne vois personne** I
can't see anybody; **je n'ai parlé à
personne** I didn't speak to anybody.

personne[2] noun F person; **vingt
personnes** twenty people; **les
personnes âgées** the elderly; **en
personne** in person.

personnel noun M **1** staff; **2 le
service du personnel** the personnel
department.
adjective (F **personnelle**) personal.

personnellement adverb
personally.

perspective noun F
1 perspective; **2** view; **3** prospect.

persuader verb [1] 1 to persuade; **persuader quelqu'un de faire** to persuade somebody to do; 2 **être persuadé** to be sure.

perte noun F 1 loss; 2 waste; une **perte de temps** a waste of time.

perturber verb [1] to disrupt.

pèse-personne noun M bathroom scales.

peser verb [50] 1 **peser quelque chose** to weigh something; 2 to weigh; **je pèse 60 kilos** I weigh 60 kilos.

pessimiste noun M & F pessimist. adjective pessimistic.

pétale noun M petal.

pétanque noun F bowls (the French version, played outdoors with metal bowls; also called 'boules').

pétard noun M firecracker, banger.

pétillant adjective sparkling (wine or mineral water).

petit adjective 1 little, small; une **petite fille** a little girl; une toute **petite maison** a tiny house; 2 short; une **petite distance** a short distance.
noun (F **petite**) little boy, little girl; les **petits** the children; ★ **petit à petit** little by little.

petit ami noun M boyfriend.

petit déjeuner noun M breakfast.

petite amie noun F girlfriend.

petite annonce noun F small ad.

petite-fille noun F granddaughter.

petit-fils noun M grandson.

petit mot noun M note.

petit pois noun M garden pea.

petits-enfants plural noun M grandchildren.

pétrole noun M 1 oil, petroleum; 2 paraffin.

peu adverb 1 not much; **il dort peu** he doesn't sleep much; **elle gagne très peu** she earns very little; 2 not very; **peu intéressant** not very interesting; 3 **peu de** not much, not many; **il reste peu de temps** there's not much time left; **peu de voitures** not many cars; 4 **un peu de** a little, a bit; **il reste un peu de café** there's a bit of coffee left; 5 **parle un peu plus fort** speak a little louder; **juste un petit peu** just a little; 6 **à peu près** about; **il y avait à peu près vingt personnes** there were about twenty people.

peuple noun M people, nation.

peuplier noun M poplar.

peur noun F fear; **avoir peur de** to be afraid of; **Nadine a peur des souris** Nadine's afraid of mice; **n'ayez pas peur!** don't be afraid!; **faire peur à quelqu'un** to frighten somebody; **tu m'as fait peur!** you gave me a fright!

peut verb SEE **pouvoir**[1].

peut-être adverb perhaps.

peuvent, peux verb SEE **pouvoir**[1].

phare noun M 1 headlight; **allumer les phares** to turn the headlights on; 2 lighthouse.

pharmacie noun F chemist's.

pharmacien, pharmacienne
noun M, F chemist, pharmacist.

phénomène noun M
phenomenon.

philo (*informal*) noun F SHORT FOR
philosophie.

philosophie noun F philosophy.

phoque noun M seal.

photo noun F 1 photo, photograph;
une photo d'identité a passport
photo; 2 photography.

photocopie noun F photocopy.

photocopier verb [1] to photocopy.

photocopieuse noun F
photocopier.

photographe noun M & F
photographer; Sean est
photographe Sean's a
photographer.

photographie noun F
1 photography; 2 photograph.

photographier verb [1] to
photograph.

photomaton™ noun M photo
booth.

phrase noun F sentence.

physique¹ noun F physics.

physique² adjective physical.

pianiste noun M & F pianist.

piano noun M piano; jouer du
piano to play the piano.

piano à queue noun M grand
piano.

pichet noun M jug.

pièce noun F 1 room; notre maison
a quatre pièces our house has four
rooms; 2 coin; une pièce de cinq
francs a five-franc coin; 3 play;
une pièce de Molière a play by
Molière; 4 bit, piece; les pièces
d'un puzzle the pieces of a jigsaw;
5 item; dix francs (la) pièce ten
francs each.

pièce détachée noun F spare
part.

pièce de théâtre noun F play.

pièce d'identité noun F
identification (*such as a passport or
identity card*).

pied noun M 1 foot; être pieds nus
to be barefoot; aller à pied to go on
foot; un coup de pied a kick; donner
un coup de pied à quelqu'un to kick
someone; 2 bottom, foot; au pied
du lit at the foot of the bed; 3 le
pied de la table the table leg.

piège noun M trap.

piéger verb [15] to trap; voiture
piégée a car bomb.

pierre noun F stone.

piéton, piétonne noun M, F
pedestrian; un passage pour
piétons a pedestrian crossing.

piétonnier (F piétonnière)
adjective pedestrian; une rue
piétonnière a pedestrian street.

pieuvre noun F octopus.

pile¹ noun F 1 battery; 2 pile; une
pile de vêtements a pile of clothes;
3 tails (*when tossing a coin*); pile ou
face? heads or tails?

pile² (*informal*) *adverb* **1** exactly; **à dix heures pile** at ten o'clock on the dot; **2 s'arrêter pile** to stop dead.

pilote *noun* M **1** pilot; **2 un pilote de course** a racing driver.

piloter *verb* [1] to fly (*a plane*).

pilule *noun* F pill.

piment *noun* M chilli.

pin *noun* M pine tree; **une pomme de pin** a pine cone.

pince *noun* F **1 une pince** a pair of pliers; **2** dart (*in a garment*); **3** pincer (*of a crab*).

pince à épiler *noun* F tweezers.

pince à linge *noun* F clothes peg.

pinceau (*plural* **pinceaux**) *noun* M paintbrush.

pincée *noun* F pinch (*of salt, for example*).

pincer *verb* [61] to pinch.

pingouin *noun* M penguin.

ping-pong *noun* M ping-pong.

pintade *noun* F guinea fowl.

pion *noun* M **1** counter (*in a board game*); **2** pawn (*in chess*); **3** piece (*in draughts*).

pipe *noun* F pipe; **fumer la pipe** to smoke a pipe.

pipi (*informal*) *noun* M wee; **faire pipi** to have a wee.

piquant *adjective* **1** prickly; **2** spicy.

pique *noun* M spades (*in a pack of cards*); **le trois de pique** the three of spades.

pique-nique *noun* M picnic.

pique-niquer *verb* [1] to have a picnic.

piquer *verb* [1] **1** to sting; **j'ai été piqué par une guêpe** I've been stung by a wasp; **2** to bite; **piqué par des moustiques** bitten by mosquitoes; **3 se piquer** to prick yourself; **je me suis piqué le doigt** I've pricked my finger; **4** (*informal*) to pinch; **quelqu'un a piqué mon stylo** somebody's pinched my pen; ★ **piquer une crise (de nerfs)** (*informal*) to throw a fit.

piquet *noun* M **1** post; **2** peg.

piqûre *noun* F **1** injection; **faire une piqûre à quelqu'un** to give somebody an injection; **2** bite, sting (*of an insect*).

pirate *noun* M pirate.

pirate informatique *noun* M computer hacker.

pire *adjective* **1** worse; **pire que** worse than; **c'est pire que ça!** it's worse than that!; **c'est encore pire** it's even worse; **2** worst; **le pire** the worst; **au pire** if the worst comes to the worst.

pis *in phrase* **tant pis** too bad; **tant pis pour lui!** that's his bad luck!

piscine *noun* F swimming-pool.

pissenlit *noun* M dandelion.

pistache *noun* F pistachio.

piste *noun* F **1** trail (*left by an animal or fugitive*); **la police est sur sa piste** the police are on his trail; **2** track (*for racing or sport*); **faire un tour de piste** to do a lap; **3** piste, trail (in skiing); **4** runway (at an airport).

piste cyclable noun F cycle lane.

pistolet noun M pistol.

pitié noun F pity; **avoir pitié de quelqu'un** to feel sorry for someone.

pittoresque adjective picturesque.

placard noun M cupboard.

place noun F **1** space, room; **il y a assez de place pour deux** there's enough room for two; **2** seat (in a theatre, cinema, train, or bus); **trois places pour ce soir** two seats for this evening's performance; **3** place; **remettez tous les livres à leur place!** put all the books back in their places!; **si j'étais à ta place** if I were you; **4** place; **en troisième place** in third place; **5** square; **la place Rouge** the Red Square; **la place du village** the village square; **6 à la place de** instead of; **il y est allé à ma place** he went instead of me; **7 être sur place** to be on the spot.

placer verb [61] **1** to place; **2** to seat (a person); **elle m'a placé à côté de Louis** she put me next to Louis.

plafond noun M ceiling.

plage noun F beach; **on va à la plage** we're going to the beach.

plaie noun F wound.

plaindre verb [31] **1** to feel sorry for; **je te plains** I feel sorry for you; **2 se plaindre** to complain; **je ne me plains pas** I'm not complaining.

plaine noun F plain.

plainte noun F complaint; **porter plainte** to complain.

plaire verb [62] **1 s'il te plaît, s'il vous plaît** please; **deux billets, s'il vous plaît** two tickets, please; **2 le tissu me plaît** I like the material; **la chambre vous plaît?** do you like your room?; **le film a beaucoup plu à mon père** my father liked the film very much.

plaisanter verb [1] to joke.

plaisanterie noun F joke.

plaisir noun M pleasure; **le plaisir de lire** the pleasure of reading; **'vous venez avec nous?' – 'oui, avec plaisir'** 'will you come too?' – 'yes, with pleasure'; **faire plaisir à quelqu'un** to please someone; **j'y suis allé pour faire plaisir à ma mère** I went to please my mother.

plan noun M **1** map (of a town or underground system); **le plan du métro** the underground map; **2** plan; **le plan du bâtiment** the plan of the building; **3 au premier plan** in the foreground, in the forefront.

planche noun F plank.

planche à repasser noun F ironing board.

planche à roulettes noun F skateboard.

planche à voile noun F windsurfing board; **faire de la planche à voile** to go windsurfing.

plancher noun M floor.

plan d'eau noun M artificial lake (often for swimming and other water sports).

planer *verb* [1] 1 to glide; 2 (*informal*) to have your head in the clouds.

planète *noun* F planet.

plante *noun* F plant; une plante verte a houseplant.

planter *verb* [1] 1 to plant (*a tree, shrub, or plant*); 2 to hammer in (*a nail*); 3 se planter (*informal*) to make a blunder.

plaque *noun* F 1 patch (*of damp or ice*); 2 plate, sheet (*of metal or glass*).

plaqué *adjective* plaqué or gold-plated; plaqué argent silver-plated.

plaque d'immatriculation *noun* F number plate (*on a car*).

plastique *noun* M plastic; un sac en plastique a plastic bag.

plat *noun* M 1 dish; un plat chaud/froid a hot/cold dish; le plat du jour the dish of the day; 2 course (*of a meal*); le plat principal the main course; ★ faire tout un plat de quelque chose (*informal*) to make a big deal of something.
adjective 1 flat; à plat ventre flat on your stomach; 2 l'eau plate still water.

platane *noun* M plane tree.

plateau (*plural* plateaux) *noun* M 1 tray; 2 plateau.

plate-bande *noun* F flower bed.

plâtre *noun* M plaster; il a une jambe dans le plâtre he has a leg in plaster.

plein *adjective* 1 full; le panier est plein the basket's full; elle est pleine

d'idées she's full of ideas; 2 en pleine nuit in the middle of the night; en plein été at the height of summer; en plein centre-ville right in the middle of town; en pleine mer on the open sea.
noun M faire le plein to fill up (*a car with petrol*); le plein, s'il vous plaît a full tank, please.
adverb plein de (*informal*) loads of; elle a plein d'amis she's got loads of friends.

pleurer *verb* [1] to cry.

pleut *verb* SEE pleuvoir.

pleuvoir *verb* [63] to rain; il pleut it's raining; il va pleuvoir it's going to rain; il a plu cette nuit it rained last night.

pli *noun* M 1 fold; 2 pleat; 3 crease (*in trousers*).

plier *verb* [1] 1 to fold; 2 to bend (*your arm or leg, or a stem*); ★ être plié en deux/en quatre (*informal*) to be doubled up (*with laughter or pain*).

plomb *noun* M 1 lead; de l'essence sans plomb unleaded petrol; 2 fuse; faire sauter les plombs to blow the fuses.

plombage *noun* M filling (*in a tooth*).

plombier *noun* M plumber.

plongée *noun* F diving; faire de la plongée to go diving.

plongeoir *noun* M diving board.

plonger *verb* [52] 1 to dive; 2 to plunge.

plongeur, plongeuse *noun* M, F 1 diver; 2 washer-up.

plu verb SEE **plaire; pleuvoir.**

pluie noun F rain; **un jour de pluie** a rainy day; **sous la pluie** in the rain.

plume noun F 1 feather; 2 ink pen.

plupart noun F **la plupart de** most; **la plupart des gens** most people; **la plupart du temps** most of the time.

pluriel noun M plural; **au pluriel** in the plural.

plus adverb 1 **plus de** more; **voulez-vous un peu plus de fromage?** would you like a little more cheese?; 2 **plus de** more than; **il y avait plus de cent personnes** there were more than a hundred people; 3 **plus que** more than; **il mange plus que moi** he eats more than I do; **le film est plus intéressant que le livre** the film's more interesting than the book; **leur maison est plus grande que la nôtre** their house is bigger than ours; 4 **le plus rapide** the fastest; **le plus joli** the prettiest; 5 **plus...plus** the more...the more; **plus je gagne, plus je dépense** the more I earn the more I spend; 6 **en plus** more; **il nous faut trois côtelettes en plus** we need three more chops; 7 **de plus** more; **trois chaises de plus** three more chairs; **une fois de plus** one more time; 8 **de plus en plus** more and more; **elle fume de plus en plus** she smokes more and more; **je deviens de plus en plus fatigué** I'm getting more and more tired; **il fait de plus en plus chaud** it's getting hotter and hotter; 9 **plus ou moins** more or less; **la cuisine est plus ou moins propre** the kitchen's more or less

clean; 10 **le plus** the most; **c'est lui qui gagne le plus** he earns the most; **au plus** at the most; 11 **ne ... plus** no longer; **elle n'habite plus ici** she no longer lives here; 12 **je ne veux plus y aller** I don't want to go there any more; 13 **il n'y a plus de lait** there's no milk left; 14 plus; **deux plus trois égalent cinq** two plus three is five.

plusieurs adjective several; **plusieurs personnes** several people; **plusieurs fois** several times.

plutôt adverb 1 rather; **prends le jaune plutôt que le vert** take the yellow one rather than the green one; 2 instead; **demande plutôt à Anne** ask Anne instead; 3 pretty; **le repas était plutôt bon** the meal was pretty good; **plutôt bien** pretty good; 4 rather; **elle est plutôt maigre** she's rather thin.

pluvieux (F **pluvieuse**) adjective rainy.

pneu noun M tyre.

poche noun F pocket; **un livre de poche** a paperback; **l'argent de poche** pocket money; ★ **c'est dans la poche** (informal) it's in the bag; ★ **je connais Paris comme ma poche** (informal) I know Paris like the back of my hand.

poêle¹ noun M stove (for heating); **un poêle à bois** a wood-burning stove.

poêle² noun F frying pan.

poème noun M poem.

poésie noun F poetry.

poète noun M poet.

poids noun M weight; **prendre du poids** to put on weight; **perdre du poids** to lose weight.

poids lourd noun M lorry.

poignée noun F 1 handful; **une poignée de cailloux** a handful of pebbles; 2 handle; 3 **une poignée de main** a handshake.

poignet noun M wrist.

poil noun M hair; **un poil** a hair; **le chat perd ses poils** the cat's moulting; ★ **être de bon/mauvais poil** to be in a good/bad mood.

poilu adjective hairy.

poing noun M fist; **un coup de poing** a punch.

point noun M 1 point; **et mon dernier point** and my last point; **un point de détail** a minor point; **un point faible** a weak point; 2 **un point de rencontre** a meeting-place; 3 **être sur le point de faire** to be just about to do; **j'étais sur le point de t'appeler** I was on the point of phoning you; 4 dot; **un petit point sur la carte** a tiny dot on the map; 5 full stop; 6 point (when scoring); **six points contre sept** six points to seven; **marquer/perdre des points** to win/lose points; 7 mark (in a test); 8 **à point** just in time; **tu es arrivé à point** you arrived just in time; **un steak cuit à point** a medium-rare steak.

point chaud noun M trouble spot.

point de départ noun M starting point.

point de vue noun M point of view; **d'un point de vue politique** from a political point of view.

point d'exclamation noun M exclamation mark.

point d'interrogation noun M question mark.

pointe noun F 1 point; **la pointe d'un couteau** the point of a knife; **sur la pointe des pieds** on tip-toe; **être en pointe** to be pointed; 2 **les heures de pointe** the rush hour, peak time; 3 **une pointe de** a touch of; **une pointe d'ail** a touch of garlic. ★ **être à la pointe du progrès** to be in the forefront of progress.

pointillé noun M dotted line.

point mort noun M neutral (gear); **tu es au point mort** you're in neutral.

pointu adjective pointed.

pointure noun F size (of shoes); **quelle est votre pointure?** what size do you take?

point-virgule noun M semi-colon.

poire noun F pear.

poireau (plural poireaux) noun M leek.

poirier noun M pear tree; **faire le poirier** to stand on your head.

pois noun M 1 pea; **des petits pois** (garden) peas; 2 **à pois** spotted; **un tissu à pois** a spotted fabric.

pois chiche noun M chick pea.

pois de senteur noun M sweet pea.

poison noun M poison.

poisson noun M fish; **j'aime le poisson** I like fish.

poisson d'avril noun M April fool; **il m'a fait un poisson d'avril** he played an April fool trick on me.

poissonnerie noun F fishmonger's.

poisson rouge noun M goldfish.

poissonnier, poissonnière noun M, F fishmonger.

Poissons plural noun M Pisces (sign of the Zodiac).

poitrine noun F 1 chest; 2 bust; **quel est votre tour de poitrine?** what is your bust size?

poivre noun M pepper; **poivre noir en grains** whole black peppercorns.

poivrier noun M pepper pot.

poivron noun M pepper (red, green, or yellow).

polar (informal) noun M detective story.

pôle noun M pole; **le pôle Nord/Sud** the North/South Pole.

poli adjective polite; **être poli avec quelqu'un** to be polite to somebody.

police noun F 1 police; **appeler la police** to call the police; 2 (insurance) policy.

policier noun M police officer; **une femme policier** a woman police officer.
adjective **un roman policier** a detective story.

poliment adverb politely.

politesse noun F politeness; **par politesse** out of politeness.

politicien, politicienne noun M, F politician.

politique noun F 1 politics; 2 policy; **la politique sociale/étrangère** social/foreign policy.
adjective 1 political; 2 **un homme politique** a politician.

polluer verb [1] to pollute.

pollution noun F pollution.

polo noun M polo shirt.

Pologne noun F Poland; **en Pologne** in (or to) Poland.

polonais noun, adjective Polish.

pommade noun F ointment.

pomme noun F 1 apple; **une tarte aux pommes** an apple tart; 2 potato; **pommes frites** chips; ★ **tomber dans les pommes** (informal) to faint (literally: to fall into the apples).

pomme de terre noun F potato.

pommier noun M apple tree.

pompe noun F pump.

pompe à essence noun F petrol pump.

pompes funèbres plural noun F undertaker's.

pompier noun M fire fighter; **appeler les pompiers** to call the fire brigade.

pompiste noun M & F petrol pump attendant.

poncer verb [61] to sand (wood).

ponctuation noun F punctuation.

poney noun M pony.

pont noun M 1 bridge; 2 deck (of a ship); ★ **faire le pont** to take a long weekend (usually when the Thursday before or the Tuesday after is a public holiday).

populaire adjective 1 working-class (family, housing, or area); 2 popular (art or writing); 3 folk; **la culture populaire** folk culture; 4 popular.

population noun F population.

porc noun M 1 pig; **un élevage de porcs** a pig farm; 2 pork; **manger un rôti de porc** to have roast pork.

porcelaine noun F china, porcelain.

port noun M 1 port; 2 harbour.

portable adjective portable; **un ordinateur portable** a laptop computer.

portail noun M gate.

portatif (F **portative**) adjective portable.

porte noun F 1 door; **la porte d'entrée** the front door; 2 gate (in an airport); **la porte numéro douze** gate number twelve; 3 **l'entreprise a fermé ses portes** the business has closed down; **mettre quelqu'un à la porte** to sack somebody.

porte-bagages noun M luggage rack.

porte-clés noun M key-ring.

portée noun F **à portée de main** within reach.

porte-fenêtre noun F French window.

portefeuille noun M wallet; **une jupe en portefeuille** a wrapover skirt.

porte-jarretelles noun M suspender belt.

portemanteau (plural **portemanteaux**) noun M coat rack.

portemine noun M propelling pencil.

porte-monnaie noun M purse.

porte-parole noun M spokesperson.

porter verb [1] 1 to carry; **porter une valise** to carry a suitcase; 2 to take; **porter un paquet à la poste** to take a parcel to the post office; 3 to wear; **elle portait une robe bleue** she was wearing a blue dress; 4 **se porter bien** to be well; **se porter mal** to be in a bad way; ★ **porter bonheur/malheur** to bring good/bad luck.

portière noun F door (of a car).

portion noun F portion, helping.

porto noun M port (wine).

portrait noun M portrait.

portugais noun M, adjective Portuguese.

Portugal noun M Portugal; **au Portugal** in (or to) Portugal.

poser verb [1] 1 to put down; **il a posé sa tasse sur la table** he put

his cup down on the table; **pose ta
valise** put your case down; **2 cela
nous pose un problème** that's a
problem for us; **3 poser une
question** to ask a question.

positif (F **positive**) *adjective*
positive.

position *noun* F position.

posséder *verb* [24] to own.

possibilité *noun* F **1** possibility;
c'est une possibilité it's a
possibility; **2** opportunity; **la
possibilité de voyager** the
opportunity to travel.

possible *adjective* possible; **aussi
grand que possible** as big as
possible; **le moins possible** as little
as possible; **dès que possible** as
soon as possible; **ce n'est pas
possible!** I don't believe it!;
★ **faire tout son possible** to do your
best.

poste¹ *noun* M **1** job, post; **un
poste de secrétaire** a job as a
secretary; **2 un poste de
radio/télévision** a radio/television
set; **3** extension (*on a telephone
system*); **le poste 578, s'il vous plaît**
extension 578, please.

poste² *noun* F post office; **il travaille
pour la poste** he works for the post
office; **mettre quelque chose à la
poste** to post something.

poste de police *noun* M police
station.

pot *noun* M **1** jar; **un pot de
confiture** a jar of jam; **2** carton; **un
pot de crème** a carton of cream;
3 un pot de peinture a tin of paint;
★ **prendre un pot** to have a drink.

potable *adjective* **eau (non)
potable** (not) drinking water.

potage *noun* M soup; **potage aux
légumes** vegetable soup.

potager *noun* M vegetable garden.

pot-au-feu *noun* M boiled beef
with vegetables.

pot d'échappement *noun* M
exhaust, silencer (*for a car*).

poteau (*plural* **poteaux**) *noun* M
post.

potelé *adjective* chubby.

poterie *noun* F **1** pottery; **2** piece
of pottery.

pou (*plural* **poux**) *noun* M louse;
★ **chercher des poux** (*informal*) to
nitpick.

poubelle *noun* F dustbin; **mettre
quelque chose à la poubelle** to
throw something in the dustbin.

pouce *noun* M **1** thumb; **2** inch;
★ **se tourner les pouces** (*informal*)
to twiddle your thumbs.

poudre *noun* F powder.

pouffer *verb* [1] **pouffer de rire** to
burst out laughing.

poulain *noun* M foal.

poule *noun* F hen; ★ **quand les
poules auront des dents** (*informal*)
when pigs can fly (*literally: when
hens have teeth*).

poulet *noun* M chicken; **une cuisse
de poulet** a chicken leg; **du poulet
rôti** roast chicken.

poulet fermier *noun* M free-
range chicken.

pouls noun M pulse.

poumon noun M lung; **crier à pleins poumons** to shout at the top of your voice.

poupée noun F doll.

pour preposition **1** for; **un cadeau pour Marie-Laure** a present for Marie-Laure; **un billet pour Calais** a ticket for Calais; **le train pour Londres** the train for London; **ce sera prêt pour samedi?** will it be ready for Saturday?; **être pour** to be in favour; **je n'y suis pour rien** I had nothing to do with it; **je n'en ai pas pour longtemps** it won't take long; **2 pour faire cela** in order to do that; **je suis allé au marché pour acheter des légumes** I went to the market to buy some vegetables; **je suis là pour t'aider** I'm here to help you; **c'était juste pour rire!** it was only meant as a joke!; **pour ainsi dire** so to speak; ★ **le pour et le contre** the pros and cons.

pour cent per cent; **dix pour cent** ten per cent.

pourboire noun M tip.

pourcentage noun M percentage.

pourquoi adverb why; **pourquoi ont-ils refusé?** why did they refuse?; **je veux savoir pourquoi** I want to know why; **pourquoi pas?** why not?

pourri adjective rotten.

pourrir verb [2] to go bad.

poursuivre verb [75] **1** to chase; **2** to continue.

pourtant adverb **1** though; **et pourtant c'est vrai** it's true

though; **2** yet; **et pourtant ça aurait pu être bien** and yet it could have been good.

pourvu que conjunction (followed by subjunctive) **1** providing, as long as; **pourvu que tu reviennes samedi** providing you come back on Saturday; **2** let's hope that; **pourvu que ça dure!** let's hope it lasts!

pousser verb [1] **1** to push; **elle a poussé la porte** she pushed the door shut (or open); **2 pousser un cri** to let out a cry, to cry out; **3** to grow (of a child, hair, or a plant); **mes tomates poussent bien** my tomatoes are growing well; **4 se pousser** to move over; **pousse-toi!** move over!

poussette noun F pushchair.

poussière noun F dust; ★ **dix francs et des poussières** ten francs something, just over 10 francs.

poutre noun F beam.

pouvez verb SEE **pouvoir**¹.

pouvoir¹ verb [12] can; **je peux être là à dix heures** I can be there at ten; **peux-tu m'aider?** can you help me?; **je ne peux pas l'ouvrir** I can't open it; **ils ne pouvaient pas téléphoner avant** they couldn't phone before; **je n'ai pas pu réserver** I wasn't able to book; **elle aurait pu nous le dire** she could have told us; **puis-je parler à Cécile, s'il vous plaît** may I speak to Cécile, please; **tu peux toujours essayer** there's no harm in trying.

pouvoir² noun M power; **après dix ans au pouvoir** after ten years in power.

pouvons verb SEE **pouvoir**[1].

prairie noun F meadow.

pratique noun F practice; **mettre quelque chose en pratique** to put something into practice; **il manque de pratique** he lacks practical experience.
adjective practical, convenient; **cet ouvre-boîte n'est pas très pratique** this can opener isn't very practical; **le nouvel appartement est très pratique pour les magasins** the new flat's very handy for the shops.

pratiquement adverb practically; **c'est pratiquement fini** it's practically finished.

pratiquer verb [1] **1** to play, to do (a sport or hobby); **je pratique le yoga** I do yoga; **2** to practise; **pendant mon séjour à Lille j'aurai la possibilité de pratiquer mon français** during my stay in Lille I'll be able to practise my French.

pré noun M meadow.

précaution noun F precaution; **par précaution** as a precaution; **prendre ses précautions** to take precautions.

précédent adjective previous; **l'année précédente** the previous year, the year before.

précieux (F **précieuse**) adjective precious, valuable; **une pierre précieuse** a precious stone; **des renseignements précieux** extremely useful information.

précipice noun M precipice.

précipitation noun F haste.

précipiter verb [1] **se précipiter** to rush; **ils se sont précipités vers la porte** they rushed for the door.

précis adjective precise.

préciser verb [1] **1** to specify (details or one's intentions); **2** to explain; **pouvez-vous préciser comment?** could you explain exactly how?

précision noun F **1** precision; **2** detail; **voici quelques précisions sur le voyage** here are some details about the journey.

précuit adjective precooked.

préfecture noun F prefecture (France is divided into 96 'départements', which are roughly equivalent to British counties. The administration of each of these is done at the local level from the prefecture.)

préférable adjective preferable.

préféré adjective favourite; **mon plat préféré** my favourite dish.

préférence noun F **1** preference; **2 de préférence** preferably; **de préférence avant le dix mai** preferably before the tenth of May.

préférer verb [24] to prefer; **elle préfère le poisson à la viande** she prefers fish to meat.

préfet noun M prefect (official with overall responsibility for running a French department); SEE ALSO **préfecture**.

préjugé noun M prejudice.

prélavage noun M prewash.

prématuré adjective premature.

premier (F **première**) *adjective*
1 first; **la première fois** the first time; **c'est la première fois que je le fais** it's the first time I've done it; **Michel, tu passes le premier** Michel, you go first; **le premier juin** the first of June; 2 top; **de première qualité** top quality; 3 **au premier étage** on the first floor; 4 **en premier** first; **arriver en premier** to arrive first.

première *noun* F 1 **première** (*of a film or play*); 2 **une première mondiale** a world first (*an important event or achievement*); 3 **voyager en première** to travel first-class; 4 (*in a French school*) the equivalent of Year 12.

premièrement *adverb* firstly.

Premier ministre *noun* M prime minister.

prendre *verb* [64] 1 to take; **prends celui-ci!** take this one!; **prendre un taxi** to take a taxi; 2 **prendre quelque chose à quelqu'un** to take something from somebody; **qui m'a pris mon vélo?** who's taken my bike?; 3 to have (*something to eat or drink*); **je prends une bière** I'll have a beer; **qu'est-ce que tu prends?** what would you like?; **est-ce que tu as pris ton parapluie?** did you bring your umbrella?; 5 **passer prendre quelqu'un** to pick somebody up; **je passerai te prendre à dix heures** I'll pick you up at ten; ★ **c'est à prendre ou à laisser** take it or leave it.

prénom *noun* M first name.

préparatifs *plural noun* M preparations; **les préparatifs du voyage** the preparations for the journey.

préparation *noun* F preparation, training.

préparer *verb* [1] 1 to prepare; **je vais préparer les légumes** I'm going to prepare the vegetables; **Françoise est en train de préparer le dîner** Françoise is busy making dinner; **as-tu préparé tes affaires pour le matin?** have you got your things ready for the morning?; **on a préparé une petite surprise pour elle** we've got a little surprise ready for her; **des plats préparés** ready-to-eat meals; 2 **se préparer** to get ready; **je vais me préparer pour partir** I'll go and get ready to leave.

préposition *noun* F preposition.

près *adverb* 1 nearby; **il y a un village tout près** there's a village nearby; 2 **près de** near; **près de la gare** near the station; **près de toi** near you; **près de chez nous** near our house, near where we live; 3 **près de** nearly, almost; **près de mille francs** nearly a thousand francs; 4 **de près** closely; **regarder quelque chose de près** to look closely at something; 5 **à peu près** more or less; **à peu près deux heures** two hours, more or less; **j'ai à peu près fini** I've more or less finished.

présence *noun* F presence.

présent *noun* M 1 present (tense); **au présent** in the present; 2 **à présent** now; **à présent je n'ai pas le temps** I haven't got time just now.

adjective present (*at an event*); **toute la famille était présente** the whole family was there.

présentateur, présentatrice *noun* M, F **1** presenter (*of a broadcast or programme*); **2** newsreader.

présentation *noun* F **1** presentation; **2** introduction (*to someone you haven't met before*).

présenter *verb* [1] **1** to introduce; **je vous présente mon père** may I introduce my father?; **Alain, je te présente Raphaël** Alain, this is Raphaël; **2** to present (*a ticket, pass, or document*); **il faut présenter votre passeport** you must show your passport; **3** présenter ses excuses to apologize; **4** se présenter to go, to come; en arrivant, présentez-vous à la réception when you get there (or here), go (or come) to reception; **5** se présenter à quelqu'un to introduce yourself to somebody.

préservatif *noun* M condom.

préserver *verb* [1] to protect, to preserve.

président *noun* M **1** president; **2** chairman.

présidente *noun* F **1** president; **2** chairwoman.

présidentielles *plural noun* F les présidentielles the presidential elections.

presque *adverb* **1** nearly; **j'ai presque fini** I've nearly finished; **2** presque rien hardly anything; **il ne reste presque rien** there's hardly anything left; **3** presque pas de

hardly any; **il ne reste presque pas de lait** there's hardly any milk left.

presqu'île *noun* F peninsula.

pressant *adjective* urgent.

presse *noun* F **la presse** the press, the newspapers; **que dit la presse?** what do the papers say?

pressé *adjective* **1** être pressé to be in a hurry; **2** urgent; **ce n'est pas pressé** it's not urgent; **3** un citron pressé a fresh lemon juice (*served with water and sugar*).

presser *verb* [1] **1** to urge (*someone to do something*); **2** to squeeze; **presser une orange** to squeeze an orange; **3** ça ne presse pas there's no hurry; **presser le pas** to hurry (on); **4** se presser to hurry.

pressing *noun* M dry cleaner's.

pression *noun* F **1** pressure; **sous pression** pressurized; **2** press stud; **3** (*informal*) draught beer; **un demi pression** a half of draught beer.

prestidigitateur, prestidigitatrice *noun* M, F conjurer.

présumer *verb* [1] to assume, to presume.

prêt *noun* M loan.
adjective ready; **le dîner est prêt!** dinner's ready!; **être prêt à partir** to be ready to leave.

prêt-à-porter *noun* M ready-to-wear (*clothes*).

prétendre *verb* [3] to claim; **elle prétend que ce n'est pas sa faute** she claims it's not her fault.

prêter verb [1] 1 to lend; prêter quelque chose à quelqu'un to lend somebody something; je te prêterai mon vélo I'll lend you my bike; 2 prêter attention to pay attention; 3 prêter l'oreille to listen.

prétexte noun M excuse.

prêtre noun M priest.

preuve noun F 1 proof; la preuve, c'est que... the proof is that...; 2 faire preuve de to show; ils ont fait preuve de beaucoup d'intelligence they showed considerable intelligence.

prévenir verb [81] 1 to tell (in advance); préviens-moi de ta visite tell me when you're coming; ils arrivent toujours sans nous prévenir they always arrive without letting us know; 2 to call (the police or a doctor); 3 to warn; je te préviens I warn you.

prévention noun F prevention.

prévision noun F forecast, forecasting; les prévisions météorologiques the weather forecast.

prévoir verb [65] 1 to predict (an event or change); 2 to plan (a journey or an arrangement); 3 tout a été prévu everything's been taken care of; 4 le départ est prévu pour huit heures departure is scheduled for eight o' clock; 5 to allow (time or money); prévoyez 50 francs pour le taxi allow 50 francs for the taxi.

prier verb [1] 1 prier quelqu'un de faire to ask someone to do; il m'a prié d'excuser son retard he asked

me to forgive him for being late; les clients sont priés de ne pas fumer customers are kindly requested not to smoke; 2 je vous en prie you're welcome, it's nothing; 'merci beaucoup' – 'je vous en prie' 'thank you very much' – 'you're welcome'; 3 to pray.

prière noun F 1 prayer; 2 request; 'prière de fermer la porte' 'please close the door'.

primaire adjective primary; l'école primaire primary school.

prime noun F 1 bonus; 2 free gift.

primevère noun F primrose.

prince noun M prince; le prince Charles Prince Charles.

princesse noun F princess.

principal (M plural principaux) adjective principal, chief.

principe noun M 1 principle; 2 en principe as a rule; en principe je rentre à six heures as a rule I get back at six; 3 en principe in theory; en principe tout le monde a été informé in theory, everybody's been informed.

printanier (F printanière) adjective spring-like (weather).

printemps noun M spring; au printemps in (the) spring.

priorité noun F 1 priority; 2 right of way; 'vous n'avez pas la priorité' 'you do not have right of way' (sign at a roundabout).

pris verb SEE prendre. adjective 1 busy; je suis très pris ce matin I'm very busy this morning;

2 taken; **toutes les places sont prises** all the seats are taken; **3** overcome (with an emotion or a feeling); **être pris de panique** to be panic-stricken.

prise noun F **1** socket, plug (for an electric appliance); **2** capture; **la prise de la Bastille** the storming of the Bastille.

prise de courant noun F power point.

prise de sang noun F blood test.

prise multiple noun F adaptor plug.

prison noun F prison.

prisonnier, prisonnière noun M, F prisoner.

privé noun M **1** private sector (of business or the school system); **2** en privé in private; off the record. adjective **1** private; 'propriété privée' 'private property'; **2** without; **nous sommes privé d'électricité** we are without electricity; **privé de sens** senseless.

priver verb [1] **1** priver quelqu'un de quelque chose to deprive someone of something; **2** se priver de quelque chose to do without something.

privilège noun M privilege.

privilégié adjective privileged, special, fortunate.

privilégier verb [1] **1** to favour; **2** to give priority to.

prix noun M **1** price; **quel est le prix des places?** what price are the seats?; **le prix a augmenté** the price

has gone up; **2** à tout prix at all costs; **3** prize; **le premier prix** first prize.

probable adjective likely; **c'est peu probable** it's unlikely.

probablement adverb probably.

problème noun M problem; **sans problème!** no problem!

procédé noun M process.

procès noun M **1** trial; **2** lawsuit.

prochain adjective next; **la prochaine fois** the next time; **le mois prochain** next month; **jeudi prochain** next Thursday; **à la prochaine!** see you soon!

prochainement adverb soon.

proche adjective **1** near; **la ville la plus proche est Valence** the nearest town is Valence; **2** close; **c'est une amie très proche de Julie** she' a very close friend of Julie's; **3** proche de near; **ils ont acheté une maison proche de Nice** they've bought a house near Nice.

Proche-Orient noun M **le Proche-Orient** the Middle East.

proches plural noun M close family and friends.

procurer verb [1] se procurer quelque chose to get something.

producteur, productrice noun M, F producer.

production noun F production.

produire verb [26] **1** to produce; **2** se produire to happen; **ça s'est produit au mois de mai** that happened in May.

produit noun M product; **les produits de beauté** beauty products; **les produits d'entretien** household products; **les produits laitiers** dairy produce.

prof noun M (*informal*) SHORT FOR **professeur** teacher; **notre prof de français** our French teacher.

professeur noun M **1** teacher; **ma sœur est professeur de physique** my sister's a physics teacher; **2** university lecturer; **3** university professor.

profession noun F profession, occupation.

professionnel (F **professionnelle**) *adjective* professional.

profil noun M profile.

profit noun M **1** profit; **les profits de la société** the company's profits; **2** **au profit de** in aid of; **au profit des sans-abri** in aid of the homeless.

profiter verb [1] **1** **profiter de** to take advantage of (*an opportunity*); **j'ai profité des soldes pour m'acheter un manteau** I took advantage of the sales to buy myself a coat; **2** to make the most of; **profite bien de tes vacances!** make the most of your holiday!; **3** **profiter à** to benefit.

profond *adjective* deep; **un trou profond de 3 mètres** a hole three metres deep; **la France profonde** provincial France.

profondément *adverb* deeply, profoundly.

profondeur noun F depth; **la piscine a une profondeur de 3 mètres** the swimming pool is 3 metres deep; **étudier quelque chose en profondeur** to study something in depth.

programme noun M **1** programme; **ce n'est pas au programme** it's not on the programme; **2** program (*for a computer*); **3** syllabus; **le programme de maths** the maths syllabus.

programmer verb [1] **1** to schedule; **2** to program (*on a computer*).

progrès noun M progress; **les progrès de l'informatique** advances in computer science; **faire des progrès** to make progress.

progresser verb [1] **1** to progress; **2** to make progress.

projecteur noun M **1** floodlight; **2** spotlight; **3** projector.

projet noun M **1** plan; **mes projets pour l'été** my plans for the summer; **2** project; **3** rough draft.

projeter verb [48] **1** to throw, to hurl; **le choc l'a projeté de sa voiture** the impact hurled him out of his car; **2** to show (*a film*); **3** to cast (*a shadow*); **4** **projeter de faire** to plan to do.

prolongation noun F continuation.

prolongé *adjective* lengthy; **une discussion prolongée** a lengthy discussion.

prolonger verb [52] **1** to extend;
elle a prolongé son congé de
maladie she's extended her sick
leave; **2** se prolonger to go on; les
discussions se sont prolongées
jusqu'à 23 h discussions went on till
11 p.m.

promenade noun F **1** walk; faire
une promenade to go for a walk;
une promenade en voiture a drive;
une promenade à vélo a bike ride;
2 promenade (by the sea).

promener verb [50] **1** promener un
enfant to take a child for a walk;
promener le chien to walk the dog;
2 promener quelque chose to
carry something around; **3** se
promener to go for a walk; se
promener en voiture to go for a
drive; se promener à vélo to go for
a bike ride.

promesse noun F promise; il m'a
fait une promesse he made me a
promise; tenir sa promesse to keep
your promise.

prometteur (F prometteuse)
adjective promising.

promettre verb [11] **1** to promise;
promettre de faire to promise to
do; il a promis de téléphoner ce
soir he promised to ring this
evening; j'ai promis à ma mère de
lui écrire une fois par semaine
I promised my mother I would write
to her once a week.

promotion noun F **1** special offer;
les fraises sont en promotion cette
semaine strawberries are on special
offer this week; **2** promotion (to a
higher job); avoir une promotion to
be promoted.

pronom noun M pronoun.

prononcer verb [61] **1** to
pronounce (a word); **2** to mention
(a name); to say (a word or phrase);
3 to make (a speech); **4** se
prononcer pour/contre quelque
chose to declare oneself
for/against something.

prononciation noun F
pronunciation.

propagande noun F propaganda.

proportion noun F proportion; en
proportion de in proportion to.

propos noun M **1** à propos by the
way; à propos, as-tu appelé
maman? by the way, did you ring
Mum?; **2** à propos de about; il n'a
rien dit à propos de son père he
said nothing about his father; **3** des
propos remarks.

proposer verb [1] **1** proposer
quelque chose à quelqu'un to
suggest something to somebody; je
leur ai proposé une petite
promenade I suggested we went for
a little walk; **2** proposer quelque
chose à quelqu'un to offer
somebody something; on lui a
proposé un poste de technicien she
(or he) has been offered a job as a
technician.

proposition noun F offer.

propre adjective **1** (when it comes
after the noun) clean; une chemise
propre a clean shirt; **2** (when it
comes before the noun) own; ma
propre voiture my own car; leurs
propres enfants their own
children.

proprement adverb 1 properly; mange proprement! eat properly!; 2 à proprement parler strictly speaking.

propreté noun F cleanliness.

propriétaire noun M & F 1 owner (usually of a building or a business); 2 landlord, landlady.

propriété noun F 1 property; propriété privée private property; 2 ownership.

prospectus noun M leaflet.

prospère adjective prosperous.

protecteur, protectrice noun M, F protector.
adjective protective; une crème protectrice protective cream.

protection noun F protection; des lunettes de protection protective goggles.

protéger verb [15] to protect; pour protéger l'environnement to protect the environment; se protéger du soleil to protect yourself from the sun.

protestant, protestante noun M, F,
adjective Protestant.

protestation noun F protest.

protester verb [1] to protest; protester contre quelque chose to protest against something.

prouver verb [1] to prove.

provenance noun F origin; du fromage en provenance de France cheese from France; un passager en provenance de Madrid a passenger arriving from Madrid.

proverbe noun M proverb.

province noun F province; en province in the provinces; une ville de province a provincial town.

provision noun F 1 supply; nous avons fait provision de bois we've laid in a supply of wood; 2 des provisions food; maman est partie prendre des provisions Mum's gone off shopping for food.

provisoire adjective temporary.

provocateur, provocatrice noun M, F agitator.
adjective provocative.

provoquer verb [1] 1 to cause; provoquer un accident to cause an accident; provoquer une discussion to spark off a discussion; 2 provoquer quelqu'un to provoke somebody.

proximité noun F nearness; à proximité de near.

prudemment adverb carefully.

prudence noun F caution; conduisez avec prudence! drive carefully!

prudent adjective 1 careful; soyez prudents par mauvais temps! be careful in bad weather!; 2 wise; il est plus prudent de réserver it's wiser to book.

prune noun F plum.

pruneau (plural pruneaux) noun M prune.

prunier noun M plum tree.

psychanalyste noun M & F psychoanalyst.

psychiatre noun M & F
psychiatrist.

psychologie noun F psychology.

psychologique adjective
psychological.

psychologue noun M & F
psychologist.

pu verb SEE **pouvoir¹**.

pub noun F (informal) SHORT FOR
publicité advert.

public noun M 1 public; **en public**
in public; **ouvert au public** open to
the public; '**interdit au public**' 'no
admission'; 2 audience,
spectators; **pour un public jeune** for
a young audience; 3 fans (of a
performer).
adjective (F **publique**) public; **dans
un lieu public** in a public place; **une
école publique** a state school.

publicitaire adjective
1 advertising; **une campagne
publicitaire** an advertising
campaign; 2 promotional
(material).

publicité noun F 1 advertising;
elle travaille dans la publicité she
works in advertising; 2 advert; ad
(in a magazine, a newspaper, on
television, or at the cinema).

publier verb [1] to publish.

puce noun F 1 **une puce
électronique** a microchip; **une
carte à puce** a smart card; 2 flea;
un marché aux puces a
fleamarket.

puer verb [1] to stink.

puis adverb then; **nous allons à
Cannes, puis à Nice** we're going to
Cannes, then Nice.

puisque, puisqu' (before a vowel or
silent 'h') conjunction since;
puisqu'il pleut je prendrai le bus
since it's raining I'll take the bus.

puissance noun F power; **un
moteur d'une forte puissance** a
high-power engine; **une puissance
étrangère** a foreign power.

puissant adjective powerful,
strong.

puits noun M well.

pull, pull-over noun M jumper.

pulvérisateur noun M spray.

punaise noun F 1 drawing-pin;
2 bug.

punir verb [2] to punish

punition noun F punishment.

pur adjective 1 pure; **un
shampooing très doux, très pur** an
ultra-mild, ultra-pure shampoo; **un
croissant pur beurre** an all-butter
croissant; 2 sheer, total; **c'est de la
folie pure** it's sheer madness.

purée noun F mashed potatoes.

puzzle noun M jigsaw puzzle.

PV noun M SHORT FOR **procès verbal**
parking ticket.

pyjama noun M (pair of) pyjamas;
où est mon pyjama? where are my
pyjamas?; **un pyjama propre** a clean
pair of pyjamas.

pyramide noun F pyramid.

Pyrénées plural noun F Pyrenees.

Q q

quai noun M 1 platform; **le train à destination de Paris va arriver au quai numéro trois** the train for Paris is about to arrive at platform number three; 2 quay.

qualifié adjective 1 qualified; 2 skilled.

qualifier verb [1] to qualify.

qualité noun F quality; **des fruits de première qualité** top quality fruit.

quand conjunction, adverb when; **quand est-ce que ton frère arrive?** when is your brother arriving?; **quand tu auras dix-sept ans, tu pourras apprendre à conduire** when you're seventeen you'll be able to learn to drive.

quand même adverb all the same; **il pleut mais je vais sortir quand même** it's raining but I'm going to go out all the same; **quand même!** honestly!

quant à preposition as for; **quant à moi, je reste** as for me, I'm staying here.

quantité noun F amount.

quarantaine noun F 1 about forty; **une quarantaine de personnes** about forty people; **j'approche la quarantaine** I'll soon be forty; 2 quarantine.

quarante number forty.

quart noun M 1 (in time expressions) quarter; **un quart d'heure** a quarter of an hour; **dix heures et quart** quarter past ten; 2 quarter; **le quart du gâteau** a quarter of the cake; **un quart d'eau minérale** a quarter-litre bottle of mineral water; **trois quarts** three quarters; **les trois quarts du temps** most of the time.

quartier noun M area (of a town); **un quartier résidentiel** a residential area; **les gens du quartier** the local people.

quartz noun M quartz.

quasi adverb almost; **quasi parfait** almost perfect.

quasiment adverb 1 practically; **c'est quasiment neuf** it's practically new; 2 **quasiment jamais** hardly ever; **il n'est quasiment jamais chez lui** he's hardly ever at home.

quatorze number fourteen; **Céline a quatorze ans** Céline's fourteen; **le quatorze juin** the fourteenth of June.

quatre number four; **Louis a quatre ans** Louis is four; **le quatre mars** the fourth of March.

quatre-vingts number eighty; **quatre-vingts personnes** eighty people; **quatre-vingt-trois** eighty-three (note that the 's' is dropped when another number is added); **quatre-vingt-seize** ninety-six.

quatre-vingt-dix number ninety; **quatre-vingt-dix-neuf** ninety-nine.

quatrième noun F (in a French school) the equivalent of Year 9.

noun M **au quatrième** on the fourth floor.
adjective fourth.

que *conjunction, pronoun, adverb*
1 that (*often left out in English*); **elle dit que c'est vrai** she says (that) it's true; **je sais qu'il y habite** I know he lives there; **je veux que tu sois heureux** I want you to be happy; 2 whether; **qu'ils arrivent demain ou mardi, n'importe** whether they come tomorrow or on Tuesday, it doesn't matter; 3 **que tout le monde se lève!** everybody stand up!; 4 **plus...que** more...than; **elle est plus grande que Marie** she's taller than Marie; 5 **aussi...que** as...as; **elle est aussi grande que moi** she's as tall as me; 6 **ne...que** only; **je n'ai que dix francs** I've only got ten francs; 7 that, which, whom (*often left out in English*); **le livre que je lis** the book (that) I'm reading; **la chemise qu'il a achetée** the shirt (which) he's bought; 8 what; **que veut-il?** what does he want?; **je ne sais pas ce qu'il veut** I don't know what he wants; 9 **qu'est-ce que...?** what...?; **qu'est-ce que tu as trouvé?** what have you found?; **qu'est-ce que c'est?** what's that? **qu'est-ce qu'il y a?** what's the matter?; **qu'est-ce qu'elle a?** what's the matter with her?; 10 how (*in an exclamation*); **que tu as grandi!** how you've grown!

quel, quelle *adjective* 1 (*in a question*) what; which; **quel livre?** which book?; **quelle voiture?** which car?; **quelle heure est-il?** what time is it?; **quel âge as-tu?** how old are you?; **dans quels pays?** in which

countries?; **pour quelles raisons?** for what reasons?; 2 (*in an exclamation*) what; **quel beau temps!** what lovely weather!; **quelle coïncidence!** what a coincidence!; **quelle horreur!** how dreadful!

quelconque *adjective* any; **si tu as un problème quelconque** if you have any sort of a problem; **si pour une raison quelconque** if for any reason.

quelle *adjective* SEE **quel.**

quelque chose *pronoun*
1 something; **il faut manger quelque chose, Claire** you must eat something, Claire; **il y a quelque chose de bizarre** there's something strange; **voulez-vous boire quelque chose?** would you like something to drink?; 2 anything; **est-ce que tu as vu quelque chose?** did you see anything?

quelquefois *adverb* sometimes.

quelque part *adverb*
1 somewhere; **quelque part dans le jardin** somewhere in the garden; 2 anywhere; **est-ce que tu as vu mes lunettes quelque part?** have you seen my glasses anywhere?

quelques *adjective* 1 some; **je vais te donner quelques cerises** I'll give you some cherries; 2 a few; **il reste quelques fraises** there are a few strawberries left; **elle est partie pour quelques jours** she's gone away for a few days.

quelques-uns, quelques-unes
plural pronoun some; **quelques-**

uns des enfants some of the children.

quelqu'un *pronoun* 1 somebody; **quelqu'un a appelé pour toi** somebody rang for you; **quelqu'un d'autre** somebody else; 2 anybody; **il y a quelqu'un?** is there anybody there?

quels, quelles *adjective* SEE **quel**.

querelle *noun* F quarrel.

qu'est-ce que SEE **que**.

qu'est-ce qui SEE **qui**.

question *noun* F 1 question; **poser une question à quelqu'un** to ask somebody a question; **elle n'a pas répondu à mes questions** she didn't answer my questions; 2 matter, question; **c'est une question de goût** it's a matter of taste; **c'est hors de question** it's out of the question; **pas question!** no way!

questionnaire *noun* M questionnaire.

questionner *verb* [1] to question.

queue *noun* F 1 tail; **la queue du chat** the cat's tail; 2 queue; **faire la queue** to queue; 3 **la queue du train** the rear of the train; 4 stalk (*of a flower or a fruit*).

queue de cheval *noun* F ponytail.

qui *pronoun* 1 who; **qui a fermé la porte?** who closed the door?; **qui voulez-vous voir?** who do you want to see?; **la personne qui vous a écrit n'est pas là aujourd'hui** the person who wrote to you is not here today; 2 that; **prends la casserole qui est**

sur l'évier take the pan that's on the sink; 3 **à qui?** whose?; **à qui est ce pull?** whose is this jumper?; 4 **à qui parles-tu?** who are you talking to?; 5 **qu'est-ce qui...?** what...?; **qu'est-ce qui t'amène?** what brings you here?

quincaillerie *noun* F hardware shop.

quinzaine *noun* F 1 about fifteen; **une quinzaine d'enfants** about fifteen children; 2 **une quinzaine de jours** a fortnight; **dans une quinzaine** two weeks from now.

quinze *number* 1 fifteen; **Marise a quinze ans** Marise is fifteen; **le quinze juillet** the fifteenth of July; 2 **quinze jours** two weeks; **tous les quinze jours** every two weeks.

quitter *verb* [1] 1 to leave; **je quitte le bureau à cinq heures** I leave the office at five; **j'ai quitté l'école à seize ans** I left school at sixteen; 2 **se quitter** to part; 3 **ne quittez pas** hold the line please (*on the telephone*).

quoi *pronoun* 1 what; **quoi encore?** what now?; **tu es sourd ou quoi?** are you deaf or what?; **à quoi penses-tu?** what are you thinking about?; **pour quoi faire?** what for?; **à quoi bon continuer?** what's the point in going on?; **il n'y a pas de quoi se fâcher** there's no reason to get angry; **il n'y a pas de quoi** don't mention it; 2 which; **après quoi, il est parti** after which, he left.

quoique *conjunction* although, though; **quoique petit, il est fort** although he's small he's strong.

quotidien (F **quotidienne**) *adjective* daily; **la vie quotidienne** daily life. *noun* M daily newspaper.

R r

rabais *noun* M discount; **au rabais** at a discount.

raccompagner *verb* [1] **raccompagner quelqu'un** to see somebody home.

raccourci *noun* M short cut.

raccrocher *verb* [1] to hang up (*telephone*).

race *noun* F **1** race; **la race humaine** the human race; **2** breed; **un chien de race** a pedigree dog.

racheter *verb* [16] **1** to buy more; **il faut racheter du pain** we'll have to buy more bread; **2 il m'a racheté ma voiture** he bought my car off me.

racine *noun* F root.

raciste *noun* M & F, *adjective* racist; **des propos racistes** racist remarks.

racler *verb* [1] to scrape.

raconter *verb* [1] to tell (*a story*); **raconte-nous ce qui s'est passé** tell us what happened.

radar *noun* M radar.

radiateur *noun* M radiator.

radio *noun* F **1** radio; **je l'ai entendu à la radio** I heard it on the radio; **2** X-ray; **passer une radio** to have an X-ray.

radiocassette *noun* M or F radio cassette player.

radio-réveil *noun* M clock radio.

radis *noun* M radish.

rafale *noun* F gust (*of wind or rain*); flurry (*of snow*).

raffoler *verb* [1] **raffoler de** to be mad about; **je ne raffole pas des huîtres** I'm not mad about oysters.

rafraîchir *verb* [2] **1 le temps se rafraîchit** the weather's getting cooler; **2** to cool (*somebody*) down.

rage *noun* F **1** rabies; **2 une rage de dents** raging toothache.

ragoût *noun* M stew.

raide *adjective* **1** stiff (*body, arm, leg*); **2** straight (*hair*); **3 une pente raide** a steep slope.

raie *noun* F **1** parting (*in your hair*); **2** skate (*the fish*).

rail *noun* M rail (*for trains*); ★ **remettre quelque chose sur les rails** to put something back on the right track.

raisin *noun* M grapes; **j'ai acheté du raisin noir** I bought some black grapes; **une grappe de raisin** a bunch of grapes; **un grain de raisin** a grape; **le jus de raisin** grape juice.

raisin de Corinthe *noun* ,M currant.

raisin sec *noun* M raisin.

raison noun F 1 reason; **pour cette raison** for this reason; **pour raisons de santé** for health reasons; 2 **avoir raison** to be right; **oui, tu as raison** yes, you're right.

raisonnable adjective sensible.

raisonnement noun M reasoning.

rajouter verb [1] to add; **on peut rajouter de l'eau si on veut** you can add water if you want.

ralentir verb [2] to slow down.

ralentissement noun M slowing down.

ralentisseur noun M speed bump.

râler (informal) verb [1] to moan; **arrête de râler!** stop moaning!

rallonge noun F 1 extension cord; 2 extra leaf (for a table).

ramasser verb [1] 1 to pick up; **est-ce que tu peux ramasser tous ces papiers, s'il te plaît** can you pick up all these papers please; 2 to pick (fruit); **ils ont déjà ramassé les framboises** they've already picked the raspberries; 3 to collect; **on va ramasser des châtaignes dans les bois** we're going to go and collect chestnuts in the woods; 4 to collect in (books, homework); **Anne, veux-tu ramasser tous les cahiers?** Anne, would you collect in all the exercise books?

rame noun F 1 oar; 2 **une rame de métro** an underground train.

rameau (plural **rameaux**) noun M branch; **le dimanche des Rameaux** Palm Sunday.

ramener verb [50] 1 **ramener quelqu'un (en voiture)** to give somebody a lift home; **tu veux que je te ramène?** do you want a lift home?; **elle m'a ramené en voiture** she gave me a lift back; 2 to take back; **je dois ramener les livres à la bibliothèque** I must take these books back to the library.

ramer verb [1] to row.

rampe noun F banister.

rançon noun F ransom.

rancune noun F resentment, grudge.

randonnée noun F **faire une randonnée pédestre** to go walking (on public footpaths); **on a fait une randonnée de vingt kilomètres** we did a twenty-kilometre walk; **faire une randonnée à cheval** to go pony-trekking; **une randonnée à vélo** a long-distance bike ride.

randonneur, randonneuse noun M, F walker, rambler.

rang noun M row; **au cinquième rang** in the fifth row.

rangée noun F row; **une rangée de maisons** a row of houses.

ranger verb [52] 1 to put away; **ranger la vaisselle** to put away the dishes; 2 to tidy; **je vais ranger ma chambre** I'm going to tidy my room; 3 to arrange; **il range ses livres par ordre alphabétique** he arranges his books alphabetically.

râper verb [1] to grate; **le fromage râpé** grated cheese.

rapide noun M express train. adjective quick; **prends le métro,**

c'est plus rapide take the underground, it's quicker.

rapidement adverb quickly, rapidly.

rappel noun M 1 reminder (for a bill); 'dernier rappel' 'final demand'; 2 booster (vaccination).

rappeler verb [18] 1 to remind; rappelle-moi de passer par la banque remind me to go to the bank; le paysage me rappelle la France the countryside reminds me of France; 2 to ring back (on the telephone); il va te rappeler dans une heure he'll ring you back in an hour; 3 se rappeler to remember; je ne me rappelle plus I can't remember; je me rappelle qu'elle avait les cheveux longs I remember she had long hair.

rapport noun M 1 report; un rapport officiel an official report; 2 connection; je ne vois pas le rapport I don't see the connection; 3 être en rapport avec quelqu'un to be in touch with someone; 4 par rapport à compared with; il a fait très beau par rapport à l'année dernière the weather's been very good compared with last year.

rapporter verb [1] 1 to bring back; est-ce que tu peux le rapporter demain? can you bring it back tomorrow?; 2 to bring in; son travail ne rapporte pas beaucoup her job doesn't bring in much money.

rapprocher verb [1] 1 to move (something) closer; peux-tu rapprocher la lampe de ma chaise? can you move the lamp closer to my chair?; 2 to bring

together (different people); des efforts pour rapprocher les deux pays efforts to bring the two countries together; 3 se rapprocher to come (or go) closer; elle s'est rapprochée de la table she moved closer to the table.

raquette noun F 1 racket (for tennis); 2 bat (for ping-pong).

rare adjective rare; une fleur rare a rare flower; il est rare qu'elle arrive à l'heure she very rarely arrives on time.

rarement adverb rarely.

ras adjective 1 short (hair or fur); il a les cheveux coupés ras his hair is cut short; 2 en rase campagne in open country; 3 au ras de l'eau/du sol at water/ground level; ★ j'en ai ras le bol! (informal) I'm fed up!

raser verb [1] 1 to shave, to shave off; il a rasé sa barbe he's shaved off his beard; la mousse à raser shaving foam; 2 se raser to shave; se raser les jambes to shave your legs.

ras-le-cou noun M crew-neck sweater.

rasoir noun M razor.

rassemblement noun M meeting, rally.

rassembler verb [1] to gather (together); j'ai rassemblé les enfants près de l'entrée I gathered all the children together by the main entrance; tout le village s'est rassemblé pour l'écouter the whole village gathered to listen to him.

rassis *adjective* du pain rassis stale bread.

rassurer *verb* [1] **1** to reassure; ah, cela me rassure! oh, that sets my mind at rest!; **2** rassure-toi don't worry.

rat *noun* M rat.

râteau (*plural* râteaux) *noun* M rake.

rater *verb* [1] **1** to fail; Sophie a raté son permis Sophie failed her driving test; **2** to miss; j'ai raté mon train I've missed my train.

rationner *verb* [1] to ration.

rattacher *verb* [1] **1** to (re)fasten; rattache ta ceinture (re)fasten your seat-belt; **2** to attach; plus rien ne me rattache ici I no longer have any ties here.

rattraper *verb* [1] **1** to catch up with (*a person*); ne t'inquiète pas, ils nous rattraperont don't worry, they'll catch up with us; **2** to make up for (*lost time*); **3** se rattraper to make up for it; j'ai très peu joué cet été mais je vais me rattraper I've played very little this summer but I'll make up for it.

rature *noun* F crossing-out.

ravi *adjective* delighted; je suis ravi de vous voir I'm delighted to see you.

ravisseur, ravisseuse *noun* M, F kidnapper.

rayé *adjective* striped (*fabric*).

rayer *verb* [59] **1** to cross out (*a mistake*); j'ai rayé ton nom de la liste I crossed your name off the list; **2** to scratch (*a surface*).

rayon *noun* M **1** shelf; un rayon pour mes livres a shelf for my books; **2** department (*in a department store*), section (*in a supermarket*); au rayon fraîcheur in the chilled foods section; **3** ray; un rayon de soleil a ray of sunshine; les rayons X X-rays; **4** radius.

rayure *noun* F **1** stripe; **2** scratch.

RC *noun* M SHORT FOR rez-de-chaussée ground floor.

réacteur *noun* M **1** un réacteur nucléaire a nuclear reactor; **2** jet engine.

réaction *noun* F reaction.

réagir *verb* [2] to react; elle n'a pas réagi she didn't react.

réalisateur, réalisatrice *noun* M, F director (*of a film or TV programme*).

réalisation *noun* F **1** carrying out (*of a plan or project*); **2** production (*of a film or a radio/TV programme*).

réaliser *verb* [1] **1** to carry out (*a project*); **2** to fulfil; réaliser un rêve to fulfil a dream; **3** to make (*a film*); **4** to realize.

réaliste *adjective* realistic.

réalité *noun* F reality; en réalité in reality.

réanimation *noun* F resuscitation; (service de) réanimation intensive care (unit).

rebondir *verb* [2] to bounce.

rebord noun M **1** le rebord de la fenêtre the window ledge; **2** edge; le rebord de la baignoire the edge of the bath.

récemment adverb recently.

récent adjective recent.

réception noun F **1** reception desk; demandez la clé à la réception ask for the key at the reception desk; **2** reception (party).

réceptionniste noun M & F receptionist.

recette noun F recipe; la recette du gâteau the recipe for the cake.

recevoir verb {66} **1** to receive, to get; j'ai reçu ta lettre I got your letter; **2** to welcome (a visitor or guest); **3** to see (a patient or client); le dentiste reçoit entre 9h et 17h the dentist sees patients between 9 a.m. and 5 p.m.; **4** être reçu à un examen to pass an exam; elle a été reçue première à l'examen she came top in the exam.

rechange noun M de rechange spare; une pièce de rechange a spare part.

recharge noun F refill.

réchaud noun M stove.

réchauffer verb {1} **1** to warm up (food); peux-tu mettre la soupe à réchauffer? can you put the soup on to warm?; **2** to warm (hands or feet); **3** se réchauffer to get warm; va te réchauffer près du feu go and get warm by the fire.

recherche noun F **1** research; **2** être à la recherche de quelque chose to be looking for something; je suis à la recherche d'un logement I'm looking for somewhere to live.

rechercher verb {1} to look for; la police le recherche the police are looking for him; elle recherche un travail plus flexible she's looking for a more flexible job.

récipient noun M container.

réciproque adjective mutual.

récit noun M story; il nous a fait le récit de son voyage he told us all about his journey.

réciter verb {1} to recite.

réclame noun F **1** advertisement; une réclame pour le nouveau modèle an advertisement for the new model; **2** en réclame on (special) offer; le jambon est en réclame cette semaine the ham is on special offer this week.

réclamer verb {1} to demand; ils réclament trois jours de plus de vacances they're demanding three more days' holiday.

récolte noun F **1** harvest; **2** crop.

récolter verb {1} **1** to harvest; récolter le blé to harvest the wheat; **2** to collect (money); **3** (informal) to get; récolter une amende to get a fine.

recommandé adjective registered; une lettre recommandée a registered letter; je voudrais l'envoyer en recommandé I'd like to send it by registered post.

recommander verb {1} **1** to advise; je te recommande de ne rien

dire I advise you to say nothing;
2 to recommend.

recommencer *verb* [61] **1** to start
again; **j'ai recommencé ma lettre** I
started my letter again; **il a
recommencé à neiger** it's started
snowing again; **2** to do it again; **si tu
ne fais pas attention, elle va
recommencer** if you don't watch
out, she'll do it again; **ça
recommence!** here we go again!

récompense *noun* F reward.

récompenser *verb* [1] to reward.

réconcilier *verb* [1] **se réconcilier
avec quelqu'un** to make it up with
somebody.

réconfortant *adjective*
comforting.

reconnaissable *adjective*
recognizable.

reconnaissance *noun* F
1 gratitude; **en reconnaissance de**
in appreciation of; **2** recognition.

reconnaissant *adjective* grateful.

reconnaître *verb* [27] **1** to
recognize; **je ne l'ai pas reconnue** I
didn't recognize her; **je l'ai reconnu
à sa voix** I recognized him by his
voice; **2** to admit; **il faut reconnaître
que c'est difficile** it must be
admitted that it's difficult; **elle
reconnaît qu'elle a menti** she
admits she lied.

reconstruire *verb* [26] to rebuild.

recopier *verb* [1] to copy out.

record *noun* M record; **un record
mondial** a world record; **battre un
record** to break a record.

recouvrir *verb* [30] to cover.

récréation *noun* F break; **la cour
de récréation** the playground.

rectangle *noun* M rectangle.

rectangulaire *adjective*
rectangular.

rectifier *verb* [1] to correct.

reçu *noun* M receipt.
verb SEE **recevoir**.

recueil *noun* M collection (*of
poems or essays*).

reculer *verb* [1] **1** to move back; **elle
a reculé de quelques pas** she moved
back a few steps; **2** to reverse (*in a
car*); **3** **reculer la date d'une
réunion** to postpone a meeting.

reculons *in phrase* **à reculons**
backwards.

récupérer *verb* [24] **1** to get back;
**je vais chez Brigitte pour récupérer
le bouquin que je lui ai prêté** I'm
going round to Brigitte's to get back
the book I lent her; **2** to recover
(*from an illness*).

recycler *verb* [1] to recycle.

rédaction *noun* F essay.

redemander *verb* [1] **1** to ask
again; **tu devrais redemander** you
should ask again; **2** to ask for more;
**il faut qu'on redemande des
cahiers** we'll have to ask for more
exercise books.

redescendre *verb* [3] **1** to go (or
come) back down; **elle est
redescendue à la cave** she went
back down to the cellar; **je monte à
Glasgow demain et je redescends
lundi** I'm going up to Glasgow

tomorrow and I'm coming back down on Monday; **2** to bring or take back down; **est-ce que tu peux redescendre ma valise?** can you bring my suitcase back down?

rédiger verb [52] to write (an article); to write up (notes).

redonner verb [1] to give again; **je leur ai redonné mon adresse** I gave them my address again; **est-ce que je te redonne un peu de salade?** can I give you a bit more salad?

redoubler verb [1] to repeat a year (at school).

réduction noun F **1** reduction; **une réduction du nombre d'étudiants** a reduction in the number of students; **2** (price) reduction; **une réduction de 20%** a 20% reduction.

réduire verb [68] to cut (prices); **réduire les impôts** to cut taxes; **des vêtements à prix réduits** cut-price clothing.

rééducation noun F physiotherapy.

réel (F **réelle**) adjective real.

réellement adverb really.

refaire verb [10] **1** to redo; **je dois refaire mon devoir de maths** I have to redo my maths homework; **c'est tout à refaire** it has to be completely redone; **il ne faut pas refaire la même erreur** we mustn't make the same mistake again; **2** to make more; **elle est en train de refaire du café** she's making some more coffee.

référence noun F reference; **faire référence à quelque chose** to refer to something;

réfléchi adjective **1** reflexive (verb); **2** considered (decision).

réfléchir verb [2] to think; **il faut bien réfléchir avant d'accepter** you should think carefully before accepting; **j'ai réfléchi au problème** I've thought about the problem.

reflet noun M **1** reflection; **2 des cheveux aux reflets blonds** hair with blond highlights.

refléter verb [24] to reflect.

réflexe noun M, adjective reflex.

réflexion noun F **1** thought; **2** comment; **il m'a fait des réflexions désagréables** he made some nasty comments to me.

refrain noun M chorus.

réfrigérateur noun M refrigerator.

refroidir verb [2] to cool down.

refroidissement noun M drop in temperature.

refuge noun M **1** mountain hut (for climbers); **2** animal sanctuary; **3** traffic island; **4** refuge.

réfugié, réfugiée noun M, F refugee.

réfugier verb [1] **se réfugier** to take shelter, to take refuge.

refus noun M refusal; ★ **ce n'est pas de refus** I wouldn't say no;

'veux-tu boire quelque chose?' – **'ce n'est pas de refus'** 'would you like a drink?' – 'I wouldn't say no'.

refuser verb [1] **1** to refuse; **refuser de faire** to refuse to do; **elle a refusé de répondre** she refused to answer; **2** to turn down; **ils ont refusé sa candidature** they turned him down for the job.

regagner verb [1] **nous avons regagné nos places** we went back to our seats.

régal noun M feast; **ça a été un véritable régal** it was a real feast.

régaler verb [1] **on s'est vraiment régalé!** the food was absolutely wonderful!

regard noun M look.

regarder verb [1] **1** to look at; **je vais regarder la carte** I'll look at the map; **2** to watch; **regarder la télé** to watch telly; **veux-tu regarder le film?** do you want to watch the film?; **3** to look; **regarder par la fenêtre** to look out of the window; **regarde!** look!; **4** to concern; **cela ne nous regarde pas** that doesn't concern us; **cela ne le regarde pas** that's none of his business.

régime noun M **1** diet; **un régime sans sel** a salt-free diet; **je fais un régime** I'm on a diet; **2** un régime de bananes a bunch of bananas; **3** régime.

région noun F region; **les vins de la région** the local wines.

régional (M plural **régionaux**) adjective regional.

registre noun M register.

réglable adjective adjustable.

règle noun F **1** ruler; **2** rule; **selon les règles** according to the rules; **les règles de sécurité** the safety regulations; **en règle générale** as a general rule; **3** en règle in order (valid); **4** les règles period (menstruation); **j'ai mes règles** I've got my period.

règlement noun M regulations.

régler verb [24] **1** to pay (a debt or a bill); **vous réglez comment, monsieur?** how would you like to pay, sir?; **2** to sort out (details or a problem); **3** to adjust; **on peut régler la hauteur** you can adjust the height.

réglisse noun F liquorice.

règne noun M reign.

régner verb [24] to reign.

regret noun M regret; **avec/sans regret** with/without regret; **mille regrets** I'm terribly sorry.

regretter verb [1] **1** to be sorry; **je regrette** I'm sorry; **nous regrettons beaucoup de partir** we're very sorry to be leaving; **2** to regret; **elles regrettent avoir quitté Paris** they regret having left Paris; **je ne regrette rien** I have no regrets; **3** to miss; **je regrette la vie à Paris** I miss the Parisian way of life.

regrouper verb [1] **1** to group together; **les débutants sont regroupés ensemble** beginners are grouped together; **2** se regrouper to regroup; **les enfants se sont regroupés autour d'elle** the children gathered around her.

régularité noun F regularity.

régulier (F **régulière**) adjective
1 regular; **à intervalles réguliers** at regular intervals; 2 **vols réguliers à New York** scheduled flights to New York.

régulièrement adverb regularly.

rein noun M 1 kidney; 2 **les reins** the back; **j'ai mal aux reins** I've got back-ache.

reine noun F queen; **la reine Elisabeth** Queen Elizabeth.

reine-claude noun F greengage.

rejeter verb [48] to reject.

rejoindre verb [49] 1 to meet up with; **je vous rejoins au bar** I'll meet you in the bar; 2 to join (other people, a group, or a movement); 3 **se rejoindre** to meet up; **alors on se rejoint à onze heures?** so shall we meet up at eleven?

relâcher verb [1] 1 to loosen (a grip or hold); 2 to set free (a prisoner, hostage, or animal); 3 to relax (your attention or discipline).

relais noun M 1 restaurant, hotel; 2 **prendre le relais (de quelqu'un)** to take over (from someone); **il a pris le relais au volant** he took over the driving; 3 relay race.

relatif (F **relative**) adjective relative.

relation noun F 1 connection; **en relation avec** in connection with; 2 acquaintance; **une relation de mon frère** an acquaintance of my brother's; 3 relationship; **il a de bonnes relations avec son patron** he has a good relationship with his boss; 4 **les relations publiques** public relations.

relativement adverb relatively; **relativement à** in relation to.

relax (informal) adjective casual, laid back.

relaxer verb [1] to relax.

relent noun M lingering smell.

relevé noun M 1 **faire le relevé de quelque chose** to make a list of something; 2 **un relevé de compte** a bank statement.

relever verb [50] 1 to raise; 2 **relever la tête** to look up; 3 to notice (details, mistakes, or interesting facts); 4 **relever le compteur** to read the meter; 5 **se relever** to pick yourself up (after a fall).

religieux, religieuse noun M, F monk, nun.
adjective religious.

religion noun F religion.

relire verb [51] to re-read, to read over.

remarquable adjective remarkable, striking.

remarque noun F remark, comment.

remarquer verb [1] 1 to notice; **je n'ai rien remarqué** I didn't notice anything; **j'ai remarqué qu'elle est arrivée en retard** I noticed she arrived late; 2 **se faire remarquer** to draw attention to yourself; **il n'aime pas se faire remarquer** he doesn't like drawing attention to himself; 3 **faire remarquer quelque**

chose à quelqu'un to point something out to somebody; **elle lui a fait remarquer que c'était déjà trop tard** she pointed out to him that it was already too late.

rembobiner verb [1] to rewind (*a tape or video*).

remboursement noun M repayment, refund.

rembourser verb [1] **1** to pay back; **je te rembourserai demain** I'll pay you back tomorrow; **2** to refund the price of; **ils m'ont remboursé les billets** they refunded me the price of the tickets; **3** to reimburse; **nous vous rembourserons le voyage** we'll pay your travelling expenses.

remède noun M remedy.

remerciement noun M thanks; **tous mes remerciements** many thanks; **une lettre de remerciement** a thank-you letter.

remercier verb [1] **1** to thank; **je l'ai remerciée pour les fleurs** I thanked her for the flowers; **2 remercier quelqu'un d'avoir fait quelque chose** to thank somebody for doing something; **il nous a remerciés de l'avoir aidé** he thanked us for helping him.

remettre verb [11] **1** to put back; **remets la bouteille au frigo** put the bottle back in the fridge; **il a remis la photo sur la table** he put the photo back on the table; **as-tu remis tous les livres à leur place?** have you put all the books back in their place?; **2** to put back on; **je vais remettre ma veste** I'm going to put my jacket back on; **3** to hand over; **pouvez-vous me remettre les clés demain?** can you hand over the keys to me tomorrow?; **4** to put off; **ils ont remis la réunion à jeudi** they've put the meeting off until Thursday; **5 se remettre** to start again; **elle s'est remise au piano** she's started playing the piano again; **il s'est remis à pleuvoir** it's started raining again; **6 se remettre de** to recover; **ils ne se sont toujours pas remis du choc** they still haven't recovered from the shock.

remise noun F **1** handing out; **la remise des prix** the prizegiving; **2** discount; **nous faisons une remise de 20% sur tous les CD** we're giving a 20% discount on all CDs; **3** garden shed.

remonte-pente M noun ski lift.

remonter verb [1] **1** to go (or come) back up; **Nathalie est remontée dans sa chambre** Nathalie's gone back up to her room; **je descends à Londres ce soir et je remonte lundi** I'm going down to London tonight and coming back up on Monday; **2** to take (or bring) back up; **veux-tu remonter les chaises?** would you take the chairs back upstairs?; **3** to put back up; **il m'a remonté ma valise au filet** he put my case up in the luggage rack for me; **4** remonter la pente to go back up the hill; **5** to get (or climb) back in; **ils sont remontés dans la car** they got back into the coach; **6 remonter quelqu'un, remonter le moral à quelqu'un** to cheer someone up.

remords noun M remorse.

remorque noun F **1** trailer (*for a car*); **2** tow-rope.

remplaçant, remplaçante noun M, F **1** replacement (*for another person*); **2** supply teacher.

remplacer verb [61] **1** to stand in for (*a person*); **2** to replace; **il faut remplacer les piles** you need to replace the batteries.

remplir verb [2] **1** to fill; **il a rempli son verre de vin** he filled his glass with wine; **la salle était remplie de jeunes** the hall was full of young people; **2** remplir un formulaire to fill in a form; **3** to carry out (*a duty or a role*).

remue-ménage noun M commotion.

remuer verb [1] **1** to move (*your head or hand, for example*); **le vent remuait les branches** the wind was shaking the branches; **2** to stir; **peux-tu remuer la sauce, s'il te plaît?** can you stir the sauce, please?

rémunérer verb [24] to pay (*a person*); to pay for (*work*).

renard noun M fox.

rencontre noun F **1** meeting; **elle est venue à ma rencontre** she came to meet me; **2** (*in sport*) match; **la rencontre entre la France et l'Allemagne** the match between France and Germany.

rencontrer verb [1] **1** to meet (*a person*); **je l'ai rencontrée en 1993** I met her in 1993; **2** to play (*an opponent or a team*); **3** se rencontrer to meet; **nous nous sommes rencontrés à Londres** we met in London.

rendez-vous noun M **1** appointment; **prendre rendez-vous** to make an appointment; **j'ai rendez-vous chez le dentiste** I've got a dentist's appointment; **le médecin voit les malades sur rendez-vous** the doctor sees patients by appointment; **2** date; **Marc a rendez-vous avec sa copine à trois heures** Marc's got a date with his girlfriend at three; **3** donner rendez-vous à quelqu'un to arrange to meet somebody; **il m'a donné rendez-vous au café** he arranged to meet me at the café.

rendormir verb [37] se rendormir to go back to sleep; **elle s'est rendormie** she went back to sleep.

rendre verb [3] **1** to give back; **je te rendrai les clés demain** I'll give you back the keys tomorrow; **2** rendre quelqu'un heureux to make somebody happy; **3** to hand in (*homework*); **4** se rendre to give oneself up; **les voleurs se sont rendus à la police** the thieves gave themselves up to the police; **5** se rendre compte de quelque chose to realize something; **je me suis rendu compte du fait que j'avais oublié mes clés** I realized I had forgotten my keys.

renifler verb [1] to sniff.

renne noun M reindeer.

renommé adjective famous.

renoncer verb [61] **1** to give up; **c'est trop difficile, je renonce!** it's too difficult, I give up!; **2** renoncer à quelque chose to give something up.

renouveler verb [18] to renew (a passport or a subscription, for example).

rénover verb [1] 1 to renovate (a house); 2 to restore (furniture).

renseignement noun M 1 un renseignement a piece of information; un renseignement utile a useful piece of information; 2 les renseignements information; je cherche des renseignements I'm looking for information; adressez-vous aux renseignements ask at the information desk; 3 renseignements directory enquiries.

renseigner verb [1] 1 renseigner quelqu'un to give someone information; la brochure vous renseigne sur les horaires the brochure gives you timetable information; il était très bien renseigné sur le projet he was very well-informed about the project; 2 se renseigner to find out; je vais me renseigner au bureau de tourisme I'm going to find out at the tourist office.

rentable adjective profitable.

rentrée noun F la rentrée (des classes) the start of the new school year.

rentrer verb [1] 1 to get home; Maman rentre à dix-huit heures Mum will be home at six; je vais rentrer chez moi I'm going home; 2 to get back; ils rentrent de Paris jeudi they'll be back from Paris on Thursday; 3 to come (or go) in; rentrez! do come in!; elles sont rentrées dans un magasin they've gone into a shop; 4 rentrer dans quelque chose to go in something; tout ça ne rentrera jamais dans ton sac! all that will never go in your bag!; 5 rentrer dans quelque chose to crash into something; la voiture est rentrée dans un mur the car crashed into a wall; 6 rentrer quelque chose to bring something in (from outside); rentre les chaises, il pleut! bring the chairs in, it's raining!

renverser verb [1] 1 to knock over; il a renversé sa chaise he knocked his chair over; 2 être renversé par une voiture to be knocked down by a car; 3 to spill; j'ai renversé mon thé I've spilled my tea.

renvoyer verb [40] 1 to send back; as-tu renvoyé le formulaire? have you sent back the form?; on m'a renvoyé à l'hôpital they sent me back to hospital; 2 to throw back (a ball); 3 to dismiss; la secrétaire a été renvoyée the secretary has been dismissed.

réouverture noun F reopening.

répandu adjective widespread.

réparation noun F repair.

réparer verb [1] to repair.

repartir verb [58] 1 to go off again; ils ont déposé les enfants et ils sont repartis they dropped the children and went off again; 2 to go again; je suis reparti chez moi I went home again; 3 repartir à zéro to start from scratch.

repas noun M meal; **le repas de midi** lunch; **le repas du soir** the evening meal.

repassage noun M ironing.

repasser verb [1] **1** to drop in again; **il a dit qu'il repasserait demain** he said he'd drop in again tomorrow; **2** to iron; **Frank est en train de repasser sa chemise** Frank's busy ironing his shirt; **une planche à repasser** an ironing board; **3** to resit (*an exam or test*).

repeindre verb [60] to repaint.

repère noun M **un point de repère** a landmark; a reference point.

repérer verb [24] **1** (*informal*) to spot; **j'ai repéré trois erreurs dans son article** I spotted three mistakes in his article; **2** to locate (*a place*).

répertoire noun M notebook (*with a thumb index*); **un répertoire d'adresses** an address book.

répéter verb [24] **1** to repeat; **elle l'a répété trois fois** she repeated it three times; **faire des essais répétés** to make repeated attempts; **2** to rehearse (*a play*); **3** to practise (*a piece of music*); **4** **se répéter** to repeat oneself; **5** **se répéter** to happen again; **espérons que cela ne se répétera pas** let's hope it doesn't happen again.

répétition noun F **1** rehearsal; **la répétition générale** the dress rehearsal; **2** repetition.

replier verb [1] **1** to fold up; **elle a replié la carte** she folded up the map (*a sheet*); **2** **elle a replié ses jambes** she tucked her legs up (under her).

répondeur noun M answering machine; **j'ai laissé un message sur le répondeur** I left a message on the answering machine.

répondre verb [3] **1** to answer; **il n'a pas répondu** he didn't answer; **je ne lui ai pas répondu** I didn't answer him; **2** **répondre à une question** to answer a question; **3** **répondre à une lettre** to reply to a letter.

réponse noun F answer; **la bonne réponse** the right answer.

reportage noun M **1** report; **un reportage sur la drogue** a report on drugs; **2** (news) story.

reporter[1] verb [1] to postpone; **on a reporté le match à jeudi** the match has been postponed until Thursday.

reporter[2] noun M reporter.

repos noun M rest; **dix jours de repos** ten days' rest.

reposant adjective restful.

reposer verb [1] **1** **reposer quelque chose** to put something back down; **elle a reposé le livre sur la table** she put the book back down on the table; **2** **se reposer** to have a rest; **j'ai besoin de me reposer** I need a rest; **repose-toi bien!** have a good rest!

repousser verb [1] **1** to grow again; **tes cheveux ont vite repoussé** your hair's grown quickly; **2** to push back; **3** to postpone; **le match a été repoussé** the match has been postponed.

reprendre verb [64] 1 to have some more (food or drink); **reprends du poulet** have some more chicken; 2 to take back; **est-ce que je peux reprendre les verres que je t'avais prêtés?** can I take back the glasses I lent you?; 3 to start again; **l'école reprend en septembre** school starts again in September; 4 **reprendre le travail** to go back to work; **j'ai repris le travail lundi** I went back to work on Monday; 5 **reprendre la route** to set off again.

représentant, représentante noun M, F sales rep.

représentation noun F performance (of a play); **prochaine représentation à 20h** next performance 8 p.m.

représenter verb [1] 1 to depict; 2 to represent.

réprimander verb [1] to tell off, to reprimand.

réprimer verb [1] to suppress.

reprise noun F 1 resumption (of work or discussions); 2 rerun (of a play or film); repeat (of a broadcast); 3 **à plusieurs reprises** on several occasions.

reproche noun M criticism; **il m'a fait des reproches** he criticized me.

reprocher verb [1] 1 to criticize; **il a reproché à son fils de ne pas travailler** he criticized his son for not working; 2 **se reprocher** to blame oneself.

reproduction noun F reproduction.

reproduire verb [26] 1 to reproduce; 2 **se reproduire** to happen again.

républicain adjective republican.

république noun F republic; **la République française** the French Republic.

répugnant adjective revolting.

réputation noun F reputation; **il a la réputation d'être très sévère** he has a reputation for being very strict.

requin noun M shark.

RER noun M SHORT FOR réseau express régional (the fast suburban network on the Paris underground).

rescousse noun F **aller à la rescousse de quelqu'un** to go to someone's rescue.

réseau (plural réseaux) noun M network.

réservation noun F reservation.

réserve noun F 1 stock; **des réserves de charbon** stocks of coal; **j'ai deux bouteilles en réserve** I have put aside two bottles; 2 reserve (for birds or animals); **une réserve ornithologique** a bird sanctuary.

réservé adjective reserved.

réserver verb [1] 1 to reserve, to book; **j'ai réservé deux places pour ce soir** I've booked two seats for this evening; 2 to keep; **Philippe t'a réservé du poulet** Philippe's kept some chicken for you.

réservoir noun M 1 tank; **réservoir à essence** petrol tank; 2 reservoir.

résidence noun F 1 home, residence; **une résidence secondaire** a holiday home; 2 block of flats.

résident, résidente noun M, F resident.

résidentiel (F résidentielle) adjective residential.

résistant, résistante noun M, F Resistance fighter (*in France during World War II*). adjective tough.

résister verb [1] **résister à** to resist.

résolu adjective 1 determined; **elle est résolue à démissionner** she is determined to resign; 2 resolved; **le problème est résolu** the problem is resolved.

résoudre verb [67] 1 to solve (*a problem*); 2 **se résoudre à faire** to make up one's mind to do; **elle s'est résolue à partir** she made up her mind to leave.

respect noun M respect.

respecter verb [1] to respect.

respectueux (F respectueuse) adjective respectful.

respiration noun F breathing.

respirer verb [1] to breathe.

responsabilité noun F 1 responsibility; 2 **avoir la responsabilité de quelque chose** to be responsible for something; **il a la responsabilité des livraisons** he's responsible for deliveries.

responsable noun M & F 1 person in charge; **le responsable du projet** the person in charge of the project;

2 person responsible; **les responsables de la catastrophe** those responsible for the disaster. adjective responsible; **il est responsable de l'accident** he's responsible for the accident.

ressemblance noun F similarity.

ressembler verb [1] 1 **ressembler à** to look like; **elle ressemble beaucoup à sa mère** she looks very like her mother; **cela ressemble à du bois mais c'est du plastique** it looks like wood but it's plastic; 2 **se ressembler** to be alike; **les deux sœurs ne se ressemblent pas du tout** the two sisters are not at all alike.

ressentiment noun M resentment.

resserrer verb [1] 1 to tighten (*a knot or screw, for example*); 2 **se resserrer** to move closer together; **resserrez-vous un peu!** squeeze up a bit!

resservir verb [58] 1 to give another helping; **je vous ressers un peu?** shall I give you a little more?; 2 **se resservir** to help yourself to more; **ressers-toi de la salade** help yourself to some more salad; **je me suis déjà resservi, merci** I've already helped myself to more, thank you.

ressort noun M spring (*in a bed or a chair*).

ressortir verb [58] to go out again; **il est revenu pour les clés et il est ressorti** he came back for the keys and went out again.

ressource noun F **1** resource; des ressources énergétiques energy resources; **2** il est sans ressources he has no means of support.

restaurant noun M restaurant; on mange au restaurant ce soir we're going out for a meal tonight.

restauration noun F **1** catering; la restauration rapide the fast-food industry; **2** restoration.

restaurer verb [1] to restore.

reste noun M **1** le reste the rest; le reste du temps the rest of the time; et tout le reste, tu le sais déjà and you know all the rest already; **2** les restes the leftovers; j'ai fait un curry avec les restes du poulet I made a curry with the leftover chicken.

rester verb [1] **1** to stay; reste là, je reviens tout de suite! stay there, I'll be right back!; Camille est restée à la maison Camille stayed at home; je ne peux pas rester longtemps I can't stay long; hier je suis resté sans manger I didn't have anything to eat yesterday; **2** rester debout to remain standing; je préfère rester debout I prefer to stand; **3** rester assis to remain seated; je suis resté assis toute la journée I've been sitting down all day; **4** to be left; il reste du fromage there's some cheese left; il nous reste combien d'argent? how much money have we got left?; il ne reste pas beaucoup à faire there's not much left to do.

restriction noun F restriction.

résultat noun M result; les résultats des examens the exam results.

résulter verb [1] résulter de to result from.

résumé noun M summary, résumé.

résumer verb [1] to summarize, to sum up.

rétablir verb [2] **1** to restore; **2** se rétablir to recover (after an illness).

retaper verb [1] to do up (a house).

retard noun M **1** delay; ils annoncent un retard d'une heure sur notre vol they say there's an hour's delay on our flight; sans retard without delay; **2** avoir du retard to be late; excusez mon retard I'm sorry I'm late; ils sont arrivés avec trois heures de retard they arrived three hours late; **3** être en retard to be late; nous sommes en retard we're late.

retarder verb [1] **1** to hold up, to delay; la grève nous a retardés the strike held us up; l'avion était retardé the plane was delayed; **2** to put off, to postpone; il a retardé son départ he put off his departure.

retenir verb [77] **1** to hold up; j'ai été retenu au bureau I was held up at the office; je ne vous retiendrai pas longtemps I won't keep you long; **2** retenir son souffle to hold your breath; elle ne pouvait pas retenir ses larmes she couldn't hold back her tears; **3** to book; j'ai retenu des places I've booked seats; **4** to remember; je ne retiens jamais leur adresse I can never remember their address.

réticence noun F 1 reluctance; 2 reticence.

retirer verb [1] 1 to take off; **je vais d'abord retirer ma veste** I'll take my jacket off first; 2 to take away; **ils ont retiré son permis** they took away his licence; 3 **retirer de l'argent** to take out some money (*from your bank account*).

retouche noun F alteration (*to a garment*).

retour noun M 1 return; **un billet aller-retour** a return ticket; **dès mon retour** as soon as I get back; 2 **être de retour** to be back; **elle sera de retour vers onze heures** she'll be back about eleven.

retourner verb [1] 1 to go back; **elle est retournée à l'école** she went back to school; **je n'y suis jamais retourné** I've never been back there again; 2 to turn over; **est-ce que je retourne les steaks?** shall I turn the steaks over?; 3 to overturn.

retraite noun F retirement; **prendre sa retraite** to retire; **une maison de retraite** an old people's home.

retraité, retraitée noun M, F pensioner.

rétrécir verb [2] to shrink.

retrouver verb [1] 1 to find; **as-tu retrouvé tes clés?** did you find your keys?; 2 to meet; **je te retrouve à la sortie** I'll meet you at the exit; 3 **se retrouver** to meet; **on se retrouve devant le cinéma?** shall we meet ouside the cinéma?; **on se retrouvera**

à Noël we'll see each other again at Christmas; 4 **se retrouver** to end up; **on s'est retrouvé chez Amanda** we ended up at Amanda's place; 5 **se retrouver** to find one's way around; **je n'arrive jamais à me retrouver à Londres** I can never find my way around London.

rétroviseur, rétro noun M rearview mirror.

réunion noun F meeting.

réunir verb [2] **se réunir** to meet; **on s'est réuni pour discuter du problème** we met to discuss the problem.

réussi adjective successful.

réussir verb [2] 1 to succeed; **j'espère qu'elle va réussir** I hope she'll succeed; **réussir un examen** to pass an exam; 3 to be successful; **ça a très bien réussi** that was very successful; 4 **réussir à faire** to manage to do; **je n'ai pas réussi à les persuader** I didn't manage to persuade them.

réussite noun F success.

revanche noun F 1 return match; 2 **prendre sa revanche** to get your own back; 3 **en revanche** on the other hand.

rêve noun M dream; **faire un rêve** to have a dream; **votre maison de rêve** your dream house.

réveil noun M alarm clock.

réveille-matin noun M alarm clock.

réveiller verb [1] 1 **réveiller quelqu'un** to wake somebody up; **elle m'a réveillé à sept heures** she woke me at seven; **2 se réveiller** to wake up; **d'habitude je me réveille à sept heures** I usually wake up at seven.

réveillon noun M **le réveillon du Nouvel An** the New Year's Eve celebrations.

réveillonner verb [1] **1** to celebrate Christmas Eve; **2** to see the New Year in.

révéler verb [24] to reveal.

revenant, revenante noun M, F ghost.

revendre verb [3] to sell, to resell.

revenir verb [81] **1** to come back; **elles sont revenues très tard** they came back very late; **tu reviendras nous voir?** will you come back and see us?; **2** to come to; **ça revient à cent francs** that comes to a hundred francs; **ça revient au même** it comes to the same thing; **3 je n'en reviens pas!** I can't get over it!

revenu noun M income.

rêver verb [1] to dream.

réverbère noun M street lamp.

revers noun M **1** lapel (on a jacket), turn-up (of trousers), cuff (on a sleeve); **2** backhand (in tennis); **3** setback; **4 le revers de la médaille** the other side of the coin.

réviser verb [1] **1** to revise; **2** to service (a car or machine).

révision noun F **1** revision; **2** service (for a car).

revoici preposition (informal) **me revoici!** here I am again!

revoir[1] verb [13] **1** to see again; **et nous ne l'avons jamais revue** and we never saw her again; **2** to revise; **je dois revoir ma chimie** I have to revise my chemistry.

revoir[2] noun M **au revoir** goodbye.

révolte noun F revolt, rebellion.

révolter verb [1] to appal.

révolution noun F revolution.

révolutionner verb [1] to revolutionize.

revolver noun M revolver, handgun.

revue noun F magazine; **une revue d'art** an art magazine; **une revue scientifique** a scientific journal.

rez-de-chaussée noun M ground floor (literally: level with the road); **la réception est au rez-de-chaussée** reception is on the ground floor.

RF SHORT FOR **République française** French Republic.

Rhin noun M **le Rhin** the Rhine.

rhinocéros noun M rhinoceros.

rhubarbe noun F rhubarb.

rhum noun M rum.

rhume noun M cold; **attraper un rhume** to catch a cold; **un rhume de cerveau** a head cold.

rhume des foins noun M hay fever.

ri verb SEE **rire**.

ricaner verb [1] to snigger, to giggle.

riche 248 FRENCH-ENGLISH

riche adjective well-off; **1 nous ne sommes pas très riches** we're not terribly well-off; **2** rich; **riche en vitamines** rich in vitamins.

richesse noun F **1** wealth; **2 les richesses naturelles** natural resources.

ride noun F wrinkle (*on skin*), ripple (*on water*).

rideau (*plural* **rideaux**) noun M curtain.

ridicule adjective ridiculous; **mais c'est totalement ridicule!** but that's completely ridiculous!

rien[1] pronoun **1** nothing; **'qu'est-ce qu'elle a dit?' – 'rien'** 'what did she say?' – 'nothing'; **il n'a rien** he has nothing; **je n'ai rien vu** I didn't see anything; **ce n'est rien** it's nothing; **il ne reste plus rien** there's nothing left; **rien du tout** nothing at all; **'merci' – 'de rien'** 'thank you' – 'it's nothing'; **rien d'autre** nothing else; **rien de bon** nothing good; **2 rien que** just; **rien que les livres pèsent 20 kilos** the books by themselves weigh 20 kilos; **'que reste-t-il à faire?' – 'rien que la vaisselle'** 'what's left to do?' – 'just the washing-up'; ★ **rien à faire!** it's no good!

rien[2] noun M little thing; **elle se met à hurler pour un rien** the slightest thing starts her shouting.

rigide adjective rigid, stiff.

rigoler (*informal*) verb [1] **1** to laugh; **elle en a beaucoup rigolé** she had a good laugh about it; **2** to have a good time; **nous avons bien rigolé** we had a great time; **3** to be

joking; **je rigolais!** I was only joking!

rigolo adjective (F **rigolote**) (*informal*) funny.

rillettes plural noun F **les rillettes de porc** potted pork.

rime noun F rhyme.

rincer verb [61] to rinse; **se rincer les cheveux** to rinse one's hair.

rire noun M laughter; **un rire** a laugh.
verb [68] **1** to laugh; **il nous fait rire** he makes us laugh; **2** to have fun; **on va rire ce soir** we'll have some fun this evening; **c'était pour rire** it was meant as a joke.

ris noun M **les ris de veau** calf's sweetbreads.

risque noun M risk; **risque d'incendie** fire risk; **c'est sans risque** it's safe.

risqué adjective risky.

risquer verb [1] **1** to risk; **vas-y, tu ne risques rien** go on, it's quite safe; **2 il risque de pleuvoir** it might well rain; **tu risques de te brûler** you might burn yourself.

rivage noun M shore.

rive noun F **1** bank (*of a river*); **la Rive gauche** the Left Bank (*when talking about the Seine in Paris and other rivers which flow through cities, the left bank is the left side of the river when you are facing downstream*); **2** shore (*by the sea*).

rivière noun F river.

riz noun M rice; **riz cantonais** fried rice; **gâteau de riz** rice pudding.

RN noun F SHORT FOR route nationale A road.

robe noun F dress; une robe d'été a summer dress; une robe de mariée a wedding dress.

robe de chambre noun F dressing gown.

robinet noun M tap; l'eau du robinet tap water.

robot noun M robot; robot ménager food processor.

robuste adjective robust, sturdy.

roche noun F rock.

rocher noun M rock.

rock noun M rock (music).

rôder verb [1] to prowl.

rognons plural noun M kidneys (for cooking).

roi noun M king; le roi Charles King Charles; les Rois mages the Three Wise Men; la fête des Rois Twelfth Night.

rôle noun M role.

romain adjective Roman.

roman noun M novel; un roman policier a detective story.

romancier, romancière noun M, F novelist.

romantique adjective romantic.

romarin noun M rosemary.

rompre verb [69] to split up; Claire et David ont rompu Claire and David have split up; Anne a rompu avec son copain Anne's broken up with her boyfriend; rompre ses

fiançailles to break off your engagement.

ronce noun F bramble.

rond noun M circle; tourner en rond to go round in circles. adjective round.

rondelle noun F 1 slice; une rondelle de tomate a slice of tomato; 2 washer (for a tap or screw).

rond-point noun M roundabout.

ronfler verb [1] to snore.

ronger verb [52] 1 to gnaw; 2 se ronger les ongles to bite one's nails.

ronronner verb [1] to purr.

rosbif noun M roast beef.

rose noun F rose. adjective pink; rose pâle pale pink.

rosé noun M rosé (wine); un verre de rosé a glass of rosé.

rosée noun F dew.

rosier noun M rosebush.

rossignol noun M nightingale.

rôti noun M roast; du rôti de bœuf roast beef; un rôti de bœuf a joint of beef.

rôtir verb [2] to roast.

roucouler verb [1] to coo.

roue noun F wheel; la roue de secours the spare wheel; ★ faire la roue to turn a cartwheel.

rouge noun M 1 (the colour) red; le rouge ne me va pas red doesn't suit me; 2 red traffic light; il est passé au rouge he jumped the lights; le feu est passé au rouge the light changed to red; **3** red wine. **un verre de rouge** a glass of red wine; *adjective* red; **tes chaussettes rouges** your red socks.

rouge à lèvres *noun* M lipstick.

rouge-gorge *noun* M robin.

rougeur *noun* F redness.

rougir *verb* [2] **1** to blush; **2** to turn red.

rouille *noun* F rust.

rouillé *adjective* rusty.

rouiller, se rouiller *verb* [1] to go rusty.

roulant *adjective* **un fauteuil roulant** a wheelchair.

rouleau (*plural* **rouleaux**) *noun* M roll; **un rouleau d'essuie-tout** a roll of kitchen towel.

rouleau à pâtisserie *noun* M rolling pin.

rouler *verb* [1] **1** to go; **nous roulons très vite** we're going very fast; **2** to drive; **il faut rouler à droite en France** in France you must drive on the right; **nous avons roulé toute la nuit** we drove all night; **3** to roll; **4** to roll up; **il faut rouler le tapis** we must roll up the carpet; **5** (*informal*) to cheat; **on m'a roulé!** I've been done!

Roumanie *noun* F Romania.

rousse *adjective* SEE **roux**.

route *noun* F **1** road; **une grande route** a main road; **un accident de la route** a road accident; **Rouen est à trois heures de route d'ici** Rouen is three hours' drive from here;

2 route; **il a changé de route à cause de la neige** he changed his route because of the snow; **3 en route** on the way; **être en route** to be on the way; **nous sommes en route pour Nice** we're on our way to Nice; **4 se mettre en route** to set off.

route départementale *noun* F secondary road, B road.

route nationale *noun* F A road.

routier, routière *noun* M, F lorry driver.
adjective road; **le transport routier** road transport; **la gare routière** the bus station.

routine *noun* F routine.

roux (F **rousse**) *adjective* red-haired, ginger.

royal (*plural* **royaux**) *adjective* royal.

royaume *noun* M kingdom.

Royaume-Uni *noun* M United Kingdom.

ruban *noun* M ribbon.

rubéole *noun* F German measles.

ruche *noun* F beehive.

rudement *adverb* (*informal*) really; **il est rudement bon ton gâteau** your cake's really good.

rue *noun* F street; **une rue piétonne** a pedestrian street; ★ **mettre quelqu'un à la rue** to put someone out on the street.

rugby *noun* M rugby; **jouer au rugby** to play rugby.

rugbyman (*plural* **rugbymen**) *noun* M rugby player.

ruine *noun* F ruin; **une maison en ruine(s)** a ruined house.

ruiner *verb* [1] to ruin.

ruisseau (*plural* **ruisseaux**) *noun* M stream.

rumeur *noun* F 1 rumour; 2 murmur.

rumsteck *noun* M rump steak.

rupture *noun* F break-up.

rural (M *plural* **ruraux**) *adjective* country; **la vie rurale** country life.

ruse *noun* F 1 trick; **les ruses du métier** the tricks of the trade; 2 cunning.

rusé *adjective* cunning, crafty.

russe *noun* M, *adjective* Russian.

Russe *noun* M & F Russian (*person*).

Russie *noun* F Russia.

rythme *noun* M rhythm; **marquer le rythme** to beat time.

S s

s' *pronoun* SEE **se**.

sa *adjective* SEE **son**.

sable *noun* M sand.

sablé *noun* M shortbread biscuit. *adjective* **la pâte sablée** shortcrust pastry.

sac *noun* M 1 bag; **un sac de sucre** a bag of sugar; **un sac de sport** a sports bag; 2 sack; **un sac de charbon** a sack of coal; ★ **vider son sac** (*informal*) to get something off one's chest (*literally: to empty one's bag*).

sac à dos *noun* M rucksack.

sac à main *noun* M handbag.

sac de couchage *noun* M sleeping bag.

sachet *noun* M sachet; **un sachet de thé** a teabag.

sacoche *noun* F 1 bag; **la sacoche du facteur** the postman's bag; 2 pannier (*for a bike*).

sacré *adjective* 1 (*informal*) **c'est un sacré problème** it's a hell of a problem; **elle a eu une sacrée chance** she's been damn lucky; 2 sacred.

sacrifier *verb* [1] to sacrifice.

sage *adjective* 1 good, well-behaved; **Tom, sois sage** be a good boy, Tom; 2 wise, sensible; **il serait sage de se renseigner sur le prix** it would be wise to enquire about the price.

sagesse *noun* F wisdom; **une dent de sagesse** a wisdom tooth.

Sagittaire *noun* M Sagittarius (*sign of the Zodiac*).

saignant *adjective* rare (*beef*).

saigner *verb* [1] to bleed.

sain *adjective* healthy; ★ **sain et sauf** safe and sound.

saint, sainte noun M, F saint; the adjective holy; **le Saint-Esprit** the Holy Spirit; **le vendredi saint** Good Friday; **la Sainte Vierge** the Virgin Mary.

Saint-Jacques noun **une coquille Saint-Jacques** a scallop.

Saint-Jean noun F Midsummer's Day (June 24th).

Saint-Sylvestre noun F New Year's Eve.

sais verb SEE savoir[1].

saisir verb [2] **1** to grab; **il m'a saisi par le bras** he grabbed my arm; **2 saisir l'occasion** to seize the opportunity; **3** to understand; **je n'ai pas tout à fait saisi...** I didn't entirely understand...; **4** to catch, (to hear); **je n'ai pas saisi votre nom** I didn't catch your name.

saison noun F season; **il fait froid pour la saison** it's cold for the time of year.

sait verb SEE savoir[1].

salade noun F **1** lettuce; **une salade** a lettuce; **2** salad; **une salade de fruits** a fruit salad.

saladier noun M salad bowl.

salaire noun M salary; wages.

salarié, salariée noun M, F salaried employee.

sale adjective **1** (after the noun) dirty; **les mains sales** dirty hands; **2** (before the noun) (informal) horrible; **quel sale temps!** what horrible weather!; **il a une sale tête** he looks awful.

salé adjective **1** salty; **la sauce est un peu trop salée** the sauce is a bit salty; **2** savoury; **des petits gâteaux salés** savoury biscuits; **3 du beurre salé** salt butter.

saler verb [1] to salt.

saleté noun F dirt.

salir verb [2] to dirty, to get (something) dirty; **tu vas salir ta robe** you'll get your dress dirty.

salle noun F **1** room ('salle' by itself is no longer used to mean a room in a house); **2** dining-room (in a restaurant); **3** hall; **4** auditorium (in a theatre or cinema).

salle à manger noun F **1** dining room; **2** dining-room suite.

salle d'attente noun F waiting room.

salle de bains noun F bathroom.

salle de classe noun F classroom.

salle d'eau noun F shower room.

salle d'embarquement noun F departure lounge.

salle de jeux noun F games room.

salle de séjour noun F living room.

salle des fêtes noun F community centre.

salon noun M **1** sitting room; **2** living-room suite; **3** trade fair; **4** salon; **salon de coiffure** hair salon.

salon de thé noun M tea-room.

salopette noun F **1** dungarees; **2** overalls.

saluer *verb* [1] **1** to say hello to; **je l'ai salué, mais il ne m'a pas entendu** I said hello to him but he didn't hear; **elle l'a salué de la main** she waved at him; **2** to say goodbye to.

salut *greeting* M Hi!

samedi *noun* M **1** Saturday; **samedi prochain** next Saturday; **samedi dernier** last Saturday; **2** on Saturday; **samedi soir** on Saturday evening; **3 le samedi** on Saturdays; **fermé le samedi** closed on Saturdays; **4 tous les samedis** every Saturday.

SAMU *noun* M SHORT FOR **Service d'assistance médicale d'urgence** ambulance service.

sandale *noun* F sandal.

sandwich *noun* M sandwich; **un sandwich au jambon** a ham sandwich.

sang *noun* M blood; **être en sang** to be covered in blood.

sang-froid *noun* M calm.

sanglier *noun* M wild boar.

sanglot *noun* M sob; **éclater en sanglots** to burst into tears.

sanisette™ *noun* F automatic public lavatory.

sanitaire *adjective* **les conditions sanitaires** sanitary conditions; **les règlements sanitaires** health regulations.
noun M **les sanitaires** the toilet block (*in a campsite*).

sans *preposition* without; **une maison sans téléphone** a house

without a telephone; **un café sans sucre** a coffee with no sugar; **sans hésiter** without hesitating.

sans-abri *noun* M & F homeless person; **les sans-abri** the homeless.

sans-emploi *noun* M & F unemployed person; **les sans-emploi** the unemployed.

santé *noun* F **1** health; **être en bonne santé** to be in good health; **2 à votre santé!** cheers!

sapeur-pompier *noun* M fireman; **appeler les sapeurs-pompiers** to call the fire brigade.

sapin *noun* M fir tree; **un sapin de Noël** a Christmas tree.

sardine *noun* F sardine.

satellite *noun* M satellite.

satin *noun* M satin.

satisfaction *noun* F satisfaction.

satisfaire *verb* [10] to satisfy.

satisfaisant *adjective* satisfactory.

satisfait *adjective* satisfied; **êtes-vous satisfaits de votre séjour?** are you satisfied with your stay?

sauce *noun* F **1** sauce; **2** gravy.

saucisse *noun* F sausage.

saucisson *noun* M salami.

sauf¹ *preposition* **1** except; **tous les jours sauf le lundi** every day except Monday; **sauf quand il pleut** except when it rains; **2 sauf si** unless; **c'est tout, sauf s'il y a des questions?** that's all, unless there are any questions?; **3 sauf que** except that; **tout va bien, sauf que ta sœur n'est pas encore arrivée**

everything's fine, except that your sister hasn't arrived yet.

sauf² *adjective* SEE **sain**.

saule *noun* M willow; **un saule pleureur** a weeping willow.

saumon *noun* M salmon.

saupoudrer *verb* [1] to sprinkle.

saut *noun* M jump.

saut à la perche *noun* M pole vault.

saut à l'élastique *noun* M bungee jumping.

saut en hauteur *noun* M high jump.

saut en longueur *noun* M long jump.

sauter *verb* [1] **1** to jump, to jump over; **elle a sauté la barrière** she jumped over the gate; **elle a sauté dans un taxi** she jumped into a taxi; **2 sauter à la corde** to skip (*with a rope*); **3** to skip; **nous avons sauté trois pages** we've skipped three pages; **4** to blow up; **les terroristes ont fait sauter l'avion** the terrorists blew up the plane; **faire sauter les plombs** to blow the fuses; ★ **ça saute aux yeux!** it's blindingly obvious!

sauterelle *noun* F grasshopper.

sauvage *adjective* wild, savage.

sauvegarder *verb* [1] **1** to safeguard; **2** to save, to back up (*on a computer*).

sauver *verb* [1] **1** to save; **vous m'avez sauvé la vie** you saved my life; **2 se sauver** to run away; **ils se**

ont sauvés they ran away; **3 je me sauve!** (*informal*) I'm off!

sauvetage *noun* M rescue, life-saving.

savent, savez *verb* SEE **savoir¹**.

savoir¹ *verb* [70] **1** to know; **je sais qu'il habite à Londres** I know he lives in London; **je ne savais pas qu'elle était médecin** I didn't know she was a doctor; **tu sais très bien que...** you know very well that...; **je n'en sais rien** I know nothing about it; **comment l'avez-vous su?** how did you find out about it?; **allez savoir!** who knows!; **2 savoir faire** to know how to do; **je ne sais pas le faire** I don't know how to do it; **savoir lire et écrire** to be able to read and write; **tu sais jouer du piano?** can you play the piano?

savoir² *noun* M knowledge.

savoir-faire *noun* M know-how.

savon *noun* M soap.

savonnette *noun* F cake of soap.

savons *verb* SEE **savoir¹**.

savoureux (F **savoureuse**) *adjective* tasty.

scandale *noun* M scandal; **le discours du ministre a fait scandale** the minister's speech caused a scandal.

scandinave *adjective* Scandinavian.

Scandinavie *noun* F Scandinavia.

scanner *noun* M scanner.

scarabée *noun* M beetle.

scénariste noun M & F
scriptwriter.

scène noun F 1 stage (*in a theatre*);
être sur scène to be on stage; **mettre
en scène** a play (*a play*); to direct
(*a film*); 2 scene; **sur la scène
politique** on the political scene; **des
scènes de panique** scenes of panic;
faire (toute) une scène to throw a
fit.

sceptique adjective sceptical.

schéma noun M diagram.

scie noun F saw.

science noun F science.

sciences naturelles plural noun
F biology.

scientifique noun M & F scientist.
adjective scientific.

scier verb [1] to saw.

scolaire adjective school; **les
vacances scolaires** the school
holidays; **le livret scolaire** the
school report.

scolarité noun F schooling,
education.

Scorpion noun M Scorpio (*sign of
the Zodiac*).

Scotch™ noun M Sellotape™.

scout, scoute noun M, F boy
scout, girl guide.

scrutin noun M 1 ballot; 2 polls;
le jour du scrutin polling day.

sculpteur noun M sculptor.

sculpture noun F sculpture.

SDF noun M & F SHORT FOR **sans
domicile fixe** of no fixed abode; **les
SDF** the homeless.

se, s' (*before a vowel or silent 'h'*)
reflexive pronoun 1 himself; **il se
regarde** he's looking at himself;
2 herself; **elle se regarde** she's
looking at herself; 3 itself; **le chien
s'est fait mal** the dog has hurt
itself; 4 themselves; **ils se sont fait
mal** they've hurt themselves;
5 each other; **ils se regardaient**
they were looking at each other;
6 yourself, oneself; **se faire mal** to
hurt yourself (or oneself);
7 (*sometimes not translated*)
Claudie se lave les cheveux
Claudie's washing her hair; **Jules se
brosse les dents** Jules is brushing
his teeth.

séance noun F 1 session;
2 showing (*of a film*); **la séance de
vingt heures** the eight o'clock
showing.

seau (*plural* **seaux**) noun M
bucket.

sec (F **sèche**) adjective 1 dry; **mes
cheveux ne sont pas secs** my hair's
not dry; **un vin blanc sec** a dry white
wine; 2 dried; **des abricots secs**
dried apricots.

sèche-cheveux noun M hair
dryer.

sèche-linge noun M tumble dryer.

sèche-mains noun M hand dryer.

sécher verb [1] to dry; **des fleurs
séchées** dried flowers.

sécheresse noun F drought.

second noun M au second on the second floor; il est arrivé en second he arrived second.
adjective second; la seconde fois the second time.

secondaire adjective secondary; une école secondaire a secondary school; des effets secondaires side effects.

seconde noun F 1 second; je reviens dans une seconde I'll be back in a moment; 2 second class; voyager en seconde to travel second class; un billet de seconde a second class ticket; 3 (in a French school) the equivalent of Year 11.

secouer verb [1] to shake; secouer la tête to shake your head.

secourir verb [29] to rescue.

secourisme noun M first aid.

secouriste noun M & F first aider.

secours noun M 1 help; au secours! help!; elle a crié au secours she shouted for help; 2 les premiers secours first aid; 3 une sortie de secours an emergency exit; 4 la roue de secours the spare wheel.

secret noun M secret; garder un secret to keep a secret; en secret in secret.
adjective (F secrète) secret.

secrétaire[1] noun M & F secretary.

secrétaire[2] noun M writing desk.

secrétariat noun M secretary's office.

secteur noun M sector; dans le secteur privé in the private sector;

dans le secteur public in the public sector.

sécu (informal) noun F SHORT FOR Sécurité sociale Social Security.

sécurité noun F 1 safety; pour votre sécurité for your own safety; les règles de sécurité safety regulations; la sécurité routière road safety; une ceinture de sécurité a seatbelt; 2 être en sécurité to be safe; 3 security; un système de sécurité a security system; la sécurité de l'emploi job security.

Sécurité sociale noun F Social Security.

séduisant adjective attractive, appealing.

seigle noun M rye; le pain de seigle rye bread.

seigneur noun M lord; le Seigneur the Lord.

sein noun M 1 breast; avoir un cancer du sein to have breast cancer; 2 within; au sein du gouvernement within the government.

seize number sixteen; Corinne a seize ans Corinne's sixteen; le seize juillet the sixteenth of July.

seizième number sixteenth.

séjour noun M 1 stay; pendant votre séjour en France during your stay in France; 2 la salle de séjour the living room.

sel noun M salt; une pincée de sel a pinch of salt.

sélection noun F selection.

sélectionner verb [1] to select.

self noun M (informal) self-service restaurant.

self-service (informal) M noun self-service restaurant.

selle noun F saddle.

selon preposition according to; **selon la météo, il va pleuvoir** according to the forecast, it's going to rain.

semaine noun F week; **cette semaine** this week; **la semaine prochaine/dernière** next/last week; **elle est payée à la semaine** she's paid by the week.

semblable adjective similar.

semblant noun M **faire semblant de faire** to pretend to do; **elle fait semblant de ne pas entendre** she's pretending not to hear.

sembler verb [1] to seem; **la maison semble vide** the house seems empty; **il semble bon d'attendre leur retour** it seems a good idea to wait till they get back.

semelle noun F sole (of a shoe).

semer verb [1] **1** to sow (seeds); **2 semer la panique** to spread panic.

semestre noun M semester.

semi-remorque noun M articulated truck.

semoule noun F semolina; **le sucre semoule** caster sugar.

sens noun M **1** direction; **dans les deux sens** in both directions; **dans le sens Calais-Paris** in the Calais-Paris direction; **dans tous les sens** in all directions; **sens dessus dessous** upside down; **mets-le dans le bon sens!** put it the right way up!; **2** meaning; **le sens d'un mot** the meaning of a word; **cela n'a pas de sens** it doesn't make sense, it's absurd.

sensation noun F **1** feeling; **2** sensation; **le film a fait sensation à Cannes** the film was a sensation at Cannes.

sensationnel (F **sensationnelle**) adjective sensational, fantastic.

sens commun noun M common sense.

sens de l'humour noun M sense of humour; **avoir le sens de l'humour** to have a sense of humour.

sensé adjective sensible.

sensibiliser verb [1] **sensibiliser les gens à un problème** to increase people's awareness of a problem.

sensible adjective **1** sensitive; **c'est une fille très sensible** she's a very sensitive girl; **je suis sensible au froid** I feel the cold; **2** noticeable; **une différence sensible** a noticeable difference.

sensiblement adverb noticeably.

sens interdit noun M no entry sign; one-way street.

sens unique noun M one-way street.

sentier noun M path.

sentier de randonnée noun M long-distance footpath (a marked route for ramblers).

sentiment noun M feeling;
sentiments affectueux best wishes;
**veuillez croire à mes sentiments les
meilleurs** yours sincerely, yours
faithfully (one of a number of fixed
formulae for ending a formal letter).

sentimental (M plural
sentimentaux) adjective
sentimental.

sentir verb [58] 1 to smell; **ça sent
bon!** that smells good!; 2 to smell
of; **ça sent les roses** it smells of
roses; **tu sens la cigarette** you smell
of cigarettes; 3 to feel; **je ne sens
rien** I can't feel anything; **on sent
que l'hiver s'approche** you can feel
it will soon be winter; **je sens qu'elle
est sincère** I feel she's sincere; 4 **se
sentir** to feel; **je ne me sens pas
bien** I don't feel well; ★ **je ne peux
pas le sentir!** I can't stand him!

séparé adjective 1 separated; **mes
parents sont séparés** my parents
are separated; 2 separate; **dans une
chambre séparée** in a separate
bedroom.

séparément adverb separately.

séparer verb [1] 1 to separate;
séparez les œufs separate the eggs;
séparer les filles des garçons to
separate the girls from the boys;
2 **se séparer** to separate, to split up;
mes parents se sont séparés my
parents have separated.

sept number seven; **Yasmin a sept
ans** Yasmin's seven; **il est sept
heures** it's seven o'clock; **le sept
mars** the seventh of March.

septante number seventy (used in
Belgium and Switzerland, instead of

soixante-dix); **septante-sept**
seventy-seven.

septembre noun M September; **en
septembre, au mois de
septembre** in September.

septième noun M **au septième** on
the seventh floor;
adjective seventh.

sera, serai, seras, serez verb
SEE **être**[1].

série noun F series.

sérieusement adverb seriously.

sérieux noun **prendre quelque
chose au sérieux** to take something
seriously.
adjective (F **sérieuse**) 1 serious;
vraiment? tu es sérieux? really? are
you serious? 2 reponsible; **Camilla
est une jeune fille sérieuse** Camilla
is a reponsible young woman;
3 reliable; **il n'est pas sérieux** he's
unreliable; 4 **un travail sérieux** a
careful piece of work; ★ **garder son
sérieux** to keep a straight face.

serin noun M canary.

seringue noun F syringe.

séronégatif adjective (F
séronégative) HIV-negative.

serons, seront verb SEE **être**[1].

séropositif (F **séropositive**)
adjective HIV-positive.

serpent noun M snake.

serpillière noun F floorcloth.

serre noun F greenhouse; **l'effet de
serre** the greenhouse effect.

serré adjective 1 tight; **ma jupe est
trop serrée** my skirt's too tight; **un**

budget serré a tight budget;
2 close (*match or competition*).

serrer *verb* [1] **1** to grip; **elle serrait
le volant** she gripped the steering
wheel; **il m'a serrée dans ses bras**
he hugged me; **2 serrer la main à
quelqu'un** to shake somebody's
hand; **nous nous sommes serré la
main** we shook hands; **3 serrer
quelqu'un dans ses bras** to hug
somebody; **4 serrer les poings** to
clench your fists; **5** to tighten (*a
screw or belt*); **6** to be too tight; **mes
chaussures me serrent** my shoes
are too tight; **7** to push closer
together; **serrez les tables** move
the tables closer together; **8 se
serrer** to squeeze up; **serrez-vous
un peu!** squeeze up a bit!

serrure *noun* F lock.

serveur, serveuse *noun* M, F
waiter, waitress.

service *noun* M **1** favour; **peux-tu
me rendre un petit service?** could
you do me a small favour?; **2** service
(*bus, train*); **service de dimanche**
Sunday service; **3 être en service**
to be working; **il n'y a qu'un
ascenseur en service** there's only
one lift working; **être hors service**
to be out of order; **l'ascenseur est
hors service** the lift is out of order;
4 duty, service; **la pharmacie de
service** the duty chemist; **je suis de
service ce soir** I am on duty this
evening; **le service militaire**
national service; **5** service (*charge*);
le service est compris service is
included; **6** department (*in a town
hall or hospital, for example*); **le
service des urgences** the casualty
department.

service après-vente *noun* M
after-sales service.

serviette *noun* F **1** towel; **une
serviette de bain** a bath towel;
2 napkin; **3** briefcase.

serviette hygiénique *noun* F
sanitary towel.

servir *verb* [71] **1** to serve (*in a shop,
for example*); **merci, on me sert**
thank you, I'm being served; **2** to
serve (*with food or drink*); **est-ce
que je peux vous servir du poulet?**
can I give you some chicken?; **'servir
frais' '**serve chilled'; **3 se servir** to
help yourself; **sers-toi de riz** help
yourself to rice; **4 se servir de** to
use; **est-ce que tu sais te servir
d'une machine à coudre?** do you
know how to use a sewing
machine?; **5** to serve (*in tennis or in
the army*); **à toi de servir!** your
service!; **6 servir à** to be used for; **à
quoi ça sert?** what's it for?; **ça ne
sert à rien!** it's no use!; **ça ne sert à
rien de pleurer** there's no point in
crying; **7 se servir** to be served
(*food or drink*); **ce vin se sert frais**
this wine should be served chilled.

ses *adjective* SEE **son**.

set de table *noun* M place mat.

seul *adjective* **1** only; **la seule
personne** the only person; **c'est le
seul Anglais que je connaisse** he's
the only English person I know;
j'étais le seul à aimer le film I was
the only one who liked the film;
2 alone; **il ne faut pas y aller seul**
you mustn't go there alone; **j'étais
tout seul à la maison** I was all alone
in the house; **3 se sentir seul** to
feel lonely; **4 tout seul** all by

yourself; **il l'a fait tout seul** he did it all by himself; **Sophie sait s'habiller toute seule maintenant** Sophie can get dressed all by herself now.

seulement *adverb* **1** only; **trois fois seulement** only three times; **2 non seulement...mais** not only...but; **non seulement elle n'est pas venue, mais elle n'a même pas appelé** not only did she not come, but she didn't even phone; **3 si seulement je l'avais su** if only I'd known.

sévère *adjective* strict.

sexe *noun* M **1** sex; **2** genitals.

sexuel (F **sexuelle**) *adjective* **1** sexual; **2 l'éducation sexuelle** sex education.

shampooing *noun* M shampoo.

short *noun* M (pair of) shorts; **où est mon short?** where are my shorts?; **trois shorts** three pairs of shorts.

si, s' (*before il or ils*) *conjunction* if; **si tu veux** if you like; **s'il pleut** if it rains.
adverb **1** so; **je suis si fatigué!** I'm so tired!; **tu chantes si bien!** you sing so well!; **2** yes (*when you are contradicting somebody*); **'tu ne viens pas avec nous?'** – **'si!'** 'you're not coming with us?' – 'yes I am!'; **'il ne reste pas manger'** – **'mais si!'** 'he's not staying for a meal' – 'of course he is!'; **elle ne les aime pas du tout, moi si** she doesn't like them at all, but I do.

Sicile *noun* F Sicily.

sida *noun* M SHORT FOR **syndrome immuno-déficitaire acquis** AIDS; **avoir le sida** to have AIDS.

siècle *noun* M century; **au vingtième siècle** in the twentieth century.

siège *noun* M **1** seat; **le siège d'avant** the front seat; **2** head office (*of a company*).

sien, sienne, siens, siennes *pronoun* **le sien, la sienne, les siens, les siennes 1** his; **j'ai prêté mon vélo à Paul, le sien est chez lui** I've lent Paul my bike, his is at home; **'est-ce que ces chaussures sont à Bernard?'** – **'oui, ce sont les siennes'** 'are these shoes Bernard's?' – 'yes, they're his'; **2** hers; **j'ai prêté mon vélo à Annie, le sien est chez elle** I've lent Annie my bike, hers is at home; **'est-ce que ces chaussures sont à Nathalie?'** – **'oui, ce sont les siennes'** 'are these shoes Nathalie's?' – 'yes, they're hers'.

sieste *noun* F nap; **faire la sieste** to have a nap.

siffler *verb* [1] to whistle.

sifflet *noun* M whistle.

signal (*plural* **signaux**) *noun* M signal.

signaler *verb* [1] **1** to point out; **je vous signale que je serai absent ce jour-là** I'd like to point out that I shall be away that day; **2** to report; **3** to indicate (*roadworks or danger, for example*).

signalisation *noun* F signalling; signals.

signalisation routière *noun* F road signs and markings.

signature *noun* F signature; **je vous demande une petite signature** just sign here, would you?

signe *noun* M signe; **c'est bon/mauvais signe** it's a good/bad sign; **faire signe à quelqu'un** to wave to someone; **il m'a fait signe de m'approcher** he beckoned me over to him; **d'un signe de main elle a montré la sortie** she pointed to the exit.

signer *verb* [1] **1** to sign; **2 se signer** to cross oneself.

signification *noun* F meaning.

signifier *verb* [1] to mean.

silence *noun* M silence; **en silence** in silence.

silencieux (F **silencieuse**) *adjective* silent.

silhouette *noun* F **1** silhouette, outline; **2** figure.

similarité *noun* F similarity.

simple *noun* M **le simple messieurs/dames** the men's/women's singles (*in tennis*). *adjective* simple; **un repas simple** a simple meal; **un simple coup de téléphone** just a telephone call.

simplement *adverb* simply.

simplicité *noun* F simplicity.

simplifier *verb* [1] to simplify.

simuler *verb* [1] to simulate.

simultané *adjective* simultaneous.

sincère *adjective* sincere.

sincérité *noun* F sincerity.

singe *noun* M monkey.

singulier *noun* M singular; **au singulier** in the singular.

sinistre *noun* M accident, disaster (*for example, a fire or flood*). *adjective* **1** sinister; **2** gloomy.

sinistré, sinistrée *noun* M, F disaster victim. *adjective* stricken; **de l'aide pour les familles sinistrées** help for the families stricken by the disaster.

sinon *conjunction* otherwise; **il faut partir, sinon on sera en retard** we must leave, otherwise we'll be late.

sirène *noun* F **1** siren; **une sirène d'alarme** a fire alarm; **2** mermaid.

sirop *noun* M **1** syrup; **sirop pectoral** cough mixture; **2 sirop de menthe** mint cordial.

site *noun* M site, area; **site touristique** place of interest (*to visit*); **site classé** conservation area.

sitôt *adverb* as soon as; **sitôt rentrée, elle s'est couchée** as soon as she got home, she went to bed; **sitôt après** immediately afterwards; ★ **sitôt dit, sitôt fait** no sooner said than done.

situation *noun* F **1** situation; **2** job; **il a perdu sa situation** he's lost his job.

situer *verb* [1] **1 être situé** to be situated; **l'hôtel est situé au bord de la mer** the hotel is situated on the edge of the sea; **bien situé** well situated; **2 se situer** to be situated; **la maison se situe dans un quartier résidentiel** the house is in a residential area; **3 se situer** to be set; **le roman se situe à Moscou** the novel is set in Moscow.

six *number* six; **Rosie a six ans** Rosie's six; **il est six heures** it's six o'clock; **le six juillet** the sixth of July.

sixième *noun* F (*in a French school*) the equivalent of Year 7.
noun M **au sixième** on the sixth floor.
adjective sixth.

ski *noun* M 1 ski; **où sont mes skis?** where are my skis? 2 skiing; **il adore le ski** he loves skiing; **on va faire du ski ce week-end** we're going skiing this weekend.

ski de fond *noun* M cross-country skiing.

ski de piste *noun* M downhill skiing.

skier *verb* [1] to ski; **il skie plutôt bien** he skis pretty well; **skier hors piste** to ski off-piste.

skieur, skieuse *noun* M, F skier.

ski nautique *noun* M water-skiing.

slip *noun* M 1 underpants; 2 knickers.

Slovaquie *noun* F Slovakia.

Slovénie *noun* F Slovenia.

SMIC *noun* M guaranteed minimum wage; **elle touche le SMIC** she's on the legal minimum wage.

smoking *noun* M dinner jacket.

SNCF *noun* F SHORT FOR **Société nationale des chemins de fer français** (*French railways*).

snob *noun* M & F snob.
adjective snobbish (*of a person*); posh (*of a restaurant*).

sobre *adjective* sober.

sociable *adjective* friendly, sociable.

social (M *plural* **sociaux**) *adjective* social.

socialiste *noun* M & F, *adjective* socialist.

société *noun* F 1 society; **dans notre société** in our society; 2 company; **il travaille pour une grande société** he works for a big company.

sociologie *noun* F sociology.

socquette *noun* F ankle sock.

sœur *noun* F sister; **ma grande sœur** my big sister, my older sister.

soi *pronoun* 1 one, oneself; **des amis autour de soi** friends around one; 2 **avoir confiance en soi** to have confidence in oneself; 3 itself; **pas très intéressant en soi** not very interesting in itself; **cela va de soi** that goes without saying.

soi-disant *adjective* 1 so-called; **c'est le soi-disant champion** he's the so-called champion; 2 supposedly; **elle est soi-disant malade** she's supposedly ill.

soie *noun* F silk; **un foulard en soie** a silk scarf; **le papier de soie** tissue paper.

soif *noun* M thirst; **avoir soif** to be thirsty.

soigner *verb* [1] to look after.

soigneusement adverb carefully.

soi-même pronoun yourself, oneself; il faut le faire soi-même you have to do it yourself.

soin noun M 1 care; 2 prendre soin de quelque chose to take care of something. 3 les soins treatment; 4 les premiers soins first aid.

soir noun M evening, night; ce soir tonight; hier soir last night; demain soir tomorrow night; je sors tous les samedis soirs I go out every Saturday night; par un beau soir d'été one fine summer's evening; à six heures du soir at six in the evening; à ce soir! see you tonight!

soirée noun F 1 evening; pendant la soirée during the evening; 2 party; elle donne une petite soirée she's having a little party; 3 en tenue de soirée in evening dress.

sois verb SEE être[1]; sois gentil be good.

soit conjunction soit...soit either...or; soit demain, soit jeudi either tomorrow or Thursday.

soixantaine noun F 1 about sixty; une soixantaine de personnes about sixty people; 2 avoir la soixantaine to be in your sixties.

soixante number sixty.

soixante-dix number seventy; soixante-dix-huit seventy-eight.

soja noun M soya bean; la sauce de soja soy sauce.

sol noun M 1 floor; 2 soil.

solaire adjective 1 solar; 2 la crème solaire sun cream.

soldat noun M soldier.

solde noun M 1 les soldes the sales; faire les soldes to go round the sales; 2 être en solde to be reduced; les pulls sont en solde the jumpers are reduced; 3 balance in a bank account.

soldé adjective reduced.

sole noun F sole (fish).

soleil noun M sun; au soleil in the sun; il fait soleil it's sunny; en plein soleil in full sun; attraper un coup de soleil to get sunburnt.

solfège noun M musical theory.

solide adjective 1 strong; 2 solid.

soliste noun M & F soloist.

solitaire adjective 1 lonely, isolated; 2 un navigateur solitaire a solo yachtsman.

solution noun F solution.

sombre adjective dark, gloomy.

somme[1] noun F sum; une somme d'argent a sum of money.

somme[2] noun M nap; faire un somme to have a nap.

sommeil noun M sleep; avoir sommeil to feel sleepy; je n'ai plus sommeil I'm not sleepy any more.

sommes verb SEE être[1].

sommet noun M summit.

somnambule noun M & F sleepwalker; être somnambule to walk in your sleep.

son[1] , **sa**, **ses** *adjective* **1** his; **son fils** his son; **sa fille** his daughter; **ses enfants** his children; **2** her; **son fils** her son; **sa fille** her daughter; **ses enfants** her children; **3** its; **le chat a perdu son collier** the cat's lost its collar.

son[2] *noun* M **1** sound; **le son d'un piano** the sound of a piano; **2** volume (*on a radio or hi-fi*); **baisser le son** to turn the volume down; **3** bran.

sondage *noun* M survey; **un sondage d'opinion** an opinion poll.

sonner *verb* [1] to ring; **le téléphone sonne** the phone's ringing; **on sonne à la porte** somebody's ringing the doorbell.

sonnerie *noun* F bell; **la sonnerie d'alarme** the alarm bell; **la sonnerie du téléphone** the ring of the telephone.

sonnette *noun* F bell, doorbell.

sono *noun* F (*informal*) sound system.

sophistiqué *adjective* sophisticated.

sorbet *noun* M sorbet; **un sorbet au cassis** a blackcurrant sorbet.

sorcière *noun* F witch.

sort *noun* M fate; ★ **tirer au sort** to draw lots.

sorte *noun* F sort; **c'est une sorte de poudre** it's a sort of powder; **toutes sortes d'activités** all sorts of activities.

sortie *noun* F **1** exit; **il nous attend à la sortie** he's waiting for us at the exit; **sortie de secours** emergency exit; **2** outing; **3** launching (*of a new product*); release (*of a film*); publication of a book.

sortir *verb* [72] **1** to go out; **tout le monde est sorti dans la rue** everybody went out into the street; **ils sont sortis déjeuner** they've gone out for lunch; **elle est sortie en courant** she ran out; **2** to come out; **c'est l'heure où les gens sortent du cinéma** it's the time when people are coming out of the cinema; **son nouveau film sortira en mai** her new film is coming out in May; **3** to go out (*for pleasure*); **mes parents sortent peu** my parents don't go out much; **4** **sortir avec** to be going out with; **il sort avec ma sœur** he's going out with my sister; **5** to take out; **elle a sorti une bouteille du frigo** she took a bottle out of the fridge; **j'ai oublié de sortir le chien** I forgot to take the dog out; **6** **s'en sortir** to manage; **je m'en sortirai d'une manière ou d'une autre** I'll manage one way or another.

sottise *noun* F **1** silliness; **2** **dire des sottises** to talk nonsense; **ne fais pas de sottises** don't do anything silly.

sou *noun* M **j'ai dépensé tous mes sous** I've spent all my money; **je n'ai pas un sou** I'm broke; **une machine à sous** a fruit machine; ★ **être près de ses sous** to be tight-fisted.

souci *noun* M **1** worry, **se faire du souci** to worry; **mon fils me donne bien des soucis** my son's a great worry to me; **j'ai d'autres soucis à présent** I've got other problems just now; **2** marigold.

soucieux (F **soucieuse**) *adjective* worried.

soucoupe *noun* F saucer.

soudain *adjective* sudden.
adverb suddenly.

souffle *noun* M breath; **être à bout de souffle** to be out of breath; **couper le souffle à quelqu'un** to take someone's breath away.

soufflé *noun* M soufflé; **un soufflé au fromage** a cheese soufflé.

souffler *verb* [1] **1** to blow; **le vent soufflait fort** there was a strong wind; **2** to blow out (*a candle*); **3** to whisper; **elle me soufflait quelque chose à l'oreille** she was whispering something in my ear; ★ **souffler dans le ballon** (*informal*) to be breathalysed.

souffrir *verb* [73] **1** to suffer; **a-t-elle beaucoup souffert?** did she suffer much?; **il souffre souvent du dos** he often has back pain; **2** **je ne peux pas le souffrir!** (*informal*) I can't stand him!

souhait *noun* M wish; ★ **à tes souhaits!** bless you! (*when somebody sneezes*).

souhaiter *verb* [1] **1** to wish; **je te souhaite bonne chance** I wish you luck; **il nous a souhaité la bienvenue** he welcomed us; **il souhaite se marier** he'd like to get married.

soûl *adjective* drunk.

soulagé *adjective* relieved.

soulagement *noun* M relief.

soulager *verb* [52] to relieve.

soulever *verb* [50] **1** to lift; **je n'arrive pas à soulever ta valise** I can't lift your case; **2** to raise (*problems, objections, or difficulties*); **personne n'a soulevé la question** nobody raised the question.

soulier *noun* M shoe.

souligner *verb* [1] **1** to underline; **2** to emphasize.

soupçon *noun* M **1** suspicion; **2** spot, drop (*of food or drink*); **juste un soupçon de lait** just a drop of milk.

soupçonner *verb* [1] to suspect.

soupe *noun* F soup; **la soupe aux oignons** onion soup.

souper *verb* [1] to have supper.

soupir *noun* M sigh.

soupirer *verb* [1] to sigh.

souple *adjective* **1** supple (*person*); **2** flexible (*system*); **3** soft (*hair or clean washing*).

source *noun* F spring; **l'eau de source** spring water.

sourcil *noun* M eyebrow.

sourd *adjective* **1** deaf; **2** dull, muffled (*noise*); ★ **faire la sourde oreille** to turn a deaf ear.

souriant *adjective* cheerful.

sourire *noun* M smile; **il faut garder le sourire** you must keep smiling. *verb* [68] to smile; **sourire à quelqu'un** to smile at somebody.

souris *noun* F mouse (*also for a computer*).

sous *preposition* under, underneath; **sous la chaise** under the chair; **sortir sous la pluie** to go out in the rain; **sous terre** underground; ★ **sous peu** before long.

sous-entendu *noun* M innuendo. *adjective* implied.

sous-estimer *verb* [1] to underestimate.

sous-marin *noun* M submarine. *adjective* under-water; deep-sea.

sous-sol *noun* M basement; **au sous-sol** in the basement.

sous-tasse *noun* F saucer.

sous-titre *noun* M subtitle.

soustraction *noun* F subtraction.

sous-vêtements *plural noun* M underwear.

soutenir *verb* [77] 1 to support; **elle m'a soutenu à la réunion** she supported me at the meeting; 2 **soutenir que** to maintain that; 3 **soutenir une conversation** to keep up a conversation; 4 to withstand (*a shock or attack*).

souterrain *adjective* underground.

soutien *noun* M support.

soutien-gorge *noun* M bra.

soutif *noun* M (*informal*) bra.

souvenir *noun* M 1 memory; **mes souvenirs de Londres** my memories of London; **garder un bon souvenir de quelque chose** to have happy memories of something; **je n'ai aucun souvenir de l'avoir rencontrée** I have no memory of meeting her; 2 souvenir.

verb [81] **se souvenir de** to remember; **je me souviens d'elle** I remember her; **je me souviens de l'avoir rencontrée** I remember meeting her; **t'en souviens-tu?** do you remember that?

souvent *adverb* often; **je ne la vois pas très souvent** I don't see her very often; **le plus souvent** more often than not

spacieux (F **spacieuse**) *adjective* spacious.

spaghettis *plural noun* M spaghetti; **manger des spaghetti** to have spaghetti.

sparadrap *noun* M sticking plaster.

speaker, speakerine *noun* M, F announcer.

spécial (M *plural* **spéciaux**) *adjective* 1 special; **rien de spécial** nothing special; **les effets spéciaux** special effects; 2 odd; **il est vraiment très spécial** he's really very odd.

spécialement *adverb* specially.

spécialiser *verb* [1] **se spécialiser** to specialize; **elle se spécialise dans la génétique** she's specializing in genetics.

spécialiste *noun* M & F specialist.

spécialité *noun* F speciality.

spécifier *verb* [1] to specify.

spectacle *noun* M show.

spectaculaire *adjective* spectacular.

spectateur, spectatrice noun M, F 1 member of the audience; 2 spectator.

spéléologie noun F potholing.

spirituel, spirituelle adjective 1 witty; 2 spiritual.

splendeur noun F splendour.

splendide adjective magnificent.

sponsoriser verb [1] to sponsor.

spontané adjective spontaneous.

sport noun M sport; sports; aimez-vous le sport? do you like sport?; il fait beaucoup de sport he does a lot of sport; mon maillot de sport my sports shirt; les sports d'hiver winter sports.

sportif, sportive noun M, F sportsman, sportswoman. adjective 1 sports; un club sportif a sports club; une rencontre sportive a sports meeting; 2 sporty, athletic.

spot noun M 1 spotlight; 2 un spot publicitaire a commercial.

square noun M public garden.

squelette noun M skeleton.

stable adjective 1 stable; 2 un emploi stable a steady job.

stade noun M stadium.

stage noun M 1 course; un stage intensif d'anglais an intensive English course; 2 un stage professionnel work experience; j'aimerais faire un stage professionnel dans une société britannique I'd like to do work experience in an British company.

stand noun M 1 stand (in a market or an exhibition); 2 stall (in a fairground).

standard noun M switchboard; il faut passer par le standard you have to go through the switchboard.

standardiste noun M & F switchboard operator.

standing noun M un appartement de standing a luxury flat.

star noun F star (in a film or show).

starter noun M choke (in a car).

station noun F 1 une station de métro an underground station; 2 une station de taxis a taxi rank; 3 resort; une station de ski a ski resort; 4 une station de radio a radio station.

station de travail noun F (computer) work station.

stationnement noun M parking; 'stationnement interdit' 'no parking'.

stationner verb [1] to park.

station-service noun F service station.

statistique noun F statistic(s).

statue noun F statue.

steak noun M steak; un steak frites steak and chips; un steak haché a burger steak.

sténodactylo noun M & F shorthand typist.

stéréo noun F, adjective stereo.

stérile adjective sterile.

stériliser verb [1] to sterilize.

stimulant adjective stimulating.

stock noun M stock; **en stock** in stock.

stop noun M **1** stop sign; **2 faire du stop** to hitch-hike.

stopper verb [1] to stop.

store noun M **1** blind; **2** awning.

strapontin noun M fold-down seat.

stratégie noun F strategy.

stratégique adjective strategic.

stress noun M stress.

stressant adjective stressful.

stressé adjective stressed; **elle avait l'air stressé** she looked stressed; **je suis très stressé en ce moment** I'm stressed out at the moment.

strict adjective **1** strict; **2** severe.

studieux (F **studieuse**) adjective studious.

studio noun M **1** studio flat; **2** studio.

stupéfait adjective astounded.

stupéfiants plural noun M narcotics.

stupeur noun F astonishment.

stupide adjective stupid.

stupidité noun F stupidity.

style noun M style; **c'est bien son style!** that's just like him!

styliste noun M & F designer.

stylo noun M fountain pen.

stylo-bille noun M ball-point pen.

stylo-feutre noun M felt pen.

stylo-plume noun M fountain pen.

su verb SEE **savoir**[1].

subir verb [2] **1** to be subjected to; (change, violence, or pressure); to suffer (defeat or damage); **2 subir une opération** to have an operation.

subitement adverb suddenly.

subjonctif noun M subjunctive; **au subjonctif** in the subjunctive.

subordonné, subordonnée noun M F subordinate.

substituer verb [1] to replace, to substitute.

subtil adjective subtle.

subvention noun F subsidy.

succès noun M success; **c'est un grand succès!** it's a big success!

succursale noun F branch (of a company).

sucer verb [61] to suck.

sucette noun F lollipop.

sucre noun M **1** sugar; **du jus d'orange sans sucre** unsweetened orange juice; **2 un sucre** a lump of sugar.

sucré adjective sweet; **c'est trop sucré pour moi** it's too sweet for me.

sucre cristallisé noun M granulated sugar.

sucre d'orge noun M barley sugar.

sucre en morceaux noun M sugar lumps.

sucre en poudre noun M caster sugar.

sucre glace noun M icing sugar.

sucrerie noun F **des sucreries** sweet things.

sucre roux noun M brown sugar.

sucrier noun M sugar bowl.

sud noun M south; **au sud de l'Écosse** in the south of Scotland; **au sud de Calais** south of Calais; **un vent du sud** a south wind. adjective 1 south; **la côte sud** the south coast; 2 southern; **la partie sud** the southern part.

sud-africain adjective South African.

sud-américain adjective South American.

sud-est noun M, adjective south-east.

sud-ouest noun M, adjective south-west.

Suède noun F Sweden.

suédois noun M, adjective Swedish.

Suédois, Suédoise noun M, F Swede.

suer verb [1] to sweat.

sueur noun F sweat; **je suis en sueur** I'm sweating.

suffire verb [74] 1 to be enough; **un kilo suffit** one kilo's enough; **ça suffit!** that's enough!; 2 **il suffit de faire** all you have to do is; **il suffit de nous téléphoner** all you have to do is give us a call.

suffisamment adverb enough; **ce n'est pas suffisamment cuit** it's not cooked enough; **il n'y a pas suffisamment de verres** there aren't enough glasses.

suffisant adjective 1 sufficient; **c'est bien suffisant!** that's quite enough!; 2 smug; **je la trouve un peu suffisante** I find her a bit smug.

suffoquer verb [1] to suffocate; to choke.

suggérer verb [24] to suggest.

suggestion noun F suggestion.

suicider verb [1] **se suicider** to commit suicide.

suis verb SEE **être**[1]; SEE **suivre**.

suisse adjective Swiss.

Suisse noun F Switzerland; **en Suisse** in (or to) Switzerland; **la Suisse romande** French-speaking Switzerland; **la Suisse allemande** German-speaking Switzerland.

suite noun F 1 rest; **je te raconterai la suite plus tard** I'll tell you the rest later; **et on connaît la suite** and we all know what happened next; 2 continuation; '**suite page 67**' 'continued on page 67'; **regardez la suite jeudi** watch the next instalment on Thursday; 3 suite (in a hotel); 4 in succession; **trois fois de suite** three times in succession; 5 **tout de suite** straightaway; **j'arrive tout de suite!** I'll be right there!; 6 **par la suite** later; **on s'est rendu compte par la suite que c'était une erreur** we realized later that it was a mistake.

suivant, suivante noun M, F next one; **pas ce lundi mais le suivant** not this Monday but the next. adjective following; **le jour suivant** the following day.

suivre verb [75] **1** to follow; **suivez-moi** follow me; **2 suivre l'actualité** to keep up with the news; **3 'à suivre'** 'to be continued'; **4 faire suivre son courrier** to have your mail forwarded; **5 suivre un cours** to do a course; **6 suivre un régime** to be on a diet.

sujet noun M **1** subject; **au sujet de** about; **c'est au sujet de votre fils** it's about your son; **c'est à quel sujet?** what's it about?; **un sujet de conversation** a topic of conversation; **2 un sujet d'examen** an exam question. adjective (F **sujette**) être sujet à to suffer from; **elle est sujette à des crises d'asthme** she suffers from asthma attacks.

super noun M four-star petrol. adjective (informal) fantastic; **mais c'est super!** but that's fantastic!

superficie noun F area.

superficiel (F **superficielle**) adjective superficial.

supérieur, supérieure noun M, F superior. adjective **1** upper; **l'étage supérieur** the upper floor; **la lèvre supérieure** the upper lip; **2** greater; **la taille supérieure** the bigger size; **à une vitesse supérieure** at a faster speed; **à une température supérieure** at a higher temperature; **un prix supérieur** a higher price;

3 better, superior (work, quality); **c'est de loin supérieur à l'autre!** it's much better than the other one! **4 supérieur à** greater than; **un nombre supérieur à trois** a number higher than three.

superlatif noun M superlative.

supermarché noun M supermarket.

superposer verb [1] **1** to stack up; **des lits superposés** bunk beds; **2** to superimpose (an image).

superstitieux (F **superstitieuse**) adjective superstitious.

superstition noun F superstition.

supplément noun M extra charge; **le vin est en supplément** wine is extra.

supplémentaire adjective **1** additional; **2 faire des heures supplémentaires** to do overtime.

supplier verb [1] to beg.

support noun M **1** support; **2** back-up (material); **un support audiovisuel** audiovisual aids.

supportable adjective bearable.

supporter verb [1] **1** to stand; **il ne supporte pas qu'on le critique** he can't stand being criticized; **je ne peux plus la supporter!** I can't stand any more of her! **2** to support (a weight).

supposer verb [1] to suppose.

supprimer verb [1] **1** to get rid of; **2 supprimer des emplois** to cut jobs; **supprimer un train** to cancel a train.

sur *preposition* 1 on; c'est sur ton lit it's on your bed; un débat sur le racisme a discussion on racism; le cinéma est sur la droite the cinema's on the right; 2 over; un pont sur la Loire a bridge over the Loire; 3 by (*in measurements*); c'est deux mètres sur trois it's two metres by three; 4 out of; trois femmes sur cinq three women out of five; 5 out of; j'ai eu douze sur vingt en géographie I got twelve out of twenty in geography.

sûr *adjective* 1 sure; tu es sûr? are you sure?; oui, bien sûr! yes, of course!; sûr et certain certain; j'en étais sûr! I knew it!; 2 il est très sûr de lui he's very self-confident; 3 safe; en lieu sûr in a safe place; le plus sûr est de tout fermer à clé the safest thing is to lock everything.

surcharger *verb* [52] to overload.

surdité *noun* F deafness.

sûrement *adverb* 1 certainly; sûrement pas! certainly not!; 2 il doit sûrement arriver à tout instant he's bound to arrive at any moment; elle est sûrement partie she's bound to have left.

sûreté *noun* F safety, security.

surf *noun* M surfing.

surface *noun* F 1 surface; 2 area; 3 une grande surface a supermarket.

surgelé *noun* M les surgelés frozen food.
adjective frozen; les légumes surgelés frozen vegetables.

sur-le-champ *adverb* right away.

surlendemain *noun* M elle est arrivée le surlendemain she arrived two days later.

surmonter *verb* [1] to overcome.

surnaturel (F surnaturelle) *adjective* supernatural.

surnom *noun* M nickname.

surnommer *verb* [1] to nickname.

surpeuplé *adjective* overpopulated.

surprenant *addjective* surprising.

surprendre *verb* [64] 1 to surprise; ça m'a beaucoup surpris I found that really surprising; 2 surprendre quelqu'un en train de faire quelque chose to catch somebody doing something; je l'ai surprise en train de lire mon courrier I caught her reading my mail.

surpris (F surprise) *adjective* surprised; je suis surpris de te voir I'm surprised to see you.

surprise *noun* F surprise; quelle surprise! what a surprise!; faire une surprise à quelqu'un to give somebody a surprise.

surréaliste *noun* M & F surrealist.
adjective surreal.

surtout *adverb* 1 especially; il y a beaucoup de touristes, surtout en été there are lots of tourists, especially in the summer; 2 above all; il faut surtout rester calme above all, we must stay calm.

surveillant, surveillante *noun* M, F supervisor (*in a school, responsible for maintaining school discipline outside the classroom*).

surveiller verb [1] **1** to watch, to keep an eye on; **est-ce que tu peux surveiller mon sac deux secondes?** can you keep an eye on my bag for a couple of minutes?; **2 surveiller une maison** to keep a house under surveillance; **3** to supervise; **surveiller le travail des élèves** to supervise the students' work (*work or progress*); **4 surveiller un examen** to invigilate an exam; **5 je surveille ma ligne** I'm watching my figure.

survêtement noun M tracksuit.

survie noun F survival.

survivant, survivante noun M, F survivor.

survivre verb [82] to survive; **survivre à un accident** to survive an accident.

survoler verb [1] to fly over.

suspect, suspecte noun M, F suspect.
adjective suspicious.

suspense noun M suspense (*as in a thriller*).

suture noun F **un point de suture** a stitch (*in a wound*).

svelte adjective slender.

SVP SHORT FOR **s'il vous plaît**; please.

syllabe noun F syllable.

symbole noun M symbol.

symbolique adjective symbolic; **un geste symbolique** a token gesture.

sympa adjective (*informal*) nice; **je le trouve très sympa, ton copain** he's really nice, your boyfriend.

sympathie noun F **j'ai beaucoup de sympathie pour elle** I like her a lot.

sympathique adjective nice; **c'est un type sympathique** he's a nice guy.

sympathiser verb [1] **sympathiser avec quelqu'un** to get on well with someone.

symptôme noun M symptom.

syndicat noun M trade union.

syndicat d'initiative noun M tourist information office.

synthétique adjective synthetic.

système noun M system; **un système d'éclairage** a lighting system.

T t

ta adjective SEE **ton**.

tabac noun M **1** tobacco; **2 un bureau de tabac** a tobacconist's.

table noun F table; **à table!** dinner's ready!; **se mettre à table** to sit down to eat; **mettre la table** to lay the table.

tableau noun M **1** painting; **un tableau de Renoir** a painting by Renoir; **2 le tableau noir** the blackboard; **3 le tableau d'affichage** the notice board.

tableau de bord noun M dashboard.

table de chevet, table de nuit noun F bedside table.

table des matières noun F (list of) contents (in a book).

tablette noun F une tablette de chocolat a bar of chocolate.

tablier noun M apron.

tabouret noun M stool.

tache noun F stain.

tâche noun F task.

tache de rousseur noun F freckle.

tacher verb [1] to stain.

tact noun M tact; il l'a fait avec beaucoup de tact he did it very tactfully.

tactique noun F tactics. adjective tactical.

taie noun F une taie d'oreiller a pillowcase.

taille noun F 1 size; qu'est-ce que vous avez à ma taille? what have you got in my size?; quelle taille faites-vous? what size are you?; 'taille unique' 'one size'; la taille au-dessus/au-dessous the next size up/down; 2 height; un homme de grande taille a tall man; 3 waist; avoir la taille fine to have a slim waist.

taille-crayon noun M pencil sharpener.

tailleur noun M 1 suit (for a woman); 2 tailor; ★ s'asseoir en tailleur to sit cross-legged (literally: like a tailor).

taire verb [76] se taire to stop talking; taisez-vous! be quiet!

talent noun M talent; c'est un jeune musicien de talent he's a talented young musician.

talon noun M 1 heel (of your foot or a shoe); 2 stub (of a ticket or cheque book).

talon aiguille noun M stiletto heel.

tambour noun M drum.

Tamise noun F la Tamise the Thames.

tampon noun M 1 pad (for sponging); un tampon à récurer a scouring pad; 2 un tampon (hygiénique) a tampon.

tamponneuse adjective les autos tamponneuses the dodgems.

tandis que conjunction while.

tant adverb 1 so much; j'ai tant mangé que... I've eaten so much that...; ce qu'elle avait tant espéré what she had so much hoped for; je ne les aime pas tant que ça I don't like them as much as that; 2 tant de so much; so many; tant d'argent so much money; tant d'amis so many friends; tant de monde so many people; 3 tant pis never mind; 4 tant mieux so much the better; 5 tant que while; tant que tu y es, passe-moi un stylo while you're there, pass me a pen; 6 tant que as long as; tant que Jacques ne sera pas rentré, je ne peux pas sortir I can't go out until Jacques gets back.

tante noun F aunt.

tantôt *adverb* sometimes; **tantôt chez elle, tantôt chez moi** sometimes at her place and sometimes at mine.

taper *verb* [1] **1 taper quelqu'un** to hit somebody; **ça tape aujourd'hui** the sun's really beating down today; **2 taper à la machine** to type; **taper une lettre** to type a letter; **3 taper des mains** to clap your hands; **taper du pied** to tap your foot; **4 taper à la porte** to knock on the door; **5** (*informal*) **se taper dessus** to knock each other about.

tapis *noun* M carpet.

tapis de bain *noun* M bathmat.

tapis roulant *noun* M **1** walkway; **2** carousel (*for airport luggage*); conveyor belt.

tapisser *verb* [1] **1** to wallpaper; **2** to upholster.

tapisserie *noun* F **1** tapestry; **2** wallpaper.

taquiner *verb* [1] to tease.

tard *adverb* late; **couche-toi, il est tard** go to bed, it's late; **plus tard** later; **trop tard** too late; **pas plus tard que mardi** no later than Tuesday; **ce sera pour plus tard** there'll be other times.

tarder *verb* [1] to be a long time; **ta mère ne va pas tarder** your mother won't be long.

tardif (F **tardive**) *adjective* late.

tarif *noun* M **1** rate; **tarif de nuit** night rate (*for the phone*); **2** fare; **plein tarif** full fare; **tarif réduit** reduced fare; **3** price list.

tarte *noun* F tart; **une tarte aux abricots** an apricot tart.

tartine *noun* F slice of bread and butter (*and/or jam*).

tartiner *verb* [1] to spread (*on bread*).

tas *noun* M **1** pile; **un tas de bois** a pile of wood; **2** (*informal*) **un tas de** stacks of; **j'ai un tas de choses à faire ce soir** I've got stacks of things to do tonight.

tasse *noun* F cup; **une tasse de thé** a cup of tea.

tatie *noun* F (*informal*) auntie.

taupe *noun* F mole (*animal*).

taureau (*plural* **taureaux**) *noun* M bull.

Taureau *noun* M Taurus (*sign of the Zodiac*).

taux *noun* M rate; **le taux mensuel** the monthly rate; **le taux de change** the exchange rate.

taxe *noun* F tax; **la boutique hors taxes** the duty-free shop.

taxi *noun* M taxi; **appeler un taxi** to call a taxi.

tchèque *adjective* Czech; **la République tchèque** the Czech Republic.

te, t' (*before a vowel or silent 'h'*) *pronoun* you; **1 Gaby te cherche** Gaby's looking for you; **il t'a vu** he saw you; **elle m'a donné son adresse** she gave me her address; **il te l'a donné** he gave it to you; **2** to you; **3** yourself; **tu peux te faire une salade** you can make yourself a salad; **tu t'es blessé?** have you hurt yourself? **tu te lèves quand?** what time do you get up?

technicien, technicienne *noun* M, F technician.

technique *noun* F technique. *adjective* technical.

technologie *noun* F technology.

teckel *noun* M dachshund.

tee-shirt *noun* M T-shirt.

teint *noun* M complexion; **avoir le teint clair** to have a fair complexion.

teinturier, teinturière *noun* M, F dry-cleaner's.

tel, telle *adjective* 1 such; **avec un tel intérêt** with such interest; **une telle aventure** such an adventure; **de tels mensonges** such lies; 2 **tel que** such as; **les grandes villes telles que Paris et Lyon** large towns such as Paris and Lyons; 3 **rien de tel que** nothing like; **il n'y a rien de tel qu'un bon repas** there's nothing like a good meal; 4 **servir le saumon tel quel** serve the salmon just as it is; **je l'ai acheté tel quel** I bought it just as it was.

télé *noun* F (*informal*) telly; **je l'ai vu à la télé** I saw it on telly.

télécarte™ *noun* F phonecard.

télécommande *noun* F remote control.

télécopie *noun* F fax.

télécopieur *noun* M fax machine, fax.

téléphérique *noun* M cable car.

téléphone *noun* M telephone; **un numéro de téléphone** a phone

number; **Bruno est au téléphone.** Bruno's on the phone.

téléphone portable *noun* M mobile phone.

téléphoner *verb* [1] to phone; **je vais téléphoner à Robert** I'll phone Robert.

téléphonique *adjective* **une cabine téléphonique** a phone box; **un appel téléphonique** a phone call.

télésiège *noun* M chairlift.

téléski *noun* M ski-tow.

téléspectateur, téléspectatrice *noun* M, F viewer (*of TV*).

téléviser *verb* [1] to televize.

téléviseur *noun* M television (set); **un téléviseur couleur** a colour television.

télévision *noun* F television; **à la télévision** on television.

telle *adjective* SEE **tel**.

tellement *adverb* 1 so; **c'est tellement compliqué!** it's so complicated!; 2 so much; **c'est tellement mieux payé** it's so much better paid; **'tu aimes lire?'** – **'pas tellement'** 'do you like reading?' – 'not much'; 3 **tellement de** so much, so many; **j'ai tellement de travail!** I've got so much work!; **il y a tellement de choses à voir!** there are so many things to see!; **il y avait tellement de monde** there were so many people there.

tels, telles *adjective* SEE **tel**.

témoignage noun M 1 story, account; **selon les témoignages de l'accident** according to accounts of the accident; 2 evidence (*in court*); 3 **un témoignage d'amitié** a token of friendship.

témoigner verb [1] to give evidence.

témoin noun M witness.

température noun F temperature.

tempête noun F storm.

temple noun M 1 temple; 2 (Protestant) church.

temporaire adjective temporary.

temps noun M 1 weather; **quel temps fait-il?** what's the weather like? **par temps de pluie** in rainy weather; 2 time; **je n'ai pas le temps** I haven't got time; **il est temps de partir** it's time to go; **arriver à temps** to arrive in (or on) time; **de temps en temps** from time to time; **en même temps** at the same time; **ça a pris beaucoup de temps** it took a long time; **il nous reste combien de temps?** how much time do we have left? **c'est du temps perdu** it's a waste of time; **il était temps!** about time too!; **ces derniers temps** recently; **un travail à plein temps** a full-time job; **un travail à temps partiel** a part-time job; 3 tense (*of a verb*).

tendance noun F 1 tendency; **avoir tendance à faire** to tend to do; 2 trend.

tendre¹ verb [3] 1 to stretch (*something elastic*); 2 to hold out; **elle m'a tendu un crayon** she held out a pencil to me; **tendre la main à**

quelqu'un to hold out one's hand to someone; 3 **tendre le bras** to reach out.

tendre² adjective tender.

tendresse noun F tenderness.

tendu adjective tense.

tenir verb [77] 1 to hold; **peux-tu tenir la corde?** can you hold the rope? **elle tenait l'enfant par la main** she was holding the child by the hand; 2 to run (*a shop, a business*); 3 to keep; **elle tenait les yeux baissés** she kept her eyes down; **'tenir hors de la portée des enfants'** 'keep out of reach of children'; 4 to take up; **cela tient la place de deux personnes** it takes up the space of two people; 5 **tenir à** to be attached to; **elle tient beaucoup à ses petits-enfants** she's very attached to her grandchildren; 6 **tenir à faire quelque chose** to be determined to do something; **je tiens à le finir aujourd'hui** I'm determined to finish it today; 7 **tiens!** oh!; **tiens, il est déjà midi!** oh, it's twelve already!; **tiens! est-ce que je t'ai raconté...?** listen! have I told you...?; **tiens, tiens, c'est toi!** well, well, it's you!; **tiens, prends le mien** here, take mine; 8 **tenir de quelqu'un** to take after someone; **elle tient de sa mère** she takes after her mother; 9 **se tenir** to hold; **ils se tenaient par la main** they were holding each other by the hand; 10 **se tenir** to stand; **elle se tenait devant l'entrée** she was standing by the entrance; **tiens-toi tranquille!** be quiet!; **tiens-toi droit!** stand up straight!; 11 **se tenir pour** to think yourself; **il se tient pour un génie** he thinks he's a genius.

tennis *noun* M 1 tennis; **jouer au tennis** to play tennis; **un terrain de tennis, un tennis** a tennis court; **tennis de table** table tennis; 2 tennis shoe.

tension *noun* F 1 tension; 2 blood pressure.

tentant *adjective* tempting.

tentation *noun* F temptation.

tentative *noun* F attempt.

tente *noun* F tent.

tenter *verb* [1] 1 to attempt; **il a tenté de s'échapper** he tried to escape; **tenter sa chance, tenter le coup** (*informal*) to give it a try; 2 to tempt.

tenu *adjective* 1 **bien/mal tenu** well/badly cared for; 2 **être tenu de faire** to be required to do.

tenue *noun* F clothes; **être en tenue de sport** to be in sports kit; **en tenue de soirée** in evening dress.

terme *noun* M 1 word, term; **un terme technique** a technical term; **les termes du contrat** the terms of the contract; 2 end; **à court terme** short-term; **à long terme** long-term.

terminale *noun* F (*in a French school*) the equivalent of Year 13.

terminer *verb* [1] 1 to finish; 2 to end; **la réunion s'est terminée à dix-huit heures** the meeting ended at six p.m.; **ça va mal se terminer!** it'll end in tears!

terminus *noun* M terminus.

terrain *noun* M 1 ground, land; **il a acheté du terrain** he's bought some land; 2 pitch, ground (*for sports*); **un terrain de football** a football pitch; **un terrain de golf** a golf course; 3 piece of ground; **un terrain à bâtir** a building plot.

terrain de camping *noun* M campsite.

terrain de jeu(x) *noun* M playground.

terrain de sport(s) *noun* M sports ground.

terrain vague *noun* M waste ground.

terrasse *noun* F terrace.

terre *noun* F 1 ground; **s'asseoir par terre** to sit on the floor; **tomber par terre** to fall down; 2 **la Terre** the Earth; 3 soil; 4 land (*not sea*); **aller à terre** to go ashore.

terre cuite *noun* F terracotta.

terrible *adjective* 1 terrible; **des événements terribles** terrible events; 2 (*informal*) terrific; **'c'était bien, le film?'** – **'pas terrible'** 'was the film any good?' – 'not great'.

terrifiant *adjective* terrifying.

terrine *noun* F pâté.

territoire *noun* M 1 territory; 2 country; **il fera beau sur l'ensemble du territoire** 'it will be fine over the whole country'.

terrorisme *noun* M terrorism.

terroriste *noun* M & F terrorist.

tes *adjective* your; SEE **ton**.

test noun M test.

testament noun M will.

tester verb [1] to test.

tétanos noun M tetanus.

têtard noun M tadpole.

tête noun F 1 head; **se laver la tête** to wash your hair; **j'ai la tête qui tourne** my head's spinning; 2 face; **je n'aime pas sa tête** I don't like his face; 3 top; **tu es en tête de la liste** you're first on the list; 4 mind; **j'ai quelque chose en tête** I have something in mind; **où avais-tu la tête?** what were you thinking of?; 5 front (of a train); **les deux wagons de tête sont à destination de Bourges** the two front coaches are for Bourges; ★ **faire la tête** to sulk; ★ **un dîner en tête à tête** a private dinner for two; ★ **j'en ai par-dessus la tête!** I'm fed up to the back teeth!

têtu adjective stubborn.

texte noun M text.

TGV noun M SHORT FOR **train à grande vitesse** high-speed train.

thalassothérapie noun F sea-water treatment (at a health spa).

thé noun M tea; **un thé au lait** tea with milk.

théâtre noun M 1 theatre; **des costumes de théâtre** stage costumes; **un coup de théâtre** a dramatic turn of events; 2 plays; **le théâtre de Molière** Molière's plays; 3 **faire du théâtre** to belong to a drama group.

théière noun F teapot.

thème noun M 1 subject; 2 prose (a text to translate into the foreign language).

théorie noun F theory.

thérapie noun F 1 (medical) treatment; 2 therapy.

thermal (M plural **thermaux**) adjective thermal; **une station thermale** a spa.

thermomètre noun M thermometer.

thon noun M tuna.

thym noun M thyme.

tibia noun M 1 shin; 2 shinbone.

tic noun M nervous twitch.

ticket noun M 1 ticket; **un ticket de métro** an underground ticket; 2 **un ticket de caisse** a till receipt.

tiède adjective 1 warm; 2 lukewarm.

tien, tienne, tiens, tiennes pronoun **le tien, la tienne, les tiens, les tiennes** yours; **est-ce que ce stylo est le tien?** is this pen yours?; **ma voiture et la tienne** my car and yours; **mes lettres et les tiennes** my letters and yours.

tiens verb SEE **tenir**. pronoun SEE **tien**.

tiers noun M third; **les deux tiers de la population** two-thirds of the population. adjective (F **tierce**) third.

tiers-monde noun M Third World.

tige noun F stem.

tigre noun M tiger.

tilleul noun M **1** lime tree; **2** lime flower tea.

timbre noun M stamp.

timide adjective shy.

timidité noun F shyness.

tiquer verb [1] **sans tiquer** without batting an eyelid.

tir noun M **1** shooting; **2** shot (in football).

tirage noun M **le tirage au sort** the draw (in a lottery, for example); **par tirage au sort** by drawing lots.

tir à l'arc noun M archery.

tire-bouchon noun M corkscrew.

tirelire noun F money box.

tirer verb [1] **1** to pull; **il m'a tiré par le bras** he pulled my arm; **elle m'a tiré les cheveux** she pulled my hair; **2** to draw; **tirer les rideaux** to draw the curtains; **il a tiré la lettre de sa poche** he drew the letter from his pocket; **tirer un trait** to draw a line; **tirer des conclusions** to draw conclusions; **tirer au sort** to draw lots; **3** to fire; **ils ont tiré sur les policiers** they fired on the police; **tirer plusieurs coups de feu** to fire several shots.

tiret noun M dash.

tiroir noun M drawer.

tisane noun F herbal tea.

tissu noun M material, fabric.

titre noun M **1** title; **2** headline; **les titres de l'actualité** the news headlines; **3** **à juste titre** quite rightly; **à titre d'exemple** as an example.

titre de transport noun M travel ticket.

tituber verb [1] to stagger.

toast noun M **1** piece of toast; **servir avec des toasts** serve with toast; **2** toast (to someone's health).

toboggan noun M slide.

toi pronoun you; **c'est toi!** it's you!; **avec toi** with you; **plus grand que toi** bigger than you; **c'est à toi de jouer** it's your turn; **assieds-toi** sit down; **est-ce que ces chaussettes sont à toi?** are these socks yours?

toile noun F **1** cloth; **toile de lin** linen; **une toile cirée** an oilcloth; **2** painting, canvas; **une toile de Picasso** a painting by Picasso.

toile d'araignée noun F spider's web, cobweb.

toilette noun F **1** **faire sa toilette** to have a wash; **2** outfit; **je me suis acheté une toilette pour le mariage de ma sœur** I've bought an outfit for my sister's wedding.

toilettes plural noun F toilet; **aller aux toilettes** to go to the toilet.

toi-même pronoun yourself; **l'as-tu fait toi-même?** did you do it yourself?

toit noun M roof.

tolérant adjective tolerant.

tolérer verb [24] to tolerate.

tomate noun F tomato; **une salade de tomates** a tomato salad.

tombe noun F grave.

tombeau (plural **tombeaux**) noun M tomb.

tomber *verb* [1] **1** to fall; **attention, tu vas tomber!** careful, you'll fall!; **la chaise est tombée** the chair fell over; **Noël tombe un lundi** Christmas falls on a Monday; **2 laisser tomber** to drop; **j'ai laissé tomber mon porte-monnaie** I've dropped my purse; **3 laisser tomber** to give up (*an activity*); **elle a laissé tomber l'espagnol** she's given up Spanish; **4 tomber malade** to fall ill; **tomber amoureux** to fall in love; **5 tomber sur** to bump into; **je suis tombé sur Georges devant la poste** I bumped into Georges outside the post office; **6 ça tombe bien** that's lucky; ★ **je tombe de sommeil** I can't keep my eyes open (*literally: I'm dropping with sleep*).

ton¹, ta, tes *adjective* your; **ton chat** your cat; **ta sœur** your sister; **tes pieds** your feet.

ton² *noun* M **1** tone of voice; **2** colour.

tondeuse *noun* F lawnmower.

tondre *verb* [3] to mow.

tonique *adjective* bracing.

tonne *noun* F tonne, metric ton (*1,000 kg*); ★ **j'ai des tonnes de choses à faire** (*informal*) I've loads of things to do.

tonneau (*plural* **tonneaux**) *noun* M barrel.

tonnerre *noun* M thunder.

tonton *noun* M (*informal*) uncle.

tonus *noun* M energy (*for a person*); tone (*for your muscles*).

toque *noun* F chef's hat.

torchon *noun* M cloth; tea towel.

tordre *verb* [3] to twist; **se tordre la cheville** to twist your ankle.

tordu *adjective* **1** bent; **2** crooked; **3** weird; **une histoire tordue** a weird story.

torrent *noun* M waterfall; mountain stream.

torse *noun* M chest, upper body; **il s'est mis torse nu** he stripped to the waist.

tort *noun* M **1 avoir tort** to be wrong; **je crois que tu as tort** I think you're wrong; **il a tort de dire ça** he's wrong to say that; **2 à tort** wrongly; **à tort ou à raison** rightly or wrongly.

torticolis *noun* M stiff neck; **avoir le torticolis** to have a stiff neck.

tortiller *verb* [1] **se tortiller** to wriggle.

tortue *noun* F tortoise, turtle.

torture *noun* F torture.

torturer *verb* [1] to torture.

tôt *adverb* **1** early; **on va partir tôt** we're leaving early; **tôt le matin** early in the morning; **2** soon; **le plus tôt possible** as soon as possible; **tôt ou tard** sooner or later.

total (*plural* **totaux**) *noun* M total; **au total** in total. *adjective* total.

totalement *adverb* totally.

totalité *noun* F **la totalité des élèves** all the pupils; **la totalité du groupe** the whole group.

touchant *adjective* touching.

touche noun F 1 key (on a piano or keyboard); 2 button (on a machine); **appuyez sur la touche** press the button marked; 3 (ligne de) touche touchline.

toucher verb [1] 1 to touch; **ne touche pas à ma peinture** don't touch my painting; 2 to touch; **cette histoire m'a beaucoup touché** that story really touched me; 3 to affect, to concern; **ce problème nous touche tous** this problem affects us all; 4 to get (money or wages); **il touche 2 000 francs par semaine** he's getting 2,000 francs a week.

touffu adjective bushy, thick.

toujours adverb 1 always; **il est toujours en retard** he's always late; **comme toujours** as always; 2 still; **nous habitons toujours au même endroit** we're still living in the same place; **ton paquet n'est toujours pas arrivé** your parcel still hasn't come; 3 pour toujours for ever.

tour[1] noun M 1 **faire le tour de** to go round; **faire le tour des magasins** to go round all the shops; **faire le tour du monde** to go round the world; 2 **faire un tour** to go for a walk; **on va faire un petit tour** we'll go for a little walk; 3 **faire un tour à vélo** to go for a bike ride; 4 **faire un tour en voiture** to go for a drive; 5 turn; **c'est ton tour de jouer** it's your turn to play; **à qui le tour?** whose turn is it?

tour[2] noun F 1 tower; **la tour Eiffel** the Eiffel Tower; 2 tower block; 3 castle, rook (in chess).

tourbillon noun M whirlwind, whirlpool.

tourisme noun M tourism.

touriste noun M & F tourist.

touristique adjective **un guide touristique** a tourist guide (book); **une ville touristique** a town which attracts tourists.

tourmenter verb [1] to tease.

tourne-disque noun M record player.

tournée noun F 1 round (of a postman or baker, for example); 2 round (of drinks); **c'est ma tournée** it's my round; 3 tour (of a performer); **être en tournée** to be on tour.

tourner verb [1] 1 to turn; **tournez à gauche à l'église** turn left at the church; 2 to toss (a salad); 3 **mal tourner** to go wrong; 4 **se tourner** to turn; **elle s'est tournée vers moi** she turned to face me; 5 **tourner le dos à quelqu'un** to have your back to somebody.

tournesol noun M sunflower.

tournevis noun M screwdriver.

tournoi noun M tournament.

tous adjective, pronoun SEE tout.

Toussaint noun F All Saints' Day (November 1st).

tousser verb [1] to cough.

tout, toute, tous, toutes adjective 1 all; **tout le pain** all the bread; **toute la classe** all the class, the whole class; **tous les garçons** all the boys; **toutes les filles** all the girls; **ils sont tous là** they're all there; **tout le monde** everybody; **toute la journée** all day; **tous les deux** both; **je les achète tous les trois** I'll buy all three of them; **pendant toute une année** for a whole year; **2** any; **à tout âge** at any age; **à tout instant** at any moment; **'service à toute heure'** 'service at any time'; **3** every; **tous les jours** every day; **prenez un comprimé toutes les quatre heures** take one pill every four hours.

pronoun **1** everything; **ils ont tout pris** they took everything; **tout va bien** everything's fine; **2** all; **54 en tout** 54 in all; **et tout ça** and all that; **tout ce que je sais, c'est que...** all I know is that...; **tous ensemble** all together; **elles étaient toutes là** they were all there; **3** pas du tout not at all.

adverb **1** **c'est tout prêt** it's all ready; **il est tout seul** he's all alone; **tout doucement** very slowly; **tout droit** straight ahead.

tout à coup *adverb* suddenly.

tout à fait *adverb* completely, absolutely; **ce n'est pas tout à fait sec** it's not absolutely dry.

tout à l'heure *adverb* **1** just now; **je l'ai vu tout à l'heure** I saw him just now; **2** in a little while; **à tout à l'heure!** see you later!

tout de même *adverb* all the same; **c'est tout de même bizarre** all the same, it is odd.

tout de suite *adverb* at once; **fais-le tout de suite!** do it at once!

tout d'un coup *adverb* suddenly.

toutefois *adverb* however.

toutes *adjective*, *pronoun* SEE **tout**.

toux *noun* F cough.

toxicomane *noun* M & F drug addict.

trac *noun* M (*informal*) **avoir le trac** to feel nervous.

trace *noun* F **1** tracks; **des traces de skis** ski-tracks; **des traces de pas** footprints; **2** mark; **des traces de doigts** finger marks.

tracer *verb* [61] to draw.

tracteur *noun* M tractor.

tradition *noun* F tradition.

traditionnel (F **traditionnelle**) *adjective* traditional.

traducteur, traductrice *noun* M, F translator.

traduction *noun* F translation.

traduire *verb* [26] to translate; **traduire en français** to translate into French.

trafic *noun* M **1** le trafic de drogue drug dealing; **2** traffic.

trafiquant, trafiquante *noun* M, F dealer (*in drugs or arms*).

tragédie *noun* F tragedy.

tragique *adjective* tragic.

trahir *verb* [2] to betray.

trahison *noun* F betrayal.

train *noun* M **1** train; **monter dans le train** to get on the train; **descendre du train** to get off the train; **le train de dix heures** the ten o'clock train; **2** être en train de faire to be (busy) doing; Henri est en train de faire la vaisselle Henri's doing the washing-up.

traîner verb [1] **1** to wander round; **2** to lie around; il laisse ses affaires traîner partout he leaves his things lying around everywhere; **3** to dawdle; ne traînez pas, le train arrive don't be long, the train's coming; **4** to drag on; j'ai des projets qui traînent I've got some projects that are dragging on; **5** to drag; elle traînait sa valise derrière elle she was dragging her suitcase behind her; **6** traîner les pieds to drag your feet.

traire verb [78] to milk.

trait noun M **1** line; **2** les traits features (of a face); avoir des traits fins to have delicate features; **3** d'un seul trait at one go; il l'a bu d'un seul trait he drank it all at one go.

trait d'union noun M hyphen.

traitement noun M **1** treatment; **2** processing; le traitement de texte word processing; **3** salary.

traiter verb [1] **1** to treat; il la traite très mal he treats her very badly; le médecin qui me traite the doctor who's treating me; **2** to deal with (a question or problem); **3** traiter de to call; il m'a traité de menteur he called me a liar.

traiteur noun M caterer.

trajet noun M **1** journey; c'est un trajet de deux heures it's a two-hour journey; **2** route.

tramway noun M tram, tramway.

tranchant adjective sharp.

tranche noun F **1** slice; deux tranches de jambon two slices of ham; **2** phase, period (of time).

trancher verb [1] **1** to slice; **2** to decide.

tranquille adjective **1** quiet; une rue tranquille a quiet street; tiens-toi tranquille! be quiet! **2** laisse-moi tranquille! leave me alone! **3** maman n'est pas tranquille si je n'appelle pas Mum worries if I don't ring.

tranquillité noun F peace.

transat noun M (informal) deck chair.

transférer verb [24] to transfer.

transfert noun M transfer.

transformer verb [1] **1** to change; ils ont transformé leur jardin they've completely changed their garden; nous avons transformé cette chambre en bureau we've turned this bedroom into a study; **2** se transformer en to change into; le têtard se transforme en grenouille the tadpole changes into a frog.

transfusion noun F une transfusion sanguine a blood transfusion.

transistor noun M transistor.

transmettre verb [11] **1** transmettre quelque chose à quelqu'un to pass something on to somebody; **2** to transmit.

transpiration noun F perspiration, sweat.

transpirer verb [1] to sweat.

transport noun M 1 transport; **les frais de transport** transport costs; 2 **les transports en commun** public transport.

transporter verb [1] 1 to transport; 2 to carry.

trappe noun F trap door.

travail (*plural* **travaux**) noun M 1 work; **j'ai beaucoup de travail à faire** I've got a lot of work to do; 2 job; **je cherche un travail** I'm looking for a job.

travailler verb [1] to work.

travailleur, travailleuse noun M, F worker.
adjective hard-working.

travailliste adjective Labour; **le parti travailliste** the Labour party (*in Britain*).

travaux plural noun M 1 work; **des travaux de construction** building work; **ils font faire des travaux chez eux** they're having some work done on the house; 2 roadworks; 3 **les travaux ménagers** housework; 4 **les travaux dirigés** classwork; **les travaux manuels** handicrafts.

travers noun M 1 **à travers** through; **j'ai regardé à travers les rideaux** I looked through the curtains; **voyager à travers le monde** to travel all over the world; 2 **de travers** crooked, wrong; **c'est boutonné de travers** it's buttoned up wrong.

traversée noun F crossing; **une traversée de l'Atlantique** an Atlantic crossing.

traverser verb [1] 1 to cross; **regarde avant de traverser la rue** look before you cross the road; 2 to go through; **traverser la France pour aller en Italie** to go through France on the way to Italy; **la pluie a traversé ma veste** the rain's gone right through my jacket; **ils ont traversé une crise** they went through a crisis.

traversin noun M bolster.

trébucher verb [1] to stumble.

trèfle noun M 1 clover; 2 clubs (*in cards*); **la dame de trèfle** the queen of clubs.

treize number thirteen; **Aurélie a treize ans** Aurélie's thirteen; **à treize heures** at one p.m.; **le treize juillet** the thirteenth of July.

treizième number thirteenth.

tremblement de terre noun M earthquake.

trembler verb [1] to shake, to tremble.

trempé adjective soaked.

tremper verb [1] to soak.

tremplin noun M springboard.

trentaine noun F 1 about thirty; **une trentaine de personnes** about thirty people; 2 **elle a la trentaine** she's in her thirties.

trente number thirty; **elle a trente ans** she's thirty; **le trente juillet** the thirtieth of July.

très adverb very; **très heureux** very happy; **j'ai très faim** I'm very hungry; **très bien fait** very well done.

trésor noun M treasure.

tresse noun F plait.

tréteau (plural **tréteaux**) noun M trestle.

tribu noun F tribe.

tribunal (plural **tribunaux**) noun M court; **paraître devant le tribunal** to appear in court (on a charge).

tricher verb [1] to cheat.

tricolore adjective three-coloured; **le drapeau tricolore** the French flag (which is three-coloured, blue, white, and red, in vertical stripes).

tricoter verb [1] to knit.

trier verb [1] to sort (out); **hier soir nous avons trié toutes les photos** last night we sorted out all the photographs.

trimestre noun M term.

triomphe noun M triumph.

triompher verb [1] to triumph.

tripes plural noun F tripe.

triple noun M **le triple** three times as much.

tripler verb [1] to treble.

triplés plural noun M triplets.

triste adjective sad.

tristesse noun F sadness.

trognon noun M **un trognon de pomme** an apple core.

trois number three; **Tom a trois ans** Tom's three; **à trois heures** at three o'clock; **le trois mars** the third of March; ★ **être haut comme trois pommes** to be knee-high to a grasshopper (literally: as tall as three apples).

troisième noun F (in a French school) the equivalent of Year 10.
noun M **au troisième** on the third floor.
adjective third.

trombone noun M 1 trombone; 2 paperclip (because of its shape).

trompe noun F trunk (elephant's).

tromper verb [1] 1 to deceive; 2 **se tromper** to make a mistake; **il s'est trompé** he made a mistake; **je me suis trompé de train** I got the wrong train; **vous vous êtes trompé de numéro** you've got the wrong number.

trompette noun F trumpet; **jouer de la trompette** to play the trumpet.

tronc noun M trunk (of a tree).

tronçonneuse noun F chain saw.

trop adverb 1 too; **c'est trop loin** it's too far; **c'est beaucoup trop cher** it's much too expensive; 2 too much; **j'ai trop mangé** I've eaten too much; **tu m'en as donné trop** you've given me too much; 3 **trop de** too much; too many; **trop de pain** too much bread; **trop de tomates** too many tomatoes; **trop de monde** too many people; 4 **de trop** too many; too much; **il y a une chaise de trop** there's one chair too many; **il y a dix francs de trop** that's ten francs too much.

tropique noun M tropic.

trottoir noun M pavement.

trou noun M hole.

troublant adjective disturbing.

trouer verb [1] to make a hole in; **des chaussettes trouées** socks with holes in them.

trouille noun F **avoir la trouille** (informal) to be scared.

troupe noun F 1 **une troupe de théâtre** a theatre company; 2 flock (of birds); 3 troop (of tourists or children).

troupeau (plural **troupeaux**) noun M herd (of cattle); flock (of sheep).

trousse noun F pencil case.

trousseau (plural **trousseaux**) noun M **un trousseau de clés** a bunch of keys.

trousse de maquillage noun F make-up bag.

trousse de toilette noun F toilet bag.

trouver verb [1] 1 to find; **as-tu trouvé ton passeport?** did you find your passport? 2 to think; **j'ai trouvé le film passionnant** I thought the film was wonderful; 3 **se trouver** to be (in a place); **les gens qui se trouvaient autour de moi** the people who were around me; **savez-vous où se trouve la gare routière?** do you know where the bus station is?

truc noun M (informal) 1 thing; **un petit truc en bois** a little thing made of wood; **il y a un truc qui ne va pas** something's wrong; **le jazz, ce n'est pas mon truc** jazz just isn't my thing; 2 trick; **il doit y avoir un truc** there must be a trick to it.

truite noun F trout.

TSVP SHORT FOR **tournez s'il vous plaît** PTO (please turn over).

TTC SHORT FOR **toutes taxes comprises** inclusive of tax.

tu pronoun you ('tu' is used when talking to family members, people you know well, and people of your own age; otherwise 'vous' is used for 'you').

tube noun M 1 tube; 2 (informal) hit (a pop song).

tuer verb [1] 1 to kill; 2 **se tuer** to be killed (accidentally); **elle s'est tuée dans un accident de voiture** she was killed in a car accident.

tue-tête in phrase **crier à tue-tête** to shout at the top of your voice.

tuile noun F 1 tile; 2 thin almond biscuit.

tulipe noun F tulip.

Tunisie noun F Tunisia.

tunisien (F **tunisienne**) adjective Tunisian.

tunnel noun M tunnel; **le tunnel sous la Manche** the Channel Tunnel.

turc noun M, adjective Turkish.

Turquie noun F Turkey.

tutoyer verb [39] to address somebody as 'tu' (rather than 'vous'); **il ne faut pas tutoyer ton professeur** you mustn't address your teacher as 'tu'; **et si on se tutoyait?** shall we say 'tu' to each other?

tuyau (*plural* **tuyaux**) *noun* M
1 pipe; 2 (*informal*) tip (*a helpful hint*).

tuyau d'arrosage *noun* M
hosepipe.

TVA *noun* F **short for** taxe à la valeur ajoutée VAT.

type *noun* M 1 kind; **quel type de papier?** what type of paper?; 2 (*informal*) guy; **le type qui a ouvert la porte** the guy who opened the door.

typique *adjective* typical.

tyranniser *verb* [1] to bully.

tzigane *noun* M & F, *adjective* gypsy.

U u

un, une (*plural* **des**) *article, pronoun, number* 1 a, an; **un lion** a lion; **une fraise** a strawberry; **des cerises** (some) cherries; 2 one; **un pour moi** one for me; **un par un** one by one; **trente et une personnes** thirty-one people; **les uns pensent que...** some think that...; **un jour sur deux** every other day; 3 **l'un(e) et l'autre** the one and the other; **l'un est français et l'autre est allemand** one's French and the other's German; 4 **l'un(e) ou l'autre** either of them; **tu peux prendre l'un ou l'autre, ça n'a pas d'importance** you can take either of them, it doesn't matter.

uni *adjective* 1 close-knit (*family or group*); 2 plain (*not patterned*); **un tissu uni** a plain fabric.

uniforme *noun* M uniform.

union *noun* F union; **l'ex-Union soviétique** the former Soviet Union.

Union européenne *noun* F European Union.

unique *adjective* 1 only; **elle est fille unique** she's an only child; **il est fils unique** he's an only child; **l'unique raison** the only reason; 2 single; **'prix unique'** 'all one price'; 3 unique.

uniquement *adverb* only.

unité *noun* F 1 unity; 2 unit (*of currency, measurement, etc*).

univers *noun* M universe.

universitaire *adjective* university (*degree, town*); academic (*work*).

université *noun* F university.

urbanisme *noun* M town planning.

urgence *noun* F 1 urgency; **il y a urgence!** it's urgent!; **il faut téléphoner d'urgence** you must phone at once; 2 emergency; **les urgences, le service des urgences** the casualty department.

urgent *adjective* urgent.

USA *plural noun* M USA; **aux USA** in (or to) the USA.

usage *noun* M 1 use; **à l'usage** with use; **en usage** in use; **à usage externe** for external use only; 2 'hors d'usage' 'not in service'.

usagé *adjective* 1 worn; 2 used.

usager *noun* M user.

usé *adjective* worn.

user verb [1] to wear out (*shoes, clothing*).

usine noun F factory.

ustensile noun M utensil.

utile adjective useful.

utiliser verb [1] to use.

utilité noun F usefulness; **un livre d'une grande utilité** a very useful book.

V v

va verb SEE aller.

vacances plural noun F holidays; **les vacances scolaires** the school holidays; **les grandes vacances** the summer holidays; **être en vacances** to be on holiday; **bonnes vacances!** have a good holiday!

vacancier, vacancière noun M, F holiday-maker.

vacarme noun M din; **ils faisaient un vacarme pas possible!** they were making an amazing din!

vaccination noun F vaccination.

vacciner verb [1] to vaccinate; **se faire vacciner** to be vaccinated.

vache noun F cow. adjective mean.

vachement adverb (*informal*) really; **c'était vachement bien!** it was really good!

va-et-vient noun M coming and going.

vagabond noun M tramp.

vagin noun M vagina.

vague[1] noun F wave (*in the sea*).

vague[2] adjective vague.

vaguement adverb vaguely.

vain adjective 1 useless; 2 **en vain** in vain.

vaincre verb [79] 1 to defeat; 2 to overcome.

vainqueur noun M winner.

vais verb SEE aller.

vaisseau (*plural* **vaisseaux**) noun M vessel.

vaisselle noun F dishes; **faire la vaisselle** to do the washing-up.

valable adjective valid.

valet noun M jack; **le valet de pique** the jack of spades.

valeur noun F value; **des objets de valeur** valuables; **c'est sans valeur** it's of no value.

valider verb [1] to stamp (*a ticket*).

valise noun F suitcase; **faire ses valises** to pack.

vallée noun F valley.

valoir verb [80] 1 to be worth; **ça vaut combien?** how much is it worth?; **ce tableau vaut cher** that painting's worth a lot; 2 **valoir la peine** to be worth it; **ça ne vaut pas la peine d'y aller s'il pleut** it's not worth going if it's raining; **ça vaudrait la peine d'essayer** it would be worth a try; 3 **il vaut mieux faire** it would be better to do; **il vaut mieux**

téléphoner avant it would be better to phone first.

valse noun F waltz.

vampire noun M vampire.

vandalisme noun M vandalism.

vanille noun F vanilla; **une glace à la vanille** a vanilla ice-cream.

vanter verb [1] **se vanter** to boast.

vapeur noun F steam; **faire cuire des légumes à la vapeur** to steam vegetables.

vaporisateur noun M (perfume) spray.

variable adjective variable, changeable.

varicelle noun F chickenpox; **avoir la varicelle** to have chickenpox.

varié adjective varied, various; **'sandwichs variés'** 'a selection of sandwiches'.

varier verb [1] to vary.

variété noun F 1 variety; 2 **un spectacle de variétés** a variety show.

vas verb SEE aller.

vase[1] noun M vase.

vase[2] noun F mud.

vaste adjective large, enormous.

va-vite adverb **à la va-vite** in a rush.

veau (plural **veaux**) noun M 1 calf; 2 veal.

vécu verb SEE vivre.

vedette noun F star; **une vedette de cinéma** a film star.

végétal adjective vegetable; **l'huile végétale** vegetable oil.

végétarien, végétarienne noun M, F, adjective vegetarian.

véhicule noun M vehicle.

veille noun F **la veille** the day before; **je l'ai rencontrée la veille** I met her the day before; **elle est arrivée la veille au soir** she arrived the evening before; **la veille de Noël** Christmas Eve; **la veille du jour de l'an** New Year's Eve.

veilleuse noun F 1 night-light; 2 pilot light.

veinard noun M (informal) **petit veinard!** you lucky little devil!

veine noun F 1 **avoir de la veine** (informal) to be lucky; 2 vein.

vélo noun M bike; **je suis venu à vélo** I came by bike; **faire du vélo** to go cycling.

vélomoteur noun M moped.

vélo tout-terrain noun M mountain bike.

velours noun M 1 velvet; 2 corduroy.

velouté noun M cream soup; **velouté de champignons** cream of mushroom soup.

vendanges plural noun F grape harvest.

vendeur, vendeuse noun M, F shop assistant.

vendre verb [3] to sell; **vendre quelque chose à quelqu'un** to sell somebody something; **j'ai vendu**

mon ordinateur à Colette I've sold my computer to Colette; **'à vendre'** 'for sale'; **'vendu'** 'sold'.

vendredi *noun* M **1** Friday; **nous sommes vendredi aujourd'hui** it's Friday today; **vendredi dernier** last Friday; **vendredi prochain** next Friday; **2** on Friday; **je l'ai vu vendredi soir** I saw him on Friday evening; **3** on Fridays; **fermé le vendredi** closed on Fridays; **4 tous les vendredis** every Friday; **le vendredi saint** Good Friday.

vénéneux (F **vénéneuse**) *adjective* poisonous (*plant*).

vengeance *noun* F revenge.

venger *verb* [52] **se venger** to have your revenge.

venimeux (F **venimeuse**) *adjective* poisonous (*snake, spider*).

venir *verb* [81] **1** to come; **il vient de Provence** he comes from Provence; **elles sont venues mardi** they came on Tuesday; **viens voir!** come and see!; **2 faire venir** to send for; **il faut faire venir le médecin** we must send for the doctor; **3 venir de faire** to have just done; **ils viennent d'arriver** they have just arrived; **elle venait de partir** she had just left.

vent *noun* M wind; **un vent du sud** a south wind.

vente *noun* F sale; **être en vente** to be on sale.

vente aux enchères *noun* F auction sale.

ventilateur *noun* M fan.

ventre *noun* M stomach; **avoir mal au ventre** to have stomachache.

venu *verb* SEE **venir**.

ver *noun* M worm.

verbe *noun* M verb.

verdict *noun* M verdict.

verger *noun* M orchard.

verglas *noun* M black ice.

vérifier *verb* [1] to check.

véritable *adjective* real.

vérité *noun* F truth.

vernir *verb* [2] to varnish.

vernis à ongles *noun* M nail varnish.

verre *noun* M **1** glass; **un verre de vin** a glass of wine; **2** glass; **un vase en verre** a glass vase; **3** lens (*of spectacles*).

verrou *noun* M bolt (*on a door*).

verrouiller *verb* [1] to bolt (*a door*).

verrue *noun* F wart.

vers¹ *preposition* **1** towards; **il montait vers l'église** he was going up towards the church; **2** about (*a time*); **vers midi** about twelve; **vers la fin du mois** around the end of the month.

vers² *noun* M line of poetry; **des vers** poetry.

Verseau *noun* M Aquarius (*sign of the Zodiac*).

versement *noun* M payment.

verser *verb* [1] to pour; **Sylvie m'a versé une tasse de thé** Sylvie poured me a cup of tea.

version noun F **1** version; **2** translation (*into your own language*).

verso noun M back (*of a piece of paper*); **voir au verso** see overleaf.

vert adjective green; ★ **avoir la main verte** to have green fingers.

vertical (M plural **verticaux**) adjective vertical, upright.

vertige noun M vertigo.

verveine noun F verbena tea.

veste noun F jacket.

vestiaire noun M **1** cloakroom (*in a theatre, restaurant, etc*); **2** changing room (*in a gym, sports ground*).

vêtement noun M garment; **les vêtements** clothes; **'vêtements pour enfants'** 'children's wear'.

vétérinaire noun M & F vet.

veuf, veuve noun M, F widower, widow.

vexer verb [1] to annoy; to offend.

viande noun F meat.

vibrer verb [1] to vibrate.

victime noun F victim.

victoire noun F victory.

vide adjective empty.
noun M **1** space; **dans le vide** in(to) space; **2** vacuum; **emballé sous vide** vacuum-packed.

vidéo noun F video; **une cassette vidéo** a video cassette; **une caméra vidéo** a video camera; **un jeu vidéo** a video game.

vidéoclip noun M music video.

vidéoclub noun M video shop.

vidéothèque noun F video library.

vider verb [1] to empty.

vie noun F life; **toute ma vie** all my life; **il est encore en vie** he's still alive; **ton mode de vie** your lifestyle; ★ **c'est la vie** that's life, that's the way it goes.

vieil adjective SEE **vieux**.

vieillard, vieillarde noun M, F old man, old woman.

vieille adjective SEE **vieux**.

vieillesse noun F old age.

vieillir verb [2] to age; **il a beaucoup vieilli récemment** he's aged a lot recently.

vierge noun F virgin; **la Sainte Vierge** the Virgin Mary.
adjective **1** blank; **une cassette vierge** a blank cassette; **2 laine vierge** pure new wool; **l'huile d'olive vierge** virgin olive oil.

Vierge noun F Virgo (*sign of the Zodiac*).

vieux, vieil (*before a vowel or silent 'h'*) (F **vieille**) (M plural **vieux**) adjective old; **une vieille ville** an old town; **un vieil arbre** an old tree.
noun M, F **un vieux** an old man; **une vieille** an old woman.

vieux garçon noun M bachelor.

vif (F **vive**) adjective **1** bright; **rose vif** bright pink; **2** lively; **une vive discussion** a lively discussion; **3 avoir l'esprit vif** to be quick-witted.

vigne noun F vine; vineyard.

vigneron, vigneronne noun M, F wine-grower.

vignette noun F 1 label; 2 tax disc.

vignoble noun M vineyard.

vilain adjective 1 ugly; 2 naughty; c'est vilain, ça! that's naughty!

villa noun F detached house; villa.

village noun M village.

ville noun F town, city; une grande ville a city; en ville in (or into) town.

vin noun M wine.

vinaigre noun M vinegar.

vinaigrette noun F French dressing.

vingt number twenty; Marion a vingt ans Marion's twenty; le vingt juillet the twentieth of July; à vingt heures at 8 p.m.; vingt et un twenty-one.

vingtaine noun F about twenty; une vingtaine de personnes about twenty people.

vingtième adjective twentieth.

viol noun M rape.

violemment adjective violently.

violence noun F violence.

violent adjective violent.

violer verb [1] to rape.

violet (F violette[1]) adjective purple.

violette[2] noun F violet (the flower).

violon noun M violin; jouer du violon to play the violin.

violoncelle noun M cello; jouer du violoncelle to play the cello.

vipère noun F adder, viper.

virage noun M bend (in the road).

virgule noun F 1 comma; 2 decimal point; sept virgule trois seven point three.

virus noun M virus.

vis[1] verb SEE vivre.

vis[2] noun F screw.

visa noun M visa.

visage noun M face.

viser verb [1] 1 to aim; 2 to aim at (a target).

visibilité noun F visibility.

visible adjective visible, obvious.

visite noun F visite; une visite chez nos cousins a visit to our cousins; rendre visite à quelqu'un to visit somebody; elle a de la visite she's got visitors.

visiter verb [1] to visit (a place); on peut visiter l'appartement? can we see round the flat?

visiteur, visiteuse noun M, F visitor.

vit verb SEE vivre.

vitamine noun F vitamin.

vite adverb 1 fast; tu conduis trop vite you drive too fast; parle moins vite speak more slowly; 2 quick; vite! le bus arrive! quick! here's the bus!; ce sera vite fait it won't take long; 3 soon; on sera vite arrivé we'll soon be there; elle a vite compris she understood immediately.

vitesse noun F 1 speed; **elle est partie à toute vitesse** she rushed off; 2 gear; **en deuxième vitesse** in second gear.

vitrail (plural **vitraux**) noun M stained glass window.

vitre noun F window.

vitrine noun F shop window.

vivant adjective 1 living; 2 lively.

vive¹ adjective SEE **vif**.

vive² exclamation **Vive le roi!** Long live the king!

vivement adverb 1 **réagir vivement** to react strongly; 2 **vivement les vacances!** roll on the holidays!

vivre verb [82] to live; **ils vivent ensemble** they live together; **ils ont vécu dans plusieurs pays différents** they've lived in several different countries.

vocabulaire noun M vocabulary.

vœu (plural **vœux**) noun M 1 wish; **faire un vœu** to make a wish; **meilleurs vœux!** best wishes! (especially at the New Year); 2 vow.

vogue noun F fashion; **en vogue** in fashion.

voici preposition 1 here is, here are; **voici l'addition** here's the bill; **voici les clés** here are the keys; **me voici!** here I am!; 2 this is; **voici ma sœur** this is my sister.

voie noun F 1 way; **être sur la bonne voie** to be on the right track; 2 track (for trains); **la voie ferrée** the railway track; **le train de Bourges entre en gare voie dix** the train from Bourges is now arriving at platform ten; 3 lane (on a main road); **une route à trois voies** a three-lane road.

voilà preposition 1 there is, there are; **voilà tes lunettes, là-bas sur la table** there are your glasses, over there on the table; **la voilà devant la boulangerie** there she is outside the baker's; 2 here is, here are; **voilà Anna qui arrive** here's Anna coming now; **voilà ton café** here's your coffee; **voilà, c'est tout** right, that's all; 3 that is; **voilà ma fille** that's my daughter; **et voilà pourquoi** and that's why.

voile¹ noun M veil.

voile² noun F sail; **des cours de voile** sailing lessons.

voilier noun M sailing boat.

voir verb [13] 1 to see; **je ne vois rien** I can't see anything; **je viendrai te voir un de ces jours** I'll come and see you one of these days; **oui, je vois, tu veux dire que…** yes, I see, you mean that…; **un film à voir** a film worth seeing; **peut-être, on verra** perhaps, we'll see; 2 to be noticeable; **ça ne se verra pas** nobody will notice; 3 **se voir** to see each other; **ils se voient à Noël** they see each other at Christmas; 4 **faire voir quelque chose à quelqu'un** to show somebody something; **je te ferai voir mes photos de vacances** I'll show you my holiday photos; **fais voir!** let's have a look!; 5 **ça n'a rien à voir avec mon problème** that's got nothing to do with my problem; ★ **il ne voit pas plus loin que le bout de son nez** he can't see any further than the end of his nose; ★ **elle ne peut pas le voir (en peinture)** she can't stand him (*literally: she can't bear to see her (in a painting)*); ★ **j'en ai vu d'autres** I've seen worse.

voisin, voisine noun M, F neighbour; **Claire est chez les voisins** Claire's round at the neighbours'; **ma voisine de table** the girl sitting next to me at table.

voisinage noun M neighbourhood.

voiture noun F 1 car; **en voiture** by car; 2 carriage (*on a train*).

voix noun F 1 voice; **à haute voix** aloud; **à voix basse** softly; 2 vote.

vol noun M 1 flight; **le vol pour Milan** the Milan flight; 2 theft; ★ **à vol d'oiseau** as the crow flies (*literally: by bird flight*).

volaille noun F poultry; **les foies de volaille** chicken livers.

volant noun M 1 steering wheel; **qui était au volant?** who was driving?; 2 shuttlecock. *adjective* flying.

volcan noun M volcano.

volée noun F volley.

voler verb [1] 1 to fly; 2 to steal; **voler quelque chose à quelqu'un** to steal something from someone; **on leur a volé leur voiture** their car's been stolen; 3 **voler quelqu'un** to rob somebody.

volet noun M shutter.

voleur, voleuse noun M, F thief.

volley noun M volleyball; **jouer au volley** to play volleyball.

volontaire noun M & F volunteer.

volonté noun F 1 will; **la bonne volonté** goodwill; 2 **à volonté** unlimited; **'pizza à volonté'** 'as much pizza as you want'.

volontiers adverb gladly; **'tu viens avec nous?' – 'volontiers'** 'will you come too?' – 'I'd love to'; **'tu me le prêtes?' – 'volontiers'** 'will you lend it to me?' – 'of course'.

volume noun M volume.

vomir verb [2] to be sick, to vomit.

vos adjective SEE **votre**.

voter verb [1] to vote.

votre (*plural* **vos**) adjective your; **nous connaissons votre fils** we know your son; **vos billets, monsieur** your tickets, sir.

vôtre pronoun **le vôtre, la vôtre, les vôtres** yours; **une maison comme la vôtre** a house like yours; **mes parents et les vôtres** my parents and yours; ★ **à la vôtre!** cheers!

vouloir verb [14] 1 to want; **elle ne veut rien** she doesn't want anything; **veux-tu venir avec nous?** do you want to come with us?; **je n'ai pas voulu arriver trop tôt** I didn't want to arrive too early; **il veut qu'elle l'appelle** he wants her to phone him; **il m'a vexé sans le vouloir** he annoyed me without meaning to; **si tu veux** if you like; **je voudrais visiter Versailles** I'd like to go to Versailles; **'encore du café?' – 'oui, je veux bien'** 'more coffee?' – 'yes, I'd love some'; 3 **voulez-vous m'excuser?** would you excuse me?; **veux-tu fermer la porte?** would you shut the door?; **veux-tu te taire!** will you be quiet!; 4 **vouloir dire** to mean; **qu'est-ce que tu veux dire?** what do you mean?; **si tu vois ce que je veux dire** if you see what I mean?; **qu'est-ce que ce mot veut dire?** what does this word mean?; 5 **en vouloir à quelqu'un** to bear a grudge against someone; **elle leur en veut** she's never forgiven them; ★ **vouloir c'est pouvoir** where there's a will there's a way (*literally*: *to want is to be able*).

voulu *verb* SEE **vouloir**.

vous *pronoun* 1 you; **avec vous** with you; **est-ce que ce sac est à vous?** is this your bag?; **à vous de jouer!** your turn to play!; 2 to you; **je vous écrirai** I'll write to you; 3 yourself; **ne vous coupez pas!** don't cut yourself!

vous-même(s) *pronoun* yourself, yourselves; **vous me l'avez dit vous-même** you told me yourself; **est-ce que vous l'avez fait vous-mêmes?** did you do it by yourselves?

voûte *noun* F vault, arch.

vouvoyer *verb* [39] to use 'vous' to mean 'you' (*rather than 'tu' which you would use only when talking to intimate friends, family, and people of your own age*); **ils se connaissent depuis des années mais ils continuent à se vouvoyer** they've known each other for years but they still address each other as 'vous'.

voyage *noun* M journey; **bon voyage!** have a good trip!

voyage organisé *noun* M package tour.

voyager *verb* [52] to travel.

voyageur, voyageuse *noun* M, F passenger.

voyelle *noun* F vowel.

voyou *noun* M hooligan.

vrac *adverb* **acheter des olives en vrac** to buy olives loose (*as opposed to pre-packaged*).

vrai *adjective* 1 true; **c'est une histoire vraie** it's a true story; 2 real; **c'est un vrai problème** it's a real problem; **c'est vrai?** really?; **pour de vrai** for real; 3 **à vrai dire** to tell the truth.

vraiment *adverb* really.

vraisemblable *adjective* likely; **peu vraisemblable** unlikely.

vraisemblablement *adverb* probably.

VTT *noun* M SHORT FOR **vélo tout-terrain** mountain bike.

vu *verb* SEE **voir**.
adjective 1 **vu que** seeing that; **vu qu'il pleut, ce n'est pas la peine d'y aller** seeing it's raining, there's no point in going; 2 **être mal vu** to be disapproved of; **il est plutôt mal vu** people don't think much of him; **c'est mal vu de faire beaucoup de bruit** they don't like people making a lot of noise; **cette critique a été mal vue** this criticism didn't go down well; 3 **être bien vu** to be well thought of; **elle est très bien vue dans la société** people in the company think highly of her.

vue *noun* F 1 eyesight; **perdre la vue** to lose your eyesight; 2 sight; **je le connais de vue** I know him by sight; **rien qu'à la vue de la viande** at the very sight of meat; **3** view; **une chambre avec vue sur le lac** a room with a view of the lake.

vulgaire *adjective* vulgar.

W w

wagon *noun* M **1** railway carriage; **2** waggon.

wagon-lit *noun* M sleeper (*on a train*).

wagon-restaurant *noun* M restaurant car.

wallon *noun* M, *adjective* (F **wallonne**) Walloon (*French-speaking Belgian*); **les Wallons** the Walloon.

WC (*pronounced 'vaysay'*) *plural noun* M toilet; **aller aux WC** to go to the toilet; **il est aux WC** he's in the loo.

X x

xylophone *noun* M xylophone; **jouer du xylophone** to play the xylophone.

Y y

y *pronoun, adverb* **1** there; **j'y vais demain** I'm going there tomorrow;

2 il y a there is, there are; **il y a un café à côté** there's a café next door; **il y a des tomates dans le frigo** there are some tomatoes in the fridge; **3 j'y pensais** I was thinking of it; **tu n'y peux rien** you can't do anything about it.

yaourt *noun* M yoghurt.

yeux *plural noun* M SEE **œil**.

yougoslave *adjective* Yugoslavian.

Yougoslavie *noun* F Yugoslavia; **l'ex-Yougoslavie** the former Yugoslavia.

Z z

zapper *verb* [1] to channel hop.

zèbre *noun* M zebra.

zéro *noun* M zero; nil; love (*in tennis*); **trois à zéro** three-nil; **zéro heure** midnight; ★ **il faut tout reprendre à zéro** we'll have to start again from scratch.

zézayer *verb* [59] to lisp.

zigzag *noun* M zigzag; **une route en zigzag** a winding road.

zodiaque *noun* M zodiac.

zone *noun* F **1** zone, area; **2 la zone** the slums.

zone industrielle *noun* F industrial estate.

zoo *noun* M zoo.

zut *exclamation* (*informal*) damn!

VERB TABLES
AND FORMS

1

aimer
to like or to love

Imperative	Past participle
aime aimons aimez	aimé

Present

j' aime
tu aimes
il aime
nous aimons
vous aimez
ils aiment

Perfect

j' ai aimé
tu as aimé
il a aimé
nous avons aimé
vous avez aimé
ils ont aimé

Future

j' aimerai
tu aimeras
il aimera
nous aimerons
vous aimerez
ils aimeront

Present subjunctive

j' aime
tu aimes
il aime
nous aimions
vous aimiez
ils aiment

Imperfect

j' aimais
tu aimais
il aimait
nous aimions
vous aimiez
ils aimaient

Conditional

j' aimerais
tu aimerais
il aimerait
nous aimerions
vous aimeriez
ils aimeraient

2

finir
to finish

Imperative	Past participle
finis	fini
finissons	
finissez	

Present

je	finis
tu	finis
il	finit
nous	finissons
vous	finissez
ils	finissent

Present subjunctive

je	finisse
tu	finisses
il	finisse
nous	finissions
vous	finissiez
ils	finissent

Perfect

j'	ai fini
tu	as fini
il	a fini
nous	avons fini
vous	avez fini
ils	ont fini

Imperfect

je	finissais
tu	finissais
il	finissait
nous	finissions
vous	finissiez
ils	finissaient

Future

je	finirai
tu	finiras
il	finira
nous	finirons
vous	finirez
ils	finiront

Conditional

je	finirais
tu	finirais
il	finirait
nous	finirions
vous	finiriez
ils	finiraient

attendre
to wait

Imperative	Past participle
attend**s**	attend**u**
attend**ons**	
attend**ez**	

Present

j'	attend**s**
tu	attend**s**
il	attend
nous	attend**ons**
vous	attend**ez**
ils	attend**ent**

Present subjunctive

j'	attend**e**
tu	attend**es**
il	attend**e**
nous	attend**ions**
vous	attend**iez**
ils	attend**ent**

Perfect

j'	ai attend**u**
tu	as attend**u**
il	a attend**u**
nous	avons attend**u**
vous	avez attend**u**
ils	ont attend**u**

Imperfect

j'	attend**ais**
tu	attend**ais**
il	attend**ait**
nous	attend**ions**
vous	attend**iez**
ils	attend**aient**

Future

j'	attend**rai**
tu	attend**ras**
il	attend**ra**
nous	attend**rons**
vous	attend**rez**
ils	attend**ront**

Conditional

j'	attend**rais**
tu	attend**rais**
il	attend**rait**
nous	attend**rions**
vous	attend**riez**
ils	attend**raient**

4

se laver
to wash
(oneself)

Imperative	**Past participle**
lave–toi	lavé
lav**ons**–nous	
lav**ez**–vous	

Present

je me lav**e**
tu te lav**es**
il se lav**e**
nous nous lav**ons**
vous vous lav**ez**
ils se lav**ent**

Present subjunctive

je me lav**e**
tu te lav**es**
il se lav**e**
nous nous lav**ions**
vous vous lav**iez**
ils se lav**ent**

Perfect

je me suis lav**é**
tu t'es lav**é**
il s'est lav**é**
nous nous sommes lav**é(s)**
vous vous êtes lav**é(s)**
ils se sont lav**é(s)**

Imperfect

je me lav**ais**
tu te lav**ais**
il se lav**ait**
nous nous lav**ions**
vous vous lav**iez**
ils se lav**aient**

Future

je me laver**ai**
tu te laver**as**
il se laver**a**
nous nous laver**ons**
vous vous laver**ez**
ils se laver**ont**

Conditional

je me laver**ais**
tu te laver**ais**
il se laver**ait**
nous nous laver**ions**
vous vous laver**iez**
ils se laver**aient**

avoir
to have

Imperative	Past participle
aie	eu
ayons	
ayez	

Present

j' ai
tu as
il a
nous av**ons**
vous av**ez**
ils ont

Present subjunctive

j' aie
tu aies
il ait
nous ayons
vous ayez
ils aient

Perfect

j' ai **eu**
tu as **eu**
il a **eu**
nous avons **eu**
vous avez **eu**
ils ont **eu**

Imperfect

j' av**ais**
tu av**ais**
il av**ait**
nous av**ions**
vous av**iez**
ils av**aient**

Future

j' aurai
tu auras
il aura
nous aurons
vous aurez
ils auront

Conditional

j' aurais
tu aurais
il aurait
nous aurions
vous auriez
ils auraient

6

être
to be

Imperative	Past participle
sois	été
soyons	
soyez	

Present

je **suis**
tu **es**
il **est**
nous **sommes**
vous **êtes**
ils **sont**

Present subjunctive

je **sois**
tu **sois**
il **soit**
nous **soyons**
vous **soyez**
ils **soient**

Perfect

j' ai **été**
tu as **été**
il a **été**
nous avons **été**
vous avez **été**
ils ont **été**

Imperfect

j' **étais**
tu **étais**
il **était**
nous **étions**
vous **étiez**
ils **étaient**

Future

je **serai**
tu **seras**
il **sera**
nous **serons**
vous **serez**
ils **seront**

Conditional

je **serais**
tu **serais**
il **serait**
nous **serions**
vous **seriez**
ils **seraient**

aller

to go

Imperative	Past participle
va	allé
allons	
allez	

Present

je	**vais**
tu	**vas**
il	**va**
nous	all**ons**
vous	all**ez**
ils	**vont**

Present subjunctive

j'	**aille**
tu	**ailles**
il	**aille**
nous	all**ions**
vous	all**iez**
ils	**aillent**

Perfect

je	suis all**é**
tu	es all**é**
il	est all**é**
nous	sommes all**és**
vous	êtes all**é(s)**
ils	sont all**és**

Imperfect

j'	all**ais**
tu	all**ais**
il	all**ait**
nous	all**ions**
vous	all**iez**
ils	all**aient**

Future

j'	**irai**
tu	**iras**
il	**ira**
nous	**irons**
vous	**irez**
ils	**iront**

Conditional

j'	**irais**
tu	**irais**
il	**irait**
nous	**irions**
vous	**iriez**
ils	**iraient**

8

devoir
to have to

Imperative	Past participle
dois	dû
dev**ons**	
dev**ez**	

Present

je **dois**
tu **dois**
il **doit**
nous dev**ons**
vous dev**ez**
ils **doivent**

Present subjunctive

je **doive**
tu **doives**
il **doive**
nous dev**ions**
vous dev**iez**
ils **doivent**

Perfect

j' ai **dû**
tu as **dû**
il a **dû**
nous avons **dû**
vous avez **dû**
ils ont **dû**

Imperfect

je dev**ais**
tu dev**ais**
il dev**ait**
nous dev**ions**
vous dev**iez**
ils dev**aient**

Future

je dev**rai**
tu dev**ras**
il dev**ra**
nous dev**rons**
vous dev**rez**
ils dev**ront**

Conditional

je dev**rais**
tu dev**rais**
il dev**rait**
nous dev**rions**
vous dev**riez**
ils dev**raient**

dire
to say

Imperative	Past participle
dis	dit
disons	
dites	

Present

je **dis**
tu **dis**
il **dit**
nous **disons**
vous **dites**
ils **disent**

Present subjunctive

je **dise**
tu **dises**
il **dise**
nous **disions**
vous **disiez**
ils **disent**

Perfect

j' ai **dit**
tu as **dit**
il a **dit**
nous avons **dit**
vous avez **dit**
ils ont **dit**

Imperfect

je **disais**
tu **disais**
il **disait**
nous **disions**
vous **disiez**
ils **disaient**

Future

je dir**ai**
tu dir**as**
il dir**a**
nous dir**ons**
vous dir**ez**
ils dir**ont**

Conditional

je dir**ais**
tu dir**ais**
il dir**ait**
nous dir**ions**
vous dir**iez**
ils dir**aient**

faire

to do
or to make

Imperative	**Past participle**
fais	fait
faisons	
faites	

Present

je	**fais**
tu	**fais**
il	**fait**
nous	**faisons**
vous	**faites**
ils	**font**

Present subjunctive

je	**fasse**
tu	**fasses**
il	**fasse**
nous	**fassions**
vous	**fassiez**
ils	**fassent**

Perfect

j'	ai **fait**
tu	as **fait**
il	a **fait**
nous	avons **fait**
vous	avez **fait**
ils	ont **fait**

Imperfect

je	**faisais**
tu	**faisais**
il	**faisait**
nous	**faisions**
vous	**faisiez**
ils	**faisaient**

Future

je	**ferai**
tu	**feras**
il	**fera**
nous	**ferons**
vous	**ferez**
ils	**feront**

Conditional

je	**ferais**
tu	**ferais**
il	**ferait**
nous	**ferions**
vous	**feriez**
ils	**feraient**

mettre
to put

Imperative	Past participle
mets	mis
mettons	
mettez	

Present

je	mets
tu	mets
il	met
nous	mettons
vous	mettez
ils	mettent

Present subjunctive

je	mette
tu	mettes
il	mette
nous	mettions
vous	mettiez
ils	mettent

Perfect

j'	ai	mis
tu	as	mis
il	a	mis
nous	avons	mis
vous	avez	mis
ils	ont	mis

Imperfect

je	mettais
tu	mettais
il	mettait
nous	mettions
vous	mettiez
ils	mettaient

Future

je	mettrai
tu	mettras
il	mettra
nous	mettrons
vous	mettrez
ils	mettront

Conditional

je	mettrais
tu	mettrais
il	mettrait
nous	mettrions
vous	mettriez
ils	mettraient

12

pouvoir
to be able

Imperative	**Past participle**
the imperative of **pouvoir** is not used	pu

Present

je **peux**
tu **peux**
il **peut**
nous pouv**ons**
vous pouv**ez**
ils **peuvent**

Present subjunctive

je **puisse**
tu **puisses**
il **puisse**
nous **puissions**
vous **puissiez**
ils **puissent**

Perfect

j' ai **pu**
tu as **pu**
il a **pu**
nous avons **pu**
vous avez **pu**
ils ont **pu**

Imperfect

je pouv**ais**
tu pouv**ais**
il pouv**ait**
nous pouv**ions**
vous pouv**iez**
ils pouv**aient**

Future

je **pourrai**
tu **pourras**
il **pourra**
nous **pourrons**
vous **pourrez**
ils **pourront**

Conditional

je **pourrais**
tu **pourrais**
il **pourrait**
nous **pourrions**
vous **pourriez**
ils **pourraient**

voir
to see

Imperative	Past participle
vois	vu
voyons	
voyez	

Present

je vois
tu vois
il voit
nous voyons
vous voyez
ils voient

Present subjunctive

je voie
tu voies
il voie
nous voyions
vous voyiez
ils voient

Perfect

j' ai vu
tu as vu
il a vu
nous avons vu
vous avez vu
ils ont vu

Imperfect

je voyais
tu voyais
il voyait
nous voyions
vous voyiez
ils voyaient

Future

je verrai
tu verras
il verra
nous verrons
vous verrez
ils verront

Conditional

je verrais
tu verrais
il verrait
nous verrions
vous verriez
ils verraient

vouloir
to want

Imperative	Past participle
veuille	vou**lu**
veuillons	
veuillez	

Present
je	**veux**
tu	**veux**
il	**veut**
nous	voul**ons**
vous	voul**ez**
ils	**veulent**

Present subjunctive
je	**veuille**
tu	**veuilles**
il	**veuille**
nous	voul**ions**
vous	voul**iez**
ils	**veuillent**

Perfect
j'	ai vou**lu**
tu	as vou**lu**
il	a vou**lu**
nous	avons vou**lu**
vous	avez vou**lu**
ils	ont vou**lu**

Imperfect
je	voul**ais**
tu	voul**ais**
il	voul**ait**
nous	voul**ions**
vous	voul**iez**
ils	voul**aient**

Future
je	**voudrai**
tu	**voudras**
il	**voudra**
nous	**voudrons**
vous	**voudrez**
ils	**voudront**

Conditional
je	**voudrais**
tu	**voudrais**
il	**voudrait**
nous	**voudrions**
vous	**voudriez**
ils	**voudraient**

French irregular verb forms

This list shows the main forms of other irregular verbs. The number before the infinitive is the number given after verbs in the dictionary which follow this pattern.

(1) = Present   (3) = Imperfect
(2) = Past participle   (4) = Future

15 **abréger** (1) j'abrège, nous abrégeons, ils abrègent (2) abrégé (3) j'abrégeais (4) j'abrégerai

16 **acheter** (1) j'achète, nous achetons, ils achètent (2) acheté (3) j'achetais (4) j'achèterai

17 **acquérir** (1) j'acquiers, il acquiert, nous acquérons, vous acquérez ils acquièrent (2) acquis (3) j'acquérais (4) j'acquerrai

18 **appeler** (1) j'appelle, nous appelons, ils appellent (2) appelé (3) j'appelais (4) j'appellerai

19 **apprendre** (1) j'apprends, nous apprenons, vous apprenez, ils apprennent (2) appris (3) j'apprenais (4) j'apprendrai

20 **s'asseoir** (1) je m'assieds, nous nous asseyons, vous vous asseyez, ils s'asseyent (2) assis (3) je m'asseyais (4) je m'assiérai

21 **battre** (1) je bats, il bat, nous battons (2) battu (3) je battais (4) je battrai

22 **boire** (1) je bois, nous buvons, ils boivent (2) bu (3) je buvais (4) je boirai

23 **bouillir** (1) je bous, nous bouillons (2) bouilli (3) je bouillais (4) je bouillirai

24 **céder** (1) je cède, nous cédons, ils cèdent (2) cédé (3) je cédais (4) je céderai

25 **conclure** (1) je conclus, nous concluons (2) conclu (3) je concluais (4) je conclurai

26 **conduire** (1) je conduis, nous conduisons (2) conduit (3) je conduisais (4) je conduirai

27 **connaître** (1) je connais, nous connaissons (2) connu (3) je connaissais (4) je connaîtrai

28 **coudre** (1) je couds, nous cousons, vous cousez, ils cousent (2) cousu (3) je cousais (4) je coudrai

29 **courir** (1) je cours, nous courons (2) couru (3) je courais (4) je courrai

30 **couvrir** (1) je couvre, nous couvrons (2) couvert (3) je couvrais (4) je couvrirai

31 **craindre** (1) je crains, nous craignons (2) craint (3) je craignais (4) je craindrai

32 **créer** (1) je crée, nous créons (2) créé (3) je créais (4) je créerai

33 **croire** (1) je crois, nous croyons, ils croient (2) cru (3) je croyais (4) je croirai

34 **croître** (1) je croîs, nous croissons (2) crû, crue (3) je croissais (4) je croîtrai

35 **cueillir** (1) je cueille, nous cueillons (2) cueilli (3) je cueillais (4) je cueillerai

36 **cuire** (1) je cuis, nous cuisons, ils cuisent (2) cuit (3) je cuisais (4) je cuirai

37 **dormir** (1) je dors, nous dormons (2) dormi (3) je dormais (4) je dormirai

38 **écrire** (1) j'écris, nous écrivons (2) écrit (3) j'écrivais (4) j'écrirai

39 **employer** (1) j'emploie, nous employons, vous employez, ils emploient (2) employé (3) j'employais (4) j'emploierai

40 **envoyer** (1) j'envoie, nous envoyons, vous envoyez, ils envoient (2) envoyé (3) j'envoyais (4) j'enverrai

41 **essuyer** (1) j'essuie, nous essuyons, vous essuyez, ils essuient (2) essuyé (3) j'essuyais (4) j'essuierai

42 **faillir** (1) je faille (2) failli

43 **falloir** (1) il faut (2) fallu (3) il fallait (4) il faudra

44 **fuir** (1) je fuis, nous fuyons, ils, fuient (2) fui (3) je fuyais (4) je fuirai

45 **geler** (1) je gèle, nous gelons, vous gelez, ils gèlent (2) gelé (3) je gelais (4) je gèlerai

46 **haïr** (1) je hais, nous haïssons, ils haïssent (2) haï (3) je haïssais (4) je haïrai

47 **interdire** (1) j'interdis, nous interdisons, vous interdisez (2) interdit (3) j'interdisais (4) j'interdirai

48 **jeter** (1) je jette, nous jetons, ils jettent (2) jeté (3) je jetais (4) je jetterai

49 **joindre** (1) je joins, nous joignons (2) joint (3) je joignais (4) je joindrai

50 **lever** (1) je lève, nous levons, ils lèvent (2) levé (3) je levais (4) je lèverai

51 **lire** (1) je lis, nous lisons (2) lu (3) je lisais (4) je lirai

52 **manger** (1) je mange, nous mangeons (2) mangé (3) je mangeais (4) je mangerai

53 **mentir** (1) je mens, nous mentons (2) menti (3) je mentais (4) je mentirai

54 **mourir** (1) je meurs, nous mourons, ils meurent (2) mort (3) je mourais (4) je mourrai

55 **naître** (1) je nais, il naît, nous naissons (2) né (3) je naissais (4) je naîtrai

56 **offrir** (1) j'offre, nous offrons (2) offert (3) j'offrais (4) j'offrirai

57 **paraître** (1) je parais, il paraît, nous paraissons (2) paru (3) je paraissais (4) je paraîtrai

58 **partir** (1) je pars, nous partons (2) parti (3) je partais (4) je partirai

59 **payer** (1) je paie/je paye, nous payons, vous payez, ils paient/ils payent (2) payé (3) je payais (4) je paierai/je payerai

60 **peindre** (1) je peins, nous peignons (2) peint (3) je peignais (4) je peindrai

61 **placer** (1) je place, nous plaçons (2) placé (3) je plaçais (4) je placerai

62 **plaire** (1) je plais, il plaît, nous plaisons (2) plu (3) je plaisais (4) je plairai

63 **pleuvoir** (1) il pleut (2) plu (3) il pleuvait (4) il pleuvra

64 **prendre** (1) je prends, nous prenons, ils prennent (2) pris (3) je prenais (4) je prendrai

65 **prévoir** (1) je prévois, nous prévoyons, vous prévoyez, ils prévoient (2) prévu (3) je prévoyais (4) je prévoirai

66 **recevoir** (1) je reçois, il reçoit, ils reçoivent (2) reçu (3) je recevais (4) je recevrai

67 **résoudre** (1) je résous, nous résolvons, vous résolvez, ils résolvent (2) résolu (3) je résolvais (4) je résoudrai

68 **rire** (1) je ris, nous rions (2) ri (3) je riais (4) je rirai

69 **rompre** (1) je romps, il rompt, nous rompons (2) rompu (3) je rompais (4) je romprai

70 **savoir** (1) je sais, nous savons, ils savent (2) su (3) je savais (4) je saurai

71 **servir** (1) je sers, nous servons (2) servi (3) je servais (4) je servirai

72 **sortir** (1) je sors, nous sortons (2) sorti (3) je sortais (4) je sortirai

73 **souffrir** (1) je souffre, nous souffrons (2) souffert (3) je souffrais (4) je souffrirai

74 **suffire** (1) je suffis, nous suffisons (2) suffi (3) je suffisais (4) je suffirai

75 **suivre** (1) je suis, nous suivons (2) suivi (3) je suivais (4) je suivrai

76 **taire** (1) je me tais, nous nous taisons (2) tu (3) je me taisais (4) je me tairai

77 **tenir** (1) je tiens, nous tenons, ils tiennent (2) tenu (3) je tenais (4) je tiendrai

78 **traire** (1) je trais, nous trayons, ils traient (2) trait (3) je trayais (4) je trairai

79 **vaincre** (1) je vaincs, il vainc, nous vainquons (2) vaincu (3) je vainquais

80 **valoir** (1) je vaux, il vaut, nous valons (2) valu (3) je valais (4) je vaudrai

81 **venir** (1) je viens, nous venons, ils viennent (2) venu (3) je venais (4) je viendrai

82 **vivre** (1) je vis, nous vivons (2) vécu (3) je vivais (4) je vivrai

A a

a *indefinite article* **1** (*before a noun which is masculine in French*) un; **a tree** un arbre; **2** (*before a noun which is feminine in French*) une; **a table** une table; **3** ten francs a kilo dix francs le kilo; **4** fifty kilometres an hour cinquante kilomètres l'heure; **5** three times a day trois fois par jour.

abandon *verb* abandonner [1].

abbey *noun* abbaye F; **Westminster Abbey** l'Abbaye de Westminster.

abbreviation *noun* abréviation F.

abide *verb* **I can't abide...** je ne supporte pas...

ability *noun* capacité F; **the ability to do** la capacité de faire.

able *adjective* **to be able to do** pouvoir [12] faire; **she wasn't able to come** elle n'a pas pu venir.

abnormal *adjective* anormal (M *plural* anormaux).

about *preposition* **1** (*on the subject of*) sur; **a film about Picasso** un film sur Picasso; **2** what's it about? de quoi s'agit-il?; **3** (*concerning or in relation to*) au sujet de; **he wants to talk to you about your exam** il veut te parler au sujet de ton examen; **4** to talk about something parler de quelque chose; **what is she talking about?** de quoi parle-t-elle?; **5** to think about something/somebody penser à quelque chose/quelqu'un; **I'm thinking about you** je pense à toi.

adverb **1** (*approximately*) environ, à peu près; **there are about sixty people** il y a environ soixante personnes, il y a à peu près soixante personnes; **2** (*when talking about the time*) vers; **about three o'clock** vers trois heures; ★ **to be about to do** être sur le point de faire; **I'm (just) about to leave** je suis sur le point de partir.

above *preposition* **1** au dessus de; **above the table** au dessus de la table; **2** above all surtout.

abroad *adverb* à l'étranger; **to go abroad** aller à l'étranger; **to live abroad** vivre à l'étranger.

abscess *noun* abcès M.

abseiling *noun* descente F en rappel.

absent *adjective* absent; **to be absent from** être absent de.

absent-minded *adjective* distrait.

absolute *adjective* complet (F complète); **an absolute disaster** un désastre complet.

absolutely *adverb* **1** absolument; **it's absolutely dreadful** c'est absolument affreux; **2** tout à fait; **you're absolutely right** tu as tout à fait raison.

absorb *verb* absorber [1].

abuse *noun* **1** alcohol abuse abus M d'alcool; **drug abuse** usage M des stupéfiants; **2** (*violent treatment of a person*) mauvais traitement M; **3** (*insults*) injures F *plural*.

verb to abuse somebody maltraiter [1] quelqu'un.

academic *adjective* the academic year l'année universitaire.

accelerate *verb* accélérer [24].

accelerator *noun* accélérateur M.

accent *noun* accent M; she has a French accent elle a un accent français.

accept *verb* accepter [1].

acceptable *adjective* acceptable.

acceptance *noun* acceptation F.

access *noun* accès M.
verb to access something accéder [24] à quelque chose.

accessory *noun* accessoire M.

accident *noun* 1 accident M; to have an accident avoir un accident; a road accident un accident de la route; a car accident un accident de voiture; 2 (*chance*) hasard M; by accident par hasard; I found it by accident je l'ai trouvé par hasard.

accidental *adjective* fortuit; an accidental discovery une découverte fortuite.

accidentally *adverb* 1 (*without meaning to*) accidentellement; I accidentally knocked over his glass j'ai accidentellement renversé son verre; 2 (*by chance*) par hasard; I accidentally discovered that... j'ai découvert par hasard que...

accommodate *verb* recevoir [66]; the centre can accommodate sixty people le centre peut recevoir soixante personnes.

accommodation *noun* logement M; I'm looking for accommodation je cherche un logement.

accompany *verb* to accompany somebody accompagner [1] quelqu'un.

according *in phrase* according to selon; according to Sophie selon Sophie.

accordion *noun* accordéon M.

account *noun* 1 (*in a bank, shop, or post office*) compte M; a bank account un compte bancaire; to open an account ouvrir un compte; I have fifty pounds in my account j'ai cinquante livres sur mon compte; 2 (*a description of an experience or event*) compte rendu M; 3 on account of à cause de; the station is closed on account of the strike la gare est fermée à cause de la grève; 4 to take something into account tenir compte de quelque chose; we will take his illness into account nous tiendrons compte de sa maladie.

accountant *noun* comptable M & F; she is an accountant elle est comptable.

accuracy *noun* précision F.

accurate *adjective* précis.

accurately *adverb* avec précision.

accuse *verb* accuser [1]; to accuse somebody of something accuser quelqu'un de quelque chose; to accuse someone of doing something accuser quelqu'un d'avoir fait quelque chose; she

accused me of stealing her pen elle m'a accusé d'avoir volé son stylo.

ace noun as M; **the ace of hearts** l'as de cœur.
adjective super (informal); **he's an ace drummer** c'est un super batteur.

ache verb **my arm aches** j'ai mal au bras; **my head aches** j'ai mal à la tête.

achieve verb **1** accomplir [2]; **she's achieved a great deal** elle a beaucoup accompli; **2 to achieve an ambition** réaliser [1] une ambition; **3 to achieve an aim** atteindre [60] un objectif; **4 to achieve success** réussir [2].

achievement noun **1** réussite F; **it's a great achievement** c'est une grande réussite; **2 a sense of achievement** un sentiment de satisfaction.

acid noun acide M.

acid rain noun pluies F plural acides.

acne noun acné F.

acorn noun gland M.

acrobat noun acrobate M & F.

across preposition **1** (over to the other side of) **to walk across something** traverser [1] quelque chose; **we walked across the park** nous avons traversé le parc; **to run across the road** traverser la route en courant; **2** (on the other side of) de l'autre côté de; **the house across the street** la maison de l'autre côté de la rue; **3 across from** en face de;

she was sitting across from me elle était assise en face de moi.

acrylic noun acrylique M.

act noun acte M.
verb **1** (in a play or film) jouer [1]; **to act the part of** jouer le rôle de; **2** (to take action) agir [2].

action noun action F.

active adjective actif (F active).

activity noun activité F.

activity holiday noun vacances F plural sportives.

actor noun acteur M; **who's your favourite actor?** qui est votre acteur préféré?

actress noun actrice F; **she's my favourite actress** c'est mon actrice préférée.

actual adjective **his actual words** ses paroles précises; ★ **in actual fact** en fait.

actually adverb **1** (in fact, as it happens) en fait; **actually, I've changed my mind** en fait, j'ai changé d'avis; **he's not actually here at the moment** en fait il n'est pas là en ce moment; **2** (really and truly) vraiment; **did she actually say that?** est-ce qu'elle a vraiment dit ça?

acupuncture noun acupuncture F.

acute adjective **1** (pain) vif (F vive); **2 an acute accent** un accent aigu.

ad noun **1** pub F (informal); **2** (in a newspaper) annonce F; **to put an ad in the paper** mettre une annonce dans le journal; **the small ads** les petites annonces.

AD après Jésus-Christ, apr. J-C; **in 400 AD** en quatre cents après Jésus-Christ.

adapt verb **1 to adapt something** adapter [1] quelque chose (a book or film); **2 to adapt to something** s'adapter [1] à quelque chose; **she's adapted to the new system** elle s'est adaptée au nouveau système.

adaptor noun adaptateur M.

add verb ajouter [1]; **add three eggs** ajoutez trois œufs.
●**to add something up** additionner [1] quelque chose.

addict noun **1** (drug addict) drogué, droguée M , F; **2** accro M & F (informal); **she's a telly addict** c'est une accro de la télé; **he's a football addict** c'est un accro du foot.

addicted adjective **1 to become addicted to heroin** former une dépendance à l'héroïne; **2 I'm addicted to tomatoes** je suis obsédé par les tomates.

addition noun **1** (adding up) addition F; **2 in addition** en plus; **3 in addition to** en plus de.

additional adjective supplémentaire; **additional costs** les frais supplémentaires.

additive noun additif M.

address noun adresse F; **what's your address?** quelle est ton adresse?; **to change address** changer d'adresse.

address book noun carnet M d'adresses.

adequate adjective suffisant.

adhesive noun colle F.
adjective collant; **adhesive tape** du papier collant.

adjective noun adjectif M.

adjust verb **1 to adjust something** régler [24] quelque chose; **to adjust the height** régler la hauteur; **2 to adjust to something** s'adapter [1] à quelque chose.

adjustable adjective réglable.

administration noun administration F.

admiral noun amiral M.

admiration noun admiration F.

admire verb admirer [1].

admission noun entrée F; 'no admission' 'entrée interdite'; 'admission free' 'entrée gratuite'.

admit verb **1** (confess) reconnaître [27]; **she admits she lied** elle reconnaît qu'elle a menti; **2** (concede) admettre [11]; **I must admit that…** j'admets que…; **3** (allow to enter) laisser [1] entrer; **to admit somebody to a restaurant** laisser entrer quelqu'un dans un restaurant; **4 to be admitted to hospital** être [6] hospitalisé.

adolescence noun adolescence F.

adolescent noun adolescent M adolescente F.

adopt verb adopter [1].

adopted adjective adoptif (F adoptive).

adoption noun adoption F.

adore verb adorer [1].

Adriatic Sea noun the Adriatic Sea la mer Adriatique.

adult noun adulte M & F.
adjective adulte; **the adult population** la population adulte.

Adult Education noun enseignement M pour adultes.

advance noun progrès M; **advances in technology** des progrès dans le domaine de la technologie.
verb 1 (make progress) progresser [1]; 2 (move forward) avancer [61].

advanced adjective avancé.

advantage noun 1 avantage M; **there are several advantages** il y a plusieurs avantages; 2 **to take advantage of something** profiter de quelque chose; **I took advantage of the sales to buy myself some shoes** j'ai profité des soldes pour m'acheter des chaussures; 3 **to take advantage of somebody** (unfairly) exploiter quelqu'un.

Advent noun Avent M.

adventure noun aventure F.

adventurous adjective aventureux (F aventureuse).

adverb noun adverbe M.

advert, advertisement noun 1 (at the cinema or on television) publicité F; 2 (commercial advertisement in a newspaper) annonce F; 3 (small ad in a newspaper advertising a job, an article for sale, etc) petite annonce F.

advertise verb 1 **to advertise something in the newspaper** (in the small ads) mettre [11] une annonce pour quelque chose dans le journal; **I saw a bike advertised in the paper** j'ai vu une annonce pour un vélo dans le journal; 2 **to advertise a product** faire [10] de la publicité pour un produit.

advertising noun publicité F.

advice noun conseils M plural; **to ask for advice about something** demander des conseils à propos de quelque chose; **a piece of advice** un conseil.

advise verb conseiller [1]; **to advise somebody to do** conseiller à quelqu'un de faire; **I advised him to stop** je lui ai conseillé d'arrêter; **I advised her not to wait** je lui ai conseillé de ne pas attendre.

aerial noun antenne F.

aerobics noun aérobic M; **to do aerobics** faire de l'aérobic.

aeroplane noun avion M.

aerosol noun **an aerosol can** une bombe.

affair noun 1 (event) affaire F; **international affairs** les affaires internationales; 2 **a love affair** une aventure amoureuse.

affect verb affecter [1].

affectionate adjective affectueux (F affectueuse).

afford verb **to be able to afford to do** avoir [5] les moyens de faire; **we**

can't afford to go out much nous n'avons pas les moyens de sortir beaucoup; **I can't afford a new bike** je n'ai pas les moyens de m'acheter un nouveau vélo.

afraid *adjective* **1 to be afraid of something** avoir peur de quelque chose; **she's afraid of dogs** elle a peur des chiens; **2 I'm afraid there's no milk left** je suis désolé mais il ne reste plus de lait; **I'm afraid so** hélas oui; **I'm afraid not** hélas non.

Africa *noun* Afrique F; **in Africa** en Afrique; **to Africa** en Afrique.

African *noun* Africain M, Africaine F.

adjective africain (F africaine).

after *preposition, adverb, conjunction* après; **after 10 o'clock** après dix heures; **after lunch** après le déjeuner; **after school** après l'école; **the day after tomorrow** après-demain; **soon after** peu après; **after I've finished my homework** après que j'aurai fini mes devoirs; **to run after somebody** courir après quelqu'un.

after all *adverb* après tout; **after all, she's only six** elle n'a que six ans après tout.

afternoon *noun* après-midi M or F; **this afternoon** cet après-midi; **tomorrow afternoon** demain après-midi; **yesterday afternoon** hier après-midi; **on Saturday afternoon** samedi après-midi; **on Saturday afternoons** le samedi après-midi; **at four o'clock in the afternoon** à quatre heures de l'après-midi; **every afternoon** tous les après-midi.

afters *noun* dessert M.

after-shave *noun* après-rasage M.

afterwards *adverb* après; **shortly afterwards** peu de temps après.

again *adverb* **1** (*one more time*) encore une fois; **try again** essaie encore une fois; **I've forgotten it again** je l'ai oublié encore une fois; **2** (*once more*) de nouveau; **she's ill again** elle est de nouveau malade; **3 I saw her again yesterday** je l'ai revue hier; **you should ask again** tu devrais redemander; **4 I don't want to see her again** je ne veux plus la revoir; **never again!** jamais plus!

against *preposition* contre; **against the wall** contre le mur; **to lean against the wall** s'appuyer contre le mur; **I'm against the idea** je suis contre l'idée; **the fight against racism** la lutte contre le racisme.

age *noun* âge M; **1 at the age of fifteen** à l'âge de quinze ans; **she's the same age as me** elle a le même âge que moi; **to be under age** être mineur; **2 I haven't seen Johnny for ages** ça fait une éternité que je n'ai pas vu Johnny; **I haven't been to London for ages** ça fait une éternité que je ne suis pas allé à Londres.

aged *adjective* âgé de; **a woman aged thirty** une femme âgée de trente ans.

agenda *noun* ordre M du jour.

agent *noun* agent M; **an estate agent** un agent immobilier; **a travel agent's** une agence de voyage.

aggressive adjective agressif (F agressive).

ago adverb **an hour ago** il y a une heure; **three days ago** il y a trois jours; **five years ago** il y a cinq ans; **a long time ago** il y a longtemps; **not long ago** il n'y a pas longtemps; **how long ago was it?** c'était il y a combien de temps?

agree verb **1 to agree with somebody** être [6] d'accord avec quelqu'un; **I agree with Laura** je suis d'accord avec Laura; **I don't agree** je ne suis pas d'accord; **2 I agree that…** je suis d'accord sur le fait que…; **I agree that it's too late now** je suis d'accord sur le fait qu'il est maintenant trop tard; **3 to agree to do** accepter [1] de faire; **Steve's agreed to help me** Steve a accepté de m'aider; **4 coffee doesn't agree with me** je ne supporte pas le café.

agreement noun accord M.

agricultural adjective agricole.

agriculture noun agriculture F.

ahead adverb **1 go ahead!** allez-y!; **2 straight ahead** tout droit; **go straight ahead until you get to the crossroads** allez tout droit jusqu'au carrefour; **3 our team was ten points ahead** notre équipe avait dix points d'avance; **4 to be ahead of time** être en avance.

aid noun **1** aide F; **aid to developing countries** l'aide aux pays en voie de développement; **2 in aid of** au profit de; **in aid of the homeless** au profit des sans-abri.

AIDS noun sida M (short for:

syndrome immunodéficitaire acquis); **to have AIDS** avoir le sida.

aim noun objectif M; **their aim is to control pollution** leur objectif est de contrôler la pollution.
verb **1 to aim to do** avoir [5] l'intention de faire; **we're aiming to finish it today** nous avons l'intention de le finir aujourd'hui; **2 a campaign aimed at young people** une campagne qui vise les jeunes; **3 to aim a gun at somebody** braquer [1] un révolver sur quelqu'un.

air noun **1** air M; **in the open air** en plein air; **to go out for a breath of air** sortir prendre l'air; **2 to travel by air** voyager en avion.

airbag noun (in a car) airbag M.

air-conditioned adjective climatisé.

air conditioning noun climatisation F.

Air Force noun Armée F de l'air.

air hostess noun hôtesse F de l'air; **she's an air hostess** elle est hôtesse de l'air.

airline noun compagnie F aérienne.

airmail noun **by airmail** par avion.

airport noun aéroport M.

aisle noun allée F centrale.

alarm noun alarme F; **a fire alarm** une alarme incendie; **a burglar alarm** une alarme contre le vol.

alarm clock noun réveil M.

album noun album M.

alcohol noun alcool M.

alcoholic *noun* alcoolique M & F.
adjective alcoolisé; **alcoholic drinks** les boissons alcoolisées.

A levels *plural noun* bac M; baccalauréat M (*Students take 'le bac'at the same age as A levels are taken in Britain. However, they are examined in many more subjects, usually around 7, and are given one overall mark out of 20*).

Algeria *noun* Algérie F; **to Algeria** en Algérie; **in Algeria** en Algérie.

alike *adjective* pareil (F pareille); **1 they're all alike** ils sont tous pareils; **2 to look alike** se ressembler; **the two brothers look alike** les deux frères se ressemblent.

alive *adjective* vivant.

all *adjective, adverb, pronoun* **1** tout (M *plural* tous); **all the knives** tous les couteaux; **all the forks** toutes les fourchettes; **all the time** tout le temps; **all day** toute la journée; **2 they've eaten it all** ils ont tout mangé; **after all** après tout; **not at all** pas du tout; **they're all there** ils sont tous là; **3 all alone** tout seul; **she's all alone at the moment** elle est toute seule en ce moment; **4 it's all I have** c'est tout ce que j'ai; **5 three all** trois partout.

all along *adverb* depuis le début; **I knew it all along** je le savais depuis le début.

allergic *adjective* allergique; **to be allergic to something** être allergique à quelque chose.

allow *verb* **1 to allow somebody to do** permettre [11] à quelqu'un de faire; **the teacher allowed them to go out** le prof leur a permis de sortir; **2 to be allowed to do** avoir [5] le droit de faire; **I'm not allowed to go out during the week** je n'ai pas le droit de sortir en semaine.

all right *adverb* **1** (*yes*) d'accord; **'come round to my house around six' – 'all right'** 'passe chez moi vers six heures' – 'd'accord'; **2** (*fine*) bien; **is everything all right?** est-ce que tout va bien?; **she's all right now** elle va bien maintenant; **it's all right by me** ça ne me dérange pas; **3** (*not bad*) pas mal; **the meal was all right** le repas n'était pas mal; **4 are you all right?** ça va?; **5 is it all right to...?** est-ce qu'on peut...?; **is it all right to leave the door open?** est-ce qu'on peut laisser la porte ouverte?

almond *noun* amande F.

almost *adverb* presque; **almost every day** presque tous les jours; **almost everybody** presque tout le monde; **she's almost five** elle a presque cinq ans.

alone *adjective* **1** seul; **he lives alone** il habite seul; **2 leave me alone!** laisse-moi tranquille! **3 leave these papers alone!** ne touche pas à ces papiers!

along *preposition* **1** le long de; **there are trees all along the road** il y a des arbres tout le long de la route; **2** (*there is often no direct translation for 'along' so the sentence has to be expressed differently*) **she lives along the road from me** elle habite dans la même rue que moi; **to go for a walk along the beach** aller se promener sur la plage.

aloud *adverb* à haute voix; **to read something aloud** lire quelque chose à haute voix.

alphabet *noun* alphabet M.

Alps *plural noun* **the Alps** les Alpes.

already *adverb* déjà; **they've already left** ils sont déjà partis; **it's six o'clock already!** il est déjà six heures!

Alsation *noun* (*dog*) berger M allemand.

also *adverb* aussi; **I've also invited Karen** j'ai aussi invité Karen.

alter *verb* changer [52].

alternate *adjective* **on alternate days** un jour sur deux.

alternative *noun* **1** possibilité F; **there are several alternatives** il y a plusieurs possibilités; **2 we have no alternative** nous n'avons pas le choix.
adjective autre; **to find an alternative solution** trouver une autre solution.

alternatively *adverb* sinon; **alternatively, we could go together on Saturday** sinon, on pourrait y aller ensemble samedi.

alternative medicine *noun* médecine F douce.

although *conjunction* bien que (*followed by subjunctive*); **although she's ill, she's willing to help us** bien qu'elle soit malade, elle est prête à nous aider.

altogether *adverb* **1** en tout; **I've spent thirty pounds altogether** j'ai dépensé trente livres en tout; **2** (*completely*) complètement; **I'm not altogether convinced** je ne suis pas complètement convaincu.

aluminium *noun* aluminium M.

always *adverb* toujours; **I always leave at five** je pars toujours à cinq heures.

am *verb* SEE be.

a.m. *abbreviation* du matin; **at 8 a.m.** à huit heures du matin.

amateur *noun* amateur M; **amateur dramatics** théâtre M amateur.

amaze *verb* surprendre [64]; **what amazes me is...** ce qui me surprend c'est...

amazed *adjective* stupéfait; **I was amazed to see her** j'étais stupéfait de la voir.

amazing *adjective* **1** (*terrific*) fantastique; **your dress is amazing!** ta robe est fantastique!; **they've got an amazing house** ils ont une maison fantastique; **2** (*extraordinary*) extraordinaire; **she has an amazing number of friends** elle a un nombre extraordinaire d'amis; **he told me an amazing story** il m'a raconté une histoire extraordinaire.

ambassador *noun* ambassadeur M, ambassadrice F.

ambition *noun* ambition F.

ambitious *adjective* ambitieux (F ambitieuse).

ambulance *noun* ambulance F.

ambulance driver *noun* ambulancier M, ambulancière F.

amenities *plural noun* équipements M *plural*.

America *noun* Amérique F; **in America** en Amérique; **to America** en Amérique.

American *noun* Américain M, Américaine F.
adjective américain (F américaine).

among, amongst *preposition* 1 parmi; **I found it amongst my books** je l'ai trouvé parmi mes livres; 2 (*between*) entre; **you can decide amongst yourselves** vous pouvez décider entre vous.

amount *noun* 1 quantité F; **an enormous amount of bread** une énorme quantité de pain; **a huge amount of work** un travail énorme; 2 (*of money*) somme F; **a large amount of money** une grosse somme d'argent.

amp *noun* 1 (*electricity*) ampère M; 2 (*amplifier*) ampli M (*informal*).

amplifier *noun* amplificateur M.

amuse *verb* amuser [1].

amusement arcade *noun* salle F de jeux électroniques.

amusing *adjective* amusant.

an *article* SEE a.

anaesthetic *noun* anesthésie F.

analyse *verb* analyser [1].

analysis *noun* analyse F.

ancestor *noun* ancêtre M & F.

anchovy *noun* anchois M.

ancient *adjective* 1 (*historic*) ancien (F ancienne); **an ancient**

abbey une abbaye ancienne; 2 (*very old*) très vieux (F très vieille); **an ancient pair of jeans** un très vieux jean; 3 **ancient Greece** la Grèce antique.

and *conjunction* 1 et; **Sean and Anna** Sean et Anna; **Rosie and I** Rosie et moi; **your shoes and socks** tes chaussures et tes chaussettes; 2 **louder and louder** de plus en plus fort.

angel *noun* ange M.

anger *noun* colère F.

angle *noun* angle M.

angrily *adverb* avec colère.

angry *adjective* **to be angry** être en colère; **she was angry with me** elle était en colère contre moi; **to get angry** se fâcher [1].

animal *noun* animal M (*plural* animaux).

ankle *noun* cheville F; **to break your ankle** se casser la cheville.

anniversary *noun* anniversaire M; **a wedding anniversary** un anniversaire de mariage.

announce *verb* annoncer [61].

announcement *noun* annonce F.

annoy *verb* agacer [61]; **to be annoyed** être [6] agacé; **to get annoyed** se fâcher [1]; **she got annoyed** elle s'est fâchée.

annoying *adjective* agaçant.

annual *adjective* annuel (F annuelle).

anorak *noun* anorak M.

anorexia *noun* anorexie F.

another *adjective* 1 un autre (F une autre); **would you like another cup of tea?** voulez-vous une autre tasse de thé?; 2 encore; **another two years** encore deux ans; **we need another three chairs** il nous faut encore trois chaises.

answer *noun* 1 réponse F; **the right answer** la bonne réponse; **the wrong answer** la mauvaise réponse; 2 **the answer to a problem** la solution à un problème. *verb* 1 répondre à [3]; **he hasn't answered our letter** il n'a pas répondu à notre lettre; 2 **to answer the door** aller [5] ouvrir la porte.

answering machine *noun* répondeur M; **to leave a message on the answering machine** laisser un message au répondeur.

ant *noun* fourmi F.

Antarctic *noun* Antarctique M.

anthem *noun* **the national anthem** l'hymne national.

antibiotic *noun* antibiotique F.

antique *noun* **antiques** les antiquités F. *adjective* ancien (F ancienne); **an antique table** une table ancienne.

antique shop *noun* magasin d'antiquités M.

antiseptic *noun* antiseptique M.

anxious *adjective* inquiet (F inquiète).

anxiously *adverb* avec inquiétude.

any *adjective, adverb, pronoun* 1 du, de l', de la, des; **is there any butter?** y a-t-il du beurre?; **is there any oil?**

y a-t-il de l'huile?; **is there any flour?** y a-t-il de la farine?; **are there any eggs?** y a-t-il des œufs?; 2 (*used in negative sentences*) **there isn't any flour** il n'y a pas de farine; **there aren't any eggs** il n'y a pas d'œufs; 3 (*when 'any' is used on its own without a noun*) **I don't want any** je n'en veux pas; 4 **not...any more** ne...plus; **there isn't any more butter** il n'y a plus de beurre; **I don't go there any more** je n'y vais plus.

anybody, anyone *pronoun* 1 (*in questions and after 'if'*) quelqu'un; **is anybody in?** est-ce qu'il y a quelqu'un?; **if anybody wants some beer, it's in the fridge** si quelqu'un veut de la bière, elle est au frigo; **does anybody want some tea?** qui veut du thé?; 2 **not...anybody** ne...personne; **there isn't anybody in her office** il n'y a personne dans son bureau; 3 (*absolutely anybody*) n'importe qui; **anybody can go** n'importe qui peut y aller.

anyhow *adverb* SEE **anyway**.

anyone *pronoun* SEE **anybody**.

anything *pronoun* 1 (*in questions*) quelque chose; **is there anything I can do to help?** est-ce que je peux faire quelque chose pour t'aider?; 2 **not...anything** ne...rien; **there isn't anything on the table** il n'y a rien sur la table; 3 (*anything at all*) n'importe quoi; **anything could happen** il pourrait arriver n'importe quoi.

anyway, anyhow *adverb* de toute façon; **anyway, I'll ring you before I**

leave de toute façon, je t'appellerai avant de partir.

anywhere adverb 1 (in questions) quelque part; **have you seen my keys anywhere?** est-ce que tu as vu mes clés quelque part?; **are you going anywhere tomorrow?** est-ce que tu vas quelque part demain?; **2 not…anywhere** ne…nulle part; **I can't find my keys anywhere** je ne trouve nulle part mes clés; **3** (absolutely anywhere) n'importe où; **put your cases down anywhere** pose tes valises n'importe où.

apart adjective, adverb 1 (separate) séparé; **we don't like being apart** nous n'aimons pas être séparés; **2 to be two metres apart** être à deux mètres l'un de l'autre; **3 apart from** à part; **apart from Judy everybody was there** à part Judy tout le monde y était.

apartheid noun apartheid M.

apartment noun appartement M.

apologize verb s'excuser [1]; **he apologizes for his behaviour** il s'excuse de son comportement; **he apologized to Tanya** il s'est excusé auprès de Tanya.

apology noun excuses F plural.

apostrophe noun apostrophe F.

apparatus noun 1 (in a gym) agrès M plural; 2 (in a lab) matériel M.

apparent adjective apparent.

apparently adverb apparemment.

appeal noun appel M.
verb 1 **to appeal for** lancer [61] un appel pour; 2 **to appeal to somebody** tenter [1] quelqu'un;

horror films don't appeal to me les films d'épouvante ne me tentent pas.

appear verb 1 apparaître [57]; **Mick appeared at the door** Mick est apparu à la porte; **2 to appear on television** passer [1] à la télévision; **3** (seem) paraître [57]; **it appears that somebody has stolen the key** il paraît que quelqu'un a volé la clé.

appendicitis noun appendicite F.

appetite noun appétit M; **it'll spoil your appetite** ça te coupera l'appétit.

applaud verb applaudir [2].

applause noun applaudissements M plural.

apple noun pomme F.

apple core noun trognon M de pomme.

apple tree noun pommier M.

applicant noun candidat M, candidate F.

application noun **a job application** une candidature.

application form noun (for a job) dossier M de candidature.

apply verb 1 **to apply for a job** poser [1] sa candidature à un poste; **2 to apply for a course** faire [10] une demande d'inscription à un cours; **3 to apply to** s'appliquer [1] à; **that doesn't apply to students** cela ne s'applique pas aux étudiants.

appointment noun rendez-vous M; **to make a dental appointment** prendre rendez-vous chez le dentiste; **I've got a hair**

appointment at four j'ai rendez-vous chez le coiffeur à seize heures.

appreciate verb **I appreciate your advice** je vous suis reconnaissant de vos conseils; **I'd appreciate it if you could tidy up afterwards** je te serais reconnaissant de ranger après.

apprentice noun apprenti M, apprentie F.

apprenticeship noun apprentissage M.

approach verb (come near to) **1** s'approcher de [1]; **we were approaching Paris** nous nous approchions de Paris; **2** (tackle) aborder [1] (a task or problem).

appropriate adjective approprié.

approval noun approbation F.

approve verb **to approve of** apprécier [1]; **they don't approve of her friends** ils n'apprécient pas ses amis.

approximate adjective approximatif (F approximative).

approximately adverb environ; **approximately fifty people** environ cinquante personnes.

apricot noun abricot M.

apricot tree noun abricotier M.

April noun avril M; **in April** en avril.

April Fool noun poisson M d'avril.

April Fool's Day noun le premier avril.

apron noun tablier M.

Aquarius noun Verseau M; **Sharon's Aquarius** Sharon est Verseau.

Arab noun Arabe M & F.
adjective arabe; **the Arab countries** les pays arabes.

arch noun arc M.

archaeologist noun archéologue M & F; **she's an archaeologist** elle est archéologue.

archaeology noun archéologie F.

archbishop noun archevêque M.

architect noun architecte M & F; **he's an architect** il est architecte.

architecture noun architecture F.

Arctic noun Arctique M.

are verb SEE be.

area noun **1** (part of a town) quartier; **a nice area** un quartier bien; **a rough area** un quartier mal fréquenté; **2** (region) région F; **in the Leeds area** dans la région de Leeds.

argue verb se disputer [1]; **1 there's no point in arguing** ce n'est pas la peine de se disputer; **2 to argue about something** discuter [1] de quelque chose; **they're arguing about the result** ils sont en train de discuter du résultat.

argument noun dispute F; **to have an argument** se disputer.

Aries noun Bélier M; **Pauline's Aries** Pauline est Bélier.

arm noun bras M; **to fold your arms** se croiser les bras; **arm in arm** bras dessus bras dessous; **to break your arm** se casser le bras.

armchair noun fauteuil M.

armed adjective armé.

army noun armée F; **to join the army** s'engager dans l'armée.

around adverb **1** (with time) vers; **we'll be there around ten** on va arriver vers dix heures; **2** (with ages or amounts) environ; **she's around fifteen** elle a environ quinze ans; **we need around six kilos** il nous faut environ six kilos; **3** (surrounding) autour de; **the countryside around Edinburgh** le paysage autour d'Édimbourg; **4** (near) **is there a post office around here?** est-ce qu'il y a un bureau de poste près d'ici?; **is Phil around?** est-ce que Phil est là?; **5** (wrapped around) autour de; **she had a scarf around her neck** elle avait une écharpe autour du cou.

arrange verb **to arrange to do** prévoir [65] de faire; **we've arranged to see a film on Saturday** nous avons prévu de voir un film samedi.

arrest noun **to be under arrest** être en état d'arrestation.
verb arrêter [1].

arrival noun arrivée F.

arrive verb arriver [1]; **they arrived at 3 p.m.** ils sont arrivés à quinze heures.

arrow noun flèche F.

art noun **1** art M; **modern art** l'art moderne; **2** (school subject) dessin M; **the art class** le cours de dessin.

artery noun artère F.

art gallery noun (public) musée M des beaux arts.

article noun article M.

artichoke noun artichaut M.

artificial adjective artificiel (F artificielle).

artist noun artiste M & F; **he's an artist** c'est un artiste.

artistic adjective artistique.

art school noun école F de beaux arts.

as conjunction, adverb **1** comme; **as you know** comme vous le savez; **as usual** comme d'habitude; **as I told you** comme je t'avais dit; **2** (because) puisque; **as there were no trains, we took the bus** puisqu'il n'y avait pas de trains, nous avons pris le bus; **3** **as…as** aussi…que; **he's as tall as his brother** il est aussi grand que son frère; **you must be as tired as I am** tu dois être aussi fatigué que moi; **4** **as much…as** autant de…que; **you have as much time as I do** tu as autant de temps que moi; **5** **as many…as** autant de…que; **we have as many problems as he does** nous avons autant de problèmes que lui; **6** **as long as** pourvu que (with subjunctive); **we'll go tomorrow, as long as it's a nice day** on va y aller demain, pourvu qu'il fasse beau; **7** **for as long as** aussi longtemps que; **you can stay for as long as you like** tu peux rester aussi longtemps que tu veux; **8** **as soon as possible** dès que possible; **9** **to work as** travailler comme; **he works as a taxi driver in the evenings** il travaille comme chauffeur de taxi le soir.

asbestos noun amiante F.

ash noun cendre F.

ashamed adjective **to be ashamed**

avoir honte; **you should be ashamed of yourself!** tu devrais avoir honte!

ashtray noun cendrier M.

Asia noun Asie F; **in Asia** en Asie.

Asian noun Asiatique M & F.
adjective asiatique.

ask verb 1 demander [1]; **you can ask at reception** tu peux demander à l'accueil; **to ask somebody something** demander quelque chose à quelqu'un; **I asked him where he lives** je lui ai demandé où il habite; **to ask for something** demander quelque chose; **I asked for three coffees** j'ai demandé trois cafés; **to ask somebody to do** demander à quelqu'un de faire; **ask Danny to give you a hand** demande à Danny de te donner un coup de main; 2 **to ask somebody a question** poser [1] une question à quelqu'un; **I asked you a question!** je t'ai posé une question!; 3 inviter [1]; **they've asked us to a party at their house** ils nous ont invité à une soirée chez eux; 4 **Paul's asked Janie out on Friday** Paul a invité Janie à sortir avec lui vendredi.

asleep adjective **to be asleep** dormir [37]; **the baby's asleep** le bébé dort; **to fall asleep** s'endormir [37].

asparagus noun asperges F plural.

aspirin noun aspirine F.

assembly noun (at school) rassemblement M.

assess verb évaluer [1].

assignment noun (at school) devoir M.

assist verb aider [1].

assistance noun aide F.

assistant noun 1 assistant M, assistante F; 2 **a shop assistant** un vendeur, une vendeuse.

association noun association F.

assorted adjective variés (F variées).

assortment noun mélange M.

assume verb supposer [1].

assure verb assurer [1].

asthma noun asthme M; **she has asthma** elle souffre de l'asthme.

astrology noun astrologie F.

astronaut noun astronaute M & F.

astronomy noun astronomie F.

at preposition 1 à (note that 'à + le' always becomes 'au' and 'à + les' always becomes 'aux') au marché; **at home** à la maison; **at school** à l'école; **at my office** à mon bureau; **at the market** au marché; **at meetings** aux réunions; 2 (talking about the time) à; **at eight o'clock** à huit heures; 3 **at night** la nuit; **at the weekend** le weekend; 4 **at Emma's house** chez Emma; **she's at her brother's this evening** elle est chez son frère ce soir; **at the hairdresser's** chez le coiffeur; 5 **at last** enfin; **he's found a job at last** il a enfin trouvé un emploi.

athlete noun athlète M & F.

athletic adjective athlétique.

athletics noun athlétisme M.

Atlantic noun Atlantique M.

atlas noun atlas M.

atmosphere noun atmosphère F.

atom noun atome M.

atomic adjective atomique.

attach verb attacher [1].

attached adjective **to be attached to** être [6] attaché à.

attack noun attaque F. verb attaquer [1].

attempt noun tentative F; **at the first attempt** à la première tentative. verb **to attempt to do** essayer [59] de faire.

attend verb assister à [1]; **to attend a class** assister à un cours.

attention noun attention F; **to pay attention to** faire attention à; **I wasn't paying atttention** je ne faisais pas attention.

attic noun grenier M; **in the attic** au grenier.

attitude noun attitude F.

attract verb attirer [1].

attraction noun attraction F.

attractive adjective séduisant.

aubergine noun aubergine F.

auction noun vente F aux enchères.

audience noun public M.

August noun août M; **in August** en août.

aunt, auntie noun tante F.

au pair noun jeune fille F au pair; **I'm looking for a job as an au pair** je cherche un emploi de jeune fille au pair.

Australia noun Australie F; **in Australia** en Australie; **to Australia** en Australie.

Australian noun Australien M, Australienne F. adjective australien (F australienne).

Austria noun Autriche F; **in Austria** en Autriche; **to Austria** en Autriche.

Austrian noun Autrichien M, Autrichienne F. adjective autrichien (F autrichienne).

author noun auteur M.

autobiography noun autobiographie F.

autograph noun autographe M.

automatic adjective automatique.

automatically adverb automatiquement.

autumn noun automne M; **in autumn** en automne.

availability noun disponibilité F.

available adjective disponible.

avenue noun avenue F.

average noun moyenne F; **on average** en moyenne; **above average** au-dessus de la moyenne. adjective moyen (F moyenne); **the average height** la hauteur moyenne.

avocado noun avocat M.

avoid verb éviter [1]; **she avoided me** elle m'a évité; **to avoid doing**

éviter de faire; **I avoid speaking to him** j'évite de lui parler.

awake *adjective* **to be awake** être réveillé; **is Lola awake?** est-ce que Lola est réveillée?; **are you still awake?** tu ne dors pas?

award *noun* prix M; **to win an award** remporter un prix.

aware *adjective* **to be aware of a noise** être conscient d'un bruit; **to be aware of a problem** être au courant d'un problème; **as far as I'm aware** à ma connaissance.

away *adverb* **1 to be away** être absent; **I'll be away next week** je serai absent la semaine prochaine; **2 to go away** partir; **Laura's gone away for a week** Laura est partie pour une semaine; **go away!** va-t-en!; **3 to run away** partir en courant; **the thieves ran away** les voleurs sont partis en courant; **4 the school is two kilometres away** l'école est à deux kilomètres; **how far away is it?** c'est à quelle distance d'ici?; **not far away** pas loin d'ici; **5 to put something away** ranger quelque chose; **I'll just put my books away** je vais juste ranger mes livres; **6 to give something away** donner quelque chose; **she's given away all her tapes** elle a donné toutes ses cassettes.

away match *noun* match M à l'extérieur.

awful *adjective* **1** affreux (F affreuse); **the film was awful!** le film était affreux!; **2 I feel awful** (*ill*) je ne me sens pas bien du tout; **3 I feel awful about it** ça m'ennuie

vraiment; **4 an awful lot of** énormément de.

awkward *adjective* **1** difficile; **it's an awkward situaion** c'est une situation difficile; **i** 's a bit awkward c'est un peu difficile; **an awkward child** un enfant difficile; **2 an awkward question** une question gênante.

axe *noun* hache F.

B b

baby *noun* bébé M.

babysit *verb* faire [10] du babysitting.

babysitter *noun* babysitter M & F.

babysitting *noun* babysitting M.

back *noun* **1** (*of a person or animal*) dos M; **to do something behind someone's back** faire quelque chose dans le dos de quelqu'un; **2** (*of a piece of paper, your hand, or a garment*) dos M; **on the back** au dos; **3** (*of a car, a plane, or a building*) arrière M; **we have seats at the back** nous avons des places à l'arrière; **a garden at the back of the house** un jardin à l'arrière de la maison; **4 the children at the back of the room** les enfants au fond de la salle; **5** (*of a chair or sofa*) dossier M; **6** (*in football or hockey*) arrière M; **left back** arrière gauche. *adjective* **1** arrière (*a wheel or seat*); **the back seat of the car** le siège arrière de la voiture; **2 the back gate** la porte de derrière; **the back**

garden le jardin de derrière.
adverb 1 **to go back** rentrer; **to go back to school** rentrer à l'école; **Lisa's gone back to London** Lisa est rentrée à Londres; 2 **to come back** rentrer; **they've come back from Italy** ils sont rentrés d'Italie; **she's back at work** elle a repris le travail; **Sue's not back yet** Sue n'est pas encore rentrée; **we went by bus and walked back** nous avons pris le bus pour y aller et nous sommes rentrés à pied; 3 **to phone back** rappeler; **I'll ring back later** je rappellerai plus tard; 4 **to give something back to somebody** rendre quelque chose à quelqu'un; **I gave him back his cassettes** je lui ai rendu ses cassettes; **give it back!** rends-le-moi!
verb 1 (*to support*) soutenir [81] (*a candidate, for example*); 2 (*to bet on*) parier [1] sur (*a horse*).
●**to back up** (*computing*) **to back up a file** sauvegarder [1] un fichier sur disquette.
●**to back somebody up** soutenir [77] quelqu'un.

backache *noun* mal M de dos.

backbone *noun* colonne F vertébrale.

back door *noun* 1 (*of a building*) porte F de derrière; 2 (*of a car*) porte F arrière.

backfire *verb* (*turn out badly*) échouer [1].

background *noun* 1 (*of a person*) (*social*) milieu M; 2 (*of events or a situation*) contexte M; 3 (*in a picture or view*) arrière-plan M; **the trees in the background** les arbres à l'arrière-plan; 4 **background music** la musique d'ambiance; 5 **background noise** les bruits M plural de fond.

backhand *noun* revers M.

backing *noun* 1 (*on sticky-back plastic, for example*) revêtement M intérieur; 2 (*moral support*) soutien M; 3 (*in music*) **a backing group** un groupe d'accompagnement.

backpack *noun* sac M à dos.
verb **to go backpacking** partir [58] en voyage avec un sac à dos.

back seat *noun* siège M arrière.

backside *noun* derrière M.

backstage *adverb* **to go backstage** aller dans les coulisses.

backstroke *noun* dos M crawlé.

back to front *adverb* à l'envers; **your jumper's back to front** ton pull est à l'envers.

backup *noun* 1 (*support*) soutien M; 2 (*in computing*) **a backup disk** un disque de sauvegarde.

backwards *adverb* (*to lean or fall*) en arrière.

bacon *noun* 1 (*French streaky bacon*) lard M; 2 (*thin-sliced British type*) bacon M; **bacon and eggs** œufs au bacon.

bad *adjective* 1 (*not good*) mauvais (*goes before the noun*); **bad work** du mauvais travail; **a bad meal** un mauvais repas; **his new film's not bad** son nouveau film n'est pas mauvais; **it's bad for your health** c'est mauvais pour la santé; **I'm bad at physics** je suis mauvais en physique; **2** (*serious*) grave; **a bad accident** un accident grave; **a bad cold** un gros rhume; **3** (*rotten*) pourri; **a bad apple** une pomme pourrie; **to go bad** se gâter. **4** (*rude*) **bad language** du langage grossier; **5** (*naughty*) vilain; **bad dog!** vilain!; **bad girl!** vilain!; ★ **too bad!** (*I'm sorry for you*) pas de chance!; (*I don't care*) tant pis!

badge noun badge M.

badly adverb **1** mal; **he writes badly** il écrit mal; **I slept badly** j'ai mal dormi; **the exam went badly** l'examen s'est mal passé; **2** (*seriously*) (*to hurt or damage*) gravement; **la voiture a été gravement endommagée** the car was badly damaged; **badly hurt** grièvement blessé.

bad-mannered adjective mal élevé.

badminton noun badminton M; **to play badminton** jouer au badminton.

bad-tempered adjective **1** (*for a little while*) irrité; **2** (*always*) **she's very bad-tempered** elle a très mauvais caractère.

bag noun sac M.

baggage noun bagages M plural.

baggage allowance noun franchise F de baggages.

baggage reclaim noun réception F des bagages.

bagpipes plural noun cornemuse F; **to play the bagpipes** jouer de la cornemuse.

bags plural noun bagages M plural;

to pack your bags faire ses bagages; ★ **to have bags under your eyes** avoir des valises sous les yeux (*informal*).

bake verb **to bake a cake** faire [10] un gâteau; **to bake vegetables** faire [10] cuire des légumes au four.

baked adjective **1** (*fish or fruit*) au four; **baked apples** les pommes au four; **2 a baked potato** une pomme de terre au four.

baked beans plural noun les haricots blancs à la sauce tomate.

baker noun boulanger M, boulangère F; **to go to the baker's** aller à la boulangerie.

bakery noun boulangerie F.

balance noun **1** équilibre M; **to lose your balance** perdre l'équilibre; **2** (*money in your bank account*) solde M.

balanced adjective équilibré.

balcony noun balcon M.

bald adjective chauve.

ball noun **1** (*for tennis or golf*) balle F; **2** (*for football or volleyball*) ballon M; **3** (*of string or wool*) pelote F.

ballet noun ballet M.

ballet dancer noun danseur M de ballet, danseuse de ballet.

ballet shoe noun chausson M de danse.

balloon noun **1** ballon M; **2** (*hot air*) montgolfière F.

ballot noun scrutin M.

ballpoint (pen) noun stylo M à bille.

ban noun interdiction F; **a ban on smoking** une interdiction de fumer.
verb interdire [47].

banana noun banane F; **a banana yoghurt** un yaourt à la banane.

band noun 1 (*playing music*) groupe M; **a rock band** un groupe de rock; **2 a jazz band** un orchestre de jazz; **3 a brass band** une fanfare; **4 a rubber band** un élastique.

bandage noun bandage M.
verb mettre [11] un bandage à.

bang noun 1 (*noise*) boum M; **2** (*of a door or window*) claquement M.
verb 1 (*to hit*) taper [1] sur (*a drum, for example*); **he banged his fist on the table** il a tapé du poing sur la table; **2** (*to knock*) cogner [1]; **bang on the door** cogner à la porte; **I banged my head on the door** je me suis cogné la tête contre la table; **I banged into the table** j'ai heurté la table; **3 to bang the door** claquer [1] la porte.
exclamation (*like a gun*) pan!

banister(s), bannister(s) (*plural*) noun rampe F (d'escalier).

bank noun 1 (*for money*) banque F; **I'm going to the bank** je vais à la banque; **2** (*of a river or lake*) bord M.

bank account noun compte M bancaire.

bank balance noun solde M bancaire.

bank card noun carte F bancaire.

bank holiday noun jour M férié.

banknote noun billet M de banque.

bank statement noun relevé M de compte.

bar noun 1 (*selling drinks*) bar M; **Janet works in a bar** Janet travaille dans un bar; **2** (*the counter*) comptoir M; **on the bar** sur le bar; **3 a bar of chocolate** une tablette de chocolat; **4 a bar of soap** une savonnette; **5** (*made of wood or metal*) barre F; **a metal bar** une barre en métal; **6** (*in music*) mesure F.
verb 1 (*to block physically*) barrer [1]; **to bar someone's way** barrer le passage à quelqu'un; **2** (*to ban from an activity*) exclure [25].

barbecue noun barbecue M; **there's a barbecue tonight** il y a un barbecue ce soir.
verb **to barbecue a chicken** faire [10] griller un poulet au barbecue; **barbecued chicken** du poulet grillé au barbecue.

barbed wire noun barbelé M.

bare adjective nu.

barefoot adjective **to be barefoot** être nu-pieds; **to walk barefoot** marcher pieds nus.

bargain noun 1 (*a good buy*) affaire F; **I got a bargain** j'ai fait une affaire; **it's a bargain!** c'est une bonne affaire!

barge noun péniche F.

bark noun 1 (*of a tree*) écorce F; **2** (*of a dog*) aboiement M.
verb aboyer [39].

barmaid noun barmaid F.

barman noun barman M.

barn noun grange F.

barrel noun tonneau M (plural tonneaux).

barrier noun barrière F.

base noun base F.

baseball noun base-ball M; **a baseball cap** une casquette de base-ball.

based adjective **1** to be based on être fondé sur; **the film is based on a true story** le film est fondé sur une histoire vraie; **2** to be based in être basé à; **he's based in Bristol** il est basé à Bristol.

basement noun sous-sol M; **in the basement** au sous-sol.

bash noun **1** bosse F; **it's got a bash on the wing** il y a une bosse à l'aile; **2** I'll have a bash je vais essayer un coup.
verb cogner [1]; **I bashed my head** je me suis cogné la tête.

basic adjective **1** de base; **basic knowledge** des connaissances de base; **her basic salary** son salaire de base; **2** the basic facts les faits essentiels; **3** (not luxurious) rudimentaire; **the flat's a bit basic** l'appartement est un peu rudimentaire.

basically adverb **1** au fond; **it's basically all right** au fond ça va; **2** à vrai dire; **basically, I don't really want to go** à vrai dire, je ne veux pas vraiment y aller.

basics noun rudiments M plural.

basin noun (washbasin) lavabo M.

basis noun **1** base F; **2** on the basis of sur la base de; **on a regular basis** régulièrement.

basket noun **1** (for shopping) panier M; **2** (other) corbeille F; **a waste-paper basket** une corbeille à papier; **a linen basket** une corbeille à linge.

basketball noun basketball M; **to play basketball** jouer au basketball.

bass noun **1** basse F; **to play bass** jouer de la basse; **2** a double bass une contrebasse.

bass drum noun grosse caisse F.

bass guitar noun guitare F basse.

bassoon noun basson M; **to play the bassoon** jouer du basson.

bat noun **1** (for cricket or baseball) batte F; **2** (for table tennis) raquette F; **3** (animal) chauve-souris F.

bath noun **1** bain M; **to have a bath** prendre un bain; **I was in the bath** j'étais dans mon bain; **2** (bathtub) baignoire F; **the bath's pink** la baignoire est rose.

bathe verb **1** laver [1] (a wound); **2** (go swimming) se baigner [1].

bathroom noun salle F de bains (plural salles de bains).

baths plural noun piscine F.

bath towel noun serviette F de bain.

batter noun **1** (for frying) pâte F à frire; **fish in batter** des beignets de poisson; **pancake batter** la pâte à crêpes.

battery noun 1 (for a torch or radio for example) pile F; 2 (for a car) batterie F.

battle noun bataillle F.

bay noun baie F.

B.C. (short for: before Christ) av. J.-C.

be verb 1 être [6]; **Melanie is in the kitchen** Melanie est dans la cuisine; **where is the butter?** où est le beurre?; **I'm tired** je suis fatigué; **when we were in France** quand nous étions en France; 2 (with jobs and professions) être; **she's a teacher** elle est professeur (note that 'a' is not translated); **he's a taxi driver** il est chauffeur de taxi; 3 (in clock times) être; **it's three o'clock** il est trois heures; **it's half past five** il est cinq heures et demie; 4 (days of the week and dates) **what day is it today?** nous sommes quel jour aujourd'hui?; **it's Tuesday today** nous sommes mardi aujourd'hui; **it's the twentieth of May** nous sommes le vingt mai; 5 (talking about age) avoir [5]; **how old are you?** quel âge as-tu?; **I'm fifteen** j'ai quinze ans; **Harry's twenty** Harry a vingt ans; 6 (cold, hot, hungry) avoir [5]; **I'm hot** j'ai chaud; **I'm cold** j'ai froid; **I'm hungry** j'ai faim; 7 (weather) faire [10]; **it's cold today** il fait froid aujourd'hui; **it's a nice day** il fait beau; 8 **I've never been to Paris** je ne suis jamais allé à Paris; **have you been to Britain before?** est-ce que tu es déjà venu en Grande Bretagne?; 9 **to be loved** être aimé; **he has been killed** il a été tué.

beach noun plage F; **to go to the beach** aller à la plage; **on the beach** sur la plage.

bead noun perle F.

beak noun bec M.

beam noun 1 (of light) rayon M; 2 (for a roof) poutre F.

bean noun haricot M; **baked beans** les haricots à la sauce tomate; **green beans** les haricots verts.

bear noun ours M.
verb 1 supporter [1]; **I can't bear him** je ne peux pas le supporter; **I can't bear the idea** je ne supporte pas l'idée; 2 **to bear something in mind** tenir [77] compte de quelque chose; **I'll bear it in mind** je ne l'oublierai pas.
● **to bear up** tenir [77] le coup.

beard noun barbe F.

bearded adjective barbu.

bearings plural noun **to get one's bearings** se repérer [24].

beast noun 1 (animal) bête F; 2 **you beast!** chameau!

beat noun rythme M.
verb 1 (defeat) battre [21]; **we beat them!** on les a battus!; 2 **to beat the eggs** battre les œufs; 3 **you can't beat a good meal** rien ne vaut un bon repas.
● **to beat somebody up** tabasser [1] quelqu'un (informal).

beautiful adjective beau (F belle) (M plural beaux) (goes before the noun); **a beautiful day** un beau jour; **a beautiful girl** une belle fille; **beautiful pictures** de beaux tableaux; **a beautiful place** un bel endroit ('*bel*' for masculine nouns beginning with a vowel or silent '*h*').

beautifully *adverb* admirablement.

beauty *noun* beauté F.

beauty spot *noun* (*for tourists*) beau site M.

because *conjunction* **1** parce que; **because it's you** parce que c'est toi; **because it's cold** parce qu'il fait froid; **2 because of** à cause de; **because of the accident** à cause de l'accident.

become *verb* devenir [81].

bed *noun* **1** lit M; **a double bed** un grand lit; **in bed** au lit; **to go to bed** aller se coucher; **2** (*flower bed*) parterre M.

bedclothes *plural noun* couvertures F *plural*.

bedding *noun* literie F.

bedroom *noun* chambre F; **bedroom furniture** les meubles de chambre; **my bedroom window** la fenêtre de ma chambre.

bedside *noun* **a bedside table** une table de chevet.

bedsit, bedsitter *noun* chambre F meublée.

bedspread *noun* dessus-de-lit M.

bedtime *noun* **it's bedtime** c'est l'heure d'aller te coucher.

bee *noun* abeille F.

beech *noun* hêtre M.

beef *noun* bœuf M; **we had roast beef** on a mangé du rôti de bœuf.

beefburger *noun* hamburger M.

beer *noun* bière F; **two beers please** deux bières s'il vous plaît; **a beer can** une canette de bière.

beetle *noun* scarabée M.

beetroot *noun* betterave F.

before *preposition* **1** avant; **before Monday** avant lundi; **he left before me** il est parti avant moi; **2 the day before** la veille; **the day before the wedding** la veille du mariage; **the day before yesterday** avant-hier; **the week before** la semaine d'avant; **3** (*already*) déjà; **I've seen him before somewhere** je l'ai déjà vu quelque part; **I had seen the film before** j'avais déjà vu le film. *conjunction* **1** avant de; **before doing** avant de faire; **I closed the windows before leaving** (or **before I left**) j'ai fermé les fenêtres avant de partir; **2** avant que; **phone me before they leave** appelle-moi avant qu'ils s'en aillent; **oh, before I forget ...** avant que j'oublie ...

beforehand *adverb* (*ahead of time*) à l'avance; **phone beforehand** appelle à l'avance.

beg *verb* **1** (*ask for money*) mendier [1]; **2** (*ask*) supplier [1]; **she begged me not to leave** elle m'a supplié de ne pas partir; **I beg your pardon** je vous demande pardon.

begin *verb* **1** commencer [61]; **the meeting begins at ten** la réunion commence à dix heures; **the words beginning with P** les mots qui commencent par un P; **to begin to do** commencer à faire; **I'm beginning to understand** je commence à comprendre.

beginner noun débutant M, débutante F.

beginning noun début M; **at the beginning** au début; **at the beginning of the holidays** au début des vacances.

behalf noun **on behalf of** pour.

behave verb 1 se comporter [1]; **he behaved badly** il s'est mal comporté; 2 **to behave yourself** être sage; **behave yourselves!** soyez sages!

behaviour noun comportement M.

behind noun derrière M. *preposition, adverb* 1 derrière; **behind the sofa** derrière le canapé; **behind them** derrière eux; **the car behind** la voiture de derrière; 2 (*not making progress*) **he's behind in class** il a du retard en classe; 3 **to leave something behind** oublier quelque chose; **I've left my keys behind** j'ai oublié mes clés.

beige *adjective* beige.

Belgian noun Belge M & F. *adjective* belge.

Belgium noun Belgique F; **to Belgium** en Belgique; **in Belgium** en Belgique.

belief noun conviction F; **his political beliefs** ses convictions politiques.

believe verb 1 croire [33]; **I believe you** je te crois; **they believed what I said** ils ont cru ce que j'ai dit; **I don't believe you!** ce n'est pas vrai!; 2 **to believe in** croire à; **to believe in**

gnosts croire aux fantômes; **to believe in God** croire en Dieu.

bell noun 1 (*in a church*) cloche F; 2 (*on a door*) sonnette F; **ring the bell!** appuyez sur la sonnette!; 3 (*for a cat or toy*) grelot M; ★ **that name rings a bell** ce nom me dit quelque chose (*literally: says something to me*).

belong verb 1 **to belong to** appartenir [81] à; **that belongs to Richard** cela appartient à Richard; 2 **to belong to a club** faire [10] partie d'un club; 3 (*go*) aller [5]; **that chair belongs in the study** cette chaise va dans le bureau; **where does this vase belong?** ce vase va où?

belongings *plural noun* affaires F *plural*; **all my belongings are in London** toutes mes affaires sont à Londres.

below *preposition* au-dessous de; **below the window** au-dessous de la fenêtre; **the flat below yours** l'appartement au-dessous du tien. *adverb* 1 (*further down*) plus bas; **shouts came from below** des cris venaient d'en bas; 2 **the flat below** l'appartement de dessous.

belt noun ceinture F.

bench noun banc M.

bend noun 1 (*in a road*) virage M; 2 (*in a river*) courbe F. *verb* 1 (*to make a bend in*) plier [1] (*your arm or leg, or a wire*); 2 (*to curve*) (*a road or path*) tourner [1]; 3 **to bend down or forwards** se pencher [1]; **she bent down to look** elle s'est penchée pour regarder.

beneath *preposition* sous.

benefit noun 1 avantage M; 2 **unemployment benefit** les allocations F plural de chômage.

bent adjective tordu.

beret noun béret M.

berth noun couchette F.

beside preposition (next to) à côté de; **she was sitting beside me** elle était assise à côté de moi; ★ **that's beside the point** ça n'a rien à voir.

besides adverb 1 (anyway) d'ailleurs; **besides, it's too late** d'ailleurs, il est trop tard; 2 (as well) en plus; **four dogs, and six cats besides** quatre chiens et six chats en plus.

best adjective 1 meilleur; **it's the best** c'est le meilleur; **that's the best car** cette voiture-là est la meilleure; **she's my best friend** c'est ma meilleure amie; 2 **she's the best at tennis** c'est elle la meilleure en tennis; **the best thing to do is to phone them** la meilleure chose à faire, c'est de les appeler.
adverb le mieux; **he plays best** il joue le mieux; **I like Paris best** c'est Paris que j'aime le mieux; **best of all** mieux que tout; ★ **all the best!** (good luck) bonne chance!; (cheers) à ta santé!; ★ **it's the best I can do** je ne peux pas faire mieux; ★ **to do your best** to do faire de son mieux pour faire; **I did my best to help her** j'ai fait de mon mieux pour l'aider.

best man noun garçon d'honneur M.

bet noun pari M.
verb parier [1]; **to bet on a horse**

parier sur un cheval; **I bet you he'll forget!** je te parie qu'il va oublier!

better adjective, adverb 1 meilleur; **she's found a better flat** elle a trouvé un meilleur appartement; **this road's better than the other one** cette route est meilleure que l'autre; 2 mieux; **this pen writes better** ce stylo écrit mieux; **it works better than the other one** ça fonctionne mieux que l'autre; 3 even better encore mieux; **it's even better than before** c'est encore mieux qu'avant; 4 (less ill) **to be better** aller mieux; **he's a bit better today** il va un peu mieux aujourd'hui; **to feel better** se sentir mieux; **I feel better** je me sens mieux; 5 **to get better** s'améliorer; **my French is getting better** mon français s'améliore; 6 **so much the better** tant mieux; **the sooner the better** le plus vite possible.
adverb 1 **you had better phone at once** tu ferais mieux d'appeler tout de suite; **he'd better not go** il ferait mieux de ne pas y aller; **I'd better go now** je dois partir maintenant.

better off adjective 1 (richer) plus riche; **they're better off than us** ils sont plus riches que nous; 2 (more comfortable) mieux; **you'd be better off in bed** tu serais mieux au lit.

between preposition 1 entre; **between London and Dover** entre Londres et Douvres; **between Monday and Friday** entre lundi et vendredi; **between the two** entre les deux.

beyond preposition 1 (in space and time) au-delà de; **beyond the**

border au-delà de la frontière;
2 it's beyond me! ça me dépasse!

Bible *noun* the Bible la Bible.

bicycle *noun* 1 vélo M; by bicycle
à vélo.

bicycle lane *noun* piste F cyclable.

big *adjective* 1 grand (*goes before the*
noun); a big house une grande
maison; a big city une grande ville;
my big sister ma grande sœur; it's
too big for me c'est trop grand pour
moi; 2 gros (F grosse) (*before the*
noun); a big dog un gros chien; a
big car une grosse voiture; a big
mistake une grosse erreur.

bigheaded *adjective* to be
bigheaded avoir la grosse tête.

big screen *noun* grand écran M.

big toe *noun* gros orteil M.

bike *noun* vélo M; by bike à vélo.

bikini *noun* bikini M.

bilingual *adjective* bilingue.

bill *noun* 1 (*in a restaurant*) addition
F; can we have the bill, please
l'addition, s'il vous plaît; 2 (*for gas,*
electricity, etc) facture F.

billiards *noun* billard M; to play
billiards jouer au billard.

billion *noun* milliard M.

bin *noun* poubelle F.

binoculars *noun* jumelles F
plural.

biochemistry *noun* biochimie F.

biography *noun* biographie F.

biology *noun* biologie F.

bird *noun* oiseau M
(*plural* oiseaux).

bird sanctuary *noun* réserve F
ornithologique.

birdwatching *noun* to go
birdwatching observer les oiseaux.

Biro™ *noun* bic™ M.

birth *noun* naissance F.

birth certificate *noun* acte M de
naissance.

birthday *noun* 1 anniversaire M;
happy birthday! joyeux
anniversaire!; 2 a birthday
present un cadeau d'anniversaire.

birthday party *noun* 1 (*for a*
child) goûter M d'anniversaire;
2 (*for an adult*) soirée F
d'anniversaire.

biscuit *noun* biscuit M.

bishop *noun* évêque M.

bit *noun* 1 (*of bread, cheese, wood*)
morceau M; a bit of chocolate un
morceau de chocolat; 2 (*of string,*
paper, garden) bout M; a bit of
string un bout de ficelle; with a little
bit of garden avec un petit bout de
jardin; 3 (*a small amount*) a bit of
un peu de; a bit of sugar un peu de
sucre; with a bit of luck avec un peu
de chance; wait a bit! attends un
peu!; a bit of news une nouvelle; to
have a bit of trouble with avoir un
petit problème avec; 4 (*in a book or*
film, for example) passage M; this
bit is brilliant! ce passage est
génial!; 5 to fall to bits tomber en
morceaux; 6 a bit un peu; a bit hot
un peu chaud; a bit early un peu

trop tôt; **7** (*for a horse*) mors M;
★ **bit by bit** petit à petit.

bite noun **1** (*snack*) morceau M; **I'll
just have a bite before I go** je vais
juste manger un morceau avant de
partir; **2** (*from an insect*) piqûre F;
a mosquito bite une piqûre de
moustique; **3** (*from a dog*) morsure
F.
verb **1** (*a person or a dog*) mordre
[3]; **2** (*an insect*) piquer [1]; ★ **to
bite one's nails** se ronger [52] les
ongles.

bitter adjective (*taste*) amer (F
amère).

black adjective **1** noir; **my black
jacket** ma veste noire; **to turn
black** noircir [2]; **2 a Black man** un
Noir; **a Black woman** une Noire;
3 a black coffee un café noir.

blackberry noun mûre F.

blackbird noun merle M.

blackboard noun tableau M noir.

blackcurrant noun cassis M.

black eye noun œil M au beurre
noir.

blade noun lame F.

blame noun responsabilité F; **to
take the blame for something**
prendre la responsabilité de quelque
chose.
verb **to blame someone for
something** tenir [77] quelqu'un
responsable de quelque chose; **they
blamed him for the accident** ils l'ont
tenu reponsable de l'accident; **she is
to blame for it** elle en est
responsable; **I blame the parents!** à
mon avis c'est la faute des parents!;

I don't blame you! je te comprends!

blank noun blanc M.
adjective (*a page or piece of paper,
or a cheque*) blanc (F blanche); (*a
tape or disk*) vierge; (*a screen*) vide;
2 my mind went blank j'ai eu un
trou de mémoire.

blanket noun couverture F.

blast noun **1** (*an explosion*)
explosion F; **2** (*of air*) souffle M;
3 to play music at full blast jouer
de la musique à plein volume.

blaze noun incendie M.
verb brûler [1].

blazer noun blazer M.

bleach noun eau F de javel.

bleed verb saigner [1]; **my nose is
bleeding** je saigne du nez.

blend noun mélange M.

blender noun mixer M.

bless verb bénir [2]; **bless you!**
(*after a sneeze*) à tes souhaits!

blind noun (*in a window*) store M.
adjective aveugle; **to go blind**
perdre la vue.

blink verb (*your eyes*) cligner [1] des
yeux.

blister noun ampoule F.

blizzard noun tempête F de neige.

blob noun goutte F.

block noun **1 a block of flats** un
immeuble; **an office block** un
immeuble de bureaux; **2** (*a square
group of buildings*) **to go round the
block** faire le tour du pâté de
maisons.
verb **1** bloquer [1] (*an exit or a*

road); **2** boucher [1] (*a drain or a hole*); **the sink's blocked** l'évier est bouché.

blonde *adjective* blond.

blood *noun* sang M.

blood test *noun* prise F de sang.

blotchy *adjective* (*skin*) marbré.

blouse *noun* chemisier M.

blow *noun* coup M.
verb **1** (*the wind or a person*) souffler [1]; **2** (*in an explosion*) **the bomb blew a hole in the wall** la bombe a fait un trou dans le mur; **3 to blow your nose** se moucher [1].
● **to blow something out** souffler [1] (*a candle*); éteindre [60] (*flames*).
● **to blow up** (*explode*) exploser [1].
● **to blow something up** gonfler [1] (*a balloon or tyre*); faire [10] sauter (*a building*); **they blew up the president's residence** ils ont fait sauter la résidence du président.

blow-dry *noun* brushing M; **a cut and blow-dry** une coupe brushing.

blue *adjective* bleu; **blue eyes** les yeux bleus.

bluebell *noun* jacinthe F des bois.

blues *plural noun* le blues M singular.

blunder *noun* gaffe F.

blunt *adjective* **1** (*a knife or scissors*) émoussé; **2** (*a pencil*) mal taillé; **3** (*person*) brusque.

blurred *adjective* **1** indistinct; **2** (*photo*) flou.

blush *verb* rougir [2].

board *noun* **1** (*plank*) planche F; **2** (*blackboard*) tableau M noir; **3** (*notice board*) panneau M d'affichage; **4** (*for a board game*) jeu M; **5 a chess board** un échiquier; **6** (*accommodation in a hotel*) **full board** pension F complète; **half board** demi-pension F; **7 on board** à bord; **they were on board the ferry** ils étaient à bord du ferry.

boarder *noun* (*in a school*) interne M & F.

board game *noun* jeu M de société (*plural* jeux de société).

boarding *noun* embarquement M.

boarding card *noun* carte F d'embarquement.

boarding school *noun* école F privée avec internat.

boast *verb* se vanter [1]; **he was boasting about his new bike** il se vantait de son nouveau vélo.

boat *noun* **1** (*in general*) bateau M; **2** (*sailing boat*) voilier M; **3** (*rowing boat*) barque F.

body *noun* **1** corps M; **2** (*corpse*) cadavre M.

bodybuilding *noun* culturisme M.

bodyguard *noun* garde M du corps.

boil *noun* **1 bring the water to the boil** portez l'eau à ébullition; **2** (*swelling*) furoncle M.
verb **1** bouillir [23]; **the water's boiling** l'eau bout; **2** faire [10] bouillir; **I'm going to boil some water** je vais faire bouillir de l'eau; **to boil vegetables** faire [10] cuire

des légumes à l'eau bouillante; **to boil an egg** faire cuire un œuf.
●**to boil over** déborder [1].

boiled egg noun œuf M à la coque.

boiler noun (for central heating) chaudière F.

boiling adjective **1** (water) bouillant; **2 it's boiling hot today!** il fait une chaleur infernale aujourd'hui!

bolt noun (on a door) verrou M.
verb (to lock) verrouiller [1] (a door).

bomb noun bombe F.
verb bombarder [1].

bombing noun **1** (in a war) bombardement M; **2** (a terrorist attack) attentat M à la bombe.

bone noun **1** os M; **2** (of a fish) arête F.

bonfire noun **1** (for rubbish) feu M de jardin; **2** (for a celebration) feu M de joie.

bonnet noun capot M (of a car).

book noun **1** (that you read) livre M; **a book about dinosaurs** un livre sur les dinosaures; **a biology book** un livre de biologie; **2 an exercise book** un cahier; **3** (of cheques, stamps, tickets, etc) carnet M; **a cheque book** un carnet de chèques.
verb réserver [1]; **I booked a table for 8 pm** j'ai réservé une table pour vingt heures.

bookcase noun bibliothèque F.

booking noun (for a theatre or a holiday, for example) réservation F.

booking office noun bureau M de location.

booklet noun brochure F.

bookshelf noun étagère F.

bookshop noun librairie F.

boot noun **1** (for football, walking, climbing, or skiing) chaussure F; **walking boots** des chaussures de randonnée; **2** (short fashion boot) bottine F; **3** (knee-high boot or wellington) botte F; **4** (of a car) coffre M.

border noun (between countries) frontière F; **at the border** à la frontière.

bore noun **1** (a boring person) raseur M, raseuse F (informal); **2** (a nuisance) **what a bore!** quelle barbe!

bored adjective **to be bored** s'ennuyer; **I'm bored** je m'ennuie; **to get bored** s'ennuyer.

boring adjective ennuyeux (F ennuyeuse).

born adjective né; **to be born** naître [55]; **she was born in June** elle est née en juin.

borrow verb **1** emprunter [1]; **can I borrow your bike?** puis-je t'emprunter ton vélo?; **to borrow something from someone** emprunter quelque chose à quelqu'un; **I'll borrow some money from Dad** je vais emprunter de l'argent à Papa.

Bosnia noun Bosnie F.

boss noun patron M, patronne F.

bossy adjective autoritaire.

both pronoun 1 (of people) tous les deux (F toutes les deux); **they both came** ils sont venus tous les deux; **both my sisters were there** mes sœurs y étaient toutes les deux; 2 (of things) les deux; **they are both sold** les deux sont vendus; **both my feet** mes deux pieds; 3 **both at home and at school** à la maison comme à l'école; **both in summer and in winter** en été comme en hiver.

bother noun ennui M; **I've had a lot of bother with the car** j'ai eu beaucoup d'ennuis avec la voiture; **it's too much bother** c'est trop de tracas; **it's no bother** ce n'est pas un problème; **without any bother** sans aucune difficulté.
verb 1 (to disturb) déranger [52]; **I'm sorry to bother you** je suis désolé de vous déranger; 2 (to worry) inquiéter [24]; **that doesn't bother me at all** ça ne m'inquiète pas du tout; **don't bother about dinner** ne t'inquiète pas pour le dîner; 3 **she didn't even bother to come** elle n'a même pas pris la peine de venir; **don't bother!** ce n'est pas la peine!

bottle noun bouteille F.

bottle bank noun conteneur M à verre.

bottle opener noun ouvre-bouteille M.

bottom noun 1 (of a hill, a wall, or steps) pied M; **at the bottom of the ladder** au pied de l'échelle; 2 (of a bag or a bottle, a hole, a stretch of water, or a garden) fond M; **at the bottom of the lake** au fond du lac; 3 **at the bottom of the page** en bas de la page; 4 (buttocks) derrière M.

adjective 1 inférieur; **the bottom shelf** le rayon inférieur; 2 (a division, team, or place) dernier (F dernière); 3 **the bottom sheet** le drap de dessous; **the bottom flat** l'appartement du rez-de-chaussée.

bounce verb rebondir [2].

bouncer noun videur M.

bound adjective (certain) **he's bound to be late** il va sûrement être en retard; **that was bound to happen** cela devait arriver.

boundary noun limite F; (for sports) limites F plural du terrain.

bow noun 1 (in a shoelace or ribbon) nœud M; 2 (for a violin) archet M; 3 **a bow and arrow** un arc et une flèche.

bowels plural noun intestins M plural.

bowl noun 1 (for cereal, for example) bol M; 2 (larger, for salad or mixing) saladier M; 3 (for washing up) cuvette F.
verb lancer [61] (a ball).

bowler noun (in cricket) lanceur M.

bowling noun (tenpin) bowling M; **to go bowling** jouer au bowling.

bow tie noun nœud M papillon.

box noun 1 boîte F; **a box of chocolates** une boîte de chocolats; 2 **a cardboard box** un carton; 3 (on an application form) case F.

boxer noun 1 (fighter) boxeur M; 2 (dog) boxer M.

boxer shorts plural noun caleçon M singular.

boxing noun 1 boxe F; 2 **a boxing match** un match de boxe.

Boxing Day noun le lendemain de Noël.

box office noun guichet M.

boy noun garçon M; **a little boy** un petit garçon.

boyfriend noun copain M.

bra noun soutien-gorge M.

brace noun (for teeth) appareil M.

bracelet noun bracelet M.

bracket noun **in brackets** entre parenthèses.

brain noun cerveau M (plural cerveaux).

brainwave noun idée F géniale.

brake noun frein M.
verb freiner [1].

bramble noun ronce F.

branch noun 1 (of a tree) branche F; 2 (of a shop) succursale F; **our Oxford branch** notre succursale à Oxford; 3 (of a bank) agence F.

brand noun marque F.

brand new adjective tout neuf (F toute neuve).

brandy noun cognac M.

brass noun 1 (the metal) laiton M; 2 (in an orchestra) **the brass** les cuivres M plural.

brass band noun fanfare F.

brave adjective courageux (F courageuse).

bread noun pain M; **a slice of bread** une tranche de pain.

break noun 1 (a short rest) pause F; **fifteen minutes' break** une pause de quinze minutes; **to take a break** faire une pause; 2 (in school) récréation F; 3 **the Christmas break** les vacances de Noël.
verb 1 casser [1]; **he broke a glass** il a cassé un verre; **I broke a tooth/my arm** je me suis cassé une dent/le bras; 2 se casser [1]; **the eggs broke** les œufs se sont cassés; 3 **to break your arm** se casser le bras; 4 **to break your promise** manquer [1] à sa promesse; **he broke the rules** il n'a pas respecté les règlements; **you mustn't break the rules** il faut respecter les règlements; 5 **to break a record** battre [21] un record; 6 **to break the news** annoncer [61] la nouvelle.
● **to break down** tomber [1] en panne; **the car broke down** la voiture est tombée en panne.
● **to break in** (a thief) entrer [1] par effraction.
● **to break out** 1 (a fire) se déclarer [1]; 2 (a fight or a storm) éclater [1]; 3 (a prisoner) s'évader [1].
● **to break up** 1 (a family or couple) se séparer [1]; 2 (a crowd or clouds) se disperser [1]; 3 (for the holidays) **we break up on Thursday** les cours finissent jeudi.

breakdown noun 1 (of a vehicle) panne F; **we had a breakdown on the motorway** nous sommes tombés en panne sur l'autoroute; 2 (in talks or negotiations) rupture F; 3 (a nervous collapse) dépression F; **to have a (nervous) breakdown** faire une dépression.

breakdown truck noun camion M de dépannage.

breakfast noun petit déjeuner M; **we have breakfast at eight** nous prenons le petit déjeuner à huit heures.

break-in noun cambriolage M.

breast noun 1 (a woman's) sein M; 2 (of a chicken or other fowl) blanc M.

breaststroke noun brasse F.

breath noun 1 (when you breathe in) souffle M; **out of breath** à bout de souffle; **to get one's breath** reprendre son souffle; **to take a deep breath** respirer profondément; 2 (when you breathe out) haleine F; **to have bad breath** avoir mauvaise haleine.

breathe verb respirer [1].

breathing noun respiration F.

breed noun (of dog, for example) race F.
verb 1 élever [50] (animals); 2 (to have babies) se reproduire [26]; **rabbits breed fast** les lapins se reproduisent vite.

breeze noun brise F.

brew verb 1 préparer [1] (tea); 2 brasser [1] (beer).

brick noun brique F; **a brick wall** un mur de briques.

bride noun mariée F; **the bride and groom** les mariés M plural.

bridegroom noun marié M.

bridesmaid noun demoiselle F d'honneur.

bridge noun 1 (over a river) pont M; **a bridge over the Thames** un pont sur la Tamise; 2 (card game) bridge M; **to play bridge** jouer au bridge.

bridle noun bride F.

brief adjective bref (F brève).

briefcase noun serviette F.

briefly adjective brièvement.

briefs plural noun slip M.

bright adjective 1 (colour, light) vif (F vive); **bright green socks** des chaussettes vert vif; 2 **bright sunshine** un soleil éclatant; 3 (clever) intelligent; **she's not very bright** elle n'est pas très intelligente; ★ **to look on the bright side** voir le bon côté des choses.

brighten up verb **the weather's brightening up** le temps s'éclaircit.

brilliant adjective 1 (very clever) brillant; **a brilliant surgeon** un chirurgien brillant; **he's brilliant at maths** il est très doué en maths; 2 (wonderful) génial (M plural géniaux) (informal); **the party was brilliant!** le boum était génial!

bring verb 1 apporter [1] (something you carry); **they brought a present** ils ont apporté un cadeau; **bring your camera!** apporte ton appareil-photo!; **it brings good luck** ça porte bonheur; 2 amener [50] (a person or an animal); **she's bringing all the children** elle va amener tous les enfants; 3 **to bring something back** rapporter [1] quelque chose; 4 **to bring up** élever [50] (children); **he was brought up by his aunt** il a été élevé par sa tante.

bristle noun poil M.

Britain, Great Britain noun Grande-Bretagne F; **in Britain** en Grande-Bretagne; **to Britain** en Grande-Bretagne; **Britain is sending aid** la Grande-Bretagne envoie de l'aide.

British plural noun **the British** les Britanniques; **the British love animals** les Britanniques adorent les animaux.
adjective britannique; **the British army** l'armée britannique; **the British Isles** les îles Britanniques.

Brittany noun Bretagne F; **in Brittany** en Bretagne; **to Brittany** en Bretagne.

broad adjective (wide) large.

broad bean noun fève F.

broadcast noun émission F.
verb diffuser [1] (a programme).

broccoli noun brocolis M plural; **to eat broccoli** manger des brocolis.

brochure noun brochure F.

broke adjective **to be broke** (no money) être fauché (informal).

broken adjective cassé; **the window's broken** la vitre est cassée; **to have a broken leg** avoir la jambe cassée.

bronchitis noun bronchite F; **to have bronchitis** avoir une bronchite.

brooch noun broche F.

broom noun 1 (for sweeping) balai M; 2 (bush) genêt M.

brother noun frère M; **my little**

brother mon petit frère; **my mother's brother** le frère de ma mère.

brother-in-law noun beau-frère M (plural beaux-frères).

brown adjective 1 marron (does not change in the feminine or plural); **my brown jacket** ma veste marron; **your brown shoes** tes chaussures marron; **light brown** marron clair; **dark brown** marron foncé; 2 châtain (hair); 3 (tanned in the sun) bronzé; **to go brown** bronzer.

brown bread noun pain M complet.

brown sugar noun sucre M brun.

bruise noun 1 (on a person) bleu M; 2 (on fruit) tache F.

brush noun 1 (for your hair, clothes, nails, or shoes) brosse F; **my hair brush** ma brosse à cheveux; 2 (for sweeping) balai M; 3 (paintbrush) pinceau M.
verb brosser [1] (the floor or your clothes); **to brush your hair** se brosser les cheveux; **she brushed her hair** elle s'est brossé les cheveux; **to brush your teeth** se brosser les dents.

Brussels noun Bruxelles.

Brussels sprout noun chou M de Bruxelles.

bubble noun bulle F.

bubble bath noun bain M moussant.

bucket noun seau M (plural seaux).

buckle noun boucle F.

Buddhism noun bouddhisme M.

Buddhist noun bouddhiste M & F.

budget noun budget M.

budgie noun perruche F.

buffet noun buffet M.

buffet car noun voiture F bar.

bug noun 1 (insect) bestiole F (informal); 2 (germ) microbe F; a stomach bug une gastroentérite; 3 (in a computer) bug M.

build verb construire [26]; they are building three houses over there ils construisent trois maisons là-bas.

builder noun maçon M.

building noun bâtiment M; (with offices or flats) immeuble M.

building site noun chantier M.

built-up adjective urbanisé; a built-up area une agglomération.

bulb noun 1 (for a light) ampoule F; 2 (that you plant) bulbe M.

bull noun taureau M (plural taureaux).

bulldozer noun bulldozer M.

bullet noun balle F.

bulletin noun bulletin M; a news bulletin un bulletin d'informations.

bully noun brute F; he's a bully c'est une brute.
verb tyranniser [1].

bum noun (bottom) derrière M.

bump noun 1 (that sticks up) bosse F; a bump on the head une bosse à la tête; a bump in the road une bosse sur la route; 2 (jolt) secousse F; 3 (noise) bruit M sourd.
verb 1 (to bang) cogner [1]; I bumped my head je me suis cogné la tête; 2 to bump into something rentrer [1] dans quelque chose; 3 to bump into somebody (meet by chance) croiser [1] quelqu'un.

bumper noun pare-chocs M.

bumpy adjective 1 accidenté (road); 2 agité (plane landing).

bun noun 1 (for a burger) petit pain M; 2 (sugary) petit cake M.

bunch noun 1 (of flowers) bouquet M; 2 (of carrots or radishes) botte F; 3 (of keys) trousseau M; 4 a bunch of grapes une grappe de raisin.

bundle noun tas M.

bungalow noun pavillon M.

bunk noun 1 (on a train or boat) couchette F; 2 bunk beds des lits superposés.

bureau noun agence F.

burger noun hamburger M.

burglar noun cambrioleur M.

burglar alarm noun sonnerie F d'alarme.

burglary noun cambriolage M.

burn noun brûlure F.
verb 1 brûler [1]; I've burned the rubbish j'ai brûlé les ordures; the fire's burning well le feu brûle bien; she burnt herself on the grill elle s'est brûlée au grill; you'll burn your finger! tu vas te brûler le doigt!; 2 laisser [1] brûler (something you're cooking); Mum's burnt her cake maman a laissé brûler son gâteau;

3 (*through sunburn*) **I burn easily** j'attrape facilement des coups de soleil.

burnt *adjective* brûlé.

burst *verb* 1 crever [50] (*a balloon or tyre, for example*); **a burst tyre** un pneu crevé; 2 **to burst out laughing** éclater [1] de rire; 3 **to burst into tears** fondre [3] en larmes; 4 **to burst into flames** prendre [64] feu.

bury *verb* enterrer [1].

bus *noun* 1 (*public transport*) autobus M, bus M; **we'll take the bus** on va prendre le bus; **on the bus** dans le bus; **a bus ticket** un ticket de bus; **a bus stop** un arrêt de bus; 2 (*coach*) car M; **to go to London by bus** aller à Londres en car.

bus driver *noun* conducteur de bus M, conductrice de bus F.

bush *noun* buisson M.

business *noun* 1 (*commercial dealings*) affaires F *plural*; **to be in business** être dans les affaires; **he's in business in Leeds** il est à Leeds en voyage d'affaires; **he's in the insurance business** il travaille dans l'assurance; **a business letter** une lettre d'affaires; 2 (*firm or company*) entreprise F; **small businesses** les petites entreprises; 3 **mind your own business!** occupe-toi de tes affaires!; **that's my business!** ça me regarde!

business class *noun* classe F d'affaires.

businessman *noun* homme M d'affaires.

business trip *noun* voyage M d'affaires.

businesswoman *noun* femme F d'affaires.

bus pass *noun* carte F de bus.

bus route *noun* ligne F d'autobus.

bus shelter *noun* abribus™ M.

bus station *noun* gare F routière.

bust *noun* **bust size** tour M de poitrine.

busy *adjective* 1 occupé (*a person*); chargé (*a day or week*); **don't disturb him, he's busy** ne le dérange pas, il est occupé; 2 **a busy day** une journée chargée; 3 (*full of cars or people*) **the shops were busy** il y avait beaucoup de monde dans les magasins; 4 (*phone*) **the line's busy** la ligne est occupée.

but *conjunction* mais; **small but strong** petit mais fort; **not Thursday but Friday** pas jeudi mais vendredi; **I'll try, but it's difficult** j'essaierai, mais c'est difficile.
preposition sauf; **anything but that** tout, sauf ça; **everyone but Roger** tout le monde sauf Roger; **the last but one** l'avant-dernier.

butcher *noun* boucher M; **he's a butcher** il est boucher; **the butcher's** la boucherie.

butter *noun* beurre M.
verb beurrer [1].

buttercup *noun* bouton M d'or.

butterfly *noun* papillon M.

button *noun* bouton M.

buttonhole noun boutonnière F.

buy noun **a good buy** une bonne affaire; **a bad buy** une mauvaise affaire.
verb **1** acheter [16]; **I bought the tickets** j'ai acheté les billets; **to buy something for somebody** acheter quelque chose à quelqu'un; **Sarah bought him a sweater** Sarah lui a acheté un pull; **to buy something from someone** acheter quelque chose à quelqu'un; **I bought a bike from Tim** j'ai acheté un vélo à Tim.

buzz verb (a fly or bee) bourdonner [1].

buzzer noun sonnerie F.

by preposition **1** par; **by telephone** par téléphone; **to take somebody by the hand** prendre quelqu'un par la main; **eaten by a dog** mangé par un chien; **by mistake** par erreur; **2** (travel) en; **to come by bus** venir en bus; **by bike** en vélo; **to leave by train** partir en train; **3** (near) à côté de; **by the fire** à côté du feu; **by the sea** au bord de la mer; **close by** tout près; **4** (before) avant; **ready by Monday** prêt avant lundi; **Kevin was back by four** Kevin est rentré avant quatre heures; **5** **by yourself** tout seul; **I was by myself in the house** j'étais tout seul chez moi; **she did it by herself** elle l'a fait toute seule; **6** **by the way** au fait; **7** **to go by** passer.

bye exclamation au revoir; **bye for now!** à bientôt!

bypass noun rocade F.

C c

cab noun **1** taxi M; **to call a cab** appeler un taxi; **2** (on a lorry) cabine F.

cabbage noun chou M (plural choux).

cable noun câble M.

cable car noun téléférique M.

cable television noun télévision F par câble.

cactus noun cactus M.

café noun café M.

cage noun cage F.

cagoule noun K-way™ M.

cake noun gâteau M (plural gâteaux); **would you like a piece of cake?** veux-tu un morceau de gâteau?

calculate verb calculer [1].

calculation noun calcul M.

calculator noun calculatrice F.

calendar noun calendrier M.

calf noun **1** (animal) veau M; **2** (of your leg) mollet.

call noun **1** (telephone) appel M; **I had several calls this morning** j'ai eu plusieurs appels ce matin; **thank you for your call** merci de votre appel; **a phone call** un coup de téléphone.
verb **1** appeler [18]; **to call a taxi** appeler un taxi; **to call the doctor**

appeler le médecin; **they called the police** ils ont appelé la police; **call this number** appelez ce numéro; **thank you for calling** merci de votre appel; **I'll call you back later** je te rappellerai plus tard; **2** appeler [18]; **they've called the baby Julie** ils ont appelé le bébé Julie; **3 to be called** s'appeler [18]; **she has a brother called Dan** elle a un frère qui s'appelle Dan; **what's he called?** il s'appelle comment?

call box noun cabine F téléphonique.

calm adjective calme.
verb calmer [1];
● **to calm down** se calmer; **he's calmed down a bit** il s'est calmé un peu;
● **to calm somebody down** calmer quelqu'un; **I tried to calm her down** j'ai essayé de la calmer.

calmly adverb calmement.

calorie noun calorie F.

camcorder noun caméscope M.

camel noun chameau M.

camera noun **1** appareil M photo (plural appareils photo); **2** (film or TV camera) caméra.

cameraman noun caméraman M.

camp noun camp M.
verb camper [1].

campaign noun campagne F.

camper van noun camping-car M.

camping noun camping M; **to go camping** faire du camping; **we're going camping in Brittany this summer** nous allons faire du camping en Bretagne cet été.

campsite noun terrain M de camping.

can[1] noun **1** boîte F; **a can of tomatoes** une boîte de tomates; **2** (for petrol or oil) bidon M.

can[2] verb **1** pouvoir [12]; **I can't be there before ten** je ne peux pas y être avant dix heures; **you can leave your bag here** tu peux laisser ton sac ici; **can you open the door, please?** peux-tu ouvrir la porte, s'il te plaît?; **can I help you?** est-ce que je peux vous aider?; **they couldn't come** ils n'ont pas pu venir; **you could ring back tomorrow** tu pourrais rappeler demain; **you could have told me** tu aurais pu me le dire; **2** (not translated) **can you hear me?** est-ce que tu m'entends?; **I can't see him** je ne le vois pas; **I can't remember** je ne me souviens pas; **I can't find my keys** je ne trouve pas mes clés; **3** (know how to) savoir [70]; **she can't drive** elle ne sait pas conduire; **can you play the piano?** est-ce que tu sais jouer du piano?

Canada noun Canada M; **to Canada** au Canada; **in Canada** au Canada.

Canadian noun Canadien M, Canadienne F.
adjective canadien (F canadienne).

canal noun canal M (plural canaux).

cancel verb annuler [1]; **the concert's been cancelled** le concert a été annulé.

cancer noun cancer M; **to have lung cancer** avoir un cancer du poumon.

Cancer noun Cancer M; **I'm Cancer** je suis Cancer.

candidate noun candidat M, candidate F.

candle noun bougie F.

candlestick noun bougeoir M.

candyfloss noun barbe F à papa.

canned adjective en conserve; **canned tomatoes** les tomates en conserve.

cannot verb SEE can[2]

canoe noun canoë M.

canoeing noun **to go canoeing** faire du canoë; **I like canoeing** j'aime faire du canoë.

can-opener noun ouvre-boîte M.

canteen noun cantine F.

canvas noun toile F.

cap noun 1 (hat) casquette F; **a baseball cap** une casquette de baseball; 2 (on a bottle or tube) bouchon M.

capable adjective capable.

capacity noun capacité F.

capital noun 1 (city) capital F; **Paris is the capital of France** Paris est la capitale de la France; 2 (letter) majuscule F; **in capitals** en majuscules.

capitalism noun capitalisme M.

Capricorn noun Capricorne M; **Linda's Capricorn** Linda est Capricorne.

capsize verb chavirer [1].

captain noun capitaine M.

capture verb capturer [1].

car noun voiture F; **in the car** dans la voiture; **to park the car** garer la voiture; **we're going by car** nous y allons en voiture; **a car crash** un accident de voiture.

caramel noun caramel M.

caravan noun caravane F.

card noun carte F; **un jeu de cartes** a card game; **a pack of cards**; **faire une partie de cartes** to have a game of cards.

cardboard noun carton M.

cardigan noun cardigan M.

cardphone noun téléphone M à carte.

care noun 1 soin M; **to take care to do** prendre soin de faire; 2 **to take care of somebody** s'occuper de quelqu'un; 3 **take care!** (be careful) fais attention!; (when saying goodbye) à bientôt!

verb 1 **to care about** se soucier de; **to care about pollution** se soucier de la pollution; 2 **she doesn't care** ça lui est égal; **I couldn't care less!** ça m'est complètement égal!

career noun carrière F.

careful adjective prudent; 1 **a careful driver** un conducteur prudent; 2 **be careful!** fais attention!

carefully adverb 1 **read the instructions carefully** lisez attentivement les instructions; **listen carefully** écoutez bien; 2 (handle) avec précaution; **she put the vase down carefully** elle a posé le vase avec précaution; 3 **to copy**

something carefully recopier soigneusement quelque chose; **4 drive carefully!** sois prudent!

careless *adjective* **1 he's very careless** il ne fait pas du tout attention à ce qu'il fait; **2 this is careless work** c'est du travail peu soigné; **a careless mistake** une faute d'inattention; **3 careless driving** la conduite imprudente.

caretaker *noun* gardien M, gardienne F.

car ferry *noun* ferry M.

car hire *noun* location F de voitures.

Caribbean *noun* **1 the Caribbean (islands)** les Caraïbes; **2 the Caribbean (sea)** la mer des Caraïbes.

carnation *noun* œillet M.

carnival *noun* carnaval M.

car park *noun* parking M.

carpenter *noun* menuisier M.

carpentry *noun* menuiserie F.

carpet *noun* **1** (*fitted*) moquette F; **2** (*loose*) tapis M.

car phone *noun* téléphone F de voiture.

car radio *noun* autoradio M.

carriage *noun* (*of a train*) voiture F.

carrier bag *noun* sac M en plastique.

carrot *noun* carotte F.

carry *verb* **1** porter [1]; **she was carrying a parcel** elle portait un paquet; **2** (*vehicle, plane*)

transporter [1]; **the coach was carrying schoolchildren** le car transportait des écoliers.

● **to carry on** continuer [1]; **they carried on talking** ils ont continué à parler.

carrycot *noun* porte-bébé M.

carsick *adjective* **to be carsick** avoir le mal de la route.

carton *noun* **1** (*of cream or yoghurt*) pot M; **2** (*of milk or orange*) brique F.

cartoon *noun* **1** (*a film*) dessin M animé; **2** (*a comic strip*) bande F dessinée; **3** (*an amusing drawing*) dessin M humoristique.

cartridge *noun* (*for a pen or a video*) cartouche F.

carve *verb* découper [1] (*meat*).

case¹ *noun* **1** (*suitcase*) valise F; **to pack a case** faire une valise; **2** (*a large wooden box, for wine for example*) caisse F; **3** (*for spectacles or small things*) étui M.

case² *noun* **1** cas M; **in that case** en ce cas; **that's not the case** ce n'est pas le cas; **a case of flu** un cas de grippe; **2** (*in case*) au cas où; **in case he's late** au cas où il serait en retard; **check first, just in case** vérifie d'abord, au cas où; **3 in any case** de toute façon; **in any case, it's too late** de toute façon, c'est trop tard.

cash *noun* **1** (*money in general*) argent M; **I haven't any cash on me** je n'ai pas d'argent sur moi; **2** (*money rather than a cheque*) espèces F *plural*; **to pay in cash**

payer en espèces; **£50 in cash** cinquante livres en espèces.

cash card *noun* carte F de retrait.

cash desk *noun* caisse F; **pay at the cash desk** payez à la caisse.

cash dispenser *noun* guichet M automatique.

cashew *noun* cajou M.

cashier *noun* caissier M, caissière F.

cash point *noun* = cash dispenser.

cassette *noun* cassette F.

cassette recorder *noun* magnétophone M à cassettes.

cast *noun* les acteurs M *plural*; **the cast were on stage** les acteurs étaient sur scène.

castle *noun* 1 château M (*plural* châteaux); 2 (*in chess*) tour F.

casual *adjective* décontracté.

casualty *noun* 1 (*in an accident*) victime F; **there are 17 casualties** il y a dix-sept victimes; 2 (*hospital department*) urgences F *plural*; **he's in casualty** il est aux urgences.

cat *noun* chat M; (*female*) chatte F; **a big black cat** un gros chat noir; ★ **it's raining cats and dogs** il pleut des cordes (*literally: it's raining in ropes*).

catalogue *noun* catalogue M.

catastrophe *noun* catastrophe F.

catch *noun* 1 (*on a door*) fermeture F; 2 (*a drawback*) piège M; **what's the catch?** où est le piège? *verb* 1 attraper [1]; **Tom caught the** ball Tom a attrapé le ballon; **you can't catch me!** vous ne m'attraperez pas!; **can you catch hold of the branch?** peux-tu attraper la branche?; 2 **to catch somebody doing** attraper quelqu'un en train de faire; **he was caught stealing money** il a été attrapé en train de voler de l'argent; 3 prendre [64] (*a bus or plane*); **did Tim catch his plane?** est-ce que Tim a pris son avion? 4 attraper [1] (*an illness*); **he's caught chickenpox** il a attrapé la varicelle; **I've caught a cold** j'ai attrapé un rhume; 5 saisir [2] (*what somebody says*); **I didn't catch your name** je n'ai pas saisi votre nom.

● **to catch up with somebody** rattraper [1] quelqu'un.

category *noun* catégorie F.

catering *noun* restauration F.

caterpillar *noun* chenille F.

cathedral *noun* cathédrale F; **Winchester cathedral** la cathédrale de Winchester.

Catholic *noun, adjective* catholique M & F.

cattle *plural noun* bétail M singular.

cauliflower *noun* chou-fleur M (*plural* choux-fleurs); **cauliflower cheese** un gratin de chou-fleur.

cause *noun* cause F; **the cause of the accident** la cause de l'accident; **for a good cause** pour une bonne cause. *verb* 1 causer [1] (*damage or problems*); **to cause problems** causer des problèmes; 2 provoquer

[1] (*chaos or disease*); **the strike caused delays** la grève a provoqué des retards.

caution *noun* prudence F.

cautious *adjective* prudent.

cave *noun* grotte F.

caving *noun* spéléologie F; **to go caving** faire de la spéléologie.

CD *noun* CD M.

CD player *noun* platine F laser.

CD-ROM *noun* CD-ROM M.

ceiling *noun* plafond M; **on the ceiling** au plafond.

celebrate *verb* fêter [1]; **I'm celebrating my birthday** je fête mon anniversaire.

celebrity *noun* célébrité F.

celery *noun* céleri M.

cell *noun* cellule F.

cellar *noun* cave F.

cello *noun* violoncelle M; **to play the cello** jouer du violoncelle.

cement *noun* ciment M.

cemetery *noun* cimetière M.

centenary *noun* centenaire M.

centigrade *adjective* centigrade; **ten degrees centigrade** dix degrés centigrade.

centimetre *noun* centimètre M.

central *adjective* central (M *plural* centraux); **central London** le centre de Londres; **the office is very central** le bureau est en plein centre-ville.

central heating *noun* chauffage M central.

centre *noun* centre M; **in the centre of** au centre de; **in the town centre** en centre-ville; **a shopping centre** un centre commercial.

century *noun* siècle M; **in the twentieth century** au vingtième siècle; **the twenty-first century** le vingt-et-unième siècle.

cereal *noun* **breakfast cereal** céréales F *plural* pour le petit déjeuner; **to have cereal for breakfast** prendre des céréales au petit déjeuner.

ceremony *noun* cérémonie F.

certain *adjective* certain; **a certain number of** un certain nombre de; **are you certain of the address?** es-tu certain de l'adresse?; **I'm certain of it** j'en suis certain; **to be certain that** être sûr que; **Nicola's certain you're wrong** Nicola est sûre que tu as tort; **nobody knows for certain** personne ne sait au juste.

certainly *adverb* certainement; **certainly not** certainement pas.

certificate *noun* **1** certificat M; **2 a birth certificate** un acte de naissance.

chain *noun* chaîne F.

chair *noun* **1** (*upright*) chaise F; **a kitchen chair** une chaise de cuisine; **2** (*with arms*) fauteuil F.

chair lift *noun* télésiège M.

chalet *noun* **1** (*in the mountains*) chalet M; **2** (*in a holiday camp*) bungalow M.

chalk noun craie F.

challenge noun 1 (*that excites you*) challenge M; **the challenge of new ideas** le challenge des nouvelles idées; 2 (*that is difficult*) épreuve F; **the exam was a real challenge** l'examen était une vraie épreuve.

champion noun champion M, championne F; **world champion** champion du monde.

chance noun 1 (*an opportunity*) occasion F; **to have the chance to do** avoir l'occasion de faire; **if you have the chance to go to New York** si tu as l'occasion d'aller à New York; **I haven't had the chance to write to him** je n'ai pas eu l'occasion de lui écrire; 2 (*likelihood*) chance F; **there's little chance of winning** il y a peu de chance de gagner; 3 (*luck*) **by chance** par hasard; **do you have her address, by any chance?** aurais-tu par hasard son adresse?

change noun 1 changement M; **a change of plan** un changement de programme; **they've made some changes to the house** ils ont fait des changements dans la maison; **for a change, let's eat out** mangeons au restaurant pour changer; **it makes a change from hamburgers** cela change un peu des hamburgers; 2 **a change of clothes** des vêtements de rechange; 3 (*cash*) monnaie F; **I haven't any change** je n'ai pas de monnaie.

verb 1 (*transform completely*) changer [52]; **it changed my life** cela m'a changé la vie; **Liz never changes** Liz ne change jamais; 2 (*to switch from one thing to*

another) changer de [52]; **we changed trains at Crewe** nous avons changé de train à Crewe; **I must change my shirt** je dois changer de chemise; **they changed places** ils ont changé de place; **to change your mind** changer d'avis; 3 (*to exchange in a shop*) échanger [52]; **can I change it for the larger size?** puis-je l'échanger contre la taille au-dessus?; 4 (*to change your clothes*) se changer [52]; **Mike's gone up to change** Mike est monté se changer.

changing room noun (*for sport or swimming*) 1 vestiaire M; 2 (*in a shop*) salon M d'essayage.

channel noun (*on TV*) chaîne F; **to change channels** changer de chaîne; 2 **the Channel** la Manche.

Channel Islands plural noun îles F plural Anglo-Normandes.

Channel Tunnel noun tunnel M sous la Manche.

chaos noun pagaille F (*informal*); **it was chaos!** c'était la pagaille!

chapel noun chapelle F.

chapter noun chapitre M; **in chapter two** au chapitre deux.

character noun 1 (*personality*) caractère M; **a house with a lot of character** une maison qui a du caractère; 2 (*somebody in a book, play, or film*) personnage M; **the main character** le personnage principal.

characteristic adjective caractéristique.

charcoal noun 1 (*for burning*)

charbon M de bois; **2** (*for drawing*) fusain M.

charge *noun* **1** (*what you pay*) frais M *plural*; **a booking charge** des frais de réservation; **an extra or additional charge** un supplément; **there's no charge** c'est gratuit; **2 to be in charge** être responsable; **who's in charge of these children?** qui est responsable de ces enfants?; **3 to be on a charge of theft** être inculpé de vol.

verb **1** (*to ask a specific sum*) prendre [64]; **they charge fifteen pounds an hour** ils vous font quinze livres de l'heure; **how much do you charge for one day?** combien prenez-vous pour une journée?; **2** (*to ask people to pay*) faire [10] payer; **we don't charge, it's free** nous ne faisons pas payer les gens, c'est gratuit; **3 to charge somebody with** inculper [1] quelqu'un de (*a crime*).

charity *noun* organisation F caritative.

charm *noun* charme M.

charming *adjective* charmant.

chart *noun* **1** (*table*) tableau M; **2 the weather chart** la carte du temps; **3 the charts** le hit-parade; **number one in the charts** numéro un au hit-parade.

charter flight *noun* vol M charter.

chase *noun* poursuite F; **a car chase** une poursuite en voiture. *verb* pourchasser [1] (*a person or animal*).

chat *noun* conversation F; **to have a chat with somebody** bavarder avec quelqu'un.

chat show *noun* talk-show M.

chatter *verb* **1** (*gossip*) bavarder [1]; **2 my teeth are chattering** je claque des dents.

cheap *adjective* pas cher (F pas chère); **cheap shoes** des chaussures pas chères; **that's very cheap!** ce n'est vraiment pas cher!

cheaper *adjective* moins cher (F moins chère).

cheaply *adverb* pas cher; **to eat cheaply** manger pas cher.

cheap rate *adjective* à tarif réduit; **a cheap rate phone call** un appel à tarif réduit.

cheat *noun* tricheur M, tricheuse F. *verb* tricher [1].

check *noun* **1** (*in a factory or at border controls*) contrôle M; **passport check** contrôle des passeports; **2** (*by a doctor*) examen M; **3** (*in chess*) **check!** échec au roi! *verb* **1** (*to make sure*) vérifier [1]; **he checked the time** il a vérifié l'heure; **check they're all back** vérifiez qu'ils sont tous rentrés; **check with your father** demande à ton père. ●**to check in** enregistrer [1] (*for a flight*).

check-in *noun* enregistrement M.

checkout *noun* caisse F; **at the checkout** à la caisse.

check-up *noun* examen M médical.

cheek *noun* **1** (*part of face*) joue

F; **2** (*nerve*) **what a cheek!** quel culot! (*informal*).

cheeky *adjective* **1** coquin; **2** (*rude*) impoli.

cheer *noun* **1** **three cheers for Tom!** faisons un ban à Tom! **2** (*when you have a drink*) **cheers!** à la vôtre!
verb (*to shout hurray*) applaudir [2].
●**to cheer up: cheer up!** courage!
●**to cheer somebody up** remonter [1] le moral à quelqu'un; **your visit's cheered me up** ta visite m'a remonté le moral.

cheerful *adjective* gai.

cheese *noun* fromage M; **blue cheese** le fromage bleu; **a cheese sandwich** un sandwich au fromage.

chef *noun* chef M cuisinier.

chemical *noun* chimie F.

chemist *noun* **1** pharmacien M, pharmacienne F; **2 chemist's pharmacie** F; **at the chemist's** à la pharmacie; **3** (*scientist*) chimiste M & F.

chemistry *noun* chimie F.

cheque *noun* chèque M; **to pay by cheque** payer par chèque; **to write a cheque** faire un chèque.

chequebook *noun* carnet M de chèques.

cherry *noun* cerise F.

chess *noun* échecs M *plural*; **to play chess** jouer aux échecs.

chessboard *noun* échiquier M.

chest *noun* **1** (*part of the body*)

poitrine F; **2** (*box*) coffre M; **3 a chest of drawers** une commode.

chestnut *noun* marrron M.

chestnut tree *noun* **1** (*horse-chestnut*) marronnier M; **2** (*sweet chestnut*) châtaignier M.

chew *verb* mâcher [1] (*food*).

chewing gum *noun* chewing-gum M.

chick *noun* (*of a hen*) poussin M.

chicken *noun* poulet M; **roast chicken** du poulet rôti; **chicken thighs** des cuisses de poulet; **a chicken sandwich** un sandwich au poulet.

chickenpox *noun* varicelle F.

chicory *noun* endive F.

child *noun* enfant M & F; **Jenny's children** les enfants de Jenny.

childish *adjective* puéril.

child-minder *noun* nourrice F.

chill *noun* fraîcheur F.

chilled *adjective* (*wine*) bien frais.

chilli *noun* piment M.

chilly *adjective* frisquet (F frisquette); **it's chilly today** il fait frisquet aujourd'hui.

chimney *noun* cheminée F.

chimpanzee *noun* chimpanzé M.

chin *noun* menton M.

china *noun* porcelaine F; **a china plate** une assiette en porcelaine.

China *noun* Chine F; **in China** en Chine.

Chinese noun 1 the Chinese (*people*) les Chinois; 2 (*language*) chinois M.
adjective chinois; a **Chinese man** un Chinois; a **Chinese woman** une Chinoise; a **Chinese meal** un repas chinois.

chip noun 1 (*fried potato*) frite F; I'd like some chips j'aimerais des frites; 2 (*microchip*) puce F; 3 (*in glass or china*) ébréchure F.

chipped adjective ébréché.

chives plural noun ciboulette F singular.

chocolate noun chocolat M; a **chocolate ice-cream** une glace au chocolat; **hot chocolate** chocolat M chaud; a **box of chocolates** une boîte de chocolats.

choice noun choix M; **you have a choice of two flights** vous avez le choix entre deux vols.

choir noun 1 (*in a school*) chorale F; **I sing in the choir** je fais partie de la chorale; 2 (*professional*) chœur M.

choke noun (*on a car*) starter M.
verb 1 (*by yourself*) s'étouffer [1]; **she was choking on a bone** elle s'étouffait avec une arête; 2 (*smoke or fumes*) étouffer [1].

choose verb choisir [2]; **you chose well** tu as bien choisi; **Cathy chose the red one** Cathy a choisi le rouge; **it's hard to choose from all these colours** il est difficile de choisir parmi toutes ces couleurs.

chop noun côtelette F; a **lamb chop** une côtelette d'agneau.
verb hacher [1].

chopstick noun baguette F.

chord noun accord M.

chorus noun 1 (*when you all join in the song*) refrain M; 2 (*a group of singers*) chœur M.

Christ noun le Christ.

christening noun baptême M.

Christian noun, adjective chrétien M, chrétienne F.

Christian name noun prénom M.

Christmas noun Noël M; at **Christmas** à Noël; Happy **Christmas!** Joyeux Noël!

Christmas card noun carte F de Noël.

Christmas carol noun chant M de Noël.

Christmas cracker noun diablotin M.

Christmas Day noun jour M de Noël.

Christmas dinner noun repas M de Noël.

Christmas Eve noun veille F de Noël; on **Christmas Eve** la veille de Noël.

Christmas present noun cadeau M de Noël.

Christmas tree noun sapin M de Noël.

chunk noun morceau M.

church noun église F; **to go to church** aller à l'église.

churchyard noun cimetière M.

chute noun (*in a swimming pool or playground*) toboggan M.

cider noun cidre M.

cigar noun cigare M.

cigarette noun cigarette F; **to light a cigarette** allumer une cigarette.

cinema noun cinéma M; **to go to the cinema** aller au cinéma.

circle noun cercle M; **to sit in a circle** s'asseoir en cercle; **to go round in circles** tourner en rond.

circuit noun 1 (*for athletes*) piste F; 2 (*for cars*) circuit M.

circumflex noun accent M circonflexe.

circumstances plural noun **under the circumstances** dans ces circonstances.

circus noun cirque M.

citizen noun citoyen M, citoyenne F.

city noun (*grande*) ville F; **the city of Paris** la ville de Paris.

city centre noun centre-ville M; **in the city centre** au centre-ville.

civilization noun civilisation F.

civil servant noun fonctionnaire M & F; **he's a civil servant** il est fonctionnaire.

civil war noun guerre civile F.

claim verb prétendre [3]; **he claimed to know** il prétendait savoir.

clap verb 1 applaudir [2]; **everyone clapped** tout le monde a applaudi; 2 **to clap your hands** battre [21] des mains.

clapping noun applaudissements M plural.

clarinet noun clarinette F; **to play the clarinet** jouer de la clarinette.

clash noun (*for example, between police and demonstrators*) affrontement M.
verb 1 (*rival groups*) s'affronter [1]; 2 (*colours*) jurer [1]; **the curtains clash with the wallpaper** les rideaux jurent avec le papier peint.

clasp noun (*of a necklace*) fermoir M.

class noun 1 (*a group of students or pupils*) classe F; **she's in the same class as me** elle est dans la même classe que moi; 2 (*a lesson*) cours M; **an art class** un cours de dessin; **in class** en cours; 3 (*division*) classe F; **a social class** une classe sociale.

classic adjective classique.

classical adjective classique; **classical music** la musique classique.

classroom noun classe F.

claw noun 1 (*of a cat or dog*) griffe F; 2 (*of a crab*) pince F.

clay noun 1 (*for modelling*) argile F; 2 **a clay court** (*in tennis*) un terrain en terre battue.

clean adjective 1 propre; **a clean shirt** une chemise propre; **my hands are clean** j'ai les mains propres; 2 (*germ-free*) pur (*air or water*).
verb nettoyer [39]; 1 **I cleaned the whole house** j'ai nettoyé toute la maison; 2 **to clean your teeth** se

laver [1] les dents; **I'm going to clean my teeth** je vais me laver les dents.

cleaner noun 1 (in a public place) agent M de nettoyage; 2 (cleaning lady) femme F de ménage; 3 a dry cleaner's un pressing.

cleaning noun to do the cleaning faire le ménage.

cleanser noun 1 (for the house) produit d'entretien; 2 (for your face) démaquillant M.

clear adjective 1 (that you can see through) transparent; **clear glass** du verre transparent; 2 (cloudless) clair; 3 (easy to understand) clair; **clear instructions** des instructions claires; **is that clear?** est-ce que c'est clair?; **it's clear that ...** il est clair que ...
verb 1 enlever [50] (papers, rubbish, or clothes); **have you cleared your stuff out of your room?** as-tu enlevé tes affaires de ta chambre?; 2 débarrasser [1] (a table or a room); **can I clear the table?** puis-je débarrasser la table?; 3 dégager [52] (a road or path); 4 (fog or snow) se dissiper [1]; **and then the fog cleared** et puis le brouillard s'est dissipé; 5 **to clear your throat** se racler [1] la gorge.
●**to clear something up** ranger [52] quelque chose; **I'll just clear up my books** je vais juste ranger mes livres.

clearly adjective 1 (to think, speak, or hear) clairement; 2 (obviously) manifestement; **she was clearly worried** manifestement, elle était inquiète.

clementine noun clémentine F.

clever adjective 1 intelligent; **their children are all very clever** leurs enfants sont tous très intelligents; 2 (ingenious) astucieux (F astucieuse); **a clever idea** une idée astucieuse.

client noun client M, cliente F.

cliff noun falaise F.

climate noun climat M.

climb verb 1 monter [1] (a hill, stairs); 2 faire [10] l'escalade de (a mountain); **we climbed Mont Blanc** nous avons fait l'escalade du Mont Blanc.

climber noun alpiniste M & F.

climbing noun escalade F; **they go climbing in Italy** ils font de l'escalade en Italie.

clinic noun centre M médical (plural centres médicaux).

clip noun 1 (from a film) extrait M; 2 (for your hair) barrette F.
verb 1 (to cut) couper [1]; 2 (to fasten) attacher [1].

cloakroom noun (for coats) vestiaire M.

clock noun (large) horloge F; (smaller) pendule F; **an alarm clock** un réveil; **to put the clocks forward an hour** avancer les pendules d'une heure; **to put the clocks back** reculer les pendules.

clock radio noun radio-réveil M.

close[1] adjective, adverb 1 (result) serré; 2 (friend or relation) proche; 3 (near) près; **the station's very close** la gare est tout près; **she lives close by** elle habite tout près;

close to the cinema près du cinéma; **not very close** pas très près.

close[2] *noun* fin F; **at the close** à la fin.
verb 1 fermer [1]; **close your eyes!** ferme les yeux!; **she closed the door** elle a fermé la porte; **the post office closes at six** la poste ferme à six heures.

closed *adjective* fermé; **'closed on Mondays'** 'fermé le lundi'.

closely *adverb* de près; **to examine something closely** regarder quelque chose de près.

closing date *noun* date F limite; **the closing date for entries** la date limite pour les inscriptions.

closing-down sale *noun* liquidation F.

closing time *noun* heure F de fermeture.

cloth *noun*
1 (*for the floor*) serpillière F;
2 (*for polishing*) chiffon M;
3 (*for drying up*) torchon M;
4 (*fabric by the metre*) tissu M.

clothes *plural noun* vêtements M *plural*; **to put your clothes on** s'habiller; **to take your clothes off** se déshabiller; **to change your clothes** se changer.

clothes hanger *noun* cintre M.

clothes line *noun* corde F à linge.

clothes peg *noun* pince F à linge.

clothing *noun* vêtements M *plural*.

cloud *noun* nuage M.

cloudy *adjective* nuageux (F nuageuse).

clove *noun* 1 clou M de girofle; 2 **a clove of garlic** une gousse d'ail.

clown *noun* clown M.

club *noun* 1 (*association*) club M; **he's in the football club** il fait partie du club de foot; 2 (*in cards*) trèfle M; **the four of clubs** le quatre de trèfle; 3 (*golfing iron*) crosse F.

clue *noun* 1 indice M; **they have a few clues** ils ont quelques indices; 2 (*in a crossword*) définition F; ★ **I haven't a clue** je n'ai aucune idée.

clumsy *adjective* maladroit.

clutch *noun* (*in a car*) embrayage M.
verb **to clutch something** tenir [77] quelque chose fermement.

coach *noun* 1 (*bus*) car M; **by coach** en car; **on the coach** dans le car; **to travel by coach** voyager en car; 2 (*sports trainer*) entraîneur M, entraîneuse F; 3 (*railway carriage*) wagon M.

coach station *noun* gare F routière.

coach trip *noun* excursion F en car; **to go on a coach trip** faire une excursion en car.

coal *noun* charbon M.

coal mine *noun* mine F de charbon.

coal miner *noun* mineur M.

coarse *adjective* grossier (F grossière).

coast *noun* côte F; **on the east coast** sur la côte est.

coat noun 1 manteau M (plural manteaux); 2 **a coat of paint** une couche de peinture.

coat hanger noun cintre M.

cobweb noun toile F d'araignée.

cockerel noun coq M.

cocoa noun (drink) chocolat M (chaud); (powder) cacoa M.

coconut noun noix F de coco.

cod noun cabillaud M.

code noun 1 code M; **the highway code** le code de la route; 2 **the dialling code for Cambridge** l'indicatif pour Cambridge.

coffee noun café M; **a cup of coffee** un café; **a black coffee, please** un café, s'il vous plaît; **a white coffee** un café au lait.

coffee break noun pause-café F.

coffee cup noun tasse F à café.

coffee machine noun cafetière F; (electric) cafetière F électrique.

coffee table noun table basse F.

coffin noun cercueil M.

coin noun pièce F de monnaie; **a pound coin** une pièce d'une livre.

coincidence noun coïncidence F.

Coke™ noun coca M; **two Cokes™ please** deux cocas s'il vous plaît.

colander noun passoire F.

cold noun 1 (cold weather) froid M; **to be out in the cold** être dehors dans le froid; 2 (illness) rhume M; **to have a cold** être enrhumé; **Carol's got a cold** Carol est enrhumée; **a bad cold** un gros rhume.

adjective 1 froid; **your hands are cold** tu as les mains froides; **cold milk** du lait froid; 2 (weather, temperature) **it's cold today** il fait froid aujourd'hui; 3 (feeling) **I'm cold** j'ai froid; **it's cold in the kitchen** il fait froid dans la cuisine.

cold sore noun bouton M de fièvre.

collapse verb 1 (a roof or a wall) s'écrouler [1]; 2 (a person) **he collapsed in his office** il a eu un malaise dans son bureau.

collar noun 1 (on a garment) col M; 2 (for a dog) collier M.

collarbone noun clavicule F.

colleague noun collègue M & F.

collect verb 1 (as a hobby) collectionner [1]; **I collect stamps** je collectionne les timbres; 2 aller [7] chercher (a person); **she collects the children from school** elle va chercher les enfants à la sortie de l'école; 3 passer [64] prendre (thing); **I have to collect a book at the library** je dois passer prendre un livre à la bibliothèque; 4 encaisser [1] (fares or money); 5 **to collect in the exercise books** ramasser [1] les cahiers.

collection noun 1 (of stamps, CDs, etc) collection F; 2 (of money) collecte F.

college noun 1 (for higher education) établissement M d'études supérieures; **to go to college** faire des études supérieures; 2 (a school) collège M.

collie noun colley M.

collision noun collision F.

colour noun couleur F; **what colour is your car?** de quelle couleur est ta voiture?; **what colour is it?** c'est de quelle couleur?; **do you have it in a different colour?** est-ce que vous l'avez dans une autre couleur?
verb (with paints or crayons) colorier [1]; **to colour something red** colorier quelque chose en rouge.

colour blind adjective daltonien (F daltonienne).

colour film noun pellicule F couleur (plural pellicules couleur).

colourful adjective en couleurs vives.

colouring book noun album M à colorier.

colour scheme noun couleurs F plural.

colour supplement noun supplément M illustré.

column noun colonne F.

comb noun peigne M.
verb **to comb your hair** se peigner [1]; **I'll just comb my hair** je vais juste me peigner.

combine verb combiner [1] (two separate things); **they don't combine well** ils ne se combinent pas bien.

come verb 1 venir [81]; **come quick!** viens vite!; **come and see!** venez voir!; **Nick came by bike** Nick est venu à vélo; **did Jess come to school yesterday?** est-ce que Jess est venue à l'école hier?; **Alan comes from Scotland** Alan vient de

l'Écosse; **can you come over for a coffee?** peux-tu venir prendre un café?; 2 arriver [1]; **coming!** j'arrive! **the bus is coming** le bus arrive; 3 **to come down** descendre [3] (the stairs or the street); 4 **to come up** monter [1]; **can you come up a moment?** peux-tu monter un instant?; 5 **to come in** entrer [1]; **come in!** entrez! **she came into the kitchen** elle est entrée dans la cuisine; 6 **to come for** passer [1] prendre (a person); **my father's coming for me** mon père passe me prendre; 7 **come along!** dépêche-toi!

● **to come back** revenir [81]; **he's coming back to collect us** il revient nous chercher.

● **to come off** (a button or handle, for example) se détacher [1]; (a lid) s'enlever [50].

● **to come out** 1 sortir [72]; **they came out when I called** ils sont sortis quand j'ai appelé; **the CD's coming out soon** le CD sort bientôt; 2 (the sun or moon) se montrer [1].

● **to come up to somebody** aborder [1] quelqu'un.

comedian noun comique M.

comedy noun comédie F.

comfortable adjective 1 confortable; **this chair's really comfortable** ce fauteuil est très confortable; 2 **to feel comfortable** (a person) se sentir à l'aise; **are you comfortable there?** êtes-vous bien là?

comfortably adverb confortablement.

comic noun (magazine) illustré M.

comic strip noun bande F dessinée.

comma noun virgule F.

command noun ordre M.

comment noun (in a conversation) remarque F; **he made some rude comments about my friends** il a fait des remarques impolies sur mes amis.

commentary noun reportage M en direct; **the commentary of the match** le reportage du match.

commentator noun commentateur M, commentatrice F; **a sports commentator** un commentateur sportif.

commercial noun spot M publicitaire.
adjective commercial (M plural commerciaux).

commit verb 1 commettre [11] (a crime); 2 **to commit yourself** s'engager [52].

committee noun comité M.

common adjective 1 courant; **it's a common problem** c'est un problème courant; 2 **in common** en commun; **they have nothing in common** ils n'ont rien en commun.

common sense noun bon sens M.

communicate verb communiquer [1].

communication noun communication F.

communion noun communion F.

communism noun communisme M.

communist noun communiste M & F.

community noun communauté F; **the European Community** la Communauté Européenne.

commute verb **to commute between Oxford and London** faire [10] le trajet entre Oxford et Londres tous les jours.

commuter noun navetteur M, navetteuse F.

compact disc noun disque compact M.

compact disc player noun platine F laser.

company noun 1 (business) société F; **an insurance company** une société d'assurances; **she's set up a company** elle a monté une société; 2 compagnie F; **an airline company** une compagnie aérienne; **a theatre company** une compagnie théâtrale; 3 **to keep somebody company** tenir compagnie à quelqu'un; **the dog keeps me company** le chien me tient compagnie.

comparatively adverb relativement.

compare verb comparer [1]; **if you compare the French with the English** si on compare les Français aux Anglais; **our house is small compared with yours** notre maison est petite par rapport à la vôtre.

comparison noun comparaison F; **in comparison with** par rapport à.

compartment noun
compartiment M.

compass noun boussole F.

compatible adjective (computing)
compatible.

compete verb 1 to compete in
something participer [1] à quelque
chose (race, event); 2 to compete
for something se disputer [1]
quelque chose (jobs, places); thirty
people competing for one job
trente personnes qui se disputent un
seul emploi.

competent adjective compétent.

competition noun concours M; a
fishing competition un concours de
pêche.

competitor noun concurrent M,
concurrente F.

complain verb se plaindre [31]; we
complained about the hotel and the
meals nous nous sommes plaints de
l'hôtel et des repas.

complete adjective complet (F
complète); the complete
collection la collection complète.
verb (to finish) compléter [24].

completely adverb complètement.

complexion noun teint M.

complicated adjective compliqué.

compliment noun compliment M;
to pay somebody a compliment
faire un compliment à quelqu'un.

compose verb composer [1];
composed of composé de.

composer noun compositeur M,
compositrice F.

compromise noun compromis M.

compulsory adjective obligatoire.

computer noun ordinateur M; to
work on a computer travailler sur
ordinateur; to have something on
computer avoir quelque chose sur
ordinateur.

computer engineer noun
technicien M en informatique,
technicienne F en informatique.

computer game noun jeu M
électronique (plural jeux
électroniques).

computer programmer noun
programmeur M, programmeuse F.

computer science noun
informatique F.

computing noun informatique F.

conceited adjective vaniteux (F
vaniteuse).

concentrate verb se concentrer [1];
I can't concentrate je n'arrive pas à
me concentrer; I was concentrating
on the film je me concentrais sur le
film.

concentration noun
concentration F.

concern noun (worry) inquiétude
F; there is no cause for concern il
n'y a pas lieu de s'inquiéter.
verb 1 (to affect) concerner [1]; this
doesn't concern you ceci ne te
concerne pas; 2 as far as I'm
concerned en ce qui me concerne.

concert noun 1 concert M; to go
to a concert aller à un concert; 2 a
concert ticket un billet de concert.

conclusion noun conclusion F.

concrete noun béton M; a
concrete floor un sol en béton.

condemn verb condamner [1].

condition noun 1 condition F; in
good condition en bonne
condition; weather conditions les
conditions météorologiques;
2 (something you agree to) condition
F; the conditions of sale les
conditions de vente; on condition
that you let me pay à condition que
tu me laisses payer.

conditional noun conditionnel M.

conditioner noun (for your hair)
après-shampooing M.

condom noun préservatif M.

conduct noun conduite F.
verb diriger [52] (an orchestra or a
piece of music).

conductor noun (of an orchestra)
chef M d'orchestre.

cone noun 1 (for ice cream) cornet
M; 2 (for traffic) balise F.

conference noun conférence F.

confess verb avouer [1].

confession noun confession F.

confidence noun 1 (self-
confidence) assurance F; to be
lacking in confidence manquer
d'assurance; 2 (faith in somebody
else) confiance F; to have
confidence in somebody avoir
confiance en quelqu'un.

confident adjective 1 (sure of
yourself) assuré; 2 (sure that
something will happen) sûr.

confirm verb confirmer [1]; we'll

confirm the date nous
confirmerons la date.

confuse verb 1 troubler [1] (a
person); 2 confondre [69]; I
confuse him with his brother je le
confonds avec son frère.

confused adjective 1 confus; he
gave us a confused story il nous a
raconté une histoire confuse; 2 I'm
confused about the holiday dates
je ne comprends pas bien les dates
des vacances; now I'm completely
confused! là je ne comprends plus
rien!

confusing adjective pas clair; the
instructions are confusing les
instructions ne sont pas claires.

confusion noun confusion F.

congratulate verb féliciter [1]; I
congratulated Tim on his success
j'ai félicité Tim de son succès; we
congratulate you on winning nous
vous félicitons d'avoir gagné.

congratulations plural noun
félicitations F plural;
congratulations on the baby!
félicitations pour le bébé!

conjurer noun prestidigitateur M.

connect verb 1 (to plug in to the
mains) brancher [1] (a dishwasher or
TV, for example).

connection noun 1 (between two
ideas or events) rapport M; there's
no connection between his letter
and my decision il n'y a aucun
rapport entre sa lettre et ma
décision; 2 (between trains or
planes) correspondance F; Sally
missed her connection Sally a raté
sa correspondance; 3 (electrical)

contact M; **a faulty conection** un mauvais contact.

conscience noun conscience F; **to have a guilty conscience** avoir mauvaise conscience.

conscious adjective conscient.

consequence noun conséquence F.

consequently adverb par conséquent.

conservation noun (of nature) protection F.

conservative noun, adjective conservateur M, conservatrice F.

conservatory noun jardin M d'hiver.

consider verb 1 (to give thought to) considérer [24] (a suggestion or idea); 2 (to think you might do) envisager [52]; **we are considering buying a flat** nous envisageons d'acheter un appartement; 3 **all things considered** tout compte fait.

considerate adjective attentionné (a person).

consideration noun considération F.

considering preposition étant donné; **considering her age** étant donné son âge; **considering he did it all himself** étant donné qu'il a tout fait lui-même.

consist verb **to consist of** être [6] composé de.

consonant noun consonne F.

constant adjective permanent.

constipated adjective constipé.

construct verb construire [26].

construction noun construction F.

consult verb consulter [1].

consumer noun consommateur M, consommatrice F.

contact noun 1 (touch) contact M; **to be in contact with somebody** être en contact avec quelqu'un; **we've lost contact** nous avons perdu contact; 2 (people you know) connaissance F; **Rob has contacts in the music business** Rob a des connaissances dans le monde de la musique.
verb contacter [1]; **I'll contact you tomorrow** je te contacterai demain.

contact lens noun lentille F de contact (plural lentilles de contact).

contain verb contenir [77].

container noun récipient M.

contemporary adjective 1 (around today) contemporain; 2 (modern) moderne.

contents plural noun contenu M; **the contents of my suitcase** le contenu de ma valise.

contest noun concours M.

contestant noun concurrent M, concurrente F.

continent noun continent M; **on the Continent** en Europe continentale.

continental adjective **a continental**

holiday des vacances en Europe continentale.

continue *verb* continuer [1]; **we continued (with) our journey** nous avons continué notre voyage; **Jill continued chatting** Jill a continué de bavarder; **'to be continued'** 'à suivre'.

continuous *adjective* continu; **continuous assessment** le contrôle continu.

contraceptive *noun* contraceptif M.

contract *noun* contrat M.

contradict *verb* contredire [47].

contradiction *noun* contradiction F.

contrary *noun* contraire M; **on the contrary** au contraire.

contrast *noun* contraste M.

contribute *verb* donner [1] (*money*).

contribution *noun* (*to charity or an appeal*) don M.

control *noun* (*of a crowd or animals*) contrôle M; **the police have lost control** la police a perdu le contrôle; **keep your dogs under control** maîtrisez vos chiens; **everything's under control** tout va bien; **the fire was out of control** on ne maîtrisait plus l'incendie.
verb **1** maîtriser [1] (*a crowd, animals, or a fire, for example*); **2** **to control oneself** se contrôler [1].

convenient *adjective* **1** commode; **frozen vegetables are very convenient** les légumes congelés sont très commodes; **2** **to be convenient for somebody** convenir à quelqu'un; **if that's convenient for you** si cela vous convient; **3** **the house is convenient for shops and schools** la maison est bien située par rapport aux magasins et aux écoles.

conventional *adjective* **1** conventionnel (F conventionnelle); **2** (*person*) conformiste.

conversation *noun* conversation F.

convert *verb* transformer [1]; **we're going to convert the garage into a workshop** nous allons transformer le garage en atelier.

convince *verb* convaincre [79]; **I'm convinced you're wrong** je suis convaincu que tu as tort.

convincing *adjective* convaincant.

cook *noun* cuisinier M, cuisinière F. *verb* **1** faire [10] la cuisine; **who's cooking tonight?** qui fait la cuisine ce soir?; **I like cooking** j'aime faire la cuisine; **2** faire [10] cuire (*vegetables, pasta, etc*); **cook the carrots for five minutes** faites cuire les carottes pendant cinq minutes; **3** préparer [1] (*a meal*); **Fran's busy cooking supper** Fran est en train de préparer le dîner; **4** (*food*) cuire [36]; **the sausages are cooking** les saucisses sont en train de cuire; **is the chicken cooked?** est-ce que le poulet est cuit?

cooker *noun* cuisinière F; **an electric cooker** une cuisinière électrique; **a gas cooker** une cuisinière à gaz.

cookery noun cuisine F.

cookery book noun livre M de cuisine.

cooking noun cuisine F; **to do the cooking** faire la cuisine; **Italian cooking** la cuisine italienne.

cool noun 1 (coldness) fraîcheur F; **stay in the cool** reste à la fraîcheur; 2 (calm) **to lose one's cool** perdre son sang-froid; **he kept his cool** il a gardé son sang-froid.
adjective 1 (cold) frais (F fraîche); **a cool drink** une boisson fraîche; **it's cool inside** il fait frais dans la maison; 2 (laid-back) décontracté; 3 (sophisticated) branché (informal).
verb refroidir [2]; **while the engine was cooling (down)** pendant que le moteur refroidissait.

cop noun flic M (informal).

cope verb 1 (to manage) se débrouiller [1]; **she copes well** elle se débrouille bien; 2 **to cope with** s'occuper [1] de (children or work); **I'll cope with the dishes** je m'occuperai de la vaisselle; 3 **faire** [10] face à (problems); **she's had a lot to cope with** elle a été obligée de faire face à beaucoup de choses; **he can't cope any more** il n'arrive plus à faire face.

copy noun 1 copie F; **make ten copies of this letter** faites dix copies de cette lettre; 2 (of a book) exemplaire M.
verb copier [1]; **I copied (down) the address** j'ai copié l'adresse.

cord noun (for a blind, for example) cordon M.

cordless telephone noun téléphone M sans fil.

core noun (of an apple or a pear) trognon M.

cork noun 1 (in a bottle) bouchon M; 2 (material) liège M.

corkscrew noun tire-bouchon M.

corn noun 1 (wheat) blé M; 2 (sweetcorn) maïs M.

corner noun coin M; **in a corner of the kitchen** dans un coin de la cuisine; **at the corner of the street** au coin de la rue; **out of the corner of your eye** du coin de l'œil; **it's just round the corner** c'est tout près.

cornflakes noun corn-flakes M plural.

Cornwall noun Cornouailles F; **in Cornwall** en Cornouailles.

corpse noun cadavre M.

correct adjective 1 exact; **yes, that's correct** oui, c'est exact; 2 bon (F bonne); **the correct sum** la bonne somme; **the correct answer** la bonne réponse; **the correct choice** le bon choix.
verb corriger [52].

correction noun correction F.

correspond verb correspondre [3].

corridor noun couloir M.

Corsica noun Corse F; **to Corsica** en Corse.

cosmetics plural noun produits M plural de beauté.

cost noun prix M; **the cost of a new**

computer le prix d'un nouvel ordinateur; **the cost of living** le coût de la vie.
verb coûter [1]; **how much does it cost?** combien est-ce que ça coûte?; **the tickets cost £10** les billets coûtent dix livres; **it costs too much** cela coûte trop cher.

costume *noun* costume M.

cosy *adjective* (*a bed or room*) douillet (F douillette); **it's cosy by the fire** on est bien à côté du feu.

cot *noun* lit M d'enfant.

cottage *noun* petite maison F.

cotton *noun* 1 (*fabric*) coton M; **a cotton shirt** une chemise en coton; 2 (*thread*) fil M de coton.

cotton wool *noun* ouate F de coton.

couch *noun* canapé M.

cough *noun* toux F; **a nasty cough** une mauvaise toux; **to have a cough** tousser.
verb tousser [1].

could *verb* 1 if he could pay s'il pouvait payer; **I couldn't open it** je ne pouvais pas l'ouvrir; **they couldn't smoke there** ils ne pouvaient pas fumer là; **she did all she could** elle a fait tout ce qu'elle pouvait; 2 (*knew how to*) **he couldn't drive** il ne savait pas conduire; **I couldn't swim** je ne savais pas nager; 3 (*with seeing, hearing, or smelling*) **I could hear the police car** j'entendais la voiture de police; **she couldn't see anything** elle ne voyait rien; 4 (*might*) **could I speak to David?** pourrais-je parler à David?;

you could try telephoning tu pourrais téléphoner.

council *noun* conseil M.

count *verb* 1 (*reckon up*) compter [1]; **I counted my money** j'ai compté mon argent; **thirty-five not counting the children** trente-cinq sans compter les enfants; 2 **to count as** être [6] considéré comme; **children over twelve count as adults** les enfants au-dessus de douze ans sont considérés comme adultes.

counter *noun* 1 (*in a shop or café*) comptoir M; 2 (*in a post office or bank*) guichet M; 3 (*in a big store*) rayon M; **on the cheese counter** au rayon fromagerie; 4 (*for board games*) jeton M.

country *noun* 1 (*France, England, etc*) pays M; **a foreign country** un pays étranger; **from another country** d'un autre pays; 2 (*not town*) campagne F; **to live in the country** vivre à la campagne; **a country walk** une promenade à la campagne; **a country road** une route de campagne.

country dancing *noun* danse F folklorique.

countryside *noun* campagne F.

county *noun* comté M.

couple *noun* 1 (*a pair*) couple M; 2 **a couple of** deux ou trois; **a couple of times** deux ou trois fois; **I've got a couple of things to do** j'ai deux ou trois choses à faire.

courage *noun* courage M.

courier *noun* 1 (*on a package holiday*) accompagnateur M, accompagnatrice F; **2** (*delivery service*) coursier M; **by courier** par coursier.

course *noun* **1** (*lessons*) cours M; **a beginners' course** un cours pour débutants; **a computer course** un cours d'informatique; **to go on a course** suivre un cours; **2** (*part of a meal*) plat M; **the main course** le plat principal; **a golf course** un golf; **3 of course** bien sûr; **yes, of course!** oui, bien sûr!; **he's forgotten, of course** il a oublié, bien sûr.

court *noun* **1** (*for tennis or squash*) court M; **2** (*for basketball*) terrain M.

courtyard *noun* cour F.

cousin *noun* cousin M, cousine F; **my cousin Sonia** ma cousine Sonia.

cover *noun* **1** (*for a book*) couverture F; **2** (*for a duvet or cushion*) housse F; **a duvet cover** une housse de couette. *verb* **1** (*to protect or cover up*) couvrir [30]; **cover the wound** couvrez la blessure; **he was covered in spots** il était couvert de boutons; **2** (*with leaves, snow, or fabric*) recouvrir [30]; **the ground was covered with snow** le sol était recouvert de neige.

cow *noun* vache F; **mad cow disease** maladie F de la vache folle.

coward *noun* lâche M & F.

cowboy *noun* cowboy M.

crab *noun* crabe M.

crack *noun* **1** (*in a wall or cup*) fêlure F; **2** (*a cracking noise*)

craquement M. *verb* **1** (*to make a crack in*) fêler [1] (*a cup, a chair, or a bone*); **2** (*to break*) casser [1] (*a nut or an egg*); **3** (*to split by itself: ice, for example*) se fêler [1]; **4** (*to make a noise*) (*a twig*) craquer [1].

cracker *noun* **1** (*biscuit*) cracker M; **2** (*Christmas cracker*) diablotin M.

crackle *verb* crépiter [1].

craft *noun* (*at school*) travaux manuels M *plural*.

cramp *noun* crampe F; **to have cramp in your leg** avoir une crampe à la jambe.

crane *noun* grue F.

crash *noun* **1** (*an accident*) accident M; **a car crash** un accident de voiture; **2** (*smashing noise*) fracas M; **a crash of broken glass** un fracas de verre brisé. *verb* **1** (*a car or plane*) s'écraser [1]; **the plane crashed** l'avion s'est écrasé; **2 to crash into something** rentrer [1] dans quelque chose; **the car crashed into a tree** la voiture est rentrée dans un arbre.

crash course *noun* cours M intensif.

crash helmet *noun* casque M.

crate *noun* **1** (*for bottles or china*) caisse F; **2** (*for fruit*) cageot M.

crawl *noun* (*in swimming*) crawl M. *verb* **1** (*a person, a baby*) marcher [1] à quatre pattes; **2** (*cars in a jam*) rouler [1] au pas; **we were crawling along** nous roulions au pas.

crayon noun 1 (wax) crayon M gras; 2 (coloured pencil) crayon M de couleur.

craze noun vogue F; the craze for rollerblades la vogue des rollers.

crazy adjective fou (F folle).

creak verb (a hinge) grincer [61]; (a floorboard) craquer [1].

cream noun crème F; strawberries and cream des fraises à la crème.

cream cheese noun fromage M à tartiner.

crease noun pli M.

creased adjective froissé.

create verb créer [32].

creative adjective créatif (F créative) (a person).

creature noun créature F.

crèche noun crèche F.

credit noun crédit M; to buy something on credit acheter quelque chose à crédit.

credit card noun carte F de crédit.

cress noun cresson M.

crew noun 1 (on a ship or plane) équipage M; 2 (rowing or filming) équipe F.

crew cut noun cheveux M plural en brosse.

cricket noun 1 (game) cricket M; to play cricket jouer au cricket; 2 (insect) grillon M.

cricket bat noun batte F de cricket.

crime noun 1 crime M; murder is a crime le meurtre est un crime; 2 (within society) criminalité F; the fight against crime la lutte contre la criminalité.

criminal noun, adjective criminel M, criminelle F.

crimson adjective pourpre.

crisis noun crise F.

crisp noun chips F; a packet of (potato) crisps un sachet de chips. adjective 1 (biscuit) croustillant; 2 (apple) croquant.

critical adjective 1 critique (a remark or somebody's condition); 2 décisif (F décisive) (a moment).

criticism noun critique F.

criticize verb critiquer [1].

Croatia noun Croatie F.

crockery noun vaisselle F.

crocodile noun crocodile M.

crook noun (criminal) escroc M.

crop noun récolte F.

cross noun croix F.
adjective fâché; she's very cross elle est très fâchée; I'm cross with you je suis fâché contre toi.
verb 1 (to cross over) traverser [1]; 2 to cross the road traverser la rue; 2 to cross your legs croiser [1] les jambes; 3 to cross into Italy passer [1] en Italie; 4 (to cross each other) se croiser [1]; the two roads cross here les deux routes se croisent ici.
●to cross out rayer [59] (a mistake, for example).

cross-Channel adjective trans-Manche; a cross-Channel ferry un ferry trans-Manche.

cross-country noun 1 cross M;
2 cross-country skiing le ski de
fond.

crossing noun 1 (from one place to
another) traversée F; a Channel
crossing une traversée trans-
Manche; a pedestrian crossing
un passage piétons; a level
crossing un passage à niveau.

cross-legged adjective to sit
cross-legged être assis en
tailleur.

crossroads noun carrefour M; at
the crossroads au carrefour.

crossword noun mots M plural
croisés; to do the crossword faire
les mots croisés.

crouch verb s'accroupir [2].

crow noun corbeau M; ★ ten
kilometres as the crow flies dix
kilomètres à vol d'oiseau.
verb (a cock) chanter [1].

crowd noun foule F; in the crowd
dans la foule; a crowd of 5,000 une
foule de cinq mille.
verb to crowd into s'entasser [1]
dans (a room or bus, for example);
we all crowded into the train nous
nous sommes tous entassés dans le
train.

crowded adjective bondé.

crown noun couronne F.

crude adjective 1 (rough and ready)
rudimentaire; 2 (vulgar) grossier
(F grossière).

cruel adjective cruel (F cruelle).

cruise noun croisière F; to go on a
cruise faire une croisière.

crumb noun miette F.

crumple verb froisser [1].

crunch verb croquer [1] (an apple).

crunchy adjective croquant.

crush verb écraser [1].

crust noun croûte F.

crusty adjective croustillant
(bread).

crutch noun béquille F; to be on
crutches marcher avec des
béquilles.

cry noun cri M.
verb 1 (weep) pleurer [1]; 2 (call
out) crier [1].

crystal noun cristal M.

cub noun 1 (animal) petit M;
2 (scout) louveteau M.

cube noun cube M; an ice cube un
glaçon.

cubic adjective (for measurements)
cube; three cubic metres trois
mètres cube.

cubicle noun 1 (in a changing
room) cabine F; 2 (in a public
lavatory) cabinet M.

cuckoo noun coucou M.

cucumber noun concombre M.

cuddle noun to give somebody a
cuddle faire un câlin à quelqu'un.
verb câliner [1].

cue noun (billiards, pool, snooker)
queue F de billard.

cuff noun (on a shirt) manchette F.

cul-de-sac noun impasse F.

culture noun culture F.

cunning *adjective* rusé.

cup *noun* 1 (*for drinking*) tasse F; a cup of tea une tasse de thé; 2 (*a trophy*) coupe F.

cupboard *noun* placard M; in the kitchen cupboard dans le placard de la cuisine.

cup tie *noun* match M de coupe.

cure *noun* remède M.
verb guérir [2].

curiosity *noun* curiosité F.

curious *adjective* curieux (F curieuse).

curl *noun* boucle F.
verb friser [1] (*hair*).

currant *noun* raisin M de Corinthe.

currency *noun* foreign currency les devises étrangères.

current *noun* (*of electricity or water*) courant M.
adjective actuel (F actuelle) (*a situation, for example*).

current affairs *noun* actualité F.

curriculum *noun* programme M.

curry *noun* curry M; chicken curry le curry de poulet.

curtain *noun* rideau M (*plural* rideaux).

cushion *noun* coussin M.

custard *noun* 1 (*runny*) crème F anglaise; 2 (*baked*) flan M.

custom *noun* coutume F.

customer *noun* client M, cliente F.

customs *plural noun* douane F

singular; to go through customs passer à la douane.

customs hall *noun* douane F.

customs officer *noun* douanier M, douanière F.

cut *noun* 1 (*injury*) coupure F; 2 (*haircut*) coupe F.
verb 1 couper [1]; I've cut the bread j'ai coupé le pain; you'll cut yourself! tu vas te couper!; Kevin's cut his finger Kevin s'est coupé le doigt; 2 to cut the grass tondre [3] le gazon; 3 to get your hair cut se faire [10] couper les cheveux; Anne's had her hair cut Anne s'est fait couper les cheveux; 4 to cut prices baisser les prix.
● **to cut down something** 1 abattre [21] (*a tree*).
● **to cut out something** 1 découper [1] (*a shape, a newspaper article*); 2 supprimer [1] (*sugar, fast food, etc.*).
● **to cut up something** couper [1] (*food*).

cutlery *noun* couverts M *plural*.

CV *noun* CV M.

cycle *noun* (*bike*) vélo M.
verb faire [10] du vélo; do you like cycling? est-ce que tu aimes faire du vélo?; we cycle to school nous allons à l'école en vélo.

cycle lane *noun* piste F cyclable.

cycle race *noun* course F cycliste.

cycling *noun* cyclisme M.

cycling holiday *noun* vacances F *plural* à vélo.

cyclist *noun* cycliste M & F.

D d

dad noun 1 père M; Anna's dad le père d'Anna; my dad works in a bank mon père travaille dans une banque; 2 (within the family) papa M; Dad's not home yet Papa n'est pas encore rentré.

daffodil noun jonquille F.

daily adjective quotidien (F quotidienne).

dairy products plural noun les produits laitiers M plural.

daisy noun pâquerette F.

dam noun barrage M.

damage noun dégâts M plural; there's no damage il n'y a pas de dégâts.
verb endommager [52].

damn noun he doesn't give a damn il s'en fiche complètement (informal).
exclamation damn! zut! (informal).

damp adjective humide.
noun humidité F; because of the damp à cause de l'humidité.

dance noun danse F; a folk dance une danse traditionnelle.
verb danser [1]; I like dancing j'aime danser.

dancer noun danseur M, danseuse F.

dancing noun danse F.

dancing class noun cours M de danse; to go to dancing classes suivre des cours de danse.

dandruff noun pellicules F plural.

danger noun danger M; to be in danger être en danger.

dangerous adjective dangereux (F dangereuse); it's dangerous to drive too fast il est dangereux de conduire trop vite.

Danish noun danois M.
adjective danois.

dare verb 1 oser [1]; to dare to do oser faire; I didn't dare suggest it je n'ai pas osé le suggérer; 2 don't you dare tell her I'm here! je t'interdis de lui dire que je suis là!; 3 I dare you! chiche que tu y vas! (informal); I dare you to tell him! chiche que tu le lui dises! (informal).

daring adjective osé; that was a bit daring! c'était un peu osé!

dark noun in the dark dans l'obscurité; after dark après la tombée de la nuit; to be afraid of the dark avoir peur du noir.
adjective 1 (colour) foncé; a dark blue skirt une jupe bleu foncé; 2 she has dark brown hair elle est brune; 3 it's dark already il fait nuit déjà; it gets dark around five la nuit commence à tomber vers cinq heures; 4 (room) sombre; the kitchen's a bit dark la cuisine est plutôt sombre; it's dark in here il fait sombre ici.

darkness noun obscurité F; in darkness dans l'obscurité.

darling noun chéri M, chérie F;

see you later, darling! à tout à l'heure, chéri!

dart noun fléchette F;   **to play darts** jouer aux fléchettes.

data plural noun données F plural.

database noun base F de données.

date noun 1 date F;   **the date of the meeting** la date de la réunion;   **to fix a date for** fixer une date pour;   2 **what's the date today?** nous sommes le combien aujourd'hui?;   3 **out of date** (passport, driving licence, etc) périmé; (technology, method, information, etc) dépassé;   **my passport's out of date** mon passeport est périmé;   4 (fruit) datte F.

date of birth noun date F de naissance.

daughter noun fille F;   **Tina's daughter** la fille de Tina.

daughter-in-law noun belle-fille F (plural belles-filles).

dawn noun aube F.

day noun 1 jour M;   **three days later** trois jours plus tard;   **the day I went to London** le jour où je suis allé à Londres;   2 (just from morning until evening) journée F;   **we spent the day in London** nous avons passé la journée à Londres;   **it rained all day** il a plu pendant toute la journée;   3 **it's going to be a nice day tomorrow** il va faire beau demain;   4 **the day after** le lendemain;   **the day after the wedding** le lendemain du mariage;   **the day after tomorrow** après-demain;   **my sister's arriving the day after tomorrow** ma sœur arrive

après-demain;   5 **the day before** la veille;   **the day before the wedding** la veille du mariage;   **the day before yesterday** avant-hier;   **my sister arrived the day before yesterday** ma sœur est arrivée avant-hier.

dead adjective, adverb 1 **her father's dead** son père est mort;   2 (really) vachement (informal);   **he's dead nice** il est vachement gentil;   **it was dead good** c'était vachement bien;   **it's dead easy** c'est vachement facile;   **you're dead right** tu as absolument raison;   **she arrived dead on time** elle est arrivée à l'heure pile.

dead end noun impasse F.

deadline noun date F limite.

deaf adjective sourd.

deafening adjective assourdissant.

deal noun 1 (involving money) affaire; **it's a good deal** c'est une bonne affaire;   2 marché M;   **I'll make a deal with you** je ferai un marché avec toi;   **it's a deal!** marché conclu!;   3 **a great deal of** beaucoup de;   **I don't have a great deal of time** je n'ai pas beaucoup de temps.
verb (in cards) donner [1];   **it's you to deal** c'est à toi de donner.
● **to deal with something** s'occuper [1] de quelque chose;   **Linda deals with the accounts** Linda s'occupe de la comptabilité;   **I'll deal with it as soon as possible** je m'en occuperai dès que possible.

dear adjective 1 cher (F chère);   **Dear Sylvie** Chère Sylvie;   2 (expensive) cher (F chère).

death noun mort F; after his father's death après la mort de son père; ★ you'll frighten him to death tu lui feras une peur bleue; ★ I'm bored to death je m'ennuie à mourir; ★ I'm sick to death of it j'en ai marre (informal).

death penalty noun peine F de mort.

debate noun débat M. verb débattre [21].

debt noun dette F; to get into debt s'endetter.

decade noun décennie F.

decaffeinated adjective décaféiné.

deceive verb tromper [1].

December noun décembre M; in December en décembre.

decent adjective 1 convenable; a decent salary un salaire convenable; 2 a decent meal un bon repas; 3 he seems a decent enough guy il semble être un type plutôt bien (informal).

decide verb décider [1]; to decide to do décider de faire; she's decided to buy a car elle a décidé d'acheter une voiture; she's decided not to buy a car elle a décidé de ne pas acheter une voiture.

decimal adjective décimal (M plural décimaux).

decimal point noun virgule F.

decision noun décision F; the right decision la bonne décision; the wrong decision la mauvaise décision; to make a decision prendre une décision.

deck noun (on a ship) pont M.

deckchair noun transat M.

declare verb déclarer [1].

decorate verb 1 décorer [1]; to decorate the Christmas tree décorer le sapin de Noël; 2 peindre; we're decorating the kitchen this weekend on va peindre la cuisine ce weekend.

decoration noun décoration F.

decrease noun diminution F; a decrease in the number of une diminution du nombre de. verb diminuer [1].

deduct verb déduire [26].

deep adjective profond; a deep feeling of gratitude un profond sentiment de reconnaissance; the river is very deep here la rivière est très profonde ici; how deep is the swimming pool? quelle est la profondeur de la piscine?; a hole two metres deep un trou de deux mètres de profondeur.

deep end noun the deep end (of a swimming pool) le grand bassin.

deep freeze noun congélateur M.

deeply adverb profondément.

deer noun 1 (red deer) cerf M; 2 (roe deer) chevreuil M; 3 (fallow deer) daim M.

defeat noun défaite F. verb battre [21].

defect noun défaut M.

defence noun défense F.

defend verb défendre [3].

defender noun défenseur.

define verb définir [2].

definite adjective **1** net (F nette) (before the noun) **a definite change** un net changement; **a definite improvement** une nette amélioration; **2** (certain) sûr; **it's not definite yet** ce n'est pas encore sûr; **3** (exact) précis; **a definite answer** une réponse précise; **I don't have a definite idea of what I want** je n'ai pas une idée précise de ce que je veux.

definitely adverb **1** (when giving your opinion about something) sans aucun doute; **the blue one is definitely the biggest** le bleu est sans aucun doute le plus grand; **your French is definitely better than mine** ton français est sans aucun doute meilleur que le mien; **'are you sure you like this one better?' – 'definitely!'** 'tu es sûr que tu préfères celui-ci?' – 'sans aucun doute!'; **2 she's definitely going to be there** elle va y être, c'est sûr; **I'm definitely not going** c'est décidé, je n'y vais pas.

definition noun définition F.

degree noun **1** degré M; **thirty degrees** trente degrés; **2 a university degree** un diplôme universitaire.

delay noun retard M; **a two-hour delay** un retard de deux heures. verb **1** (make late) retarder [1]; **the flight was delayed by bad weather** le vol a été retardé pas le mauvais temps; **2** (postpone) différer [24];

the decision has been delayed until Thursday la décision a été différée jusqu'à jeudi.

delete verb effacer [61].

deliberate adjective délibéré.

deliberately adverb exprès; **you did it deliberately** tu l'as fait exprès; **he left it there deliberately** il a fait exprès de le laisser là.

delicate adjective délicat.

delicatessen noun épicerie F fine.

delicious adjective délicieux (F délicieuse).

delighted adjective ravi; **they're delighted with their new flat** ils sont ravis de leur nouvel appartement; **I'm delighted to hear you can come** je suis ravi d'apprendre que vous pouvez venir.

deliver verb **1** livrer [1]; **they're delivering the washing machine tomorrow** ils vont livrer la machine à laver demain; **2** distribuer [1] (mail).

delivery noun livraison F.

demand noun demande F. verb exiger [52].

demo noun (protest) manif F (informal).

democracy noun démocratie F.

democratic adjective démocratique.

demolish verb démolir [2].

demonstrate verb **1** faire [10] la démonstration de (a machine, product, or technique); **2** (protest) manifester [1]; **to demonstrate**

against something manifester contre quelque chose.

demonstration noun 1 (of machine, product, technique) démonstration F; 2 (protest) manifestation.

demonstrator noun (in protest) manifestant M, manifestante F.

denim noun jean M; a denim jacket un blouson en jean.

Denmark noun Danemark M; in Denmark au Danemark; to Denmark au Danemark.

dense adjective dense.

dent noun bosse F. verb cabosser [1].

dental adjective 1 dentaire; dental floss du fil dentaire; dental hygiene l'hygiène dentaire; 2 a dental appointment un rendez-vous chez le dentiste.

dental surgeon noun chirurgien-dentiste M.

dentist noun dentiste M & F; my mum's a dentist ma mère est dentiste.

deny verb nier [1].

deodorant noun déodorant M.

depart verb partir [58].

department noun 1 (in school, university) département M; the language department le département de langues; 2 (in a shop) rayon M; the men's department le rayon hommes.

department store noun grand magasin M.

departure noun départ M.

departure lounge noun salle F d'embarquement.

depend verb to depend on dépendre [3] de; it depends on the price ça dépend du prix; it depends on what you want ça dépend de ce que tu veux; it depends ça dépend.

deposit noun 1 (when renting or hiring) caution F; 2 (when booking a holiday or hotel room) arrhes F plural; to pay a deposit verser des arrhes; 3 (on a bottle) consigne F.

depressed adjective déprimé.

depressing adjective déprimant.

depth noun profondeur F.

deputy noun adjoint M, adjointe F.

deputy head noun directeur adjoint M, directrice adjointe F.

descend verb descendre [3].

describe verb décrire [38].

description noun description F.

desert noun désert M; in the desert dans le désert.

desert island noun île F déserte.

deserve verb mériter [1].

design noun 1 conception F; the design of the plane la conception de l'avion; 2 (artistic design) design M; fashion design le stylisme; 3 (pattern) motif M; a floral design un motif floral. verb 1 concevoir [66] (a machine, plane, system); 2 créer [32] (costumes, clothes, fabric, scenery).

designer noun 1 (fashion designer)

styliste M & F; 2 (*graphic designer*)
graphiste M & F.

desire *noun* désir M.
verb désirer [1].

desk *noun* 1 (*in office or at home*)
bureau M; 2 (*pupil's*) table F;
3 **the reception desk** la réception;
the information desk le bureau des
renseignements.

despair *noun* désespoir M.
verb **to despair of doing** désespérer
[24] de faire.

desperate *adjective* 1 désespéré; **a
desperate attempt** une tentative
désespérée; 2 **to be desperate to
do** avoir très envie de faire; **I'm
desperate to see you** j'ai très envie
de te voir.

despise *verb* mépriser [1].

dessert *noun* dessert M; **what's for
dessert?** qu'est-ce qu'il y a comme
dessert?

destination *noun* destination F.

destroy *verb* détruire [26].

destruction *noun* destruction F.

detached house *noun* maison F
individuelle.

detail *noun* détail M.

detailed *adjective* détaillé.

detective *noun* 1 (*police*)
inspecteur de police M; 2 **a
private detective** un détective.

detective story *noun* roman M
policier.

detention *noun* retenue F.

detergent *noun* détergent M.

determined *adjective* résolu; **he's
determined to leave** il est résolu de
partir.

detour *noun* détour M.

develop *verb* 1 développer [1]; **to
get a film developed** faire
développer une pellicule; 2 se
développer; **how children develop**
comment les enfants se
développent.

developing country *noun* pays
M en voie de développement.

development *noun*
développement M.

devil *noun* diable M.

devoted *adjective* dévoué.

diabetes *noun* diabète M.

diabetic *noun*, *adjective* diabète
M & F; **to be (a) diabetic** être
diabète.

diagonal *adjective* diagonal (M
plural diagonaux).

diagram *noun* schéma M.

dial *verb* composer [1] le numéro; **lift
the receiver and dial 142** décrochez
et composez le 142.

dialling tone *noun* tonalité F.

dialogue *noun* dialogue M.

diamond *noun* 1 diamant M;
2 (*in cards*) carreau; **the jack of
diamonds** le valet de carreau;
3 (*shape*) losange M.

diarrhoea *noun* diarrhée F; **to
have diarrhoea** avoir la diarrhée.

diary *noun* 1 agenda M; **j'ai
marqué la date de la réunion dans
mon agenda** I've noted the date of

the meeting in my diary; **2** journal intime; **to keep a diary** tenir un journal (intime).

dice noun dé M; **to throw the dice** jeter le dé.

dictation noun dictée F.

dictionary noun dictionnaire M; **to look up a word in the dictionary** chercher un mot dans le dictionnaire.

did verb SEE do.

die verb **1** mourir [54]; **my grannie died in January** ma grand-mère est morte en janvier; **2 to be dying to do** mourir d'envie de faire; **I'm dying to see them!** je meurs d'envie de les voir!

diesel noun **1** gazole M; **2 a diesel engine** un moteur diesel; **a diesel car** une voiture diesel.

diet noun **1** alimentation F; **to have a healthy diet** avoir une alimentation saine; **2** (slimming or special) régime M; **to be on a diet** être au régime; **a salt-free diet** un régime sans sel.

difference noun **1** différence F; **I can't see any difference between the two** je ne vois pas la différence entre les deux; **what's the difference between...?** quelle est la différence entre...?; **2 it makes a difference** ça change quelque chose; **it makes no difference** ça ne change rien; **it makes no difference what I say** je peux dire ce que je veux, ça ne change rien.

different adjective différent; **the two sisters are very different** les deux sœurs sont très différentes;

she's very different from her sister elle est très différente de sa sœur.

difficult adjective difficile; **it's really difficult** c'est vraiment difficile; **it's difficult to decide** il est difficile de décider.

difficulty noun **1** difficulté F; **2 to have difficulty doing** avoir du mal à faire; **I had difficulty finding your house** j'ai eu du mal à trouver ta maison.

dig verb **to dig a hole** creuser [1] un trou.

digestion noun digestion F.

digital adjective numérique; **a digital recording** un enregistrement numérique; **a digital watch** une montre à affichage numérique.

dim adjective **1 a dim light** une lumière faible; **2 she's a bit dim** elle est un peu bouchée (informal).

dimension noun dimension F.

din noun vacarme M; **they were making a dreadful din** ils faisaient un vacarme aussi possible; **stop making such a din!** arrêtez de faire ce vacarme!

dinghy noun **1 a sailing dinghy** un dériveur; **2 a rubber dinghy** un canot pneumatique.

dining room noun salle à manger F; **in the dining room** dans la salle à manger.

dinner noun **1** (evening) dîner M; **to invite somebody to dinner** inviter quelqu'un à dîner; **2** (midday) déjeuner M; **to have school dinner** manger à la cantine.

dinner party noun dîner M.

dinner time noun 1 (*evening*) l'heure du dîner; 2 (*midday*) l'heure du déjeuner.

dinosaur noun dinosaure M.

diploma noun diplôme M.

direct adjective direct.
verb 1 réaliser [1] (*programme*, *film*); 2 mettre en scène (*play*); 3 régler (*traffic*).

direction noun 1 direction F; **in the other direction** dans l'autre direction; 2 **to ask somebody for directions** demander son chemin à quelqu'un; 3 **directions for use** mode M d'emploi.

directly adverb 1 directement; 2 **directly afterwards** immédiatement après.

director noun 1 (*of a company*) directeur M, directrice F; 2 (*of a programme or film*) réalisateur M, réalisatrice F; 3 (*of a play*) metteur M en scène.

directory noun annuaire M; **to be ex-directory** être sur la liste rouge.

dirt noun saleté F.

dirty adjective sale; **my hands are dirty** j'ai les mains sales; **to get something dirty** salir quelque chose; **you'll get your dress dirty** tu vas salir ta robe; **to get dirty** se salir; **the curtains get dirty quickly** les rideaux se salissent vite.

disabled adjective handicapé; **disabled people** les handicapés.

disadvantage noun

1 désavantage M; 2 **to be at a disadvantage** être désavantagé.

disagree verb **I disagree** je ne suis pas d'accord; **I disagree with James** je ne suis pas d'accord avec James.

disappear verb disparaître [27].

disappearance noun disparition F.

disappointed adjective déçu; **I disappointed with my marks** j'ai été déçu par mes notes.

disappointment noun déception F.

disaster noun désastre M; **it was a complete disaster** ça a été un désastre complet.

disastrous adjective désastreux (F désastreuse).

discipline noun discipline F.

disc noun 1 **a compact disc** un disque compact; 2 **a slipped disc** une hernie discale; 3 **a tax disc** (*for a vehicle*) une vignette.

disc-jockey noun disc-jockey M.

disco noun 1 soirée F disco; **they're having a disco** ils font une soirée disco; 2 (*club*) discothèque.

discount noun réduction F.

discourage verb décourager [52].

discover verb découvrir [30].

discovery noun découverte F.

discreet adjective discret (F discrète).

discrimination noun discrimination F; **racial**

discrimination la discrimination raciale.

discuss *verb* to discuss something discuter [1] de quelque chose; **we'll discuss the problem tomorrow** nous allons discuter du problème demain; **I'm going to discuss it with Phil** je vais en discuter avec Phil.

discussion *noun* discussion F.

disease *noun* maladie F.

disgraceful *adjective* scandaleux (F scandaleuse).

disguise *noun* déguisement M; **to be in disguise** être déguisé. *verb* déguiser [1]; **disguised as a woman** déguisé en femme.

disgust *noun* dégoût M.

disgusted *adjective* dégoûté.

disgusting *adjective* dégoûtant.

dish *noun* 1 plat M; **a large white dish** un grand plat blanc; **he cooked my favourite dish** il a préparé mon plat favori; 2 **to do the dishes** faire la vaisselle.

dishcloth *noun* (*for drying up*) torchon M.

dishonest *adjective* malhonnête.

dishonesty *noun* malhonnêteté F.

dish towel *noun* torchon M.

dishwasher *noun* lave-vaisselle M.

disinfect *verb* désinfecter [1].

disinfectant *noun* désinfectant M.

disk *noun* disque M; **a floppy disk** une disquette; **the hard disk** le disque dur.

diskette *noun* disquette F.

dislike *verb* ne pas aimer [1]; **I dislike sport** je n'aime pas le sport.

dismay *noun* consternation F.

dismiss *verb* licencier [1] (*an employee*).

disobedient *adjective* désobéissant.

display *noun* 1 exposition F; **a handicrafts display** une exposition d'artisanat; **to be on display** être exposé; 2 **a window display** une vitrine; 3 **a firework display** un feu d'artifice. *verb* exposer [1].

disposable *adjective* jetable.

disqualify *verb* disqualifier [1].

disrupt *verb* perturber [1].

dissolve *verb* dissoudre [67].

distance *noun* distance F; **from a distance** de loin; **in the distance** au loin; **it's within walking distance** on peut y aller à pied.

distant *adjective* lointain.

distinct *adjective* net (F nette).

distinctly *adverb* 1 distinctement; 2 **it's distinctly odd** c'est vraiment bizarre.

distract *verb* distraire [78].

distribute *verb* distribuer [1].

district *noun* 1 (*in town*) quartier M; **a poor district of Paris** un quartier pauvre de Paris; 2 (*in the country*) région F.

disturb verb déranger [52]; **sorry to disturb you** je suis désolé de vous déranger.

ditch noun fossé M.
verb **to ditch somebody** plaquer [1] quelqu'un (informal).

dive noun plongeon M.
verb plonger [52].

diver noun plongeur M, plongeuse F.

diversion noun (traffic) déviation F.

divide verb diviser [1].

diving noun plongée F.

diving board noun plongeoir M.

division noun division F.

divorce noun divorce M.

divorced adjective divorcé.

DIY noun bricolage M; **to do DIY** faire du bricolage; **a DIY shop** un magasin de bricolage.

dizzy adjective **I feel dizzy** j'ai la tête qui tourne.

DJ noun disc-jockey M.

do verb 1 faire [10]; **what are you doing?** qu'est-ce que tu fais?; **I'm doing my homework** je fais mes devoirs; **what have you done with the hammer?** qu'est-ce que tu as fait du marteau?; 2 (questions in French are formed either with 'est-ce que' or by putting the subject after the verb and a hyphen between them) **do you want some strawberries?** est-ce que tu veux des fraises?, veux-tu des fraises?; **when does it start?** quand est-ce que ça commence?; **how did**

you open the door? comment as-tu ouvert la porte?; 3 (in negative sentences) **don't, doesn't, didn't** ne. . .pas; **I don't like mushrooms** je n'aime pas les champignons; **Rosie doesn't like spinach** Rosie n'aime pas les épinards; **you didn't shut the door** tu n'as pas fermé la porte; **it doesn't matter** ça ne fait rien;
4 (when it refers back to another verb, 'do' is not translated) **'do you live here?'** – **'yes, I do'** 'est-ce que tu habites ici?' – 'oui'; **she has more money than I do** elle a plus d'argent que moi; **'I live in Oxford'** – **'so do I'** 'j'habite à Oxford' – 'moi aussi'; **'I didn't phone Gemma'** – **'neither did I'** 'je n'ai pas appelé Gemma' – 'ni moi non plus';
5 **don't you?, doesn't he?** etc. n'est-ce pas? **you know Helen, don't you?** tu connais Helen, n'est-ce pas?; **she left on Thursday, didn't she?** elle est partie jeudi, n'est-ce pas?; 6 **that'll do** ça ira; **it'll do like that** ça ira comme ça.
● **to do something up** 1 lacer [61] (shoes); 2 boutonner [1] (cardigan, jacket); 3 retaper [1] (house).
● **do without** se passer [1] de; **we can do without knives** on peut se passer de couteaux.

doctor noun médecin M; **her mother's a doctor** sa mère est médecin.

document noun document M.

documentary noun documentaire M.

dodgems plural noun **the dodgems** les autos F plural tamponneuses.

dog noun chien M; (female) chienne F.

do-it-yourself noun bricolage M.

dole noun allocations chômage F plural; **to be on the dole** être au chômage.

doll noun poupée F.

dollar noun dollar M.

dolphin noun dauphin M.

domino noun domino M; **to play dominoes** jouer aux dominos.

donkey noun âne M.

don't SEE do.

door noun 1 porte F; **to open the door** ouvrir la porte; **to shut the door** fermer la porte; 2 (of a vehicle or train) portière F.

doorbell noun sonnerie F; **to ring the doorbell** sonner à la porte; **there's the doorbell!** on sonne!

doorstep noun pas M de la porte.

dot noun 1 (written) point M; 2 (on fabric) pois M; 3 **at ten on the dot** à dix heures pile.

double adjective, adverb 1 double; **a double helping** une double portion; **a double whisky** un double whisky; 2 **le double**; **double the time** le double du temps; **double the price** le double du prix; 3 **a double room** une chambre pour deux personnes; 4 **a double bed** un grand lit.

double bass noun contrebasse F; **to play the double bass** jouer de la contrebasse.

double-breasted adjective a

double-breated jacket une veste croisée.

double-decker bus noun autobus M à impériale.

double glazing noun double vitrage M.

doubles noun (in tennis) double M; **to play a game of doubles** faire un double.

doubt noun doute M; **there's no doubt about it** il n'y a aucun doute là-dessus; **I have my doubts** j'ai des doutes.
verb **to doubt something** douter [1] de quelque chose; **I doubt it** j'en doute; **to doubt that** douter que (+ subjunctive); **I doubt they'll do it** je doute qu'ils le fassent.

doubtful adjective 1 pas sûr; **it's doubtful** ce n'est pas sûr; 2 **to be doubtful about doing** hésiter à faire; **I'm doubtful about inviting them together** j'hésite à les inviter ensemble.

dough noun pâte F.

doughnut noun beignet M.

Dover noun Douvres; **to Dover** à Douvres.

down adverb, preposition 1 en bas; **he's down in the cellar** il est en bas dans la cave; 2 **down the road** (nearby) à côté; **there's a chemist's just down the road** il y a une pharmacie juste à côté; 3 **to go down** descendre; **I went down to the kitchen** je suis descendu dans la cuisine; **to walk down the street** descendre la rue; **to run down the stairs** descendre les escaliers en courant; 4 **to come down**

descendre; **she came down from her bedroom** elle est descendue de sa chambre; **5 to sit down** s'asseoir; **she sat down on the sofa** elle s'est assise sur le canapé.

downstairs adverb **1** en bas; **she's downstairs in the sitting-room** elle est en bas dans le salon; **the dog sleeps downstairs** le chien dort en bas; **2** du dessous; **the flat downstairs** l'appartement du dessous; **the people downstairs** les voisins du dessous.

doze verb sommeiller [1].

dozen noun douzaine F; **a dozen eggs** une douzaine d'œufs.

drag noun **what a drag!** quelle barbe! (informal); **she's a bit of a drag** elle n'est pas marrante (informal).
verb traîner [1].

dragon noun dragon M.

drain noun égout M.
verb égoutter [1] (vegetables).

drama noun **1** (subject) art M dramatique; **2 he made a big drama about it** il en a fait tout un cinéma (informal).

dramatic adjective spectaculaire.

draught noun courant d'air M.

draughts noun dames F plural; **to play draughts** jouer aux dames.

draw noun **1** (in a match) match nul M; **it was a draw** ils ont fait match nul; **2** (lottery) tirage M au sort.
verb **1** dessiner [1]; **I can't draw horses** je ne sais pas dessiner les chevaux; **she can draw really well** elle dessine vraiment bien; **2 to**

draw a picture faire [10] un dessin; **3 to draw the curtains** tirer [1] les rideaux; **4 to draw a crowd** attirer [1] une foule de spectateurs; **5** (in a match) faire [10] match nul; **we drew three all** nous avons fait match nul trois à trois; **6 to draw lots** tirer [1] au sort.

drawback noun inconvénient M.

drawer noun tiroir M.

drawing noun dessin M.

drawing pin noun punaise F.

dreadful adjective affreux (F affreuse).

dreadfully adverb terriblement; **I'm dreadfully late** je suis terriblement en retard; **I'm dreadfully sorry** je suis vraiment navré.

dream noun rêve M; **to have a dream** faire un rêve; **I had a horrible dream last night** j'ai fait un rêve horrible cette nuit.
verb rêver [1]; **to dream about something** rêver de quelque chose.

drenched adjective trempé; **to get drenched** se faire tremper; **we got drenched on the way home** on s'est fait tremper en rentrant.

dress noun robe F.
verb **to dress a child** habiller [1] un enfant.
●**to dress up** se déguiser [1]; **to dress up as a vampire** se déguiser en vampire.

dressed adjective **1** habillé; **is Tom dressed yet?** est-ce que Tom est habillé?; **she was dressed in black trousers and a yellow shirt** elle était habillée d'un pantalon noir et une chemise jaune; **2 to get dressed** s'habiller; **I got dressed quickly** je me suis vite habillé.

dresser noun (*for dishes*) vaisselier M.

dressing gown noun robe de chambre F.

dressing table noun coiffeuse F.

drier noun **a hair drier** un sèche-cheveux; **a tumble drier** un sèche-linge.

drift noun **a snow drift** une congère.

drill noun perceuse F.

drink noun **1** boisson F; **a hot drink** une boisson chaude; **a cold drink** une boisson fraîche; **2 would you like a drink?** tu veux boire quelque chose?; **3 to go out for a drink** aller prendre un pot (*informal*).
verb boire [22]; **he drank a glass of water** il a bu un verre d'eau.

drive noun **1 to go for a drive** faire un tour en voiture; **2** (*up to a house*) allée F.
verb **1** conduire [26]; **she drives very fast** elle conduit très vite; **to drive a car** conduire une voiture; **I'd like to learn to drive** j'aimerais apprendre à conduire; **can you drive?** tu sais conduire?; **2** aller en voiture; **we drove to Paris** nous somes allés à Paris en voiture; **3 to drive somebody** (*to a place*) emmener [50] quelqu'un en voiture; **Mum drove me to the station** Maman m'a emmené en voiture à la gare; **to drive somebody home** raccompagner [1] quelqu'un;

★ **she drives me mad!** elle me rend folle!

driver noun **1** conducteur M, conductrice F; **2** (*of a taxi or bus*) chauffeur M.

driving instructor noun moniteur M d'auto-école.

driving lesson noun leçon F de conduite.

driving licence noun permis M de conduire.

driving test noun permis M de conduire; **to take your driving test** passer son permis; **Jenny's passed her driving test** Jenny a eu son permis.

drop noun goutte F.
verb **1 to drop something** laisser [1] tomber quelque chose; **I dropped my glasses** j'ai laissé tomber mes lunettes; **I'm going to drop history next year** je vais laisser tomber l'histoire l'année prochaine; **drop it!** laisse tomber!; **2** déposer [1] (*a person*); **could you drop me at the station?** est-ce que tu peux me déposer à la gare?

drown verb se noyer [39]; **she drowned in the lake** elle s'est noyée dans le lac.

drug noun **1** (*medicine*) médicament M; **2** (*illegal*) **drugs** la drogue.

drug abuse noun usage M des stupéfiants.

drug addict noun toxicomane M & F.

drug addiction noun toxicomanie F.

drum noun 1 tambour M;
2 drums la batterie; **to play drums**
jouer de la batterie.

drum kit noun batterie F.

drummer noun batteur M,
batteuse F.

drunk noun ivrogne M & F.
adjective ivre.

dry adjective sec (F sèche).
verb 1 sécher [1]; **to let something
dry** laisser [1] sécher quelque
chose; 2 **to dry your hair** se sécher
les cheveux; 3 **to dry your hands**
essuyer [41] les mains; **to dry the
dishes** s'essuyer [41] la vaisselle;
4 **to dry the washing** faire [10]
sécher le linge.

dry cleaner's noun pressing M.

dryer noun SEE drier.

dubbed adjective **a dubbed film** un
film doublé.

duck noun canard M.

due adjective, adverb 1 **to be due to
do** devoir faire; **we're due to leave
on Thursday** nous devons partir
jeudi; **Paul's due back soon** Paul
doit bientôt revenir; 2 **due to** en
raison de; **the match has been
cancelled due to bad weather** le
match a été annulé en raison du
mauvais temps.

duke noun duc M.

dull adjective 1 **dull weather** un
temps maussade; **it's a dull day
today** il fait un temps maussade
aujourd'hui; 2 (boring) ennuyeux
(F ennuyeuse).

dumb adjective 1 muet (F muette);

to be deaf and dumb être sourd-
muet; 2 (stupid) bête; **he asked
some dumb questions** il a posé des
questions bêtes.

dummy noun (for a baby) tétine F.

dump verb 1 jeter [48] (rubbish);
2 plaquer [1] (a person) (informal);
she's dumped her boyfriend elle a
plaqué son copain.

dungarees plural noun salopette F
singular.

dungeon noun cachot M.

Dunkirk noun Dunkerque.

during preposition pendant; **during
the night** pendant la nuit; **I saw her
during the holidays** je l'ai vue
pendant les vacances.

dusk noun **at dusk** à la nuit
tombante.

dust noun poussière F.
verb épousseter [48].

dustbin noun poubelle F; **to put
something in the dustbin** jeter
quelque chose à la poubelle.

dustman noun éboueur M.

dusty adjective poussiéreux (F
poussiéreuse).

Dutch noun 1 (language)
hollandais M; 2 **the Dutch**
(people) les Hollandais M plural.
adjective hollandais.

duty noun 1 devoir M; **to have a
duty to do** avoir le devoir de faire;
you have a duty to inform us vous
avez le devoir de nous informer;
2 **to be on duty** être de service; **to
be on night duty** être de service de

nuit; **I'm off duty tonight** je ne suis pas de service ce soir.

duty-free *adjective* hors taxes; **the duty-free shops** les boutiques hors taxes; **duty-free purcheses** les achats hors taxes.

duvet *noun* couette F.

duvet cover *noun* housse F de couette.

dwarf *noun* nain M, naine F.

dye *noun* teinture F.
verb teindre [60]; **to dye your hair** se teindre les cheveux; **I'm going to dye my hair pink** je vais me teindre les cheveux en rose.

dynamic *adjective* dynamique.

dyslexia *noun* dyslexie F.

dyslexic *adjective* dyslexique.

E e

each *adjective* chaque; **each time** chaque fois; **curtains for each window** des rideaux pour chaque fenêtre.
pronoun chacun (F chacune); **my sisters each have a computer** mes sœurs ont chacune un ordinateur; **she gave us an apple each** elle nous a donné une pomme à chacun; **each of you** chacun de vous, chacune de vous; **we each got a present** chacun de nous a reçu un cadeau; **the tickets cost ten pounds each** les billets coûtent dix livres chacun.

each other *pronoun* ('each other' is usually translated using a reflexive pronoun) **they love each other** ils s'aiment; **we know each other** nous nous connaissons; **do you often see each other?** est-ce que vous vous voyez souvent?

eagle *noun* aigle M.

ear *noun* oreille F.

earache *noun* **to have earache** avoir une otite.

earlier *adverb* 1 (*a while ago*) tout à l'heure; **your brother phoned earlier** ton frère a appelé tout à l'heure; 2 (*not as late*) plus tôt; **we should have started earlier** nous aurions dû commencer plus tôt; **earlier in the morning** plus tôt le matin.

early *adverb* 1 (*in the morning*) tôt; **to get up early** se lever tôt; **it's too early** il est trop tôt; 2 (*for an appointment*) en avance; **we're early, the train doesn't leave until ten** nous sommes en avance, le train ne part qu'à dix heures; **Grandma likes to be early** Grand-mère aime être en avance.
adjective 1 (*one of the first*) premier (F première); **in the early months** pendant les premiers mois; **I'm getting the early train** je prends le premier train; 2 **to have an early lunch** déjeuner tôt; **Jan's having an early night** Jan va se coucher tôt; **we're making an early start** nous partons tôt; 3 **in the early afternoon** en début d'après-midi; **in the early hours** au petit matin.

earn *verb* gagner [1] (*money*); **Richard earns four pounds an**

hour Richard gagne quatre livres de l'heure.

earnings *plural noun* salaire M.

earring *noun* boucle F d'oreille.

earth *noun* terre F; **life on earth** la vie sur terre; ★ **what on earth are you doing?** mais qu'est-ce que tu fais là?

earthquake *noun* tremblement M de terre.

easily *adverb* 1 (*to do something*) facilement; 2 (*by far*) de loin; **he's easily the best** il est de loin le meilleur.

east *noun* est M; **in the east** à l'est. *adjective, adverb* est; **the east side** le côté est; **an east wind** un vent d'est; **east of Paris** à l'est de Paris.

Easter *noun* Pâques M; **they're coming at Easter** ils viennent à Pâques; **Happy Easter** Joyeuses Pâques.

Easter Day *noun* dimanche M de Pâques.

Easter egg *noun* œuf M de Pâques.

Eastern Europe *noun* Europe F de l'Est.

easy *adjective* facile; **it's easy!** c'est facile!; **it was easy to decide** c'était facile à décider.

eat *verb* 1 manger [52]; **he was eating a banana** il mangeait une banane; **we're going to have something to eat** nous allons manger quelque chose; 2 prendre [64] (*a meal*); **we were eating**

breakfast nous prenions le petit déjeuner; 3 **to eat out** manger au restaurant.

EC *noun* (*short for European Community*) CE F, Communauté F européenne.

echo *noun* écho M. *verb* retentir [2].

ecological *adjective* écologique.

ecology *noun* écologie F.

economical *adjective* 1 économe (*a person*); 2 économique (*way of doing something*); **it's more economical to buy a big one** c'est plus économique d'acheter un grand.

economics *noun* économie F.

economy *noun* économie F.

eczema *noun* eczéma M.

edge *noun* 1 bord M; **the edge of the table** le bord de la table; **at the edge of the lake** au bord du lac; 2 **to be on edge** être énervé.

edible *adjective* comestible.

Edinburgh *noun* Édimbourg.

edit *verb* éditer [1].

editor *noun* (*of a newspaper*) rédacteur en chef M, rédactrice en chef F.

educate *verb* (*a teacher*) instruire [26].

education *noun* éducation F.

educational *adjective* éducatif (F éducative).

effect *noun* effet M; **the effect of the accident** l'effet de l'accident; **to**

have an effect on avoir un effet sur; **it had a good effect on the whole family** ça a eu un bon effet sur toute la famille; **special effects** les effets spéciaux.

effective *adjective* efficace.

efficient *adjective* efficace.

effort *noun* effort M; **to make an effort** faire un effort; **David made an effort to help us** David a fait un effort pour nous aider; **he didn't even make the effort to apologize** il n'a même pas fait l'effort pour s'excuser.

e.g. par ex.

egg *noun* œuf M; **a dozen eggs** une douzaine d'œufs; **a fried egg** un œuf au plat; **two boiled eggs** deux œufs à la coque; **a hard-boiled egg** un œuf dur; **scrambled eggs** les œufs brouillés.

egg-cup *noun* coquetier M.

eggshell *noun* coquille F d'œuf.

egg-white *noun* blanc M d'œuf.

egg-yolk *noun* jaune M d'œuf.

eight *number* huit M; **Maya's eight** Maya a huit ans; **at eight o'clock** à huit heures.

eighteen *number* dix-huit M; **Jason's eighteen** Jason a dix-huit ans.

eighth *number* **1** huitième; **2 the eighth of July** le huit juillet; **on the eighth floor** au huitième étage.

eighty *number* quatre-vingts; **eighty-five** quatre-vingt-cinq (*note that the 's' disappears when another number follows*).

Eire *noun* la République d'Irlande; **in Eire** en République d'Irlande.

either *pronoun* **1** (*one or the other*) l'un ou l'autre; **choose either (of them)** choisis l'un ou l'autre; **I don't like either (of them)** je n'aime ni l'un ni l'autre; **2** (*both*) les deux; **either is possible** tous les deux sont possibles.
conjunction **1 either ... or ...** ou ... ou; **either Thursday or Friday** ou jeudi ou vendredi; **either Susie or Judy** ou Susie ou Judy; **he either wrote or phoned** il a ou écrit ou appelé; **2** (*with a negative*) non plus; **he doesn't want to either** il ne veut pas non plus; **I don't know them either** je ne les connais pas non plus.

elastic *noun, adjective* élastique M.

elastic band *noun* élastique M.

elbow *noun* coude M.

elder *adjective* aîné; **her elder brother** son frère aîné.

elderly *adjective* âgé; **the elderly** les personnes F *plural* âgées.

eldest *adjective* aîné; **her eldest brother** son frère aîné.

elect *verb* élire [51]; **she has been elected** elle a été élue.

election *noun* élection F; **in the election** aux élections.

electric *adjective* électrique.

electrical *adjective* électrique.

electrician *noun* électricien M, électricienne F.

electricity *noun* électricité F; **to**

turn off the electricity couper le courant.

electronic *adjective* électronique.

electronics *noun* électronique F.

elegant *adjective* élégant.

elephant *noun* éléphant M.

eleven *number* onze M; **Josh is eleven** Josh a onze ans; **at eleven o'clock** à onze heures; **a football eleven** une équipe de football.

eleventh *number* onzième; **the eleventh of May** le onze mai; **on the eleventh floor** à l'onzième étage.

eliminate *verb* éliminer [1].

else *adverb* 1 d'autre; **somebody else** quelqu'un d'autre; **did you see anyone else?** as-tu vu quelqu'un d'autre?; **nothing else** rien d'autre; **I don't want anything else** je ne veux rien d'autre; 2 **something else** autre chose; **would you like something else?** désirez-vous autre chose?; 3 **somewhere else** ailleurs; 4 **or else** sinon; **hurry up, or else we'll be late** dépêche-toi, sinon nous serons en retard.

e-mail *noun* courrier électronique M.

embankment *noun* 1 (*by a river*) quai M; 2 (*by a railway*) remblai M.

embarrassed *adjective* gêné; **I was terribly embarrassed** j'étais très gêné.

embarrassing *adjective* gênant.

embassy *noun* ambassade F; **the**

French Embassy l'ambassade de France.

embroider *verb* broder [1].

embroidery *noun* broderie F.

emergency *noun* cas M d'urgence; **in an emergency, break the glass** en cas d'urgence, cassez la vitre; **it's an emergency!** c'est urgent!

emergency exit *noun* sortie F de secours.

emergency landing *noun* atterrissage M d'urgence.

emotion *noun* émotion F.

emotional *adjective* 1 ému (*a person*); **she was quite emotional** elle était tout émue; 2 (*a speech or an occasion*) chargé d'émotion.

emperor *noun* empereur M.

emphasize *verb* **he emphasized that it wasn't compulsory** il a insisté [1] sur le fait que ce n'était pas obligatoire.

empire *noun* empire M; **the Roman Empire** l'Empire Romain.

employ *verb* employer [39].

employee *noun* salarié M, salariée F.

employer *noun* employeur M, employeuse F.

employment *noun* travail M.

empty *adjective* vide; **an empty bottle** une bouteille vide; **the room was empty** la pièce était vide.
verb vider [1]; **I emptied the teapot into the sink** j'ai vidé la théière dans l'évier.

enchanting *adjective* ravissant.

enclose verb (in a letter) joindre
[49]; **please find enclosed a
cheque** veuillez trouver ci-joint un
chèque.

encore noun bis M; **to give an
encore** jouer un bis.

encourage verb encourager [52]; **to
encourage somebody to do
something** encourager quelqu'un à
faire quelque chose; **Mum
encouraged me to try again**
Maman m'a encouragé à essayer
encore une fois.

encouragement noun
encouragement M.

encouraging adjective
encourageant.

encyclopedia noun encyclopédie
F.

end noun 1 (last part) fin F; **'The
End'** 'Fin'; **at the end of the film** à la
fin du film; **by the end of the day** à la
fin de la journée; **in the end I went
home** finalement je suis rentré chez
moi; **Sally's coming at the end of
June** Sally viendra fin juin; 2 (of a
table, garden, stick, or road, for
example) bout M; **hold the other
end** tiens l'autre bout; **at the end of
the street** au bout de la rue; 3 (in
tennis or football) côté M; **to
change ends** changer de côté.
verb 1 (to put an end to) mettre [11]
fin à (an arrangement); **they've
ended the strike** ils ont mis fin à la
grève; 2 (to come to an end) se
terminer [1]; **the day ended with a
dinner** la journée s'est terminée par
un dîner.
●**to end up** 1 **to end up doing** finir
[2] par faire; **we ended up taking a**

taxi nous avons fini par prendre un
taxi; 2 **to end up somewhere** se
retrouver [1] quelque part; **Rob
ended up in San Francisco** Rob
s'est retrouvé à San Francisco.

ending noun fin F.

endless adjective interminable (a
day or a journey, for example).

enemy noun ennemi M, ennemie
F; **to make enemies** se faire des
ennemis.

energetic adjective énergique.

energy noun énergie F.

engaged adjective 1 (to be
married) fiancé; **they're engaged**
ils sont fiancés; **to get engaged** se
fiancer [61]; 2 (a phone or toilet)
occupé; **it's engaged, I'll ring
later** c'est occupé, j'appellerai plus
tard.

engagement noun (to marry)
fiançailles F plural.

engagement ring noun bague F
de fiançailles.

engine noun 1 (in a car) moteur
M; 2 (pulling a train) locomotive
F.

engineer noun 1 (who comes for
repairs) technicien M; 2 (who
builds roads and bridges) ingénieur
M.

England noun Angleterre F; **in
England** en Angleterre; **to England**
en Angleterre; **I am from England** je
suis anglais.

English noun 1 (the language)
anglais M; **do you speak English?**
parlez-vous anglais?; **he answered in**

English il a répondu en anglais;
2 (*English people*) **the English** les
Anglais M *plural*.
adjective 1 (*of or from England*)
anglais; **the English team** l'équipe
anglaise; 2 **an English lesson** un
cours d'anglais; **our English
teacher** notre professeur d'anglais.

English Channel *noun* **the
English Channel** la Manche.

Englishman *noun* Anglais M.

Englishwoman *noun* Anglaise F.

enjoy *verb* 1 aimer [1]; **did you enjoy
the party?** as-tu aimé la soirée?; **we
really enjoyed the concert** nous
avons beaucoup aimé le concert;
2 **to enjoy doing** aimer faire; **I enjoy
swimming** j'aime nager; **do you
enjoy living in York?** aimez-vous
vivre à York?; 3 **to enjoy oneself**
s'amuser [1]; **we really enjoyed
ourselves** nous nous sommes très
bien amusés; **enjoy yourselves!**
amusez-vous bien!; **did you enjoy
yourself?** tu t'es bien amusé?

enjoyable *adjective* agréable.

enlarge *verb* agrandir [2] (*a photo,
for example*).

enlargement *noun* (*of a photo*)
agrandissement M.

enormous *adjective* énorme.

enough *adverb, pronoun* 1 assez;
there's enough for everyone il y en
a assez pour tout le monde;
2 (*followed by a noun*) assez de; **is
there enough bread?** est-cé qu'il y a
assez de pain?; 3 (*followed by an
adjective or adverb*) suffisamment;
big enough suffisamment grand;
slowly enough suffisamment

lentement; 4 **that's enough** ça
suffit.

enquire *verb* se renseigner [1]; **I'm
going to enquire about the trains**
je vais me renseigner sur les
trains.

enquiry *noun* demande F de
renseignements; **to make enquiries
about something** demander des
renseignements sur quelque chose.

enrol *verb* s'inscrire [38]; **I want to
enrol on the course** je veux
m'inscrire au cours.

enter *verb* 1 (*to go inside*) entrer [1]
dans (*a room or building*); **we all
entered the church** nous sommes
tous entrés dans l'église; 2 **to enter
for** s'inscrire [38] à (*an exam or
competition*); s'inscrire pour (*a
race*).

entertain *verb* 1 (*to keep amused*)
divertir [2]; **something to entertain
the children** quelque chose pour
divertir les enfants; 2 (*to have
people round*) recevoir [66]; **they
don't entertain much** ils reçoivent
peu.

entertaining *noun* **they do a lot of
entertaining** ils reçoivent
beaucoup.
adjective amusant.

entertainment *noun* (*fun*)
distractions F *plural*; **there wasn't
much entertainment in the
evenings** il n'y avait pas beaucoup
de distractions le soir.

enthusiasm *noun* enthousiasme
M.

enthusiast *noun* passionné M,
passionnée F; **he's a rugby**

enthusiast c'est un passionné de rugby.

enthusiastic *adjective* enthousiaste.

entire *adjective* entier (F entière); **the entire class** la classe entière.

entirely *adverb* complètement.

entrance *noun* entrée F.

entry *noun* (*the way in*) entrée F; **'no entry'** 'défense d'entrer'.

entry phone *noun* interphone M.

envelope *noun* enveloppe F.

environment *noun* environnement M.

environmental *adjective* écologique.

environment-friendly *adjective* écologique.

envy *noun* envie F.

epidemic *noun* épidémie F.

epileptic *noun* épileptique M & F.

episode *noun* épisode M.

equal *adjective* égal (M *plural* égaux); **in equal quantities** en quantités égales.
verb égaler [1].

equally *adjective* (*to share*) en parts égales; **we divided it equally** nous l'avons divisé en parts égales.

equality *noun* égalité F.

equator *noun* équateur M.

equip *verb* équiper [1]; **well equipped for the hike** bien équipé pour la randonnée; **equipped with rucksacks** équipés de sacs à dos.

equipment *noun* 1 (*for sport*) équipement M; 2 matériel M; **laboratory equipment** le matériel de laboratoire; 3 (*for sports*) équipement M.

equivalent *adjective* **to be equivalent to** être équivalent à.

error *noun* 1 (*in spelling or typing*) faute F; **a spelling error** une faute d'orthographe; 2 (*in maths or on a computer*) erreur F.

error message *noun* message M d'erreur.

escalator *noun* escalier M mécanique.

escape *noun* (*from prison*) évasion F.
verb 1 (*a person*) s'évader [1]; 2 (*an animal*) s'échapper [1].

escort *noun* escorte F; **a police escort** une escorte de police.

especially *adjective* 1 (*above all*) surtout; **there are lots of tourists, especially in August** il y a beaucoup de touristes, surtout en août; 2 (*unusually*) particulièrement; **'is he rich?'** – **'not especially'** 'est-il riche?' – 'pas particulièrement'.

essay *noun* rédaction F; **an essay on pollution** une rédaction sur la pollution.

essential *adjective* essentiel (F essentielle); **it's essential to reply quickly** il est essentiel de répondre vite.

establishment *noun* (*an organization*) établissement M.

estate *noun* 1 (*a housing estate*)

cité F; **2** (*a big house and grounds*) domaine M.

estate agent's *noun* agence F immobilière.

estate car *noun* break M.

estimate *noun* **1** (*a quote for work*) devis M; **2** (*a rough guess*) estimation F.
verb évaluer [1].

etc etc.

ethnic *adjective* ethnique; **an ethnic minority** une minorité ethnique.

EU *noun* (SHORT FOR European Union); Union européenne F.

Europe *noun* Europe F; **in Europe** en Europe; **to Europe** en Europe.

European *noun* Européen M, Européennne F.
adjective européen (F européenne).

European Union *noun* Union F européenne.

eve *noun* **Christmas Eve** la veille de Noël; **New year's Eve** la Saint-Sylvestre.

even[1] *adverb* **1** même; **even Lisa didn't like it** même Lisa, elle ne l'a pas aimé; **without even asking** sans même demander; **2 even if** même si; **even if they arrive** même s'ils arrivent; **3 not even** même pas; **I don't like animals, not even dogs** je n'aime pas les animaux, même pas les chiens; **4 even bigger** encore plus grand; **even more embarrassing** encore plus gênant; **even faster** encore plus vite; **5 even more than** encore plus que; **I liked the song even more than their last one** j'ai aimé la chanson

encore plus que leur dernière; **6 even so** quand même; **even so, we had a good time** nous nous sommes bien amusés quand même.

even[2] *adjective* **1** (*a surface or layer*) régulier (F régulière); **2** (*a number*) pair; **six is an even number** six est un numéro pair; **3** (*with the same score*) à égalité (*competitors*); **Lee and Blair are even** Lee et Blair sont à égalité.

evening *noun* **1** soir M; **this evening** ce soir; **at six o'clock in the evening** à six heures du soir; **tomorrow evening** demain soir; **on Thursday evening** jeudi soir; **the evening before** la veille au soir; **every evening** tous les soirs; **I work in the evening(s)** je travaille le soir; **the evening meal** le repas du soir; **2** (*from beginning to end*) soirée F; **during the evening** pendant la soirée; **an evening with Pavarotti** une soirée avec Pavarotti.

evening class *noun* cours M du soir.

event *noun* **1** (*a happening*) événement M; **2** (*in athletics*) épreuve F; **track events** les épreuves de vitesse; **3 in any event, at all events** de toute façon.

eventful *adjective* mouvementé (*a day or an outing*).

eventually *adverb* finalement.

ever *adverb* **1** (*at any time*) jamais; **hardly ever** presque jamais; **have you ever noticed that?** as-tu jamais remarqué ça?; **no-one ever came** personne n'est jamais venu; **hotter than ever** plus chaud que jamais;

more slowly than ever plus
lentement que jamais; **2** (*always*)
toujours; **as cheerful as ever**
toujours aussi gai; **the same as
ever** toujours le même; **3 ever
since** depuis; **and it's been raining
ever since** et depuis il pleut tout le
temps.

every *adjective* **1** tous (F toutes);
every house has a garden toutes
les maisons ont un jardin; **every day**
tous les jours; **every Monday** tous
les lundis; **every ten kilometres** tous
les dix kilomètres; **I've seen every
one of his films** j'ai vu tous ses
films; **2** (*each*) chaque; **every time**
chaque fois; **3 every now and then**
de temps en temps.

everybody, everyone *pronoun*
tout le monde; **everybody knows
that ...** tout le monde sait que ...;
everyone else tous les autres.

everything *pronoun* tout;
everything is ready tout est prêt;
everything's fine tout va bien;
everything else tout le reste;
everything you said tout ce que tu
as dit.

everywhere *adverb* partout; **there
was mud everywhere** il y avait de la
boue partout; **everywhere she
went** partout où elle allait;
everywhere else partout ailleurs.

evidently *adverb* manifestement.

evil *noun* mal M.
adjective mauvais.

exact *adjective* exact; **the exact
amount** la somme exacte; **it's the
exact opposite** c'est exactement le
contraire.

exactly *adverb* exactement; **they're
exactly the same age** ils ont
exactement le même âge; **yes,
exactly** oui, exactement.

exaggerate *verb* exagérer [24].

exaggeration *noun* exagération F.

exam *noun* examen M; **a history
exam** un examen d'histoire; **to sit
an exam** passer un examen; **to pass
an exam** réussir un examen; **to fail
an exam** échouer à un examen.

examination *noun* examen M.

examine *verb* examiner [1].

examiner *noun* examinateur M,
examinatrice F.

example *noun* exemple M; **for
example** par exemple; **to set a good
example** donner l'exemple.

excellent *adjective* excellent.

except *preposition* **1** sauf; **except in
March** sauf au mois de mars; **every
day except Tuesday** tous les jours
sauf le mardi; **except when it rains**
sauf quand il pleut; **2 except for**
sauf; **except for the children** sauf
les enfants.

exception *noun* exception F;
without exception sans exception;
with the exception of à l'exception
de.

exchange *noun* échange M; **in
exchange for his help** en échange
de son aide; **an exchange visit** un
voyage d'échange.
verb échanger [52]; **can I exchange
this shirt for a smaller one?** puis-je
échanger cette chemise contre une
plus petite?

exchange rate noun taux M d'échange.

excite verb exciter [1].

excited adjective **1** excité (*a person or animal*); **the children are excited** les enfants sont excités; **2 to get excited** s'exciter; **the dogs get excited when they hear the car** les chiens s'excitent quand ils entendent la voiture.

exciting adjective passionnant; **a really exciting film** un film vraiment passionnant.

exclamation mark noun point M d'exclamation.

excursion noun excursion F.

excuse noun excuse F; **Gary has a good excuse** Gary a une bonne excuse; **that's no excuse** ce n'est pas une excuse.
verb (*apologizing*) **excuse me!** excusez-moi!

exercise noun exercice M; **a maths exercise** un exercice de maths; **physical exercise** l'exercice physique.

exercise bicycle noun vélo M d'appartement.

exercise book noun cahier M; **my French exercise book** mon cahier de français.

exhausted adjective épuisé.

exhaust fumes plural noun gaz M plural d'échappement.

exhaust (pipe) noun pot M d'échappement.

exhibition noun exposition F; the

Cézanne exhibition l'exposition Cézanne.

exist verb exister [1].

exit noun sortie F.

expect verb **1** attendre [3] (*guests or a baby*); **we're expecting thirty people** nous attendons trente personnes; **2** s'attendre à [3] (*something to happen*); **I didn't expect that** je ne m'attendais pas à ça; **I didn't expect it at all** je ne m'y attendais pas du tout; **3** (*as a supposition*) imaginer [1]; **I expect you're tired** j'imagine que tu es fatigué; **I expect she'll bring her boyfriend** j'imagine qu'elle amènera son copain; **yes, I expect so** oui, j'imagine.

expedition noun expédition F.

expel verb **to be expelled** (*from school*) se faire [10] renvoyer.

expenses plural noun frais M plural.

expensive adjective cher (F chère); **those shoes are too expensive for me** ces chaussures sont trop chères pour moi; **the most expensive CDs** les CDs les plus chers.

experience noun expérience F.

experienced adjective expérimenté.

experiment noun expérience F; **to do an experiment** faire une expérience.

expert noun spécialiste M & F; **he's a computer expert** c'est un spécialiste en informatique.

expire verb expirer [1].

expiry date noun date F
d'expiration.

explain verb expliquer [1].

explanation noun explication F.

explode verb exploser [1].

explore verb explorer [1].

explosion noun explosion F.

exposure noun (of a film) pose F;
a 24-exposure film une pellicule de
vingt-quatre poses.

express noun (a train) rapide M.
verb 1 exprimer [1]; 2 to express
yourself s'exprimer.

expression noun expression F.

extend verb agrandir [2] (a
building).

extension noun 1 (to a house)
addition F; 2 (telephone) poste
M; can I have extension 2347
please? est-ce que je peux avoir le
poste vingt-trois quarante-sept, s'il
vous plaît? (note that in spoken
French telephone numbers are
usually broken down into groups of
two figures; this applies to longer
numbers as well); 3 (electrical)
rallonge F.

extension lead noun rallonge F.

extension number noun numéro
M de poste.

exterior adjective extérieur.

extinguish verb éteindre [60].

extinguisher noun (fire
extinguisher) extincteur M.

extra adjective 1 supplémentaire;
extra homework des devoirs
supplémentaires; wine is extra le

vin est en supplément; you have to
pay extra il faut payer un
supplément; at no extra charge
sans supplément.
adverb extra hot extra-chaud;
extra large extra-grand.

extraordinary adjective
extraordinaire.

extra-special adjective
exceptionnel (F exceptionnelle).

extra time noun (in football)
prolongation F; to go into extra
time jouer les prolongations.

extravagant adjective dépensier (F
dépensière) (a person).

extreme noun extrême M; to go to
extremes pousser les choses à
l'extrême.
adjective extrême.

extremely adverb extrêmement;
extremely fast extrêmement vite.

eye noun œil M (plural yeux); my
left eye mon œil gauche; a girl with
blue eyes la fille aux yeux bleus;
shut your eyes! ferme les yeux!;
★ to keep an eye on something
surveiller quelque chose; ★ to
make eyes at somebody faire des
yeux doux à quelqu'un.

eyebrow noun : sourcil M.

eyelash noun cil M.

eyelid noun paupière F.

eyeliner noun eye-liner M.

eye make-up noun maquillage M
pour les yeux.

eyesight noun vue F.

F f

fabric noun (cloth) tissu M.

fabulous adjective sensationnel (F sensationnelle).

face noun 1 (of a person) visage M; you've got chocolate on your face tu as du chocolat sur le visage; 2 to pull a face faire une grimace; 3 (of a clock or watch) cadran M.
verb 1 (a person) faire [10] face à; she faced her attacker elle a fait face à son agresseur; 2 the house faces the park la maison donne sur le jardin public; 3 (to stand the idea of) avoir [5] le courage de; I can't face going back je n'ai pas le courage de rentrer; 4 to face up to something faire face à quelque chose.

facilities plural noun 1 the school has good sport facilities l'école dispose d'un bon ensemble sportif; 2 the flat has cooking facilities l'appartement a une cuisine équipée.

fact noun fait M; the fact is that ... le fait est que ... ; in fact en fait; is that a fact? vraiment?

factory noun usine F.

fade verb 1 (fabric) se décolorer [1]; faded jeans un jean délavé; 2 the colours have faded les couleurs ont passé.

fail verb 1 rater [1] (a test or exam); I failed my driving test j'ai raté mon permis; 2 échouer [1]; three students failed trois étudiants ont échoué; 3 (not to do) to fail to do manquer [1] de faire; he failed to contact us il a manqué de nous contacter; ★ without fail sans faute; ring me without fail appelle-moi sans faute.

failure noun 1 échec M; it was a terrible failure c'était un échec terrible; 2 (a breakdown in a machine) panne F; a power failure une panne de courant.

faint adjective 1 to feel faint se sentir mal; 2 (slight) léger (F légère); a faint smell of gas une légère odeur de gaz; I haven't the faintest idea je n'en ai pas la moindre idée; 3 (a voice or sound) faible.
verb s'évanouir [2]; Lisa fainted Lisa s'est évanouie.

fair noun foire F.
adjective 1 (not unfair) juste; it's not fair! ce n'est pas juste!; 2 (hair) blond; he's fair-haired il a les cheveux blonds; 3 (skin) clair; people with fair skin les gens qui ont la peau claire; 4 (fairly good) assez bon (F assez bonne) (a chance, condition, or performance); her history is fair son histoire est assez bonne; 5 (weather) if it's fair tomorrow s'il ne pleut pas demain.

fairground noun champ M de foire.

fairly adverb (quite) assez; she's fairly happy elle est assez contente.

fairy noun fée F.

fairy tale noun conte M de fées.

faith noun 1 (trust) confiance F; to

have faith in somebody avoir
confiance en quelqu'un;
2 (*religious belief*) foi F.

faithful *adjective* fidèle.

faithfully *adverb* **yours faithfully**
veuillez agréer, Monsieur (or
Madame) mes salutations
distinguées.

fake *noun* faux M; **the diamonds
were fakes** les diamants étaient des
faux.
adjective faux (F fausse) (*goes before
the noun*); **a fake passport** un faux
passeport.

fall *noun* chute F; **to have a fall**
tomber.
verb **1** tomber [1]; **mind, you'll fall**
attention, tu vas tomber; **Tony fell
off his bike** Tony est tombé de son
vélo; **she fell downstairs** elle est
tombée dans l'escalier; **my jacket fell
on the floor** ma veste est tombée par
terre; **2** (*the temperature*)
descendre [3]; **it fell to minus eleven
last night** il est descendu à moins
onze cette nuit; **3** (*prices*) baisser
[1].

false *adjective* faux (F fausse) (*goes
before the noun*); **a false alarm** une
fausse alerte.

false teeth *plural noun* dentier M.

fame *noun* renommée F.

familiar *adjective* familier (F
familière); **your face is familiar**
votre visage m'est familier.

family *noun* famille F; **a family of
six** une famille de six personnes;
Ben's one of the family Ben fait
partie de la famille; **the Barnes
family** la famille Barnes.

famous *adjective* célèbre.

fan *noun* **1** fan M & F (*informal*);
Diana's an Oasis fan Diana est une
fan de Oasis; **2** (*of a team*)
supporter M; **Brian's a Chelsea
fan** Brian est un supporter de
Chelsea; **3** (*electric, for cooling*)
ventilateur M; **4** (*that you hold in
your hand*) éventail M.

fanatic *noun* fanatique M & F.

fancy *noun* **to take someone's
fancy** faire envie à quelqu'un; **the
picture took his fancy** le tableau lui
a fait envie.
adjective (*equipment*) sophistiqué.
verb **1** (*to want*) **do you fancy a
coffee?** tu veux un café?; **do you
fancy going to the new film?** ça te
dirait d'aller voir le nouveau film?;
2 I really fancy him il me plaît
beaucoup; **3** (*just*) **fancy that!** pas
possible!; **fancy you being here!**
tiens donc, toi ici!

fancy dress *noun* **in fancy dress**
déguisé; **a fancy-dress party** une
soirée déguisée.

fantastic *adjective* génial (M *plural*
géniaux) (*informal*); **really? that's
fantastic!** vraiment? c'est génial!; **a
fantastic holiday** des vacances
géniales.

far *adverb, adjective* **1** loin; **it's not
far** ce n'est pas loin; **is it far to
Carlisle?** est-ce que Carlisle est loin
d'ici?; **how far is it to Bristol?** Bristol
est à quelle distance d'ici?; **he took
us as far as Newport** il nous a
accompagnés jusqu'à Newport;
2 by far de loin; **the prettiest by
far** de loin le plus joli; **3** (*much*)
beaucoup; **far better** beaucoup

mieux; **far faster** beaucoup plus vite; **far too many people** beaucoup trop de gens; **4 so far** jusqu'ici; **so far everything's going well** jusqu'ici tout va bien; ★ **as far as I know** pour autant que je sache.

fare *noun* **1** (*on a bus or the underground*) prix M du ticket; **2** (*on a train or plane*) prix M du billet; **half fare** demi-tarif M; **full fare** plein tarif M; **the return fare to Cardiff** le prix d'un aller-retour à Cardiff.

Far East *noun* Extrême-Orient M.

farm *noun* ferme F.

farmer *noun* agriculteur M, agricultrice F.

farmhouse *noun* ferme F.

farming *noun* agriculture F.

fascinating *adjective* fascinant.

fashion *noun* mode F; **in fashion** à la mode; **out of fashion** démodé.

fashionable *adjective* à la mode.

fashion model *noun* mannequin M.

fashion show *noun* présentation F de collection.

fast *adjective* **1** rapide; **a fast car** une voiture rapide; **2 my watch is fast** ma montre avance; **you're ten minutes fast** ta montre avance de dix minutes.
adverb **1** vite; **he swims fast** il nage vite; **2** **to be fast asleep** être profondément endormi.

fast forward *noun* avance F rapide.

fat *noun* **1** (*butter, cream, etc*) matières F *plural* grasses; **2** (*on meat*) gras M; **3** (*on your body*) graisse F.
adjective gros (F grosse) (*goes before the noun*); **a fat man** un gros monsieur; **to get fat** grossir.

fatal *adjective* mortel (F mortelle).

father *noun* père M; **my father's office** le bureau de mon père.

Father Christmas *noun* le père Noël.

father-in-law *noun* beau-père M.

fault *noun* **1** (*when you are responsible*) faute F; **it's Stephen's fault** c'est la faute de Stephen; **it's not my fault** ce n'est pas ma faute; **2** (*a defect*) défaut M; **there's a fault in this sweater** il y a un défaut dans ce pull; **3** (*in tennis*) faute F.

favour *noun* **1** (*a kindness*) service M; **to do somebody a favour** rendre service à quelqu'un; **can you do me a favour?** peux-tu me rendre service?; **to ask a favour of somebody** demander un service à quelqu'un; **2** **to be in favour of something** être pour quelque chose.

favourite *adjective* préféré; **my favourite band** mon groupe préféré.

fear *noun* peur F.
verb craindre [31]; **to fear the worst** craindre le pire.

feather *noun* plume F.

feature *noun* **1** (*of your face*) trait M; **to have delicate features** avoir des traits délicats; **2** (*of a car or a machine*) caractéristique F.

February *noun* février M; **in February** en février.

fed up *adjective* **I'm fed up** j'en ai marre (*informal*); **I'm fed up with working every day** j'en ai marre de travailler tous les jours.

feed *verb* donner [1] à manger à; **have you fed the dog?** est-ce que tu as donné à manger au chien?

feel *verb* **1** se sentir [58]; **I feel tired** je me sens fatigué; **I don't feel well** je ne me sens pas bien; **2** sentir [58]; **I didn't feel a thing** je n'ai rien senti; **3** to **feel afraid** avoir [5] peur; **to feel cold** avoir froid; **to feel thirsty** avoir soif; **4** to **feel like doing** avoir envie de faire; **I feel like going to the cinema** j'ai envie d'aller au cinéma; **5** (*touch*) toucher [1].

feeling *noun* **1** (*in your mind*) sentiment M; **a feeling of embarrassment** un sentiment de gêne; **to show your feelings** montrer ses sentiments; **to hurt somebody's feelings** blesser quelqu'un; **2** (*in your body*) sensation F; **a dizzy feeling** une sensation de vertige; **3** (*an impression or intuition*) impression F; **I have the feeling James doesn't like me** j'ai l'impression que James ne m'aime pas.

felt-tip (pen) *noun* feutre M.

female *noun* (*animal*) femelle F. *adjective* **1** féminin (*person, population*); **2** femelle (*animal, insect*).

feminine *adjective* féminin.

feminist *noun, adjective* féministe M & F.

fence *noun* (*round a field*) clôture F.

fern *noun* fougère F.

ferry *noun* ferry M.

fertilizer *noun* engrais M.

festival *noun* (*for films, art, or music*) festival M.

fetch *verb* aller [7] chercher; **Tom's fetching the children** Tom est allé chercher les enfants; **fetch me the other knife!** va me chercher l'autre couteau!

fever *adjective* fièvre F.

few *adjective, pronoun* **1** peu de; **few people think that …** peu de gens pensent que …; **very few houses have a swimming-pool** très peu de maisons ont une piscine; **2** **a few** (*followed by a noun*) quelques; **a few weeks earlier** quelques semaines plus tôt; **in a few minutes** dans quelques minutes; **3** **a few** (*by itself*) quelques-uns (F quelques-unes); **have you any tomatoes? we want a few for the salad** avez-vous des tomates? nous en voulons quelques-unes pour la salade; **4** **quite a few** pas mal de; **there were quite a few questions** il y avait pas mal de questions.

fewer *adjective* moins de; **there are fewer tourists this year** il y a moins de touristes cette année.

fiction *noun* **I read a lot of fiction** je lis beacoup de romans.

field noun 1 (*with grass or crops*) champ M; **a field of wheat** un champ de blé; 2 (*for sport*) terrain M; 3 (*the kind of work you do*) domaine M.

fierce adjective 1 féroce (*an animal or person*); 2 violent (*a storm or a battle*).

fifteen number quinze; **Lara's fifteen** Lara a quinze ans.

fifth number cinquième; **the fifth of January** le cinq janvier; **on the fifth floor** au cinquième étage.

fifty number cinquante M; **my uncle's fifty** mon oncle a cinquante ans.

fig noun figue F.

fight noun 1 (*a scuffle*) bagarre F; 2 (*in boxing*) combat M; 3 (*against illness*) lutte F.
verb 1 (*to have a fight*) se battre [21]; **they were fighting** ils se battaient; 2 (*to quarrel*) se disputer [1]; **they're always fighting** ils sont toujours en train de se disputer; 3 (*struggle against*) lutter [1] contre (*poverty or a disease*).

fighting noun 1 (*in the streets or a pub, for example*) bagarre F; 2 (*in war*) combat M.

figure noun 1 (*number*) chiffre M; **a four-figure number** un nombre de quatre chiffres; 2 (*body shape*) ligne F; **good for your figure** bon pour la ligne; 3 (*a person*) personnage M; **a familiar figure** un personnage familier; 4 (*diagram*) figure F.

file noun 1 (*for records of a person or case*) dossier M; 2 (*ring binder*) classeur M; 3 (*cardboard folder*)

chemise F; 4 (*on a computer*) fichier M; 5 (*a nail file*) une lime.
verb 1 classer [1] (*documents*); 2 **to file your nails** se limer [1] les ongles.

fill verb remplir [2] (*a container*); **she filled my glass** elle a rempli mon verre; **a smoke-filled room** une pièce remplie de fumée.
●**to fill in** remplir [2] (*a form*).
●**to fill in for someone** remplacer [61] quelqu'un.

film noun 1 (*in a cinema*) film M; **shall we go and see a film?** si on allait voir un film?; **the new film about Picasso** le nouveau film au sujet de Picasso; 2 (*for a camera*) pellicule F; **a 24-exposure colour film** une pellicule couleur de 24 poses.

film star noun vedette F de cinéma.

filter noun filtre M.

filthy adjective dégoûtant.

fin noun nageoire F.

final noun (*in sport*) finale F.
adjective dernier (F dernière); **the final instalment** le dernier épisode; **the final result** le résultat final.

finally adverb finalement.

find verb trouver [1]; **did you find your passport?** as-tu trouvé ton passeport?; **I can't find my keys** je ne trouve pas mes clefs.
●**to find out** 1 (*to enquire*) se renseigner [1]; **I don't know, I'll find out** je ne sais pas, je me renseignerai; 2 **to find something out** découvrir [30] (*the facts or an answer*); **when Lucy found out the truth** quand Lucy a découvert la vérité.

fine noun amende F; (for parking or speeding) contravention F.
adjective 1 (in good health) bien; 'how are you?' – 'fine, thanks' 'comment ça va?' – 'très bien merci'; 2 (very good) excellent; she's a fine athlete c'est une excellente athlète; 3 (convenient) très bien; ten o'clock? yes, that's fine dix heures? oui, très bien; Friday will be fine vendredi sera très bien; 4 (sunny) beau (F belle) (weather or a day); if it's fine s'il fait beau; 5 (not coarse or thick) fin; in fine wool en laine fine.

finely adjective (chopped or grated) finement.

finger noun doigt M; ★ I'll keep my fingers crossed for you je croise les doigts pour toi.

fingernail noun ongle M.

finish noun 1 (end) fin F; 2 (in a race) arrivée F.
verb 1 finir [2]; wait, I haven't finished attends, je n'ai pas fini; when does school finish? à quelle heure finit l'école?; 2 (to finish off) terminer [1] (work or a project); have you finished the book? est-ce que tu as terminé le livre?; 3 to finish doing finir de faire; have you finished telephoning? as-tu fini de téléphoner?
●to finish with finir avec; have you finished with the computer? as-tu fini avec l'ordinateur?

Finland noun Finlande F; in Finland en Finlande; to Finland en Finlande.

Finnish noun finnois M (the language).
adjective finlandais.

fir tree noun sapin M.

fire noun 1 (in a grate) feu M; to light a fire allumer un feu; sitting by the fire assis près du feu; 2 to catch fire prendre feu; 3 (accidental) incendie M; a fire in a factory un incendie dans une usine.
verb 1 (to shoot) tirer [1]; the soldiers were firing les soldats tiraient; to fire at somebody tirer sur quelqu'un; 2 décharger (a gun).

fire alarm noun alarme F incendie.

fire brigade noun pompiers M plural.

fire engine noun voiture F des pompiers.

fire escape noun escalier M de secours.

fire extinguisher noun extincteur M.

fire fighter noun pompier M.

fireplace noun cheminée F.

fire station noun caserne F de pompiers.

firework noun feu M d'artifice (plural feux d'artifice); there will be a firework display il y aura un feu d'artifice.

firm noun (business) entreprise F.
adjective ferme.

first adjective, adverb 1 premier (F première); Susan's the first Susan est la première; the first of May le premier mai; for the first time pour la première fois; I came first in the

200 metres je suis arrivé premier aux 200 mètres; **2** (*to begin with*) d'abord; **first, I'm going to make some tea** d'abord je vais faire du thé; **3** (*at first*) au début; **at first; at first he was shy** au début il était timide.

first aid *noun* premiers secours M *plural*.

first class *adjective* **1** de première classe (*a ticket, carriage, or hotel*); **a first-class compartment** un compartiment de première classe; **he always travels first class** il voyage toujours en première; **2** au tarif rapide (*a letter or stamp*); **six first-class stamps** six timbres au tarif rapide.

first floor *noun* premier étage M; **on the first floor** au premier étage.

firstly *adverb* premièrement.

first name *noun* prénom M.

fish *noun* poisson M; **do you like fish?** aimez-vous le poisson? *verb* pêcher [1]; **Dad was fishing for trout** Papa pêchait la truite.

fish and chips *noun* poisson M frit avec des frites.

fisherman *noun* pêcheur M.

fishing *noun* pêche F; **I love fishing** j'adore la pêche; **to go fishing** aller à la pêche.

fishing rod *noun* canne F à pêche.

fishing tackle *noun* matériel M de pêche.

fist *noun* poing M.

fit *noun* **1** (*of rage*) **to have a fit** piquer une crise; **your dad'll have a**

fit when he sees your hair! ton père va piquer une crise quand il va voir tes cheveux!; **2** *an epileptic fit* une crise d'épilepsie.
adjective (*healthy*) en forme; **I feel really fit** je me sens vraiment en forme; **to keep fit** se maintenir en forme.
verb **1** (*to be the right size for*) (*a garment*) être [6] de la taille de (*a person*); (*shoes*) être à la pointure de; **this skirt doesn't fit me** cette jupe n'est pas à ma taille; **2** (*be able to be put into*) aller [7] dans; **will my cases all fit in the car?** est-ce que mes valises iront dans la voiture?; **the key doesn't fit in the lock** la clé ne va pas dans la serrure; **3** (*install*) installer [1]; **they've fitted an alarm** ils ont installé une alarme.

fitted carpet *noun* moquette F.

fitted kitchen *noun* cuisine F intégrée.

fitting room *noun* cabine F d'essayage.

five *number* cinq M; **Belinda's five** Belinda a cinq ans; **it's five o'clock** il est cinq heures.

fix *verb* **1** (*repair*) réparer [1]; **Mum's fixed the computer** Maman a réparé l'ordinateur; **2** (*to decide on*) fixer [1]; **to fix a date** fixer une date; **at a fixed price** à prix fixe; **3** préparer [1] (*a meal*); **I'll fix supper** c'est moi qui vais préparer le repas du soir.

fizzy *adjective* gazeux (F gazeuse); **fizzy water** eau F gazeuse.

flag *noun* drapeau M (*plural* drapeaux).

flame noun flamme F.

flamingo noun flamant M rose.

flan noun tarte F; **an onion flan** une tarte à l'oignon.

flap verb battre [21]; **the bird flapped its wings** l'oiseau battait des ailes.

flash noun 1 **a flash of lightning** un éclair; 2 **to do something in a flash** faire quelque chose en un clin d'œil; 3 (on a camera) flash M.
verb 1 (a light) clignoter [1]; 2 **to flash by or past** passer [1] comme un éclair; 3 **to flash your headlights** faire [10] un appel de phares.

flashback noun flash-back M.

flat noun appartement M; **a third-floor flat** un appartement au troisième étage.
adjective 1 plat; **flat shoes** des chaussures plates; **a flat landscape** un paysage plat; 2 **a flat tyre** un pneu crevé.

flatmate noun colocataire M & F.

flatter verb flatter [1].

flattering adjective flatteur (F flatteuse).

flavour noun 1 (taste) goût M; **the sauce had no flavour** la sauce n'avait aucun goût; 2 (of drink, ice cream, etc) parfum M; **what flavour of ice cream would you like?** tu veux quel parfum de glace?
verb 1 parfumer [1]; **vanilla-flavoured** parfumé à la vanille.

flea noun puce F.

flea market noun marché M aux puces.

flesh noun chair F.

flex noun fil M.

flexible adjective flexible (an arrangement).

flight noun 1 vol M; **a charter flight** un vol charter; **the flight from Moscow is delayed** le vol de Moscou est retardé; 2 **a flight of stairs** un escalier; **four flights of stairs** quatre étages.

fling verb lancer [61].

flipper noun (for a swimmer) palme F.

flirt verb flirter [1].

float verb flotter [1].

flood noun 1 (of water) inondation F; **the floods in the south** les inondations au sud; **to be in floods of tears** verser des torrents de larmes; 2 (of letters or complaints) déluge M.
verb inonder [1]

floodlight noun projecteur M.

floor noun 1 (wooden) plancher M; (concrete) sol M; **to sweep the floor** balayer; **to sweep the kitchen floor** balayer la cuisine; **your glasses are on the floor** tes lunettes sont par terre; 2 (a storey) étage M; **on the second floor** au deuxième étage.

floppy disk noun disquette F.

florist noun fleuriste M & F.

flour noun farine F.

flow verb couler [1].

flower noun fleur F; **a bunch of**

flowers un bouquet.
verb fleurir [2].

flu *noun* grippe F; **to have flu** avoir la grippe.

fluent *adjective* **she speaks fluent Italian** elle parle couramment l'italien.

fluently *adverb* couramment.

flush *verb* **1** (*to go red*) rougir [2]; **2 to flush the lavatory** tirer [1] la chasse.

flute *noun* flûte F; **to play the flute** jouer de la flûte.

fly *noun* mouche F.
verb **1** (*a bird, a bee, or a plane*) voler [1]; **2** (*in a plane*) prendre [64] l'avion; **we flew to Edinburgh** nous sommes allés à Édimbourg en avion; **we flew from Gatwick** nous sommes partis de Gatwick; **3** faire [10] voler (*a kite*); **4** (*to pass quickly*) (*time*) passer [1] très vite.

fly spray *noun* bombe F insecticide.

foam *noun* **1** (*foam rubber*) mousse F; **a foam mattress** un matelas mousse; **2** (*on a drink*) mousse F.

focus *noun* **to be in focus** être au point; **to be out of focus** être flou.
verb mettre [1] au point (*a camera*).

fog *noun* brouillard M.

foggy *adjective* brumeux (F brumeuse) (*weather*); **it was foggy** il y avait du brouillard.

foil *noun* (*kitchen foil*) papier M aluminium.

fold *noun* pli M.
verb **1** plier [1]; **to fold something**

up plier quelque chose; **2 to fold your arms** croiser [1] les bras.

folder *noun* chemise F.

folding *adjective* pliant; **a folding table** une table pliante.

follow *verb* suivre [75]; **follow me!** suivez-moi!; **followed by a dinner** suivi d'un dîner; **do you follow me?** vous me suivez?

following *adjective* suivant; **the following year** l'année suivante.

fond *adjective* **to be fond of somebody** aimer beaucoup quelqu'un; **I'm very fond of him** je l'aime beaucoup.

food *noun* **1** nourriture F; **to buy food** acheter à manger; **I like French food** j'aime la cuisine française; **2** (*stocks*) provisions F *plural*; **we bought food for the holiday** nous avons acheté des provisions pour les vacances.

fool *noun* idiot M, idiote F.

foot *noun* **1** pied M; **Lucy came on foot** Lucy est venue à pied; **2** (*the bottom*) **at the foot of the stairs** en bas de l'escalier.

football *noun* **1** (*the game*) football M; **to play football** jouer au football; **2** (*ball*) ballon M de football.

footballer *noun* joueur de football M, joueuse de football F.

footpath *noun* sentier M.

footprint *noun* empreinte F.

footstep *noun* pas M.

for *preposition* **1** pour; **a present for**

my mother un cadeau pour ma mère; **petrol for the car** de l'essence pour la voiture; **sausages for lunch** des saucisses pour le déjeuner; **it's for cleaning** c'est pour nettoyer; **what's it for?** c'est pour quoi faire?
2 (*time expressions in the past or future*) pendant; **I studied French for six years** (*but I no longer do*) j'ai étudié le français pendant six ans; **I'll be away for four days** je serai absent pendant quatre jours;
3 (*time expressions in the past but continuing in the present*) depuis; **I've been waiting here for an hour** (*and I'm still waiting*) j'attends ici depuis une heure; **my brother's been living in Paris for three years** (*and he still lives there*) mon frère habite à Paris depuis trois ans; 4 **I sold my bike for fifty pounds** j'ai vendu mon vélo cinquante livres; 5 **what's the French for 'bee'?** comment dit-on 'bee' en français?

forbid *verb* défendre [3]; **to forbid somebody to do something** défendre à quelqu'un de faire quelque chose; **I forbid you to go out** je te défends de sortir.

forbidden *adjective* défendu.

force *noun* force F.
verb forcer [61]; **to force somebody to do** forcer quelqu'un à faire.

forecast *noun* (*weather forecast*) météo F.

forefinger *noun* index M.

foreground *noun* premier plan M; **in the foreground** au premier plan.

forehead *noun* front M.

foreign *adjective* étranger (F

étrangère); **in a foreign country** dans un pays étranger.

foreigner *noun* étranger M, étrangère F.

foresee *verb* prévoir [65].

forest *noun* forêt F.

forever *adverb* 1 pour toujours; **I'd like to stay here forever** j'aimerais rester là pour toujours; 2 (*non-stop*) sans arrêt; **he's forever asking questions** il pose sans arrêt des questions.

forget *verb* oublier [1]; **I forget his name** j'oublie son nom; **we've forgotten the bread!** nous avons oublié le pain!; **to forget to do** oublier de faire; **I forgot to phone** j'ai oublié d'appeler; **to forget about something** oublier quelque chose.

forgive *verb* pardonner [1] à; **to forgive somebody** pardonner à quelqu'un; **I forgave him** je lui ai pardonné; **to forgive somebody for doing** pardonner à quelqu'un d'avoir fait; **I forgave her for losing my ring** je lui ai pardonné d'avoir perdu ma bague.

fork *noun* fourchette F.

form *noun* 1 formulaire M; **to fill in a form** remplir un formulaire; 2 (*shape or kind*) forme F; **in the form of** sous forme de; 3 **to be on form** être en forme; 4 (*in school*) classe F.
verb former [1].

formal *adjective* officiel (F officielle) (*invitation, event, complaint, etc*).

format *noun* format M.

former *adjective* ancien (F

ancienne) (*goes before the noun*); a former pupil un ancien élève.

fortnight *noun* quinze jours M *plural*; **we're going to Spain for a fortnight** nous allons passer quinze jours en Espagne.

fortunately *adverb* heureusement.

forty *number* quarante; **my aunt's forty** ma tante a quarante ans.

forward *noun* (*in sport*) avant M. *adverb* **to move forward** avancer; **a seat further forward** une place plus en avant.

foster child *noun* enfant adoptif M, enfant adoptive F.

foul *noun* (*in sport*) faute F. *adjective* infect; **the weather's foul** il fait un temps infect.

fountain *noun* fontaine F.

fountain pen *noun* stylo M à encre.

four *number* quatre M; **Simon's four** Simon a quatre ans; **it's four o'clock** il est quatre heures; ★ **on all fours** à quatre pattes.

fourteen *number* quatorze M; **Susie's fourteen** Susie a quatorze ans.

fourth *number* quatrième; **the fourth of July** le quatre juillet; **on the fourth floor** au quatrième étage.

fox *noun* renard M.

fragile *adjective* fragile.

frame *noun* cadre M.

franc *noun* franc M; **a fifty-franc note** un billet de cinquante francs.

France *noun* France F; **in France** en France; **to France** en France; **I like France** j'aime la France; **Nadine's from France** Nadine est française.

frantic *adjective* **1** (*very upset*) fou (F folle); **Mum was frantic with worry** Maman était folle d'inquiétude; **2** (*desperate*) désespéré (*efforts or a search*).

freckle *noun* tache F de rousseur.

free *adjective* **1** (*when you don't pay*) gratuit; **the bus is free** le bus est gratuit; **a free ticket** un billet gratuit; **2** (*not occupied*) libre; **are you free on Thursday?** es-tu libre jeudi?; **3** sugar-free sans sucre; lead-free sans plomb. *verb* libérer [24].

freedom *noun* liberté F.

free gift *noun* cadeau M (*plural* cadeaux).

freeze *verb* **1** (*in a freezer*) congeler [45]; **frozen peas** des petits pois congelés; **2** (*in cold weather*) geler [45]; **it's freezing outside** il gèle dehors.

freezer *noun* congélateur M.

freezing *noun* zéro M; **three degrees below freezing** trois degrés en-dessous de zéro. *adjective* **I'm freezing** je suis gelé (*informal*); **it's freezing outside** il fait très froid dehors.

French *noun* **1** (*the language*) français M; **to speak French** parler français; **say it in French** dis-le en français; **to learn French** apprendre le français; **2** (*the people*) **the French** les Français M *plural*; **most

of the French la plupart des Français.
adjective **1** français; **Jean-Marc is French** Jean-Marc est français; **2** de français (*a teacher or a lesson*); **the French class** le cours de français.

French bean *noun* haricot M vert.

French dressing *noun* vinaigrette F.

French fries *plural noun* frites F plural.

Frenchman *noun* Français M.

French window *noun* porte-fenêtre F (*plural* portes-fenêtres).

Frenchwoman *noun* Française F.

frequent *adjective* fréquent.

fresh *adjective* frais (F fraîche); **fresh eggs** des œufs frais; **I'm going out for some fresh air** je vais prendre de l'air.

Friday *noun* vendredi M; **next Friday** vendredi prochain; **last Friday** vendredi dernier; **on Friday** vendredi; **I'll phone you on Friday evening** je t'appellerai vendredi soir; **on Fridays** le vendredi; **closed on Fridays** fermé le vendredi; **every Friday** tous les vendredis; **Good Friday** le Vendredi saint.

fridge *noun* frigo M (*informal*); **put it in the fridge** mets-le au frigo.

friend *noun* ami M, amie F; **a friend of mine** un ami (or une amie) à moi; **to make friends** (*in a general way*) se faire des amis; **he made friends with Danny** il est devenu ami avec Danny.

friendly *adjective* sympathique.

friendship *noun* amitié F.

fries *plural noun* frites F plural.

fright *noun* peur F; **get a fright** avoir peur; **you gave me a fright!** tu m'as fait peur!

frighten *verb* effrayer [59].

frightened *adjective* **to be frightened** avoir peur; **Martin's frightened of snakes** Martin a peur des serpents.

frightening *adjective* effrayant.

fringe *noun* frange F.

frog *noun* grenouille F.

from *preposition* de; **a letter from Tom** une lettre de Tom; **100 metres from the cinema** à cent mètres du cinéma; **from Monday to Friday** du lundi jusqu'au vendredi; **he comes from Dublin** il vient de Dublin; **two years from now** d'ici deux ans; **from seven o'clock onwards** à partir de sept heures.

front *noun* **1** (*of a building, a garment, or a cupboard*) devant M; **2** (*of a car*) avant M; **sitting in the front** assis à l'avant; **3** (*of a train or a queue*) tête F; **there are seats at the front of the train** il y a des places en tête du train; **4** (*of a card or envelope*) recto M; **the address is on the front** l'adresse est au recto; **5** (*in a theatre, cinema, or class*) premier rang M; **seats at the front** des places au premier rang; **6 in front of** devant; **in front of the TV** devant la télé; **in front of me** devant moi.
adjective **1** de devant; **his front**

paw sa patte de devant; **in the front row** au premier rang; **2** avant; **the front seat** (of a car) le siège avant; **the front wheel** la roue avant.

front door noun porte F d'entrée.

frontier noun frontière F.

frost noun gel M.

frosty adjective **1** **it's frosty this morning** il gèle ce matin; **2** couvert de givre (windscreen, grass, etc).

frown verb froncer [61] les sourcils; **he frowned at us** il nous a regardés en fronçant les sourcils.

frozen adjective (in a freezer) surgelé; **a frozen pizza** une pizza surgelée.

fruit noun fruits M plural (note that in French 'un fruit' is a piece of fruit, whereas 'fruit' in English meaning several pieces of fruit always has to be 'fruits' in the plural in French); **we bought cheese and fruit** nous avons acheté du fromage et des fruits; **fruit juice** le jus de fruits.

fruit machine noun machine F à sous.

fruit salad noun salade F de fruits.

frustrated adjective frustré.

fry verb faire [10] frire; **we fried the fish** nous avons fait frire les poissons; **a fried egg** un œuf au plat.

frying pan noun poêle F.

fuel noun **1** (for a vehicle or plane) carburant M.

full adjective **1** plein; **this glass is full** ce verre est plein; **the train was**

full of tourists le train était plein de touristes; **2** complet (F complète) (a hotel or flight); **3** (top) **at full speed** à toute vitesse; **at full volume** à plein volume; **4** **I'm full** j'ai assez mangé; **5** **to write something out in full** écrire quelque chose en toutes lettres.

full stop noun point M.

full-time noun **a full-time job** un travail à plein temps.

fully adjective entièrement.

fun noun plaisir M; **to have fun** s'amuser; **have fun!** amusez-vous bien!; **we had fun catching the ponies** nous nous sommes beaucoup amusés en attrapant les poneys; **skiing is fun** c'est amusant de faire du ski; **I do it for fun** je le fais pour m'amuser; ★ **to make fun of somebody** se moquer de quelqu'un.

funds plural noun fonds M plural.

funeral noun enterrement M.

funfair noun fête F foraine.

funny adjective **1** (when you laugh) drôle; **how funny you are!** que tu es drôle!; **a funny story** une histoire drôle; **2** (strange) bizarre; **that's funny, I'm sure I paid** c'est bizarre, je suis certain que j'ai payé; **a funny noise** un bruit bizarre.

fur noun **1** (on an animal) poils M plural; **2** (for a coat) fourrure F; **a fur coat** un manteau de fourrure.

furious adjective furieux (F furieuse); **she was furious with Steve** elle était furieuse contre Steve.

furniture noun meubles M plural; to buy some furniture acheter des meubles; a piece of furniture un meuble.

further adverb plus loin; further than the station plus loin que la gare; ten kilometres further on dix kilomètres plus loin; further forward plus en avant; further back plus en arrière.

fuse noun fusible M.

fuss noun histoires F plural; to make a fuss faire des histoires; to make a fuss about the bill faire toute une histoire à propos de l'addition.

fussy adjective to be fussy about something être difficile sur quelque chose (food, for example).

future noun 1 avenir M; in future à l'avenir; in the future dans l'avenir; 2 (in grammar) futur M; a verb in the future un verbe au futur.

G g

gadget noun gadget M.

gain verb 1 gagner [1]; in order to gain time pour gagner du temps; we have nothing to gain nous n'avons rien à gagner; 2 to gain speed prendre de la vitesse; to gain weight prendre du poids.

gale noun vent M violent.

gallery noun an art gallery (public) un musée; (private) une galerie.

gamble verb jouer [1].

game noun 1 jeu M; children's games les jeux d'enfant; a game of chance un jeu de hasard; a board game un jeu de société; 2 a game of une partie de; to have a game of cards faire une partie de cartes; 3 match M; a game of football un match de foot.

gang noun bande F; all the gang were there toute la bande y était.

gangster noun gangster M.

gap noun 1 (hole) trou M; 2 (in time) intervalle M; a two-year gap un intervalle de deux ans; 3 an age gap une différence d'âge.

garage noun garage M.

garden noun jardin M.

gardener noun jardinier M; he wants to be a gardener il veut être jardinier.

gardening noun jardinage M.

garlic noun ail M.

garlic mayonnaise noun aïoli M.

garment noun vêtement M.

gas noun gaz M.

gas cooker noun cuisinière F à gaz.

gas fire noun radiateur M à gaz.

gas meter noun compteur M à gaz.

gate noun 1 (garden) portail M; 2 (field) barrière F; 3 (at the airport) porte F.

gather verb 1 (people) se rassembler [1]; a crowd gathered une foule s'est rassemblée;

2 cueillir [35] (*fruit, vegetables, flowers*); **3 as far as I can gather** autant que je sache.

gay *adjective* homosexuel (F homosexuelle).

gaze *verb* **to gaze at something** regarder [1] quelque chose.

gear *noun* **1** (*in a car*) vitesse F; **to change gear** changer de vitesse; **2** (*equipment*) matériel M; **camping gear** du matériel de camping; **3** (*things*) affaires; **I've left all my gear at Gary's** j'ai laissé toutes mes affaires chez Gary.

gear lever *noun* levier M de vitesses.

gel *noun* **hair gel** le gel pour les cheveux.

Gemini *noun* Gémeaux M *plural*; **Steph's Gemini** Steph est Gémeaux.

gender *noun* (*of a word*) genre M; **what is the gender of 'maison'?** quel est le genre de 'maison'?

general *noun* général M (*plural* généraux). *adjective* général (M *plural* généraux); **in general** en général.

general election *noun* élections législatives F *plural*.

general knowledge *noun* connaissances générales F *plural*.

generally *adverb* généralement.

generation *noun* génération F.

generator *noun* générateur M.

generous *adjective* généreux (F généreuse).

genetics *noun* génétique F.

Geneva *noun* Genève; **to Geneva** à Genève; **in Geneva** à Genève; **Lake Geneva** le lac Léman.

genius *noun* génie M; **Lisa, you're a genius!** Lisa, tu es un génie!

gentle *adjective* doux (F douce).

gentleman *noun* monsieur M (*plural* messieurs); **ladies and gentlemen** mesdames et messieurs.

gently *adverb* doucement.

gents *noun* toilettes F *plural*; (*marked on the door*) 'Messieurs'; **where's the gents?** où sont les toilettes?

genuine *adjective* **1** (*real*) véritable; **a genuine diamond** un véritable diamant; **2** (*authentic*) authentique; **a genuine signature** une signature authentique; **3** *sincere* (*person*); **she's very genuine** elle est très sincère.

geography *noun* géographie F.

germ *noun* microbe M.

German *noun* **1** Allemand M, Allemande F; **2** (*language*) allemand. *adjective* le allemand.

Germany *noun* Allemagne F; **to Germany** en Allemagne; **in Germany** en Allemagne.

get *verb* **1** (*have, receive*) avoir [5]; **he's got lots of money** il a beaucoup d'argent; **she's got long hair** elle a les cheveux longs; **I got a bike for my birthday** j'ai eu un vélo pour mon anniversaire; **I got your letter yesterday** j'ai eu ta lettre hier; **I got fifteen for my French homework** j'ai eu quinze pour mon devoir français; 2 (*fetch*) chercher [1]; **I'll go and get some bread** j'irai chercher du pain; **I'll get your bag for you** je te chercherai ton sac; 3 (*obtain*) trouver [1]; **Fred's got a job** Fred a trouvé un emploi; **where did you get that jacket?** où est-ce que tu as trouvé cette veste?; 4 **to have got to do** devoir [8] faire; **I've got to phone before midday** je dois appeler avant midi; 5 **to get to somewhere** arriver [1] quelque part; **when we got to London** quand nous sommes arrivés à Londres; **to get here** (or **there**) arriver; **we got here this morning** nous sommes arrivés ce matin; **what time did they get there?** ils sont arrivés à quelle heure?; 6 (*become*) commencer [61] à être; **I'm getting tired** je commence à être fatigué; **it's getting late** il commence à être tard; **it's getting dark** il commence à faire nuit; **I'm getting hungry** je commence à avoir faim; 7 **to get something done** faire [10] faire quelque chose; **I'm getting my hair cut this afternoon** je vais me faire couper les cheveux cet après-midi.

●**to get back** rentrer [1]; **Mum gets back at six** Maman rentre à six heures.

●**to get something back** récupérer [24] quelque chose; **did you get your books back?** est-ce que tu as récupéré tes livres?

●**to get into something** monter [1] dans quelque chose (*a vehicle*); **he got into the car** il est monté dans la voiture.

●**to get off something** descendre [3] de quelque chose; **I got off the train at Banbury** je suis descendu du train à Banbury.

●**to get on** aller [7]; **how's Amanda getting on?** comment va Amanda?

●**to get on something** monter [1] dans quelque chose (*vehicle*); **she got on the train at Reading** elle est montée dans le train à Reading.

●**to get on with somebody** s'entendre [3] avec quelqu'un; **she doesn't get on with her brother** elle ne s'entend pas avec son frère.

●**to get out of something** descendre [3] de quelque chose (*vehicle*); **Laura got out of the car** Laura est descendue de la voiture.

●**to get something out** sortir [72] quelque chose; **Robert got his guitar out** Robert a sorti sa guitare.

●**to get together** se voir; [13] **we must get together soon** il faut qu'on se voie bientôt.

●**to get up** se lever; [50] **I get up at seven** je me lève à sept heures.

ghost *noun* fantôme M.

giant *noun* géant M, géante F. *adjective* énorme; **a giant lorry** un énorme camion.

gift *noun* 1 cadeau M (*plural* cadeaux); **a Christmas gift** un cadeau de Noël; 2 **to have a gift for something** être doué pour quelque chose; **Jo has a real gift for languages** Jo est vraiment douée pour les langues.

gifted *adjective* doué.

gigantic *adjective* gigantesque.

gin *noun* gin M.

ginger *noun* gingembre M.

giraffe *noun* girafe F.

girl *noun* 1 fille F; **three boys and four girls** trois garçons et quatre filles; **a little girl** une petite fille; **when I was a little girl** quand j'étais petite; **2** (*a teenager or young woman*) jeune fille F; **an eighteen-year-old girl** une jeune fille de dix-huit ans.

girlfriend *noun* copine F; **Darren's gone out with his girlfriend** Darren est sorti avec sa copine; **Lizzie and her girlfriends have gone to the cinema** Lizzie et ses copines sont allées au cinéma.

give *verb* donner [1]; **to give something to somebody** donner quelque chose à quelqu'un; **I'll give you my address** je te donnerai mon adresse; **give me the key** donne-moi la clé; **Yasmin's dad gave her the money** le père de Yasmin lui a donné l'argent.

●**to give something away** donner quelque chose; **she's given away all her books** elle a donné tous ses livres.

●**to give something back to somebody** rendre [3] quelque chose à quelqu'un; **I gave her back the keys** je lui ai rendu les clés.

●**to give in** céder [24]; **my mum said no but she gave in in the end** maman a dit non, mais elle a fini par céder.

●**to give up** abandonner [1] **I give up!** j'abandonne!

●**to give up doing** arrêter [1] de faire; **she's given up smoking** elle a arrêté de fumer.

glad *adjective* content; **I'm glad to hear he's better** je suis content d'apprendre qu'il va mieux; **I'm glad to be back** je suis content d'être de retour.

glance *noun* coup d'œil M.

verb **to glance at something** jeter [48] un coup d'œil à quelque chose; **Sara glanced at the envelope** Sara a jeté un coup d'œil à l'enveloppe.

glass *noun* verre M; **a glass of water** un verre d'eau; **a glass table** une table en verre.

glasses *plural noun* lunettes F *plural*; **to wear glasses** porter des lunettes.

glider *noun* planeur M.

global *adjective* mondial (M *plural* mondiaux).

global warming *noun* le réchauffement de la planète.

globe *noun* globe M.

glove *noun* gant M; **a pair of gloves** une paire de gants.

glove compartment *noun* boîte F à gants.

glue *noun* colle F.

go *noun* **1** (*in a game*) whose go is it? c'est à qui de jouer?; **it's my go** c'est à moi de jouer; **2** **to have a go at doing** essayer de faire; **I'll have a go at mending it for you** j'essaierai de le réparer pour toi.

verb **1** aller [7]; **we're going to London tomorrow** nous allons à Londres demain; **Mark's gone to the dentist's** Mark est allé chez le dentiste; **to go for a walk** aller se promener; **2** (*with another verb*) aller; **I'm going to make some tea** je vais faire du thé; **he was going to phone me** il allait m'appeler; **3** (*leave*) partir [58]; **Pauline's already gone** Pauline est déjà partie; **we're going on holiday** tomorrow nous partons en vacances demain; **4** (an event) se passer [1]; **did the party go well?** est-ce que la soirée s'est bien passée?

● **to go away** s'en aller [7]; **go away!** va-t-en!

● **to go back 1** retourner [1]; **I'm going back to France in March** je retourne en France en mars; **I'm not going back there again!** je n'y retourne plus! **2** (to home, school, office) rentrer [1]; **I went back home** je suis rentré chez moi.

● **to go down 1** descendre [3]; **she's gone down to the kitchen** elle est descendue dans la cuisine; **to go down the stairs** descendre l'escalier; **2** (price, temperature) baisser [1]; **prices have gone down** les prix ont baissé; **3** (tyre, balloon, airbed) se dégonfler [1].

● **to go in** entrer [1]; **he went in and shut the door** il est entré et il a fermé la porte.

● **to go into 1** (person) entrer dans; **Fran went into the kitchen** Fran est entrée dans la cuisine; **2** (object) rentrer [1] dans; **this file won't go into my bag** ce classeur ne rentre pas dans mon sac.

● **to go off 1** (bomb) exploser [1]; **2** (alarm clock) sonner [1]; **my alarm clock went off at six** mon réveil a sonné à six heures; **3** (fire or burglar alarm) se déclencher [1]; **the fire alarm went off** l'alarme d'incendie s'est déclenchée.

● **to go on 1** se passer [1]; **what's going on?** qu'est-ce qui se passe?; **2 to go on doing** continuer [1] à faire; **she went on talking** elle a continué à parler. **3 to go on about something** ne pas arrêter [1] de

parler de quelque chose; **he's always going on about his dog** il n'arrête pas de parler de son chien.

● **to go out 1** sortir [72]; **I'm going out tonight** je sors ce soir; **she went out of the kitchen** elle est sortie de la cuisine; **2 to be going out with somebody** sortir avec quelqu'un; **she's going out with my brother** elle sort avec mon frère; **3** (light, fire) s'éteindre [60]; **the light went out** la lumière s'est éteinte.

● **to go past something** passer [1] devant quelque chose; **we went past your house** nous sommes passés devant chez toi.

● **to go round to: go round to somebody's house** aller [7] chez quelqu'un; **I went round to Fred's last night** je suis allé chez Fred hier soir.

● **to go round something 1** faire [10] le tour de (building, park, garden); **2** visiter [1] (museum, monument).

● **to go through** passer [1] par; **the train went through Dijon** le train est passé par Dijon; **you can go through my office** tu peux passer par mon bureau.

● **to go up 1** (person) monter [1]; **she's gone up to her room** elle est montée dans sa chambre; **to go up the stairs** monter l'escalier; **2** (prices) augmenter [1]; **the price of petrol has gone up** le prix de l'essence a augmenté.

goal noun but M; **to score a goal** marquer un but.

goalkeeper noun gardien M de but.

goat noun chèvre F; **goat's cheese** le fromage de chèvre.

god noun dieu M (plural dieux).

God noun Dieu M; **to believe in God** croire en Dieu.

godchild noun filleul M, filleule F.

goddaughter noun filleule F.

goddess noun déesse F.

godfather noun parrain M.

godmother noun marraine F.

godson noun filleul M.

goggles plural noun lunettes F plural; **swimming goggles** les lunettes de plongée; **skiing goggles** les lunettes de ski.

go-karting noun karting M; **to go go-karting** faire du karting.

gold noun or M; **a gold bracelet** un bracelet en or.

goldfish noun poisson rouge M.

golf noun golf M; **to play golf** jouer au golf.

golf club noun 1 (place) club M de golf; 2 (iron) crosse F de golf.

golf course noun terrain M de golf.

good adjective 1 bon (F bonne); **she's a good teacher** c'est un bon professeur; **the cherries are very good** les cerises sont très bonnes; 2 **to be good for you** être bon pour la santé; **tomatoes are good for you** les tomates sont bonnes pour la santé; 3 **to be good at** être bon en; **she's good at art** elle est bonne en dessin; 4 (well-behaved) sage; **be good!** sois sage!; 5 (kind) gentil (F gentille); **she's been very good to me** elle a été très gentille avec moi; 6 **for good** pour de bon; **I've**

stopped smoking for good j'ai arrêté de fumer pour de bon.

good afternoon exclamation bonjour.

goodbye exclamation au revoir.

good evening exclamation bonsoir.

Good Friday noun le Vendredi saint.

good-looking adjective beau (F belle) (M plural beaux); **Maya's boyfriend's really good-looking** le copain de Maya est très beau.

good morning exclamation bonjour.

goodness exclamation mon Dieu!; **for goodness sake!** au nom du ciel!

goodnight exclamation bonne nuit.

goods plural noun marchandises F plural.

goods train noun train M de marchandises.

goose noun oie F.

goose pimples noun chair F de poule.

gorgeous adjective superbe; **a gorgeous dress** une robe superbe; **it's a gorgeous day** il fait un temps superbe.

gorilla noun gorille M.

gorse noun ajoncs M plural.

gosh exclamation ça alors!

gossip noun 1 (person) bavard M, bavarde F; 2 (news) nouvelles F plural; **what's the latest gossip?**

quoi de neuf?
verb bavarder [1].

government *noun* gouvernement M.

grab *verb* **1** saisir [2]; **she grabbed my arm** elle m'a saisi par le bras; **2 to grab something from somebody** arracher [1] quelque chose à quelqu'un; **he grabbed the book from me** il m'a arraché le livre.

graceful *adjective* élégant.

grade *noun* (*mark*) note F; **to get good grades** avoir de bonnes notes.

gradual *adjective* progressif (F progressive).

gradually *adverb* petit à petit; **the weather got gradually better** le temps s'est amélioré petit à petit.

graffiti *plural noun* graffiti M *plural*.

grain *noun* grain M.

grammar *noun* grammaire F.

grammar school *noun* (*from age 11 to 15*) collège M; (*from age 15 to 18*) lycée M.

grammatical *adjective* **a grammatical error** une faute de grammaire.

gramme *noun* gramme M.

gran *noun* mamie F (*informal*).

grandchildren *plural noun* petits-enfants M *plural*.

granddad *noun* papy M (*informal*).

granddaughter *noun* petite-fille F.

grandfather *noun* grand-père M.

grandma *noun* mamie F (*informal*).

grandmother *noun* grand-mère F.

grandpa *noun* papi M (*informal*).

grandparents *plural noun* grandparents M *plural*.

grandson *noun* petit-fils M.

granny *noun* mamie F (*informal*).

grape *noun* **a grape** un grain de raisin; **to buy some grapes** acheter du raisin; **do you like grapes?** est-ce que tu aimes le raisin?; **a bunch of grapes** une grappe de raisin.

grapefruit *noun* pamplemousse M.

graph *noun* graphique M.

grasp *verb* saisir [2].

grass *noun* **1** herbe F; **sitting on the grass** assis sur l'herbe; **2** (*lawn*) pelouse F; **to cut the grass** tondre la pelouse.

grasshopper *noun* sauterelle F.

grate *verb* râper [1]; **grated cheese** du fromage râpé.

grateful *adjective* reconnaissant.

grater *noun* râpe F.

grave *noun* tombe F.

gravel *noun* gravillons M *plural*.

graveyard *noun* cimetière M.

gravy *noun* sauce F au jus de rôti.

grease *noun* graisse F.

greasy *adjective* gras (F grasse); **to have greasy skin** avoir la peau grasse; **I hate greasy food** je déteste la nourriture grasse.

great *adjective* **1** grand; **a great poet** un grand poète; **2** (*terrific*) génial (M *plural* géniaux); **it was a great party!** ça a été une soirée géniale!; **great!** génial!; **3 a great deal of** beaucoup de; **a great many** beaucoup de; **there are a great many things still to be done** il reste beaucoup de choses à faire.

Great Britain *noun* Grande-Bretagne F; **in Great Britain** en Grande-Bretagne; **to Great Britain** en Grande-Bretagne; **to be from Great Britain** être britannique.

Greece *noun* Grèce F; **to Greece** en Grèce; **in Greece** en Grèce.

greedy *adjective* (*with food*) gourmand.

Greek *noun* **1** (*person*) Grec M, Grecque F; **2** (*language*) grec M. *adjective* grec (F grecque).

green *noun* **1** (*colour*) vert M; **a pale green** un vert pâle; **2 greens** (*vegetables*) les légumes verts; **3 the Greens** (*ecologists*) les Verts M *plural*. *adjective* **1** vert; **a green door** une porte verte; **2** écologiste; **the Green Party** le parti écologiste.

greengrocer *noun* marchand M de fruits et légumes.

greenhouse *noun* serre F.

greenhouse effect *noun* effet M de serre.

greetings *plural noun* **Season's Greetings** meilleurs vœux M *plural*.

greetings card *noun* carte F de vœux.

grey *adjective* gris; **a grey skirt** une jupe grise; **to have grey hair** avoir les cheveux gris.

greyhound *noun* lévrier M.

grid *noun* **1** (*grating*) grille F; **2** (*network*) réseau M (*plural* réseaux).

grief *noun* chagrin M.

grill *noun* (*of a cooker*) gril M. *verb* **to grill something** faire [10] griller quelque chose; **I grilled the sausages** j'ai fait griller les saucisses.

grim *adjective* sinistre.

grin *noun* sourire M. *verb* sourire [68].

grip *noun* prise F. *verb* serrer [1].

grit *noun* (*for roads*) gravillons M *plural*.

groan *noun* **1** (*of pain*) gémissement M; **2** (*of disgust, boredom*) grognement M. *verb* **1** (*in pain*) gémir [2]; **2** (*in disgust, boredom*) grogner [1].

grocer *noun* épicier M; **my dad's a grocer** mon père est épicier.

groceries *plural noun* provisions F *plural*; **to buy some groceries** acheter des provisions.

grocer's *noun* épicerie F; **I met Jake in the grocer's** j'ai rencontré Jake à l'épicerie.

groom *noun* (*bridegroom*) marié

M; **the bride and groom** les jeunes mariés.

gross *adjective* **1 a gross injustice** une injustice flagrante; **2 a gross error** une erreur grossière; **3** (*disgusting*) dégoûtant; **the food was gross!** la nourriture était dégoûtante!

ground *noun* **1** terre F; **to sit on the ground** s'asseoir par terre; **to throw something on the ground** jeter quelque chose par terre; **2** (*for sport*) terrain M; **a football ground** un terrain de foot.
adjective moulu; **ground coffee** du café moulu.

ground floor *noun* rez-de-chaussée M; **they live on the ground floor** ils habitent au rez-de-chaussée.

group *noun* groupe M.

grow *verb* **1** (*plant, hair*) pousser [1]; **you hair's grown!** tes cheveux ont poussé!; **2** (*person*) grandir [2]; **my little sister's grown a lot this year** ma petite sœur a beaucoup grandi cette année; **3** (*number*) augmenter [1]; **the number of students has grown** le nombre d'étudiants a augmenté; **4 hair** [10] pousser (*fruit, vegetables*); **our neighbours grow strawberries** nos voisins font pousser des fraises; **5 to grow a beard** se laisser [1] pousser la barbe; **6 to grow old** vieillir [2].
●**to grow up** grandir [2]; **the children are growing up** les enfants grandissent; **she grew up in Scotland** elle a grandi en Écosse.

growl *verb* grogner [1].

grown-up *noun* adulte M & F.

growth *noun* croissance F.

grudge *noun* **to bear a grudge against somebody** en vouloir à quelqu'un; **she bears me a grudge** elle m'en veut.

gruesome *adjective* horrible.

grumble *verb* se plaindre [31]; **she's always grumbling** elle est toujours en train de se plaindre; **to grumble about something** se plaindre de quelque chose.

guarantee *noun* garantie F; **a year's guarantee** une garantie d'un an.
verb garantir [2].

guard *noun* **1 a prison guard** un gardien de prison; **2** (*on a train*) chef M de train; **3 a security guard** un vigile.
verb surveiller [1].

guard dog *noun* chien M de garde.

guess *noun* **have a guess!** devine!; **it's a good guess** tu as deviné.
verb deviner [1]; **guess who I saw last night!** devine qui j'ai vu hier soir!; **you'll never guess!** tu ne devineras jamais!

guest *noun* **1** invité M, invitée F; **we've got guests coming tonight** nous avons des invités ce soir; **2** (*in a hotel*) client M, cliente F; **3 a paying guest** un hôte payant.

guide *noun* **1** (*person or book*) guide M; **2** (*girl guide*) guide F; (*belonging to a church company of girl guides*) éclaireuse F.

guidebook *noun* guide M.

guide dog noun chien M d'aveugle.

guideline noun indication F.

guilty adjective coupable; **to feel guilty** se sentir coupable.

guinea pig noun 1 (pet) cochon M d'Inde; (in an experiment) cobaye M; **they want me to be a guinea pig** ils veulent que je serve de cobaye.

guitar noun guitare F; **to play the guitar** jouer de la guitare; **on the guitar** à la guitare.

gum noun 1 (in mouth) gencive F; **2** (chewing gum) chewing-gum M.

gun noun 1 revolver M; **2** (rifle) fusil M.

gust noun **a gust of wind** une rafale de vent.

gutter noun (in the street) caniveau M (plural caniveaux).

guy noun type M (informal); **he's a nice guy** c'est un type sympa; **a guy from Newcastle** un type qui vient de Newcastle.

gym noun gym F; **to go to the gym** aller à la gym.

gymnasium noun gymnase M.

gymnast noun gymnaste M & F.

gymnastics noun gymnastique F.

gym shoe noun tennis M.

H h

habit noun habitude F; **to have a habit of doing** avoir l'habitude de faire; **it's a bad habit** c'est une mauvaise habitude.

haddock noun églefin M; **smoked haddock** haddock M.

hail noun grêle F.

hailstone noun grêlon M.

hailstorm noun averse F de grêle.

hair noun 1 cheveux M plural; **to have short hair** avoir les cheveux courts; **to brush your hair** se brosser les cheveux; **to wash your hair** se laver les cheveux; **to have your hair cut** se faire couper les cheveux; **she's had her hair cut** elle s'est fait couper les cheveux; **2 a hair** (from the head) un cheveu; (from the body) un poil.

hairbrush noun brosse F à cheveux.

haircut noun 1 coupe F; **I like your new haircut** j'aime bien ta nouvelle coupe; **2 to have a haircut** se faire couper les cheveux.

hairdresser noun coiffeur M, coiffeuse F; **she's a hairdresser** elle est coiffeuse; **at the hairdresser's** chez le coiffeur.

hair drier noun sèche-cheveux M.

hair gel noun gel M pour les cheveux.

hairgrip noun pince F à cheveux.

hair remover noun crème F dépilatoire.

hairslide noun barrette F.

hairspray noun laque F.

hairstyle noun coiffure F.

hairy adjective poilu.

half noun 1 moitié F; **half of** la
moitié de; **I gave him half of the
money** je lui ai donné la moitié de
l'argent; **half an apple** la moitié
d'une pomme; **you've only eaten
half of it** tu n'en as mangé que la
moitié; **half the people** la moitié des
gens; 2 **to cut something in half**
couper quelque chose en deux; 3
(as a fraction) demi; **three and a
half** trois et demi; **she's five and a
half** elle a cinq ans et demi; 4 (in
time) demi, demie; **half an hour** une
demi-heure; **an hour and a half** une
heure et demie; **it's half past three**
il est trois heures et demie; 5 (in
weights and measures) demi, demie;
half a litre un demi-litre; **half a cup**
une demi-tasse.

half hour noun demi-heure F;
every half hour toutes les demi-
heures.

half price adjective, adverb à moité
prix; **half-price CDs** des CD à moité
prix; **I bought it half price** je l'ai
acheté à moitié prix.

half-time noun mi-temps F; **at
half-time** à la mi-temps.

halfway adverb 1 à mi-chemin;
halfway between Paris and Dijon à
mi-chemin entre Paris et Dijon; 2 **to
be halfway through doing** avoir à
moitié fini de faire; **I'm halfway
through my homework** j'ai à moitié
fini mes devoirs.

hall noun 1 (in a house) entrée F;
2 (public) salle F; **the village hall**
la salle des fêtes; **a concert hall** une
salle de concert.

Hallowe'en noun la veille de la
Toussaint (the French do not have

any particular customs for this date).

ham noun jambon M; **a slice of
ham** une tranche de jambon; **a ham
sandwich** un sandwich au jambon.

hamburger noun hamburger M.

hammer noun marteau M
(plural marteaux).

hamster noun hamster M.

hand noun 1 main F; **to have
something in your hand** avoir
quelque chose à la main; **to hold
somebody's hand** tenir quelqu'un
par la main; 2 **to give somebody a
hand** donner un coup de main à
quelqu'un; **can you give me a hand
to move the table?** est-ce que tu
peux me donner un coup de main
pour déplacer la table?; **do you need
a hand?** est-ce que tu as besoin d'un
coup de main?; 3 **on the other
hand...** par contre...; 4 (of a watch
or clock) aiguille F; **the hour hand**
l'aiguille des heures.

verb 1 **to hand something to
somebody** passer [1] quelque chose
à quelqu'un; **I handed him the keys**
je lui ai passé les clés.

●**to hand something in** rendre [3]
quelque chose; **I've handed in my
homework** j'ai rendu mon devoir.

●**to hand something out** distribuer
quelque chose [1]; **Claire handed out
the exercise books** Claire a
distribué les cahiers.

handbag noun sac M à main
(plural sacs à main).

handcuffs plural noun menottes F
plural.

handful noun **a handful of** une
poignée de.

handkerchief noun mouchoir M.

handicapped adjective handicapé.

handle noun 1 (of a door or drawer) poignée F; 2 (on a cup or basket) anse F; 3 (of a knife, tool, or saucepan) manche M; 4 (of a frying pan) queue F.
verb s'occuper [1] de; **Gina handles the accounts** Gina s'occupe de la comptabilité; **2 she's good at handling people** elle a un bon contact avec les gens; **3 I can't handle any more problems!** j'en ai assez de problèmes comme ça!

handlebars plural noun guidon M.

hand luggage noun bagages M plural à main.

handmade adjective fait à la main.

handsome adjective beau (F belle); **he's a handsome guy** c'est un beau type.

handwriting noun écriture F.

handy adjective 1 pratique; **this little knife's very handy** ce petit couteau est très pratique; **2 sous la main; I always keep a notebook handy** je garde toujours un calepin sous la main.

hang verb 1 être [6] accroché; **there was a mirror hanging on the wall** il y avait un miroir accroché au mur; **2 to hang something** accrocher [1] quelque chose; **we hung the mirror on the wall** nous avons accroché le miroir au mur.
●**to hang around** traîner [1]; **we were hanging around outside the cinema** on traînait devant le cinéma.

●**to hang down** pendre [3].
●**to hang on** attendre [3]; **hang on a second!** attends une seconde!
●**to hang up** (on the phone) raccrocher [1]; **she hung up on me** elle m'a raccroché au nez (literally: she hung up on my nose).
●**to hang something up** accrocher [1] quelque chose; **you can hang your coat up in the hall** tu peux accrocher ton manteau dans l'entrée.

hang-gliding noun deltaplane M; **to go hang-gliding** faire du deltaplane.

hangover noun gueule F de bois; **to have a hangover** avoir la gueule de bois.

happen verb 1 se passer [1]; **what's happening?** qu'est-ce qui se passe?; **it happened in June** ça s'est passé en juin; **2 what's happened to the can-opener?** où est l'ouvre-boîte?; **3 if you happen to see Jill** si par hasard tu vois Jill.

happily adverb 1 joyeusement; **she smiled happily** elle a souri joyeusement; **2** (willingly) volontiers; **I'll happily do it for you** je le ferai pour toi volontiers.

happiness noun bonheur M.

happy adjective heureux (F heureuse); **a happy child** un enfant heureux; **Happy Birthday!** Bon anniversaire!

harbour noun port M.

hard adjective 1 dur; **to go hard** durcir [2]; 2 (difficult) difficile; **a difficult question** une question difficile; **it's hard to know...** il est difficile de savoir...

hard *adverb* **1 to work hard** travailler dur; **2 to try hard** faire beaucoup d'efforts.

hard disk *noun* (*in a computer*) disque dur M.

hardly *adverb* **1** à peine; **I can hardly hear him** je l'entends à peine; **2 hardly any** presque pas de; **there's hardly any milk** il n'y a presque pas de lait; **3 hardly ever** presque jamais; **I hardly ever see them** je ne les vois presque jamais; **4 there was hardly anybody** il n'y avait presque personne.

hard up *adjective* fauché (*informal*).

hare *noun* lièvre M.

harm *noun* **it won't do you any harm** ça ne te fera pas de mal. *verb* **to harm somebody** faire [10] du mal à quelqu'un; **they did not harm him** ils ne lui ont pas fait de mal; **a cup of coffee won't harm you** une tasse de café ne te fera pas de mal.

harmful *adjective* nuisible.

harmless *adjective* inoffensif (F inoffensive).

hat *noun* chapeau M (*plural* chapeaux).

hate *verb* détester [1]; **I hate geography** je déteste la géographie.

hatred *noun* haine F.

have *verb* **1** avoir [5]; **Anna has three brothers** Anna a trois frères; **how many sisters do you have?** tu as combien de sœurs?; **2 to have got** avoir [5]; **we've got a dog** nous avons un chien; **what have you got in your hand?** qu'est-ce que tu as à la main?; **3** (*to form past tenses, some verbs in French take 'avoir' and some 'être'*) **I've finished** j'ai fini; **have you seen the film?** est-ce que tu as vu le film?; **Rosie hasn't arrived yet** Rosie n'est pas encore arrivée; **he had left** il était parti; **4 to have to do** devoir [8] faire; **I have to phone my mum** je dois appeler ma mère; **5** prendre [64] (*food, drink, a shower*); **we had a coffee** nous avons pris un café; **what will you have?** qu'est-ce que tu prends?; **I'll have an omelette** je prends une omelette; **I'm going to have a shower** je vais prendre une douche; **to have lunch** déjeuner [1]; **to have dinner** (*in the evening*) dîner [1]; **7 to have something done** faire [10] faire quelque chose; **I'm going to have my hair cut** je vais me faire couper les cheveux.

hay *noun* foin M.

hay fever *noun* rhume M des foins.

hazelnut *noun* noisette F.

he *pronoun* il; **he lives in Manchester** il habite à Manchester.

head *noun* **1** tête F; **he had a cap on his head** il avait une casquette sur la tête; **at the head of the queue** à la tête de la queue; **2** (*of school*) directeur M, directrice F; **3** (*when tossing a coin*) **'heads or tails?'** – **'heads'** 'pile ou face?' – 'face'. (*note that it is in fact 'tails or heads' in French*).

●**to head for something** se diriger [52] vers quelque chose; **Liz headed for the door** Liz s'est dirigée vers la porte.

headache noun I've got a headache j'ai mal à la tête.

headlight noun phare M.

headline noun gros titre M; to hit the headlines faire la une.

headmaster noun directeur M.

headmistress noun directrice F.

headphones noun casque M singular.

headteacher noun directeur M, directrice F.

health noun santé F.

health centre noun centre médico-social M

healthy adjective 1 (person) to be healthy être en bonne santé; 2 a healthy diet une alimentation saine.

heap noun tas M; I've got heaps of things to do j'ai un tas de choses à faire.

hear verb 1 entendre [3]; I can't hear you je ne t'entends pas; I can't hear anything je n'entends rien; 2 apprendre [64] (news); I hear you've bought a dog j'apprends que tu as acheté un chien.

●to hear about something entendre [3] parler de quelque chose; have you heard about the concert? as-tu entendu parler du concert?

●to hear from somebody avoir [5] des nouvelles de quelqu'un; have you heard from Amanda? as-tu des nouvelles d'Amanda?

heart noun 1 cœur M; to learn something by heart apprendre quelque chose par cœur; 2 (in cards) cœur; the jack of hearts le valet de cœur.

heart attack noun crise cardiaque F.

heat noun chaleur F.
verb 1 chauffer [1]; the soup's heating la soupe est en train de chauffer; 2 to heat something faire [10] chauffer quelque chose; I'll go and heat the soup je vais faire chauffer la soupe.

●to heat something up faire [10] réchauffer quelque chose; I'm heating up the sauce je fais réchauffer la sauce.

heater noun radiateur M.

heather noun bruyère F.

heating noun chauffage M.

heatwave noun vague F de chaleur.

heaven noun paradis M.

heavy adjective 1 lourd; my rucksack's really heavy mon sac à dos est très lourd; 2 (busy) chargé; I've got a heavy day tomorrow j'ai une journée chargée demain; 3 heavy rain des pluies fortes.

heavy metal noun (music) hard rock M.

hectic adjective a hectic day une journée mouvementée.

hedge noun haie F.

hedgehog noun hérisson M.

heel noun talon M.

height noun 1 (of a person) taille F; 2 (of a building) hauteur F; 3 (of a mountain) altitude F.

helicopter noun hélicoptère M.

hell noun enfer M; **it's hell here!** c'est infernal ici!

hello exclamation 1 (polite) bonjour!; 2 (informal) salut!; 3 (on the telephone) allô!

helmet noun casque M.

help noun aide F; **do you need any help?** est-ce que tu as besoin d'aide?
verb 1 aider [1]; **to help somebody to do** aider quelqu'un à faire; **can you help me move the table?** peux-tu m'aider à déplacer la table?; 2 **to help yourself to something** se servir [71] de quelque chose; **help yourselves to vegetables** servez-vous de légumes; **help yourself!** sers-toi!; 3 **help!** au secours!

helpful adjective (person) serviable.

hem noun ourlet M.

hen noun poule F.

her pronoun 1 la, l' (before a vowel or silent 'h'); **I know her** je la connais; **I can hear her** je l'entends; **listen to her!** écoute-la!; **I saw her last week** je l'ai vue la semaine dernière; 2 (to her) lui; **I gave her my address** je lui ai donné mon adresse; 3 (after a preposition) elle; **with her** avec elle; **without her** sans elle; (in comparisons) **he's older than her** il est plus âgé qu'elle.
adjective 1 (before a masculine noun) son; **her brother** son frère; **her book** son livre; 2 (before a feminine noun) sa; **her sister** sa sœur; **her house** sa maison (but 'sa' becomes 'son' before a feminine noun beginning with a vowel or silent 'h'); **her address** son adresse; 3 (before

a plural noun) ses; **her children** ses enfants; 4 (with parts of the body) le, la, les; **she had a glass in her hand** elle avait un verre à la main; **she's washing her hands** elle se lave les mains.

herb noun herbe F.

here adverb 1 ici; **not far from here** pas loin d'ici; 2 là; **Tom isn't here at the moment** Tom n'est pas là en ce moment; 3 **here is** voilà; **here's my address** voilà mon adresse; 4 **here are** voilà; **here are the photos** voilà les photos; **and here they are!** et les voilà!

hero noun héros M.

heroin noun héroïne F.

heroine noun héroïne F.

herring noun hareng M.

hers pronoun 1 (for a masculine noun) le sien; **I took my hat and she took hers** j'ai pris mon chapeau et elle a pris le sien; 2 (for a feminine noun) la sienne; **I gave her my address and she gave me hers** je lui ai donné mon adresse et elle m'a donné la sienne; 3 (for a masculine plural noun) les siens; **I've invited my parents and Karen's invited hers** j'ai invité mes parents et Karen a invité les siens; 4 (for a feminine plural noun) les siennes; **I showed her my photos and she showed me hers** je lui ai montré mes photos et elle m'a montré les siennes; 5 à elle; **the green one's hers** le vert est à elle; **it's hers** c'est à elle.

herself pronoun 1 **she's hurt herself** elle s'est blessée; 2 **she said it herself** elle l'a dit elle-même; **3 she did it by herself** elle l'a fait toute seule.

hesitate *verb* hésiter [1]; **to hesitate to do** hésiter à faire.

heterosexual *noun* hétérosexuel M, hétérosexuelle F.

hi *exclamation* salut!

hiccups *plural noun* **to have the hiccups** avoir le hoquet.

hidden *adjective* caché.

hide *verb* (*person*) se cacher [1]; **1 she hid behind the door** elle s'est cachée derrière la porte; **2 to hide something** cacher [1] quelque chose; **who's hidden the chocolate?** qui a caché le chocolat?

hide-and-seek *noun* **to play hide-and-seek** jouer à cache-cache.

hi-fi *noun* chaîne F hi-fi.

high *adjective* **1** haut; **on a high shelf** sur une étagère haute; **the wall is very high** le mur est très haut; **how high is the wall?** quelle est la hauteur du mur?; **the wall is two metres high** le mur fait deux mètres de hauteur; **2** (*number, price, temperature*) élevé; **food prices are very high** les prix de la nourriture sont très élevés; **3 at high speed** à grande vitesse; **4 high winds** des vents violents; **5 a high voice** une voix aiguë.

high-heeled *adjective* à hauts talons; **high-heeled shoes** des chaussures à hauts talons.

high jump *noun* saut M en hauteur.

highly *adverb* extrêmement.

hijack *verb* **to hijack a plane** détourner [1] un avion.

hijacker *noun* pirate M de l'air.

hike *noun* randonnée F; **to go on a hike** faire une randonnée.

hilarious *adjective* hilarant.

hill *noun* **1** (*in landscape*) colline F; **you can see the hills** on voit les collines; **2** (*hillside*) coteau M (*plural* coteaux); **the houses on the hill** les maisons sur le coteau; **3** (*sloping street or road*) colline F; **to go up the hill** monter; **you go up the hill to the church and then turn right** vous montez jusqu'à l'église et vous tournez à droite.

him *pronoun* **1** le, l' (*before a vowel or silent 'h'*); **I know him** je le connais; **I can hear him** je l'entends; **listen to him!** écoute-le!; **I saw him last week** je l'ai vu la semaine dernière; **2** (*to him*) lui; **I gave him my address** je lui ai donné mon adresse; **3** (*after a preposition*) lui; **with him** avec lui; **without him** sans lui; (*in comparisons*) **she's older than him** elle est plus âgée que lui.

himself *pronoun* **1 he's hurt himself** il s'est blessé; **2 he said it himself** il l'a dit lui-même; **3 he did it by himself** il l'a fait tout seul.

Hindu *adjective* hindou.

hip *noun* hanche F.

hippie *noun* hippie M & F.

hippopotamus *noun* hippopotame M.

hire *noun* location F; **car hire** location de voitures; **for hire** à louer.

verb louer [1]; **we're going to hire a car** nous allons louer une voiture.

his *adjective* **1** (*before a masculine noun*) son; **his brother** son frère; **his book** son livre; **2** (*before a feminine noun*) sa; **his sister** sa sœur; **his house** sa maison (*but 'sa' becomes 'son' before a feminine noun beginning with a vowel or silent 'h'*); **his address** son adresse; **3** (*before a plural noun*) ses; **his children** ses enfants; **4** (*with parts of the body*) le, la, les; **he had a glass in his hand** il avait un verre à la main; **he's washing his hands** il se lave les mains.

pronoun **1** (*for a masculine noun*) le sien; **I took my hat and he took his** j'ai pris mon chapeau et il a pris le sien; **2** (*for a feminine noun*) la sienne; **I gave him my address and he gave me his** je lui ai donné mon adresse et il m'a donné la sienne; **3** (*for a masculine plural noun*) les siens; **I've invited my parents and Steve's invited his** j'ai invité mes parents et Steve a invité les siens; **4** (*for a feminine plural noun*) les siennes; **I showed him my photos and he showed me his** je lui ai montré mes photos et il m'a montré les siennes; **5** à lui; **the green car's his** la voiture verte est à lui; **it's his** c'est à lui.

history *noun* histoire F.

hit *noun* **1** (*song*) tube M (*informal*); **their latest hit** leur dernier tube; **2** (*success*) succès M; **the film is a huge hit** le film a un succès fou.

verb **1** frapper [1]; **to hit the ball** frapper la balle; **2** **to hit your head on something** se cogner [1] la tête contre quelque chose; **3** heurter [1]; **the car hit a tree** la voiture a heurté un arbre; **4** **to be hit by a car** (*person*) être [6] renversé par une voiture.

hitch *noun* problème M; **there's been a slight hitch** il y a eu un petit problème.

verb **to hitch a lift** faire [10] du stop (*informal*).

hitchhike *verb* faire [10] du stop (*informal*); **we hitchhiked to Dijon** nous sommes allés à Dijon en stop.

hitchhiker *noun* autostoppeur M, autostoppeuse F.

HIV-negative *adjective* séronégatif (F séronégative).

HIV-positive *adjective* séropositif (F séropositive).

hobby *noun* passe-temps M.

hockey *noun* hockey M; **to play hockey** jouer au hockey.

hockey stick *noun* crosse F de hockey.

hold *verb* **1** tenir [77]; **to hold something in your hand** tenir quelque chose à la main; **can you hold the torch?** est-ce que tu peux tenir la lampe? **2** (*contain*) contenir [77]; **a jug which hold a litre** un pichet qui contient un litre; **3** **to hold a meeting** organiser [1] une réunion; **4** **can you hold the line, please** ne quittez pas, s'il vous plaît; **5** **hold on!** (*wait*) attends!; (*on telephone*) ne quittez pas!

● **to hold somebody up** (*delay*) retenir [77] quelqu'un; **I was held up at the**

dentist's j'ai été retenu chez le dentiste.

●**to hold something up** (*raise*) lever [50] quelque chose; **he held up his glass** il a levé son verre.

hold-up *noun* 1 retard M; 2 (*traffic jam*) bouchon M; 3 (*robbery*) hold-up M.

hole *noun* trou M.

holiday *noun* 1 vacances F *plural*; **where are you going for your holiday?** où est-ce que vous partez en vacances?; **have a good holiday!** bonnes vacances!; **to be away on holiday** être en vacances; **to go on holiday** partir en vacances; **the school holidays** les vacances scolaires; 2 (*from work*) congé M; **I'm taking two days' holiday next week** je prends deux jours de congé la semaine prochaine; 3 **a public holiday** un jour férié; **Monday's a holiday** lundi est férié.

holiday home *noun* résidence F secondaire.

Holland *noun* Hollande F; **to Holland** en Hollande; **in Holland** en Hollande.

hollow *adjective* creux (F creuse).

holy *adjective* saint.

home *noun* maison F; **I was at home** j'étais à la maison; **to stay at home** rester à la maison; **make yourself at home** fais comme chez toi.
adverb 1 chez soi; **Susie's gone home** Susie est rentrée chez elle; **I'll call in and see you on my way home** je passerai te voir en rentrant chez moi; 2 **to get home** rentrer;

we got home at midnight nous sommes rentrés à minuit.

homeless *adjective* sans abri; **the homeless** les sans-abri M *plural*.

homemade *adjective* fait maison; **homemade cakes** des gâteaux faits maison.

home match *noun* match M à domicile.

homeopathic *adjective* homéopathique.

homesick *adjective* **to be homesick** avoir le mal du pays.

homework *noun* devoirs M *plural*; **I did my homework** j'ai fait mes devoirs; **my French homework** mes devoirs de français; (*written*) mon devoir de français.

homosexual *adjective, noun* homosexuel (F homosexuelle).

honest *adjective* honnête.

honestly *adverb* franchement.

honesty *noun* honnêteté F.

honey *noun* miel M.

honeymoon *noun* voyage M de noces; **they're going to Paris on their honeymoon** ils partent à Paris en voyage de noces.

honeysuckle *noun* chèvrefeuille M.

honour *noun* honneur M.

hood *noun* capuchon M.

hook *noun* 1 crochet M; 2 **to take the phone of the hook** décrocher le téléphone.

hooligan noun voyou M.

hooray exclamation hourra!

hoover verb passer [1] l'aspirateur; **I hoovered my bedroom** j'ai passé l'aspirateur dans ma chambre.

Hoover™ noun aspirateur M.

hope noun espoir M; **to give up hope** perdre espoir.
verb espérer [24]; **we hope you'll be able to come** nous espérons que vous allez pouvoir venir; **hoping to see you on Friday** en espérant de te voir vendredi; **here's hoping!** espérons que ça marche!; **I hope so** je l'espère; **I hope not** j'espère que non.

hopefully adverb avec un peu de chance; **hopefully, the film won't have started** avec un peu de chance, le film n'aura pas commencé.

hopeless adjective nul (F nulle) (informal); **I'm completely hopeless at geography** je suis complètement nul en géographie.

horizontal adjective horizontal (M plural horizontaux).

horn noun 1 (of an animal) corne F; 2 (of a car) klaxon M; **to sound your horn** klaxonner; 3 (musical instrument) cor M; **to play the horn** jouer du cor.

horoscope noun horoscope M.

horrible adjective 1 affreux (F affreuse); **the weather was horrible** il a fait un temps affreux; 2 (person) désagréable; **she's really horrible!** elle est vraiment désagréable; **he was really horrible to me** il a été vraiment désagréable avec moi.

horror noun horreur F.

horror film noun film M d'épouvante.

horse noun cheval M (plural chevaux).

horse chestnut noun 1 (tree) marronnier M; 2 (nut) marron M.

horseshoe noun fer M à cheval.

hose noun tuyau M (plural tuyaux).

hosepipe noun tuyau M d'arrosage.

hospital noun hôpital M (plural hôpitaux); **to be in hospital** être à l'hôpital; **to be taken into hospital** être hospitalisé.

hospitality noun hospitalité F.

hostage noun otage M.

hostel noun youth hostel auberge F de jeunesse.

hostess noun hôtesse F; **an air hostess** une hôtesse de l'air.

hot adjective 1 chaud; **a hot drink** une boisson chaude; **be careful, the plates are hot!** fais attention, les assiettes sont très chaudes!; 2 (a person) **to be hot** avoir chaud; **I'm hot** j'ai chaud; **I'm very hot** j'ai très chaud; **I'm too hot** j'ai trop chaud; 3 (the weather or temperature in a room) **it's hot today** il fait chaud aujourd'hui; **it's very hot in the kitchen** il fait très chaud dans la cuisine; 4 (food: spicy) épicé; **the curry's too hot for me** le curry est trop épicé pour moi.

hot dog noun hot-dog M.

hotel noun hôtel M.

hour noun heure F; **two hours later** deux heures plus tard; **we waited for two hours** nous avons attendu pendant deux heures; **two hours ago** il y a deux heures; **to be paid by the hour** être payé à l'heure; **every hour** toutes les heures; **half an hour** une demi-heure; **a quarter of an hour** un quart d'heure; **an hour and a half** une heure et demie.

house noun 1 maison F; **to buy a house** acheter une maison; 2 **at somebody's house** chez quelqu'un; **I'm at Judy's house** je suis chez Judy; **I'm going to Judy's house tonight** je vais chez Judy ce soir; **I phoned from Judy's house** j'ai téléphoné de chez Judy.

housewife noun femme F au foyer.

housework noun ménage M; **to do the housework** faire le ménage.

hovercraft noun aéroglisseur M.

how adverb 1 comment; **how did you do it?** comment l'as-tu fait?; **how are you?** comment allez-vous?; 2 **how much?** combien?; **how much money do you have?** tu as combien d'argent?; **how much is it?** (price) ça coûte combien?; 3 **how many?** combien?; **how many brothers do you have?** tu as combien de frères?; 4 **how old are you?** quel âge as-tu?; 5 **how far is it?** c'est à quelle distance?; **how far is it to Paris?** Paris est à quelle distance d'ici?; 6 **how long will it take?** ça va prendre combien de temps?; **how long have you known**

ho [obscured]

hug [obscured]
serr[obscured]
ses br[obscured]

huge ad[obscured]

hum verb [obscured]

human ad[obscured] humain.

human being noun être humain M.

humour noun humour M; **to have a sense of humour** avoir le sens de l'humour.

hundred number 1 cent; **two hundred** deux cents; **two hundred and ten** deux cent dix (note that there is no 's' on 'cent' when it is followed by another number); **a hundred people** cent personnes; 2 **about a hundred** une centaine; **about a hundred people** une centaine de personnes; **hundreds of people** des centaines de personnes.

Hungary noun Hongrie F.

hunger noun faim F.

hungry adjective **to be hungry** avoir faim; **I'm hungry** j'ai faim.

hunt verb 1 chasser [1] (an animal); 2 rechercher [1] (person).

hunting noun chasse F; **fox-hunting** la chasse au renard.

hurry noun **to be in a hurry** être pressé; **I'm in a hurry** je suis pressé. verb se dépêcher [50]; **I must hurry** je dois me dépêcher; **he hurried**

home il s'est dépêch[obscured]
chez lui; [10] ma[obscured]

hurt

...e rentrer
dépêche-toi!

...hurt somebody faire
...quelqu'un; you're hurting
...me fais mal!; that hurts! ça
...mal!; 2 my back hurts j'ai mal
au dos; 3 to hurt yourself se faire
[10] mal; did you hurt yourself? est-
ce que tu t'es fait mal?
adjective 1 (in an accident) blessé;
three people were hurt trois
personnes ont été blessées; 2 (in
feelings) blessé; she felt hurt elle
était blessée.

husband noun mari M.

hutch noun clapier M.

hymn noun cantique M.

hypermarket noun hypermarché
M.

hyphen noun trait M d'union.

I i

I pronoun 1 je, j' (before a vowel or a
silent 'h'); **I am Scottish** je suis
écossais; **I have two sisters** j'ai deux
sœurs; 2 moi; **Robert and I** Robert
et moi; **Tony and I left before you**
Tony et moi sommes partis avant
vous.

ice noun 1 glace F; 2 (on the
roads) verglas M; 3 (in a drink)
glaçons M plural.

ice cream noun glace F; **a
chocolate ice cream** une glace au
chocolat.

ice-cube noun glaçon M.

ice hockey noun hockey M sur
glace.

ice rink noun patinoire F.

ice-skating noun to go ice-
skating faire [10] du patin à glace.

icy adjective 1 verglacé (a road);
2 (very cold) glacial; **an icy wind** un
vent glacial.

idea noun idée F; **what a good
idea!** quelle bonne idée!; **I've no
idea** je n'ai aucune idée.

ideal adjective idéal (M plural
idéaux).

identical adjective identique.

identification noun identification
F.

identify verb identifier [1].

identity card noun carte F
d'identité.

idiom noun idiome M.

idiot noun idiot M, idiote F.

idiotic adjective bête.

idyllic adjective idyllique.

i.e. c-à-d (short for: c'est-à-dire).

if conjunction 1 si, s' (before 'il' and
'ils'); **if Sue's there** si Sue est là; **if it
rains** s'il pleut; **if I won the lottery**
si je gagnais la loterie; **if not** sinon;
2 **if only ...** si seulement...; **if only
you'd told me** si seulement tu me
l'avais dit; 3 **even if** même si; **even
if it snows** même s'il neige; 4 **if I
were you...** à ta place ...; **if I were
you, I'd forget it** à ta place je
l'oublierais.

ignore verb 1 ignorer [1] (a person); 2 ne pas écouter [1] (what somebody says); 3 **just ignore it** ne fais pas attention.

ill adjective malade; **to fall ill, to be taken ill** tomber malade; **I feel ill** je ne me sens pas bien.

illegal adjective illégal (M plural illégaux).

illegible adjective illisible.

illness noun maladie F.

illusion noun illusion F.

illustrated adjective illustré.

illustration noun illustration F.

image noun image F; ★ **he's the spitting image of his father** c'est son père tout craché.

imagination noun imagination F; **to show imagination** faire preuve d'imagination.

imaginative adjective plein d'imagination.

imagine verb imaginer [1]; **imagine that you're very rich** imagine que tu es très riche; **you can't imagine how hard it was!** tu ne peux pas t'imaginer combien c'était difficile!

imitate verb imiter [1].

imitation noun imitation F.

immediate adjective immédiat.

immediately adverb immédiatement; **I rang them immediately** je les ai appelés immédiatement; **immediately before** juste avant; **immediately after** juste après.

immigrant noun immigré M, immigrée F.

immigration noun immigration F.

impatience noun impatience F.

impatient adjective 1 impatient; 2 **to get impatient with somebody** s'impatienter contre quelqu'un.

impatiently adverb avec impatience.

imperfect noun (of a verb) imparfait M; **in the imperfect** à l'imparfait.

importance noun importance F.

important adjective important.

impossible adjective impossible; **it's impossible to find a telephone** il est impossible de trouver un téléphone.

impressed adjective impressionné.

impression noun impression F; **to make a good impression on somebody** faire bonne impression sur quelqu'un; **I got the impression he was hiding something** j'avais l'impression qu'il cachait quelque chose.

impressive adjective impressionnant.

improve verb 1 **to improve something** améliorer [1] quelque chose; 2 (get better) s'améliorer [1]; **the weather is improving** le temps s'améliore.

improvement noun 1 (a clear change for the better) amélioration F. 2 (gradual progress) progrès M plural (in schoolwork, for example).

in *preposition, adverb* 1 dans; **in my pocket** dans ma poche; **in the newspaper** dans le journal; **in the kitchen** dans la cuisine; **I was in the bath** j'étais dans mon bain; 2 à; **in Oxford** à Oxford; **a house in the country** une maison à la campagne; **in school** à l'école; **in the sun** au soleil; **the girl in the pink shirt** la fille à la chemise rose; 3 en; **in France** en France (*BUT*) **in Portugal** au Portugal ('en' *for feminine countries,* 'au' *for most masculine countries*); **in town** en ville; **in French** en français; 4 (*time expressions*) **in May** en mai; **in '94** en quatre-vingt-quatorze; **in winter** en hiver; **in summer** en été; (*BUT*) **in spring** au printemps; **in the morning** le matin; **at eight in the morning** à huit heures du matin; **in the night** pendant la nuit; **I'll phone you in ten minutes** je t'appellerai dans dix minutes; **she did it in five minutes** elle l'a fait en cinq minutes; 5 (*talking about a group*) de; **the tallest boy in the class** le garçon le plus grand de la classe; **the biggest city in the world** la ville la plus grande du monde; 6 **in time** à temps; 7 **in the photo** sur la photo; 8 **in the rain** sous la pluie; 9 **dressed in white** habillé en blanc; 10 **to come in** entrer; **to go in** entrer; **we went into the cinema** nous sommes entrés dans le cinéma; **to run in** entrer en courant; 11 **to be in** être là; **Mick's not in at the moment** Mick n'est pas là en ce moment.

incident *noun* incident M.

include *verb* comprendre [64]; **dinner is included in the price** le dîner est compris dans le prix; **service included** service compris.

including *preposition* (y) compris; **£50 including VAT** cinquante livres TVA comprise; **everyone, including children** tout le monde, y compris les enfants; **including Sundays** y compris les dimanches; **not including Sundays** sans compter les dimanches.

income *noun* revenu M.

income tax *noun* impôt M sur le revenu.

inconvenient *adjective* 1 incommode (*a place or an arrangement*); 2 inopportun (*a time*).

increase *noun* augmentation F (*in price, for example*).
verb augmenter [1]; **the price has increased by £10** le prix a augmenté de dix livres.

incredible *adjective* incroyable.

incredibly *adverb* (*very*) extrêmement; **the film's incredibly boring** le film est extrêmement ennuyeux.

indeed *adverb* 1 (*to emphasize*) vraiment; **she's very pleased indeed** elle est vraiment très contente; **I'm very hungry indeed** j'ai vraiment très faim; **thank you very much indeed** merci beaucoup; 2 (*certainly*) bien sûr; **'can you hear his radio?' – 'indeed I can!'** 'entends-tu sa radio?' – 'bien sûr que oui!'

indefinite article *noun* (*in grammar*) article indéfini M.

independence noun
indépendance F.

independent adjective
indépendant; **an independent school** une école privée.

index noun index M.

India noun Inde F; **in India** en Inde; **to India** en Inde.

Indian noun Indien M, Indienne F.
adjective indien (F indienne).

indicate verb indiquer [1].

indication noun indication F.

indigestion noun indigestion F; **to have indigestion** avoir une indigestion.

individual noun individu M.
adjective 1 individuel (F individuelle) (a serving or a contribution, for example); 2 **individual tuition** des cours particuliers.

indoor adjective couvert; **an indoor swimming pool** une piscine couverte.

indoors adverb à l'intérieur; **it's cooler indoors** il fait plus frais à l'intérieur; **to go indoors** rentrer.

industrial adjective industriel (F industrielle).

industrial estate noun zone industrielle F.

industry noun industrie F; **the advertising industry** l'industrie de la publicité.

inefficient adjective inefficace.

inevitable adjective inévitable.

inevitably adverb inévitablement.

inexperienced adjective inexpérimenté.

infant school noun école F maternelle.

infection noun infection F; **an eye infection** une infection de l'œil; **a throat infection** une angine.

infectious adjective contagieux (F contagieuse).

infinitive noun infinitif M; **in the infinitive** à l'infinitif.

inflammable adjective inflammable.

inflatable adjective pneumatique (a mattress or a boat).

inflate verb gonfler [1] (a mattress or boat).

inflation noun inflation F.

influence noun influence F; **to be a good influence on somebody** avoir une bonne influence sur quelqu'un.
verb influencer [61].

inform verb informer [1]; **to inform somebody that** informer quelqu'un du fait que; **they informed us that there was a problem** ils nous ont informés du fait qu'il y avait un problème; **to inform somebody of something** informer quelqu'un de quelque chose.

informal adjective 1 simple (a meal or event, for example); 2 (language) familier (F familière); **an informal expression** une expression familière.

information noun renseignements M plural; **I need some information**

about flights to Paris j'ai besoin de quelques renseignements sur les vols vers Paris; **a piece of information** un renseignement.

information desk, information office *noun* bureau M des renseignements.

information technology, IT *noun* informatique F.

infuriating *adjective* exaspérant.

ingredient *noun* ingrédient M.

inhabitant *noun* habitant M, habitante F.

initials *plural noun* initiales F *plural*; **put your initials here** marquez vos initiales ici.

initiative *noun* initiative F.

injection *noun* piqûre F; **to give somebody an injection** faire une piqûre à quelqu'un.

injure *verb* blesser [1].

injured *adjective* blessé.

injury *noun* blessure F.

ink *noun* encre F.

in-laws *plural noun* beaux-parents M *plural*.

inner *adjective* intérieur.

innocent *adjective* innocent.

insane *adjective* fou (F folle).

inscription *noun* inscription F.

insect *noun* insecte M; **an insect bite** une piqûre d'insecte.

insect repellent *noun* insectifuge M.

inside *noun* intérieur M; **the inside**

of the oven l'intérieur du four. *preposition* à l'intérieur de; **inside the cinema** à l'intérieur du cinéma. *adverb* à l'intérieur; **she's inside, I think** elle est à l'intérieur, je crois; **to go inside** rentrer.

inside out *adjective, adverb* à l'envers.

insincere *adjective* peu sincère.

insist *verb* 1 insister [1]; **if you insist** puisque tu insistes; **to insist on doing** insister pour faire; **he insisted on paying** il a insisté pour payer; 2 **to insist that** affirmer [1] que; **Ruth insisted I was wrong** Ruth a affirmé que j'avais tort.

insomnia *noun* insomnie F.

inspector *noun* inspecteur M, inspectrice F.

install *verb* installer [1].

instalment *noun* (*of a story or serial*) épisode M.

instance *noun* **for instance** par exemple.

instant *noun* instant M; **come here this instant!** viens ici tout de suite! *adjective* 1 instantané (*coffee or soup*); 2 (*immediate*) immédiat (*an effect or a success, for example*).

instantly *adverb* immédiatement.

instead *adverb* 1 **Ted couldn't go, so I went instead** Ted ne pouvait pas y aller, donc je suis allé à sa place; **we didn't go to the concert, we went to Lucy's instead** au lieu d'aller au concert, nous sommes allés chez Lucy; 2 **instead of** au lieu de; **instead of pudding I had cheese** j'ai pris le fromage au lieu d'un dessert; **instead of playing tennis we went swimming** au lieu de jouer au tennis nous sommes allés à la piscine.

instinct noun instinct M.

institute noun institut M.

institution noun institution F.

instruct verb **to instruct somebody to do** donner [1] l'ordre à quelqu'un de faire; **the teacher instructed us to stay together** le professeur nous a donné l'ordre de rester en groupe.

instructions plural noun instructions F plural; **follow the instructions on the packet** suivez les instructions sur l'emballage; **'instructions for use'** 'mode d'emploi'.

instructor noun moniteur M, monitrice F; **my skiing instructor** mon moniteur de ski.

instrument noun instrument M; **to play an instrument** jouer d'un instrument.

insulin noun insuline F.

insult noun insulte F.
verb insulter [1].

insurance noun assurance F; **travel insurance** l'assurance voyage.

intelligence noun intelligence F.

intelligent adjective intelligent.

intend verb 1 vouloir [14]; **as I intended** comme je le voulais; 2 **to intend to do** avoir [5] l'intention de faire; **we intend to spend the night in Rome** nous avons l'intention de passer la nuit à Rome.

intensive care noun **in intensive care** en réanimation.

intention noun intention F; **I have no intention of paying** je n'ai aucune intention de payer.

interest noun 1 (hobby) centre M d'intérêt; **what are your interests?** quels sont vos centres d'intérêts?; 2 (keenness) intérêt M; **he has an interest in jazz** il a un intérêt pour le jazz.
verb intéresser [1]; **that doesn't interest me** ça ne m'intéresse pas.

interested adjective 1 **to be interested in** s'intéresser à; **Sean's very interested in cooking** Sean s'intéresse beaucoup à la cuisine.

interesting adjective intéressant.

interfere verb 1 **to interfere with something** (to fiddle with it) toucher [1] quelque chose; **don't interfere with my computer!** ne touche pas mon ordinateur; 2 **to interfere in** se mêler [1] à (someone else's affairs).

interior designer noun designer M & F.

international adjective international (M plural internationaux).

Internet noun Internet M; **on the internet** sur Internet.

interpret verb (act as an interpreter) faire [10] l'interprète.

interpreter noun interprète M & F.

interrupt verb interrompre [69].

interruption noun interruption F.

interval noun entracte M (in a play or concert).

interview noun 1 (for a job) entretien M; **a job interview** un entretien; 2 (in a newspaper, on TV or radio) interview F.
verb interviewer [1] (on TV, radio).

interviewer noun interviewer M.

into preposition 1 dans; **he's gone into the bank** il est entré dans la banque; **I put the cat into his basket** j'ai mis le chat dans son panier; **we all got into the car** nous sommes tous montés dans la voiture; 2 **to go into town** aller en ville; **Mum's gone into the office** Maman est allée au bureau; **to get into bed** se mettre au lit; **to translate into French** traduire en français; **to change pounds into francs** changer des livres sterling en francs; 3 **to be into jazz** être fana du jazz (informal).

introduce verb présenter [1]; **she introduced me to her brother** elle m'a présenté à son frère; **can I introduce you to my mother?** je te présente ma mère.

introduction noun (in a book) introduction F.

intuition noun intuition F.

invade verb envahir [2].

invalid noun malade M et F.

invent verb inventer [1].

invention noun invention F.

inventor noun inventeur M, inventrice F.

inverted commas plural noun

guillemets M plural; **in inverted commas** entre guillemets.

investigation noun (by police) enquête F; **an investigation into the fire** une enquête sur l'incendie.

invisible adjective invisible.

invitation noun invitation F; **an invitation to dinner** une invitation à dîner.

invite verb inviter [1]; **Kirsty invited me to lunch** Kirsty m'a invité à déjeuner; **he's invited me out on Tuesday** il m'a invitée à sortir avec lui mardi.

inviting adjective 1 appétissant (a meal); 2 accueillant (a room).

involve verb 1 nécessiter [1]; **it involves a lot of work** cela nécessite beaucoup de travail; 2 (to affect) concerner [1]; **the play will involve everybody** le spectacle va concerner tout le monde; **two cars were involved** deux voitures ont été concernées; 3 **to be involved in** participer [1] à; **I am involved in the new project** je participe au nouveau projet.

Iran noun Iran M.

Iraq noun Iraq M.

Ireland noun Irlande F; **in Ireland** en Irlande; **to Ireland** en Irlande; **the Republic of Ireland** la République d'Irlande.

Irish noun 1 (the language) irlandais M; 2 (the people) **the Irish** les Irlandais M plural.
adjective irlandais.

Irishman noun Irlandais M.

Irish Sea noun mer F d'Irlande.

Irishwoman noun Irlandaise F.

iron noun 1 (for clothes) fer M à repasser; 2 (the metal) fer M.
verb repasser [1].

ironing noun repassage M; **to do the ironing** faire le repassage.

ironing board noun planche F à repasser.

ironmonger's noun quincaillerie F.

irregular adjective irrégulier (F irrégulière).

irritable adjective irritable.

irritate verb irriter [1].

irritating adjective irritant.

Islam noun Islam M.

Islamic adjective islamique.

island noun île F.

isolated adjective isolé.

Israel noun Israël M.

Israeli noun Israélien M, Israélienne F.
adjective israélien (F israélienne).

issue noun 1 (something you discuss) question F; **a political issue** une question politique; 2 (of a magazine) numéro M.
verb (hand out) distribuer [1].

it pronoun 1 (as the subject) il (when it stands for a masculine noun); elle (when it stands for a feminine noun); **'where is my bag?'** – **'it's in the kitchen'** 'où est mon sac?' – 'il est dans la cuisine'; **'how old is your car?'** – **'it's five years old'** 'quel

âge a ta voiture?' – 'elle a cinq ans'; 2 (as the object) le (when it stands for a masculine noun); la (when it stands for a feminine noun); l' (before a vowel or silent 'h'); **is that her brother? I know him** c'est son frère? je le connais; **is that his sister? I know her** c'est sa sœur? je la connais; **where's my book? I've lost it** où est mon livre? je l'ai perdu; 3 **yes, it's true** oui, c'est vrai; **it doesn't matter** ça ne fait rien; 4 **who is it?** qui c'est?; **it's me** c'est moi; **what is it?** qu'est-ce que c'est?; 5 **it's raining** il pleut; **it's a nice day** il fait beau; **it's two o'clock** il est deux heures.

IT noun (short for information technology) informatique F.

Italian noun 1 (the language) italien M; 2 (person) Italien M, Italienne F.
adjective 1 italien (F italienne); **Italian cooking** la cuisine italienne; 2 d'italien (a teacher or a lesson); **my Italian class** mon cours d'italien.

italics noun italique M; **in italics** en italique.

Italy noun Italie F; **in Italy** en Italie; **to Italy** en Italie.

itch verb **my back is itching** j'ai le dos qui me démange; **this sweater itches** ce pull me gratte.

item noun article M.

its determiner son (before a masculine noun or a feminine noun beginning with a vowel or silent 'h'); sa (before a feminine noun); ses (before a plural noun); **the dog has lost its collar** le chien a perdu son collier; **the dog's in its kennel** le chien est dans sa niche; **its ear** son oreille; **its toys** ses jouets.

itself *pronoun* **1** se, s' (*before a vowel or silent 'h'*); **the cat is washing itself** le chat se lave; **2 he left the dog by itself** il a laissé le chien tout seul.

ivy *noun* lierre M.

J j

jack *noun* **1** (*in cards*) valet M; **the jack of clubs** le valet de trèfle; **2** (*for a car*) cric M.

jacket *noun* veste F.

jacket potato *noun* pomme F de terre en robe des champs.

jackpot *noun* gros lot M; **to win the jackpot** gagner le gros lot.

jail *noun* prison F.
verb emprisonner.

jam *noun* **1** (*that you eat*) confiture F; **raspberry jam** la confiture de framboises; **2 a traffic jam** un embouteillage.

jammed *adjective* coincé.

January *noun* janvier M; **in January** en janvier.

Japan *noun* Japon M; **in Japan** au Japon.

Japanese *noun* **1** (*the language*) japonais M; **2** (*person*) Japonais M, Japonaise F; **the Japanese** les Japonais M *plural*.
adjective japonais.

jar *noun* (*small*) pot M; (*large*) bocal M (*plural* bocaux); **a jar of jam** un pot de confiture.

javelin *noun* javelot M.

jaw *noun* mâchoire F.

jazz *noun* jazz M.

jealous *adjective* jaloux (F jalouse).

jeans *noun* jean M; **my jeans** mon jean; **a pair of jeans** un jean.

jelly *noun* gelée F.

jellyfish *noun* méduse F.

jersey *noun* **1** (*a pullover*) pull-over M; **2** (*for football*) maillot M.

Jersey *noun* Jersey F.

Jesus *noun* Jésus M; **Jesus Christ** Jésus-Christ.

jet *noun* jet M.

jet lag *noun* décalage M horaire.

jetty *noun* jetée F.

Jew *noun* Juif M, Juive F.

jewel *noun* bijou M (*plural* bijoux).

jeweller *noun* bijoutier M, bijoutière F.

jeweller's *noun* bijouterie F.

jewellery *noun* bijoux M *plural*.

Jewish *adjective* juif (F juive).

jigsaw *noun* puzzle M.

job *noun* **1** (*paid work*) emploi M; **a job as a secretary** un emploi comme secrétaire; **he's got a job** il a trouvé un emploi; **out of a job** sans emploi; **what's your job?** qu'est-ce que vous faites comme travail?; **a job**

offer une offre d'emploi; 2 (*a task*) travail M; **it's not an easy job** ce n'est pas un travail facile; **she made a good job of it** elle a fait un bon travail.

jobless *adjective* sans emploi.

jockey *noun* jockey M.

jog *verb* **to go jogging** faire [10] du jogging.

join *verb* 1 (*become a member of*) s'inscrire [38] à; **I've joined the judo club** je me suis inscrit au club de judo; 2 (*to meet up with*) rejoindre [49]; **I'll join you later** je vous rejoindrai plus tard.

● **to join in** 1 participer [1]; **Ruth never joins in** Ruth ne participe jamais; 2 **to join in something** participer [1] à quelque chose; **won't you join in the game?** veux-tu participer au jeu?

joiner *noun* menuisier M.

joint *noun* 1 (*of meat*) rôti M; **a joint of beef** un rôti de bœuf; 2 (*in your body*) articulation F.

joke *noun* (*a funny story*) plaisanterie F; **to tell a joke** raconter une plaisanterie.
verb plaisanter [1]; **you must be joking!** tu plaisantes!

joker *noun* (*in cards*) joker M.

Jordan *noun* Jordanie F.

journalism *noun* journalisme M.

journalist *noun* journaliste M & F; **Sean's a journalist** Sean est journaliste.

journey *noun* 1 (*a long one*) voyage M; **our journey to Turkey** notre voyage en Turquie; 2 (*shorter: to work or school*) trajet M; **a bus journey** un trajet en bus.

joy *noun* joie F.

joy-riding *noun* rodéo M à la voiture volée.

joystick *noun* (*for computer games*) manette F de jeu.

judge *noun* juge M.
verb estimer [1] (*a time or distance*).

judo *noun* judo M; **he does judo** il fait du judo.

jug *noun* pot M.

juice *noun* jus M; **two orange juices please** deux jus d'orange s'il vous plaît.

juicy *adjective* juteux (F juteuse).

jukebox *noun* jukebox M.

July *noun* juillet M; **in July** en juillet.

jumble sale *noun* vente F de charité.

jumbo jet *noun* gros-porteur M.

jump *noun* saut M; **a parachute jump** un saut en parachute.
verb sauter [1].

jumper *noun* pull M.

June *noun* juin M; **in June** en juin.

jungle *noun* jungle F.

junior *adjective* primaire; **a junior school** une école primaire; **the juniors** les élèves du primaire.

junk *noun* (*real rubbish*) bric-à-brac M.

junk food *noun* **you shouldn't eat**

junk food tu devrais manger correctement (*there is no word for junk food in French, so you will need to express it differently, according to the context*).

junk shop *noun* magasin M de brocante.

jury *noun* jury M.

just *adjective* 1 juste; **just before midday** juste avant midi; **just after the church** juste après l'église; **just for fun** juste pour rire; 2 **to have just done** venir de faire; **Tom has just arrived** Tom vient d'arriver; **Helen had just called** Helen venait d'appeler; 3 **to be just doing** être en train de faire; **I'm just finishing the ironing** je suis en train de finir le repassage; 4 (*only*) ne...que; **he's just a child** il n'est qu'un enfant; **there's just me and Justine** il n'y a que moi et Justine; 5 **just coming!** j'arrive!

justice *noun* justice F.

justify *verb* justifier [1].

K k

kangaroo *noun* kangourou M.

karaoke *noun* karaoké M.

karate *noun* karaté M.

kebab *noun* brochette F.

keen *adjective* 1 (*enthusiastic*) enthousiaste; **you don't look too keen** tu n'as pas l'air très enthousiaste; 2 (*committed*)

passionné; **he's a keen photographer** c'est un photographe passionné; 3 **I'm not keen on fish** je n'aime pas trop le poisson; 4 **to be keen on doing** (*or to do*) avoir très envie de faire; **I'm not keen on camping** je n'ai pas très envie de faire du camping.

keep *verb* 1 garder [1]; **I kept the letter** j'ai gardé la lettre; **will you keep my seat?** veux-tu garder ma place?; **they kept her in hospital** ils l'ont gardée à l'hôpital; **to keep a secret** garder un secret; 2 **to keep somebody waiting** faire [10] attendre quelqu'un; 3 (*to store*) ranger [52]; **I keep my bike in the garage** je range mon vélo dans le garage; **where do you keep saucepans?** où rangez-vous les casseroles?; 4 **to keep on doing** continuer [1] à faire; **she kept on talking** elle a continué à parler; **keep straight on** continuez tout droit; 5 **to keep on doing** (*time after time*) he keeps on ringing me up; 6 il n'arrête pas de m'appeler; 7 (*stay*) rester [1]; **keep calm!** restez calme!; **keep out of the sun** reste à l'abri du soleil; 8 **to keep a promise** tenir [77] sa promesse.

keep fit *noun* gymnastique F d'entretien.

kennel *noun* 1 (*for one dog*) niche F; 2 (*for boarding*) **kennels** chenil M.

kerb *noun* bord M du trottoir.

kettle *noun* bouilloire F; **to put the kettle on** mettre l'eau à chauffer.

key *noun* 1 (*for a lock*) clé F; **a bunch of keys** un trousseau de clés; **2** (*on a piano or typewriter*) touche F.

keyboard *noun* (*for a piano or a computer*) clavier M.

keyring *noun* porte-clés M.

kick *noun* **1** (*from a person or a horse*) coup M de pied; **to give somebody a kick** donner un coup de pied à quelqu'un; **2** (*in football*) tir M; ★ **to get a kick out of doing** prendre plaisir à faire.
verb **to kick somebody** donner [1] un coup de pied à quelqu'un; **to kick the ball** donner un coup de pied dans le ballon.
●**to kick off** donner [1] le coup d'envoi.

kick-off *noun* coup M d'envoi.

kid *noun* gosse M & F (*child*); **Dad's looking after the kids** Papa s'occupe des gosses.

kidnap *verb* enlever [50].

kidney *noun* **1** (*part of your body*) rein M; **2** (*for eating*) rognon M.

kill *verb* tuer [1]; **she was killed in an accident** elle a été tuée dans un accident.

killer *noun* (*murderer*) meurtrier M, meurtrière F.

kilo *noun* kilo M; **a kilo of sugar** un kilo de sucre; **fifteen francs a kilo** quinze francs le kilo.

kilogramme *noun* kilogramme M.

kilometre *noun* kilomètre M.

kilt *noun* kilt M.

kind *noun* sorte F; **all kinds of people** toutes sortes de gens.
adjective gentil (F gentille); **Marion was very kind to me** Marion a été très gentille avec moi.

kindness *noun* gentillesse F.

king *noun* roi M; **King George** le roi Georges; **the king of hearts** le roi de cœur.

kingdom *noun* royaume M; **the United Kingdom** le Royaume-Uni.

kiosk *noun* **1** (*for newspapers or snacks*) kiosque M; **2** (*for a phone*) cabine F.

kipper *noun* hareng fumé M.

kiss *noun* baiser M; **to give somebody a kiss** embrasser quelqu'un.
verb embrasser [1]; **kiss me!** embrasse-moi!; **we kissed each other** nous nous sommes embrassés.

kit *noun* **1** (*of tools*) trousse F; **a tool kit** une trousse à outils; **2** (*clothes*) affaires F *plural*; **where's my football kit?** où sont mes affaires de foot?; **3** (*for making a model, a piece of furniture, etc*) kit M.

kitchen *noun* cuisine F; **the kitchen table** la table de la cuisine.

kitchen foil *noun* papier M d'aluminium.

kitchen garden *noun* jardin M potager.

kitchen roll *noun* essuie-tout M.

kite *noun* (*toy*) cerf-volant M; **to fly a kite** faire voler un cerf-volant.

kitten *noun* chaton M.

kiwi fruit *noun* kiwi M.

knee *noun* genou M

kneel (*plural* genoux); on (your) hands and knees à quatre pattes.

kneel *verb* se mettre [11] à genoux.

knickers *plural noun* petite culotte F.

knife *noun* couteau M (*plural* couteaux).

knight *noun* (*in chess*) cavalier M.

knit *verb* tricoter [1].

knitting *noun* tricot M.

knob *noun* bouton M.

knock *noun* coup M; a knock on the head un coup à la tête; a knock at the door un coup à la porte.
verb 1 (*to bang*) cogner [1]; I knocked my arm on the table je me suis cogné le bras contre la table;
2 to knock on something (*a person*) frapper [1] à (*the door*).
● **to knock down** 1 (*in a traffic accident*) renverser [1] (*a person*);
2 (*to demolish*) démolir [2] (*an old building*).
● **to knock out** 1 (*to make unconscious*) assommer [1]; 2 (*in sport, to eliminate*) éliminer [1].

knot *noun* nœud M; to tie a knot in something nouer quelque chose.

know *verb* 1 (*know a fact*) savoir [70]; do you know where Tim is? sais-tu où est Tim?; I know they've moved house je sais qu'ils ont déménagé; he knows it by heart il le sait par cœur; yes, I know oui, je sais; you never know! on ne sait jamais!; 2 (*be personally acquainted with*) connaître [27] (*a person, place, book, or music, for example*); do you know the Jacksons? est-ce que tu connais les Jackson?; all the people I know tous les gens que je connais; I don't know his mother je ne connais pas sa mère; 3 to know how to do savoir [70] faire; Steve knows how to make couscous Steve sait faire du couscous; Liz knows how to mend it Liz sait le réparer; 4 to know about être [6] au courant de (*the latest news*); 5 to know about s'y connaître [27] en (*machines, cooking, etc*); Lindy knows about computers Lindy s'y connaît en informatique.

knowledge *noun* connaissance F.

Koran *noun* Coran M.

kosher *adjective* kascher.

L l

lab *noun* labo M.

label *noun* étiquette F.

laboratory *noun* laboratoire M.

Labour *noun* les travaillistes M *plural*; to vote for the Labour party voter pour les travaillistes; the Labour Party le parti travailliste.

lace *noun* 1 (*for a shoe*) lacet M;
2 (*for curtains, for example*) dentelle F.

lad *noun* gars M.

ladder *noun* (*for climbing, or in your tights*) échelle F.

ladies *noun* (*lavatory*) toilettes F

plural; (on a sign) **'Ladies' 'Dames'**.

lady noun dame F; **ladies and gentlemen** mesdames et messieurs.

ladybird noun coccinelle F.

lager noun bière F blonde.

laid-back adjective relaxe.

lake noun lac M; **Lake Geneva** le lac Léman.

lamb noun agneau M (plural agneaux); **a leg of lamb** un gigot.

lame adjective boiteux (F boiteuse); **he is lame** il boite.

lamp noun lampe F.

lamp-post noun réverbère M.

lampshade noun abat-jour M (plural abat-jour).

land noun 1 terre F; **I can see land** je vois la terre; 2 (property) terrain M; **a piece of land** un terrain.
verb 1 (plane, passenger) atterrir [2]; 2 (leave a ship) débarquer [1].

landing noun 1 (on the stairs) palier M; 2 (of a plane) atterrissage M; 3 (from a boat) débarquement M.

landlady noun propriétaire F.

landlord noun propriétaire M.

landscape noun paysage M.

lane noun 1 (a country path) chemin M; 2 (of a motorway) voie F.

language noun 1 (French, Italian, etc) langue F; **a foreign language** une langue étrangère; 2 (way of speaking) langage M; **bad language** un langage grossier.

language lab noun laboratoire M de langues.

lap noun 1 (your knees) genoux M plural; **on my lap** sur mes genoux; 2 (in races) tour M de piste.

laptop noun portable M.

larder noun garde-manger M.

large adjective 1 grand (goes before the noun); **a large number** un grand nombre; **a large house** une grande maison; 2 gros (F grosse) (a piece, part, animal) (goes before the noun); **a large piece of cake** un gros morceau de gâteau; 3 nombreux (F nombreuse) (crowd or family); **I come from a large family** je viens d'une famille nombreuse.

laser noun laser M.

last adjective dernier (F dernière); **the last time** la dernière fois; **last week** la semaine dernière; **last night** (in the evening) hier soir; (in the night) cette nuit.
adverb 1 (in final position) (to arrive or leave) en dernier; **Rob arrived last** Rob est arrivé en dernier; **at last!** enfin!; 2 (most recently) **I last saw him in May** la dernière fois que je l'ai vu était en mai.
verb durer [1]; **the play lasted two hours** le spectacle a duré deux heures.

late adjective, adverb 1 en retard; **we're late** nous sommes en retard; **they arrived late** ils sont arrivés en retard; **to be late for something** être en retard pour quelque chose; **we were late for the film** nous étions en retard pour le film; **2 to be late** (*a bus or train*) avoir du retard; **the train was an hour late** le train a eu une heure de retard; **3** (*late in the day*) tard; **we got up late** nous nous sommes levés tard; **the chemist is open late** la pharmacie est ouverte tard; **late last night** tard hier soir; **too late!** trop tard!

lately *adverb* ces derniers temps.

later *adverb* plus tard; **I'll explain later** j'expliquerai plus tard; **see you later!** à tout à l'heure!

latest *adjective* **1** dernier (F dernière); **the latest news** les dernières nouvelles; **2 at the latest** au plus tard.

Latin *noun* latin M.

laugh *noun* rire M; **to do something for a laugh** faire quelque chose pour rigoler (*informal*).
verb **1** rire [68]; **everybody laughed** tout le monde a ri; **2 to laugh at** se moquer [1] de; **I tried to explain but they laughed at me** j'ai essayé d'expliquer mais ils se sont moqués de moi.

launderette *noun* laverie F automatique.

lavatory *noun* toilettes F *plural*; **to go to the lavatory** aller aux toilettes.

lavender *noun* lavande F.

law *noun* **1** loi F; **it's against the law** c'est interdit; **2** (*subject of study*) droit M.

lawn *noun* pelouse F.

lawnmower *noun* tondeuse F à gazon.

lawyer *noun* avocat M, avocate F.

lay *verb* **1** (*put*) poser [1]; **she laid the card on the table** elle a posé la carte sur la table; **2** (*spread out*) étaler [1]; **we laid newspaper on the floor** nous avons étalé du papier journal sur le parquet; **3 to lay the table** mettre [11] la table.

lay-by *noun* aire F de stationnement.

layer *noun* couche F.

lazy *adjective* paresseux (F paresseuse).

lead[1] *noun* **1** (*when you are ahead*) **to be in the lead** être en tête; **Baxter's in the lead** Baxter est en tête; **we have a lead of three points** nous avons trois points d'avance; **2** (*electric*) fil M; **3** (*for a dog*) laisse F; **on a lead** en laisse.
adjective (*a role or a singer*) principal (M *plural* principaux).
verb **1** mener [50]; **the path leads to the sea** le chemin mène à la mer; **2 to lead the way** mo ıtrer [1] le chemin; **3 to lead to something** entraîner [1] quelque chose (*an accident or problems, for example*).

lead[2] *noun* (*the metal*) plomb M.

leader *noun* **1** (*of a gang*) chef M; **2** (*of a political party*) dirigeant M, dirigeante F; **3** (*in a competition*) premier M, première F.

lead-free petrol *noun* essence F sans plomb.

lead singer *noun* chanteur

principal M, chanteuse principale F.

leaf noun feuille F.

leaflet noun dépliant M.

league noun (*in sport*) championnat M.

leak noun fuite F; **a gas leak** une fuite de gaz.
verb (*a bottle or a roof*) fuir [44].

lean adjective (*meat*) maigre.
verb **1 to lean on something** s'appuyer [41] contre quelque chose; **2** (*prop*) appuyer [41]; **lean the ladder against the tree!** appuie l'échelle contre l'arbre!; **3** (*a person*) se pencher [1]; **to lean out of the window** se pencher par la fenêtre; **lean forward a bit** penche-toi un peu en avant.

leap verb sauter [1].

leap year noun année F bissextile.

learn verb apprendre [64]; **to learn Russian** apprendre le russe; **to learn (how) to drive** apprendre à conduire.

learner noun apprenant M, apprenante F; **to be a fast learner** apprendre vite.

learner driver noun élève M & F d'auto-école.

least adverb, adjective, pronoun **1 le** moins; **I like the blue shirt least** c'est la chemise bleue que j'aime le moins; **2** (*followed by a noun*) le moins de; **Tony has the least money** c'est Tony qui a le moins d'argent; **3** (*followed by an adjective*) le moins, la moins, les moins (*according to the gender and number of the noun*

going with the adjective) **the least expensive hotel** l'hôtel le moins cher; **the least expensive car** la voiture la moins chère; **the least expensive shoes** les chaussures les moins chères; **4** (*the slightest*) le moindre, la moindre (*according to the gender of the noun that follows*); **I haven't the least idea** je n'ai pas la moindre idée; **5 at least** (*at a minimum*) au moins; **at least twenty people** au moins vingt personnes; **6 at least** (*at any rate*) du moins; **at least, I think she's a teacher** du moins, je crois qu'elle est professeur.

leather noun cuir M; **a leather jacket** un blouson en cuir.

leave noun congé M; **three days' leave** trois jours de congé.
verb **1** (*go away*) partir [58]; **they're leaving tomorrow** ils vont partir demain; **we left at six** nous sommes partis à six heures; **2** (*go away from*) quitter [1]; **I left the office at five** j'ai quitté le bureau à cinq heures; **Guy left school at sixteen** Guy a quitté l'école à seize ans; **3** (*go out of*) sortir [72] de; **she left the cinema at ten** elle est sortie du cinéma à dix heures; **4** (*deposit*) laisser [1]; **you can leave your coats in the hall** vous pouvez laisser vos manteaux dans l'entrée; **5** (*not do*) laisser [1]; **let's leave the washing up!** laissons la vaisselle!; **6** (*forget*) oublier [1]; **he left his umbrella on the train** il a oublié son parapluie dans le train; **7 be left** rester [1]; **there are two pancakes left** il reste deux crêpes; **we have ten minutes left** il nous reste dix minutes; **I don't**

have any money left il ne me reste plus d'argent.

lecture noun 1 (at university) cours magistral M (plural cours magistraux); 2 (public) conférence F.

lecturer noun professeur M à l'université.

leek noun poireau M (plural poireaux).

left noun gauche F; **to drive on the left** conduire à gauche; **turn left at the church** tournez à gauche à l'église; **on my left** à ma gauche. adjective gauche; **his left foot** son pied gauche.

left-hand noun **the left-hand side** la gauche.

left-handed adjective gaucher M, gauchère F.

left luggage office noun consigne F.

leftovers plural noun restes M plural.

leg noun 1 (of a person or a horse) jambe F; **my left leg** ma jambe gauche; **to break your leg** se casser la jambe; 2 (of other animals) patte F; 3 (of a table or chair) pied M; 4 (in cooking) **a leg of chicken** une cuisse de poulet; **a leg of lamb** un gigot; ★ **to pull somebody's leg** faire [10] marcher quelqu'un.

legal adjective légal (M plural légaux).

leggings plural noun caleçon M.

leisure noun loisirs M plural; **in my leisure time** pendant mes loisirs.

lemon noun citron M; **a lemon yoghurt** un yaourt au citron.

lemonade noun limonade F.

lemon juice noun jus M de citron.

lend verb prêter [1]; **to lend something to somebody** prêter quelque chose à quelqu'un; **I lent Judy my bike** j'ai prêté mon vélo à Judy; **will you lend it to me?** veux-tu me le prêter?

length noun longueur F.

lens noun 1 (in a camera) objectif M; 2 (in spectacles) verre M; 3 **contact lenses** les lentilles F plural de contact.

Lent noun Carême M.

lentil noun lentille F.

Leo noun Lion M; **I'm Leo** je suis Lion.

leotard noun justaucorps M.

lesbian noun lesbienne F.

less pronoun, adjective, adverb 1 moins; **Richard eats less** Richard mange moins; 2 (before a noun) moins de; **less traffic** moins de circulation; **less time** moins de temps; 3 (before an adjective or adverb) moins; **less interesting** moins intéressant; **less quickly than us** moins vite que nous; 4 **less than** moins de; **less than three hours** moins de trois heures; **less than a kilo** moins d'un kilo; 5 **less than** (in comparisons) moins que; **you spent less than me** tu as dépensé moins que moi.

lesson noun 1 (class) cours M; **the**

history lesson le cours d'histoire; **to take tennis lessons** prendre des cours de tennis; **2** (*one in a planned series*) leçon F; **a driving lesson** une leçon de conduite.

let¹ *verb* (*allow*) **to let somebody do** laisser [1] quelqu'un faire; **she lets me borrow my bike** elle me laisse emprunter son vélo; **will you let me go alone?** veux-tu me laisser y aller toute seule?; **the police let us through** la police nous a laissés passer; **let me see** (*show me*) laisse-moi voir; **2** (*as a suggestion or a command*) **let's go!** allons-y!; **let's not talk about it** n'en parlons pas; **let's see, if Tuesday is the trois ...; let's eat out** si on mangeait au restaurant?

● **to let off 1** tirer [1] (*fireworks*); **2** faire [10] exploser (*a bomb*); **3** (*to excuse from*) dispenser [1] de (*homework*).

let² *verb* (*to rent out*) louer [1]; **'flat to let'** 'appartement à louer'.

letter *noun* lettre F; **a letter for you from Delia** une lettre pour toi de Delia; **G is the letter after F** G est la lettre après F.

letter box *noun* boîte F à lettres.

lettuce *noun* salade F; **two lettuces** deux salades.

leukaemia *noun* leucémie F.

level *noun* niveau M (*plural* niveaux); **at street level** au niveau de la rue.
adjective **1** droit (*a shelf or floor*); **2** plat (*ground*).

level crossing *noun* passage M à niveau.

lever *noun* levier M.

liar *noun* menteur M, menteuse F.

liberal *adjective* libéral (M *plural* libéraux); **the Liberal Democrats** le parti libéral-démocrate.

Libra *noun* Balance F; **Sean's Libra** Sean est Balance.

librarian *noun* bibliothécaire M & F; **Mark's a librarian** Mark est bibliothécaire.

library *noun* bibliothèque F; **the public library** la bibliothèque municipale.

licence *noun* **1** (*for driving or fishing*) permis M; **a driving licence** un permis de conduire; **2** (*for a TV*) redevance F.

lick *verb* lécher [1].

lid *noun* couvercle M; **she took the lid off** elle a enlevé le couvercle.

lie *noun* mensonge M; **to tell a lie** (*or lies*) mentir.
verb **1** (*to be stretched out*) être [6] allongé; **Jimmy was lying on the bed** Jimmy était allongé sur le lit; **my coat lay on the bed** mon manteau était sur le lit; **to lie down** se coucher [1]; (*for a little while*) s'allonger [52]; **come and lie down in the sun** viens t'allonger au soleil; **3** (*not to tell the truth*) mentir [53].

lie-in *noun* **to have a lie-in** faire la grasse matinée.

life *noun* vie F; **all her life** toute sa vie; **full of life** plein de vie; **that's life!** c'est la vie!

lifebelt noun bouée F de sauvetage.

lifeboat noun canot M de sauvetage.

life jacket noun gilet M de sauvetage.

life-style noun style M de vie.

lift noun 1 ascenseur M; let's take the lift prenons l'ascenseur; 2 (a ride) to give somebody a lift to the station déposer quelqu'un à la gare; Tom gave me a lift home Tom m'a déposé chez moi; can I give you a lift? puis-je vous déposer quelque part?
verb soulever [50]; he lifted the box il a soulevé le carton.

light noun 1 (electric) lumière F; will you turn the light on? veux-tu allumer la lumière?; to turn off the light éteindre la lumière; 2 (streetlight) réverbère M; 3 (a headlight for a car) phare M; are your lights on? as-tu allumé tes phares?; 4 (an indicator on a machine) voyant M; 5 traffic lights les feux M plural; the lights were green le feu était au vert; ★ have you got a light? tu as du feu?
adjective 1 (in colour) clair; light blue eyes des yeux bleu clair; 2 (not night) it gets light at six il fait jour à six heures; 3 (not heavy) léger (F légère); a light sweater un pull léger; a light breeze une brise légère.
verb 1 allumer [1] (the oven, the fire, or a cigarette); we lit a fire nous avons fait un feu; 2 craquer [1] (a match).

light bulb noun ampoule F.

lighter noun briquet M.

lighthouse noun phare M.

lightning noun éclairs M plural; a flash of lightning un éclair; to be struck by lightning être frappé par la foudre.

light switch noun interrupteur M.

like[1] preposition, conjunction 1 comme; like me comme moi; like this comme ça; like a duck comme un canard; like I said comme j'ai dit; what's it like? c'est comment?; what was the weather like? quel temps faisait-il?; 2 to look like ressembler [1] à; Cindy looks like her father Cindy ressemble à son père.

like[2] verb 1 aimer [1] (bien); I like fish j'aime bien le poisson; I don't like snakes je n'aime pas les serpents; Mum likes travelling Maman aime bien voyager; I like Renoir best je préfère Renoir; 2 I would like je voudrais; would you like a coffee? est-ce que tu voudrais un café?; what would you like to eat? qu'est-ce que tu veux manger?; yes, if you like oui, si tu veux.

likely adjective probable; it's not very likely ce n'est pas très probable; she's likely to phone elle va probablement appeler.

lilac noun lilas M.

lily noun lys M.

lily of the valley noun muguet M.

lime noun citron vert M.

limit noun limitation F; the speed limit la limitation de vitesse.

limp *noun* **to have a limp** boiter [1].

line *noun* **1** ligne F; **a straight line** une ligne droite; **six lines of text** six lignes de texte; **to draw a line** tirer un trait; **2 a railway line** (*from one place to another*) une ligne de chemin de fer; **on the railway line** (*the track*) sur la voie ferrée; **3** (*a queue of people or cars*) file F; **to stand in line** faire la queue; **4** (*telephone*) ligne F; **the line's bad** la ligne est mauvaise; **hold the line, please** ne quittez pas.
verb doubler [1] (*a coat*).

linen *noun* lin M; **a linen jacket** une veste en lin.

lining *noun* doublure F.

link *noun* **1** rapport M; **what's the link between the two?** quel est le rapport entre les deux?
verb relier [1] (*two places*); **the terminals are linked by a shuttle service** les terminaux sont reliés par une navette.

lion *noun* lion M.

lino *noun* linoléum M.

lip *noun* lèvre F.

lip-read *verb* lire [51] sur les lèvres.

lipstick *noun* rouge M à lèvres.

liquid *noun, adjective* liquide M.

liquidizer *noun* mixer M.

list *noun* liste F.

listen *verb* **1** écouter [1]; **I wasn't listening** je n'écoutais pas; **2 to listen to** écouter [1]; **listen to the music** écoutez la musique; **you're**

not listening to me** tu ne m'écoutes pas.

listener *noun* (*to the radio*) auditeur M, auditrice F.

literally *adverb* littéralement.

literature *noun* littérature F.

litre *noun* litre M; **a litre of milk** un litre de lait.

litter *noun* (*rubbish*) détritus M *plural.*

litter bin *noun* poubelle F.

little *adjective, pronoun* **1** (*small*) petit (*goes before the noun*); **a little boy** un petit garçon; **a little break** une petite pause; **2** (*not much*) peu (de); **they have little money** ils ont peu d'argent; **we have very little time** nous avons très peu de temps; **3 a little** un peu (de); **4 we have a little money** nous avons un peu d'argent; **just a little, please** juste un peu, s'il vous plaît; **it's a little late** c'est un peu tard; **a little more** un peu plus; **a little less** un peu moins; ★ **little by little** petit à petit.

little finger *noun* petit doigt M.

live[1] *verb* **1** (*in a house or town*) habiter [1]; **Susan lives in York** Susan habite à York; **we live in a flat** nous habitons dans un appartement; **they live at number 57** ils habitent au numéro cinquante-sept; **we're living in the country now** nous habitons à la campagne maintenant; **2** (*be or stay alive, spend one's life*) vivre [82]; **lions live in Africa** les lions vivent en Afrique; **they live on fruit** ils vivent de fruits; **they live together** ils vivent ensemble.

live² *adjective* **1** en direct (*a broadcast*); **a live concert** un concert en direct; **a broadcast live from Wembley** une émission en direct de Wembley; **2** (*alive*) vivant.

lively *adjective* animé (*a party or restaurant, for example*).

liver *noun* foie M.

living *noun* vie F; **to earn a living** gagner sa vie.

living room *noun* salle F de séjour.

lizard *noun* lézard M.

load *noun* **1** (*on a lorry*) chargement M; **a (lorry-) load of bricks** un camion de briques; **2** a bus-load of tourists un autobus plein de touristes; **3** loads of des tas de (*informal*); **loads of people** des tas de gens; **they've got loads of money** ils sont bourrés de fric (*informal*).
verb charger [52]; **a lorry loaded with wood** un camion chargé de bois.

loaf *noun* pain M; **a loaf of wholemeal bread** un pain complet.

loan *noun* prêt M.
verb prêter.

loathe *verb* détester [1]; **I loathe getting up early** je déteste me lever tôt.

lobster *noun* homard M.

local *noun* **1** (*a pub*) pub M du coin; **2 the locals** (*people*) les gens du coin.
adjective **the local library** la

bibliothèque du coin; **the local newspaper** le journal local.

lock *noun* **1** (*with a key*) serrure F; **2** (*on a canal*) écluse F.
verb **to lock the door** fermer [1] la porte à clé; **the door was locked** la porte était fermée à clé.

locker *noun* casier M.

locker room *noun* vestiaire M.

lodger *noun* locataire M & F.

loft *noun* grenier M.

log *noun* bûche F; **a log fire** un feu de bois.

logical *adjective* logique.

lollipop *noun* sucette F.

London *noun* Londres; **to London** à Londres; **a day in London** une journée à Londres; **the London streets** les rues de Londres.

Londoner *noun* Londonien M, Londonienne F.

lonely *adjective* **1** seul; **to feel lonely** se sentir seul; **2** (*a place*) isolé.

long *adjective, adverb* **1** long (F longue); **a long film** un film long; **a long day** une longue journée; **it's an hour long** ça dure une heure; **2 a long time** longtemps; **he stayed for a long time** il est resté longtemps; **I've been here for a long time** je suis là depuis longtemps; **a long time ago** il y a longtemps; **this won't take long** ça ne prendra pas longtemps; **3 how long?** combien de temps?; **how long have you been here?** tu es là depuis combien de temps?; **long ago** il y a longtemps; **4 a long way**

loin; **it's a long way to the cinema**
le cinéma est loin d'ici; **5 all night
long** toute la nuit; **6 he doesn't
work here any longer** il ne travaille
plus ici.
verb to long **to do** avoir [5] **très
envie de faire; I'm longing to see
you** j'ai très envie de te voir.

long-distance call *noun* (*within
the country*) appel M interurbain.

longer *adverb* **no longer** ne…plus; **I
no longer know** je ne sais plus; **they
no longer live here** ils n'habitent
plus ici.

long jump *noun* saut M en
longueur.

longlife milk *noun* lait M longue
conservation.

loo *noun* toilettes F *plural*.

look *noun* 1 (*a glance*) coup M
d'œil; **to have a look at something**
jeter un coup d'œil à quelque chose;
2 (*a tour*) **to have a look round the
town** une tour dans la ville; **to
have a look round the shops** faire
les magasins; 3 **to have a look for**
chercher (*something you've lost*).
verb 1 regarder [1]; **I wasn't
looking** je ne regardais pas; **to look
out of the window** regarder par la
fenêtre; 2 **to look at** regarder [1];
Andy was looking at the photos
Andy regardait les photos; 3 (*to
seem*) avoir [5] l'air; **Melanie looks
pleased** Melanie a l'air contente;
the salad looks delicious la salade
a l'air délicieuse; 4 **to look like**
ressembler [1] à; **Sally looks like her
aunt** Sally ressemble à sa tante; **they
look like each other** ils se

ressemblent; **what does the house
look like?** comment est la maison?

● **to look after** 1 s'occuper [1] de;
Dad's looking after the baby Papa
s'occupe du bébé; 2 surveiller [1]
(*luggage*).

● **to look for** chercher [1]; **I'm looking
for the keys** je cherche les clés.

● **to look forward to something**
attendre [3] quelque chose avec
impatience (*a party or a trip, for
example*).

● **to look out** (*to be careful*) faire [10]
attention; **look out, it's hot!** (fais)
attention, c'est chaud!

● **to look something up** chercher [1]
quelque chose (*in a dictionary or
directory*); **you can look it up in the
dictionary** tu peux le chercher dans
le dictionnaire.

loose *adjective* 1 (*a screw or knot*)
desserré; 2 (*a garment*) ample;
3 **loose change** la petite monnaie;
★ **I'm at a loose end** je ne sais pas
trop quoi faire.

lorry *noun* camion M.

lorry driver *noun* routier M.

lose *verb* 1 perdre [3]; **we lost** nous
avons perdu; **we lost the match**
nous avons perdu le match; **Sam's
lost his watch** Sam a perdu sa
montre; 2 **to get lost** se perdre [3];
we got lost in the woods nous nous
sommes perdus dans les bois.

loss *noun* perte F.

lost *adjective* perdu.

lost property *noun* objets M
plural trouvés.

lot *noun* 1 **a lot** beaucoup; **Jason
eats a lot** Jason mange beaucoup;

I spent a lot j'ai beaucoup dépensé; **he's a lot better** il va beaucoup mieux; **2 a lot of** beaucoup de; **a lot of coffee** beaucoup de café; **lots of people** beaucoup de gens; **'what are you doing tonight?' – 'not a lot'** 'qu'est-ce que tu fais ce soir?' – 'pas grand-chose'.

lottery noun loterie F; **to win the lottery** gagner à la loterie.

loud adjective **1** fort; **in a loud voice** d'une voix forte; **2 to say something out loud** dire quelque chose à haute voix.

loudly adverb fort.

loudspeaker noun haut-parleur M (plural haut-parleurs).

lounge noun **1** (in a house or hotel) salon M; **2** (in an airport) **the departure lounge** la salle d'embarquement.

love noun **1** amour M; **to be in love with somebody** être amoureux de quelqu'un; **she's in love with Jake** elle est amoureuse de Jake; **Gina sends her love** Gina t'embrasse; **with love from Charlie** amitiés, Charlie; **2** (in tennis) zéro M. verb **1** aimer [1] (a person); **I love you** je t'aime; **2** aimer beaucoup (place, suggestion); **she loves London** elle aime beaucoup Londres; **I'd love to come** j'aimerais beaucoup venir; **3** adorer [1] (activity, thing); **I love dancing** j'adore danser; **Wayne loves seafood** Wayne adore les fruits de mer.

lovely adjective **1** (to look at) joli; **a lovely dress** une jolie robe; **their garden is lovely** leur jardin est très joli; **a lovely house** une belle maison; **2 it's a lovely day** il fait très beau; **we had lovely weather** il a fait très beau; **3** (food, meal) délicieux (F délicieuse).

low adjective **1** bas (F basse); **a low table** une table basse; **at a low price** à prix bas; **in a low voice** à voix basse.

lower adjective (not as high) inférieur. verb baisser [1].

low-fat milk noun lait écrémé M.

luck noun chance F; **good luck!** bonne chance!; **bad luck!** pas de chance!; **with a bit of luck** avec un peu de chance.

luckily adverb heureusement; **luckily for them** heureusement pour eux.

lucky adjective **1 to be lucky** (a person) avoir de la chance; **we were lucky** nous avons eu de la chance; **2 to be lucky** (bringing luck) porter bonheur; **it's supposed to be lucky** c'est censé porter bonheur; **my lucky number** mon numéro porte-bonheur.

luggage noun bagages M plural; **my luggage is in the boot** mes bagages sont dans le coffre.

lump noun morceau M (plural morceaux).

lunch noun déjeuner M; **to have lunch in Oxford** déjeuner [1]; **we had lunch in Oxford** nous avons déjeuné à Oxford.

lunch break noun pause-déjeuner F.

lunch hour, lunch time noun heure F du déjeuner.

lung noun poumon M.

Luxembourg noun 1 (country) Luxembourg M; **to Luxembourg** au Luxembourg; **in Luxembourg** au Luxembourg; 2 (city) Luxembourg; **in Luxembourg** à Luxembourg.

luxurious adjective luxueux (F luxueuse).

luxury noun luxe M.

lyrics plural noun paroles F plural.

M m

mac noun imper M (informal).

macaroni noun macaronis M plural; **we had macaroni** nous avons mangé des macaronis.

machine noun machine F.

machinery noun machines F plural.

mackerel noun maquereau M (plural maquereaux).

mad adjective 1 fou (F folle); **she's completely mad!** elle est complètement folle!; 2 (angry) furieux (F furieuse); **my mum will be mad!** ma mère sera furieuse!; 3 **to be mad about something** adorer quelque chose; **she's mad about horses** elle adore les chevaux.

madam noun madame F.

madman noun fou M.

madness noun folie F.

magazine noun magazine M.

maggot noun asticot M.

magic noun magie F.
adjective 1 magique; **a magic wand** une baguette magique; 2 (great) super.

magician noun 1 (wizard) magicien M; 2 (conjurer) prestidigitateur M.

magnificent adjective magnifique.

magnifying glass noun loupe F.

magnolia noun magnolia M.

mahogany noun acajou M.

maiden name noun nom M de jeune fille.

mail noun courrier M; **e-mail** (electronic mail) courrier M électronique.

mail order noun **to buy something by mail order** acheter quelque chose par correspondance; **a mail order catalogue** un catalogue de vente par correspondance.

main adjective principal (M plural principaux); **the main entrance** l'entrée principale.

mainly adverb principalement.

main road noun route F principale.

maize noun maïs M.

major adjective majeur.

Majorca noun Majorque F.

majority noun majorité F.

make noun marque F; **what make is your bike?** de quelle marque est ton vélo?
verb 1 faire [10]; **I made an omelette** j'ai fait une omelette; **she made her bed** elle a fait son lit; **he made me wait** il m'a fait attendre; **she makes me laugh** elle me fait rire; **two and three make five** deux et trois font cinq; 2 fabriquer [1]; **they make computers** ils fabriquent des ordinateurs; **'made in France'** 'fabriqué en France'; 3 rendre [3]; **to make somebody happy** rendre quelqu'un heureux; **that makes me hungry** ça me donne faim; 4 gagner [1] (money); **he makes forty pounds a day** il gagne quarante livres par jour; **to make a living** gagner sa vie; 5 (force) **to make somebody do something** obliger [52] quelqu'un à faire quelque chose; **she made him give the money back** elle l'a obligé à rendre l'argent; 6 **to make a meal** préparer [1] un repas; 7 **to make a phone call** passer [1] un coup de fil; **I have to make a few phone calls** je dois passer quelques coups de fil; 8 **I can't make it tonight** je ne peux pas venir ce soir.

● **to make something up** 1 inventer [1] quelque chose; **she made up an excuse** elle a inventé une excuse; 2 **to make it up** (after a quarrel) se réconcilier [1]; **they've made it up now** ils se sont maintenant réconciliés.

make-up noun maquillage M; **to put on your make-up** se maquiller [1]; **Jo's putting on her make-up** Jo est en train de se maquiller; **I don't wear make-up** je ne me maquille pas.

male adjective 1 mâle (animal); **a male rat** un rat mâle; 2 (sex : on a form) masculin; 3 **a male rôle** un rôle pour homme; **a male voice** une voix d'homme; **a male student** un étudiant.

male chauvinist noun macho M.

Malta noun Malte F.

man noun homme M.

manage verb 1 diriger [52] (business, team); **she manages a travel agency** elle dirige une agence de voyages; 2 (cope) se débrouiller [1]; **I can manage** je me débrouille; 3 **to manage to do** réussir [2] à faire; **he managed to open the door** il a réussi à ouvrir la porte; **I didn't manage to get in touch with her** je n'ai pas réussi à la contacter.

management noun 1 gestion F; **a management course** un cours de gestion; 2 direction; **a meeting with management** une réunion avec la direction.

manager noun 1 (of a company or a bank) directeur M, directrice F; 2 (of a shop or restaurant) gérant M, gérante F; 3 (in sport and entertainment) manager M.

manageress noun gérante F.

mandarin (orange) noun mandarine F.

mango noun mangue F.

mania noun manie F.

maniac noun fou M, folle F; **she drives like a maniac!** elle conduit comme une folle!

mankind noun humanité F.

man-made adjective (fibre) synthétique.

manner noun 1 in a manner of speaking pour ainsi dire; 2 to have good manners être poli; it's bad manners to talk like that ce n'est pas poli de parler comme ça.

manpower noun main-d'œuvre F.

mantelpiece noun cheminée F.

manual noun manuel M.

manufacture verb fabriquer [1].

manufacturer noun fabricant M.

manure noun fumier M.

many adjective, pronoun
1 beaucoup de; does she have many friends? est-ce qu'elle a beaucoup d'amis?; we didn't see many people nous n'avons pas vu beaucoup de gens; there aren't many onions left il ne reste pas beaucoup d'oignons; not many pas beaucoup; many of them forgot beaucoup d'entre eux ont oublié; 2 very many beaucoup; there aren't very many glasses il n'y a pas beaucoup de verres; 3 so many tant; I have so many things to do! j'ai tant de choses à faire!; 4 so many autant de; I've never eaten so many strawberries je n'ai jamais mangé autant de fraises; 5 as many as autant que; you can take as many as you like tu peux en prendre autant que tu veux; 6 too many trop (de); I've got too many things to do j'ai trop de choses à faire; there were too many people il y avait trop de monde; that's far too many! c'est beaucoup trop! 7 how many?

combien?; how many are there? il y en a combien?; how many sisters have you got? tu as combien de sœurs?; how many are there left? il en reste combien?

map noun 1 carte F; a road map une carte routière; 2 (of a town) plan M.

marathon noun marathon M.

marble noun 1 marbre M; a marble fireplace une cheminée en marbre; 2 bille F; to play marbles jouer aux billes.

March noun mars M; in March en mars.

march noun (demonstration) manifestation F.
verb (demonstrators) défiler [1].

mare noun jument F.

margarine noun margarine F.

margin noun marge F.

marijuana noun marijuana F.

mark noun 1 (at school) note F; I got a good mark for my French homework j'ai eu une bonne note pour mon devoir de français; what mark did you get for French? tu as eu combien en français?; 2 (stain) tache F.
verb corriger [52]; the teacher marks our homework le professeur corrige nos devoirs.

market noun marché M.

marketing noun marketing M.

marmalade noun confiture F d'oranges amères.

maroon adjective bordeaux; a maroon jumper un pull bordeaux.

marriage noun mariage M.

married adjective a married couple un couple marié; they've been married for twenty years ils sont mariés depuis vingt ans.

marry verb 1 to marry somebody épouser [1] quelqu'un; she married a Frenchman elle a épousé un Français; 2 to get married se marier [1]; they got married in July ils se sont mariés en juillet.

marvellous adjective merveilleux (F merveilleuse); the weather's marvellous il fait un temps merveilleux.

marzipan noun pâte F d'amandes.

mascara noun mascara M.

masculine noun (in French and other grammars) masculin M; in the masculine au masculin.

mash verb écraser [1] (vegetables).

mashed potatoes plural noun purée F de pommes de terre.

mask noun masque M.

mass noun 1 a mass of une masse de; 2 masses of beaucoup de; they've got masses of money ils ont beaucoup d'argent; there's masses left over il en reste beaucoup; 3 (religious) messe F; to go to mass aller à la messe.

massage noun massage M.

massive adjective énorme.

master verb maîtriser [1].

masterpiece noun chef-d'œuvre M (plural chefs-d'œuvre).

mat noun 1 (doormat) paillasson M; 2 (to put under a hot dish) dessous-de-plat M; 3 a table mat un set de table.

match noun 1 allumette F; a box of matches une boîte d'allumettes; 2 (sports) match M (plural matchs); a football match un match de foot; to watch the match regarder le match; to win the match gagner le match; to lose the match perdre le match.
verb être [6] assorti à; the jacket matches the skirt la veste est assortie à la jupe.

matching adjective matching curtains and cushions des rideaux et des coussins assortis.

mate noun copain M, copine F (informal); I'm going out with my mates tonight je sors avec mes copains ce soir.

material noun 1 (fabric) tissu M; 2 (information) documentation F; 3 (substance) matière F; raw materials les matières premières plural.

mathematics noun mathématiques F plural.

maths noun maths F plural; I like maths j'aime bien les maths; Anna's good at maths Anna est forte en maths.

matter noun what's the matter? qu'est-ce qu'il y a?
verb 1 the things that matter les choses importantes; it matters a lot to me c'est très important pour

moi; **2 it doesn't matter** ça ne fait rien; **it doesn't matter if it rains** ça ne fait rien s'il pleut; **3 it doesn't matter** (whether one thing or another) you can write it in French or English, it doesn't matter tu peux l'écrire en français ou en anglais, ça n'a pas d'importance.

mattress noun matelas M.

mature adjective mûr.

maximum noun maximum M; **the maximum possible** le maximum possible.
adjective maximum (does not change in the feminine or plural); **the maximum temperature** la température maximum; **maximum profits** les bénéfices maximum.

May noun mai M; **in May** en mai.

May Day noun le Premier Mai.

may verb **1 she may be ill** elle est peut-être malade; **we may go to Spain** nous irons peut-être en Espagne; **2** (asking permission) **may I close the door?** est-ce que je peux fermer la porte?

maybe adverb peut-être; **maybe not** peut-être pas; **maybe he's forgotten** il a peut-être oublié; **maybe they've got lost** ils se sont peut-être perdus.

mayonnaise noun mayonnaise F.

mayor noun maire M.

me pronoun **1** me, m' (before a vowel or silent 'h'); **she knows me** elle me connaît; **can you help me, please?** est-ce que tu peux m'aider, s'il te plaît?; **can you lend me a pen?** peux-tu me prêter un stylo?; **can you give me your address?** peux-tu me donner ton adresse?; **2** (after a preposition) moi; **I took her with me** je l'ai emmenée avec moi; **they left without me** ils sont partis sans moi; **3** (in commands) moi; **listen to me!** écoute-moi!; **wait for me!** attends-moi!; **excuse me!** excusez-moi!; **4** (in comparisons) **than me** que moi; **she's older than me** elle est plus âgée que moi; **5 me too!** moi aussi!

meal noun repas M.

mean verb **1** vouloir [14] dire; **what do you mean?** qu'est-ce que tu veux dire?; **what does that mean?** qu'est-ce que ça veut dire?; **that's not what I meant** ce n'est pas ce que je voulais dire; **2 to mean to do** avoir [5] l'intention de faire; **I meant to phone my mother** j'avais l'intention d'appeler ma mère; **3 to be meant to do** être [6] censé faire; **she was meant to be here at six** elle était censée être là à six heures.
adjective **1** (with money) radin (informal); **2** (unkind) méchant; **she's really mean to her brother** elle est vraiment méchante avec son frère; **what a mean thing to do!** c'est vraiment méchant!

meaning noun sens M.

means noun moyen M; **a means of transport** un moyen de transport; **a means of doing** un moyen de faire; **we have no means of contacting him** nous n'avons aucun moyen de le contacter; **by means of** au moyen de; **by all means** certainement.

meantime adverb **for the**

meantime pour le moment; **in the meantime** pendant ce temps.

measles noun rougeole F.

measure verb mesurer [1].

measurements plural noun 1 (of a room or an object) dimensions F plural; **the measurements of the room** les dimensions de la pièce; 2 (of a person) mensurations F plural; **my chest measurement** mon tour de poitrine; **my waist measurement** mon tour de taille.

meat noun viande F.

mecca noun Mecque F.

mechanic noun mécanicien M; **he's a mechanic** il est mécanicien.

mechanical adjective mécanique.

medal noun médaille F; **the gold medal** la médaille d'or.

media noun **the media** les médias M plural.

medical noun visite F médicale; **to have a medical** passer une visite médicale.
adjective médical (M plural médicaux).

medicine noun 1 médicament M; **I'd like some cough medicine** je voudrais un médicament pour la toux; 2 (subject of study) médecine; **she's studying medicine** elle fait des études de médecine; 3 **alternative medicine** la médecine douce.

Mediterranean noun **the Mediterranean** la Méditerranée.

medium adjective moyen (F moyenne).

medium-sized noun de taille moyenne.

meet verb 1 (by chance) rencontrer [1]; **I met Rosie outside the baker's** j'ai rencontré Rosie devant la boulangerie; 2 (by appointment) retrouver [1]; **I'll meet you outside the cinema at six** je te retrouverai devant le cinéma à six heures; 3 se retrouver [1]; **we're meeting at six** nous allons nous retrouver à six heures; 4 (get to know) faire [10] la connaissance de; **I met a French girl last week** j'ai fait la connaissance d'une Française la semaine dernière; 5 **Tom, have you met Oskar?** Tom, est-ce que tu connais Oskar?; 6 (off a train, bus, etc) venir [81] chercher; **my dad's meeting me at the station** mon père vient me chercher à la gare.

meeting noun réunion F; **there's a meeting at ten o'clock** il y a une réunion à dix heures; **she's in a meeting** elle est en réunion.

megabyte noun mégaoctet M.

melody noun mélodie F.

melon noun melon M.

melt verb 1 fondre [3]; **it melts in your mouth** ça fond dans la bouche; 2 **to melt something** faire [10] fondre quelque chose; **melt the butter in a saucepan** faites fondre le beurre dans une casserole.

member noun membre M; **she's a member of the Labour Party** elle est membre du parti travailliste.

Member of Parliament noun député M.

membership noun adhésion F.

membership card noun carte F de membre.

membership fee noun cotisation F.

memorial noun a war memorial un monument aux morts.

memorial service noun messe F commémorative.

memorize verb to memorize something apprendre [64] quelque chose par cœur.

memory noun 1 (of a person or computer) mémoire F; you have a good memory! tu as bonne mémoire!; I have a bad memory je n'ai pas de mémoire; 2 (of the past) souvenirs m; I have good memories of my stay in France j'ai de bons souvenirs de mon séjour en France.

mend verb réparer [1].

meningitis noun méningite F.

mental adjective mental (M plural mentaux); a mental illness une maladie mentale; a mental hospital un hôpital psychiatrique.

mention verb mentionner [1].

menu noun menu M; on the menu au menu.

mercy noun pitié F.

meringue noun meringue F.

merit noun mérite M.

mermaid noun sirène F.

merry adjective 1 joyeux (F joyeuse); Merry Christmas Joyeux Noël; 2 (from drinking) éméché (informal).

merry-go-round noun manège M.

mess noun désordre M; my papers are in a mess mes papiers sont dans le désordre; to make a mess mettre du désordre; to clear up the mess mettre de l'ordre; what a mess! quelle pagaille! (informal).
● to mess about faire [10] l'imbécile; stop messing about! arrête de faire l'imbécile!
● to mess about with something jouer [1] avec quelque chose; it's dangerous to mess about with matches il est dangereux de jouer avec les allumettes.
● to mess something up mettre [11] la pagaille dans quelque chose (informal); you've messed up all my papers tu as mis la pagaille dans toutes mes papiers.

message noun message M; a telephone message un message téléphonique.

messenger noun messager M.

messy adjective 1 it's a messy job c'est un travail salissant; 2 he's a messy eater il mange n'importe comment; her writing's really messy elle écrit n'importe comment.

metal noun métal M (plural métaux).

meter noun 1 (electricity, gas, taxi) compteur M; to read the meter relever le compteur; 2 a parking meter un parcmètre.

method noun méthode F.

Methodist noun méthodiste M &

F; **I'm a Methodist** je suis méthodiste.

metre *noun* mètre M.

metric *adjective* métrique.

Mexico *noun* Mexique M; **in Mexico** au Mexique; **to Mexico** au Mexique.

microchip *noun* puce F.

microphone *noun* microphone M.

microscope *noun* microscope M.

microwave oven *noun* four M à micro-ondes.

midday *noun* midi M; **at midday** à midi.

middle *noun* 1 milieu M; **in the middle of the room** au milieu de la pièce; **in the middle of the night** au milieu de la nuit; 2 **to be in the middle of doing** être en train de faire; **when she phoned I was in the middle of washing my hair** quand elle a appelé j'étais en train de me laver les cheveux.

middle-aged *adjective* d'un certain âge; **a middle-aged lady** une dame d'un certain âge.

middle-class *adjective* de la classe moyenne; **a middle-class family** une famille de la classe moyenne.

Middle-East *noun* Moyen-Orient M; **in the Middle East** au Moyen-Orient.

midge *noun* moucheron M.

midnight *noun* minuit M; **at midnight** à minuit.

Midsummer's Day *noun* la Saint Jean.

might *verb* **'are you going to phone him?' – 'I might'** 'est-ce que tu vas l'appeler?' – 'peut-être'; **I might invite Jo** j'inviterai peut-être Jo; **Amanda might know** Amanda le saurait peut-être; **he might have forgotten** il a peut-être oublié.

migraine *noun* migraine F.

mike *noun* micro M (*informal*).

mild *adjective* doux (F douce); **it's quite mild today** il fait plutôt doux aujourd'hui.

mile *noun* 1 mille M (*the French use kilometres for distances; to convert miles roughly to kilometres, multiply by 8 and divide by 5*); **the village is ten miles from Oxford** le village est à seize kilomètres d'Oxford; 2 **it's miles better!** c'est dix fois meilleur!

military *adjective* militaire.

milk *noun* lait M; **full-cream milk** le lait entier; **skimmed milk** le lait écrémé; **semi-skimmed milk** le lait demi-écrémé.
verb traire [78].

milk chocolate *noun* chocolat M au lait.

milk jug *noun* pot M à lait.

milkman *noun* laitier M.

milk shake *noun* milk-shake M.

millimetre *noun* millimètre M.

million *noun* million M; **a million people** un million de personnes; **two million people** deux millions de personnes.

millionaire noun millionnaire M.

mimic verb imiter [1].

mince noun viande hachée F.

mind noun 1 esprit M; **it crossed my mind that...** il m'est venu à l'esprit que...; 2 **to change your mind...** changer d'avis; **I've changed my mind** j'ai changé d'avis; 3 **to make up your mind** se décider; **I can't make up my mind** je n'arrive pas à me décider.
verb 1 surveiller [1]; **can you mind my bag for me?** est-ce que tu peux surveiller mon sac?; 2 s'occuper [1] de (baby); **could you mind the baby for ten minutes?** est-ce que tu peux t'occuper du bébé pendant dix minutes?; 3 **do you mind if...?** est-ce que cela vous dérange si...?; **do you mind if I close the door?** est-ce que cela vous dérange si je ferme la porte?; **I don't mind** cela ne me dérange pas; **I don't mind the heat** la chaleur ne me dérange pas; 4 **mind the step!** attention à la marche!; 5 **never mind!** tant pis!

mine[1] noun mine F; **a coal mine** une mine de charbon.

mine[2] pronoun 1 (for a masculine noun) le mien; **she took her hat and I took mine** elle a pris son chapeau et j'ai pris le mien; 2 (for a feminine noun) la mienne; **she gave me her address and I gave her mine** elle m'a donné son adresse et je lui ai donné la mienne; 3 (for a masculine plural noun) les miens; **Karen's invited her parents and I've invited mine** Karen a invité ses parents et j'ai invité les miens; 4 (for a feminine plural noun) les miennes;

she showed me her photos and I showed her mine elle m'a montré ses photos et je lui ai montré les miennes; 5 à moi; **the green one's mine** le vert est à moi; **it's mine** c'est à moi.

miner noun mineur M.

mineral water noun eau minérale F.

miniature noun, adjective miniature F.

minibus noun minibus M.

minimum noun minimum M; **a minimum of** un minimum de. adjective minimum (does not change in the feminine or plural); **the minimum age** l'âge minimum; **minimum safety measures** des mesures de sécurité minimum; **the minimum amount** le minimum.

miniskirt noun mini-jupe F.

minister noun 1 (in government) ministre M; 2 (of a church) pasteur M.

ministry noun ministère M.

minor adjective mineur.

minority noun minorité F.

mint noun 1 (herb) menthe F; 2 (sweet) bonbon M à la menthe.

minus preposition moins; **seven minus three is four** sept moins trois égale quatre; **it was minus ten this morning** il a fait moins dix ce matin.

minute[1] noun minute F; **just a minute!** une minute!; **I'll be ready in two minutes** je serai prêt dans deux minutes; **it's five minutes' walk from**

here c'est à cinq minutes à pied d'ici.

minute² *adjective* minuscule; **the bedrooms are minute** les chambres sont minuscules.

miracle *noun* miracle M.

mirror *noun* 1 glace F; **I looked at myself in the mirror** je me suis regardé dans la glace; 2 (*rearview mirror in a car*) rétroviseur M.

misbehave *verb* se conduire [26] mal.

mischief *noun* **to get up to mischief** faire des bêtises.

mischievous *adjective* coquin.

miser *noun* avare M & F.

miserable *adjective* 1 malheureux (F malheureuse); **he was miserable without her** il était malheureux sans elle; **I feel really miserable today** je n'ai vraiment pas le moral aujourd'hui; 2 **it's miserable weather** il fait un sale temps; 3 **she gets paid a miserable wage** elle gagne un salaire de misère.

misfire *verb* tomber [1] à plat; **our plans misfired** nos projets sont tombés à plat.

misfortune *noun* malheur M.

misjudge *verb* 1 mal évaluer [1]; **she misjudged the distance** elle a mal évalué la distance; 2 mal juger [52] (*a person*); **everybody had misjudged her** tout le monde l'avait mal jugée.

mislay *verb* égarer [1]; **I've mislaid my keys** j'ai égaré mes clés.

misleading *adjective* trompeur (F

trompeuse); **it's a misleading advertisement** c'est une publicité trompeuse.

miss *verb* 1 rater [1]; **she missed her train** elle a raté son train; **I missed the film** j'ai raté le film; **the ball missed the goal** le ballon a raté le but; **missed!** raté! [1]; 2 manquer [1]; **he's missed several classes** il a manqué plusieurs cours; **to miss an opportunity** manquer une occasion; 3 **I miss you** tu me manques; **she's missing her sister** sa sœur lui manque; **I miss France** la France me manque.

Miss *noun* Mademoiselle; **Miss Jones** Mademoiselle Jones; (*written as*) Mlle Jones.

missing *adjective* 1 manquant; **she's found the missing pieces** elle a trouvé les pièces manquantes; **the missing link** le chaînon manquant; 2 **there's a plate missing** il manque une assiette; **there are three forks missing** il manque trois fourchettes; 3 **to go missing** disparaître; **several things have gone missing lately** plusieurs choses ont disparu récemment; **three people are missing** trois personnes ont disparu.

missionary *noun* missionnaire M & F.

mist *noun* brume F.

mistake *noun* 1 erreur F; **by mistake** par erreur; **it was my mistake** c'était une erreur de ma part; 2 faute F; **a spelling mistake** une faute d'orthographe; **you've made lots of mistakes** tu as fait beaucoup de fautes; 3 **to make**

a mistake (*be mistaken*) se
tromper; **sorry, I made a mistake** je
suis désolé, je me suis trompé.
verb **I mistook you for your brother**
je vous ai pris pour votre frère.

mistaken *adjective* **to be mistaken**
se tromper; **you're mistaken** tu te
trompes.

mistletoe *noun* gui M.

misty *adjective* brumeux (F
brumeuse); **a misty morning** un
matin brumeux; **it's misty this
morning** il y a de la brume ce matin.

misunderstand *verb* mal
comprendre [64]; **I misunderstood**
j'ai mal compris.

misunderstanding *noun*
malentendu M; **there's been a
misunderstanding** il y a eu un
malentendu.

mix *noun* 1 mélange M; **a good mix
of people** un bon mélange de gens;
2 **a cake mix** une préparation pour
gâteau.
verb 1 mélanger [52]; **mix all the
ingredients together** mélangez tous
les ingrédients; 2 **to mix with**
fréquenter [1]; **she mixes with lots of
interesting people** elle fréquente
beaucoup de gens intéressants.
●**to mix up 1** mélanger [52]; **you've
mixed up all my papers** tu as
mélangé tous mes papiers; **you've
got it all mixed up!** tu mélanges
tout! (*story*) 2 (*confuse*) confondre
[69]; **I get him mixed up with his
brother** je le confonds avec son
frère.

mixed *adjective* varié; **a mixed
programme** un programme varié.

mixed salad *noun* salade
composée F.

mixed school *noun* école mixte F.

mixture *noun* mélange M; **it's a
mixture of jazz and rock** c'est un
mélange de jazz et de rock.

moan *verb* râler [1] (*informal*); **stop
moaning!** arrête de râler!

mobile home *noun* mobile home
M.

mobile phone *noun* téléphone
portatif M.

mock *noun* (*mock exam*) examen
blanc M.
verb se moquer [1] de; **stop mocking
me!** arrête de te moquer de moi!

model *noun* 1 (*type*) modèle M;
the latest model le dernier
modèle; 2 (*fashion model*)
mannequin M; **she's a model** elle
est mannequin de luxe; 3 (*of a
plane, car, etc*) modèle réduit M; **he
makes models** il fait des modèles
réduits; 4 (*of a building*) maquette
F; **a model of Westminster Abbey**
une maquette de l'Abbaye de
Westminster.

model aeroplane *noun* modèle
réduit d'avion M.

model railway *noun* chemin de fer
miniature M.

model village *noun* village
miniature M.

modem *noun* modem M.

moderate *adjective* modéré.

modern *adjective* moderne.

modern languages *noun* langues vivantes F *plural*.

modernize *verb* moderniser [1].

modest *adjective* modeste.

modify *verb* modifier [1].

moisture *noun* humidité F.

moisturizer *noun* **1** (*lotion*) lait hydratant M; **2** (*cream*) crème hydratante F.

mole *noun* **1** (*animal*) taupe F; **2** (*on skin*) graine F de beauté.

molecule *noun* molécule F.

molehill *noun* taupinière F.

moment *noun* **1** instant M; **he'll be here in a moment** il sera là dans un instant; **at any moment** à tout instant; **2 at the moment** en ce moment; **at the right moment** au bon moment.

Monaco *noun* Monaco.

monarchy *noun* monarchie F.

monastery *noun* monastère M.

Monday *noun* lundi M; **on Monday** lundi; **I'm going out on Monday** je sors lundi; **see you on Monday!** à lundi!; **on Mondays** le lundi; **the museum is closed on Mondays** le musée est fermé le lundi; **every Monday** tous les lundis; **last Monday** lundi dernier; **next Monday** lundi prochain.

money *noun* argent M; **I don't have enough money** je n'ai pas assez d'argent; **to make money** gagner de l'argent; **they gave me my money back** (*in a shop*) ils m'ont remboursé.

money box *noun* tirelire F.

mongrel *noun* chien bâtard M.

monitor *noun* (*on computer*) moniteur M.

monk *noun* moine M.

monkey *noun* **1** singe M; **2 you little monkey!** petit galopin! (*informal*).

monotonous *adjective* monotone.

monster *noun* monstre M.

month *noun* mois M; **in the month of May** au mois de mai; **this month** ce mois-ci; **next month** le mois prochain; **we're leaving next month** nous allons partir le mois prochain; **last month** le mois dernier; **every month** tous les mois; **in two months' time** dans deux mois; **at the end of the month** à la fin du mois.

monthly *adjective* mensuel (F mensuelle); **a monthly payment** une mensualité.

monument *noun* monument M.

mood *noun* humeur F; **to be in a good mood** être de bonne humeur; **to be in a bad mood** être de mauvaise humeur; **I'm not in the mood** ça ne me dit rien.

moody *adjective* lunatique.

moon *noun* lune F; **by the light of the moon** au clair de lune; ★ **to be over the moon** être aux anges (*literally: to be at the level of the angels*).

moonlight *noun* clair M de lune; **by moonlight** au clair de lune.

moor noun lande F; **the Yorkshire moors** les landes du Yorkshire.
verb amarrer [1] (*a boat*).

moped noun mobylette™ F.

moral noun morale F; **the moral of the story** la morale de l'histoire.
adjective moral (M *plural* moraux).

morals *plural noun* moralité F.

morale noun moral M; **to boost somebody's morale** remonter le moral à quelqu'un; **he's been trying to boost their morale** il essaie de leur remonter le moral.

more adverb 1 plus; **more interesting** plus intéressant; **more difficult** plus difficile; **more slowly** plus lentement; **more easily** plus facilement; **2 more...than** plus...que; **the book's more interesting than the film** le livre est plus intéressant que le film.
adjective 1 plus de; **they have more money than we do** ils ont plus d'argent que nous; **I'll have a little more milk** je prendrai un peu plus de lait; **2** (*of something you have already*) encore de; **would you like some more cake?** voulez-vous encore du gâteau?; **a few more glasses** encore quelques verres.
pronoun 1 plus; **he eats more than me** il mange plus que moi; **I'll have a little more** je prendrai un peu plus; **I don't want any more** je n'en veux plus; **2** (*of something you have already*) encore; **we need three more** il nous en faut encore trois; **3 more and more** de plus en plus; **books are getting more and more expensive** les livres coûtent de plus en plus cher; **it takes more and more**

morning noun 1 matin M; **this morning** ce matin; **tomorrow morning** demain matin; **yesterday morning** hier matin; **in the morning** le matin; **she doesn't work in the morning** elle ne travaille pas le matin; **on Friday mornings** le vendredi matin; **at six o'clock in the morning** à six heures du matin; **2** (*as a period of time spent doing something*) matinée F; **I spent the whole morning doing the washing-up** j'ai passé toute la matinée à faire la vaisselle.

Morocco noun Maroc M; **to Morocco** au Maroc; **in Morocco** au Maroc.

Moscow noun Moscou; **in Moscow** à Moscou.

Moslem noun musulman M, musulmane F.

mosque noun mosquée F.

mosquito noun moustique M; **a mosquito bite** une piqûre de moustique.

most adjective, adverb, pronoun 1 (*followed by a plural noun*) la plupart de; **most children like chocolate** la plupart des enfants aiment le chocolat; **most of my friends** la plupart de mes amis; **2** (*followed by a singular noun*) presque tout; **they've eaten most of the chocolate** ils ont mangé presque tout le chocolat; **3 most of**

time ça prend de plus en plus de temps; **4 more or less** plus ou moins; **it's more or less finished** c'est plus ou moins fini.

the time la plupart du temps; **4 the most** (followed by adjective) le plus, la plus, les plus; **the most interesting film** le film le plus intéressant; **the most exciting story** l'histoire la plus passionnante; **the most boring books** les livres les plus ennuyeux; **5 the most** (followed by noun) le plus de; **I've got the most time** c'est moi qui ai le plus de temps; **6 the most** (after verb) le plus; **what I hate most is the noise** ce que je déteste le plus, c'est le bruit.

moth noun **1** (butterfly) papillon M de nuit; **2** (clothes moth) mite F.

mother noun mère F; **my mother** ma mère; **Kate's mother** la mère de Kate.

mother-in-law noun belle-mère F (plural belles-mères).

Mother's Day noun la fête des Mères (in France the last Sunday in May).

motion noun mouvement M.

motivated adjective motivé.

motivation noun motivation F.

motor noun moteur M.

motorbike noun moto F.

motorcyclist noun motocycliste M & F.

motorist noun automobiliste M & F.

motor racing noun course F automobile.

motorway noun autoroute F.

mouldy adjective moisi.

mountain noun montagne F; **in the mountains** à la montagne.

mountain bike noun VTT M (short for 'vélo tout-terrain').

mountaineer noun alpiniste M & F.

mountaineering noun alpinisme M; **to go mountaineering** faire de l'alpinisme.

mountainous adjective montagneux (F montagneuse).

mouse noun souris F (both the animal and for a computer).

mousse noun mousse F; **chocolate mousse** la mousse au chocolat.

moustache noun moustache F; **a man with a moustache** un moustachu.

mouth noun bouche F.

mouthful noun bouchée F.

mouth organ noun harmonica M; **to play the mouth organ** jouer de l'harmonica.

move noun **1** (to a different house) déménagement M; **2** (in a game) your move! à toi de jouer!
verb **1** bouger [52]; **she didn't move** elle n'a pas bougé; **2 move up a bit** pousse-toi un peu; **3** enlever [50] (an object); **can you move your bag, please?** peux-tu enlever ton sac, s'il te plaît? **4** (car, traffic) avancer [61]; **the traffic was moving slowly** la circulation avançait lentement; **5 to move forward** avancer [61]; **he moved forward a step** il s'est avancé d'un pas; **6** (move house) déménager [52];

we're moving on Tuesday nous déménageons mardi; **they've moved to France** ils se sont installés en France.

movement *noun* mouvement M.

movie *noun* film M; **to go to the movies** aller au cinéma.

moving *adjective* 1 en marche; **a moving vehicle** un véhicule en marche; 2 (*emotionally*) émouvant; **it's a very moving film** c'est un film très émouvant.

mow *verb* tondre [3]; **to mow the grass** tondre la pelouse.

mower *noun* tondeuse F à gazon.

MP *noun* député M; **she is an MP** elle est député.

Mr *noun* Monsieur (*usually abbreviated to 'M.'*); **Mr Angus Brown** M. Angus Brown.

Mrs *noun* Madame (*usually abbreviated to 'Mme'*); **Mrs Mary Hendry** Mme Mary Hendry.

Ms *noun* Madame (*usually abbreviated to 'Mme'; note that there is no direct equivalent to 'Ms' in French, but 'Madame' may be used whether the woman is married or not*).

much *adjective, adverb, pronoun* 1 beaucoup; **she doesn't eat much** elle ne mange pas beaucoup; **we don't go out much** nous ne sortons pas beaucoup; **much more** beaucoup plus; **much shorter** beaucoup plus court; 2 (*followed by a noun*) beaucoup de; **we don't have much time** nous n'avons pas beaucoup de temps; **there isn't much**

butter left il ne reste pas beaucoup de beurre; 3 **very much** beaucoup; **thank you very much** merci beaucoup; **I don't watch television very much** je ne regarde pas beaucoup la télé; 4 **very much** (*followed by a noun*) beaucoup de; **there isn't very much milk** il n'y a pas beaucoup de lait; 5 **not much** pas beaucoup; **'do you have a lot of homework?' – 'no, not much'** 'est-ce que tu as beaucoup de devoirs?' – 'non, pas beaucoup'; 6 **so much** tellement; **we liked it so much!** nous l'avons tellement aimé!; **I have so much to do!** j'ai tellement de choses à faire!; 7 **so much** autant; **you shouldn't have given me so much** tu n'aurais pas dû m'en donner autant; 8 **as much as** autant que; **you can take as much as you like** tu peux en prendre autant que tu veux; 9 **too much** trop (de); **her parents give her too much money** ses parents lui donnent trop d'argent; **that's far too much!** c'est beaucoup trop!; 10 **how much?** combien (de)?; **how much is it?** ça coûte combien?; **how much do you want?** tu en veux combien?; **how much sugar do you want?** tu veux combien de sucre?

mud *noun* boue F.

muddle *noun* désordre M; **to be in a muddle** être en désordre.

muddy *adjective* 1 (*path, road*) boueux (F boueuse); 2 (*shoes, clothes*) couverts de boue; **your boots are all muddy** tes bottes sont couvertes de boue.

mug noun grande tasse F; a mug of coffee une grande tasse de café. verb to mug somebody agresser [1] quelqu'un; to be mugged se faire [10] agresser; my brother was mugged in the park mon frère s'est fait agresser au parc.

mugging noun agression F.

multiplication noun multiplication F.

multiply verb mulitplier [1]; to multiply six by four multiplier six par quatre.

mum, mummy noun 1 mère F; Tom's mum la mère de Tom; I'll ask my mum je vais demander à ma mère; 2 (within the family or as a name) maman F; mum's not back yet maman n'est pas encore rentrée.

mumps noun oreillons M plural.

murder noun meurtre M. verb assassiner [1].

murderer noun assassin M.

muscle noun muscle M.

muscular adjective musclé.

museum noun musée M; to go to the museum aller au musée.

mushroom noun champignon M; a mushroom salad une salade aux champignons.

music noun musique F; pop music la musique pop; classical music la musique classique.

musical noun comédie musicale F. adjective 1 a musical instrument un instrument de musique; 2 they're a very musical family ils sont très musiciens dans la famille.

musician noun musicien M, musicienne F.

Muslim noun musulman M, musulmane F.

mussel noun moule F.

must verb 1 falloir [43] (to express obligation 'falloir' is used as an impersonal verb); we must leave now il faut partir maintenant; (the construction 'il faut que' is followed by a verb in the subjunctive) I must tell you something il faut que je te dise quelque chose; you must be there at eight il faut que tu sois là à huit heures; you must learn the vocabulary il faut que tu apprennes le vocabulaire; 2 (expressing probability) devoir [8]; you must be tired tu dois être fatigué; it must be five o'clock il doit être cinq heures; he must have forgotten il a dû oublier.

mustard noun moutarde F.

mutter verb marmonner [1].

my adjective 1 (before a masculine noun) mon; my brother mon frère; my book mon livre; 2 (before a feminine noun) ma; my sister ma sœur; my house ma maison (but 'ma' becomes 'mon' before a feminine noun beginning with a vowel or silent 'h'); my address mon adresse; 3 (before a plural noun) mes; my children mes enfants; 4 (with parts of the body) le, la, les; I had a glass in my hand j'avais un verre à la main; I'm washing my hands je me lave les mains.

myself pronoun 1 I've hurt myself je me suis blessé; 2 I said it myself

je l'ai dit moi-même; **3 by myself**
tout seul; **I did it by myself** je l'ai fait
tout seul.

mysterious *adjective* mystérieux
(F mystérieuse).

mystery *noun* **1** mystère M;
2 (*book*) roman policier M.

myth *noun* mythe M.

mythology *noun* mythologie F.

N n

nail *noun* **1** (*on finger or toe*) ongle
M; **to bite your nails** se ronger les
ongles; **2** (*metal*) clou M.
verb clouer [1].

nailbrush *noun* brosse F à ongles.

nailfile *noun* lime F à ongles.

nail scissors *noun* ciseaux M
plural à ongles.

nail varnish *noun* vernis M à
ongles.

nail varnish remover *noun*
dissolvant M.

naked *adjective* nu.

name *noun* **1** nom M; **I've
forgotten her name** j'ai oublié son
nom; **what's your name?** comment
vous appelez-vous?; **my name is
Joy** je m'appelle Joy; **2** (*of a book or
film*) titre M.

nap *noun* petit somme M; **to have a
nap** faire un petit somme.

napkin *noun* serviette F.

nappy *noun* couche F.

narrow *adjective* étroit; **a narrow
street** une rue étroite.

nasty *adjective* **1** (*mean*) méchant;
that was a nasty thing to do c'était
méchant; **2** (*unpleasant*)
désagréable; **that's a nasty job** c'est
une tâche désagréable; **3** (*bad*)
mauvais; **a nasty smell** une
mauvaise odeur.

nation *noun* nation F.

national *adjective* national (M
plural nationaux).

national anthem *noun* hymne M
national.

nationality *noun* nationalité F.

national park *noun* parc national
M (*plural* parcs nationaux).

natural *adjective* naturel (F
naturelle).

naturally *adverb* naturellement.

nature *noun* nature F.

nature reserve *noun* réserve F
naturelle.

naughty *adjective* vilain.

navy *noun* marine F; **my uncle's in
the navy** mon oncle est dans la
marine.

navy-blue *adjective* bleu marine;
navy-blue gloves des gants bleu
marine.

near *adjective* proche; **the nearest
shop** le magasin le plus proche.
adverb, *preposition* **1** près; **they live
quite near** ils habitent tout près; **to
come nearer** s'approcher; **2 near**

(to) près de; **near the station** près de la gare.

nearby adverb tout près; **there's a park nearby** il y a un parc tout près.

nearly adverb presque; **nearly empty** presque vide; **we're nearly there** nous sommes presque arrivés.

neat adjective 1 (well-organized) bien rangé; **a neat desk** un bureau bien rangé; 2 soigné (a garden, your clothes, or the way you look).

neatly adverb avec soin.

necessarily adverb **not necessarily** pas forcément.

necessary adjective nécessaire; **if necessary** si besoin est.

neck noun 1 (of a person) cou M; 2 (of a garment) encolure F.

necklace noun collier M.

need noun **there's no need, I've done it already** inutile, c'est fait; **there's no need to wait** inutile d'attendre.
verb 1 avoir [5] besoin de; **we need bread** nous avons besoin de pain; **they need help** ils ont besoin d'aide; **everything you need** tout ce qu'il vous faut; 2 (to have to) devoir [8]; **I need to drop in at the bank** je dois passer à la banque; 3 **you needn't decide today** tu n'es pas obligé de décider aujourd'hui; **you needn't wait** tu n'es pas obligé d'attendre.

needle noun aiguille F.

negative noun (of a photo) négatif M.

neglected adjective mal entretenu.

neighbour noun voisin M, voisine F; **we're going round to the neighbours'** on va chez les voisins.

neighbourhood noun quartier M; **a nice neighbourhood** un quartier agréable.

neither conjunction 1 **neither... nor** ni...ni; **I have neither the time nor the money** je n'ai ni le temps ni l'argent; 2 **neither do I** moi non plus; **'I don't like fish'** – **'neither do I'** 'je n'aime pas le poisson' – 'moi non plus'; (translations using 'non plus' can be used for many similar replies) **'I wasn't invited'** – **'neither was I'** 'je n'ai pas été invité' – 'moi non plus'; **'I didn't like the film'** – **'neither did Kirsty'** 'je n'ai pas aimé le film' – 'Kirsty non plus'; 3 **'which do you like?'** – **'neither'** 'lequel aimes-tu?' – 'ni l'un ni l'autre'.

nephew noun neveu M (plural neveux).

nerve noun 1 (in the body) nerf M; 2 **to lose one's nerve** perdre son courage; 3 **you've got a nerve!** tu as un sacré culot! (informal); ★ **he gets on my nerves** il me tape sur les nerfs (informal).

nervous adjective nerveux (F nerveuse); **to feel nervous** (before a performance or an exam) avoir le trac (informal).

nest noun nid M.

net noun 1 (for fishing or in tennis) filet M; 2 (in football) filets M plural.

Netherlands noun Pays-Bas M plural; **in the Netherlands** aux Pays-Bas.

nettle noun ortie F.

network noun réseau M (plural réseaux).

neutral noun (in a gearbox) point mort M; **to be in neutral** être au point mort.
adjective 1 neutre.

never adverb 1 ne ... jamais; **Ben never smokes** Ben ne fume jamais; **I've never seen the film** je n'ai jamais vu le film; 2 jamais; 'have you ever been to Spain?' – 'no, never' 'est-ce que tu es déjà allé en Espagne?' – 'non, jamais'; 3 **never again** plus jamais; 4 **never mind** ça ne fait rien.

new adjective 1 (different or unknown to you) nouveau (F nouvelle); **have you seen their new house?** as-tu vu leur nouvelle maison?; **Debbie's new boyfriend** le nouveau copain de Debbie; 2 (brand new) neuf (F neuve); **it's a new car** c'est une voiture neuve.

newcomer noun nouveau venu M (plural nouveaux venus), nouvelle venue F (plural nouvelles venues).

news plural noun 1 (everyday gossip) nouvelles F plural; **a piece of good news** une bonne nouvelle; **I've got good news** j'ai de bonnes nouvelles; **any news?** y a-t-il des nouvelles?; 2 (on TV) journal M; **the midday news** le journal de midi; 3 (on the radio) the news les informations.

newsagent noun marchand M de journaux; **at the newsagent's** chez le marchand de journaux.

newspaper noun journal M (plural journaux).

newsreader noun présentateur M, présentatrice F.

New Year noun le Nouvel An; **Happy New Year!** Bonne Année!

New Year's Day noun le jour de l'An.

New Year's Eve noun la Saint-Sylvestre.

New Zealand noun Nouvelle-Zélande F.

next adjective 1 prochain; **the next train is at ten** le prochain train est à dix heures; **next week** la semaine prochaine; **next Thursday** jeudi prochain; **next year** l'année prochaine; **the next time I see you** la prochaine fois que je te verrai; 2 (following) suivant; **I saw her the next week** je l'ai vue la semaine suivante; **the next day** le lendemain; **the letter arrived the next day** la lettre est arrivée le lendemain; 3 (next-door) voisin; **in the next room** dans la pièce voisine.
adverb 1 (afterwards) ensuite; **what did he say next?** qu'est-ce qu'il a dit ensuite?; 2 (now) maintenant; **what shall we do next?** qu'est-ce qu'on fait maintenant?; 3 **next to** à côté de; **the girl next to Pat** la fille à côté de Pat; **it's next to the baker's** c'est à côté de la boulangerie.

next door adverb à côté; **they live next door** ils habitent à côté; **the girl next door** la fille d'à côté.

nice adjective 1 (pleasant) agréable; **we had a nice evening** nous avons

passé une soirée agréable;
Brighton's a nice town Brighton est
une ville agréable; **have a nice time!**
amusez-vous bien!; 2 (*attractive to
look at*) joli; **that's a nice dress** elle
est jolie, cette robe; 3 (*kind,
friendly*) sympathique (*a person*);
she's really nice elle est vraiment
sympathique; **to be nice to
somebody** être gentil avec
quelqu'un; **she's been very nice to
me** elle a été très gentille avec moi;
5 (*tasting good*) bon (F bonne); **let's
have a nice cup of tea** si on prenait
une bonne tasse de thé; 6 (*weather*)
it's a nice day il fait beau; **we had
nice weather** il a fait beau.

nick verb (*steal*) piquer [1]
(*informal*).

nickname noun surnom M.

niece noun nièce F.

night noun 1 (*before you go to bed*)
soir M; **what did you do last
night?** qu'est-ce que tu as fait hier
soir?; **see you tomorrow night!** à
demain soir!; **I saw Greg last night**
j'ai vu Greg hier soir; 2 (*after
bedtime*) nuit F; **it's cold at night** il
fait froid la nuit; **to stay the night
with somebody** coucher chez
quelqu'un.

night club noun boîte F de nuit.

nightie noun chemise F de nuit.

nightingale noun rossignol M.

nightmare noun cauchemar M; **to
have a nightmare** faire un
cauchemar.

night-time noun nuit F.

nil noun zéro M; **they won four-nil**
ils ont gagné quatre à zéro.

nine number neuf M; **Jake's nine**
Jake a neuf ans.

nineteen number dix-neuf M;
Kate's nineteen Kate a dix-neuf ans.

ninety number quatre-vingt-dix M.

ninth number neuvième; **on the
ninth floor** au neuvième étage; **the
ninth of June** le neuf juin.

no adverb non; **I said no** j'ai dit non;
no thank you non merci.
adjective 1 pas de; **we've got no
bread** nous n'avons pas de pain; **no
problem!** pas de problème!; 2 (*on
a notice*) **'no smoking'** 'défense de
fumer'; **'no parking'** 'stationnement
interdit'.

nobody pronoun personne; **'who's
there?'** – **'nobody'** 'qui est là?' –
'personne'; **there's nobody in the
kitchen** il n'y a personne dans la
cuisine; **nobody knows me**
personne ne me connaît; **nobody
answered** personne n'a répondu.

nod verb (*to say yes*) faire [10] oui de
la tête; **he nodded** il a fait oui de la
tête.

noise noun bruit M; **to make a
noise** faire du bruit.

noisy adjective bruyant.

none pronoun 1 (*not one*) aucun (F
aucune); **'how many students failed
the exam?'** – **'none'** 'combien
d'étudiants ont raté l'examen?' –
'aucun'; **none of the girls knows
him** aucune des filles ne le connaît;
2 **there's none left** il n'y en a plus;
there are none left il n'y en a plus.

nonsense noun bêtises F plural; **to talk nonsense** dire des bêtises; **nonsense! she's at least thirty!** tu dis des bêtises! elle a au moins trente ans!

non-smoker noun non-fumeur M.

non-stop adjective direct (a train or flight).
adverb sans arrêt; **she talks non-stop** elle parle sans arrêt.

noodles plural noun nouilles F plural.

noon noun midi M; **at (twelve) noon** à midi.

no-one pronoun personne; 'who's there?' – 'no-one' 'qui est là?' – 'personne'; **there's no-one in the kitchen** il n'y a personne dans la cuisine; **no-one knows me** personne ne me connaît; **no-one answered** personne n'a répondu.

nor conjunction 1 ne...nor ni...ni; **I have neither the time nor the money** je n'ai ni le temps ni l'argent; 2 **nor do I** moi non plus; **'I don't like fish'** – **'nor do I'** 'je n'aime pas le poisson' – 'moi non plus'; (translations using 'non plus' can be used for many similar replies) **'I wasn't invited'** – **'nor was I'** 'je n'ai pas été invité' – 'moi non plus'.

normal adjective 1 normal (M plural normaux); 2 (usual) habituel (F habituelle).

normally adverb normalement.

Normandy noun Normandie F; **in Normandy** en Normandie.

north noun nord M; **in the north** au nord.
adjective, adverb nord (never agrees); **the north side** le côté nord; **a north wind** un vent du nord; **north of Paris** au nord de Paris.

North America noun Amérique F du Nord.

northeast noun nord-est M.
adjective **in northeast England** au nord-est de l'Angleterre.

Northern Ireland noun Irlande F du Nord.

North Pole noun pôle Nord M.

North Sea noun **the North Sea** la mer du Nord.

northwest noun nord-ouest M.
adjective **in northwest England** au nord-ouest de l'Angleterre.

Norway noun Norvège F; **in Norway** en Norvège.

Norwegian noun 1 (person) Norvégien M, Norvégienne F; 2 (language) norvégien M.
adjective norvégien (F norvégienne).

nose noun nez M; **to blow your nose** se moucher.

nosebleed noun **to have a nosebleed** saigner du nez.

not adverb 1 pas; **not on Saturdays** pas le samedi; **not all alone!** pas tout seul!; **not bad** pas mal!; **not at all** pas du tout; **not yet** pas encore; 2 (when used with a verb) ne...pas; **it's not my car** ce n'est pas ma voiture; **I don't know** je ne sais pas; **Sam didn't phone** Sam n'a pas appelé; **we decided not to wait** nous avons décidé de ne pas attendre; **3 I hope not** j'espère que non.

note noun **1** (a short letter) mot M; **she left me a note** elle m'a laissé un mot; **2 to take notes** prendre [64] des notes; **3** (a banknote) billet M; **a ten-pound note** un billet de dix livres; **4** (in music) note F; (on the keyboard) touche F.

notebook noun carnet M.

notepad noun bloc-notes M (plural blocs-notes).

nothing pronoun **1** rien; 'what did you say?' – 'nothing' 'qu'est-ce que tu as dit?' – 'rien'; **2** (with an adjective) **nothing new** rien de nouveau; **nothing special** rien de particulier; **3** (when used with a verb) **she knows nothing** elle ne sait rien; **but there was nothing there** mais il n'y avait rien; **I saw nothing** je n'ai rien vu; **there's nothing happening** il ne se passe rien; **4 there's nothing new** il n'y a rien de nouveau.

notice noun **1** (a sign) panneau M (plural panneaux); **2** (an advertisement) annonce F; **3 don't take any notice of her!** ne fais pas attention à elle!; **4 to do something at short notice** faire quelque chose à la dernière minute.
verb remarquer [1]; **I didn't notice anything** je n'ai rien remarqué.

noticeable adjective visible.

notice board noun panneau M d'affichage.

nought noun zéro M.

noun noun nom M.

novel noun roman M.

novelist noun romancier M, romancière F.

November noun novembre M; **in November** en novembre.

now adverb **1** maintenant; **where is he now?** il est où maintenant?; **they've got six children now** ils ont six enfants maintenant; **2 he's busy just now** il est occupé en ce moment; **I saw her just now in the corridor** je viens de la voir dans le couloir; **3 do it right now!** fais-le tout de suite!; **4 now and then** de temps en temps.

nowhere adverb **1** nulle part; **nowhere in France** nulle part en France; **2 there's nowhere to park** il n'y a pas d'endroit pour se garer.

nuclear adjective nucléaire; **a nuclear power station** une centrale nucléaire.

nude noun **in the nude** nu.
adjective nu.

nuisance noun **it's a nuisance** c'est embêtant.

numb adjective **1** (with cold) engourdi; **2** (with an anaesthetic) insensible.

number noun **1** (of a house, telephone, or account) numéro M; **I live at number thirty-one** j'habite au numéro trente-et-un; **my new phone number** mon nouveau numéro de téléphone; **2** (a written figure) chiffre M; **the third number is a 7** le troisième chiffre est un 7; **3** (an amount) nombre M; **a large number of visitors** un grand nombre de visiteurs.

number plate *noun* plaque F d'immatriculation.

nun *noun* religieuse F.

nurse *noun* infirmier M, infirmière F; **Janet's a nurse** Janet est infirmière.

nursery *noun* **1** (*for children*) crèche F; **2** (*for plants*) pépinière F.

nursery school *noun* école F maternelle.

nut *noun* **1** (*walnut*) noix F; **2** (*almond*) amande F; **3** (*peanut*) cacahuète F; **4** (*for a bolt*) écrou M.

nutmeg *noun* noix F de muscade.

nylon *noun* nylon M.

O o

oak *noun* chêne M.

oar *noun* rame F.

oats *noun* avoine F; **porridge oats** les flocons d'avoine.

obedient *adjective* obéissant.

obey *verb* **1** obéir [2] à (*a person*); **to obey the rules** respecter [1] les règlements.

object *noun* objet M.
verb soulever [50] des objections; **if you don't object** si vous n'avez pas d'objection.

objection *noun* objection F.

oblong *adjective* rectangulaire.

oboe *noun* hautbois M; **to play the oboe** jouer du hautbois.

obscene *adjective* obscène.

observe *verb* observer [1].

obsessed *adjective* obsédé; **she's obsessed with her diet** elle est obsédée par son régime.

obstacle *noun* obstacle M.

obstinate *adjective* têtu.

obstruct *verb* gêner [1] (*people or the traffic*).

obtain *verb* obtenir [77].

obvious *adjective* évident.

obviously *adverb* **1** (*of course*) évidemment; **'do you want to come too?' – 'obviously, but it's a bit difficult'** 'veux-tu nous accompagner?' – 'évidemment, mais c'est un peu difficile'; **2** (*looking at something*) manifestement; **the house is obviously empty** la maison est manifestement vide.

occasion *noun* occasion F; **a special occasion** une grande occasion.

occasionally *adverb* de temps en temps.

occupation *noun* profession F.

occupied *adjective* occupé.

occur *verb* **1** **it occurs to me that my cousins live nearby** il me vient à l'esprit que mes cousins habitent tout près; **it never occurred to me** cela ne m'est pas venu à l'idée; **2** (*happen*) avoir [5] lieu; **the**

accident occurred on Monday
l'accident a eu lieu lundi.

ocean *noun* océan M.

o'clock *adverb* **at ten o'clock** à dix
heures; **it's three o'clock** il est trois
heures.

October *noun* octobre M; **in
October** en octobre.

octopus *noun* pieuvre F.

odd *adjective* **1** (*strange*) bizarre;
**that's odd, I'm sure I heard the
phone** c'est bizarre, je suis sûr
d'avoir entendu le téléphone;
2 (*number*) impair; **three is an odd
number** trois est un chiffre impair;
3 **to be the odd one out** être
l'exception.

odds and ends *plural noun*
bricoles F *plural*.

of *preposition* **1** de; **a kilo of
tomatoes** un kilo de tomates; **the
end of my work** la fin de mon
travail; **2** (*note that 'de le' becomes
'du' and 'de les' becomes 'des'*) **the
beginning of the concert** le début
du concert; **the name of the flower**
le nom de la fleur; **the parents of the
children** les parents des enfants;
3 **Ray has four horses but he's
selling three of them** Ray a trois
chevaux mais il en vend trois; **we ate
a lot of it** nous en avons mangé
beaucoup; **4** **two of us** deux d'entre
nous; **5** **the sixth of June** le six
juin; **6** *made of* en; **a bracelet
made of silver** un bracelet en
argent.

off *adverb, adjective, preposition*
1 (*switched off*) éteint; **is the telly

off?** est-ce que la télé est éteinte?; **to
turn off the lights** éteindre la
lumière; **2** (*tap, water, gas*) fermé;
to turn off the tap fermer le
robinet; **3** (*turned off at the meter*)
coupé; **the gas and electricity were
off** le gaz et l'électricité étaient
coupés; **4** **to be off** (*to leave*) s'en
aller [7]; **I'm off** je m'en vais; **5** **a day
off** un jour de congé; **Caroline took
three days off work** Caroline a pris
trois jours de congé; **to be off sick**
être malade; **Maya's off school
today** Maya n'est pas à l'école
aujourd'hui; **6** (*cancelled*) annulé;
the match is off le match est
annulé; **7** **'20% off shoes'** '20% de
remise sur les chaussures'.

offence *noun* **1** (*crime*) délit M;
2 **to take offence** s'offenser [1]; **he
takes offence easily** il s'offense
facilement.

offer *noun* **1** offre F; **a job offer**
une offre d'emploi; **2** **'on (special)
offer'** 'en promotion'.
verb **1** offrir [56] (*a present, a
reward, or a job*); **he offered her a
chair** il lui a offert une chaise; **2** **to
offer to do** proposer [1] de faire;
**Blake offered to drive me to the
station** Blake m'a proposé de me
conduire à la gare.

office *noun* bureau M
(*plural* bureaux); **he's still at the
office** il est toujours au bureau; **Sue
works in the same office** Sue
travaille dans le même bureau.

office block, office building
noun immeuble M de bureaux.

official *adjective* officiel (F

officielle); **the official version** la
version officielle.

off-licence noun magasin M de
vins et de spiritueux.

often adverb souvent; **he's often
late** il est souvent en retard; **how
often do you see Rosie?** est-ce que
tu vois Rosie souvent?; **I'd like to see
Eric more often** j'aimerais voir Eric
plus souvent.

oil noun 1 olive oil l'huile d'olive;
suntan oil l'huile solaire; 2 (crude
oil) pétrole M.

oil painting noun peinture F à
l'huile (both the activity and the
object).

oil rig noun plateforme pétrolière F.

ointment noun pommade F.

okay adjective 1 d'accord; **okay,
tomorrow at ten** d'accord, demain
à dix heures; **is it okay with you if I
don't come till Friday?** tu es
d'accord si je ne viens que
vendredi?; 2 (person) sympa
(informal); **Daisy's okay** Daisy est
sympa; 3 (nothing special) pas mal;
the film was okay le film n'était pas
mal; 4 (not ill) are you okay? ça
va?; **I've been ill but I'm okay now**
j'ai été malade, mais ça va mieux
maintenant.

old adjective 1 (not young, not new)
vieux, vieil (before a vowel or silent
'h') (F vieille); **an old man** un vieux
monsieur; **an old lady** une vieille
dame; **an old tree** un vieil arbre; **old
people** les personnes âgées; **bring
some old clothes** apporte de vieux
vêtements; 2 (previous) ancien (F
ancienne); **our old car was a Rover**

notre ancienne voiture était une
Rover; **I've only got their old
address** je n'ai que leur ancienne
adresse; 3 (talking about age) how
old are you? tu as quel âge?; **James
is ten years old** James a dix ans; a
two-year-old child un enfant de
deux ans; 4 **my older sister** ma
sœur aînée; **she's older than me**
elle est plus âgée que moi; **he's a year
older than me** il a un an de plus que
moi.

old age noun vieillesse F.

old age pensioner noun retraité
M, retraitée F.

old-fashioned noun 1 (clothes,
music, style) démodé; 2 (a person)
vieux jeu (never agrees); **my parents
are so old-fashioned** mes parents
sont si vieux jeu.

olive noun olive F.

olive oil noun huile F d'olive.

Olympic Games, Olympics
plural noun Jeux Olympiques M
plural.

omelette noun omelette F; a
cheese omelette une omelette au
fromage.

on preposition 1 sur; **on the desk**
sur le bureau; **on the road** sur la
route; **on the beach** sur la plage;
2 (in expressions of time) on March
21st le 21 mars; **he's arriving on
Tuesday** il arrive mardi; **it's shut on
Saturdays** c'est fermé le samedi; **on
rainy days** quand il pleut; 3 (for
buses, trains, etc) she arrived on the
bus elle est arrivée en bus; **I met
Jackie on the bus** j'ai vu Jackie dans
le bus; **I slept on the plane** j'ai

dormi dans l'avion; **let's go on our bikes!** allons-y à vélo!; **4 on TV** à la télé; **on the radio** à la radio; **on video** en vidéo; **5 on holiday** en vacances; **on strike** en grève.

adjective **1** (*switched on*) to be on (*TV, light, oven*) être [6] allumé; (*radio, machine*) être en marche; **all the lights were on** toutes les lumières étaient allumées; **is the radio on?** est-ce que la radio est en marche?; **I've put the oven on** j'ai allumé le four; **2** (*happening*) **what's on TV?** qu'est-ce qu'il y a à la télé?; **what's on this week at the cinema?** qu'est-ce qui passe cette semaine au cinéma?

once *adverb* **1** une fois; **I've tried once already** j'ai déjà essayé une fois; **try once more** essaie encore une fois; **once a day** une fois par jour; **more than once** plus d'une fois; **2 at once** (*immediately*) tout de suite; **the doctor came at once** le médecin est venu tout de suite; **3 at once** (*at the same time*) à la fois; **I can't do two things at once** je ne peux pas faire deux choses à la fois.

one *number* un (F une); **one son** un fils; **one apple** une pomme; **if you want a pen I've got one** si tu veux un stylo j'en ai un; **at one o'clock** à une heure.

pronoun **1** on; **one never knows** on ne sait jamais; **2 this one** celui-ci (F celle-ci); **I like that bike, but this one's cheaper** j'aime bien ce vélo-là, mais celui-ci est moins cher; **do you want the red tie or this one?** veux-tu la cravate rouge ou celle-ci?; **3 that one** celui-là (F celle-là); **'which video?' – 'that one'** quelle

vidéo?' – 'celle-là'; **4 which one?** lequel? (F laquelle?); **'my foot's hurting' – 'which one?'** 'j'ai mal au pied' – 'lequel?' **'she borrowed a skirt from me' – 'which one?'** 'elle m'a emprunté une jupe' – 'laquelle?'

one's *determiner* son, sa, ses; **one does one's best** on fait de son mieux; **to pay for one's car** payer sa voiture; **to love one's children** aimer ses enfants; **to wash one's hands** se laver les mains.

oneself *noun* **1 to wash oneself** se laver; **to hurt oneself** se blesser; **2** (*for emphasis*) soi-même; **one has to do everything oneself** il faut tout faire soi-même; **3** (*all*) **by oneself** tout seul (F toute seule).

one-way street *noun* sens unique M.

onion *noun* oignon M; **onion soup** la soupe à l'oignon.

only *adjective* **1** seul; **the only free seat** la seule place libre; **the only thing to do** la seule chose à faire; **2 an only child** un enfant unique. *adverb* **conjunction 1** (*with a verb*) ne…que; **they've only got two bedrooms** ils n'ont que deux chambres; **Anne's only free on Fridays** Anne n'est libre que le vendredi; **there are only three left** il n'en reste que trois; **2** seulement; **'how long did they stay?' – 'only two days'** 'ils sont restés combien de temps?' – 'deux jours seulement'; **3** (*but*) mais; **I'd walk, only it's raining** j'irais à pied, mais il pleut.

onto preposition sur.

open noun **in the open** en plein air.
adjective **1** (not shut) ouvert; **the door's open** la porte est ouverte; **the baker's is not open** la boulangerie n'est pas ouverte; **2 in the open air** en plein air.
verb **1** ouvrir [30]; **can you open the door for me?** est-ce que tu peux ouvrir la porte?; **Sam opened his eyes** Sam a ouvert les yeux; **the bank opens at nine** la banque ouvre à neuf heures; **2 the door opened slowly** la porte s'est ouverte lentement.

open-air adjective en plein air; **an open-air swimming pool** une piscine en plein air.

opera noun opéra M.

operation noun opération F; **to have an operation** se faire opérer; **she's had an operation** elle s'est fait opérer.

opinion noun avis M; **in my opinion** à mon avis.

opinion poll noun sondage M.

opponent noun adversaire M & F.

opportunity noun occasion F; **to have the opportunity of doing** avoir l'occasion de faire; **I took the opportunity to visit the museum** j'ai profité de l'occasion pour visiter le musée.

opposite noun contraire M; **no, quite the opposite** non, tout le contraire.
adjective **1** opposé (a direction, side, or view, for example); **she went off in the opposite direction** elle est partie dans la direction opposée;
2 (facing) d'en face; **in the house opposite** dans la maison d'en face.
adverb en face; **they live opposite** ils habitent en face.
preposition en face de; **opposite the station** en face de la gare.

optician noun opticien M, opticienne F.

optimistic adjective optimiste.

option noun choix M; **we have no option** nous n'avons pas le choix.

optional adjective facultatif (F facultative).

or conjunction **1** ou; **English or French?** anglais ou français?; **today or Tuesday?** aujourd'hui ou mardi?; **2** (in negatives) **I don't have a cat or a dog** je n'ai ni un chat ni un chien; **not in June or July** ni en juin ni en juillet; **3** (or else) sinon; **phone Mum, or she'll worry** appelle maman, sinon elle va s'inquiéter.

oral noun (an exam) oral M (plural oraux); **the French oral** l'oral de français.

orange noun (the fruit) orange F; **an orange juice** un jus d'orange.
adjective orange (never changes); **my orange socks** mes chaussettes orange.

orchestra noun orchestre M.

order noun **1** (arrangement) ordre M; **in the right order** dans le bon ordre; **in the wrong order** dans le mauvais ordre; **in alphabetical order** dans l'ordre alphabétique; **2** (in a restaurant or café) commande F; **can I take your orders?** puis-je prendre vos commandes?; **3** 'out of order' en panne'; **4** (in order to do) pour faire; **we hurried in order to be on time** nous nous sommes dépêchés pour arriver à l'heure.

verb **1** (in a restaurant or a shop) commander [1]; **we ordered steaks** nous avons commandé des steaks; **2** réserver [1] (a taxi).

ordinary *adjective* ordinaire.

organ *noun* (the instrument) orgue M; **to play the organ** jouer de l'orgue.

organic *adjective* biologique (food).

organization *noun* organisation F.

organize *verb* organiser [1].

orienteering *noun* course F d'orientation.

original *adjective* **1** original (M *plural* originaux); **the original version was better** la version originale était meilleure; **it's a really original novel** c'est un roman très original.

originally *adverb* à l'origine; **originally we wanted to take the car** à l'origine nous voulions prendre la voiture.

Orkneys *plural noun* **the Orkneys** les Orcades F *plural*.

ornament *noun* bibelot M.

orphan *noun* orphelin M, orpheline F.

ostrich *noun* autruche F.

other *adjective* **1** autre; **the other day** l'autre jour; **we took the other road** nous avons pris l'autre route;

give me the other one donne-moi l'autre; **where are the others?** où sont les autres?; **the other two cars** les deux autres voitures; **2 every other week** une semaine sur deux; **3 somebody or other** quelqu'un; **something or other** quelque chose; **somewhere or other** quelque part.

otherwise *adverb* (in other ways) à part ça; **the flat's a bit small but otherwise it's lovely** l'appartement n'est pas très grand mais à part ça il est très bien.

conjunction (or else) sinon; **I'll phone home, otherwise they'll worry** je vais appeler chez moi, sinon ils vont s'inquiéter.

ought *verb* ('ought' is translated by the conditional tense of 'devoir' [8]) **I ought to go now** je devrais partir maintenant; **they ought to know the address** ils devraient savoir l'adresse; **you oughtn't to have any problems** vous ne devriez pas avoir des problèmes.

our *adjective* **1** notre; **our house** notre maison; **2** (before a plural noun) nos; **our parents** nos parents; **3** (with parts of the body) le, la, les; **we'll go and wash our hands** on va se laver les mains.

ours *pronoun* **1** (for a masculine noun) le nôtre; **their garden's bigger than ours** leur jardin est plus grand que le nôtre; **2** (for a feminine noun) la nôtre; **their house is smaller than ours** leur maison est plus petite que la nôtre; **3** (for a plural noun) les nôtres; **they've invited their friends and we've invited ours** ils ont invité leurs amis et nous avons invité les nôtres; **4** à nous; **the green one's ours** le vert est à nous; **it's ours** c'est à nous; **a friend of ours** un ami à nous.

ourselves *pronoun* **1** nous; **we introduced ourselves** nous nous sommes présentés; **2** (*for emphasis*) nous-mêmes; **in the end we did it ourselves** finalement nous l'avons fait nous-mêmes.

out *adverb* **1** (*outside*) dehors; **it's cold out there** il fait froid dehors; **out in the rain** sous la pluie; **they're out in the garden** ils sont dans le jardin; **2 to go out** sortir [72]; **he went out of the room** il est sorti de la pièce; **Mr. Barnes is out** Monsieur Barnes est sorti; **are you going out this evening?** est-ce que tu sors ce soir?; **Alison's going out with Danny at the moment** Alison sort avec Danny en ce moment; **he's asked me out** il m'a invitée à sortir avec lui; **3** (*light, fire*) éteint; **are all the lights out?** est-ce que toutes les lumières sont éteintes?; **the fire was out** le feu était éteint; **4 to go out of the room** sortir de la pièce; **he threw it out of the window** il l'a jeté par la fenêtre; **to drink out of a glass** boire dans un verre; **she took the photo out of her bag** elle a pris la photo dans son sac.

outdoor *adjective* (*an activity or sport*) de plein air; **an outdoor restaurant** un restaurant en plein air.

outdoors *adverb* en plein air.

outing *noun* sortie F; **to go on an outing** faire une sortie.

outline *noun* (*of an object*) contour M.

out-of-date *noun* **1** (*no longer valid*) périmé; **my passport's out of date** mon passeport est périmé; **2** (*old-fashioned*) démodé; **they played out-of-date music** ils ont joué la musique démodée.

outside *noun* extérieur M; **it's blue on the outside** c'est bleu à l'extérieur.
adjective extérieur.
adverb dehors; **it's cold outside** il fait froid dehors.
preposition devant (*a building*); **I'll meet you outside the cinema** on se retrouve devant le cinéma.

outskirts *noun* périphérie F; **on the outskirts of York** à la périphérie de York.

oval *adjective* ovale.

oven *noun* four M; **I've put it in the oven** je l'ai mis au four.

over *preposition* **1** (*above*) au-dessus de; **there's a mirror over the sideboard** il y a un miroir au-dessus du buffet; **2** (*involving movement*) par-dessus; **she jumped over the fence** elle a sauté par-dessus la clôture; **he threw the ball over the wall** il a jeté la balle par-dessus le mur; **3 over here** par ici; **the drinks are over here** les boissons sont par ici; **4 over there** là-bas; **she's over there talking to Julian** elle est là-bas en train de discuter avec Julian; **5** (*more than*) plus de; **it will cost over a hundred pounds** ça coûtera plus de cent livres; **he's over sixty** il a plus de soixante ans; **6** (*during*) pendant; **over the weekend** pendant le weekend; **over Christmas** à Noël; **7** (*finished*)

terminé; when the meeting's over quand la réunion sera terminée; **it's all over now** c'est terminé maintenant; **8** over the phone par téléphone; **to ask someone over** inviter quelqu'un; **can you come over on Saturday?** peux-tu venir chez moi samedi?; **9 all over the place** partout; **all over the house** partout dans la maison.

overseas *adverb* à l'étranger; **Dave works overseas** Dave travaille à l'étranger.

oversleep *verb* se réveiller [1] trop tard.

overtake *verb* doubler [1] (*another car*).

overtime *noun* **to work overtime** faire [10] des heures supplémentaires.

overweight *adjective* (*a person*) trop gros (F trop grosse).

owe *verb* devoir [8]; **I owe Rick ten pounds** je dois dix livres à Rick.

owing *adjective* **1** (*to pay*) à payer; **there's five pounds owing** il y a cinq livres à payer; **2** owing to en raison de; **owing to the snow** en raison de la neige.

owl *noun* hibou M (*plural* hiboux).

own *adjective* **1** propre (*goes before the noun*); **my own computer** mon propre ordinateur; **I've got my own room** j'ai une chambre à moi; **2 on your own** tout seul (F toute seule); **Annie did it on her own** Annie l'a fait toute seule.
verb posséder [24].

owner *noun* propriétaire M & F.

oxygen *noun* oxygène M.

oyster *noun* huître F.

ozone layer *noun* couche F d'ozone.

P p

pace *noun* **1** (*a step*) pas M; **2** (*the speed you walk at*) allure F; **at a brisk pace** à vive allure.

Pacific *noun* **the Pacific ocean** l'océan M Pacifique.

pack *noun* **1** paquet M; **2 a pack of cards** un jeu de cartes.
verb **1** faire [10] ses bagages; **I haven't packed yet** je n'ai pas encore fait mes bagages; **2 I'll pack my case tonight** je ferai ma valise ce soir; **have you packed my red shirt?** as-tu mis ma chemise rouge dans la valise?

package *noun* paquet M.

package holiday, package tour *noun* voyage M organisé.

packed lunch *noun* panier-repas M.

packet *noun* **1** paquet M; **a packet of biscuits** un paquet de biscuits; **2** (*bag*) sachet M; **a packet of crisps** un sachet de chips.

packing *noun* **to do your packing** faire [10] ses bagages.

pad *noun* (*of paper*) bloc-notes M.

paddle *noun* (*for a canoe*) pagaie F.
verb (*at the seaside*) **to go paddling** faire [10] trempette.

padlock noun cadenas M.

page noun page F; **on page seven** à la page sept.

pain noun douleur F; **I've got a pain in my leg** j'ai mal à la jambe; **to be in pain** souffrir [73]; ★ **Eric's a real pain (in the neck)** Eric est vraiment pénible.

painful adjective douloureux (F douloureuse).

paint noun peinture F; **'wet paint'** 'peinture fraîche'.
verb peindre [60]; **to paint something pink** peindre quelque chose en rose.

paintbrush noun pinceau M (plural pinceaux).

painter noun peintre M.

painting noun 1 (picture) tableau M (plural tableaux); **a painting by Monet** un tableau de Monet.

pair noun 1 paire F; **a pair of socks** une paire de chaussettes; **a pair of scissors** une paire de ciseaux; 2 **a pair of jeans** un jean; **a pair of trousers** un pantalon; **a pair of knickers** un slip; 3 **to work in pairs** travailler en groupes de deux.

Pakistan noun Pakistan M; **in Pakistan** au Pakistan; **to Pakistan** au Pakistan.

Pakistani noun Pakistanais M, Pakistanaise F.
adjective pakistanais.

palace noun palais M.

pale adjective pâle; **pale green** vert pâle (never changes); **pale green**

curtains des rideaux vert pâle; **to turn pale** pâlir [2].

palm noun 1 (of your hand) paume F; 2 (a palm tree) palmier M.

pan noun 1 (saucepan) casserole F; **a pan of water** une casserole d'eau; 2 (frying-pan) poêle F.

pancake noun crêpe F.

panel noun 1 (on radio or TV) (for a discussion) invités M plural (i.e. guests); (for a quiz show) jury M; 2 (for a wall or a bath, for example) panneau M (plural panneaux).

panel game noun jeu M (plural jeux).

panic noun panique F.
verb s'affoler [1]; **don't panic!** pas de panique!

panther noun panthère F.

pannier noun (on a bike) sacoche F.

pantomime noun spectacle M pour enfants.

pants plural noun slip M.

paper noun 1 papier M; **a sheet of paper** une feuille de papier; 2 **a paper cup** un gobelet en carton; **a paper hanky** un mouchoir en papier; 3 (newspaper) journal M (plural journaux); **it was in the paper** c'était dans le journal.

paperback noun livre M de poche.

paperclip noun trombone M (because of its shape).

paper shop noun magasin M de journaux.

paper towel noun essuie-tout M.

parachute noun parachute M.

parachuting noun parachutisme M; **to go parachuting** faire du parachutisme.

parade noun défilé M.

paradise noun paradis M.

paraffin noun pétrole M.

paragraph noun paragraphe M; **'new paragraph'** 'à la ligne'.

parallel adjective parallèle.

paralysed adjective paralysé.

parcel noun paquet M.

pardon noun **I beg your pardon** pardon; **pardon?** pardon?

parent noun parent M; **my parents are Scottish** mes parents sont écossais; **a parents' evening** une réunion pour les parents d'élèves.

Paris noun Paris; **Marie lives in Paris** Marie habite à Paris.

Parisian noun Parisien M, Parisienne F.
adjective parisien (F parisienne).

park noun 1 parc M; **a theme park** un parc à thème; 2 **a car park** un parking.
verb 1 se garer [1]; **you can park outside the house** vous pouvez vous garer devant la maison; 2 **to park a car** garer [1] une voiture; **where did you park the car?** où as-tu garé la voiture?

parking noun stationnement M; **'no parking'** 'stationnement interdit'.

parking meter noun parcmètre M.

parking space noun place F.

parking ticket noun PV M (informal).

parliament noun parlement M.

parrot noun perroquet M.

parsley noun persil M.

part noun 1 partie F; **part of the garden** une partie du jardin; **the last part of the concert** la dernière partie du concert; **that's part of your job** ça fait partie de votre travail; 2 **to take part in something** participer à quelque chose; 3 (a role in a play) rôle M; 4 **spare parts** pièces F plural détachées.

particular adjective particulier (F particulière); **nothing in particular** rien de particulier.

particularly adverb 1 (unusually) spécialement; **not particularly interesting** pas spécialement intéressant; 2 (in particular) surtout; **particularly since it's our last day** surtout que c'est notre dernier jour.

parting noun (in your hair) raie F.

partly adverb en partie.

partner noun 1 (in a game) partenaire M; 2 (the person you live with) partenaire M & F; 3 (in business) associé M, associée F.

part-time adjective, adverb à temps partiel; **part-time work** du travail à temps partiel; **to work part-time** travailler à temps partiel.

party noun 1 fête F; **a Christmas party** une fête de Noël; **to have a**

birthday party faire une fête d'anniversaire; **2** (*more formal, in the evening*) soirée F; **we've been invited to a party at the Smiths' house** nous sommes invités à une soirée chez les Smith; **3** (*group*) groupe M; **a party of schoolchildren** un groupe d'élèves; **a rescue party** une équipe de secouristes; **4** (*in politics*) parti M; **the Labour party** le parti travailliste.

party game noun jeu M de société (*plural* jeux de société).

pass noun **1** (*to let you in*) laisser-passer M (*plural* laisser-passer); **2 a bus pass** une carte de bus; **3** (*a mountain pass*) col M; **4** (*in an exam*) **to get a pass in history** être reçu en histoire.
verb **1** (*go past*) passer [1] devant (*a place or building*); **we passed your house** nous sommes passés devant chez toi; **2** (*to overtake*) doubler [1] (*a car*); **3** (*give*) passer [1]; **could you pass me the paper please?** peux-tu me passer le journal s'il te plaît?; **4** (*time*) passer [1]; **the time passed slowly** le temps passait lentement; **5** (*in an exam*) être reçu [6]; **did you pass?** as-tu été reçu?; **to pass an exam** être reçu à un examen.

passage noun **1** (*a corridor*) couloir M; **2** (*a piece of text*) passage M.

passenger noun **1** (*in a car, plane, or ship*) passager M, passagère F; **2** (*in a train, bus, or underground*) voyageur M, voyageuse F.

passerby noun passant M, passante F.

passion noun passion F.

passionate adjective passionné.

passive noun passif M.
adjective passif (F passive).

Passover noun Pâque juive F.

passport noun passeport M; **an EU passport** un passeport de l'UE.

password noun mot M de passe.

past noun passé M; **in the past** dans le passé.
adjective **1** (*recent*) dernier (F dernière) (*goes before the noun*); **in the past few weeks** pendant les dernières semaines; **2** (*over*) fini; **winter is past** l'hiver est fini.
preposition, adverb **1 to walk or drive past something** passer devant quelque chose; **we went past the school** nous sommes passés devant l'école; **Ray went past in his new car** Ray est passé dans sa nouvelle voiture; **2** (*the other side of*) après; **it's just past the post office** c'est juste après la poste; **3** (*talking about time*) **ten past six** six heures dix; **half past four** quatre heures et demie; **a quarter past two** deux heures et quart.

pasta noun pâtes F plural; **I don't like pasta** je n'aime pas les pâtes.

pasteurized adjective pasteurisé.

pastry noun pâte F.

patch noun **1** (*fabric, for mending*) pièce F; **2** (*of snow or ice*) plaque F; **3** (*of blue sky*) coin M.

path noun chemin M; (*very narrow*) sentier M.

pathetic adjective (useless, hopeless) lamentable.

patience noun 1 patience F; 2 (card game) réussite F.

patient noun patient M, patiente F. adjective patient.

patiently adverb avec patience.

patio noun terrasse F.

patrol car noun voiture F de police.

pattern noun 1 (on wallpaper or fabric) motif M; 2 (dressmaking) patron M; 3 (knittting) modèle M.

pause noun pause F.

pavement noun trottoir M; on the pavement sur le trottoir.

paw noun patte F.

pawn noun pion M.

pay noun salaire M.
verb 1 payer [59]; I'm paying c'est moi qui paie; to pay cash payer comptant; 2 to pay for something payer [59] quelque chose; Tony paid for the drinks Tony a payé les boissons; it's all paid for c'est tout payé; 3 to pay by credit card régler [24] par carte de crédit; to pay by cheque régler par chèque; 4 to pay somebody back (money) rembourser [1] quelqu'un; 5 to pay attention faire [10] attention; 6 to pay a visit to somebody rendre [3] visite à quelqu'un.

paydesk noun caisse F.

payment noun paiement M; (of a bill) règlement M.

pay phone noun téléphone public M.

PC noun (computer) PC M.

pea noun petit pois M.

peace noun paix F.

peaceful adjective paisible (day, scene).

peach noun pêche F.

peacock noun paon M.

peak noun (of a mountain) pic M.

peak period (for holidays) période F de pointe.

peak rate noun (for phoning) tarif rouge M.

peak time noun (for traffic) heures F plural de pointe.

peanut noun cacahuète F.

peanut butter noun beurre M de cacahuètes.

pear noun poire F.

pearl noun perle F.

pebble noun 1 (on the road) caillou M (plural cailloux); 2 (on a beach) galet M.

peculiar adjective bizarre.

pedal noun pédale F.
verb pédaler [1].

pedal boat noun pédalo™ M.

pedestrian noun piéton M.

pedestrian crossing noun passage M pour piétons.

pedestrian precinct noun zone F piétonne.

pee noun to have a pee faire [10] pipi (informal).

peel noun 1 (of an apple) peau F; 2 (of an orange) écorce F. verb éplucher [1] (fruit, vegetables).

peer verb to peer at something regarder [1] quelque chose attentivement.

peg noun 1 (hook) patère F; 2 a clothes peg une pince à linge; 3 a tent peg un piquet.

pen noun stylo M; a felt pen un stylo-feutre.

penalty noun 1 (a fine) amende F; 2 (in football) penalty M; 3 (in rugby) pénalité F.

pence plural noun pence M plural.

pencil noun crayon M; to write in pencil écrire au crayon.

pencil case noun trousse F.

pencil sharpener noun taille-crayon M.

pendant noun pendentif M.

penfriend noun correspondant M, correspondante F; my French pen-friend is called Christelle ma correspondante française s'appelle Christelle.

penguin noun pingouin M.

penis noun pénis M.

penknife noun canif M.

penny noun penny M.

pension noun retraite F.

pensioner noun retraité M, retraitée F.

people plural noun 1 gens M plural: **people round here** les gens d'ici; **nice people** des gens sympathiques; 2 (when you're counting them) personnes F plural; **ten people** dix personnes; **several people** plusieurs personnes; **how many people have you asked?** tu as invité combien de personnes?; 3 **people say he's very rich** on dit qu'il est très riche.

pepper noun 1 (spice) poivre M; 2 (vegetable) poivron M; **a green pepper** un poivron vert.

peppermill noun moulin M à poivre.

peppermint noun menthe F; **peppermint tea** le thé à la menthe.

per preposition par; **ten pounds per person** dix livres par personne.

per cent adverb pour cent; **sixty per cent of students** soixante pour cent des étudiants.

percentage noun pourcentage M.

percussion noun percussion F; **to play percussion** jouer des percussions.

perfect adjective 1 parfait; **she speaks perfect English** elle parle un anglais parfait; 2 (ideal) idéal (M plural idéaux); **the perfect place for a picnic** l'endroit idéal pour un pique-nique.

perfectly adverb parfaitement.

perform verb 1 jouer [1] (a piece of music or a play); 2 chanter [1] (a song).

performance noun 1 (playing or acting) interprétation F; **a wonderful performance of**

Macbeth une superbe interprétation de Macbeth; **2** (*show*) spectacle M; **the performance starts at eight** le spectacle commence à huit heures; **3** (*the results of a team or company*) performance F.

performer *noun* artiste M & F.

perfume *noun* parfum M.

perhaps *adverb* peut-être; **perhaps it's in the drawer?** c'est peut-être dans le tiroir?; **perhaps he's missed the train** il a peut-être raté le train.

period *noun* **1** période F; **a two-year period** une période de deux ans; **2** (*in school*) cours M; **a forty-five-minute period** un cours de quarante-cinq minutes; **3** (*menstruation*) règles F *plural*; **during your period** pendant vos règles.

perm *noun* permanente F.

permanent *adjective* permanent.

permanently *adverb* en permanence.

permission *noun* permission F; **to get permission to do** obtenir la permission de faire.

permit *noun* permis M. *verb* permettre [11]; **to permit somebody to do** permettre à quelqu'un de faire; **smoking is not permitted** il est interdit de fumer; **weather permitting** si le temps le permet.

person *noun* personne F; **there's room for one more person** il y a de la place pour une autre personne; **in person** en personne.

personal *adjective* personnel (F personnelle).

personality *noun* personnalité F.

personally *adverb* personnellement; **personally, I'm against it** personnellement, je suis contre.

perspiration *noun* transpiration F.

persuade *verb* persuader [1]; **to persuade somebody to do** persuader quelqu'un de faire; **we persuaded Tim to wait a bit** nous avons persuadé Tim d'attendre un peu.

pessimistic *adjective* pessimiste.

pest *noun* **1** (*greenfly for example*) insecte M nuisible; **2** (*annoying person*) casse-pieds M & F.

pet *noun* **1** animal M de compagnie (*plural* animaux de compagnie); **do you have a pet?** avez-vous un animal de compagnie?; **a pet dog** un chien; **2** (*favourite person*) chouchou M, chouchoute F; **Julie is teacher's pet** Julie est la chouchoute du prof.

petal *noun* pétale M.

pet name *noun* petit nom M.

petrol *noun* essence F; **to fill up with petrol** faire le plein d'essence; **to run out of petrol** tomber en panne d'essence.

petrol station *noun* station F d'essence.

pharmacy *noun* pharmacie F.

pheasant *noun* faisan M.

philosophy noun philosophie F.

phone noun téléphone M; **she's on the phone** elle est au téléphone; **I was on the phone to Sophie** j'étais au téléphone avec Sophie; **you can book by phone** on peut réserver par téléphone.
verb 1 téléphoner [1]; **while I was phoning** pendant que je téléphonais; 2 to **phone somebody** appeler [18] quelqu'un; **I'll phone you tonight** je t'appellerai ce soir.

phone book noun annuaire M.

phone box noun cabine F téléphonique.

phone call noun appel M; **phone calls are free** les appels sont gratuits; **to make a phone call** téléphoner.

phone card noun télécarte F.

phone number noun numéro M de téléphone.

photo noun photo F; **to take a photo** prendre une photo; **to take a photo of somebody** prendre quelqu'un en photo; **I took a photo of their house** j'ai pris leur maison en photo.

photocopier noun photocopieuse F.

photocopy noun photocopie F.
verb photocopier [1].

photograph noun photo F; **to take a photograph** prendre une photo; **to take a photograph of somebody** prendre quelqu'un en photo.
verb photographier [1].

photographer noun photographe M & F.

photography noun photographie F.

phrase noun expression F.

phrase-book noun manuel M de conversation.

physical adjective physique.

physicist noun physicien M, physicienne F.

physics noun physique F.

physiotherapist noun kinésithérapeute M & F.

physiotherapy noun kinésithérapie F.

pianist noun pianiste M & F.

piano noun piano M; **to play the piano** jouer du piano; **Steve played it on the piano** Steve l'a joué au piano; **a piano lesson** une leçon de piano.

pick noun **take your pick!** choisis!
verb 1 (to choose) choisir [2]; **pick a card** choisis une carte; 2 (for a team) sélectionner [1]; **I've been picked for Saturday** j'ai été sélectionné pour samedi; 3 cueillir [35] (fruit or flowers).
● **to pick up** 1 (lift) prendre [64]; **he picked up the papers and went out** il a pris les papiers et il est sorti; 2 (collect together) ramasser [1]; **I'll pick up the toys** je ramasserai les jouets; 3 (to collect) venir [81] chercher; **I'll pick you up at six** je viendrai te chercher à six heures; **I'll pick up the keys tomorrow** je viendrai chercher les clés demain;

4 (*learn*) apprendre [64]; **you'll soon pick it up** tu vas vite l'apprendre.

picnic *noun* pique-nique M; **to have a picnic** pique-niquer.

pickpocket *noun* pickpocket M.

picture *noun* 1 (*a painting*) tableau M (*plural* tableaux); **a picture by Renoir** une tableau de Renoir; **he painted a picture of a horse** il a peint un cheval; 2 (*a drawing*) dessin M; **draw me a picture of your little sister** dessine-moi ta petite sœur; 3 (*in a book*) illustration F; **a book with lots of pictures** un livre avec beaucoup d'illustrations; 4 (*the cinema*) **the pictures** le cinéma; **to go to the pictures** aller au cinéma.

pie *noun* 1 (*sweet*) tarte F; **an apple pie** une tarte aux pommes; 2 (*savoury*) tourte F; **a meat pie** une tourte à la viande.

piece *noun* 1 (*a bit*) morceau M (*plural* morceaux); **a big piece of cheese** un gros morceau de fromage; 2 (*that you fit together*) pièce F; **the pieces of a jigsaw** les pièces d'un puzzle; **to take something to pieces** démonter [1] quelque chose; 3 **a piece of furniture** un meuble; **four pieces of luggage** quatre valises; **a piece of information** un renseignement; **that's a piece of luck!** c'est un coup de chance!; 4 (*coin*) pièce F; **a five-franc piece** une pièce de cinq francs.

pier *noun* jetée F.

pierced *adjective* percé; **to have**

pierced ears avoir les oreilles percées.

pig *noun* cochon M.

pigeon *noun* pigeon M.

piggy bank *noun* tirelire F.

pigtail *noun* natte F.

pile *noun* 1 (*a neat stack*) pile F; **a pile of plates** une pile d'assiettes; 2 (*a heap*) tas M; **a pile of dirty shirts** un tas de chemises sales.
● **to pile something up** (*neatly*) empiler [1] quelque chose; (*in a heap*) entasser [1] quelque chose.

pill *noun* comprimé M; **the pill** (*contraceptive*) la pilule.

pillar *noun* pilier M.

pillar box *noun* boîte F aux lettres.

pillow *noun* oreiller M.

pilot *noun* pilote M.

pimple *noun* bouton M.

pin *noun* 1 (*for sewing*) épingle F; 2 **a three-pin plug** une prise à trois fiches.
● **to pin up** 1 épingler [1] (*a hem*); 2 accrocher [1] (*a notice*).

PIN *noun* (*personal identification number*) code confidentiel M.

pinball *noun* flipper M; **to play pinball** jouer au flipper; **a pinball machine** un flipper.

pinch *noun* (*of salt, for example*) pincée F.
verb 1 (*steal*) piquer [1]; **somebody's pinched my bike** on m'a piqué mon vélo; 2 **to pinch somebody** pincer [61] quelqu'un.

pine noun pin M; **a pine table** une table en pin.

pineapple noun ananas M.

pine cone noun pomme F de pin.

ping-pong noun ping-pong M; **to play ping-pong** jouer au ping-pong.

pink adjective rose.

pip noun (in a fruit) pépin M.

pipe noun 1 (for gas or water) tuyau M (plural tuyaux); 2 (to smoke) pipe F; **he smokes a pipe** il fume la pipe.

pirate noun pirate M.

pirated adjective piraté; **a pirated video** une vidéo piratée.

Pisces noun Poissons M plural; **Amanda is Pisces** Amanda est Poissons.

pit noun fosse F.

pitch noun terrain M; **a football pitch** un terrain de foot.
verb **to pitch a tent** dresser [1] une tente.

pity noun 1 **what a pity!** quel dommage!; **it would be a pity to miss the beginning** ce serait dommage de rater le début;
2 (feeling sorry for somebody) pitié F.
verb **to pity somebody** plaindre [31] quelqu'un.

pizza noun pizza F.

place noun 1 endroit M; **in a warm place** dans un endroit chaud; **Rome is a wonderful place** Rome est un endroit merveilleux; **all over the place** partout; 2 (a space) place F;

a place for the car une place pour la voiture; **is there a place for me?** y a-t-il une place pour moi?; **will you keep my place?** veux-tu me garder ma place?; **to change places** changer de place; 3 (in a race) place F; **in first place** à la première place; 4 **at your place** chez toi; **we'll go round to Zafir's place** on ira chez Zafir; 5 **to take place** avoir [5] lieu; **the competition will take place at four** le concours aura lieu à quatre heures.
verb mettre [11]; **he placed his cup on the table** il a mis sa tasse sur la table.

plain noun plaine F.
adjective 1 simple; **plain cooking** une cuisine simple;
2 (unflavoured) nature; **a plain yoghurt** un yaourt nature; 3 (not patterned) uni; **plain curtains** des rideaux unis.

plait noun natte F.

plan noun 1 projet M; **what are your plans for this summer?** quels sont vos projets pour cet été?; **to go according to plan** se passer comme prévu; **everything went according to plan** tout s'est passé comme prévu; 2 (a map) plan M.
verb **to plan to do** avoir [5] l'intention de faire; **we're planning to leave at eight** nous avons l'intention de partir à huit heures; 2 (make plans for) préparer [1]; **Ricky's planning a trip to Italy** Ricky prépare un voyage en Italie; 3 (organize) organiser [1]; **I'm planning my day** j'organise ma journée; 4 (to design) concevoir [66] (a house or garden); **a well-**

planned kitchen une cuisine bien conçue.

plane noun avion M; **we went by plane** nous avons pris l'avion.

planet noun planète F.

plank noun planche F.

plant noun plante F; **a house plant** une plante d'intérieur.
verb planter [1].

plaster noun 1 (sticking plaster) pansement adhésif M; 2 (for walls) plâtre M; 3 **to have your leg in plaster** avoir la jambe dans le plâtre.

plastic noun plastique M; **a plastic bag** un sac en plastique.

plate noun assiette F.

platform noun 1 (in a station) quai M; **the train arriving at platform six** le train qui entre en gare quai numéro six; 2 (for lecturing or performing) estrade F.

play noun pièce F; **a play by Molière** une pièce de Molière; **our school is putting on a play** notre école monte une pièce.
verb 1 jouer [1]; **the children were playing with a ball** les enfants jouaient avec un ballon; **they play all kinds of music** ils jouent toutes sortes de musique; **who's playing Hamlet?** qui est-ce qui joue Hamlet?; 2 jouer [1] à (a game); **to play tennis** jouer au tennis; **they were playing cards** ils jouaient aux cartes; 3 jouer [1] de (a musical instrument); **Helen plays the violin** Helen joue du violon; 4 mettre [11] (a tape, CD, or record); **play me your new CD** mets-moi ton nouveau CD.

player noun 1 (in sport) joueur M, joueuse F; **a football player** un joueur de foot; 2 (musician) musicien M, musicienne F.

playground noun cour F de récréation.

playgroup noun halte-garderie F.

playing field noun terrain M de sport.

playroom noun salle F de jeux.

plaza noun **a shopping plaza** un centre commercial.

pleasant adjective agréable.

please adverb s'il vous plaît; (less formal), s'il te plaît; **two coffees, please** deux cafés, s'il vous plaît; **could you turn the TV off, please?** est-ce que tu peux éteindre la télé s'il te plaît?

pleased adjective content; **I was really pleased!** j'étais très content!; **she was pleased with her present** elle était contente de son cadeau; **pleased to meet you!** enchanté!

pleasure noun plaisir M.

plenty pronoun 1 (lots) beaucoup; **there's plenty of bread** il y a beaucoup de pain; **he's got plenty of money** il a beaucoup d'argent; 2 (quite enough) **we've got plenty of time for a coffee** nous avons largement le temps de prendre un café; **thank you, that's plenty!** merci, ça suffit largement!

plot noun (of a film or novel) intrigue F.

plough verb labourer [1].

plug noun 1 (electrical) prise F;

2 (*in a bath or sink*) bonde F; **to pull out the plug** retirer la bonde.

plum *noun* prune F; **a plum tart** une tarte aux prunes.

plumber *noun* plombier M; **he's a plumber** il est plombier.

plump *adjective* potelé.

plunge *verb* plonger [52].

plural *noun* pluriel M; **in the plural** au pluriel.

plus *preposition* plus; **three children plus the baby** trois enfants plus le bébé.

p.m. *adverb* (*French people usually express times after midday in terms of the 24-hour clock*) **1 at two p.m.** à quatorze heures; **at nine p.m.** à vingt-et-une heures; **2** (*however, you can also use 'de l'après-midi', for times up to 6 p.m. and 'du soir' for times after that*) **at two p.m.** à deux heures de l'après-midi; **at nine p.m.** à neuf heures du soir.

poached egg *noun* œuf M poché.

pocket *noun* poche F.

pocket money *noun* argent M de poche.

poem *noun* poème M.

poet *noun* poète M.

poetry *noun* poésie F.

point *noun* **1** (*tip*) pointe F; **the point of a nail** la pointe d'un clou; **2** (*in time*) moment M; **at that point the police arrived** à ce moment là, la police est arrivée; **3 to get the point** comprendre; **I don't get the point** je ne comprends pas;

what's the point of waiting? à quoi bon attendre?; **there's no point phoning, he's out** ça ne sert à rien d'appeler, il est sorti; **that's not the point** il ne s'agit pas de ça; **4 that's a good point!** c'est vrai!; **5 from my point of view** de mon point de vue; **6 her strong point** son point fort; **7** (*in scoring*) point M; **fifteen points to eleven** quinze points à onze; **8** (*in decimals*) (*in French, a comma is used for the decimal point, so 6,75*) **6 point 4** 6 virgule 4 (*this is how you say it aloud*).

verb **1** indiquer [1]; **a notice pointing to the station** un panneau qui indiquait la gare; **James pointed out the cathedral** James nous a montré la cathédrale; **2** (*with finger*) montrer [1] du doigt; **he pointed at one of the children** il a montré l'un des enfants du doigt; **3 I'd like to point out that I'm paying** je vous signale que c'est moi qui paie.

pointless *adjective* inutile; **it's pointless to keep on ringing** c'est inutile de continuer de sonner.

poison *noun* poison M.
verb empoisonner [1].

poisonous *adjective* **1** toxique (*chemical or gas*); **2** vénéneux (F vénéneuse) (*toadstools or berries*); **3** venimeux (F venimeuse) (*snake or insect*).

Poland *noun* Pologne F; **in Poland** en Pologne.

polar bear *noun* ours M polaire.

pole *noun* **1** (*for a tent*) mât M; **2** (*for skiing*) bâton M; **3 the North Pole** le pôle Nord.

Pole noun (a Polish person) Polonais M, Polonaise F.

police noun the police la police; the police are coming la police arrive (note that a singular verb is used after 'la police').
verb surveiller [1].

police car noun voiture F de police.

policeman noun agent M de police.

police station noun commissariat M de police.

policewoman noun femme F policier.

polish noun 1 (for furniture) cire F; 2 (for shoes) cirage M.
verb cirer [1] (shoes or furniture).

Polish noun, adjective polonais M.

polite adjective poli; to be polite to somebody être poli avec quelqu'un.

political adjective politique.

politician noun homme politique M, femme politique F.

politics noun politique F.

polluted adjective pollué.

pollution noun pollution F.

polo-necked adjective à col roulé; a polo-necked jumper un pull à col roulé.

polythene bag noun sac M en plastique.

pond noun 1 (large) étang M; 2 (smaller) mare F; 3 (in a garden) bassin M.

pony noun poney M.

ponytail noun queue F de cheval.

poodle noun caniche M.

pool noun 1 (swimming pool) piscine F; 2 (in the country) étang M; 3 (puddle) flaque F; 4 (game) billard M américain; to have a game of pool jouer au billard américain; 5 the football pools le loto sportif; to do the pools jouer au loto sportif.

poor adjective pauvre; a poor area un quartier pauvre; a poor family une famille pauvre; poor Tanya's failed her exam la pauvre Tanya a raté son examen; 2 (bad) mauvais; this is poor work c'est du mauvais travail; the weather was pretty poor le temps était assez mauvais.

pop noun pop M; a pop concert un concert de pop; a pop star un pop star; a pop song une chanson pop.
●to pop into faire [10] un saut à; I'll just pop into the bank je vais juste faire un saut à la banque.

popcorn noun pop-corn M.

pope noun pape M.

poppy noun coquelicot M.

popular adjective populaire.

population noun population F.

porch noun porche M.

pork noun porc M; a pork chop une côtelette de porc.

porridge noun porridge M.

port noun 1 port M; the ferry was in port le ferry était au port; 2 (wine) porto M.

porter noun 1 (at a station or airport) porteur M; 2 (in a hotel) portier M.

portion noun (*of food*) portion F.

portrait noun portrait M.

Portugal noun Portugal M; **to Portugal** au Portugal; **in Portugal** au Portugal.

Portuguese noun 1 (*language*) portugais M; 2 (*a person*) Portugais M, Portugaise F. adjective portugais.

posh adjective chic (*never changes*); **a posh house** une maison chic.

position noun position F.

positive adjective 1 (*sure*) sûr; **I'm positive he's left** je suis sûr qu'il est parti; 2 (*enthusiastic*) positif (F positive); **her reaction was very positive** sa réaction était très positive; **try to be more positive** essaie d'être plus positif.

possess verb posséder [24].

possessions plural noun affaires F plural; **all my possessions are in the flat** toutes mes affaires sont dans l'appartement.

possibility noun possibilité F.

possible adjective possible; **it's possible** c'est possible; **if possible** si possible; **as quickly as possible** le plus vite possible.

possibly adverb 1 (*maybe*) peut-être; **'will you be at home at midday?'** – **'possibly'** 'est-ce que tu seras chez toi à midi?' – 'peut-être'; 2 (*for emphasis*) **how can you possibly believe that?** mais comment donc peux-tu croire ça?; **I can't possibly arrive before Thursday** je ne peux vraiment pas arriver avant jeudi.

post noun 1 poste F; **to send something by post** envoyer quelque chose par la poste; 2 (*letters*) courrier M; **is there any post for me?** y a-t-il du courrier pour moi?; 3 (*a pole*) poteau M (*plural* poteaux); 4 (*a job*) poste M.
verb **to post a letter** mettre [11] une lettre à la poste.

postbox noun boîte F à lettres.

postcard noun carte postale F.

postcode noun code postal M.

poster noun 1 (*for decoration*) poster M; **I've bought an Oasis poster** j'ai acheté un poster d'Oasis; 2 (*advertising*) affiche F; **I saw a poster for the concert** j'ai vu une affiche pour le concert.

postman noun facteur M; **has the postman been?** est-ce que le facteur est passé?

post office noun poste F; **the post office is on the right** la poste est à droite.

postpone verb **to postpone something** remettre [11] quelque chose à plus tard.

postwoman noun factrice F.

pot noun 1 (*jar*) pot M; **a pot of honey** un pot de miel; 2 (*teapot*) théière F; **I'll make a pot of tea** je vais faire du thé; 3 **the pots and pans** les casseroles F plural; ★ **to take pot luck** manger à la fortune du pot.

potato noun pomme F de terre; **fried**

potatoes des pommes de terre sautées; **mashed potatoes** de la purée.

potato crisps *plural noun* chips M *plural*.

pottery *noun* poterie F.

pound *noun* 1 (*money*) livre F; **fourteen pounds** quatorze livres; **how much is that in pounds?** c'est combien en livres sterling?; 2 (*in weight*) livre F; **a pound of apples** une livre de pommes.

pour *verb* 1 verser [1] (*liquid*); **he poured the milk into the pan** il a versé le lait dans la casserole; 2 servir [71] (*a drink*); **to pour the tea** servir le thé; **I poured him a drink** je lui ai servi à boire; 3 (*with rain*) **it's pouring** il pleut à verse.

poverty *noun* pauvreté F.

powder *noun* poudre F.

power *noun* 1 (*electricity*) courant M; **a power cut** une coupure de courant; 2 (*energy*) énergie F; **nuclear power** l'énergie nucléaire; 3 (*over other people*) pouvoir M; **to be in power** être au pouvoir.

powerful *adjective* puissant.

power point *noun* prise F de courant.

power station *noun* centrale F électrique.

practical *adjective* pratique.

practically *adverb* pratiquement.

practice *noun* 1 (*for sport*) entraînement M; **a hockey practice** l'entraînement de hockey; 2 (*for an instrument*) **to do your piano**

practice travailler [1] son piano; 3 **to be out of practice** être rouillé; 4 **in practice** en pratique.

practise *verb* 1 travailler [1] (*music, language, etc*); **a week in Berlin to practise my German** une semaine à Berlin pour travailler mon allemand; 2 (*in a sport*) s'entraîner [1]; **the team practises on Wednesdays** l'équipe s'entraîne le mercredi.

praise *verb* **to praise somebody for something** féliciter [1] quelqu'un de quelque chose.

pram *noun* landau M.

prawn *noun* crevette F.

pray *verb* prier [1].

prayer *noun* prière F.

precaution *noun* précaution F; **to take precautions** prendre ses précautions.

precinct *noun* **a shopping precinct** un quartier commerçant; **a pedestrian precinct** une zone piétonne.

precious *adjective* précieux (F précieuse).

precisely *adverb* précisément; **at eleven o'clock precisely** à onze heures précises.

preface *noun* préface F.

prefer *verb* préférer [24]; **I prefer coffee to tea** je préfère le café au thé.

pregnant *adjective* enceinte.

prejudice *noun* préjugé M; **a prejudice** un préjugé; **to fight**

against racial prejudice lutter contre les préjugés raciaux.

prejudiced *adjective* **to be prejudiced** avoir des préjugés.

preliminary *adjective* préliminaire.

première *noun* première F (*of a play or film*).

prep *noun* devoirs M *plural*; **my English prep** mes devoirs d'anglais.

preparation *noun* 1 préparation F; 2 **the preparations for** les préparatifs M *plural* pour; **our preparations for Christmas** nos préparatifs pour Noël.

prepare *verb* préparer [1]; **to prepare somebody for** préparer quelqu'un à (*a surprise or shock*); **to be prepared for the worst** s'attendre [3] au pire.

prepared *adjective* prêt; **I'm prepared to pay half** je suis prêt à en payer la moitié.

preposition *noun* préposition F.

prep school *noun* école primaire privée F.

prescription *noun* ordonnance F; **on prescription** sur ordonnance.

presence *noun* présence F; **in my presence** en ma présence.

presence of mind *noun* présence F d'esprit.

present *noun* 1 (*a gift*) cadeau M (*plural* cadeaux); **to give somebody a present** offrir un cadeau à quelqu'un; 2 (*the time now*) présent M; **in the present (tense)** au présent; **that's all for the present** c'est tout pour le moment.

adjective 1 (*attending*) présent; **is Tracy present?** est-ce que Tracy est présente? à [1] à; **fifty people were present at the funeral** cinquante personnes ont assisté à l'enterrement; 2 (*existing now*) actuel (F actuelle); **the present situation** la situation actuelle; 3 **at the present time** actuellement.

verb 1 remettre [11] (*a prize*); 2 (*introduce*) présenter [1].

presenter *noun* (*on TV*) présentateur M, présentatrice F.

presently *adverb* (*soon*) bientôt.

president *noun* président M, présidente F.

press *noun* **the press** la presse. *verb* 1 (*to push*) appuyer [41]; **press here to open** appuyez ici pour ouvrir; 2 appuyer [41] sur (*a button, switch, or pedal*); **he pressed the button** il a appuyé sur le bouton.

press conference *noun* conférence F de presse.

pressure *noun* pression F.

pressure group *noun* groupe M de pression.

pretend *verb* **to pretend to do** faire [10] semblant de faire; **he's pretending not to hear** il fait semblant de ne pas entendre.

pretty *adjective* joli (*goes before the noun*); **a pretty dress** une jolie robe. *adverb* plutôt; **it was pretty silly** c'était plutôt bête.

prevent *verb* **to prevent somebody from doing** empêcher [1] quelqu'un de faire; **there's nothing to prevent**

you from leaving rien ne vous
empêche de partir.

previous adjective précédent.

previously adverb auparavant.

price noun prix M; **the price per
kilo** le prix du kilo; **CDs have gone
up in price** les CD ont augmenté.

price list noun liste F des prix.

price ticket noun étiquette F.

prick verb piquer [1]; **to prick your
finger** se piquer le doigt.

pride noun fierté F.

priest noun prêtre M.

primary school noun école F
primaire.

primary (school) teacher noun
instituteur M, institutrice F.

prime minister noun Premier
ministre M.

primrose noun primevère F.

prince noun prince M; **Prince
Charles** le prince Charles.

princess noun princesse F;
Princess Anne la princesse Anne.

principal noun (of a college)
directeur M, directrice F.
adjective (main) principal (M plural
principaux).

principle noun principe M; **on
principle** par principe; **that's true in
principle** cela est vrai en principe.

print noun 1 (letters) caractères M
plural; **in small print** en petits
caractères; 2 (a photo) tirage M; **a
colour print** un tirage en couleur.

printer noun imprimante F.

print-out noun copie F papier.

prison noun prison F; **in prison** en
prison.

prisoner noun prisonnier M,
prisonnière F.

private adjective 1 privé; **a private
school** une école privée; **'private
property'** 'propriété privée';
2 particulier (F particulière)
(lesson); **to have private lessons**
prendre des cours particuliers.

privately adverb en privé.

prize noun prix M; **to win a prize**
gagner un prix.

prize-giving noun distribution F
des prix.

prizewinner noun gagnant M,
gagnante F.

probable adjective probable.

probably adverb probablement.

problem noun problème M; **it's a
serious problem** c'est un grave
problème; **no problem!** pas de
problème!

process noun 1 processus M;
2 **to be in the process of doing** être
en train de faire.

produce noun (food) produits M
plural.
verb produire [26]; **I produced my
passport** j'ai produit mon
passeport; **it produces a lot of heat**
ça produit beaucoup de chaleur.

producer noun (of a film or
programme) metteur M en scène.

product noun produit M.

production noun 1 (of a film or

opera) production F;   **2** (*of a play*) mise F en scène; **a new production of Hamlet** une nouvelle mise en scène de Hamlet; **3** (*by a factory*) production F.

profession *noun* profession F.

professional *noun* professionnel M, professionnelle F; **he's a professional** c'est un professionnel. *adjective* professionnel (F professionnelle); **she's a professional singer** c'est une chanteuse professionnelle.

professor *noun* professeur M.

profile *noun* profil M.

profit *noun* bénéfice M.

profitable *adjective* rentable.

program *noun* **a computer program** un programme informatique.

programme *noun* **1** (*for a play or an event*) programme M;   **2** (*on TV or radio*) émission F.

progress *noun* **1** progrès M; **to make progress** faire des progrès; **2 to be in progress** être en cours.

project *noun* **1** (*at school*) dossier M;   **2** (*a plan*) projet M; **a project to build a bridge** un projet pour construire un pont.

projector *noun* projecteur M.

promise *noun* promesse F; **to make a promise** faire une promesse; **to break a promise** manquer à sa promesse; **it's a promise!** c'est promis! *verb* **to promise to do** promettre [11] de faire; **I've promised to be**

home by ten** j'ai promis de rentrer avant dix heures.

promote *verb* **to be promoted** être [6] promu.

promotion *noun* promotion F.

promptly *adjective* **1** (*at once*) immédiatement; **he promptly fell off again** il est retombé immédiatement;   **2** (*quickly*) rapidement; **please reply promptly** répondez rapidement s'il vous plaît; **3 promptly at five o'clock** à cinq heures précises.

pronoun *noun* pronom M.

pronounce *verb* prononcer [61]; **it's hard to pronounce** c'est difficile à prononcer.

pronunciation *noun* prononciation F.

proof *noun* preuve F; **there's no proof that ...** rien ne prouve que ...

propaganda *noun* propagande F.

propeller *noun* hélice F.

proper *adjective* **1** (*real, genuine*) vrai; **a proper doctor** un vrai médecin; **I need a proper meal** j'ai besoin d'un vrai repas;   **2** (*correct*) bon (F bonne); **the proper answer** la bonne réponse; **the proper tool** le bon outil; **in its proper place** à sa place.

properly *adverb* comme il faut; **hold it properly** tiens-le comme il faut; **is it properly wrapped?** est-ce que c'est emballé comme il faut?

property *noun* **1** (*your belongings*) affaires F *plural*; propriété F; **'private property'** 'propriété privée'.

proposal noun proposition F.

propose verb 1 (suggest) proposer [1]; 2 (marriage) he proposed to her il l'a demandée en mariage.

protect verb protéger [15].

protection noun protection F.

protein noun protéine F.

protest noun protestation F; in spite of their protests malgré leurs protestations.
verb 1 (to grumble) protester [1]; he protested, but ... il a protesté, mais ...; 2 (demonstrate) manifester [1].

Protestant noun, adjective protestant M, protestante F.

protester noun manifestant M, manifestante F.

protest march noun manifestation F.

proud adjective fier (F fière).

prove verb prouver [1].

proverb noun proverbe M.

provide verb fournir [2].

provided conjunction à condition que; provided you do it now à condition que tu le fasses maintenant (note that a verb in the subjunctive is needed).

prune noun pruneau M (plural pruneaux).

psychiatrist noun psychiatre M & F; he's a psychiatrist il est psychiatre.

psychological adjective psychologique.

psychologist noun psychologue M & F; she's a psychologist elle est psychologue.

psychology noun psychologie F.

PTO TSVP (= tournez s'il vous plaît).

pub noun pub M.

public noun the public le public; in public en public.
adjective 1 public (F publique); 2 the public library la bibliothèque municipale.

public address system noun sonorisation F.

public holiday noun jour M férié; January 1 is a public holiday le premier janvier est férié.

publicity noun publicité F.

public school noun école F privée.

public transport noun transports M plural en commun.

publish verb publier [1].

publisher noun éditeur M.

pudding noun (dessert) dessert M; for pudding we've got strawberries comme dessert nous avons des fraises.

puddle noun flaque F.

puff noun (of smoke) bouffée F.

puff pastry noun pâte feuilletée F.

pull verb tirer [1]; pull hard! tire fort!; to pull a rope tirer sur une corde; he pulled a letter out of his pocket il a tiré une lettre de sa poche; ★ you're pulling my leg! tu me fais marcher.
●to pull down baisser [1] (a blind).
●to pull in (at the roadside) s'arrêter [1].

pullover noun pull-over M.

pump noun pompe F; a bicycle pump une pompe à vélo.
verb **1** pomper [1]; **they were pumping the water out of the cellar** ils pompaient l'eau de la cave.
●**to pump up** gonfler [1] (a tyre).

pumpkin noun citrouille F.

punch noun **1** (in boxing) coup M de poing; **2** (drink) punch M.
verb **1 to punch somebody** donner [1] un coup de poing à quelqu'un; **he punched me** il m'a donné un coup de poing; **2** composter [1] (a ticket).

punctual adjective ponctuel (F ponctuelle).

punctuation noun ponctuation F.

punctuation mark noun signe M de ponctuation.

puncture noun crevaison F; we had a puncture on the way nous avons crevé en route.

punish verb punir [2].

punishment noun punition F.

pupil noun élève M & F.

puppet noun marionnette F.

puppy noun chiot M; a labrador puppy un chiot labrador.

pure adjective pur.

purple adjective violet (F violette).

purpose noun **1** but M; what was the purpose of her call? quel était le but de son appel?; **2** on purpose exprès; **she did it on purpose** elle l'a fait exprès; **he closed the door on purpose** il a fait exprès de fermer la porte.

purr verb ronronner [1].

purse noun porte-monnaie M (plural porte-monnaie).

push noun **to give something a push** pousser [1] quelque chose.
verb **1** pousser [1]; **he pushed me** il m'a poussé; **2** (to press) appuyer [41] sur (a bell or button); **3 to push somebody to do** pousser [1] quelqu'un à faire; **his teacher is pushing him to sit the exam** son prof le pousse à passer l'examen.
●**to push something away** repousser [1] quelque chose; **she pushed her plate away** elle a repoussé son assiette.

pushchair noun poussette F.

put verb mettre [11]; **you can put the cream in the fridge** tu peux mettre la crème au frigo; **where did you put my bag?** où est-ce que tu as mis mon sac?; **put your suitcase here** mets ta valise ici; **2** (write) écrire [38]; **put your address here** écris ton adresse ici.
●**to put away** ranger [52]; **I'll put the shopping away** je vais ranger les courses.
●**to put back 1** remettre [11]; **I put it back in the drawer** je l'ai remis dans le tiroir; **2** (postpone) remettre [11]; **the meeting has been put back until Thursday** la réunion a été remise à jeudi.
●**to put down** poser [1]; **she put the vase down on the table** elle a posé le vase sur la table.
●**to put off 1** (postpone) remettre [11]; **he's put off my lesson till Thursday** il a remis ma leçon à jeudi; **2** (turn off) éteindre [60] (a light or TV); **don't forget to put off**

the lights n'oublie pas d'éteindre la lumière; **3 to put somebody off something** dégoûter [1] quelqu'un de quelque chose; **it really put me off Chinese food!** ça m'a vraiment dégoûté de la nourriture chinoise! **4 to be put off** *(doing something)* se décourager [52]; **don't be put off!** ne te décourage pas!

●**to put on 1** mettre [11] *(clothing, make-up, CD);* **I'll just put my shoes on** je vais juste mettre mes chaussures; **he's put on Oasis** il a mis Oasis; **2** *(switch on)* allumer [1] *(a light or heating);* **could you put the lamp on?** est-ce que tu peux allumer la lampe?; **3** monter [1] *(a play);* **we're putting on a French play** nous sommes en train de monter une pièce française.

●**to put out 1** *(put outside)* sortir [72]; **have you put the rubbish out?** as-tu sorti les ordures?; **2** éteindre [60] *(a fire, light, or cigarette);* **I've put the lights out** j'ai éteint la lumière; **3 to put out your hand** tendre [3] la main.

●**to put up 1** lever [50] *(your hand);* **I put up my hand** j'ai levé la main; **2** mettre [11] *(picture);* **I've put up some photos in my room** j'ai mis des photos dans ma chambre; **3** afficher [1] *(a notice);* **4** augmenter [1] *(the price);* **they've put up the price of the tickets** ils ont augmenté le prix des billets; **5** *(for the night)* héberger [52]; **can you put me up on Friday?** est-ce que tu peux m'héberger vendredi?

●**to put up with something** supporter [1]; **I don't know how she puts up with it** je ne sais pas comment elle le supporte.

puzzle noun *(jigsaw)* puzzle M.

puzzled adjective perplexe.

pyjamas plural noun pyjama M singular; **a pair of pyjamas** un pyjama; **where are my pyjamas?** où est mon pyjama?

Pyrenees noun les Pyrénées F plural; **in the Pyrenees** dans les Pyrénées.

Q q

qualification noun **1** diplôme M *(certificate, exam, degree);* **2 qualifications** qualifications F plural; **vocational qualifications** les qualifications professionnelles.

qualify verb **1** *(to be eligible)* avoir [5] droit à; **we don't qualify for a reduction** nous n'avons pas droit à une réduction; **2** *(in sport)* se qualifier [1].

qualified adjective **1** qualifié; **she's a qualified ski instructor** c'est une monitrice de ski qualifiée; **2** *(having a degree or a diploma)* diplômé; **a qualified architect** un architecte diplômé.

quality noun qualité F; **good quality vegetables** des légumes de bonne qualité.

quantity noun quantité F.

quarantine noun quarantaine F.

quarrel noun dispute F; **to have a quarrel** se disputer [1].
verb se disputer [1]; **they're always**

quarrelling ils sont tout le temps en train de se disputer.

quarter *noun* 1 quart M; **a quarter of the class** le quart de la classe; **three quarters of the class** les trois quarts de la classe; 2 **a quarter past ten** dix heures et quart; **a quarter to ten** dix heures moins le quart; **a quarter of an hour** un quart d'heure; **three quarters of an hour** trois quarts d'heure; **an hour and a quarter** une heure et quart.

quartet *noun* quatuor M; **a jazz quartet** un quatuor de jazz.

quay *noun* quai M.

queen *noun* reine F; **Queen Elizabeth** la reine Elizabeth; **the Queen Mother** la reine mère.

query *noun* question F; **are there any queries?** y a-t-il des questions?

question *noun* question F; **to ask a question** poser une question; **I asked her a question** je lui ai posé une question; **it's a question of time** c'est une question de temps; **it's out of the question!** c'est hors de question!
verb interroger [52].

question mark *noun* point M d'interrogation.

questionnaire *noun* questionnaire M; **to fill in a questionnaire** remplir un questionnaire.

queue *noun* 1 (*of people*) queue F; **to stand in a queue** faire la queue; 2 (*of cars*) file F.
verb faire [10] la queue; **we were queueing for check-in** nous

faisions la queue pour l'enregistrement.

quick *adjective* 1 rapide; **a quick lunch** un déjeuner rapide; **it's quicker on the motorway** c'est plus rapide par l'autoroute; **to have a quick look at something** jeter un coup d'œil rapide à quelque chose; 2 **quick! there's the bus!** vite! voilà le bus!; **be quick!** dépêche-toi!

quickly *adverb* vite; **I'll just quickly phone my mother** je vais vite appeler ma mère.

quiet *adjective* 1 (*silent*) silencieux (F silencieuse); **the children are very quiet** les enfants sont très silencieux; 2 **to keep quiet** se taire [76]; **please keep quiet** taisez-vous, s'il vous plaît; 3 (*gentle*) doux (F douce); **some quiet music** de la musique douce; **in a quiet voice** à voix basse; 4 (*peaceful*) tranquille; **a quiet street** une rue tranquille; **a quiet day at home** une journée tranquille à la maison.

quietly *adverb* 1 (*to move*) sans bruit; **he got up quietly** il s'est levé sans bruit; 2 (*speak*) doucement; 3 (*read or play*) en silence.

quilt *noun* couette F.

quite *adverb* 1 assez; **it's quite cold outside** il fait assez froid dehors; **that's quite a good idea** c'est une assez bonne idée; **he sings quite well** il chante assez bien; **quite often** assez souvent; 2 **not quite** pas tout à fait; **the meat's not quite cooked** la viande n'est pas tout à fait cuite; 3 **quite a lot of** pas mal de; **we've got quite a lot of friends here** nous avons pas mal d'amis ici;

quite a few people pas mal de gens.

quiz noun quiz M.

quotation noun (from a book) citation F.

quotation marks plural noun guillemets M plural; **in quotation marks** entre guillemets.

quote verb 1 (from a book) citation F; 2 (estimate) devis M; 3 **in quotes** entre guillemets.
verb citer [1].

R r

rabbi noun rabbin M.

rabbit noun lapin M.

rabbit hutch noun clapier M.

rabies noun rage F.

race noun 1 (a sports event) course F; **a cycle race** une course cycliste; **to have a race** faire la course; 2 (an ethnic group) race F.

racer noun (bike) vélo M de course.

racetrack noun 1 (for horses) champ M de course; 2 (for cars) circuit M; 3 (for cycles) piste F.

racing noun courses F plural.

racing car noun voiture F de course.

racing driver noun pilote M de course.

racial adjective racial (M plural raciaux); **racial discrimination** la discrimination raciale.

racism noun racisme M.

racist noun, adjective raciste M & F.

rack noun (for luggage) porte-bagages M.

racket noun 1 (for tennis) raquette F; **here's your tennis racket** voici ta raquette de tennis; 2 (noise) vacarme M.

radiation noun radiation F.

radiator noun radiateur M.

radio noun radio F; **to listen to the radio** écouter la radio; **to hear something on the radio** entendre quelque chose à la radio.

radioactive adjective radioactif (F radioactive).

radio-controlled adjective téléguidé.

radio station noun station F de radio.

radish noun radis M.

rag noun chiffon M.

rage noun colère F; **she's in a rage** elle est furieuse; ★ **it's all the rage** ça fait fureur.

raid noun 1 hold-up M; 2 (by the police) rafle F.

rail noun 1 (the railway) **to go by rail** prendre le train; 2 (on a balcony or bridge) balustrade F; 3 (on stairs) rampe F; 4 (for a train) rail M.

rail strike noun grève F des cheminots.

railing(s) (plural) noun grille F.

railway noun 1 (the system) chemin M de fer; **the railways** les chemins de fer; 2 **a railway line** une ligne de chemin de fer (from one place to another); 3 **on the railway line** sur la voie ferrée (the rails).

railway carriage noun wagon M.

railway station noun gare F; **opposite the railway station** en face de la gare.

rain noun pluie F; **in the rain** sous la pluie.
verb pleuvoir [63]; **it's raining** il pleut; **it's going to rain** il va pleuvoir.

rainbow noun arc-en-ciel M (plural arcs-en-ciel).

raincoat noun imperméable M.

raindrop noun goutte F de pluie.

rainy adjective pluvieux (F pluvieuse).

raise verb 1 (lift up) lever [50]; **she raised her head** elle a levé la tête; 2 (increase) augmenter [1] (a price or a salary); 3 **to raise money for something** collecter [1] des fonds pour quelque chose; 4 (to raise the alarm) donner [1] l'alarme; 5 (to raise somebody's spirits) remonter [1] le moral à quelqu'un.

raisin noun raisin M sec.

rake noun rateau M (plural rateaux).

rally noun 1 (a meeting) rassemblement M; 2 (for sport) rallye M; 3 (in tennis) échange M.

rambler noun randonneur M, randonneuse F.

rambling noun randonnée F.

ramp noun (for a wheelchair, for example) rampe F.

ranch noun ranch M.

range noun 1 (a choice) gamme F; **we offer a range of sports** nous vous proposons une gamme de sports; **in a wide range of colours** dans un grand choix de coloris; **a top-of-the-range computer** un ordinateur haut de gamme; 2 (of mountains) chaîne F.

rap noun rap M (music).

rape noun viol M.
verb violer [1].

rare adjective 1 rare; **a rare bird** un oiseau rare; 2 saignant (a steak); **medium-rare** à point.

rarely adverb rarement.

rash noun rougeurs F plural; **I've got a rash on my arms** j'ai des rougeurs sur les bras.
adjective irréfléchi; **a rash decision** une décision irréfléchie.

raspberry noun framboise F; **raspberry jam** la confiture de framboises; **a raspberry tart** une tarte aux framboises.

rat noun rat M.

rate noun 1 (a charge) tarif M; **what are the rates for children?** quels sont les tarifs pour les enfants?; **reduced rates** les tarifs réduits; 2 (a level) taux M; **a high cancellation rate** un taux élevé d'annulation; 3 **at any rate** en tout cas.

rather adverb 1 plutôt; **I'm rather**

busy je suis plutôt occupé;
2 **rather than** plutôt que; **in
summer rather than winter** en été
plutôt qu'en hiver; 3 **I'd rather
wait** je préfère attendre; **they'd
rather come on Thursday** ils
préfèrent venir jeudi; 4 **rather a lot
of** pas mal de; **I've got rather a lot
of shopping to do** j'ai pas mal de
courses à faire.

rave noun rave M (a party).

raw adjective cru.

razor noun rasoir M.

razor blade noun lame F de rasoir.

RE noun éducation religieuse F.

reach noun portée F; **out of reach**
hors de portée; **within reach** (of
your hand) à portée de main; **within
easy reach of the sea** à proximité
de la mer.
verb 1 arriver [1] à; **when you reach
the church** quand vous arrivez à
l'église; **to reach a decision** arriver
à une décision; 2 **to reach the final**
arriver [1] à la finale.

react verb réagir [2].

reaction noun réaction F.

read verb lire [51]; **what are you
reading at the moment?** qu'est-ce
que tu lis en ce moment? **I'm reading
a detective novel** je lis un roman
policier; **he read out the list** il a lu la
liste à haute voix.

reading noun lecture F; **I don't
much like reading** je n'aime pas
beaucoup la lecture; **some easy
reading for the beach** de la lecture
facile pour la plage.

ready adjective prêt; **supper's not**

ready yet le dîner n'est pas encore
prêt; **are you ready to leave?** est-ce
que tu es prêt à partir? **to get ready**
se préparer [1]; **I'm getting ready to
go out** je me prépare pour sortir; **I
was getting ready for bed** je me
préparais pour me coucher; **I'll get
your room ready** je vais préparer ta
chambre.

real adjective vrai; **it's a real
diamond** c'est un vrai diamant; **he's
a real bore** c'est un vrai casse-pieds;
is that his real name? est-ce que
c'est son vrai nom?; **her real father is
dead** son vrai père est mort.

realistic adjective réaliste.

reality noun réalité F.

realize verb se rendre [3] compte; **I
hadn't realized** je ne m'en étais pas
rendu compte; **I didn't realize he
was French** je ne me suis pas rendu
compte qu'il était français; **do you
realize what time it is?** tu te rends
compte de l'heure qu'il est?

really adverb vraiment; **not really**
pas vraiment; **is it midnight?**
est-il vraiment minuit?; **the film was
really good** le film était vraiment
très bon; **really?** c'est vrai?

rear noun arrière M.
adjective arrière; **the rear door** la
porte arrière.

reason noun raison F; **the reason
for the delay** la raison du retard; **the
reason why I phoned** la raison pour
laquelle j'ai appelé.

reasonable adjective raisonnable.

reassure verb rassurer [1].

reassuring adjective rassurant.

ebuild *verb* reconstruire [26].

eceipt *noun* reçu M.

eceive *verb* recevoir [66].

eceiver *noun* combiné M; **to pick up the receiver** décrocher [1].

ecent *adjective* récent.

ecently *adverb* récemment.

eception *noun* 1 réception F; **he's waiting at reception** il attend à la réception; **a big wedding reception** une grande réception de mariage; 2 **to get a good reception** avoir un bon accueil.

eceptionist *noun* réceptionniste M & F.

recipe *noun* recette F; **can I have the recipe for your salad?** est-ce que je peux prendre la recette de ta salade?

reckon *verb* penser [1]; **I reckon it's a good idea** je pense que c'est une bonne idée.

recognize *verb* reconnaître [27].

recommend *verb* conseiller [1]; **can you recommend a dentist?** est-ce que vous pouvez me conseiller un dentiste?; **I recommend the fish soup** je vous conseille la soupe de poisson.

record *noun* 1 record M; **it's a world record** c'est un record mondial; **record sales for the CD** des ventes record pour le CD; **the hottest summer on record** l'été le plus chaud qu'on ait jamais enregistré; 2 **to keep a record of something** noter quelque chose; 3 (*music*) disque M; **a Miles Davis**

record un disque de Miles Davis; 4 (*office files*) dossier M; **I'll just check your records** je vais juste vérifier votre dossier.
verb (*on tape or CD*) enregistrer [1]; **they're recording a new album** ils sont en train d'enregistrer un nouvel album.

recorder *noun* 1 flûte F à bec; **to play the recorder** jouer de la flûte à bec; 2 **a cassette recorder** un magnétophone à cassettes; **a video recorder** un magnétoscope.

recording *noun* enregistrement M.

record player *noun* tourne-disque M.

recover *verb* 1 se remettre [11]; **she's recovered now** elle s'est maintenant remise.

recovery *noun* (*from an illness*) rétablissement M.

recovery vehicle *noun* camion M de dépannage.

rectangle *noun* rectangle M.

rectangular *adjective* rectangulaire.

recycle *verb* recycler [1].

red *adjective* 1 rouge; **a red shirt** une chemise rouge; **a bright red car** une voiture rouge vif; **to go red** rougir [2]; 2 roux (F rousse) (*hair*); **to have red hair** avoir les cheveux roux.

Red Cross *noun* **the Red Cross** la Croix-Rouge.

redcurrant *noun* groseille F;

redcurrant jelly la gelée de groseilles.

redecorate verb refaire [10]; **they've redecorated the kitchen** ils ont refait la cuisine.

redo verb refaire [10].

reduce verb réduire [68]; **they've reduced the price** ils ont réduit le prix; **to reduce speed** ralentir [2].

reduction noun réduction F.

redundant adjective **to be made redundant** être licencié.

reel noun (of cotton) bobine F.

referee noun (in sport) arbitre M.

reference noun références F plural (for a job); **she gave me a good reference** elle m'a fourni de bonnes références.

reference book noun ouvrage M de référence.

refill noun recharge F.

reflect verb refléter [24].

reflection noun 1 (in a mirror) image F; 2 (thought) réflexion F; **on reflection** à la réflexion.

reflexive adjective **a reflexive verb** un verbe réfléchi.

refreshing adjective rafraîchissant.

refrigerator noun réfrigérateur M.

refugee noun réfugié M, réfugiée F.

refund noun remboursement M. verb rembourser [1].

refusal noun refus M.

refuse noun (rubbish) ordures F plural.
verb refuser [1]; **I refused** j'ai refusé; **he refuses to help** il refuse de nous aider.

regards plural noun amitiés F plural; **'regards to your parents'** 'mes amitiés à vos parents'; **Nat sends his regards** tu as le bonjour de Nat.

reggae noun reggae M.

region noun région F.

regional adjective régional (M plural régionaux).

register noun (in school) cahier M des absences.
verb s'inscrire [38].

registered letter noun lettre F recommandée.

registration number noun numéro M d'immatriculation (of a vehicle).

regret verb regretter [1].

regular adjective régulier (F régulière); **regular visits** des visites régulières.

regularly adverb régulièrement.

regulation noun règlement M.

rehearsal noun répétition F.

rehearse verb répéter [24].

reheat verb réchauffer [1].

rein noun rêne F.

reject verb rejeter [48].

related adjective apparenté; **we're not related** nous ne sommes pas apparentés.

relation noun my relations ma famille; there were just relations and close friends il n'y avait que la famille et des amis proches; she's got relations in France elle a de la famille en France.

relationship noun relations F plural; we have a good relationship nous avons de bonnes relations.

relative noun membre M de la famille; there were a few relatives at the funeral il y avait quelques membres de la famille à l'enterrement; all my relatives toute ma famille.

relatively adverb relativement.

relax verb se détendre [3]; I'm going to relax and watch telly tonight je vais me détendre en regardant la télé ce soir.

relaxed adjective détendu.

relaxing adjective reposant.

relay race noun course F de relais.

release noun 1 nouveauté F; this week's new releases les nouveautés de la semaine; 2 (of a prisoner or hostage) libération F. verb 1 sortir [72] (a record or a video); 2 libérer [24] (a person).

relevant adjective pertinent.

reliable adjective fiable.

relief noun soulagement M; what a relief! quel soulagement!

relieve verb soulager [52] (pain).

relieved adjective soulagé; I was relieved to hear you'd arrived j'ai été soulagé d'apprendre que tu étais arrivé.

religion noun religion F.

religious adjective 1 croyant (a person); Jane's not religious Jane n'est pas croyante; 2 religieux (F religieuse) (art or music, for example).

rely verb to rely on somebody compter [1] sur quelqu'un; I'm relying on you for Saturday je compte sur toi pour samedi.

remain verb rester [1].

remains plural noun restes M plural; the remains of the chicken les restes du poulet; the remains of a castle les restes d'un château.

remark noun remarque F; to make remarks about faire des remarques sur.

remarkable adjective remarquable.

remarkably adverb remarquablement.

remember verb 1 se souvenir [81]; I don't remember je ne me souviens plus; 2 to remember something se souvenir [81] de quelque chose; I can't remember the number je ne me souviens pas du numéro; 3 to remember to do ne pas oublier [1] de faire; remember to shut the door n'oublie pas de fermer la porte; I remembered to bring the CDs je n'ai pas oublié d'apporter les CD.

remind verb 1 rappeler [18]; to remind somebody to do rappeler à quelqu'un de faire; remind your mother to pick me up rappelle à ta mère de venir me chercher; **2 it reminds me of Paris** ça me fait penser [1] à Paris; **he reminds me of Frank** il me fait penser à Frank; **oh, that reminds me...** oh, ça me fait penser...

remote *adjective* isolé.

remote control *noun* télécommande F.

remove *verb* enlever [50]; **he removed his jacket** il a enlevé sa veste; **the chairs had all been removed** quelqu'un avait enlevé toutes les chaises.

renew *verb* renouveler [18] (*a passport or licence*).

rent *noun* loyer M.
verb **1** louer [1]; **Simon's rented a flat** Simon a loué un appartement.

rental *noun* location F.

reorganize *verb* réorganiser [1].

repair *noun* réparation F.
verb réparer [1]; **to get something repaired** faire [10] réparer quelque chose; **we've had the television repaired** nous avons fait réparer la télévision.

repay *verb* rembourser [1]; **he repaid me the money he owed me** il m'a remboursé l'argent qu'il me devait.

repeat *noun* reprise F (*of a programme*).
verb répéter [24].

repeatedly *adverb* à plusieurs reprises.

repertoire *noun* répertoire M.

repetitive *adjective* répétitif (F répétitive).

replace *verb* remplacer [61].

reply *noun* réponse F; **I didn't get a reply to my letter** je n'ai pas reçu de réponse à ma lettre; **there's no reply** ça ne répond pas (*on the telephone*).
verb répondre [3]; **I still haven't replied to the letter** je n'ai toujours pas répondu à la lettre.

report *noun* **1** (*of an event*) compte rendu M; **2** (*school report*) bulletin M scolaire.
verb **1** signaler [1] (*a problem or accident*); **we've reported the theft** nous avons signalé le vol; **2 se présenter** [1]; **I had to report to reception** je devais me présenter à la réception.

reporter *noun* journaliste M & F.

represent *verb* représenter [1].

representative *noun* représentant M, représentante F.

reproach *noun* reproche M.
verb reprocher [1].

reproduction *noun* reproduction F.

reptile *noun* reptile M.

republic *noun* république F.

reputation *noun* réputation F; **a good reputation** une bonne réputation; **she has a reputation for honesty** elle a la réputation d'être honnête.

request *noun* demande F; **on request** sur demande.
verb demander [1].

rescue *noun* secours M; **to come to somebody's rescue** venir au secours de quelqu'un.

verb sauver [1]; **they rescued the dog** ils ont sauvé le chien.

rescue party noun équipe F de secours.

rescue worker noun secouriste M & F.

research noun recherche F; **for research into Aids** pour la recherche sur le Sida; **to do research** faire des recherches. verb **to research into** faire [10] des recherches sur; **a well-researched programme** un programme bien documenté.

resemblance noun ressemblance F.

reservation noun (a booking) réservation F; **to make a reservation** faire une réservation.

reserve noun 1 réserve F; **we have some in reserve** nous en avons en réserve; 2 **a nature reserve** une réserve naturelle; 3 (for a match) remplaçant M, remplaçante F. verb réserver [1]; **this table is reserved** cette table est réservée.

reservoir noun réservoir M.

resident noun résident M, résidente F.

residential adjective résidentiel (F résidentielle); **a residential area** un quartier résidentiel.

resign verb démissionner [1].

resignation noun (from a post) démission F.

resist verb résister [1] à (an offer or temptation); **I can't resist!** je ne peux pas résister!

resit verb repasser [1] (an exam).

resort noun 1 (for holidays) **a holiday resort** un lieu de villégiature; **a ski resort** une station de ski; **a seaside resort** une station balnéaire; 2 **as a last resort** en dernier recours.

respect noun respect M. verb respecter [1].

respectable adjective respectable.

respectful adjective respectueux (F respectueuse).

responsibility noun responsabilité F.

responsible adjective 1 (to blame) responsable; **he's responsible for the delay** il est responsable du retard; 2 (in charge) responsable; **I'm responsible for booking the rooms** je suis responsable de la réservation des chambres; 3 (reliable) sérieux (F sérieuse); **he's not very responsible** il n'est pas très sérieux.

rest noun 1 **the rest** le reste; **the rest of the day** le reste du jour; **the rest of the bread** le reste du pain; 2 (the others) les autres; **the rest have gone home** les autres sont rentrés; 3 repos M; **ten days' complete rest** dix jours de repos total; 4 (a short break) pause F; **to have a rest** se reposer [1]; **to stop for a rest** faire une pause. verb (have a rest) se reposer [1].

restaurant noun restaurant M.

restful adjective reposant.

restless adjective nerveux (F nerveuse).

restrain verb retenir [77].

restrict verb limiter [1].

restriction noun limitation F.

result noun 1 résultat M; **the exam results** les résultats des examens; 2 **as a result** par conséquent; **as a result we missed the ferry** par conséquent nous avons raté le ferry.

retire verb (from work) prendre [64] sa retraite; **she retires in June** elle prend sa retraite en juin; **for retired people** pour les retraités.

retirement noun retraite F.

return noun 1 retour M; **the return journey** le voyage de retour; **by return of post** par retour de courrier; 2 **in return** en échange; **in return for his help** en échange de son aide; ★ **many happy returns!** bon anniversaire!

verb 1 (come back) revenir [81]; **he returned ten minutes later** il est revenu dix minutes plus tard; 2 (get home) rentrer [1]; **to return from holiday** rentrer de vacances; **I'll ask her to phone as soon as she returns** je lui demanderai de vous appeler dès qu'elle rentre; 3 (to give back) rendre [3]; **Gemma's never returned the video** Gemma n'a jamais rendu la vidéo.

return fare noun prix M d'un billet aller-retour.

return ticket noun billet M aller-retour.

reveal verb révéler [24].

reverse verb 1 (in a car) faire [10] marche arrière; 2 **to reverse the charges** faire [10] un appel en PCV.

review noun (of a book, play, or film) critique F.

verb faire [10] la critique de (a play or concert); **the film was well reviewed** le film a eu une bonne critique.

revise verb réviser [1]; **Tessa's busy revising for her exams** Tessa est en train de réviser pour ses examens.

revision noun révision F.

revive verb ranimer [1].

revolting adjective infect; **the sausages are revolting** les saucisses sont infectes.

revolution noun révolution F; **the Fench Revolution** la Révolution française.

revolving door noun porte F à tambour.

reward noun récompense F; **a £100 reward** cent livres de récompense. verb récompenser [1].

rewarding adjective enrichissant.

rewind verb rembobiner [1] (a cassette or video).

rhinoceros noun rhinocéros M.

rhubarb noun rhubarbe F.

rhyme noun rime F.

rhythm noun rythme M.

rib noun côte F.

ribbon noun ruban M.

rice noun riz M; **chicken and rice** du poulet au riz; **rice pudding** le riz au lait.

rich adjective riche; **we're not very rich** nous ne sommes pas très riches; **the rich and the poor** les riches et les pauvres.

rid *adjective* **to get rid of something** se débarrasser de quelque chose; **we got rid of the car** nous nous sommes débarrassés de la voiture.

riddle *noun* devinette F.

ride *noun* tour M; **to go for a ride (on a bike)** faire un tour à vélo; **to go for a ride (on a horse)** faire une promenade à cheval.
verb **1 to learn to ride a bike** apprendre [64] à faire du vélo; **can you ride a bike?** sais-tu faire [10] du vélo?; **2 to learn to ride (a horse)** apprendre [3] à monter à cheval; **I've never ridden a horse** je ne suis jamais monté à cheval.

rider *noun* **1** (*on a horse*) cavalier M, cavalière F; **2** (*on a bike*) cycliste M & F.

ridiculous *adjective* ridicule.

riding *noun* équitation F; **to go riding** faire [10] de l'équitation.

riding school *noun* école F d'équitation.

rifle *noun* fusil M.

right *noun* **1** (*not left*) droite F; **on the right** à droite; **on my right** à ma droite; **2** (*to do something*) droit M; **the right to strike** le droit de grève; **you have no right to say that** tu n'as pas le droit de dire ça.
adjective, adverb **1** (*not left*) droit; **my right hand** ma main droite; **2** (*correct*) bon (F bonne); **the right answer** la bonne réponse; **the right telephone number** le bon numéro de téléphone; **the right amount of**

la bonne quantité de; **is this the right address?** est-ce que c'est la bonne adresse?; **3 to be right** (*a person*) avoir raison; **you see, I was right** tu vois, j'avais raison; **4 you were right to stay at home** tu as bien fait de rester chez toi; **he was right not to say anything** il a bien fait de ne rien dire; **5** (*moral*) bien; **it's not right to talk like that** ce n'est pas bien de parler comme ça.
adverb **1** (*direction*) à droite; **turn right at the lights** tournez à droite aux feux; **2** (*correctly*) comme il faut; **you're not doing it right** tu ne le fais pas comme il faut; **3** (*completely*) tout; **right at the bottom** tout au fond; **right at the beginning** tout au début; **right now** tout de suite; **right in the middle** en plein milieu; **4** (*okay*) bon; **right, let's go** bon, allons-y.

right-hand *adjective* **on the right-hand side** à droite.

right-handed *adjective* droitier (F droitière).

rind *noun* **1** (*on fruit*) peau F; **2** (*on cheese*) croûte F.

ring *noun* **1** (*on the phone*) **to give somebody a ring** appeler [18] quelqu'un; **2** (*for your finger*) bague F; **3** (*circle*) cercle M; **4 there was a ring at the door** on a sonné à la porte.
verb **1** (*a bell or phone*) sonner [1]; **the phone rang** le téléphone a sonné; **2** (*phone*) appeler [18]; **I'll ring you tomorrow** je t'appellerai demain; **could you ring for a taxi?** est-ce que tu peux appeler un taxi?
●**to ring back** rappeler [18]; **I'll ring**

you back later je te rappellerai tout à l'heure.
- to ring off raccrocher [1].

ring road noun rocade F.

rinse verb rincer [61].

riot noun émeute F.

rioting noun émeutes F plural.

rip verb déchirer [1].

ripe adjective mûr; are the tomatoes ripe? est-ce que les tomates sont mûres?

rip-off noun it's a rip-off! c'est de l'arnaque!

rise noun 1 hausse F; a rise in price une hausse de prix; 2 a pay rise une augmentation.
verb 1 (the sun) se lever [50]; when the sun rose quand le soleil s'est levé; 2 (prices) augmenter [1].

risk noun risque F; to take risks prendre des risques.
verb risquer [1]; he risks losing his job il risque de perdre son emploi.

river noun 1 rivière F; we picnicked on the edge of a river nous avons pique-niqué au bord d'une rivière; 2 fleuve M; the rivers of Europe les fleuves de l'Europe ('fleuve' is only used for a river which flows directly into the sea like the Thames in Britain or the Seine in France).

Riviera noun the French Riviera la Côte d'Azur.

road noun 1 route F; the road to London la route de Londres; 2 (in a town) rue F; the butcher's is on the other side of the road la

boucherie est de l'autre côté de la rue; 3 across the road en face; they live across the road from us ils habitent en face de chez nous.

road accident noun accident M de la route.

road map noun carte F routière.

roadside noun by the roadside au bord de la route.

road sign noun panneau M de signalisation (plural panneaux de signalisation).

roadworks plural noun travaux M plural.

roast noun rôti M.
adjective rôti; roast potatoes les pommes de terre rôties; roast beef le rôti de bœuf.

rob verb 1 voler [1] (a person); 2 dévaliser [1] (a bank).

robber noun voleur M, voleuse F.

robbery noun vol M; a bank robbery un hold-up.

robot noun robot M.

rock noun 1 (a big stone) rocher M; she was sitting on a rock elle était assise sur un rocher; 2 (the material) roche F; 3 (music) rock M; a rock band un groupe de rock; to dance rock and roll danser le rock.

rock climbing noun escalade F; to go rock climbing faire de l'escalade.

rock star noun rock-star F.

rocket noun fusée F.

rocking horse noun cheval M à bascule.

rocky adjective rocailleux (F rocailleuse).

rod noun **a fishing rod** une canne à pêche.

role noun rôle M; **to play the role of** jouer le rôle de.

roll noun 1 rouleau M (plural rouleaux); **a roll of fabric** un rouleau de tissu; **a roll of sellotape™** un rouleau de scotch™; **a toilet roll** un rouleau de papier hygiénique; **2 a bread roll** un petit pain.
verb rouler [1].

roller noun rouleau M (plural rouleaux).

rollerblades plural noun rollers M plural.

rollercoaster noun montagnes russes F plural (literally: Russian mountains).

roller skates plural noun patins M plural à roulettes.

Roman Catholic noun, adjective catholique M & F.

romantic adjective romantique.

roof noun toit M.

roof rack noun galerie F.

room noun 1 pièce F; **she's in the other room** elle est dans l'autre pièce; **it's the biggest room in the house** c'est la pièce la plus grande de la maison; **a three-room flat** un appartement à trois pièces; **2** (a bedroom) chambre F; **Freda's in her room** Freda est dans sa chambre; **I**

tidied my room last night j'ai rangé ma chambre hier soir; **3** (space) **place** F; **enough room for two** assez de place pour deux; **very little room** très peu de place.

roommate noun camarade M & F de chambre.

root noun racine F.

rope noun corde F.

rose noun rose F.

rosebush noun rosier M.

rot verb pourrir [2].

rota noun tableau M de service.

rotten adjective pourri.

rough adjective 1 (scratchy) rugueux (F rugueuse); **2** (vague) approximatif (F approximative); **a rough idea** une idée approximative; **3** (stormy) agité; **a rough sea** une mer agitée; **in rough weather** par gros temps; **4** (difficult) **to have a rough time** passer par une période difficile; **5** (to sleep rough) dormir à la dure.

roughly adjective (approximately) **roughly ten per cent** à peu près dix pour cent; **it takes roughly three hours** ça prend à peu près trois heures.

round noun 1 (in a tournament) manche F; **2** (of cards) partie F; **3 a round of drinks** une tournée; **it's my round** c'est ma tournée.
adjective rond; **a round table** une table ronde.
preposition 1 autour de; **round the city** autour de la ville; **round my arm** autour de mon bras; **they were sitting round the table** ils étaient

assis autour de la table; **2 to go
round the shops** faire les magasins;
to go round a museum visiter un
musée; **it's just round the corner**
c'est tout près.
adverb **1 to go round to
somebody's house** aller chez
quelqu'un; **we invited Sally round
for lunch** nous avons invité Sally à
déjeuner; **2 all the year round**
toute l'année.

roundabout *noun* **1** (*for traffic*)
rond-point M; **2** (*in a fairground*)
manège M.

route *noun* **1** (*that you plan*)
itinéraire M; **the best route is via
Calais** le meilleur itinéraire est par
Calais; **2 a bus route** un parcours
de bus.

routine *noun* routine F.

row¹ *noun* **1** rang M; **in the front
row** au premier rang; **in the back
row** au dernier rang; **2** rangée F; **a
row of books** une rangée de livres;
3 four times in a row quatre fois de
suite.

row² *verb* (*in a boat*) ramer [1]; **it's
your turn to row** c'est à toi de ramer;
we rowed across the lake nous
avons traversé le lac à la rame.

row³ *noun* **1** (*a quarrel*) dispute F;
to have a row se disputer; **they've
had a row** ils se sont disputés; **I had
a row with my parents** je me suis
disputé avec mes parents; **2** (*noise*)
vacarme M; **they were making a
terrible row** ils faisaient un
vacarme pas possible!

rowing *noun* aviron M; **to go
rowing** faire de l'aviron.

rowing boat *noun* barque F.

royal *adjective* royal (M *plural*
royaux); **the royal family** la famille
royale.

rub *verb* frotter [1]; **to rub your eyes**
se frotter les yeux.
●**to rub something out** effacer [61]
quelque chose.

rubber *noun* **1** (*an eraser*) gomme
F; **2** (*material*) caoutchouc M;
rubber soles des semelles en
caoutchouc.

rubbish *noun* **1** (*for the bin*)
ordures F *plural*; **2** (*nonsense*)
bêtises F *plural*; **you're talking
rubbish!** tu dis des bêtises!
adjective nul (F nulle); **the film was
rubbish** le film était nul; **they're a
rubbish band** c'est un groupe nul.

rubbish bin *noun* poubelle F.

rucksack *noun* sac M à dos.

rude *adjective* **1** impoli; **that's rude**
c'est impoli; **2 a rude joke** une
plaisanterie grossière; **a rude word**
un gros mot.

rug *noun* **1** tapis M; **2** (*a blanket*)
couverture F.

rugby *noun* rugby M; **to play
rugby** jouer au rugby; **a rugby
match** un match de rugby.

ruin *noun* ruine F; **in ruins** en
ruines.
verb **1** abîmer [1]; **you'll ruin your
jacket** tu vas abîmer ta veste;
2 gâcher [1] (*day, holiday*); **it ruined
my evening** ça m'a gâché la soirée.

rule *noun* **1** règle F; **the rules of the
game** les règles du jeu; **2 the**

school rules le règlement de l'école; **3 as a rule** en général.

ruler noun règle F; **I've lost my ruler** j'ai perdu ma règle.

rum noun rhum F.

rumour noun rumeur F.

run noun **1 to go for a run** courir; **2** (in cricket) point M; **to score fifteen runs** marquer quinze points; **3 in the long run** à long terme.

verb **1** courir [29]; **I ran ten kilometres** j'ai couru dix kilomètres; **he ran across the pitch** il a traversé le terrain en courant; **Kitty ran for the bus** Kitty a couru pour attraper le bus; **2** (organize) organiser [1]; **who's running this concert?** qui est-ce qui organise ce concert?; **3** diriger [52] (a business); **he ran the firm for forty years** il a dirigé l'entreprise pendant quarante ans; **4** (a train or bus) circuler [1]; **the buses don't run on Sundays** les bus ne circulent pas le dimanche; **5 to run a bath** faire [10] couler un bain.

●**to run away** s'enfuir [44].

●**to run into** rentrer [1] dans; **the car ran into a lamp-post** la voiture est rentrée dans un réverbère.

●**to run out of something: we've run out of bread** il ne reste plus de pain; **I'm running out of money** je n'ai presque plus d'argent.

●**to run somebody over** écraser [1] quelqu'un; **you'll get run over!** tu vas te faire écraser!

runner noun coureur M, coureuse F.

runner-up noun second M, seconde F.

running noun (for exercise) course F.

adjective **1 running water** l'eau courante; **2 three days running** trois jours de suite; **six times running** six fois de suite.

runway noun piste F.

rush noun (a hurry) **to be in a rush** être pressé; **sorry, I'm in a rush** désolé, je suis pressé.

verb **1** (hurry) se dépêcher [50]; **I must rush!** il faut que je me dépêche!; **2** (run) se précipiter [1]; **she rushed into the street** elle s'est précipitée dans la rue; **3 Louise was rushed to hospital** on a emmené Louise d'urgence à l'hôpital.

rush hour noun heures F plural de pointe; **in the rush hour** aux heures de pointe.

Russia noun Russie F; **in Russia** en Russie.

Russian noun **1** (a person) Russe M & F; **2** (the language) russe M. adjective russe.

rust noun rouille F.

rusty adjective rouillé.

rye noun seigle M.

S s

Sabbath noun **1** (Jewish) sabbat M; **2** (Christian) dimanche M.

sack noun **1** sac M; **2 to get the**

sack être mis à la porte.
verb to sack somebody mettre [11] quelqu'un à la porte.

sad *adjective* triste.

saddle *noun* selle F.

saddlebag *noun* sacoche F.

sadly *adverb* 1 tristement; she looked at me sadly elle m'a regardé tristement; 2 (*unfortunately*) malheureusement.

safe *adjective* 1 (*out of danger*) hors de danger; to feel safe se sentir en sécurité; 2 (*not dangerous*) pas dangereux (F pas dangereuse); the path is safe le sentier n'est pas dangereux; it's not safe c'est dangereux.

safety *noun* sécurité F.

safety belt *noun* ceinture F de sécurité.

safety pin *noun* épingle F de nourrice.

Sagittarius *noun* Sagittaire M; Kylie's Sagittarius Kylie est Sagittaire.

sail *noun* voile F.

sailing *noun* voile F; to go sailing faire de la voile; she's does a lot of sailing elle fait beaucoup de voile.

sailing boat *noun* voilier M.

sailor *noun* marin M.

saint *noun* saint M, sainte F.

sake *noun* 1 for your mother's sake par égard pour ta mère; 2 for heaven's sake! nom de Dieu!

salad *noun* salade F; a tomato salad une salade de tomates.

salad dressing *noun* vinaigrette F.

salami *noun* saucisson M.

salary *noun* salaire M.

sale *noun* 1 (*selling*) vente F; the sale of the house la vente de la maison; 'for sale' 'à vendre'; 2 the sales les soldes F *plural*; I bought it in the sales je l'ai acheté en solde.

sales assistant *noun* vendeur M, vendeuse F.

salesman *noun* représentant M; he's a salesman il est représentant.

saleswoman *noun* représentante F.

salmon *noun* saumon M.

salt *noun* sel M.

salty *adjective* salé.

Salvation Army *noun* armée F du Salut.

same *adjective* 1 même; she said the same thing elle a dit la même chose; her birthday's the same day as mine son anniversaire est le même jour que le mien; at the same time en même temps; their car's the same as ours ils ont la même voiture que nous; 2 the same (*after verb*) pareil; the two bikes are not the same les deux vélos ne sont pas pareils; it's not the same ce n'est pas pareil.

sample *noun* échantillon M; a free sample un échantillon gratuit.

sand *noun* sable M.

sandal *noun* sandale F; a pair of sandals une paire de sandales.

sand castle noun château M de sable (plural châteaux de sable).

sandpaper noun papier M de verre.

sandwich noun sandwich M; **a ham sandwich** un sandwich au jambon.

sanitary towel noun serviette hygiénique F.

Santa Claus noun le père Noël.

sarcastic adjective sarcastique.

sardine noun sardine F.

satchel noun cartable M.

satellite noun satellite M.

satellite dish noun antenne parabolique F.

satellite television noun télévision F par satellite.

satisfactory adjective satisfaisant.

satisfied adjective satisfait.

satisfy verb satisfaire [10].

satisfying adjective 1 (pleasing) satisfaisant; 2 **a satisfying meal** un repas consistant.

Saturday noun samedi M; **on Saturday** samedi; **I'm going out on Saturday** je sors samedi; **see you on Saturday!** à samedi!; **on Saturdays** le musée est fermé le samedi; **every Saturday** tous les samedis; **last Saturday** samedi dernier; **next Saturday** samedi prochain; **to have a Saturday job** travailler le samedi.

sauce noun sauce F.

saucepan noun casserole F.

saucer noun soucoupe F.

sausage noun 1 saucisse F; 2 (salami) saucisson M.

save verb 1 (rescue) sauver [1]; **to save somebody's life** sauver la vie à quelqu'un; **the doctors saved his life** les médecins lui ont sauvé la vie; 2 mettre [11] de côté (money, food); **I've saved £60** j'ai mis soixante livres de côté; 3 (avoid spending) économiser [1]; **I walk to school to save money** je vais à l'école à pied pour économiser de l'argent; 4 **to save time** gagner [1] du temps; **we'll take a taxi to save time** on va prendre un taxi pour gagner du temps; 5 (on a computer) sauvegarder [1].
●**to save up** mettre [11] de l'argent à côté; **I'm saving up to go to Spain** je mets de l'argent à côté pour aller en Espagne.

savings plural noun économies F plural; **I've spent all my savings** j'ai dépensé toutes mes économies.

savoury adjective salé; **I prefer savoury things to sweet things** j'aime mieux les choses salées que les choses sucrées.

saw noun scie F.

sawdust noun sciure F.

sax noun saxo M (informal); **to play the sax** jouer du saxo.

saxophone noun saxophone M; **to play the saxophone** jouer du saxophone.

say verb 1 dire [9]; **what did you say?** qu'est-ce que tu as dit?; **she says she's tired** elle dit qu'elle est fatiguée; **he said to wait here** il a dit d'attendre ici; **as they say** comme on dit; **that goes without saying** cela va sans dire; **2 to say something again** répéter [24] quelque chose.

saying noun dicton M; **as the saying goes** comme on dit.

scale noun 1 (of a map or model) échelle F; **large-scale** à grande échelle; **2** (extent) ampleur F; **the scale of the disaster** l'ampleur du désastre; **3** (in music) gamme F; **4** (of a fish) écaille F.

scales noun 1 balance F singular; **kitchen scales** une balance de cuisine; **2 bathroom scales** un pèse-personne M singular.

scallop noun coquille F Saint-Jacques.

scandal noun 1 scandale M; **2** (gossip) ragots M plural.

Scandinavia noun Scandinavie F.

Scandinavian adjective scandinave.

scar noun cicatrice F.

scarce adjective rare.

scare noun 1 panique F; **it caused a scare** cela a provoqué une panique; **2 a bomb scare** une alerte à la bombe.
verb **to scare somebody** faire [10] peur à quelqu'un; **you scared me!** tu m'as fait peur!

scarecrow noun épouvantail M.

scared adjective **to be scared** avoir [5] peur; **I'm scared!** j'ai peur; **to be scared of** avoir [5] peur de; **he's scared of dogs** il a peur des chiens;

I'm scared of falling j'ai peur de tomber.

scarf noun 1 (silky) foulard M; **2** (long, warm) écharpe F.

scary adjective effrayant.

scene noun 1 (of an incident or a crime) lieux M plural; **to be on the scene** être sur les lieux; **the scene of the crime** le lieu du crime; **2** (world) monde M; **on the music scene** dans le monde de la musique; **3 scenes of violence** des incidents violents; **4 to make a scene** faire une scène.

scenery noun 1 (landscape) paysage M; **2** (theatrical) décors M plural.

scent noun parfum M.

scented adjective parfumé.

schedule noun programme M.

scheduled flight noun vol régulier M.

scheme noun projet M.

scholarship noun bourse F.

school noun école F; **at school** à l'école; **to go to school** aller à l'école.

schoolbook noun livre scolaire M.

schoolboy noun écolier M.

schoolchildren plural noun écoliers M plural.

schoolfriend noun camarade M & F de classe.

schoolgirl noun écolière F.

science noun science F; **I like science** j'aime la science; **the**

science teacher le prof de sciences.

science fiction noun science-fiction F.

scientific adjective scientifique.

scientist noun scientifique M & F.

scissors plural noun ciseaux M plural; **a pair of scissors** une paire de ciseaux.

scoff verb (eat) bouffer [1] (informal).

scooter noun 1 (motor scooter) scooter M; 2 (for a child) trottinette F.

score noun score M; **the score was three two** le score était trois à deux.
verb 1 marquer [1]; **Lenny scored a goal** Lenny a marqué un but; **I scored three points** j'ai marqué trois points; 2 (keep score) compter [1] les points.

Scorpio noun Scorpion M; **Jess is Scorpio** Jess est Scorpion.

Scot noun Écossais M, Écossaise F; **the Scots** les Écossais M plural.

Scotland noun Écosse F; **in Scotland** en Écosse; **to Scotland** en Écosse; **Pauline's from Scotland** Pauline est écossaise.

Scots adjective écossais; **a Scots accent** un accent écossais.

Scotsman noun Écossais M.

Scotswoman noun Écossaise F.

Scottish adjective écossais; **a Scottish accent** un accent écossais.

scout noun scout M.

scrambled eggs plural noun œufs brouillés M plural.

scrap noun **a scrap of paper** un bout de papier.

scrapbook noun album M.

scrape verb gratter [1].

scratch noun 1 (on your skin) égratignure F; 2 (on a surface) rayure F; ★ **to start from scratch** partir de zéro.
verb (scratch yourself) se gratter [1]; **to scratch your head** se gratter la tête.

scream noun cri M.
verb crier [1].

screen noun écran M; **on the screen** à l'écran.

screw noun vis F.
verb visser [1].

screwdriver noun tournevis M.

scribble verb griffonner [1].

scrub verb récurer [1] (a saucepan); **to scrub your nails** se brosser [1] les ongles.

sculpture noun sculpture F.

sculptor noun sculpteur M; **Rebecca's a sculptor** Rebecca est sculpteur.

sea noun mer F.

seafood noun fruits M plural de mer; **I love seafood** j'adore les fruits de mer.

seagull noun mouette F.

seal noun (animal) phoque M.
verb coller [1] (envelope).

seaman noun marin M.

search verb 1 fouiller [1]; **I've searched my desk but I can't find the letter** j'ai fouillé dans mon bureau mais je ne trouve pas la lettre; 2 **to search for** chercher [1]; **I've been searching everywhere for the scissors** j'ai cherché les ciseaux partout.

seashell noun coquillage M.

seasick adjective **to be seasick** avoir le mal de mer.

seaside noun **at the seaside** au bord de la mer.

season noun saison F; **the rugby season** la saison de rugby; **strawberries are not in season at the moment** ce n'est pas la saison des fraises en ce moment; **off-season prices** des prix hors saison.

season ticket noun carte F d'abonnement.

seat noun 1 siège M; **the front seat** (in a car) le siège avant; **the back seat** le siège arrière; **take a seat** assieds-toi; 2 (in a cinema, theatre, etc) place F; **to book a seat** réserver une place; **can you keep my seat?** est-ce que tu peux garder ma place?

seatbelt noun ceinture F de sécurité.

seaweed noun algues F plural.

second noun seconde F; **can you wait a second?** est-ce que tu peux attendre une seconde? adjective 1 deuxième; **for the second time** pour la deuxième fois; 2 **the second of July** le deux juillet.

secondary school noun 1 collège M (up to the end of the equivalent of Year 10); 2 lycée M (for the equivalent of Years 11 to 13).

secondhand adjective, adverb d'occasion; **a secondhand bike** un vélo d'occasion; **I bought it secondhand** je l'ai acheté d'occasion.

secondly adverb deuxièmement.

secret noun secret M; **to keep a secret** garder un secret; **in secret** en secret. adjective secret (F secrète); **a secret plan** un projet secret.

secretarial college noun école F de secrétariat.

secretary noun secrétaire M & F; **she's a secretary** elle est secrétaire; **the secretary's office** le secrétariat.

secretly adverb secrètement.

sect noun secte F.

section noun section F.

security noun sécurité F.

security guard noun vigile M; **he's a security guard** il est vigile.

see verb 1 voir [13]; **I saw Lindy yesterday** j'ai vu Lindy hier; **have you seen the film?** est-ce que tu as vu le film?; **I haven't see her for ages** ça fait une éternité que je l'ai pas vue; **I'll see what I can do** je vais voir ce que je peux faire; 2 **to be able to see** voir [13]; **I can't see anything** je ne vois rien; 3 **see you!** salut! **see you on Saturday!** à samedi!; **see you soon!** à bientôt!

● **to see to something** s'occuper [1] de

quelque chose; **Jo's seeing to the drinks** Jo s'occupe des boissons.

seed noun graine F; **to plant seeds** semer des graines.

seem verb 1 paraître [57]; **it seems odd to me** ça me paraît bizarre; **it seems he's left** il paraît qu'il est parti; 2 (look, appear to be) avoir [5] l'air; **he seems a bit shy** il a l'air un peu timide; **the museum seems to be closed** le musée a l'air d'être fermé.

seesaw noun tapecul M.

select verb sélectionner [1].

self-confidence noun confiance F en soi; **she doesn't have much self-confidence** elle n'a pas beaucoup de confiance en elle.

self-contained noun **a self-contained flat** un appartement indépendant.

self-employed noun **the self-employed** les travailleurs indépendants M plural. adjective **to be self-employed** travailler à son compte; **my parents are self-employed** mes parents travaillent à leur compte.

selfish adjective égoïste.

self-service adjective **a self-service restaurant** un self (informal).

sell verb vendre [3]; **to sell something to somebody** vendre quelque chose à quelqu'un; **I sold him my bike** je lui ai vendu mon vélo; **the house has been sold** la maison a été vendue; **the concert's sold**

out il ne reste plus de billets pour le concert.

sell-by date noun date F limite de vente.

Sellotape™ noun Scotch™ M. verb **to sellotape something** scotcher [1] quelque chose (informal).

semi noun maison jumelée F (literally: a twinned house); **we live in a semi** nous habitons dans une maison jumelée.

semicircle noun demi-cercle M.

semicolon noun point-virgule M.

semi-detached house noun maison jumelée F (literally: a twinned house); **we live in a semi-detached house** nous habitons dans une maison jumelée.

semi-final noun demi-finale F.

semi-skimmed milk noun lait demi-écrémé M.

send verb envoyer [40]; **to send something to somebody** envoyer quelque chose à quelqu'un; **I sent her a present for her birthday** je lui ai envoyé un cadeau pour son anniversaire.
- **to send somebody back** renvoyer [40] quelqu'un.
- **to send something back** renvoyer [40] quelque chose.

sender noun expéditeur M, expéditrice F.

senior citizen noun personne F du troisième âge.

sensational adjective sensationnel (F sensationnelle).

sense noun 1 sens M; **common sense** le bon sens; **it doesn't make sense** ça n'a pas de sens; **it makes sense** ça paraît logique; **to have a sense of humour** avoir le sens de l'humour; **she has no sense of humour** elle n'a aucun sens de l'humour; 2 **the sense of smell** l'odorat M; **the sense of touch** le toucher.

sensible adjective raisonnable; **she's very sensible** elle est très raisonnable; **it's a sensible decision** c'est une décision raisonnable.

sensitive adjective sensible; **for sensitive skin** pour peaux sensibles.

sentence noun 1 phrase F; **écris une phrase en français** write a sentence in French; 2 **the death sentence** la peine de mort. verb condamner [1]; **to be sentenced to death** être condamné à mort.

sentimental adjective sentimental (M plural sentimentaux).

separate adjective 1 à part; **in a separate pile** dans une pile à part; **on a separate sheet of paper** sur une feuille à part; 2 (different) autre; **that's a separate problem** c'est un autre problème; 3 **they have separate rooms** ils ont chacun leur chambre. verb 1 séparer [1]; 2 (a couple) se séparer [1].

separately adverb séparément.

separation noun séparation F.

September noun septembre M; **in September** en septembre.

sequel noun suite F.

sequence noun 1 série F; **a sequence of events** une série d'événements; 2 **in sequence** dans l'ordre; 3 (in a film) séquence F.

sergeant noun 1 (in the police) brigadier M; 2 (in the army) sergent M.

serial noun feuilleton M.

series noun série F; **a television series** une série télévisée.

serious adjective 1 sérieux (F sérieuse); **a serious discussion** une discussion sérieuse; **are you serious?** sérieusement?; 2 grave (illness, injury, mistake, problem); **we have a serious problem** nous avons un grave problème.

seriously adverb 1 sérieusement; **seriously, I have to go now** sérieusement je dois partir maintenant; **seriously?** vraiment?; 2 **to take somebody seriously** prendre quelqu'un au sérieux; 3 gravement (ill, injured); **she is seriously ill** elle est gravement malade.

servant noun domestique M & F.

serve noun (in tennis) service M; **it's my serve** c'est à moi de servir. verb 1 (in tennis) servir [71]; 2 **can you serve the vegetables, please?** est-ce que tu peux servir les légumes, s'il te plaît?; **they served the fish with a lemon sauce** ils ont servi le poisson accompagné d'une sauce au citron; ★ **it serves him right** c'est bien fait pour lui.

service noun 1 (*in a restaurant, from a company, etc*) service M; **the service is very slow** le service est très lent; **service is included** le service est compris; **2 the emergency services** les services des urgences; 3 (*church service*) office M; 4 (*of a car or machine*) révision F.
verb réviser [1] (*a car or a machine*).

service area noun aire F de services.

service charge noun service M; **what is the service charge?** le service est de combien?; **there is no service charge** le service est compris.

service station noun station-service F (*plural* stations-service).

serviette noun serviette F.

session noun séance F.

set noun 1 (*for playing a game*) jeu M (*plural* jeux); **a chess set** un jeu d'échecs; **2 a train set** un petit train; 3 (*in tennis*) set M.
adjective fixe; **at a set time** à une heure fixe; **a set menu** un menu fixe.
verb 1 fixer [1] (*date, time*); 2 établir [2] (*record*); **3 to set the table** mettre [11] la table; **to set an alarm clock** mettre [11] un réveil; **I've set my alarm for seven** j'ai mis mon réveil à sept heures; 4 **to set a watch** régler [24] une montre; 5 (*sun*) se coucher [1].
● **to set off** partir [58]; **we're setting off at ten** nous allons partir à dix heures; **they set off for Paris**

yesterday ils sont partis pour Paris hier.
● **to set off something** 1 faire [10] partir (*firework*); 2 faire [10] exploser (*bomb*); 3 déclencher [1] (*alarm*).
● **to set out** partir [58]; **they set out for Paris yesterday** ils sont partis pour Paris hier.

settee noun canapé M.

settle verb régler [24] (*a bill or a problem*).

seven number sept; **Rosie's seven** Rosie a sept ans.

seventeen number dix-sept; **Jonny's seventeen** Jonny a dix-sept ans.

seventh adjective septième; **on the seventh floor** au septième étage; **the seventh of July** le sept juillet.

seventies plural noun **the seventies** les années soixante-dix; **in the seventies** aux années soixante-dix.

seventieth adjective soixant-dixième; **it's her seventieth birthday** elle fête ses soixante-dix ans.

seventy number soixante-dix; **my grandma's seventy** ma grand-mère a soixante-dix ans.

several adjective, pronoun plusieurs; **I've seen her several times** je l'ai vue plusieurs fois; **I've read several of her novels** j'ai lu plusieurs de ses romans; **he took several** il en a pris plusieurs.

sew verb coudre [28].

sewing noun couture F; **I like sewing** j'aime la couture.

sewing machine noun machine F à coudre.

sex noun sexe M.

sex education noun éducation sexuelle F.

sexism noun sexisme M.

sexist adjective sexiste; **sexist remarks** des propos sexistes.

sexual adjective sexuel (F sexuelle).

sexual harassment noun harcèlement sexuel M.

sexuality noun sexualité F.

sexy adjective sexy.

shabby adjective miteux (F miteuse).

shade noun 1 (of a colour) ton M; **a pretty shade of green** un joli vert; 2 **in the shade** à l'ombre.

shadow noun ombre F.

shake verb 1 (tremble) trembler [1]; **my hands are shaking** j'ai les mains qui tremblent; 2 **to shake something** secouer [1] quelque chose; 3 **to shake hands with somebody** serrer [1] la main à quelqu'un; **she shook hands with me** elle m'a serré la main; **we shook hands** nous nous sommes serré la main; 4 **to shake your head** (meaning no) faire [10] non de la tête.

shaken adjective bouleversé; **I was shaken by the news** j'ai été bouleversé par la nouvelle.

shall verb **shall I come with you?**

est-ce que tu veux que je t'accompagne?; **shall we stop now?** si on s'arrêtait maintenant?

shallow adjective peu profond; **the water's very shallow here** l'eau est très peu profonde ici.

shambles noun pagaille F (informal); **it was a total shambles!** ça a été la pagaille complète!

shame noun 1 honte F; **shame on you!** tu devrais avoir honte!; 2 **what a shame!** quel dommage!; **it's a shame she can't come** c'est dommage qu'elle ne puisse pas venir (note that 'c'est dommage que' is followed by a verb in the subjunctive).

shameful adjective honteux (F honteuse).

shampoo noun shampooing M; **I bought some shampoo** j'ai acheté du shampooing.

shamrock noun trèfle M.

shandy noun panaché M; **a half of shandy** un demi panaché.

shape noun forme F.

share noun 1 part F; **your share of the money** ta part de l'argent; **he paid his fair share** il a payé sa part; 2 (in a company) action F. verb partager [52]; **I'm sharing a room with Emma** je partage une chambre avec Emma.

shark noun requin M.

sharp adjective 1 (knife) bien aiguisé; **this knife isn't very sharp** ce couteau ne coupe pas très bien; 2 **a sharp pencil** un crayon bien taillé; 3 **a sharp bend** un virage brusque; 4 (*clever*) intelligent.

shave *verb* 1 (*have a shave*) se raser [h]; **he's just shaving** il est en train de se raser; 2 **to shave your legs** se raser [1] les jambes; **to shave off your beard** se raser la barbe.

shaver *noun* **an electric shaver** un rasoir électrique.

shaving cream *noun* crème F à raser.

shaving foam *noun* mousse F à raser.

she *pronoun* elle; **she's in her room** elle est dans sa chambre; **she's a student** elle est étudiante; **she's a very good teacher** c'est un très bon prof; **here she is!** la voici!; **there she is!** la voilà!

shed *noun* remise F.

sheep *noun* mouton M.

sheepdog *noun* chien M de berger (*plural* chiens de berger).

sheer *adjective* 1 pur; **it's sheer stupidity!** c'est de la pure bêtise!; 2 (*tights*) extra-fin.

sheet *noun* 1 (*for a bed*) drap M; 2 **a sheet of paper** une feuille de papier; **a blank sheet** une feuille blanche; 3 (*of glass or metal*) plaque; ★ **to be as white as a sheet** être blanc comme un linge; **she was as white as a sheet** elle était blanche comme un linge.

shelf *noun* 1 (*in the home*) étagère F; **a set of shelves** une étagère; 2 (*in a shop, in a fridge*) rayon M.

shell *noun* 1 (*of an egg or a nut*)

coquille F; 2 (*seashell*) coquillage M; 3 (*explosive*) obus M.

shellfish *noun* fruits M *plural* de mer.

shelter *noun* 1 abri M; **in the shelter of** à l'abri de; **to take shelter from the rain** se mettre à l'abri de la pluie; 2 **a bus shelter** un abribus™.

shepherd *noun* berger M.

sheriff *noun* shérif M.

sherry *noun* sherry M.

Shetland Islands *plural noun* îles Shetland F *plural*.

shield *noun* bouclier M.

shift *noun* service M; **the night shift** le service de nuit; **to be on night shift** être de nuit.
verb **to shift something** déplacer [61] quelque chose; **can you help me shift this table?** est-ce que tu peux m'aider à déplacer cette table?

shifty *adjective* louche; **he looks a bit shifty** il a l'air un peu louche; **a shifty-looking guy** un type un peu louche.

shin *noun* tibia M.

shine *verb* briller [1].

shiny *adjective* brillant.

ship *noun* 1 bateau M; 2 **a passenger ship** un paquebot; 3 (*large naval vessel*) navire M.

shipbuilding *noun* construction navale F.

shipyard *noun* chantier naval M.

shirt *noun* 1 (*man's*) chemise F; 2 (*woman's*) chemisier M.

shiver verb frissonner [1].

shock noun 1 choc M; **it was a shock** ça a été un choc; **it gave me a shock** j'ai eu un choc; 2 **an electric shock** une décharge; **to get an electric shock** prendre une décharge.
verb choquer [1].

shocked adjective choqué.

shocking adjective choquant.

shoe noun chaussure F; **a pair of shoes** une paire de chaussures.

shoelace noun lacet M.

shoe polish noun cirage M.

shoe shop noun magasin M de chaussures.

shoot verb 1 (fire) tirer [1]; **to shoot at somebody** tirer sur quelqu'un; **she shot him in the leg** elle lui a tiré une balle dans la jambe; **he was shot in the arm** il a reçu une balle dans le bras; 2 (kill) abattre [21]; **he was shot by terrorists** il a été abattu par des terroristes; 3 (execute) fusiller [1]; 4 (in football, hockey) shooter [1]; 5 **to shoot a film** tourner [1] un film.

shop noun magasin M; **a shoe shop** un magasin de chaussures; **to go round the shops** faire les magasins.

shop assistant noun vendeur M, vendeuse F; **Brad's a shop assistant** Brad est vendeur.

shopkeeper noun commerçant M, commerçante F.

shoplifter noun voleur à l'étalage M, voleuse à l'étalage F.

shoplifting noun vol M à l'étalage.

shopping noun courses F plural; **can you put the shopping away?** est-ce que tu peux ranger les courses?; **I've got a lot of shopping to do** j'ai beaucoup de courses à faire; **to go shopping** (for food) faire des courses; (for fun, to buy clothes or presents) faire du shopping.

shopping bag noun sac M à provisions.

shopping trolley noun 1 (in a supermarket) chariot M; 2 (personal) caddie™ M.

shop window noun vitrine F.

short adjective 1 court; **a short dress** une robe courte; **she has short hair** elle a les cheveux courts; 2 **a short break** une petite pause; **to go for a short walk** faire une petite promenade; **it's a short walk from the station** c'est à quelques minutes à pied de la gare; 3 **to be short of something** ne pas avoir beaucoup de quelque chose; **we're a bit short of money at the moment** nous n'avons pas beaucoup d'argent en ce moment; **we're getting short of time** il ne nous reste pas beaucoup de temps.

shortage noun pénurie F.

shortbread noun sablé M.

shortcrust pastry noun pâte brisée F.

short cut noun raccourci M; **we took a short cut** nous avons pris un raccourci.

shortly adverb bientôt.

shorts plural noun short M singular;

a pair of shorts un short; **my red shorts** mon short rouge.

short-sighted adjective myope; **I'm short-sighted** je suis myope.

short story noun nouvelle F.

shot noun 1 (from a gun) coup M de feu (plural coups de feu); 2 (a photo) photo F; **I took several shots of the garden** j'ai pris plusieurs photos du jardin.

shotgun noun fusil M de chasse (plural fusils de chasse).

should verb 1 ('should' is translated by the conditional tense of 'devoir') devoir [8]; **you should ask Simon** tu devrais demander à Simon; **the potatoes should be cooked now** les pommes de terre devraient être cuites maintenant; 2 ('should have' is translated by the past conditional tense of 'devoir') **you should have told me** tu aurais dû me le dire; **I shouldn't have stayed** je n'aurais pas dû rester; 3 ('should' meaning 'would' is translated by the conditional tense of the verb) **I should forget it if I were you** à ta place je l'oublierais; 4 **I should think** à mon avis; **I should think he's forgotten** à mon avis, il a oublié.

shoulder noun épaule F.

shoulder bag noun sac M à bandoulière.

shout noun cri M.
verb crier [1]; **stop shouting!** arrêtez de crier!; **they shouted at us to come back** ils nous ont crié de revenir.

shovel noun pelle F.

show noun 1 (on stage) spectacle M; **we went to see a show** nous sommes allés voir un spectacle; 2 (on TV) émission F; **he has a TV show** il a une émission à la télé; 3 (exhibition) salon M; **the motor show** le salon des automobiles.
verb 1 montrer [1]; **to show something to somebody** montrer quelque chose à quelqu'un; **I'll show you my photos** je te montrerai mes photos; **to show somebody how to do** montrer à quelqu'un comment on fait; **he showed me how to make pancakes** il m'a montré comment on fait les crêpes; 2 **it shows!** ça se voit!

● **to show off** frimer [1] (informal).

shower noun 1 (in a bathroom) douche F; **to have a shower** prendre une douche; 2 (of rain) averse F.

show-jumping noun saut M d'obstacles.

show-off noun frimeur M, frimeuse F (informal).

shriek verb hurler [1].

shrimp noun crevette F.

shrink verb rétrécir [2].

Shrove Tuesday noun mardi gras M.

shrug verb **to shrug your shoulders** hausser [1] les épaules.

shuffle verb **to shuffle the cards** battre [21] les cartes.

shut adjective fermé; **the shops are shut** les magasins sont fermés.
verb fermer [1]; **can you shut the door please?** est-ce que tu peux

shutter

fermer la porte, s'il te plaît?; **the shops shut at six** les magasins ferment à six heures.

● **to shut up** (*be quiet*) se taire [76]; **shut up!** tais-toi!

shutter *noun* volet M.

shuttle *noun* navette F; **there's a shuttle service from the airport** il y a une navette de l'aéroport.

shuttlecock *noun* volant M.

shy *adjective* timide.

shyness *noun* timidité F.

Sicily *noun* Sicile F; **to Sicily** en Sicile; **in Sicily** en Sicile.

sick *adjective* 1 (*ill*) malade; 2 **to be sick** (*vomit*) vomir [2]; **I was sick several times** j'ai vomi plusieurs fois; **to feel sick** avoir envie de vomir; 3 **a sick joke** une plaisanterie malsaine; 4 **to be sick of something** en avoir assez de quelque chose; **I'm sick of staying at home every night** j'en ai assez de rester à la maison tous les soirs.

sickness *noun* maladie F.

side *noun* 1 côté M; **on the other side of the street** de l'autre côté de la rue; **on the wrong side** du mauvais côté; **I'm on your side** (*I agree with you*) je suis de ton côté; 2 (*edge*) bord M; **at the side of the road** au bord de la route; **by the side of the pool** au bord de la piscine; 3 (*team*) équipe F; **she plays on our side** elle joue dans notre équipe; 4 **to take sides** prendre parti; 5 **side by side** côte à côte.

sideboard *noun* buffet M.

sideburns *noun* pattes F *plural*.

side-effect *noun* effet secondaire M.

side street *noun* petite rue F.

sieve *noun* passoire F.

sigh *noun* soupir M. *verb* pousser [1] un soupir.

sight *noun* 1 spectacle M; **it was a marvellous sight** c'était un spectacle merveilleux; 2 **at the sight of** à la vue de; 3 (*eyesight*) vue F; **to have poor sight** avoir une mauvaise vue; **to know somebody by sight** connaître quelqu'un de vue; **out of sight** caché; 4 **to see the sights** visiter les attractions touristiques.

sightseeing *noun* tourisme M; **to do some sightseeing** faire du tourisme.

sign *noun* 1 (*notice*) panneau M (*plural* panneaux); **there's a sign on the door** il y a un panneau sur la porte; 2 (*trace, indication*) signe M; 3 (*of the Zodiac*) signe M; **what sign are you?** tu es de quel signe? *verb* 1 signer [1]; **to sign a cheque** signer un chèque; 2 (*using sign language*) communiquer [1] en langage par signes.

● **to sign on** (*as unemployed*) s'inscrire [38] au chômage.

signal *noun* signal M (*plural* signaux).

signature *noun* signature F.

significance *noun* importance F.

significant *adjective* important.

sign language *noun* langage M par signes.

signpost noun poteau indicateur M (*plural* poteaux indicateurs).

silence noun silence M.

silent adjective silencieux (F silencieuse).

silicon chip noun puce électronique F.

silk noun soie F.
adjective en soie; **a silk shirt** une chemise en soie.

silky adjective soyeux (F soyeuse).

silly adjective idiot; **it was a really silly thing to do** c'était vraiment idiot.

silver noun argent M.
adjective **a silver spoon** une cuillère en argent; **a silver medal** une médaille d'argent.

similar adjective semblable.

similarity noun ressemblance F.

simmer verb **to simmer something** faire [10] mijoter quelque chose.

simple adjective facile.

simply adverb simplement.

sin noun péché M.

since preposition, adverb, conjunction **1** depuis (*notice that French uses the present tense where English uses 'have done' or 'have been doing'*) **I have been in Paris since Saturday** je suis à Paris depuis samedi; **I've been learning French since last year** j'apprends le français depuis l'année dernière; **2** depuis que (*the same thing happens with tenses here as above*)

since I have known him depuis que je le connais; **since I've been learning French** depuis que j'apprends le français; **3 I haven't seen her since** je ne l'ai pas revue depuis; **I haven't seen her since Monday** je ne l'ai pas revue depuis lundi; **since when?** depuis quand?; **4** (*because*) puisque; **since it was raining, the match was cancelled** puisqu'il pleuvait le match a été annulé.

sincere adjective sincère.

sincerely adverb **Yours sincerely** (*in a business letter*) Veuillez agréer Madame (or Monsieur) l'expression de mes sentiments distingués; (*to somebody you know*) Cordialement (*in French there are very formal and rigid formulae for signing letters*).

sing verb chanter [1].

singer noun chanteur M, chanteuse F.

singing noun **1** chant M; **a singing lesson** une leçon de chant; **2 I like singing** j'aime chanter.

single noun aller simple M; **a single to Lyons, please** un aller simple pour Lyon, s'il vous plaît.
adjective **1** (*not married*) célibataire; **2 a single room** une chambre pour une personne; **a single bed** un lit pour une personne; **3 not a single** pas un seul, pas une seule; **I haven't had a single reply** je n'ai pas reçu une seule réponse.

single parent noun **she's a single parent** elle élève ses enfants toute seule; **a single-parent family** une famille monoparentale.

singles *plural noun* (*in tennis*) simple M singular; **the women's singles** le simple dames; **the men's singles** le simple messieurs.

singular *noun* singulier M; **in the singular** au singulier.

sink *noun* évier M.
verb couler [1].

sir *noun* monsieur M; **yes, sir** oui, Monsieur.

siren *noun* sirène F.

sister *noun* sœur F; **my sister's ten** ma sœur a dix ans.

sister-in-law *noun* belle-sœur F (*plural* belles-sœurs).

sit *verb* **1** s'asseoir [20]; **you can sit on the sofa** tu peux t'asseoir sur le canapé; **I can sit on the floor** je peux m'asseoir par terre; **2 to be sitting** être [6] assis; **Leila was sitting on the sofa** Leila était assise sur le canapé; **3 to sit an exam** passer [1] un examen; **she's sitting her driving test on Thursday** elle passe son permis jeudi.

● **to sit down** s'asseoir [20]; **he sat down on a chair** il s'est assis sur une chaise; **do sit down** asseyez-vous.

sitcom *noun* comédie F de situation (*plural* comédies de situation).

site *noun* **1 a building site** un chantier; **2 a camping site** un camping; **3 an archaeological site** un site archéologique.

sitting room *noun* salon M.

situated *adjective* **to be situated**

être situé; **the house is situated in a small village** la maison est située dans un petit village.

situation *noun* situation F.

six *number* six; **Harry's six** Harry a six ans.

sixteen *number* seize; **Alice is sixteen** Alice a seize ans.

sixth *adjective* sixième; **on the sixth floor** au sixième étage; **the sixth of July** le six juillet.

sixty *number* soixante; **she's sixty** elle a soixante ans.

size *noun* **1** grandeur F; **it depends on the size of the house** ça dépend de la grandeur de la maison; **2** (*precise measurements*) dimensions F *plural*; **what size is the window?** quelles sont les dimensions de la fenêtre?; **3** (*in clothes*) taille F; **what size do you take?** quelle taille est-ce que vous faites?; **4** (*of shoes*) pointure F; **I take a size thirty-eight** je fais du trente-huit.

skate *noun* **1 an ice skate** un patin à glace; **2 a roller skate** un patin à roulettes.
verb **1** (*ice-skate*) faire [10] du patin à glace; **2** (*roller-skate*) faire [10] du patin à roulettes.

skateboard *noun* skateboard M.

skateboarding *noun* skateboard M; **to go skateboarding** faire du skateboard.

skating *noun* **1** (*ice*) patin M à glace; **to go skating** faire du patin à glace; **2** roller-skating le patin à roulettes; **to go roller-skating** faire du patin à roulettes.

skating rink noun patinoire F.

skeleton noun squelette M.

sketch noun 1 (drawing) croquis M; 2 (comedy routine) sketch M.

ski noun ski M.
verb faire [10] du ski; **he can ski** il sait faire du ski.

ski boot noun chaussure F de ski.

skid verb déraper [1]; **the car skidded** la voiture a dérapé.

skiing noun ski M; **to go skiing** faire du ski.

ski lift noun remonte-pente M.

skimmed milk noun lait écrémé M.

skin noun peau F (plural peaux).

skinhead noun skinhead M & F.

skinny adjective maigre.

skip noun (for rubbish) benne F.
verb 1 sauter [1] (a meal, part of a book); **I skipped a few chapters** j'ai sauté quelques chapitres; 2 **to skip a lesson** sécher un cours (informal).

ski pants noun fuseau M singular; **I bought some ski pants** j'ai acheté un fuseau.

ski suit noun combinaison F de ski.

skirt noun jupe F; **a long skirt** une jupe longue; **a straight skirt** une jupe droite; **a mini-skirt** une mini-jupe.

skittles plural noun quilles F

plural; **to play skittles** jouer aux quilles.

skull noun crâne M.

sky noun ciel M.

skyscraper noun gratte-ciel M (plural gratte-ciel).

slam verb claquer [1]; **she slammed the door** elle a claqué la porte.

slang noun argot M.

slap noun claque F.
verb **to slap somebody** donner [1] une claque à quelqu'un.

slate noun ardoise F.

sledge noun luge F.

sledging noun **to go sledging** faire [10] de la luge.

sleep noun sommeil M; **I had a good sleep** j'ai bien dormi; **to go to sleep** s'endormir [37].
verb dormir [37]; **she's sleeping** elle dort.

sleeping bag noun sac M de couchage.

sleeping pill noun somnifère M.

sleepy adjective **to be sleepy** avoir sommeil; **I feel sleepy** j'ai sommeil; **he was getting sleepy** il commençait à avoir sommeil.

sleet noun neige fondue F.

sleeve noun manche F; **a long-sleeved jumper** un pull à manches longues; **a short-sleeved shirt** une chemise à manches courtes; **to roll up your sleeves** retrousser ses manches.

slice noun tranche F; **a slice of ham** une tranche de jambon.

verb **to slice something** couper [1] quelque chose en tranches.

slide *noun* 1 (*photo*) diapositive F; 2 (*hairslide*) barrette F; 3 (*for sliding down*) toboggan M.

slight *adjective* léger (F légère); **there is a slight problem** il y a un léger problème.

slightly *adverb* légèrement.

slim *adjective* mince.
verb **I'm slimming** je fais un régime.

sling *noun* écharpe F; **to have your arm in a sling** avoir le bras en écharpe.

slip *noun* 1 (*mistake*) erreur F; 2 (*petticoat*)(*from waist*) jupon M; (*full-length*) combinaison F.
verb 1 (*slide*) glisser [1]; 2 **it had slipped my mind** j'avais oublié.

slipper *noun* pantoufle F.

slippery *adjective* glissant.

slope *noun* pente F.

slot *noun* fente F.

slot machine *noun* 1 (*games machine*) machine F à sous; 2 (*vending machine*) distributeur automatique M.

slow *adjective* 1 lent; **the service is a bit slow** le service est un peu lent; 2 **my watch is slow** ma montre retarde.
●**to slow down** ralentir [2].

slowly *adverb* 1 lentement; **he got up slowly** il s'est levé lentement; 2 (*speak, drive*) doucement; **can you speak more slowly, please?** est-ce que vous pouvez parler plus doucement, s'il vous plaît?

slug *noun* limace F.

slush *noun* neige fondue F.

sly *adjective* (*person*) rusé; ★ **on the sly** en douce.

smack *noun* claque F.
verb **to smack somebody** donner [1] une claque à quelqu'un.

small *adjective* petit (*goes before the noun*); **a small dog** un petit chien.

smart *adjective* 1 (*well-dressed, posh*) chic; **a smart restaurant** un restaurant chic; 2 (*clever*) intelligent.

smash *noun* **a car smash** un accident de voiture.
verb casser [1]; **they smashed a window** ils ont cassé une vitre.

smashing *adjective* formidable.

smell *noun* odeur F; **a nasty smell** une mauvaise odeur; **there's a smell of burning** ça sent le brûlé.
verb 1 sentir [58]; **I can't smell anything** je ne sens rien; **I can smell lavender** ça sent la lavande; 2 (*smell bad*) sentir [58] mauvais; **the drains smell** les égouts sentent mauvais.

smelly *adjective* qui sent mauvais; **her smelly dog** son chien qui sent mauvais.

smile *noun* sourire M.
verb sourire [68].

smoke *noun* fumée F.
verb fumer [1]; **she doesn't smoke** elle ne fume pas; **he smokes a pipe** il fume la pipe.

smoker *noun* fumeur M, fumeuse F.

smoking noun 'no smoking'
'défense de fumer'; **to give up
smoking** arrêter de fumer.

smooth adjective **1** lisse; **a smooth
surface** une surface lisse;
2 (person) mielleux (F mielleuse).

smug adjective suffisant.

smuggle verb **to smuggle
something** faire [10] passer quelque
chose en contrebande.

smuggler noun **1** contrebandier
M, contrebandière F; **2 a drugs
smuggler** un passeur de drogue.

smuggling noun **1** contrebande
F; **2** (of drugs or arms) trafic M.

snack noun casse-croûte M.

snail noun escargot M.

snake noun serpent M.

snap noun (card game) bataille F.
verb **1** (break) casser [1]; **2 to snap
your fingers** faire [10] claquer ses
doigts.

snapshot noun photo F.

snarl verb gronder [1].

snatch verb arracher [1]; **to snatch
something from somebody**
arracher quelque chose à quelqu'un;
he snatched my book il m'a arraché
mon livre; **she had her bag
snatched** on lui a arraché son sac.

sneak verb **to sneak in** entrer [1]
furtivement; **to sneak out** sortir [72]
furtivement; **he sneaked up on me**
il s'est approché de moi sans faire de
bruit.

sneeze verb éternuer [1].

sniff verb renifler [1].

snob noun snob M & F.

snobbery noun snobisme M.

snooker noun snooker M; **to play
snooker** jouer au snooker.

snooze noun somme M; **to have a
snooze** faire un petit somme.

snore verb ronfler [1].

snow noun neige F.
verb neiger [52]; **it's snowing** il
neige; **it's going to snow** il va
neiger.

snowball noun boule F de neige
(plural boules de neige).

snowman noun bonhomme M de
neige (plural bonshommes de
neige).

so conjunction, adverb **1** tellement;
he's so lazy il est tellement
paresseux; **the coffee's so hot I can't
drink it** le café est tellement chaud
que je n'arrive pas à le boire; **2 not
so** moins; **our house is a bit like
yours, but not so big** notre maison
est un peu comme la vôtre, mais
moins grande; **3 so much**
tellement; **I hate it so much!** je le
déteste tellement!; **4 so much, so
many** tellement de; **I have so much
work to do** j'ai tellement de travail à
faire; **we've got so many problems**
nous avons tellement de
problèmes; **5** (therefore) donc; **he
got up late, so he missed his train**
il s'est levé tard, donc il a raté son
train; **6** (starting a sentence) alors;
so what's your name? alors, tu
t'appelles comment?; **so what shall
we do?** alors, qu'est-ce qu'on fait?;
so what? et alors?; **7 so do I, so
did I** moi aussi; **'I live in Leeds'** –

'**so do I**' 'j'habite à Leeds' – 'moi
aussi'; '**I hated the film**' – 'so did
I' 'j'ai détesté le film' – 'moi aussi
so am I' moi aussi; **so do we** nous
aussi; **8 I think so** je crois; **I hope
so** j'espère.

soak verb tremper [1].

soaked adjective trempé; ★ **to be
soaked to the skin** être trempé
jusqu'aux os (literally: to be soaked to
the bones).

soaking adjective trempé; **soaking
wet** trempé.

soap noun 1 savon M; **a cake of
soap** un savon; 2 (soap opera: on
TV) feuilleton M.

soap powder noun lessive F.

sober adjective **to be sober** ne pas
avoir bu; **he's sober** il n'a pas bu;
are you sure she's sober? tu es sûr
qu'elle n'a pas bu?

soccer noun football M; **to play
soccer** jouer au football.

social adjective social (M plural
sociaux).

socialism noun socialisme M.

socialist noun, adjective socialiste
M & F.

social security noun 1 aide
sociale F; **to be on social security**
recevoir de l'aide sociale; 2 **the
social security** (the system)
sécurité sociale F.

social worker noun travailleur
social M (plural travailleurs
sociaux), travailleuse sociale F; **she's
a social worker** elle est travailleuse
sociale.

society noun société F.

sociology noun sociologie F.

sock noun chaussette F; **a pair of
socks** une paire de chaussettes.

socket noun (power point) prise F
de courant (plural prises de
courant).

sofa noun canapé M.

sofa bed noun canapé-lit M.

soft adjective doux (F douce); ★ **to
have a soft spot for somebody** avoir
un faible pour quelqu'un.

soft drink noun boisson non
alcoolisée F.

software noun logiciel M.

soft toy noun peluche F.

soil noun terre F.

solar energy noun énergie solaire
F.

soldier noun soldat M.

solicitor noun 1 (dealing with
property or documents) notaire M;
she's a solicitor elle est notaire;
2 (dealing with lawsuits) avocat M,
avocate F; **she's a solicitor** elle est
avocate.

solid adjective 1 massif (F massive);
a table made of solid pine une table
en pin massif; **a solid gold ring** une
bague en or massif; **solid silver**
argent massif; 2 (not flimsy) solide;
a solid structure une structure
solide.

solo noun solo M; **a guitar solo** un
solo de guitare.
adjective, adverb en solo; **a solo**

album un album en solo; **to play solo** jouer en solo.

soloist noun soliste M & F.

solution noun solution F.

solve verb résoudre [67].

some adjective, adverb 1 (followed by a singular noun) du (with a masculine noun), de la (with a feminine noun), de l' (with a noun beginning with a vowel or silent 'h'); **would you like some butter?** voulez-vous du beurre?; **may I have some salad?** puis-je prendre de la salade?; **can you lend me some money?** est-ce que tu peux me prêter de l'argent?; 2 (followed by a plural noun) des; **I've bought some apples** j'ai acheté des pommes; 3 (referring to something that has been mentioned) en; 'would you like butter?' – 'thanks, I've got some' 'veux-tu du beurre?' – 'merci, j'en ai'; **he's eaten some of it** il en a mangé un peu; 4 **some people think he's wrong** il y a des gens qui pensent qu'il a tort; 5 **some day** un de ces jours.

somebody, someone pronoun quelqu'un; **there's somebody in the garden** il y a quelqu'un dans le jardin.

somehow adverb 1 d'une manière ou d'une autre; **I've got to finish this essay somehow** je dois finir cette rédaction d'une manière ou d'une autre; 2 **I somehow think they won't come** quelque chose me dit qu'ils ne viendront pas.

something pronoun quelque chose; **I've got something to tell you** j'ai quelque chose à te dire; **something pretty** quelque chose de joli; **something interesting** quelque chose d'intéressant; **there's something wrong** il y a quelque chose qui ne va pas; **their house is really something!** leur maison c'est vraiment quelque chose!; **a guy called Colin something or other** un type qui s'appelle Colin quelque chose.

sometime adverb un de ces jours; **give me a ring sometime** appelle-moi un de ces jours; **I'll ring you sometime next week** je t'appellerai dans le courant de la semaine prochaine.

sometimes adverb quelquefois; **I sometimes take the train** quelquefois je prends le train.

somewhere adverb quelque part; **I've put my bag down somewhere** j'ai posé mon sac quelque part; **I've met you somewhere before** je vous ai déjà vu quelque part.

son noun fils M.

song noun chanson F.

son-in-law noun gendre M.

soon adverb 1 bientôt!; **it will soon be the holidays** c'est bientôt les vacances; **see you soon!** à bientôt!; 2 **as soon as** dès que; **as soon as she arrives** dès qu'elle arrive; **as soon as possible** dès que possible; 3 **it's too soon** c'est trop tôt.

sooner adverb 1 plus tôt; **we should have started sooner** nous aurions dû commencer plus tôt; 2 **I'd sooner wait** je préfère attendre; ★ **sooner or later** tôt ou tard.

soprano noun soprano M & F.

sore noun plaie F.
adjective **to have a sore leg** avoir mal à la jambe; **to have a sore throat** avoir mal à la gorge; **my arm's sore** j'ai mal au bras; ★ **it's a sore point** c'est un sujet délicat.

sorry *adjective* **1** désolé; **I'm really sorry** je suis vraiment désolé; **sorry to disturb you** je suis désolé de vous déranger; **I'm sorry I forgot your birthday** je suis désolé d'avoir oublié ton anniversaire; **2** sorry! excusez-moi! **3** sorry? comment?; **4 to feel sorry for somebody** plaindre [31] quelqu'un.

sort noun sorte F; **what sort of music do you like?** tu aimes quelle sorte de musique?; **all sorts of** toutes sortes de; **for all sorts of reasons** pour toutes sortes de raisons.
●**to sort something out 1** mettre [11] de l'ordre dans (*room, desk, papers, possessions*); **I must sort out my room tonight** je dois mettre de l'ordre dans ma chambre ce soir; **2** s'occuper [1] de (*problem, arrangement*); **Liz is sorting it out** Liz s'en occupe.

so-so *adjective* moyen (F moyenne); **'how was the film?'** – **'so-so'** 'c'était comment le film?' – 'moyen'.

soul noun **1** âme F; **2** (*music*) soul M.

sound noun **1** (*noise*) bruit; **the sound of voices** le bruit des voix; **2** (*volume*) volume M; **to turn down the sound** baisser le volume.
verb **it sounds easy** ça a l'air facile;

it sounds as if she's happy elle a l'air d'être heureuse.

sound asleep *adjective* profondément endormi.

sound effect noun effet sonore M.

soundtrack noun bande sonore F.

soup noun soupe F; **mushroom soup** la soupe aux champignons.

soup plate noun assiette creuse F.

soup spoon noun cuillère F à soupe.

sour *adjective* **1** (*taste*) aigre; **2 the milk has gone sour** le lait a tourné.

south noun sud M; **in the south** au sud.
adjective, adverb sud (*never agrees*); **the south side** le côté sud; **a south wind** un vent du sud; **south of Paris** au sud de Paris.

South Africa noun Afrique F du Sud.

South America noun Amérique F du Sud.

southeast noun sud-est M.
adjective **in southeast England** au sud-est de l'Angleterre.

South Pole noun pôle Sud M.

southwest noun sud-ouest M.
adjective **in southwest England** au sud-ouest de l'Angleterre.

souvenir noun souvenir M.

soya noun soja M.

soy sauce noun sauce F de soja.

space noun **1** (*room*) place F; **is**

there enough space? est-ce qu'il y a de la place?; **there's enough space for two** il y a de la place pour deux; **2** (gap) espace M; **leave a space** laissez un espace; **3** (outer space) espace M; **in space** dans l'espace.

spacecraft noun engin spatial M.

spade noun **1** pelle F; **2** (in cards) pique M; **the queen of spades** la reine de pique.

Spain noun Espagne F; **in Spain** en Espagne; **to Spain** en Espagne.

Spaniard noun Espagnol M, Espagnole F.

spaniel noun épagneul M.

Spanish noun **1** (language) espagnol M; **I'm learning Spanish** j'apprends l'espagnol; **2 the Spanish** (people) les Espagnols M plural;
adjective espagnol; **Pedro is Spanish** Pedro est espagnol.

spank verb **to spank somebody** donner [1] une fessée à quelqu'un.

spanner noun clé anglaise F.

spare adjective (part, battery) de rechange; **we have a spare ticket** nous avons un billet de trop.
verb **I can't spare the time** je n'ai pas le temps; **can you spare a moment?** est-ce que tu as un instant?

spare part noun pièce F de rechange.

spare room noun chambre F d'amis.

spare time noun temps libre M; **in**

my spare time dans mon temps libre.

spare wheel noun roue F de secours.

sparkling adjective **sparkling (mineral) water** l'eau (minérale) pétillante; **sparkling wine** le vin mousseux.

sparrow noun moineau M (plural moineaux).

speak verb **1** parler [1]; **do you speak French?** est-ce que vous parlez français?; **spoken French** le français parlé; **2 to speak to somebody** parler [1] à quelqu'un; **she's speaking to Mike** elle parle à Mike; **I've never spoken to her** je ne lui ai jamais parlé; **I'll speak to him about it** je vais lui en parler; **3 who's speaking?** (on the phone) c'est qui à l'appareil?

speaker noun **1** (on a music system) enceinte F; **2** (at a public lecture) conférencier M, conférencière F; **3** (of a language) a **French speaker** un/une francophone; **an English speaker** un/une anglophone.

special adjective spécial (M plural spéciaux).

specialist noun spécialiste M & F.

specialize verb **to specialize in** être [6] spécialisé dans; **we specialize in French cars** nous sommes spécialisés dans les voitures françaises.

specially adverb **1** spécialement; **not specially** pas spécialement; **the poems have been specially chosen for small children** les poèmes ont été spécialement choisis pour les petits enfants; **2** (*specifically*) exprès; **I came specially in order to see you** je suis venu exprès pour te voir; **I made this cake specially for you** j'ai fait ce gâteau exprès pour toi.

species *noun* espèce F.

specific *adjective* précis.

spectacles *plural noun* lunettes F *plural*.

spectacular *adjective* spectaculaire.

spectator *noun* spectateur M, spectatrice F.

speech *noun* discours M; **to make a speech** faire un discours.

speechless *adjective* muet (F muette); **to be speechless with rage** rester muet de colère; **I was speechless** j'étais stupéfait.

speed *noun* vitesse F; **at top speed** à toute vitesse; **what speed was he doing?** il roulait à quelle vitesse?; **a twelve-speed bike** un vélo à douze vitesses.

●**to speed up** accélérer [24].

speeding *noun* excès M de vitesse; **he was fined for speeding** il a reçu une contravention pour excès de vitesse.

speed limit *noun* limitation F de vitesse.

spell *noun* (*of time*) période F; **a cold spell** une période de temps froid; **sunny spells** des éclaircies F *plural*.
verb **1** (*in writing*) écrire [38]; **how do you spell it?** ça s'écrit

comment?; **how do you spell your surname?** ça s'écrit comment, ton nom de famille?; **2** (*out loud*) épeler [18].

spelling *noun* orthographe F; **a spelling mistake** une faute d'orthographe.

spend *verb* **1** dépenser [1] (*money*); **I've spent all my money** j'ai dépensé tout mon argent; **2** passer [1] (*time*); **we spent three days in Paris** nous avons passé trois jours à Paris; **she spends her time writing letters** elle passe son temps à écrire des lettres.

spice *noun* épice F.

spicy *adjective* épicé; **he doesn't like spicy food** il n'aime pas les choses épicées.

spider *noun* araignée F.

spill *verb* renverser [1]; **I've spilled my wine on the carpet** j'ai renversé mon vin sur la moquette.

spinach *noun* épinards F *plural*; **do you like spinach?** est-ce que tu aimes les épinards?

spine *noun* colonne vertébrale F.

spiral *noun* spirale F.

spiral staircase *noun* escalier M en colimaçon.

spire *noun* flèche F.

spirit *noun* **1** (*energy*) énergie F; **2 to get into the spirit of the occasion** se mettre dans l'ambiance.

spirits *noun* **1** (*alcohol*) alcools forts M *plural*; **2 to be in good spirits** être de bonne humeur.

spit verb cracher [1]; **to spit something out** cracher quelque chose.

spite noun 1 **in spite of** malgré; **we decided to go in spite of the rain** nous avons décidé d'y aller malgré la pluie; 2 (*nastiness*) méchanceté F; **to do something out of spite** faire quelque chose par méchanceté.

spiteful adjective méchant.

splash noun 1 (*noise*) plouf M; 2 **a splash of colour** une touche de couleur.
verb éclabousser [1].

splendid adjective splendide.

splinter noun écharde F.

split verb 1 (*with an axe or a knife*) fendre [3]; **to split a piece of wood** fendre un morceau de bois; 2 (*come apart*) se fendre [3]; **the lining has split** la doublure s'est fendue; 3 (*divide up*) partager [52]; **they split the money between them** ils ont partagé l'argent entre eux.
• **to split up** 1 (*a couple or group*) se séparer [1]; 2 **she's split up with her boyfriend** elle a rompu avec son copain.

spoil verb 1 gâcher [1]; **it completely spoiled the evening** ça a complètement gâché la soirée; **to spoil the surprise** gâcher la surprise; 2 gâter [1] (*a child*).

spoiled adjective gâté; **a spoiled child** un enfant gâté.

spoilsport noun trouble-fête M & F.

spoke noun (*of a wheel*) rayon M.

spokesman noun porte-parole M (*plural* porte-parole).

spokeswoman noun porte-parole M (*plural* porte-parole).

sponge noun éponge F.

sponge bag noun trousse F de toilette.

sponge cake noun génoise F.

sponsor noun sponsor M.
verb sponsoriser [1].

spontaneous adjective spontané.

spooky adjective 1 (*atmosphere*) sinistre; 2 **a spooky story** une histoire qui fait froid dans le dos.

spoon noun cuillère F; **a soup spoon** une cuillère à soupe; **a teaspoon** une petite cuillère.

spoonful noun cuillère F.

sport noun sport M; **to be good at sport** être bon en sport; **my favourite sport** mon sport préféré.

sports bag noun sac M de sport.

sports car noun voiture F de sport.

sports centre noun centre sportif M.

sports club noun club M sportif.

sportsman noun sportif M.

sportswear noun vêtements M *plural* de sport.

sportswoman noun sportive F.

sporty adjective sportif (F sportive); **she's very sporty** elle est très sportive.

spot noun 1 (*in fabric*) pois M; **a red tie with black spots** une cravate

rouge aux pois noirs; **2** (*on your skin*) bouton M; **I've got spots** j'ai des boutons; **to be covered in spots** être couvert de boutons; **3** (*stain*) tache F; **you've got a spot on your tie** tu as une tache sur ta cravate; **4** (*spotlight*) projecteur M; (*in the home*) spot M; **5 on the spot** (*immediately*) sur-le-champ; **we'll do it for you on the spot** nous le ferons sur-le-champ; **6** (*at hand*) sur place; **they have experts on the spot** ils ont des experts sur place.
verb repérer [24]; **I spotted her in the crowd** je l'ai repérée dans la foule.

spotless *adjective* impeccable.

spotlight *noun* **1** projecteur F; **2** (*in the home*) spot M.

spotty *adjective* (*pimply*) boutonneux (F boutonneuse).

spouse *noun* époux M, épouse F.

sprain *noun* entorse F.
verb **to sprain your ankle** se faire [10] une entorse à la cheville.

spray *noun* (*spray can*) bombe F.
verb vaporiser [1] (*liquid*).

spread *noun* pâte à tartiner F; **cheese spread** le fromage à tartiner.
verb **1** (*news or a disease*) se propager [52]; **2** étaler [1] (*butter, jam, cement, glue, etc*).

spreadsheet *noun* (*on a computer*) tableur M.

spring *noun* **1** (*the season*) printemps M; **in the spring** au printemps; **spring flowers** les fleurs du printemps; **2** (*made of metal*) ressort M; **3** (*providing water*) source F.

spring-cleaning *noun* grand nettoyage M de printemps.

springtime *noun* printemps M; **in springtime** au printemps.

spring water *noun* eau F de source.

sprint *noun* sprint M.
verb courir [2] à toute vitesse.

sprinter *noun* sprinteur M, sprinteuse F.

sprout *noun* (*Brussels sprout*) chou M de Bruxelles (*plural* choux de Bruxelles).

spy *noun* espion M, espionne F.
verb **to spy on somebody** espionner [1] quelqu'un.

spying *noun* espionnage M.

squabble *verb* se disputer [1].

square *noun* **1** (*shape*) carré; **2** (*in a town or village*) place F; **the village square** la place du village; ★ **to go back to square one** retourner à la case départ.
adjective carré; **a square box** une boîte carrée; **three square metres** trois mètres carrés; **the room is four metres square** la pièce fait quatre mètres carrés.

squash *noun* **1** (*drink*) sirop M; **orange squash** le sirop d'orange; **2** (*sport*) squash M; **to play squash** jouer au squash.

squeak *verb* **1** (*door, hinge*) grincer [61]; **2** (*person, animal*) pousser [1] un petit cri.

squeeze *verb* **1** serrer [1] (*somebody's arm, hand, etc*); **2** presser [1] (*toothpaste*).

squirrel noun écureil M.

stab verb poignarder [1].

stable noun écurie F.
adjective stable.

stack noun 1 (pile) pile F;
2 **stacks of them she's got
stacks of CDs** elle a plein de CD.

stadium noun stade M.

staff noun 1 (of a company)
personnel M; 2 (in a school)
professeurs M plural.

stage noun 1 (for a performance)
scène F; **on stage** sur scène;
2 (phase) stade M; **at this stage of
the project** à ce stade du projet; **at
this stage it's hard to know** pour
l'instant il est difficile de savoir.

staggered adjective (amazed)
stupéfié.

stain noun tache F.
verb tacher [1].

stainless steel noun inox M; **a
stainless steel sink** un évier en inox.

stair noun 1 (step) marche F;
2 **stairs** escalier M; **I met her on
the stairs** je l'ai croisée dans
l'escalier.

staircase noun escalier M.

stale adjective (bread) rassis.

stalemate noun (in chess) pat M.

stall noun 1 (at a market or fair)
stand M; 2 **the stalls** (in a
theatre) l'orchestre M singular.

stammer noun **to have a stammer**
bégayer [59].
verb bégayer [59].

stamp noun timbre M.

verb 1 affranchir [2] (a letter); 2 **to
stamp your foot** taper [1] du pied.

stamp album noun album M de
timbres.

stamp collection noun collection
F de timbres.

stand verb 1 être [6] debout; **several
people were standing** plusieurs
personnes étaient debout; 2 (when
you say somebody is standing
somewhere 'standing' is not usually
translated) **we were standing
outside the cinema** nous étions
devant le cinéma; **I'm standing here
waiting for you** je suis là en train de
t'attendre; 3 (bear) supporter [1];
I can't stand her je ne la supporte
pas; **I can't stand waiting** je ne
supporte pas d'attendre.

● **to stand for something** (be short for)
être [6] l'abréviation de; **'UN' stands
for 'United Nations'** 'UN' est
l'abréviation de 'United Nations'.

● **stand up** se lever [50]; **everybody
stood up** tout le monde s'est levé.

standard noun niveau M; **her work
is of a high standard** son travail est
d'un bon niveau; **the standard of
living** le niveau de vie.
adjective standard; **the standard
price** le prix standard.

stands plural noun (in a stadium)
tribune F plural.

staple noun agrafe F.
verb agrafer [1]; **to staple the pages
together** agrafer les feuilles.

stapler noun agrafeuse F.

star noun 1 (in the sky) étoile F;
2 (person) vedette; **he's a film star**
c'est une vedette de cinéma.

verb **to star in a film** être [6] la vedette d'un film.

stare *verb* regarder [1] fixement; **he was staring at me** il me regardait fixement; **what are you staring at?** qu'est-ce que tu regardes?

start *noun* **1** début M; **at the start** au début; **at the start of the book** au début du livre; **from the start** dès le début; **we knew from the start that it was dangerous** nous savions dès le début que c'était dangereux; **2 to make a start on something** commencer à faire quelque chose; **I've made a start on my homework** j'ai commencé à faire mes devoirs; **3** (*of a race*) départ M.
verb **1** commencer [61]; **the film starts at eight** le film commence à huit heures; **I've started the book** j'ai commencé le livre; **2 to start doing** commencer [61] à faire; **I've started learning Spanish** j'ai commencé à apprendre l'espagnol; **3 to start a business** créer [32] une entreprise; **4 to start a car** faire [10] démarrer une voiture; **she started the car** elle a fait démarrer la voiture; **the car wouldn't start** la voiture n'a pas voulu démarrer.

starter *noun* (*in a meal*) entrée F; **what would you like as a starter?** qu'est-ce que vous voulez comme entrée?

starve *verb* mourir [54] de faim; **I'm starving!** je meurs de faim!

state *noun* **1** état M; **the house is in a very bad state** la maison est en très mauvais état; **2** (*administrative*) état M; **the state** l'État; **3 the States** les États-

Unis M *plural*; **they live in the States** ils habitent aux États-Unis.
verb **1** déclarer [1] (*intention, opinion*); **2** indiquer [1] (*address, income, occupation, reason, etc*).

stately home *noun* château M (*plural* châteaux).

statement *noun* déclaration F.

station *noun* gare F; **the railway station** la gare; **the bus station** la gare routière; **the police station** le commissariat; **a radio station** une station de radio.

stationer's *noun* papeterie F.

statistics *noun* **1** (*subject*) statistique F; **2 the statistics** (*figures*) les statistiques.

statue *noun* statue F.

stay *noun* séjour M; **our stay in Paris** notre séjour à Paris; **enjoy your stay!** bon séjour!
verb **1** rester [1]; **I'll stay here** je reste ici; **how long are you staying?** vous restez combien de temps?; **2** (*with time*) **we're going to stay in Berlin for three days** nous allons passer trois jours à Berlin; **3** (*at somebody's house*) **to stay with somebody** aller [7] chez quelqu'un; **I'm going to stay with my sister this weekend** je vais chez ma sœur ce weekend; **4** (*be temporarily lodged*) loger [52]; **where are you staying?** où est-ce que vous logez?
● **to stay in** rester [1] à la maison; **I'm staying in tonight** je reste à la maison ce soir.

steady *adjective* **1** stable; **a steady job** un emploi stable; **2** régulier (F régulière); **a steady increase** une augmentation régulière; **3** (*hand, voice*) ferme; **4 to hold something steady** bien tenir quelque chose.

steak *noun* steak M; **steak and chips** un steak frites.

steal *verb* voler [1].

steam *noun* vapeur F.

steam engine *noun* locomotive F à vapeur.

steam iron *noun* fer M à vapeur.

steel *noun* acier M.

steep *adjective* raide; **a steep slope** une pente raide.

steeple *noun* **1** (*spire*) flèche F; **2** (*bell tower*) clocher M.

steering wheel *noun* volant M.

step *noun* **1** pas M; **to take a step forwards** faire un pas en avant; **to take a step backwards** faire un pas en arrière; **2** (*stair*) marche F; **'mind the step'** 'attention à la marche'.

to step back faire [10] un pas en arrière.

to step forward faire [10] un pas en avant.

to step into entrer [1] dans (*a lift*).

stepbrother *noun* demi-frère M (*plural* demi-frères).

stepdaughter *noun* belle-fille F (*plural* belles-filles).

stepfather *noun* beau-père M.

stepladder *noun* escabeau M (*plural* escabeaux).

stepmother *noun* belle-mère F.

stepsister *noun* demi-sœur F (*plural* demi-sœurs).

stepson *noun* beau-fils M (*plural* beaux-fils).

stereo *noun* chaîne F stéréo (*plural* chaînes stéréo).

sterling *noun* sterling M; **in sterling** en livres sterling.

stew *noun* ragoût M.

steward *noun* steward M.

stewardess *noun* hôtesse F.

stick *noun* **1** bâton M; **2 a walking stick** une canne; **3 a hockey stick** une crosse de hockey.
verb **1** (*with glue*) coller [1]; **2** (*put*) mettre [11]; **stick them on my desk** mets-les sur mon bureau.

sticker *noun* autocollant M.

sticky *adjective* **1** poisseux (F poisseuse); **my hands are sticky** j'ai les mains poisseuses; **2** adhésif (F adhésive); **sticky paper** le papier adhésif.

sticky tape *noun* Scotch™ M.

stiff *adjective* **1 to feel stiff** avoir des courbatures; **to have stiff legs** avoir des courbatures dans les jambes; **2 to be bored stiff** s'ennuyer à mourir; **to be scared stiff** être mort de peur.

still *adjective* **1 sit still!** tiens-toi tranquille!; **keep still!** ne bouge pas!; **2 still mineral water** l'eau minérale non-gazeuse.
adverb **1** toujours; **do you still live in London?** est-ce que tu habites toujours à Londres?; **I've still not finished** je n'ai toujours pas fini; **he's still working** il est toujours en train de travailler; **2** encore; **there's still a lot of beer left** il reste encore

beaucoup de bière; **3 better still** encore mieux.

sting noun piqûre F; **a wasp sting** une piqûre de guêpe.
verb piquer [1]; **I was stung by a bee** je me suis fait piquer par une abeille.

stink noun odeur F; **what a stink!** ça pue!
verb puer [1]; **it stinks of cigarette smoke in here** ça pue la cigarette ici.

stir verb remuer [1].

stitch noun **1** (in sewing) point M; **2** (in knitting) maille F; **3** (surgical) point M de suture (plural points de suture).

stock noun **1** (in a shop) stock M; **to have something in stock** avoir quelque chose en stock; **2** (supply) réserve F; **I always have a stock of pencils** j'ai toujours une réserve de crayons; **3** (for cooking) bouillon M; **chicken stock** le bouillon de poulet.
verb **1** (in a shop) vendre [3]; **they don't stock dictionaries** ils ne vendent pas les dictionnaires.
●**to stock up on something** s'approvisionner [1] en quelque chose.

stock cube noun bouillon-cube M.

stocking noun bas M.

stomach noun estomac M.

stomachache noun **to have stomachache** avoir mal au ventre.

stone noun **1** pierre F; **a stone wall** un mur en pierre; **2** (pebble)

caillou M (plural cailloux); **3** (in fruit) noyau M (plural noyaux).

stool noun tabouret M.

stop noun arrêt M; **the bus stop** l'arrêt de bus.
verb **1** s'arrêter [1]; **he stopped in front of the shop** il s'est arrêté devant le magasin; **the music stopped** la musique s'est arrêtée; **does the train stop in Dijon?** est-c que le train s'arrête à Dijon?; **2 to stop somebody/something** arrête [1] quelqu'un/quelque chose; **she stopped me in the street** elle m'a arrêté dans la rue; **3 to stop doing** arrêter [1] de faire; **he's stopped smoking** il a arrêté de fumer; **she never stops asking questions** elle n'arrête pas de poser des questions; **4 to stop somebody doing** empêcher [1] quelqu'un de faire; **there's nothing to stop you going c your own** rien ne t'empêche d'y aller tout seul.

stopwatch noun chronomètre M.

store noun (shop) magasin M.
verb **1** garder [1]; **2** (on a computer) mémoriser [1].

storey noun étage M; **a three-storey house** une maison à trois étages.

storm noun **1** (wind) tempête F; **a snowstorm** une tempête de neige; **rainstorm** une tempête de pluie; **2** (thunderstorm) orage M.

stormy adjective orageux (F orageuse).

story noun histoire F; **to tell a story** raconter une histoire.

stove noun (cooker) cuisinière F.

straight adjective **1** droit; **a straight line** une ligne droite; **2 to have straight hair** avoir les cheveux raides.
adverb **1** (in direction) droit; **go straight ahead** continuez tout droit; **2** (in time) directement; **he went straight to the doctor's** il est allé directement chez le médecin; **3 straight away** tout de suite.

straightforward adjective simple.

strain noun stress M; **the strain of the last few weeks** le stress de ces dernières semaines; **to be a strain** être stressant.
verb se faire [10] mal à (part of the body); **he's strained his back** il s'est fait mal au dos.

strange adjective bizarre; **a strange situation** une situation bizarre.

stranger noun inconnu M, inconnue F.

strangle verb étrangler [1].

strap noun **1** (on case, bag, camera) courroie F; **2** (on a garment) bretelle F; **3** (of a watch) bracelet M; **a watchstrap** un bracelet de montre; **4** (on a shoe) lanière F.

strapless adjective sans bretelles.

straw noun paille F (both the material and for drinking with); **a straw hat** un chapeau de paille.

strawberry noun fraise F; **strawberry jam** la confiture de fraises; **a strawberry yoghurt** un yaourt à la fraise.

stray adjective **a stray dog** un chien perdu.

stream noun (small river) ruisseau M (plural ruisseaux).

street noun rue F; **I met Simon in the street** j'ai croisé Simon dans la rue.

streetlamp noun réverbère M.

street map noun plan M de la ville.

streetwise adjective dégourdi.

strength noun force F.

stress noun stress M.
verb (emphasize) souligner [1]; **to stress the importance of something** souligner l'importance de quelque chose.

stretch verb **1** (garment) se déformer [1]; **this jumper has stretched** ce pull s'est déformé; **2** (shoes) s'élargir [2].

stretcher noun brancard M.

stretchy adjective élastique.

strict adjective strict.

strike noun grève F; **to go on strike** faire grève; **to be on strike** être en grève.
verb **1** (hit) frapper [1]; **2** (clock) sonner [1]; **the clock struck six** l'horloge a sonné six heures; **3** (go on strike) faire [10] grève.

striker noun **1** (in football) buteur M; **2** (person on strike) gréviste M & F.

striking adjective frappant; **a striking resemblance** une ressemblance frappante.

string noun **1** (for tying) ficelle F; **2** (for a musical instrument) corde F.

strip noun bande F.
verb (undress) se déshabiller [1].

strip cartoon noun bande
dessinée F.

stripe noun rayure F.

striped adjective rayé.

stroke noun 1 (style of swimming)
nage F; 2 (medical) attaque F; **to
have a stroke** avoir une attaque;
★ **a stroke of luck** un coup de
chance.
verb caresser [1].

stroll noun **to go for a stroll** faire
une petite promenade.
verb se promener [50].

strong adjective 1 (person, drink)
fort; 2 (feeling) puissant;
3 (material) solide.

strongly adverb 1 (believe)
fermement; 2 (support)
fortement; 3 (advise, oppose)
vivement.

struggle noun 1 lutte F; **the
struggle for independence** la lutte
pour l'indépendance; **a power
struggle** une lutte pour le pouvoir;
2 **it's been a struggle** ça a été très
dur.
verb 1 (to obtain something) se
battre [21]; **they have struggled to
survive** ils se sont battus pour
survivre; 2 (physically, in order to
escape or reach something) se
débattre [21]; 3 (have difficulty in
doing) avoir [5] du mal à faire; **I'm
struggling to finish my homework**
j'ai du mal à finir mes devoirs.

stub noun **a cigarette stub** un
mégot.
●**to stub out** écraser [1] (a cigarette).

stubborn adjective têtu.

stuck adjective 1 (jammed) coincé;
the drawer's stuck le tiroir est
coincé; 2 (person) **to get stuck**
rester coincé (in a lift, traffic jam, or
place).

stud noun 1 (on a belt or jacket) clou
M; 2 (on a boot) clou M;
3 (earring) boucle F d'oreille.

student noun étudiant M,
étudiante F.

studio noun 1 (film, TV) studio
M; 2 (artist's) atelier M.

studio flat noun studio M.

study verb 1 réviser [1]; **he's busy
studying for his exams** il est en
train de réviser pour ses examens;
2 faire [10] des études de (a subject);
she's studying medicine elle fait
des études de médecine.

stuff noun 1 (things) trucs M
plural (informal); **we can put all
that stuff in the attic** on peut mettre
tous ces trucs au grenier;
2 (personal belongings) affaires F
plural; **you can leave your stuff at
my house** tu peux laisser tes affaires
chez moi; 3 (substance) truc M
(informal); **some antiseptic stuff**
un truc antiseptique.
verb 1 (shove) fourrer [1]
(informal); **she stuffed some
things into a suitcase** elle a fourré
quelques affaires dans une valise;
2 farcir [2] (chicken, turkey,
vegetables); **stuffed aubergines** des
aubergines farcies.

stuffing noun (for cooking) farce F.

stuffy adjective (airless) étouffant.

stumble verb (trip) trébucher [1].

stunned adjective (amazed) stupéfait.

stunning adjective sensationnel (F sensationnelle).

stunt noun (in a film) cascade F.

stuntman noun cascadeur M.

stuntwoman noun cascadeuse F.

stupid adjective bête; **that was really stupid** c'était vraiment bête; **to do something stupid** faire une bêtise.

stutter noun **to have a stutter** bégayer [59].
verb bégayer [59].

style noun 1 style M; **a style of living** un style de vie; **he has his own style** il a son propre style; 2 (fashion) mode F; **it's the latest style** c'est la dernière mode.

subject noun 1 sujet M; **the subject of my talk** le sujet de mon exposé; 2 (at school) matière F; **my favourite subject is biology** ma matière préférée c'est la biologie.

submarine noun sous-marin M (plural sous-marins).

subscription noun abonnement M; **to take out a subscription to** s'abonner à.

subsidy noun subvention F.

substance noun substance F.

substitute noun (person) remplaçant M, remplaçante F.
verb substituer [1].

subtitled adjective (film) sous-titré.

subtitles plural noun sous-titres M plural.

subtle adjective subtil.

subtract verb soustraire [78].

suburb noun banlieue F; **a suburb of Edinburgh** une banlieue d'Édimbourg; **in the suburbs of London** dans la banlieue de Londres.

suburban adjective de banlieue.

subway noun (underpass) passage souterrain M.

succeed verb réussir [2]; **to succeed in doing** réussir à faire; **we've succeeded in contacting her** nous avons réussi à la contacter.

success noun succès M; **a great success** un grand succès.

successful adjective 1 réussi; **he's a successful writer** c'est un écrivain réussi; 2 **to be successful in doing** réussir à faire.

successfully adverb avec succès.

such adjective, adverb 1 tellement; **they're such nice people!** ils sont tellement gentils!; **I've had such a busy day!** j'ai eu une journée tellement chargée!; **it's such a long way** c'est tellement loin; **it's such a pity** c'est tellement dommage; 2 **such a lot of** tellement de; **I've got such a lot of things to tell you!** j'ai tellement de choses à te dire!; 3 **such as** comme; **in big cities such as Glasgow** dans les grandes villes comme Glasgow; 4 **there's no such thing** ça n'existe pas.

suck verb sucer [61].

sudden adjective soudain; ★ all of a sudden tout d'un coup.

suddenly adverb 1 tout d'un coup; he suddenly started to laugh tout d'un coup il s'est mis à rire; suddenly the light went out tout d'un coup la lumière s'est éteinte; 2 to die suddenly mourir subitement.

suede noun daim M; a suede jacket une veste en daim.

suffer verb souffrir [73].

sufficiently adverb suffisamment.

sugar noun sucre M; would you like sugar? est-ce que tu veux du sucre?; brown sugar le sucre roux.

suggest verb suggérer [24]; he suggested I should speak to you about it il m'a suggéré de vous en parler.

suggestion noun suggestion F; to make a suggestion faire une suggestion.

suicide noun suicide M; to commit suicide se suicider.

suit noun 1 (man's) costume M; 2 (woman's) tailleur M.

suitable adjective 1 (clothing) approprié; I don't have any suitable shoes je n'ai pas de chaussures appropriées. 2 convenable; a suitable hotel un hôtel convenable; 3 to be suitable for convenir à.

suitcase noun valise F.

sulk verb bouder [1].

sum noun 1 somme F; a sum of money une somme d'argent; a large

sum une grosse somme; 2 (calculation) calcul M.
● to sum up résumer [1].

summarize verb résumer [1].

summary noun résumé M.

summer noun été M; in summer en été; summer clothes les vêtements d'été; the summer holidays les grandes vacances.

summertime noun été M; in summertime en été.

summit noun sommet M.

sun noun soleil M; in the sun au soleil.

sunbathe verb se bronzer [1].

sunblock noun crème F écran total.

sunburn noun coup M de soleil.

sunburned adjective 1 (tanned) bronzé; 2 to get sunburned (burned) attraper un coup de soleil.

Sunday noun dimanche M; on Sunday dimanche; I'm going out on Sunday je sors dimanche; see you on Sunday! à dimanche!; on Sundays le dimanche; the museum is closed on Sundays le musée est fermé le dimanche; every Sunday tous les dimanches; last Sunday dimanche dernier; next Sunday dimanche prochain.

sunflower noun tournesol M; sunflower oil l'huile F de tournesol.

sunglasses plural noun lunettes F plural de soleil.

sunlight noun soleil M.

sunny adjective 1 it's a sunny day il fait du soleil; it's going to be

sunny il va faire du soleil; **2** (*place*) ensoleillé; **in a sunny corner of the garden** dans un coin ensoleillé du jardin.

sunrise *noun* lever M du soleil.

sunroof *noun* toit ouvrant M.

sunset *noun* coucher M du soleil.

sunshine *noun* soleil M.

sunstroke *noun* insolation F; **to get sunstroke** attraper une insolation.

suntan *noun* bronzage M; **to get a suntan** bronzer.

suntan lotion *noun* lotion solaire F.

suntan oil *noun* huile solaire F.

super *adjective* formidable; **we had a super time!** c'était formidable!

supermarket *noun* supermarché M.

supernatural *adjective* surnaturel (F surnaturelle).

superstitious *adjective* superstitieux (F superstitieuse).

supervise *verb* surveiller [1].

supper *noun* dîner M; **I had supper at Sandy's** j'ai dîné chez Sandy.

supplement *noun* supplément M.

supplies *plural noun* (*of food*) provisions F plural.

supply *noun* **1** (*stock*) réserves F plural; **2 to be in short supply** être difficile à trouver.
verb fournir [1]; **the school supplies the paper** c'est l'école qui fournit le papier; **to supply somebody with**

something fournir quelque chose à quelqu'un.

supply teacher *noun* suppléant M, suppléante F.

support *noun* soutien M; **he has a lot of support** il a beaucoup de soutien.
verb **1** (*back up*) soutenir [77]; **her teachers have really supported her** ses professeurs l'ont vraiment soutenue; **2** être [6] supporter de (*a team*); **Graeme supports Liverpool** Graeme est supporter de Liverpool; **3** (*financially*) **to support a family** subvenir [81] aux besoins d'une famille.

supporter *noun* supporter M; **a Manchester United supporter** un supporter de Manchester United.

suppose *verb* **I suppose she's forgotten** elle a sans doute oublié.

supposed *adjective* **to be supposed to do** être censé faire; **you're supposed to wear a helmet** on est censé porter un casque; **he was supposed to be here at six** il était censé être là à six heures.

sure *adjective* sûr; **are you sure?** tu es sûr?; **are you sure you've had enough to eat?** tu es sûr que tu as assez mangé?; **are you sure you saw her?** tu es sûr de l'avoir vue?; **'can you shut the door?' – 'sure!'** 'peux-tu fermer la porte?' – 'bien sûr!'

surely *adverb* quand même; **surely she couldn't have forgotten!** elle ne peut quand même pas avoir oublié!

surface *noun* surface F.

surfboard noun planche F de surf
(*plural* planches de surf).

surfing noun surf M; **to go surfing**
faire du surf.

surgeon noun chirurgien M; **she's
a surgeon** elle est chirurgien.

surgery noun 1 **to have surgery** se
faire opérer; 2 (*doctor's*) cabinet
médical M; **the dentist's surgery** le
cabinet dentaire.

surname noun nom M de famille
(*plural* noms de famille).

surprise noun surprise F; **what a
surprise!** quelle surprise!

surprised adjective surpris; **I was
surprised to see her** j'ai été surpris
de la voir.

surprising adjective surprenant.

surround verb 1 encercler [1]; 2 **to
be surrounded by** être [6] entouré
de; **she's surrounded by friends** elle
est entourée d'amis.

survey noun enquête F.

survive verb survivre [82].

survivor noun survivant M,
survivante F.

suspect noun suspect M, suspecte
F.
adjective douteux (F douteuse).
verb soupçonner [1].

suspend verb 1 (*hang*) suspendre
[3]; 2 **to be suspended** (*from
school*) être [6] exclu.

suspense noun suspense M.

suspicious adjective 1 méfiant; **to
be suspicious of** se méfier de; 2 **a
suspicious parcel** un paquet

suspect; 3 **a suspicious-looking
individual** un individu louche.

swallow noun (*bird*) hirondelle F.
verb avaler [1].

swan noun cygne M.

swap verb 1 échanger [52]; **do you
want to swap?** tu veux qu'on
échange? **he's swapped his bike for
a computer** il a échangé son vélo
contre un ordinateur; 2 **to swap
seats with somebody** changer [52]
de place avec quelqu'un.

swear verb (*use bad language*)
utiliser [1] des gros mots; **he swears
a lot** il utilise beaucoup de gros
mots.

swearword noun gros mot M.

sweat noun transpiration F.
verb transpirer [1].

sweater noun pull M.

Swede noun Suédois M, Suédoise
F.

swede noun (*vegetable*) rutabaga
M.

Sweden noun Suède F; **in Sweden**
en Suède; **to Sweden** en Suède.

Swedish noun (*language*) suédois
M.
adjective suédois.

sweep verb balayer [59].

sweet noun 1 bonbon M; **I bought
her some sweets** je lui ai acheté des
bonbons; 2 (*dessert*) dessert M.
adjective 1 (*food*) sucré; **I try not to
eat sweet things** j'essaie d'éviter
les choses sucrées; 2 (*kind*) gentil
(F gentille); **she's a really sweet
person** elle est vraiment gentille; **it**

was really sweet of him c'était vraiment gentil de sa part; **3** (*cute*) mignon (F mignonne); **he looks really sweet in that hat!** il est mignon avec ce chapeau!

●**sweetcorn** *noun* maïs M.

●**swell** *verb* (*part of the body*) enfler [1].

●**swim** *noun* **to go for a swim** aller [7] se baigner;
verb nager [52]; **can he swim?** est-ce qu'il sait nager?; **to swim across something** traverser [1] quelque chose à la nage.

●**swimmer** *noun* nageur M, nageuse F; **she's a strong swimmer** c'est une bonne nageuse.

●**swimming** *noun* natation F; **to go swimming** faire de la natation.

●**swimming cap** *noun* bonnet M de bain.

●**swimming costume** *noun* maillot M de bain.

●**swimming pool** *noun* piscine F.

●**swimming trunks** *noun* maillot M de bain.

●**swimsuit** *noun* maillot M de bain.

●**swing** *noun* balançoire F.

●**Swiss** *noun* (*person*) Suisse M & F; **the Swiss** les Suisses M *plural*
adjective suisse.

●**switch** *noun* **1** (*button type*) bouton M; **2** (*up-down type*) interrupteur M.
verb (*change*) changer [52] de; **to switch places** changer de place.
●**to switch something off** éteindre [60] quelque chose.

●**to switch something on** allumer [1] quelque chose.

●**Switzerland** *noun* Suisse F; **in Switzerland** en Suisse; **to Switzerland** en Suisse.

●**swollen** *adjective* enflé.

●**swop** *verb* SEE swap.

●**sword** *noun* épée F.

●**sycamore** *noun* sycomore M.

●**syllabus** *noun* programme M; **to be on the syllabus** être au programme.

●**symbol** *noun* symbole M.

●**symbolic** *adjective* symbolique.

●**sympathetic** *adjective* compréhensif (F compréhensive).

●**sympathize** *verb* **to sympathize with somebody** comprendre [64] quelqu'un; **I sympathize with her** je la comprends.

●**sympathy** *noun* compassion F.

●**symphony** *noun* symphonie F.

●**symphony orchestra** *noun* orchestre symphonique M.

●**symptom** *noun* symptôme M.

●**synthesizer** *noun* synthétiseur M.

●**synthetic** *adjective* synthétique.

●**syringe** *noun* seringue F.

●**system** *noun* système M.

T t

●**table** *noun* table F; **on the table** sur

la table; **to lay the table** mettre la table; **to clear the table** débarrasser la table.

tablecloth noun nappe F.

tablespoon noun grande cuillère F; (in recipes) **a tablespoon of flour** une cuillère à soupe de farine.

tablet noun comprimé M.

table tennis noun ping-pong™ M; **to play table tennis** jouer au ping-pong.

tabloid noun quotidien populaire M.

tackle verb 1 (in football or hockey) tacler [1]; 2 s'attaquer [1] à (a job or problem).

tact noun tact M.

tactful adjective plein de tact; **that wasn't very tactful** ça a manqué un peu de tact.

tadpole noun têtard M.

tail noun 1 queue F; 2 **'heads or tails?'** – **'tails'** 'pile ou face?' – 'pile'.

take verb 1 prendre [64]; **he took a chocolate** il a pris un chocolat; **take my hand** prends ma main; **I took the bus** j'ai pris le bus; **to take a holiday** prendre des vacances; **do you take sugar?** est-ce que vous prenez du sucre?; **who's taken my keys?** qui a pris mes clefs?; **it takes two hours** ça prend deux heures; **he took the news badly** il a mal pris la nouvelle; 2 (to accompany) emmener [50] (a person); **I'm taking Jake to the doctor's** j'emmène Jake chez le médecin; **I must take the car to the garage** je dois emmener la

voiture au garage; 3 (carry away) emporter [1]; **she's taken some work to do at home** elle a emporté du travail pour faire chez elle; 4 **to take something up(stairs)** monter [1] quelque chose; **could you take these towels up?** est-ce que tu peux monter ces serviettes?; 5 **to take something down(stairs)** descendre [3] quelque chose; **Cheryl's taken the cups down** Cheryl a descendu les tasses; 6 accepter [1] (a credit card or a cheque); **do you take cheques?** est-ce que vous acceptez les chèques?; 7 passer [1] (an exam); **she's taking her driving test tomorrow** elle passe son permis demain; 8 **it takes a lot of courage** il faut beaucoup de courage; 9 **what size do you take?** quelle taille faites-vous?

●**to take something apart** démonter [1] quelque chose.

●**to take something back** rapporter [1] quelque chose.

●**to take off** 1 (a plane) décoller [1]; 2 enlever [50] (clothes or shoes); **he took off his shirt** il a enlevé sa chemise; 3 déduire [26] (money); **he took five pounds off the price** il a déduit cinq livres du prix.

●**to take out** 1 (from a bag or pocket) sortir [72]; **Eric took out his wallet** Eric a sorti son porte-feuille; 2 **he's taking me out to lunch** il m'emmène déjeuner; **she took me out to the theatre** elle m'a emmenée au théâtre.

takeaway noun 1 (a meal) repas M à emporter; **an Indian takeaway** un repas indien à emporter; 2 (where you buy it) restaurant M qui fait des plats à emporter.

take-off noun décollage M (of a plane).

talent noun talent M; **to have a talent for something** être doué pour quelque chose.

talented adjective doué; **he's really talented** il est vraiment doué.

talk noun 1 (a chat) conversation F; **I had a talk with Roy about it** j'ai eu une conversation avec Roy à ce sujet; 2 exposé M; **she's giving a talk on Hungary** elle fait un exposé sur la Hongrie.
verb 1 parler [1]; **I was talking to Jeevan about football** je parlais du foot avec Jeevan; **what's he talking about?** il parle de quoi?; **we'll talk about it later** on en parlera plus tard; 2 (to gossip) bavarder [1]; **they're always talking** ils n'arrêtent pas de bavarder.

talkative adjective bavard; **he's not exactly talkative!** on ne pourrait pas dire qu'il est bavard!

tall adjective 1 grand; **she's very tall** elle est très grande; **I'm 1.7 metres tall** je mesure un virgule sept mètres; 2 haut (a building or tree).

tame adjective apprivoisé (an animal).

tampon noun tampon M.

tan noun bronzage M; **to get a tan** bronzer.
verb bronzer [1]; **I tan easily** je bronze facilement.

tank noun 1 (for petrol or water) réservoir M; 2 **a fish tank** un aquarium; 3 (military) char M.

tanned adjective bronzé.

tap noun 1 robinet M; **to turn on the tap** ouvrir le robinet; **to turn off the tap** fermer le robinet; **the hot tap** le robinet d'eau chaude; 2 (a pat) petite tape F.
verb taper [1].

tap-dancing noun claquettes F plural; **to do tap-dancing** faire des claquettes.

tape noun 1 cassette F; **my tape of the Stones** ma cassette des Stones; **I've got it on tape** je l'ai en cassette; 2 **sticky tape** Scotch™ M.
verb enregistrer [1]; **I want to tape the film** je veux enregistrer le film.

tape measure noun mètre M à ruban.

tape recorder noun magnétophone M.

tapestry noun tapisserie F.

target noun cible F.

tart noun tarte F; **a raspberry tart** une tarte aux framboises.

tartan adjective écossais; **a tartan skirt** une jupe écossaise.

task noun tâche F.

taste noun goût M; **the taste of onions** le goût des oignons; **in bad taste** de mauvais goût.
verb 1 goûter [1]; **do you want to taste?** tu veux goûter?; **the soup tastes horrible** la soupe a un goût infect; 2 **to taste of** avoir [5] un goût de; **it tastes of strawberries** ça a un goût de fraises.

tasty adjective savoureux (F savoureuse).

tattoo noun tatouage M; **he's got a**

tattoo on his arm il a un tatouage sur le bras.

Taurus noun Taureau M; **Josephine's Taurus** Josephine est Taureau.

tax noun **1** impôts M plural; **2** (on goods) taxe F.

taxi noun taxi M; **by taxi** en taxi; **to take a taxi** prendre un taxi.

taxi driver noun chauffeur M de taxi.

taxi rank noun station F de taxis.

TB noun tuberculose F.

tea noun **1** thé M; **a cup of tea** une tasse de thé; **to have tea** prendre le thé; **2** (evening meal) dîner M.

teabag noun sachet M de thé.

teach verb **1** apprendre [64]; **she's teaching me Italian** elle m'apprend l'italien; **that'll teach you!** ça t'apprendra!; **2** enseigner [1]; **her mum teaches maths** sa mère enseigne les maths; **3** **to teach yourself something** apprendre [64] quelque chose tout seul; **Anne taught herself Italian** Anne a appris l'italien toute seule.

teacher noun **1** (in a secondary school) professeur M; **my mother's a teacher** ma mère est professeur; **our biology teacher** notre professeur de biologie; **2** (in primary school) instituteur M, institutrice F; **she's a primary school teacher** elle est institutrice.

teaching noun enseignement M.

team noun équipe F; **a football**

team une équipe de foot; **our team won** notre équipe a gagné.

teapot noun théière F.

tear[1] noun (a rip) accroc M; **I've got a tear in my jeans** j'ai un accroc dans mon jean.
verb **1** déchirer [1]; **you've torn your shirt** tu as déchiré ta chemise; **she tore up my letter** elle a déchiré ma lettre; **2** se déchirer [1]; **be careful, it tears easily** attention, ça se déchire facilement.
● **to tear off, to tear open 1** (carefully) détacher [1]; **2** (violently) arracher [1].

tear[2] noun (when you cry) larme F; **to be in tears** être en larmes; **to burst into tears** fondre en larmes.

tease verb **1** taquiner [1] (a person); **2** tourmenter [1] (an animal).

teaspoon noun petite cuillère F; (in recipes) **a teaspoonful of...** une cuillère à café de...

teatime noun l'heure F du dîner (evening meal).

tea towel noun torchon M.

technical adjective technique.

technical college noun lycée technique M.

technician noun technicien M, technicienne F.

technique noun technique F.

techno noun techno F (music).

technological adjective technologique.

technology noun technologie F;

information technology l'informatique F.

teddy bear noun nounours M.

teenage adjective 1 adolescent (F adolescente); **they have a teenage son** ils ont un fils adolescent; 2 (films, magazines, etc) pour les jeunes; **a teenage magazine** un magazine pour les jeunes.

teenager noun 1 jeune M & F; **a group of teenagers** une bande de jeunes; 2 (more precisely) adolescent M, adolescente F; **when I was a teenager** quand j'étais adolescent.

teens plural noun adolescence F; **he's in his teens** c'est un adolescent.

tee-shirt noun tee-shirt M.

telephone noun téléphone M; **on the telephone** au téléphone. verb appeler [18]; **I'll telephone the bank** je vais appeler la banque.

telephone box noun cabine F téléphonique.

telephone call noun coup M de téléphone.

telephone directory noun annuaire M.

telephone number noun numéro M de téléphone.

telescope noun télescope M.

televise verb téléviser [1]; **they're televising the match** on va téléviser le match.

television noun télévision F; **she was watching television** elle regardait la télévision; **I saw it on television** je l'ai vu à la télévision.

television programme noun émission F de télévision.

tell verb 1 **to tell somebody something** dire [9] quelque chose à quelqu'un; **that's what she told me** c'est ce qu'elle m'a dit; **I told him it was silly** je lui ai dit que c'était idiot; **have you told Sara?** est-ce que tu l'as dit à Sara?; 2 **to tell somebody to do** dire [9] à quelqu'un de faire; **he told me to do it myself** il m'a dit de le faire moi-même; **she told me not to wait** elle m'a dit de ne pas attendre; 3 (explain) **can you tell me how to do it?** est-ce que vous pouvez m'expliquer comment on le fait? 4 raconter [1] (a story); **tell me about your holiday** raconte-moi tes vacances; 5 (to see) voir [13]; **you can tell it's old** on voit bien que c'est ancien; **you can tell she's cross** on voit bien qu'elle est fâchée; **I can't tell them apart** je n'arrive pas à les distinguer.

telly noun télé F; **to watch telly** regarder la télé; **I saw her on telly** je l'ai vue à la télé.

temp noun intérimaire M & F.

temper noun **to be in a temper** être en colère; **to lose your temper** se mettre en colère.

temperature noun 1 température F; **the oven temperature** la température du four; 2 **to have a temperature** avoir de la fièvre.

temple noun temple M.

temporary adjective temporaire.

temptation noun tentation F.

tempted adjective tenté; I'm really tempted to go je suis vraiment tenté d'y aller.

tempting adjective tentant.

ten number dix M; Harry's ten Harry a dix ans.

tend verb to tend to do avoir [5] tendance à faire; he tends to talk a lot il a tendance à beaucoup parler.

tender adjective tendre.

tennis noun tennis M; to play tennis jouer au tennis.

tennis ball noun balle F de tennis.

tennis court noun tennis M.

tennis player noun joueur de tennis M, joueuse de tennis F.

tennis racket noun raquette F de tennis.

tenor noun ténor M.

tenpin bowling noun bowling M; to go tenpin bowling jouer au bowling.

tense noun the present tense le présent; in the future tense au futur.
adjective tendu.

tent noun tente F.

tenth number dixième M; on the tenth floor au dixième étage; the tenth of April le dix avril.

term noun 1 (in school) trimestre M; 2 to be on good terms with somebody être en bons termes avec quelqu'un.

terminal noun 1 (at an airport) aérogare F; terminal two l'aérogare numéro deux; 2 a ferry

terminal une gare maritime; 3 (a computer terminal) terminal M (plural terminaux).

terrace noun 1 (of a house or hotel) terrasse F; 2 the terraces (at a stadium) les gradins M plural.

terrible adjective épouvantable; the weather was terrible il a fait un temps épouvantable.

terribly adverb 1 (very) très; not terribly clean pas très propre; 2 (badly) affreusement mal; I played terribly j'ai joué affreusement mal.

terrific adjective 1 at a terrific speed à une vitesse folle; a terrific amount une quantité énorme; 2 terrific! formidable!

terrified adjective terrifié.

terrorism noun terrorisme M.

terrorist noun terroriste M & F.

test noun 1 (in school) contrôle M; we've got a maths test tomorrow nous avons un contrôle de maths demain; 2 (of your skills or patience) test M; 3 (medical) analyse F; a blood test une analyse de sang; 4 a driving test un examen de permis de conduire; she's doing her driving test on Friday elle passe son permis vendredi; he passed his driving test il a eu son permis.
verb 1 (in school) contrôler [1]; 2 to test something out quelque chose.

test tube noun éprouvette F.

text noun texte M.

textbook noun manuel M.

Thames noun the Thames la Tamise.

than preposition, conjunction 1 que; their new album's better than the last one leur nouveau CD est meilleur que le dernier; they have more money than we do ils ont plus d'argent que nous; 2 (for quantities) de; more than forty plus de quarante; more than thirty years plus de trente ans.

thank verb remercier [1].

thanks plural noun 1 merci; no thanks non merci; thanks a lot merci beaucoup; thanks for your letter merci pour ta lettre; 2 with thanks for avec mes remerciements pour; 3 thanks to grâce à; it was thanks to Micky c'était grâce à Micky.

thank you adverb merci; thank you very much for the cheque merci beaucoup pour le chèque; no thank you merci; a thank-you letter une lettre de remerciements.

that adjective 1 ce (F cette) (but 'ce' becomes 'cet' before a masculine noun beginning with a vowel or a silent 'h'); that dog ce chien; that man cet homme; that blue car cette voiture bleue; 2 that one celui-là M, celle-là F; 'which cake would you like?' – 'that one, please' 'tu veux quel gâteau?' – 'celui-là, s'il te plaît; I like all the dresses but I'm going to buy that one j'aime toutes les robes mais je vais acheter celle-là.

adverb 1 it's not that silly ce n'est pas si idiot que ça; your house isn't that big leur maison n'est pas si grande que ça; 2 it was that high c'était haut comme ça.

pronoun 1 ce, c' (before a vowel or a silent 'h'); that's not true ce n'est pas vrai; that's not what you told me ce n'est pas ce que tu m'as dit; what's that? qu'est-ce que c'est?; who's that? c'est qui?; where's that? c'est où?; is that Mandy? c'est Mandy?; 2 ça; did you see that? est-ce que tu as vu ça?; that's my bedroom ça c'est ma chambre; 3 qui; the book that's on the table le livre qui est sur la table; 4 que, qu' (before a vowel or a silent 'h'); the book that I lent you le livre que je t'ai prêté.

conjunction que, qu' (before a vowel or a silent 'h'); I knew that he was wrong je savais qu'il avait tort.

the definite article 1 (before a noun which is masculine in French) le, l' (before a vowel or silent 'h'); the cat le chat; the tree l'arbre; 2 (before a noun which is feminine in French) la, l' (before a vowel or silent 'h'); the table la table; the orange l'orange; 3 les (before all plural nouns); the windows les fenêtres.

theatre noun théâtre M; to go to the theatre aller au théâtre.

theft noun vol M.

their adjective leur (plural leurs); their flat leur appartement; their mother leur mère; their presents leurs cadeaux.

theirs pronoun 1 le leur (when standing for a masculine noun); our garden's smaller than theirs notre jardin est plus petit que le leur; 2 la leur (when standing for a feminine *noun*); **your house is bigger than theirs** votre maison est plus grande que la leur; **3** les leurs (*when standing for a plural noun*); **our children are older than theirs** nos enfants sont plus âgés que les leurs; **4** à eux; **the yellow car's theirs** la voiture jaune est à eux; **it's theirs** c'est à eux.

them *pronoun* **1** les; **I know them** je les connais; **I don't know them** je ne les connais pas; **listen to them!** écoute-les!; **I saw them last week** je les ai vus la semaine dernière; **2** (*to them*) leur; **I gave them my address** je leur ai donné mon adresse; **3** (*after a preposition*) eux (F elles); **I'll go with them** j'irai avec eux; (*if they are all female*) j'irai avec elles; **without them** sans eux; sans elles; (*in comparisons*) **she's older than them** elle est plus âgée qu'eux; (*if all female*) elle est plus âgée qu'elles.

theme *noun* thème F.

theme park *noun* parc M de loisirs.

themselves *pronoun* **1** se; **they've helped themselves** ils se sont servis; **2** (*for emphasis*) eux-mêmes M, elles-mêmes F; **the boys can do it themselves** les garçons peuvent le faire eux-mêmes; **the girls will tell you themselves** les filles vous le diront elles-mêmes.

then *adverb* **1** (*next*) ensuite; **I wash up and then I make the bed** je fais la vaisselle et ensuite je fais le lit; **I went to the post office and then the bank** je suis allé à la poste et ensuite à la banque; **2** (*at that time*) à l'époque; **we were living in York**

then nous habitions à York à l'époque; **3** (*in that case*) alors; **then why worry?** alors pourquoi s'inquiéter?; **that's all right then** ça va alors; **4** by then déjà; **by then it was too late** il était déjà trop tard.

theory *noun* théorie F; **in theory** en théorie.

there *adverb* **1** là; **put it there** mets-le là; **stand there** mettez-vous là; **they're in there** ils sont là; **look up there!** regarde là-haut!; **2** over there là-bas; **she's over there talking to Mark** elle est là-bas en train de discuter avec Mark; **down there** là-bas; **3** up there là-haut; **4** y (*when the place 'there' stands for has already been mentioned*) **I've seen photos of Oxford but I've never been there** j'ai vu des photos d'Oxford mais je n'y suis jamais allé; **yes, I'm going there on Tuesday** oui, j'y vais mardi; **5** there is il y a; **there's a cat in the garden** il y a un chat dans le jardin; **there was no bread** il n'y avait pas de pain; **yes, there's enough** oui, il y en a assez; **6** there are il y a; **there are plenty of seats** il y a beaucoup de places; **7** there they are! les voilà!; **there she is!** la voilà!; **there's the bus coming!** voilà le bus qui arrive!

therefore *adverb* donc.

thermometer *noun* thermomètre M.

these *adjective* ces.

they *pronoun* **1** ils (*when standing for a masculine noun*); **'where are the knives?'** – **'they're in the drawer'** 'où sont les couteaux?' – 'ils sont dans le tiroir'; **2** elles (*when* *standing for a feminine noun)*; **I bought some apples but they're not very nice** j'ai acheté des pommes mais elles ne sont pas très bonnes.

thick *adjective* épais (F épaisse); **a thick layer of butter** une couche épaisse de beurre.

thief *noun* voleur M, voleuse F.

thigh *noun* cuisse F.

thin *adjective* 1 mince (*a slice or a person*); 2 (*too thin, skinny*) maigre; **she's got terribly thin** elle a beaucoup maigri.

thing *noun* 1 (*an object*) chose F; **shops full of pretty things** des magasins remplis de jolies choses; **she told me some surprising things** elle m'a raconté des choses étonnantes; 2 (*a whatsit*) truc M (*informal*); **you can use that thing to open it** tu peux utiliser ce truc-là pour l'ouvrir; **that thing next to the hammer** ce truc à côté du marteau; 3 **things** (*belongings*) affaires F *plural*; **you can put your things in my room** tu peux mettre tes affaires dans ma chambre; 4 **the best thing to do is ...** ce qu'il faut faire, c'est ...; **the thing is, I've lost her address** ce qu'il y a, c'est que j'ai perdu son adresse; **how are things with you?** comment ça va?

think *verb* 1 (*believe*) croire [33]; **do you think they'll come?** tu crois qu'ils vont venir?; **no, I don't think so** non, je ne crois pas; **I think he's already left** je crois qu'il est déjà parti; 2 penser [1]; **I'm thinking about you** je pense à toi; **Tony thinks it's silly** Tony pense que c'est bête; **what do you think of my new

jacket?** qu'est-ce que tu penses de ma nouvelle veste?; **what do you think of that?** qu'en penses-tu?; 3 (*to think carefully*) réfléchir [2]; **he thought for a moment** il a réfléchi un instant; **I've thought it over carefully** j'y ai bien réfléchi; 4 (*imagine*) imaginer [1]; **just think! we'll soon be in Spain!** imagine! on va bientôt être en Espagne!; **I never thought it would be like this!** je n'ai jamais imaginé que ce serait comme ça!

third *noun* tiers M; **a third of the population** un tiers de la population.
adjective troisième; **on the third floor** au troisième étage; **the third of March** le trois mars.

thirdly *adverb* troisièmement.

Third World *noun* tiers-monde M.

thirst *noun* soif M.

thirsty *adjective* **to be thirsty** avoir soif; **I'm thirsty** j'ai soif; **we were all thirsty** nous avions tous soif.

thirteen *number* treize M; **Ahmed's thirteen** Ahmed a treize ans.

thirty *number* trente M.

this *adjective* 1 ce (*before a masculine noun*), cet (*before a masculine noun beginning with a vowel or a silent 'h'*), cette (*before a feminine noun*); **this paintbrush** ce pinceau; **this tree** cet arbre; **this cup** cette tasse; **this morning** ce matin; **this evening** ce soir; **this afternoon** cet après-midi; 2 **this one** celui-ci M, celle-ci F; **if you need a pen you can use this one** si

tu as besoin d'un stylo tu peux utiliser celui-ci; **if you want a lamp you can borrow this one** si tu veux une lampe tu peux emprunter celle-ci.
pronoun **1** ça; **can you hold this for a moment?** est-ce que tu peux prendre ça un instant?; **2 what's this?** qu'est-ce que c'est?; **this is Tracy speaking** (*on the phone*) c'est Tracy à l'appareil; **3** (*in introductions*) **this is my sister Carla** je te présente ma sœur Carla.

thistle *noun* chardon M.

thorn *noun* épine F.

those *adjective* ces; **those books** ces livres.
pronoun ceux-là M, celles-là F; **if you want some knives you can take those** si tu veux des couteaux tu peux prendre ceux-là; **if you want some plates you can take those** si tu veux des assiettes tu peux prendre celles-là.

though *conjunction* **1** bien que (*followed by a verb in the subjunctive*); **though it's cold** bien qu'il fasse froid; **though he's older than she is** bien qu'il soit plus âgé qu'elle; **2 it was a good idea, though** et pourtant, c'était une bonne idée.

thought *noun* pensée F.

thoughtful *adjective* **1** (*considerate*) gentil (F gentille); **it was really thoughtful of you** c'était vraiment gentil de ta part; **2** (*deep in thought*) pensif (F pensive).

thoughtless *adjective* irréfléchi.

thousand *number* **1** mille M; **a**

thousand mille; **three thousand** trois mille; **2 thousands of** des milliers de; **there were thousands of tourists in Venice** il y avait des milliers de touristes à Venise.

thread *noun* fil M.
verb enfiler [1] (*a needle*).

threat *noun* menace F.

threaten *verb* menacer [61]; **to threaten to do** menacer de faire.

three *number* trois M; **Oskar's three** Oskar a trois ans.

three-quarters *noun* trois-quarts M *plural*; **three-quarters full** plein aux trois-quarts.

thrilled *adjective* ravi; **I was thrilled to hear from you** j'ai été ravi d'avoir de tes nouvelles.

thriller *noun* thriller M.

thrilling *adjective* palpitant.

throat *noun* gorge F; **to have a sore throat** avoir mal à la gorge.

through *preposition* **1** (*across*) à travers; **through the forest** à travers la forêt; **the water went right through** l'eau est passée à travers; **the police let us through** la police nous a laissés passer; **2** (*via*) par; **the train went through Leeds** le train est passé par Leeds; **through the window** par la fenêtre; **I know them through my cousins** je les connais par mes cousins; **3** (*to go through something*) traverser quelque chose; **we went through the park** nous avons traversé le parc; **4 right through the day** toute la journée.
adjective direct (*a train or flight*).

throw verb 1 jeter [48]; **I threw the letter into the bin** j'ai jeté la lettre dans la poubelle; **he threw the book on the floor** il a jeté le livre par terre; 2 (taking aim) lancer [61]; **throw me the ball!** lance-moi le ballon!; **we were throwing snowballs** on lançait des boules de neige.

●**to throw something away** jeter [48] quelque chose; **I've thrown away the old newspapers** j'ai jeté les vieux journaux.

●**to throw somebody out** expulser [1] quelqu'un.

●**to throw something out** jeter [48] quelque chose (rubbish).

●**to throw up** vomir [2].

thumb noun pouce M.

thump verb taper [1].

thunder noun tonnerre M; **a peal of thunder** un roulement de tonnerre.

thunderstorm noun orage M.

thundery adjective orageux (F orageuse).

Thursday noun jeudi M; **on Thursday** jeudi; **I'm going out on Thursday** je sors jeudi; **see you on Thursday!** à jeudi!; **on Thursdays** le jeudi; **the museum is closed on Thursdays** le musée est fermé le jeudi; **every Thursday** tous les jeudis; **last Thursday** jeudi dernier; **next Thursday** jeudi prochain.

thyme noun thym M.

tick verb 1 (tick-tock) faire [10] tic-tac; 2 (on paper) cocher [1]; **tick the box** cochez la case.

ticket noun 1 billet M; (for a plane, a train, an exhibition, a theatre or cinema) two tickets for the concert deux billets pour le concert; 2 (for the underground, the bus, or left luggage) ticket M; **a bus ticket** un ticket de bus; 3 **a parking ticket** un PV (informal).

ticket inspector noun contrôleur M.

ticket office noun (at a station) guichet M.

tickle verb chatouiller [1].

tide noun marée F; **at high tide** à marée haute; **the tide is out** c'est la marée basse.

tidy adjective 1 bien rangé (a room); 2 soigné (homework); 3 ordonné (a person).
verb ranger [52]; **I'll tidy (up) the kitchen** je rangerai la cuisine.

tie noun 1 cravate F; **a red tie** une cravate rouge; 2 (in a match) match M nul.
verb 1 nouer [1]; **to tie your shoelaces** nouer ses lacets; 2 **to tie a knot in something** faire [10] un nœud à quelque chose; 3 (in a match) **we tied two all** nous avons fait match nul, deux partout.

tiger noun tigre M.

tight adjective 1 juste; **the skirt's a bit tight** la jupe est un peu juste; **these shoes are too tight** ces chaussures me serrent; 2 (close-fitting) moulant; **she was wearing a tight dress** elle portait une robe moulante.

tighten verb serrer [1].

tightly adverb fermement.

tights *plural noun* collant M
singular; **a pair of purple tights** un
collant violet.

tile *noun* **1** (*on a floor or wall*)
carreau M (*plural* carreaux);
2 (*on a roof*) tuile F.

till[1] *preposition, conjunction*
1 jusqu'à; **they're here till Sunday**
ils sont là jusqu'à dimanche; **till
then** jusque-là; **till now** jusqu'à
présent; **2 not till** pas avant; **she
won't be back till ten** elle ne sera
pas rentrée avant dix heures; **we
won't know till Monday** nous ne le
saurons pas avant lundi.

till[2] *noun* caisse F; **pay at the till**
payez à la caisse.

time *noun* **1** (*on the clock*) heure F;
what time is it? quelle heure est-il?;
it's time for lunch c'est l'heure du
déjeuner; **on time** à l'heure; **ten
o'clock French time** dix heures
heure française; **2** (*an amount of
time*) temps M; **we've got lots of
time** nous avons beaucoup de
temps; **there's not much time left** il
ne reste plus beaucoup de temps; **for
a long time** longtemps; **from time to
time** de temps en temps;
3 (*moment*) moment M; **is this a
good time to phone?** est-ce que
c'est le bon moment pour vous
appeler?; **at times** par moments; **for
the time being** pour le moment; **any
time now** d'un moment à l'autre;
4 (*in a series*) fois F; **six times** six
fois; **the first time** la première fois;
the first time I saw you la première
fois que je t'ai vu; **three times a year**
trois fois par an; **three times two is
six** trois fois deux égale six; **5 to
have a good time** bien s'amuser [1];
we had a really good time nous

nous sommes très bien amusés; **have
a good time!** amusez-vous bien!

time off *noun* **1** (*free time*) temps
M libre; **2** (*leave*) congé M.

timetable *noun* **1** (*in school*)
emploi M du temps; **2** (*for trains or
buses*) horaire M; **the bus
timetable** l'horaire des bus.

tin *noun* boîte F; **a tin of tomatoes**
une boîte de tomates.

tinned *adjective* en conserve; **tinned
peas** des petits pois en conserve.

tin opener *noun* ouvre-boîte M.

tinted *adjective* teinté.

tiny *adjective* minuscule.

tip *noun* **1** (*the end*) bout M; **the tip
of my finger** le bout de mon doigt;
2 (*money*) pourboire M; **3** (*a
useful hint*) tuyau M
(*plural* tuyaux) (*informal*).
verb **1** (*to give money to*) donner [1]
un pourboire à; **we tipped the
waiter** nous avons donné un
pourboire au garçon; **2** verser [1]
(*liquid*).

tiptoe *noun* **on tiptoe** sur la pointe
des pieds.

tired *adjective* **1** fatigué; **I'm tired** je
suis fatigué; **you look tired** tu as l'air
fatigué; **2 to be tired of** en avoir
assez de; **I'm tired of London** j'en ai
assez de Londres; **I'm tired of
watching TV** j'en ai assez de
regarder la télé.

tiring *adjective* fatigant.

tissue *noun* (*a paper hanky*)
kleenex™ M; **do you have a
tissue?** est-ce que tu as un kleenex?

tissue paper noun papier M de soie.

title noun titre M.

to preposition 1 (to a place or person) à (note that 'à + le' becomes 'au' and 'à + les' becomes 'aux'); to go to London aller à Londres; give the book to Leila donne le livre à Leila; I'm going to school je vais à l'école; she's gone to the office elle est partie au bureau; a letter to parents une lettre aux parents; from Monday to Friday du lundi au vendredi; 2 (with names of countries) they're going to Spain ils vont en Espagne; (BUT) they're going to Japan ils vont au Japon ('en' with feminine countries, 'au' with most masculine countries); 3 à; I have nothing to do je n'ai rien à faire; I had a lot of homework to do j'avais beaucoup de devoirs à faire; we're ready to go nous sommes prêts à partir; it's easy to do c'est facile à faire; 4 (to somebody's house, shop, surgery) chez; I went round to Paul's house je suis allé chez Paul; we're going to the Browns' for supper on va dîner chez les Brown; I'm going to the dentist's tomorrow je vais chez le dentiste demain; she's gone to the hairdresser's elle est allée chez le coiffeur; 5 (talking about the time) it's ten to nine il est neuf heures moins dix; it's twenty to il est moins vingt; 6 (in order to) pour; he gave me some money to buy a sandwich il m'a donné de l'argent pour acheter un sandwich.

toad noun crapaud M.

toadstool noun champignon M; a poisonous toadstool un champignon vénéneux.

toast noun 1 pain grillé M; two slices of toast deux tranches de pain grillé; 2 (to your health) toast M; to drink a toast to the future lever un verre à l'avenir.

toaster noun grille-pain M.

tobacco noun tabac M.

tobacconist's noun bureau M de tabac.

today noun aujourd'hui M; today's her birthday c'est son anniversaire aujourd'hui.

toe noun doigt M de pied; my big toe mon gros orteil.

toffee noun caramel M.

together adverb 1 ensemble; Kate and Lenny arrived together Kate et Lenny sont arrivés ensemble; 2 (at the same time) en même temps; they all left together ils sont tous partis en même temps.

toilet noun toilettes F plural; where's the toilet? où sont les toilettes?; she's gone to the toilet elle est allé aux toilettes.

toilet paper noun papier M hygiénique.

toilet roll noun rouleau M de papier hygiénique.

token noun 1 (for a machine or game) jeton M; 2 a record token un chèque-cadeaux pour disque.

tolerant adjective tolérant.

toll noun péage M.

tomato noun tomate F; a tomato

salad une salade de tomates; **tomato sauce** la sauce tomate.

tomorrow *adverb* demain; **I'll do it tomorrow** je le ferai demain; **tomorrow afternoon** demain après-midi; **tomorrow morning** demain matin; **tomorrow night** demain soir; **the day after tomorrow** après-demain.

tone *noun* 1 (*on an answerphone*) tonalité F; **speak after the tone** parlez après la tonalité; 2 (*of a voice or a letter*) ton M.

tongue *noun* langue F; **to stick your tongue out** tirer la langue; ★ **it's on the tip of my tongue** je l'ai sur le bout de la langue.

tonic *noun* Schweppes™ M; **a gin and tonic** un gin tonic.

tonight *adverb* 1 (*this evening*) ce soir; **I'm going out with my mates tonight** je sors avec les copains ce soir; 2 (*after bedtime*) cette nuit.

tonsillitis *noun* angine F.

too *adverb* 1 trop; **it's too expensive** c'est trop cher; **too often** trop souvent; 2 **too much, too many** trop; **it takes too much time** ça prend trop de temps; **there are too many accidents** il y a trop d'accidents; **he eats too much** il mange trop; 3 (*as well*) aussi; **Karen's coming too** Karen vient aussi; **me too!** moi aussi!

tool *noun* outil M.

tool box *noun* boîte F à outils.

tool kit *noun* trousse F à outils.

tooth *noun* dent F; **to brush your teeth** se brosser les dents.

toothache *noun* mal M de dents; **to have toothache** avoir mal aux dents.

toothbrush *noun* brosse F à dents.

toothpaste *noun* dentifrice M.

top *noun* 1 haut M (*of a page, a ladder, or stairs*); **at the top of the stairs** en haut de l'escalier; 2 (*of a container or box*) dessus M; **it's on top of the chest-of-drawers** c'est sur la commode; 3 (*of a mountain*) sommet M; 4 (*a lid*) (*of a pen*) capuchon M; (*of a bottle*) capsule F; 5 **to be at the top of the list** être en tête de la liste.
adjective 1 (*a step or floor*) dernier (F dernière); **it's on the top floor** c'est au dernier étage; 2 **de haut** (*a bunk*); 3 **du haut** (*a shelf*); 4 **in the top left-hand corner** en haut à gauche; ★ **and on top of all that** et par-dessus le marché; ★ **it was a bit over the top** c'était un peu exagéré.

topic *noun* sujet M.

torch *noun* lampe F de poche.

torn *adjective* déchiré.

tortoise *noun* tortue F.

torture *noun* torture F.
verb torturer [1].

Tory *noun* conservateur M, conservatrice F.

total *noun* total M.
adjective total (M *plural* totaux).

totally *adverb* complètement.

touch *noun* 1 (*contact*) **to get in touch with somebody** prendre contact avec quelqu'un; **to stay in touch with somebody** rester en contact avec quelqu'un; 2 **we've**

lost touch on s'est perdu de vue; **I've lost touch with her recently** je l'ai perdue de vue récemment; 3 (*a little bit*) petit peu M; **a touch of vanilla** un petit peu de vanille; **it was a touch embarrassing** c'était un petit peu gênant.
verb toucher [1].

touched adjective touché.

touching adjective touchant.

tough adjective 1 dur; **the meat's a bit tough** la viande est un peu dure; **it's a tough area** c'est un quartier dur; **things are a bit tough at the moment** la vie est un peu dure en ce moment; **a tough guy** un dur; 2 robuste; **you need to be tough to survive** il faut être robuste pour survivre!; **a tough fabric** un tissu robuste; 3 (*tough luck*) tant pis; **tough, you're too late** tant pis pour toi, tu arrives trop tard.

tour noun 1 visite F; **we did the tour of the castle** nous avons fait la visite du château; **a tour of the city** une visite de la ville; 2 (*a package tour*) un voyage organisé; 3 (*by a band or theatre group*) tournée F; **to go on tour** partir en tournée.
verb 1 (*performer*) être [6] en tournée; **they're touring the States** ils sont en tournée aux États-Unis.

tourism noun tourisme M.

tourist noun touriste M & F.

tourist information office noun syndicat M d'initiative.

tournament noun tournoi M; **a tennis tournament** un tournoi de tennis.

tow verb **to be towed away** (*by the police*) être [6] emmené à la fourrière; (*by a breakdown truck*) être [6] remorqué.

towards adverb en direction de; **she went off towards the lake** elle est parti en direction du lac.

towel noun serviette F.

tower noun tour F; **the Eiffel Tower** la tour Eiffel.

tower block noun tour F.

town noun ville F; **to go into town** aller en ville.

town centre noun centre-ville M.

town hall noun mairie F.

toy noun jouet M; **a toy car** une petite voiture.

toyshop noun magasin M de jouets.

trace noun trace F; **there was no trace of it** il n'en restait aucune trace.
verb retrouver [1].

tracing paper noun papier calque M.

track noun 1 (*for sport*) piste F; **a track event** une épreuve de vitesse; **a racing track** (*for cars*) un circuit; 2 (*a path*) chemin M; 3 (*song*) chanson; **this is my favourite track** c'est ma chanson préférée.

track suit noun survêtement M.

tractor noun tracteur M.

trade noun (*a profession*) métier M.

trade union noun syndicat M.

tradition noun tradition F.

traditional adjective traditionnel (F traditionnelle).

traffic noun circulation F.

traffic island noun refuge M.

traffic jam noun embouteillage M.

traffic lights plural noun feux M plural.

traffic warden noun contractuel M, contractuelle F.

tragedy noun tragédie F.

tragic adjective tragique.

trail noun (a path) sentier M; a nature trail un sentier écologique.

trailer noun remorque F.

train noun train M; he's coming by train il prend le train; I met her on the train je l'ai rencontrée dans le train; the train for York le train pour York.
verb **1** former [1] (a student); **2** to train to be something suivre [75] une formation de quelque chose; he's training to be a nurse il suit une formation d'infirmier; **3** (in sport) s'entraîner [1]; the team trains on Saturdays l'équipe s'entraîne le samedi.

train ticket noun billet M de train.

train timetable noun horaire M des trains.

trainee noun stagiaire M & F.

trainer noun **1** (of an athlete or a horse) entraîneur M, entraîneuse F; **2** (shoe) basket M; my new trainers mes nouveaux baskets.

training noun **1** (for a career) formation F; **2** (for sport) entraînement M.

tram noun tramway M.

tramp noun clochard M, clocharde F.

transfer noun (sticker) décalcomanie F.

transform verb transformer [1].

transistor noun transistor M.

translate verb traduire [26]; to translate something into French traduire quelque chose en français.

translation noun traduction F.

translator noun traducteur M, traductrice F; I'd like to be a translator j'aimerais être traducteur.

transparent adjective transparent.

transport noun transport M; air transport le transport aérien; public transport les transports en commun.

trap noun piège M.

travel noun voyages M plural; foreign travel les voyages à l'étranger; a travel brochure une brochure de voyages.
verb voyager [52].

travel agency noun agence F de voyages.

travel agent noun agent M de voyages.

traveller noun **1** voyageur M, voyageuse F. **2** (gypsy) nomade M & F.

traveller's cheque noun chèque-voyage M (plural chèques-voyage).

travelling noun voyages M plural;

like travelling j'aime partir en voyage.

travel-sick noun **to be** or **get travel-sick** souffrir [73] du mal de voyage.

tray noun plateau M (plural plateaux).

tread verb **to tread on something** marcher [1] sur quelque chose.

treasure noun trésor M.

treat noun **1 I took them to the circus as a treat** je les ai emmenés au cirque pour leur faire plaisir; **2** (food) gâterie F; **it's a little treat** c'est une petite gâterie. verb **1** traiter [1]; **he treats his dog well** il traite bien son chien; **the doctor who treated you** le médecin qui vous a traité; **2 to treat somebody to something** offrir [56] quelque chose à quelqu'un; **I'll treat you to a drink** je vous offre à boire; **I treated myself to a new dress** je me suis offert une nouvelle robe.

treatment noun traitement M.

tree noun arbre M.

tree trunk noun tronc M d'arbre.

tremble verb trembler [1].

trend noun **1** (a fashion) mode F; **2** (a tendency) tendance F.

trendy adjective branché.

trial noun procès M (legal).

triangle noun triangle M.

trick noun **1** (by a conjuror, or as a joke) tour M; **to play a trick on somebody** jouer un tour à quelqu'un; **2** (a knack) astuce F; **it**

doesn't work, there must be a trick to it ça ne marche pas, il doit y avoir une astuce. verb rouler [1]; **he tricked me!** il m'a roulé!

tricky adjective délicat; **it's a tricky situation** c'est une situation délicate.

tricycle noun tricycle M.

trim verb couper [1] (hair or fabric).

trip noun voyage M; **a trip to Florida** un voyage en Floride; **he's on a business trip** il est en voyage d'affaires; **a day trip to France** une excursion d'une journée en France. verb (to stumble) trébucher [1]; **Nicky tripped over a stone** Nicky a trébuché sur un gros caillou.

triumph noun triomphe M.

trolley noun chariot M.

trombone noun trombone M; **to play the trombone** jouer du trombone.

troops plural noun troupes M plural.

trophy noun trophée M.

tropical adjective tropical (M plural tropicaux).

trot verb trotter [1].

trouble noun **1** problèmes M plural; **we've had trouble with the car** nous avons eu des problèmes avec la voiture; **the trouble is, I've forgotten the number** c'est que j'ai oublié le numéro; **2** (personal problems) ennuis M plural; **Steph's in trouble** Steph a des ennuis; **what's the trouble?** qu'est-ce qui ne va pas?;

3 (*difficulty*) **to have trouble doing**
avoir du mal à faire; **I had trouble
finding a seat** j'ai eu du mal à
trouver une place; **it's not worth the
trouble** cela ne vaut pas la peine; **it's
no trouble!** ça ne me dérange pas!

trousers *plural noun* pantalon M
singular; **my old trousers** mon
vieux pantalon; **a new pair of
trousers** un pantalon neuf.

trout *noun* truite F.

truck *noun* camion M.

true *adjective* vrai; **a true story** une
histoire vraie; **is that true?** c'est
vrai?; **it's true she's absent-minded**
c'est vrai qu'elle est distraite.

trump *noun* atout M; **spades are
trumps** atout pique.

trumpet *noun* trompette F; **to play
the trumpet** jouer de la trompette.

trunk *noun* **1** (*of a tree*) tronc M;
2 (*of an elephant*) trompe F; **3** (*a
suitcase*) malle F.

trunks *plural noun* **swimming
trunks** maillot M singular de bain.

trust *noun* confiance F.
verb **I trust her** je lui fais confiance.

truth *noun* vérité F; **to tell the truth,
I'd completely forgotten** à vrai dire,
j'avais complètement oublié.

try *noun* **1** essai M; **it's my first try**
c'est mon premier essai; **to have a
try** essayer [59]; **you should give it a
try** tu devrais l'essayer.
verb essayer [59]; **to try to do**
essayer de faire; **I'm trying to open
the door** j'essaie d'ouvrir la porte; **to
try hard to do** faire [10] de gros
efforts pour faire.

●**to try something on** essayer [59]
quelque chose (*a garment*).

T-shirt *noun* tee-shirt M.

tube *noun* tube M.

tuberculosis *noun* tuberculose F.

Tuesday *noun* mardi M; **on
Tuesday mardi**; **I'm going out on
Tuesday** je sors mardi; **see you on
Tuesday!** à mardi!; **on Tuesdays** le
mardi; **the museum is closed on
Tuesdays** le musée est fermé le
mardi; **every Tuesday** tous les
mardis; **last Tuesday** mardi dernier;
next Tuesday mardi prochain.

tug *verb* tirer [1].

tuition *noun* cours M *plural*; **piano
tuition** les cours de piano; **private
tuition** des cours particuliers.

tulip *noun* tulipe F.

tumble-drier *noun* sèche-linge
M.

tumbler *noun* verre M droit.

tuna *noun* thon M.

tune *noun* air M.

Tunisia *noun* Tunisie F; **in Tunisia**
en Tunisie.

tunnel *noun* tunnel M; **the Channel
Tunnel** le tunnel sous la Manche.

turf *noun* gazon M.

turkey *noun* dinde F.

Turkey *noun* Turquie F; **in Turkey**
en Turquie; **to Turkey** en Turquie.

Turkish *noun* turc M (*language*).
adjective turc (F turque).

turn *noun* **1** (*in a game*) tour M; **it's
your turn** c'est ton tour; **whose turn**

is it? c'est à qui le tour?; **it's Jane's turn to play** c'est à Jane de jouer; **to take turns driving** conduire à tour de rôle; 2 (*in a road*) virage M.

verb 1 tourner [1]; **turn your chair round** tourne ta chaise; **turn left at the next set of lights** tournez à gauche aux prochains feux; 2 (*become*) devenir [81]; **she turned red** elle est devenue rouge.

to turn back faire [10] demi-tour; **we turned back** nous avons fait demi-tour.

to turn off 1 (*from a road*) tourner [1]; 2 (*switch off*) éteindre [60] (*a light, an oven, a TV or radio*); fermer [1] (*a tap*); couper [1] (*gas or electricity*).

to turn on allumer [1] (*the oven, TV, radio, or a light*); ouvrir [30] (*a tap*).

to turn out 1 **to turn out well** bien se terminer [1]; **the holiday turned out badly** les vacances se sont mal terminées; **it all turned out alright in the end** finalement tout s'est arrangé; 2 **it turned out that I was wrong** il s'est avéré que j'avais tort.

to turn over 1 (*roll over*) se retourner [1]; 2 tourner [1] (*a page*).

to turn up 1 (*to arrive*) arriver [1]; **they turned up an hour later** ils sont arrivés une heure plus tard; 2 augmenter [1] (*the gas or the heating*); 3 (*make louder*) **can you turn up the volume?** est-ce que tu peux monter le son?

turnip *noun* navet M.

turquoise *adjective* turquoise.

turtle *noun* tortue F.

TV *noun* télé F; **I saw her on TV** je l'ai vue à la télé.

tweezers *plural noun* pince à épiler F singular.

twelfth *number* douzième; **on the twelfth floor** au douzième étage; **the twelfth of May** le douze mai.

twelve *number* 1 douze M; **Tara's twelve** Tara a douze ans; 2 **at twelve o'clock** (*midday*) à midi; (*midnight*) à minuit.

twenty *number* vingt M; **Marie's twenty** Marie a vingt ans; **twenty-one** vingt-et-un; **twenty-five** vingt-cinq.

twice *adverb* deux fois; **I've asked him twice** je lui ai demandé deux fois; **twice as much** deux fois plus.

twig *noun* brindille F.

twin *noun* jumeau M (*plural* jumeaux), jumelle F; **Helen and Tim are twins** Helen et Tim sont jumeaux; **her twin sister** sa sœur jumelle.

verb **Oxford is twinned with Grenoble** Oxford est jumelée avec Grenoble.

twist *verb* tordre [3].

two *number* deux M; **Ben's two** Ben a deux ans; **two by two** deux par deux.

type *noun* type M; **what type of computer is it?** c'est quel type d'ordinateur?

verb (*on a typewriter*) taper [1]; **I'm learning to type** j'apprends à taper à la machine; **I was busy typing**

some letters j'étais en train de taper des lettres.

typewriter noun machine F à écrire.

typical adjective typique.

tyre noun pneu M.

U u

ugly adjective laid.

UK noun (short for United Kingdom) Royaume-Uni M.

Ulster noun Irlande du Nord F.

umbrella noun parapluie M.

umpire noun arbitre M.

UN noun ONU F (short for Organisation des Nations Unies).

unable adjective **to be unable to do** ne pas pouvoir faire; **he's unable to come** il ne peut pas venir.

unanimous adjective unanime.

unattractive adjective peu attrayant (person, place).

unavoidable adjective inévitable.

unbearable adjective insupportable.

unbelievable adjective incroyable.

uncertain adjective **1** (not sure) incertain; **2** (unpredictable) variable (weather, for example).

unchanged adjective inchangé.

uncivilized adjective barbare.

uncle noun oncle M; **my Uncle Julian** mon oncle Julian.

uncomfortable adjective **1** inconfortable (shoes or a chair); **2** pénible (a journey or a situation)

uncommon adjective rare.

unconscious adjective (out cold) sans connaissance; **Tessa's still unconscious** Tessa est toujours sans connaissance.

under preposition **1** (underneath) sous; **under the bed** sous le lit; **perhaps it's under there** c'est peut être là-dessous; **2** (less than) moins de; **under £20** moins de vingt livres **children under five** les enfants de moins de cinq ans.

under-age noun **to be under-age** être mineur (F mineure).

underclothes plural noun sous-vêtements M plural.

undercooked adjective pas assez cuit.

underestimate verb sous-estimer [1].

underground noun (a railway) métro M; **I saw her on the underground** je l'ai vue dans le métro; **shall we go by underground?** on prend le métro? adjective souterrain; **an underground carpark** un parking souterrain.

underline verb souligner [1].

underneath preposition sous; **it's underneath these papers** c'est sous ces papiers. adverb dessous; **look underneath** cherche dessous.

underpants plural noun slip M singular; **my underpants** mon slip.

underpass noun 1 (pedestrian) passage souterrain M; 2 (for traffic) passage inférieur M.

understand verb comprendre [64]; **I don't understand** je ne comprends pas; **I didn't understand what he was saying** je n'ai pas compris ce qu'il disait.

understandable adjective **that's understandable** ça se comprend.

understanding noun compréhension F.
adjective compréhensif (F compréhensive); **he was very understanding** il a été très compréhensif.

underwear noun sous-vêtements M plural.

undo verb 1 défaire [10] (a button or a lock); 2 ouvrir [30] (a parcel).

undone adjective **to come undone** se défaire [10].

undress verb **to get undressed** se déshabiller [1]; **I got undressed** je me suis déshabillé.

unemployed noun **work for the unemployed** du travail pour les chômeurs.
adjective au chômage; **she's unemployed** elle est au chômage; **the unemployed** les chômeurs.

unemployment noun chômage M.

uneven adjective irrégulier (F irrégulière).

unexpected adjective imprévu.

unexpectedly adverb (to happen, arrive) à l'improviste.

unfair adjective injuste; **it's unfair to young people** c'est injuste pour les jeunes.

unfashionable adjective démodé.

unfasten verb défaire [10].

unfit adjective **I'm terribly unfit** je ne suis pas du tout en forme.

unfold verb déplier [1].

unfortunate adjective regrettable.

unfortunately adverb malheureusement.

unfriendly adjective pas très sympathique.

unfurnished adjective non meublé.

ungrateful adjective ingrat.

unhappy adjective malheureux (F malheureuse).

unhealthy adjective 1 maladif (F maladive) (a person); 2 malsain (food).

uniform noun uniforme M; **in school uniform** en uniforme scolaire.

union noun (a trade union) syndicat M.

Union Jack noun **the Union Jack** le drapeau du Royaume-Uni.

unique adjective unique.

unit noun 1 (for measuring, for example) unité F; 2 (in a kitchen) élément M; 3 (a hospital department) service M.

United Kingdom noun Royaume-Uni M.

United Nations noun O.N.U. (*Organisation des Nations Unies*).

United States (of America) plural noun États-Unis M plural; **in the United States** aux États-Unis; **to the United States** aux États-Unis.

universe noun univers M.

university noun université F; **to go to university** aller à l'université.

unkind adjective pas gentil (F pas gentille).

unknown adjective inconnu.

unleaded petrol noun essence F sans plomb.

unless conjunction unless he does it à moins qu'il ne le fasse; **unless you tell her** à moins que tu ne le lui dises (*note that 'à moins que' is followed by a subjunctive*).

unlike adjective 1 unlike me, she hates dogs contrairement à moi, elle déteste les chiens; 2 **it's unlike her to be late** ce n'est pas son genre d'être en retard.

unlikely adjective peu probable; **it's unlikely** c'est peu probable.

unlimited adjective illimité.

unload verb décharger [52].

unlock verb ouvrir [30]; **the car's unlocked** la voiture est ouverte.

unlucky adjective 1 **to be unlucky** (*a person*) ne pas avoir de chance; **I was unlucky, it was shut** je n'ai pas eu de chance, c'était fermé;

2 **thirteen is an unlucky number** le treize porte malheur.

unmarried adjective célibataire.

unnatural adjective anormal (M plural anormaux).

unnecessary adjective inutile; **it's unnecessary to book** il est inutile de réserver.

unpack verb défaire [10]; **I unpacked my rucksack** j'ai défait mon sac à dos; **I'll just unpack and then come down** je vais juste défaire ma valise et puis je descendrai.

unpaid adjective 1 impayé (*a bill*); 2 non rémunéré (*work*).

unpleasant adjective désagréable.

unplug verb débrancher [1].

unpopular adjective impopulaire.

unreasonable adjective pas raisonnable; **he's being really unreasonable** il n'est vraiment pas raisonnable.

unrecognizable adjective méconnaissable.

unreliable adjective peu fiable (*information or equipment*); **he's unreliable** on ne peut pas compter sur lui.

unroll verb dérouler [1].

unsafe adjective dangereux (F dangereuse) (*wiring, for instance*).

unsatisfactory adjective insatisfaisant.

unscrew verb dévisser [1].

unshaven adjective pas rasé.

unsuccessful adjective to be

unsuccessful ne pas réussir; **I tried, but I was unsuccessful** j'ai essayé mais je n'ai pas réussi; **an unsuccessful attempt** un essai vain.

unsuitable *adjective* inapproprié.

untidy *adjective* en désordre; **the house is always untidy** la maison est toujours en désordre.

until *preposition* **1** jusqu'à; **until Monday** jusqu'à lundi; **until the tenth** jusqu'au dix; **until now** jusqu'à présent; **until then** jusque-là; **2 not until** pas avant; **not until September** pas avant septembre; **it won't be finished until Friday** ce ne sera pas fini avant vendredi.

unusual *adjective* peu commun; **an unusual beetle** un scarabée peu commun; **storms are unusual in June** c'est rare d'avoir des orages au mois de juin.

unwilling *adjective* **to be unwilling to do** ne pas vouloir faire; **he's unwilling to wait** il ne veut pas attendre.

unwrap *verb* déballer [1].

up *preposition, adverb* **1** (*out of bed*) **to be up** être levé; **Liz isn't up yet** Liz n'est pas encore levée; **to get up** se lever [50]; **we got up at six** nous sommes levés à six heures; **I was up late last night** je me suis couché tard hier soir; **2** (*higher up*) en haut; **hands up!** haut les mains!; **up on the roof** en haut sur le toit; **up here** ici; **up there** là-haut; **we went up the road** nous avons remonté la rue; **it's just up the road** c'est tout près; **up in Glasgow** à Glasgow;

3 (*wrong*) **what's up?** qu'est-ce qui se passe?; **what's up with him?** qu'est-ce qu'il a?; **4** **up to** jusqu'à; **up to here** jusqu'ici; **up to fifty people** jusqu'à cinquante personnes; **she came up to me** elle s'est approchée de moi; **5** **what's she up to?** qu'est-ce qu'elle fait?; **it's up to you (to decide)** c'est à toi de décider; ★ **time's up!** c'est l'heure!

update *noun* mise F à jour; **here's an update on the delays** voici une mise à jour des retards.
verb **1** (*revise*) mettre [11] à jour (*timetables or information*); **2** moderniser [1] (*styles or furnishings*).

upheaval *noun* bouleversement M.

upright *adjective* droit; **put it upright** mets-le droit; **to stand upright** se tenir droit.

upset *noun* **a stomach upset** une indigestion.
adjective contrarié; **he's upset** il est contrarié.
verb **to upset somebody** contrarier [1] quelqu'un.

upside down *adjective* à l'envers.

upstairs *adverb* en haut; **Mum's upstairs** maman est en haut; **to go upstairs** monter [1].

up-to-date *adjective* **1** (*in fashion*) moderne; **2** (*information*) à jour.

upwards *adjective* vers le haut.

urgent *adjective* urgent.

US *noun* U.S.A. M *plural*.

us *pronoun* nous; **she knows us** elle

nous connaît; **they saw us** ils nous ont vus; **he gave us a cheque** il nous a donné un chèque; **with us** avec nous.

USA noun U.S.A. M plural.

use noun 1 emploi M; **the instructions for use** le mode d'emploi; 2 **it's no use** ça ne sert à rien; **it's no use phoning** ça ne sert à rien de téléphoner.
verb 1 utiliser [1]; **we used the dictionary** nous avons utilisé le dictionnaire; **to use something to do** se servir [71] de quelque chose pour faire; **I used a knife to open the parcel** je me suis servi d'un couteau pour ouvrir le paquet.
● **to use up** 1 consommer [1] (food or petrol); 2 dépenser [1] (money).

used adjective 1 **to be used to something** avoir l'habitude de quelque chose; **I'm not used to cats** je n'ai pas l'habitude des chats; **I'm not used to it** je n'ai pas l'habitude; **I'm not used to eating in restaurants** je n'ai pas l'habitude de manger au restaurant; 2 **to get used to** s'habituer à; **I've got used to living here** je me suis habitué à habiter ici; **you'll get used to it!** tu t'y habitueras!
verb **they used to live in the country** ils habitaient à la campagne avant; **she used to smoke** elle fumait avant.

useful adjective utile.

useless adjective 1 nul (F nulle); **this knife's useless** ce couteau est nul; **you're completely useless!** tu es complètement nul!

user-friendly adjective convivial (M plural conviviaux).

usual adjective habituel (F habituelle); **it's the usual problem** c'est le problème habituel; **as usual** comme d'habitude; **it's colder than usual** il fait plus froid que d'habitude.

usually adjective d'habitude; **I usually leave at eight** d'habitude je pars à huit heures.

V v

vacancy noun 1 (in a hotel) 'vacancies' 'chambres libres'; 'no vacancies' 'complet'; 2 **a job vacancy** un poste vacant.

vacant adjective libre.

vaccinate verb vacciner [1].

vaccination noun vaccination F.

vacuum verb passer [1] l'aspirateur; **I'm going to vacuum my room** je vais passer l'aspirateur dans ma chambre.

vacuum cleaner noun aspirateur M.

vagina noun vagin M.

vague adjective vague.

vaguely adverb vaguement.

vain adjective vaniteux (F vaniteuse); **in vain** en vain.

Valentine's Day noun la Saint-Valentin.

valid adjective valable.

valley noun vallée F.

valuable adjective 1 de valeur; to be valuable avoir de la valeur; that watch is very valuable cette montre a une grande valeur; 2 (appreciated) précieux (F précieuse); he gave us some valuable information il nous a donné des renseignements précieux.

value noun valeur F. verb apprécier [1] (somebody's help, opinion, or friendship).

van noun (small) fourgon M; (large) camionnette F.

vandal noun vandale M & F.

vandalism noun vandalisme M.

vandalize verb vandaliser [1].

vanilla noun vanille F; a vanilla ice-cream une glace à la vanille.

vanish verb disparaître [27].

variety noun variété F.

various adjective plusieurs; there are various ways of doing it il y a plusieurs façons de le faire.

vary verb varier [1]; it varies a lot ça varie beaucoup.

vase noun vase M.

VAT noun TVA F.

VCR noun magnétoscope M.

VDU noun console F.

veal noun veau M.

vegan noun végétalien M, végétalienne F.

vegetable noun légume M.

vegetarian noun, adjective végétarien M, végétarienne F; he's vegetarian il est végétarien.

vehicle noun véhicule M.

vein noun veine F.

velvet noun velours M.

vending machine noun distributeur M automatique.

verb noun verbe M.

verdict noun verdict M.

verge noun 1 (the roadside) accotement M; 2 to be on the verge of doing être [6] sur le point de faire; I was on the verge of leaving j'étais sur le point de partir.

version noun version F.

versus preposition contre; Bath versus Chelsea Bath contre Chelsea.

vertical adjective vertical (M plural verticaux).

vertigo noun vertige M.

very adverb 1 it's very difficult c'est très difficile; very well très bien; very much beaucoup. adjective 1 the very person I need! exactement la personne qu'il me faut!; the very thing he was looking for exactement ce qu'il cherchait; 2 in the very middle en plein milieu; at the very end tout à la fin; at the very front tout devant.

vest noun maillot M de corps.

vet noun vétérinaire M & F; she's a vet elle est vétérinaire.

via preposition to go via passer par;

we're going **via Dover** nous allons passer par Douvres; **we'll go via the bank** on va passer par la banque.

vicar noun pasteur M.

vicious adjective **1** méchant (a dog); **2** brutal (M plural brutaux) (an attack).

victim noun victime F.

victory noun victoire F.

video noun **1** (film) vidéo F; **to watch a video** regarder une vidéo; **I've got it on video** je l'ai en vidéo; **2** (cassette) cassette vidéo F; **I bought a video** j'ai acheté une cassette vidéo F; **3** (video recorder) magnétoscope M.
verb enregistrer [1]; **I'll video it for you** je te l'enregistrerai.

video cassette noun cassette F vidéo.

video game noun jeu M vidéo (plural jeux vidéo).

video recorder noun magnétoscope M.

video shop noun vidéoclub M.

view noun **1** vue F; **a room with a view of the lake** une chambre avec vue sur le lac; **2** (opinion) avis M; **in my view** à mon avis; **a point of view** un point de vue.

viewer noun (on TV) téléspectateur M, téléspectatrice F.

viewpoint noun point M de vue.

vigorous adjective vigoureux (F vigoureuse).

vile adjective abominable.

villa noun villa F.

village noun village M.

vine noun vigne F.

vinegar noun vinaigre M.

vineyard noun vignoble M.

violence noun violence F.

violent adjective violent.

violin noun violon M; **to play the violin** jouer du violon.

violinist noun violoniste M & F.

virgin noun vierge F.

Virgo noun Vierge F; **Robert's Virgo** Robert est Vierge.

virtual reality noun réalité F virtuelle.

virus noun virus M.

visa noun visa M.

visible adjective visible.

visit noun **1** (stay) séjour M; **my last visit to France** mon dernier séjour en France; **2** visite F (to a house, museum).
verb **1** visiter [1] (museum, castle, town); **2** aller [7] voir (a person); **we visited Auntie Pat at Christmas** nous sommes allés voir tante Pat à Noël.

visitor noun **1** invité M, invitée F; **we've got visitors tonight** on a des invités ce soir; **2** (a tourist) visiteur M, visiteuse F.

visual adjective visuel (F visuelle).

vital adjective indispensable; **it's vital to book** il est indispensable de réserver.

vitamin noun vitamine F.

vivid adjective **1** (colour) vif (F vive); **2 to have a vivid imagination** exagérer.

vocabulary noun vocabulaire M.

vocational adjective professionnel (F professionnelle).

vodka noun vodka M.

voice noun voix F.

volcano noun volcan M.

volleyball noun volley-ball M; **to play volleyball** jouer au volley-ball.

volume noun volume M; **could you turn down the volume?** est-ce que tu peux baisser le volume?

voluntary adjective **1** (not compulsory) volontaire; **2 to do voluntary work** travailler bénévolement.

volunteer noun **1** (for a job) volontaire M & F; **2** (in charity work) bénévole M & F.

vomit verb vomir [2].

vote verb voter [1].

voucher noun bon M.

vowel noun voyelle F.

vulgar adjective vulgaire.

W w

waffle noun (to eat) gaufre F.

wage(s) (plural) noun salaire M.

waist noun taille F.

waistcoat noun gilet M.

waist measurement noun tour M de taille.

wait noun attente F; **an hour's wait** une heure d'attente.
verb **1** attendre [3]; **they're waiting in the car** ils attendent dans la voiture; **she kept me waiting** elle m'a fait attendre; **2 to wait for** attendre [3]; **wait for me!** attends-moi!; **wait for the signal** attendez le signal; **3 I can't wait to open it!** j'ai hâte de l'ouvrir!

waiter noun serveur M.

waiting list noun liste F d'attente.

waiting room noun salle F d'attente.

waitress noun serveuse F.

wake verb **1** réveiller [1] (somebody else); **Jess woke me at six** Jess m'a réveillé à six heures; **2** se réveiller [1]; **I woke (up) at six** je me suis réveillé à six heures; **wake up!** réveille-toi!

Wales noun pays M de Galles; **in Wales** au pays de Galles; **to Wales** au pays de Galles.

walk noun promenade F; (a little stroll) tour M; **to go for a walk** faire une promenade; **we went for a walk in the woods** nous avons fait une promenade dans la forêt; **we'll go for a little walk round the village** on va faire un petit tour au village; **to take the dog for a walk** promener [50] le chien; **it's about five minutes' walk from here** c'est à environ cinq minutes à pied d'ici.
verb **1** marcher [1]; **I like walking on sand** j'aime marcher sur le sable; **2** (walk around) se promener [50];

we walked around the old town
nous nous sommes promenés dans
la vieille ville; **3** (*go*) aller [7]; **I'll
walk to the bus stop with you** j'irai
avec toi jusqu'à l'arrêt de bus; **4** (*on
foot rather than by car or bus*) aller
[7] à pied; **it's not far, we can walk**
ce n'est pas loin, on peut y aller à
pied.

walkie-talkie *noun* talkie-walkie
M (*plural* talkies-walkies).

walking *noun* (*hiking*) randonnée
F; **we're going walking in
Scotland** nous allons faire de la
randonnée en Écosse.

walking distance *noun* **it's within
walking distance of the sea** c'est à
quelques minutes à pied de la mer.

walking stick *noun* canne F.

walkman™ *noun* walkman™ M.

wall *noun* mur M.

wallet *noun* portefeuille M.

wallpaper *noun* papier M peint.

walnut *noun* noix F (*plural* noix).

wander *verb* **to wander around
town** se balader [1] en ville; **to
wander off** s'éloigner [1].

want *noun* **all our wants** tous nos
besoins.
 verb vouloir [14]; **do you want some
coffee?** est-ce que tu veux du café?;
what do you want to do? qu'est-ce
que tu veux faire?; **I don't want to
bother him** je ne veux pas le
déranger.

war *noun* guerre F.

ward *noun* salle F (*in a hospital*).

wardrobe *noun* **1** (*cupboard*)
armoire F; **2** (*clothes*) garde-robe
F.

warm *adjective* **1** chaud; **a warm
drink** une boisson chaude; **it's
warm today** il fait chaud
aujourd'hui; **I am warm** j'ai chaud;
are you warm enough? as-tu assez
chaud?; **I'll keep your dinner warm**
je tiendrai ton dîner au chaud;
2 (*friendly*) chaleureux (F
chaleureuse); **a warm welcome** un
accueil chaleureux.
 verb chauffer [1]; **warm the plates**
chauffez les assiettes.
●**to warm up 1** (*the weather*)
s'adoucir [2]; **2** (*an athlete*)
s'échauffer [1]; **3** (*to heat up*)
réchauffer [1] (*food*); **I'll warm up
some soup for you** je vous
réchaufferai de la soupe.

warmth *noun* chaleur F.

warn *verb* prévenir [81]; **I warn you,
it's expensive** je vous préviens que
c'est cher; **to warn somebody to do**
conseiller [1] à quelqu'un de faire; **he
warned me to lock the car** il m'a
conseillé de fermer la voiture.

warning *noun* avertissement M.

wart *noun* verrue F.

wash *noun* **to give something a
wash** laver [1] quelque chose; **to
have a wash** se laver.
 verb laver [1]; **I've washed your
jeans** j'ai lavé ton jean; **to wash
your hands** se laver les mains;
I washed my hands je me suis lavé
les mains; **to wash your hair** se laver
les cheveux; **to get washed** se laver;
to wash the dishes faire [10] la
vaisselle.

●**to wash up** faire [10] la vaisselle.

washbasin noun lavabo M.

washing noun 1 (dirty) linge M sale; 2 (clean) linge M.

washing machine noun machine F à laver.

washing powder noun lessive F.

washing-up noun vaisselle F; to do the washing-up faire la vaisselle.

washing-up liquid noun liquide M à vaisselle.

wasp noun guêpe F.

waste noun 1 (of food, money, paper) gaspillage M; 2 (of time) perte F; it's a waste of time c'est une perte de temps.
verb 1 gaspiller [1] (food, money, paper); 2 perdre [3] (time); you're wasting your time tu perds ton temps.

waste-bin noun poubelle F.

wastepaper-basket noun corbeille F à papier.

watch noun montre F; my watch is fast ma montre avance; my watch is slow ma montre retarde.
verb 1 (to look at) regarder [1]; I was watching TV je regardais la télé; 2 (keep a check on) surveiller [1]; watch the time surveille l'heure; 3 (to be careful) faire [10] attention; watch you don't spill it fais attention de ne pas le renverser; watch out for black ice faites attention au verglas; watch out! attention!

water noun eau F.

verb arroser [1]; **to water the plants** arroser les plantes.

waterfall noun cascade F.

watering can noun arrosoir M.

water melon noun pastèque F.

waterproof adjective imperméable.

water-skiing noun ski M nautique; to go water-skiing faire du ski nautique.

water sports plural noun sports M plural nautiques.

wave noun 1 (in the sea) vague F; 2 (with your hand) signe M; she gave him a wave from the bus elle lui a fait signe du bus.
verb 1 (with your hand) saluer [1] de la main; 2 (flap) agiter [1] (your ticket or the newspaper, for example).

wax noun cire F.

way noun 1 (a route or road) chemin M; the way to town le chemin pour aller en ville; we asked the way to the station nous avons demandé le chemin pour aller à la gare; on the way back sur le chemin de retour; 'way in' 'entrée'; 'way out' 'sortie'; 2 (direction) direction F; which way did he go? en quelle direction est-il parti? come this way venez par ici; to be in the way gêner le passage; 3 (side) sens M; the right way up dans le bons sens; the wrong way round dans le mauvais sens; 4 (distance) it's a long way c'est loin; Terry went all the way to York Terry est allé jusqu'à York; 5 (manner) façon F; a way of talking une façon de parler; he does it his way il le fait à sa façon; **either way, she's wrong** de toute façon elle a tort; **do it this way** fais-le comme ceci; **6 no way!** pas question!; **7 by the way** à propos.

we *pronoun* nous; (*informally*) on; **we live in Carlisle** nous habitons Carlisle; **we're going to the cinema tonight** on va au cinéma ce soir.

weak *adjective* 1 (*feeble*) faible; **her voice was weak** sa voix était faible; **2 léger** (F légère) (*coffee or tea*).

wealthy *adjective* riche.

weapon *noun* arme F.

wear *noun* **children's wear** vêtements M *plural* pour enfants; **sports wear** vêtements de sport. *verb* porter [1]; **Tamsin's wearing her trainers** Tamsin porte ses baskets; **she often wears red** elle est souvent en rouge; **to wear make-up** se maquiller [1].

weather *noun* temps M; **what's the weather like?** quel temps fait-il?; **in fine weather** quand il fait beau; **the weather was cold** il faisait froid; **the weather here is terrible** il fait un temps affreux ici.

weather forecast *noun* météo F; **the weather forecast says it will rain** selon la météo il va pleuvoir.

wedding *noun* mariage M.

Wednesday *noun* mercredi M; **on Wednesday** mercredi; **I'm going out on Wednesday** je sors mercredi; **see you on Wednesday!** à mercredi!; **on Wednesdays** le mercredi; **the museum is closed on Wednesdays** le musée est fermé le

mercredi; **every Wednesday** tous les mercredis; **last Wednesday** mercredi dernier; **next Wednesday** mercredi prochain.

weed *noun* mauvaise herbe F.

week *noun* semaine F; **last week** la semaine dernière; **next week** la semaine prochaine; **this week** cette semaine; **for weeks** pendant des semaines; **a week today** aujourd'hui en huit.

weekday *noun* **on weekdays** en semaine.

weekend *noun* week-end M; **last weekend** le week-end dernier; **next weekend** le week-end prochain; **they're coming for the weekend** ils vont passer le week-end chez nous; **I'll do it at the weekend** je le ferai pendant le week-end; **have a nice weekend!** bon week-end!

weigh *verb* peser [50]; **to weigh something** peser quelque chose; **how much do you weigh?** combien pèses-tu?; **I weigh 50 kilos** je pèse cinquante kilos; **to weigh yourself** se peser.

weight *noun* poids M; **to put on weight** prendre du poids; **to lose weight** perdre du poids.

weird *adjective* bizarre.

welcome *noun* accueil M; **they gave us a warm welcome** ils nous ont fait un accueil chaleureux; **welcome to Oxford!** bienvenue à Oxford!
adjective bienvenu; **you're welcome any time** vous êtes toujours les bienvenus; **'thank you!' – 'you're welcome!'**

'merci!' – 'de rien!'
verb accueillir [35].

well[1] *noun* puits M.

well[2] *adverb* **1** to feel well se sentir bien; **I'm very well, thank you** ça va très bien, merci; **2** bien; **Terry played well** Terry a bien joué; **the operation went well** l'opération s'est bien passée; **well done!** bravo!; **3** as well aussi; **Kevin's coming as well** Kevin vient aussi; **4** alors; **5** well then, what's the problem? alors, quel est le problème?; **6** very well then, you can go très bien, tu peux y aller.

well-behaved *adjective* sage.

well-done *adjective* bien cuit (*a steak*).

wellington (boot) *noun* botte F en caoutchouc.

well-known *adjective* célèbre.

well-off *adjective* aisé.

Welsh *noun* **1** the Welsh (*people*) les Gallois M *plural*; **2** (*language*) gallois M.
adjective gallois.

Welshman *noun* Gallois M.

Welshwoman *noun* Galloise F.

west *noun* ouest M; **in the west** à l'ouest.
adjective, adverb ouest (*never agrees*); **the west side** le côté ouest; **a west wind** un vent d'ouest; **west of Paris** à l'ouest de Paris.

western *noun* (*a film*) western M.

West Indian *noun* Antillais M,

Antillaise F.
adjective antillais.

West Indies *plural noun* Antilles F *plural*; **in the West Indies** aux Antilles.

wet *adjective* **1** (*damp*) mouillé; **the grass is wet** l'herbe est mouillée; **we got wet** nous nous sommes fait mouiller; **2** a wet day un jour de pluie.

whale *noun* baleine F.

what *pronoun, adjective* **1** qu'est-ce que (*in questions*); **what did you say?** qu'est-ce que tu as dit?; **what's she doing?** qu'est-ce qu'elle fait?; **what did you buy?** qu'est-ce que tu as acheté?; **what is it?** qu'est-ce que c'est?; **what's the matter?** qu'est-ce qu'il y a?; **2** qu'est-ce qui (*in questions as the subject of the verb*); **what's happening?** qu'est-ce qui se passe?; **3** ce que (*relative pronoun*); **tell me what you bought** dis-moi ce que tu as acheté; **4** ce qui (*relative pronoun as subject of a verb*); **she told me what had happened** elle m'a dit ce qui s'était passé; **5** quel (F quelle); **what's your address?** quelle est ton adresse?; **what country is it in?** c'est dans quel pays?; **what colour is it?** c'est de quelle couleur?; **what make is it?** c'est quelle marque?; **6** what's her name? elle s'appelle comment?; **what?** comment?

wheat *noun* blé M.

wheel *noun* roue F; **the spare wheel** la roue de rechange; **the steering wheel** le volant.

wheelbarrow noun brouette F.

wheelchair noun fauteuil roulant M.

when adverb, conjunction quand;
when is she arriving? quand est-ce
qu'elle arrive?; when's your
birthday? c'est quand, ton
anniversaire?; it was raining when I
went out il pleuvait quand je suis
sorti.

where adverb, conjunction où;
where are the plates? où sont les
assiettes?; where do you live? tu
habites où?; where are you going?
où vas-tu?; I don't know where they
live je ne sais pas où ils habitent.

whether conjunction si; I don't
know whether he's back or not je
ne sais pas s'il est rentré ou non.

which adjective quel (F quelle);
which CD did you buy? quel CD as-
tu acheté?
pronoun 1 (which one) lequel,
laquelle (depending on whether it is
standing for a masculine or a
feminine noun); 'I saw your
brother' – 'which one?' 'j'ai vu ton
frère' – 'lequel?'; 'I saw your
sister' – 'which one?' 'j'ai vu ta
sœur' – 'laquelle?'; which of these
jackets is yours? laquelle de ces
vestes est à toi?; 2 (relative
pronoun) qui (as subject of the verb);
the lamp which is on the table la
lampe qui est sur la table; 3 (relative
pronoun) que (as object of the verb);
the book which you borrowed from
me le livre que tu m'as emprunté.

while noun for a while pendant

quelque temps; she worked here for
a while elle a travaillé ici pendant
quelque temps; after a while au
bout d'un moment.
conjunction pendant que; you can
make some tea while I'm finishing
my homework tu peux faire du thé
pendant que je finirai mes devoirs.

whip noun (for a horse) cravache F.
verb fouetter [1]; whipped cream la
crème fouettée.

whiskers plural noun moustaches
F plural.

whisky noun whisky M.

whisper noun chuchotement M; to
speak in a whisper chuchoter [1].
verb chuchoter [1].

whistle noun sifflet M.
verb siffler [1].

white noun blanc M; an egg white
un blanc d'œuf.
adjective blanc (F blanche); a white
shirt une chemise blanche.

white coffee noun café M au lait.

Whitsun noun Pentecôte F.

who pronoun 1 (in questions) qui;
who wants some chocolate? qui
veut du chocolat?; 2 (relative
pronoun) qui (as subject of the verb);
my friend who lives in Paris mon
ami qui habite à Paris; 3 (relative
pronoun) que (as object of the verb);
the friends who we invited les amis
que nous avons invités.

whole noun the whole of the class
la classe tout entière; on the whole
dans l'ensemble.
adjective tout; the whole family
toute la famille; the whole morning

toute la matinée; **the whole time** tout le temps; **the whole world** le monde entier.

holemeal adjective complet (F complète); **wholemeal bread** le pain complet.

hom pronoun 1 que; **the person whom I saw** la personne que j'ai vue; 2 (after a preposition) qui; **the person to whom I wrote** la personne à qui j'ai écrit.

hose pronoun, adjective 1 à qui; **whose is this jacket?** à qui est cette veste?; **whose shoes are these?** à qui sont ces chaussures?; **whose is it?** 1 à qui c'est?; **I know whose it is** je sais à qui c'est; 2 dont; **the man whose car has been stolen** le monsieur dont la voiture a été volée.

hy adverb pourquoi; **why did she phone?** pourquoi est-ce qu'elle a appelé?; **nobody knows why he did it** personne ne sait pourquoi il l'a fait.

wicked adjective 1 (bad) méchant; 2 (brilliant) génial (M plural géniaux).

wide adjective 1 large; **the Thames is very wide here** la Tamise est très large ici; **a piece of paper 20 cm wide** une feuille de papier de vingt centimètres de large; 2 **a wide range** une vaste gamme.
adverb **the door was wide open** la porte était grande ouverte.

wide awake adjective complètement éveillé.

widow noun veuve F.

widower noun veuf M.

width noun largeur F.

wife noun femme F.

wig noun perruque F.

wild adjective 1 sauvage (an animal or plant); **wild birds** les oiseaux sauvages; 2 (crazy) fou (F folle) (idea, party, person); 3 **to be wild about something** être un fana de quelque chose.

wild life noun **a programme on wild life in Africa** un programme sur la nature en Afrique.

wild life park noun réserve F naturelle.

will verb 1 (if you are unsure of the future tense of a French verb, you can check in the verb tables in the centre of the dictionary); **I'll see you soon** je te reverrai bientôt; **he'll be pleased to see you** il sera content de te voir; **it won't rain** il ne pleuvra pas; **there won't be a problem** il n'y aura pas de problème; 2 aller [7](can be used for the immmediate future); **I'll phone them at once** je vais les appeler tout de suite; 3 (in questions and requests) **will you have a drink?** est-ce que vous prenez quelque chose à boire?; **will you help me?** est-ce que tu peux m'aider?; **'will you write to me?'** – 'of course I will!' 'est-ce que tu m'écriras?' – 'bien sûr que oui!'; 4 **he won't open the door** il ne veut pas ouvrir la porte; **the car won't start** la voiture ne veut pas démarrer; **the drawer won't open** je n'arrive pas à ouvrir le tiroir.

willing adjective **to be willing to do**

être prêt à faire; **I'm willing to pay half** je suis prêt à payer la moitié.

willingly *adverb* volontiers.

willow *noun* saule M; **a weeping willow** un saule pleureur.

win *noun* victoire F; **our win over Everton** notre victoire sur Everton.
verb gagner [1]; **we won!** nous avons gagné!; **Rovers won by two goals** Rovers ont gagné de deux buts.

wind[1] *noun* vent M; **the North wind** le vent du nord.

wind[2] *verb* 1 enrouler [1] (*a wire or a rope, for example*); 2 remonter [1] (*a clock*).

wind instrument *noun* instrument M à vent.

window *noun* 1 (*in a building*) fenêtre F; **to look out of the window** regarder par la fenêtre; 2 (*in a car, bus, train*) vitre F.

windscreen *noun* pare-brise M (*plural* pare-brise).

windscreen wipers *plural noun* essuie-glace M.

windy *adjective* 1 venteux (F venteuse) (*a place*); 2 **it's windy today** il fait du vent aujourd'hui.

wine *noun* vin M; **a glass of white wine** un verre de vin blanc.

wing *noun* 1 aile F; 2 (*in sport*) ailier M.

wink *verb* **to wink at somebody** faire [10] un clin d'œil à quelqu'un.

winner *noun* gagnant M, gagnante F.

winning *adjective* gagnant.

winnings *plural noun* gains M plural.

winter *noun* hiver M; **in winter** en hiver.

wipe *verb* essuyer [41]; **I'll just wipe the table** je vais juste essuyer la table; **to wipe your nose** se moucher [1].
to wipe up (*dishes*) essuyer [41] la vaisselle.

wire *noun* fil M; **an electric wire** un fil électrique.

wire netting *noun* grillage M.

wise *adjective* sage.

wish *noun* 1 vœu M (*plural* vœux); **make a wish!** fais un vœu!; 2 (*a desire*) désir M; 3 **best wishes on your birthday** meilleurs vœux pour ton anniversaire.
verb 1 **I wish he were here** si seulement il était ici; 2 **I wished him happy birthday** je lui ai souhaité un bon anniversaire.

wit *noun* esprit M.

with *preposition* 1 avec; **with James** avec James; **with me** avec moi; **with pleasure** avec plaisir; **beat the eggs with a fork** battez les œufs avec une fourchette; **he took his umbrella with him** il a pris son parapluie; 2 (*at the house of*) chez; **we're staying the night with Frank** on va passer la nuit chez Frank; 3 (*in descriptions*) **a girl with red hair** une fille aux cheveux roux; **the boy with the broken arm** le garçon au bras cassé; 4 de; **filled with water** rempli d'eau; **covered with mud**

couvert de boue; **red with rage** rouge de colère.

without *preposition* sans; **without you** sans toi; **without sugar** sans sucre; **without a sweater** sans pull; **without looking** sans regarder.

witness *noun* témoin M.

witty *adjective* spirituel (F spirituelle).

wolf *noun* loup M.

woman *noun* femme F; **a woman friend** une amie; **a woman doctor** une femme médecin.

wonder *noun* 1 merveille F; 2 **it's no wonder you're tired** ce n'est pas étonnant si tu es fatigué.
verb se demander [1]; **I wonder why** je me demande pourquoi; **I wonder where Jake is** je me demande où est Jake.

wonderful *adjective* merveilleux (F merveilleuse).

wood *noun* bois M; **the lamp is made of wood** la lampe est en bois.

wooden *adjective* en bois.

woodwork *noun* menuiserie F.

wool *noun* laine F.

word *noun* 1 mot M; **a long word** un mot long; **what's the French word for 'window'?** comment dit-on 'window' en français?; **in other words** autrement dit; **to have a word with somebody** parler avec quelqu'un; 2 (*promise*) **to give somebody your word** donner sa parole à quelqu'un; **he broke his word** il n'a pas tenu parole; 3 **the**

words of a song les paroles d'une chanson.

word processing *noun* traitement M de texte.

word processor *noun* machine F à traitement de texte.

work *noun* travail M (*plural* travaux); **Mum's at work** maman est au travail; **I've got some work to do** j'ai du travail à faire; **he's out of work** il est sans emploi; **Ben's off work** (*sick*) Ben est en arrêt de travail; (*on holiday*) Ben est en congé.
verb 1 travailler [1]; **she works in an office** elle travaille dans un bureau; **Dad works at home** papa travaille à domicile; **Ruth works in advertising** Ruth travaille dans la publicité; **he works nights** il travaille de nuit; 2 (*to operate*) se servir [71] de; **can you work the video?** sais-tu te servir du magnétoscope?; 3 (*function*) marcher [1]; **the dishwasher's not working** le lave-vaisselle est en panne; **that worked really well!** ça a bien marché!

●**to work out** 1 (*understand*) comprendre [64]; **I can't work out why** je ne comprends pas pourquoi; 2 (*exercise*) s'entraîner [1]; 3 (*to make*) (*a plan*) marcher [1]; 4 (*calculate*) calculer [1]; **I'll work out how much it would cost** je vais calculer combien ça coûterait.

worked up *adjective* **to get worked up** s'énerver [1].

worker *noun* ouvrier M, ouvrière F.

work experience *noun* stage M; **to do work experience** faire un stage; **to be on work experience** être en stage.

worker noun (in a factory) ouvrier M, ouvrière F.

working-class adjective ouvrier (F ouvrière); **a working-class background** un milieu ouvrier.

work of art noun œuvre F d'art.

workshop noun atelier M.

workstation noun (computer) poste M de travail (plural postes de travail).

world noun monde M; **the best in the world** le meilleur du monde; **the Western world** les pays occidentaux.

World Cup noun the World Cup la Coupe du Monde.

world war noun guerre F mondiale; **the Second World War** la Seconde Guerre mondiale.

worm noun ver M.

worn out adjective 1 (a person) épuisé; 2 (clothes or shoes) complètement usé.

worried adjective inquiet (F inquiète); **they're worried** ils s'inquiètent; **to be worried about** s'inquiéter pour; **we're worried about Susan** nous nous inquiétons pour Susan.

worry noun soucis M plural. verb s'inquiéter [24]; **don't worry!** ne t'inquiète pas!; **there's nothing to worry about** il n'y a pas de quoi s'inquiéter.

worrying adjective inquiétant.

worse adjective pire; **it was even worse than the last time** c'était encore pire que la dernière fois; **to get worse** empirer [1]; **the weather's getting worse** le temps empire; **things are getting worse and worse** ça va de pire en pire.

worst adjective **the worst** le plus mauvais; **it was the worst day of my life** ça a été la journée la plus mauvaise de ma vie; **if the worst comes to the worst** au pire.

worth adjective **to be worth** valoir [80]; **how much is it worth?** ça vaut combien?; **to be worth doing** valoir la peine de faire; **it's worth trying** ça vaut la peine d'essayer; **it's not worth it** ça ne vaut pas la peine.

would verb 1 **would you like something to eat?** voulez-vous quelque chose à manger?; 2 **he wouldn't answer** il n'a pas voulu répondre; **the car wouldn't start** la voiture n'a pas voulu démarrer; 3 **I would like an omelette** je voudrais une omelette; **I'd like to go to the cinema** j'aimerais aller au cinéma; **that would be a good idea** ce serait une bonne idée; **if we asked her she would help us** elle nous aiderait, si nous le lui demandions.

wound noun blessure F. verb blesser [1].

wrap verb emballer [1]; **I'm going to wrap (up) my presents** je vais emballer mes cadeaux; **could you wrap it for me please?** voulez-vous me faire un paquet cadeau, s'il vous plaît?

wrapping paper noun papier cadeau M.

wreck noun 1 (of a crashed car or plane) épave F; 2 I feel a wreck! je suis une loque!
verb 1 détruire [26]; 2 gâcher [1] (plans, occasion); it completely wrecked my evening! ça m'a complètement gâché la soirée!

wrestler noun catcheur M, catcheuse F.

wrestling noun catch M.

wrinkled adjective ridé.

wrist noun poignet M.

write verb 1 écrire [38] (a letter or a story); I'll write her a letter je lui écrirai une lettre; to write to somebody écrire à quelqu'un; I wrote to Jean yesterday j'ai écrit à Jean hier.
● to write down noter [1]; I wrote down her name j'ai noté son nom.

writer noun écrivain M.

writing noun écriture F.

wrong adjective 1 (not correct) mauvais; the wrong answer la mauvaise réponse; it's the wrong address ce n'est pas la bonne adresse; I've brought the wrong file je n'ai pas apporté le bon classeur; you've got the wrong number vous vous êtes trompé de numéro; 2 to be wrong (mistaken) se tromper; I was wrong je me suis trompé; I was wrong when I said it was finished je me suis trompé en disant que c'était fini; 3 what's wrong? qu'est-ce qu'il y a?; 4 (false) faux (F fausse); the information was wrong les renseignements étaient faux.

X x

xerox™ noun photocopie F.
verb photocopier [1].

X-ray noun radio F; I saw the X-rays j'ai vu les radios.
verb faire [10] une radio de; they X-rayed her ankle ils ont fait une radio de sa cheville.

Y y

yacht noun 1 (sailing boat) voilier M; 2 (large luxury boat) yacht M.

yawn verb bâiller [1].

year noun 1 an M; (the whole period) année F; six years ago il y a six ans; the whole year toute l'année; they lived in Moscow for years ils ont habité Moscou pendant des années; 2 (for someone's age) an M; he's seventeen years old il a dix-sept ans; a two-year-old child un enfant de deux ans; 3 (in secondary schools in France the years go from 'sixième', the equivalent of Year 7, to 'terminale', the equivalent of Year 13); I'm in Year 10 je suis en troisième; I'm in Year 11 je suis en seconde.

yell verb hurler [1].

yellow adjective jaune.

yes adverb 1 oui; yes, I know oui, je

sais; **'is Tom in his room?'** – **'yes, he is'** 'est-ce que Tom est dans sa chambre?' – 'oui'; **2** (*answering a negative*) si; **'you don't want to go, do you?'** – **'yes I do!'** 'tu ne veux pas y aller, n'est-ce pas?' – 'mais si!'; **'you haven't finished, have you?'** – **'yes, I have'** 'tu n'as pas fini?' – 'si si'.

yesterday *adverb* hier; **I saw her yesterday** je l'ai vue hier; **yesterday afternoon** hier après-midi; **yesterday morning** hier matin; **the day before yesterday** avant-hier.

yet *adverb* not yet pas encore; **it's not ready yet** ce n'est pas encore prêt.

yoghurt *noun* yaourt M; **a banana yoghurt** un yaourt à la banane.

yolk *noun* jaune d'œuf M (*plural* jaunes d'œuf).

you *pronoun* **1** tu (*'tu' is the familiar way of talking to family members, close friends, and people of your own age; 'vous' is more polite*); **do you want to go to the cinema tonight?** est-ce que tu veux aller au cinéma ce soir?; **2** te (*the object form of 'tu'*); **I'll lend you my bike** je te prêterai mon vélo; **I'll invite you** je t'inviterai; **I'll write to you** je t'écrirai; **3** toi (*after prepositions and in comparisons*); **I'll go with you** j'irai avec toi; **he's older than you** il est plus âgé que toi; **4** (*more polite or to several people*) vous; **can you tell me where the station is, please?** est-ce que vous pouvez m'indiquer la gare, s'il vous plaît?; **I'll invite you all!** je vous inviterai tous!

young *adjective* jeune; **he's younger than me** il est plus jeune que moi; **Tessa's two years younger than me** Tessa a deux ans de moins que moi; **young people** les jeunes.

your *adjective* **1** ton (F ta) (*plural* tes) (*this is the familiar way of talking to family members, close friends, and people of your own age; 'vous' is more polite*); **I met your Dad** j'ai rencontré ton père; **I like your skirt!** j'aime bien ta jupe!; **you've forgotten your CDs!** tu as oublié tes CD; **2** (*more polite or to several people*) votre (*plural* vos); **thank you for your hospitality** merci pour votre hospitalité; **you can all bring your friends** vous pouvez tous amener vos amis.

yours *pronoun* **1** le tien (*plural* les tiens), la tienne (*plural* les tiennes) (*this is the familiar way of talking to somebody of your own age or belonging to your own family; otherwise you should use 'vôtre'*); **my brother's younger than yours** mon frère est plus jeune que le tien; **2** (*formally or to several people*) le vôtre (F la vôtre) (*plural* les vôtres); **my children are younger than yours** mes enfants sont plus jeunes que les vôtres; **3** à toi; à vous (*polite form*); **is this pen yours?** est-ce que ce stylo est à toi?

yourself *pronoun* **1** te; (*formally*) vous; **you'll hurt yourself** tu vas te faire mal; **2** (*for emphasis*) toi-même; (*formally*) vous-même; **did you do it yourself?** est-ce que tu l'as fait toi-même?; **3** **all by yourself** tout seul (F toute seule).

yourselves *pronoun* **1** vous; **help yourselves** servez-vous; **2** (*for*

emphasis) vous-mêmes; **did you do
it yourselves?** est-ce que vous
l'avez fait vous-mêmes?

outh hostel *noun* auberge F de
jeunesse (*plural* auberges de
jeunesse).

ugoslavia *noun* Yougoslavie F;
the former Yugoslavia ex-
Yougoslavie

Z z

any *adjective* loufoque.

ebra *noun* zèbre M.

zebra crossing *noun* passage M
pour piétons.

zero *noun* zéro M.

zigzag *verb* zigzaguer [1].

zip *noun* fermeture F éclair™.

zodiac *noun* zodiaque M; **the signs
of the zodiac** les signes du
zodiaque.

zone *noun* zone F.

zoo *noun* zoo M.

zoom lens *noun* zoom M.